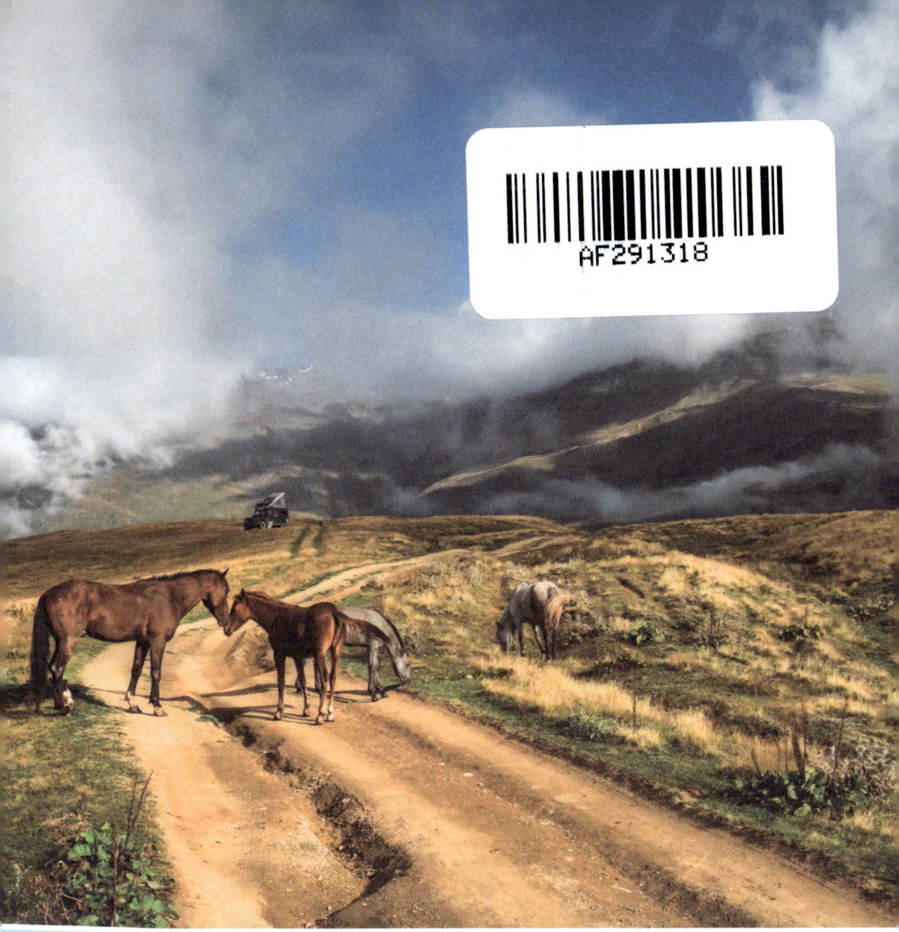

THE ROUGH GUIDE TO
GEORGIA, ARMENIA & AZERBAIJAN

This first edition was written and researched by
Owen Morton, Adam Prince and Natalie Taylor

Contents

STAINED GLASS WINDOW AT SHEKI KHAN'S PALACE, AZERBAIJAN

Introduction to
Georgia, Armenia & Azerbaijan

Where east meets west and north meets south, the three Caucasian republics of Georgia, Armenia and Azerbaijan stand at the crossroads of Europe and Asia, and have spent their history interacting with Byzantines, Turks, Persians and Russians, resulting in a rich, vibrant and unique heritage. Even without the draw of their fantastic history these small countries are blessed with stunning natural beauty, including some of the highest mountains in Europe, amid countryside ideal for trekking and other outdoor activities. But the main memory of your visit may well be the incredible hospitality of the welcoming people, to whom hosting guests is a matter of honour and pride.

The land to the south of the Caucasus Mountains has been of strategic importance for thousands of years. **Ancient empires**, including the Persians, Greeks and Romans, fought over this territory long ago, and over the following centuries it's been a target for Byzantines, Seljuk Turks, Iranians and Russians. Despite the constant flow of conquerors, the native inhabitants of the region established independent kingdoms, which at times became serious political heavyweights. After years of push-and-pull, they were all incorporated into the Russian Empire in the early nineteenth century, which led to them spending the twentieth century as the southernmost territories of the USSR.

Following the collapse of the Soviet Union, however, the three newly **independent nations** have followed their own paths. Georgia, the most pro-Western of the three, has aspirations of EU membership and is cautious of its northern Russian neighbour, while Armenia largely remains closely allied to Russia. Azerbaijan, meanwhile, has grown rich from its oil reserves in the Caspian Sea, but its society is considerably more

KHOR VIRAP MONASTERY AND MOUNT ARARAT, ARMENIA

authoritarian when compared to the parliamentary democracies established in Georgia and Armenia.

From the late 1980s until 2023, the region remained splintered over the thorny issue of **Nagorno-Karabakh**, a territory in between Armenia and Azerbaijan that declared itself an independent republic. Following a devastating war in the early 1990s, the two countries settled into a frozen conflict in which Azerbaijan maintained ownership of Nagorno-Karabakh, while Armenia recognised its independence. Eventually, in 2020 and 2023, Azerbaijan launched successful offensives against the self-declared republic, resulting in its Armenian populace fleeing and Azerbaijan regaining control over the territory. Georgia has territorial issues of its own with the regions of Abkhazia and South Ossetia having effectively seceded.

Despite the unresolved issues in the region, all three countries are extremely attractive tourist destinations. The mighty Caucasus Mountains in the north of both Georgia and Azerbaijan offer fantastic opportunities for **hiking** trips, and winter sports such as **skiing** are also on the up. Fans of history and culture will love the region's heady blend of beautiful medieval **monasteries, palaces** of eighteenth-century khans, stolid Soviet concrete, and innovative 21st-century **architecture**. For foodies, the area has a distinct and delicious cuisine, which pairs beautifully with the excellent local **wine**. But whatever your reason for travelling here, you're sure to be met with a sincere welcome from the local people.

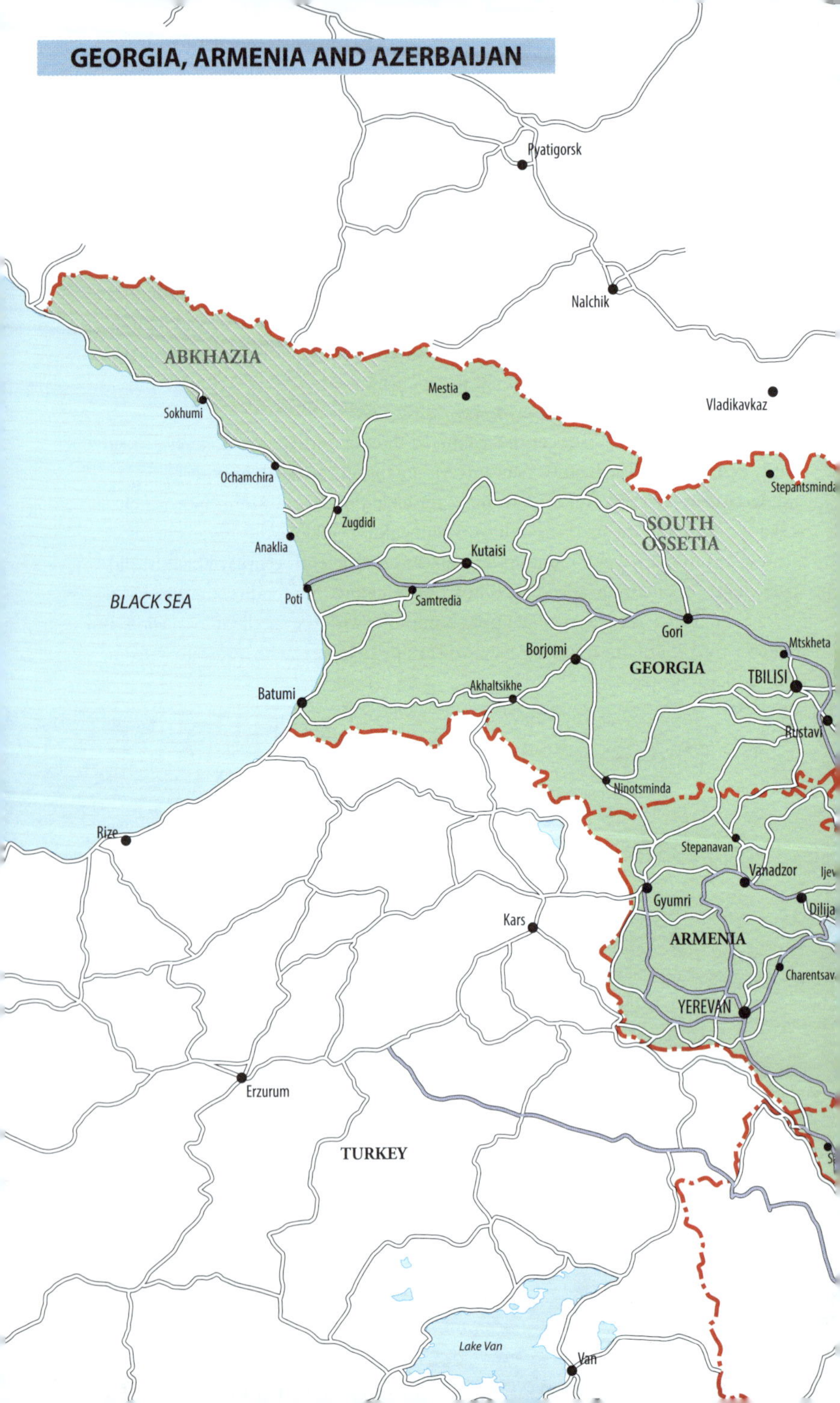

GEORGIA, ARMENIA AND AZERBAIJAN
Pyatigorsk
Nalchik
Vladikavkaz
ABKHAZIA
Mestia
Sokhumi
Ochamchira
Stepantsminda
SOUTH OSSETIA
Zugdidi
Kutaisi
Anaklia
Poti
Samtredia
Gori
Mtskheta
BLACK SEA
Borjomi
GEORGIA
TBILISI
Akhaltsikhe
Batumi
Rustavi
Ninotsminda
Rize
Stepanavan
Vanadzor
Ijev
Gyumri
Dilija
Kars
ARMENIA
Charentsav
YEREVAN
Erzurum
TURKEY
Lake Van
Van

N
RUSSIA
Grozny
Makhachkala
CASPIAN SEA
Quba
Lavi
Lagodekhi
Sighnaghi
Sheki
Qabala
Mingəçevir
Ganja
Shamakhi
Lake
Sevan
Küdämir
AZERBAIJAN
BAKU
Vardenis
Sabirabad
Jermuk
Stepanakert
Yeghegnadzor
NAGORNO-
KARABAKH
Goris
Sisian
Nakhchivan
Kapan
Meghri
Lankaran
IRAN
0   80
kilometres

FACT FILE

- Georgia, Armenia and Azerbaijan are small countries, with a combined area of 186,000 sq km – about the size of Syria and considerably smaller than the UK.
- All three countries are constitutionally parliamentary democracies, although Azerbaijan is becoming increasingly autocratic.
- Armenia was the world's first country to adopt Christianity as its state religion, in 301 AD and Georgia was the third, in 326. Azerbaijan is an Islamic country. All three are politically secular.
- Baku, in Azerbaijan, is the world's lowest capital city at 28m below sea level. Azerbaijan is also home to Xinaliq, which, at 2,350m, is arguably Europe's highest village.
- Georgia and Armenia both claim to have invented wine, with traditions dating back at least 8000 years.
- Economically, the Caucasian republics were reliant on industry in the Soviet era. Now, Azerbaijan relies on oil production, while the economies of Georgia and Armenia are predominantly agricultural and tourist-focused.

Where to go

Georgia's capital, **Tbilisi**, is an ideal introduction to the Caucasus – an ancient city which wears its history on its sleeve. Check out the churches, the baths district, the nineteenth-century town houses, and the winding streets of the Old Town before zipping forward in time to see the ambitious architecture of the 21st century, such as the Bridge of Peace and the Public Services Hall. The city's museums are perfect for getting a handle on the history and art of the country – and in the evening, when you're all cultured out, you can eat and drink great food and wine in the vibrant restaurant and bar scene. If you're a party animal, it's the nightlife capital of the Caucasus, boasting in internationally renowned electronic clubs.

North of Tbilisi is **Mtskheta**, the former capital of Georgia and still its holiest city, as well as the Georgian Military Highway which leads up into the Caucasus to the town of **Stepantsminda**, the starting point for many hikes in the mountains. Further to the west, **Svaneti** is renowned for its beautiful mountain scenery and distinctive stone towers, an architectural legacy of the region's history of blood feuds. Heading south from Svaneti will bring you to **Kutaisi**, Georgia's second city and home to some of its most impressive medieval monasteries.

In Georgia's far southwest corner is **Batumi**, a beach city on the Black Sea that's likely to be your first stop in the Caucasus if you're entering the region overland from Turkey. The south of the country is also home to the utterly remarkable **Vardzia** cave monastery, which dates from the twelfth century, and the attractive town of **Borjomi**, where you'll find a beautiful national park perfect for hiking trips.

To Tbilisi's east is the large Kakheti region, home to the beautiful **Davit Gareja** monastery on the Azerbaijani border, as well as the country's wine heartland. Taking it slow and visiting the vineyards around **Sighnaghi** and **Telavi** will delight any oenophile, and the gorgeous scenery and attractive monasteries make this region an essential stop on any visit to Georgia.

To Georgia's south is Armenia, which, despite being the smallest of the three Caucasian nations, packs a huge amount into its diminutive size. Most visitors will start in the capital, **Yerevan**, which is a lively city with striking and unusual Soviet

PROMETHEUS CAVE (ALSO KUMISTAVI CAVE) NEAR TSKALTUBO IN THE IMERETI REGION, GEORGIA architecture – notably the remarkable open-air art museum, The Cascade, a huge staircase packed with innovative sculpture. From the top, on a clear day, Armenia's sacred mountain, Mount Ararat, is visible beyond the city spread out below. While in Yerevan, be sure to visit the National Museum, a fascinating and sobering walk through Armenia's history, and don't miss the Genocide Memorial, which is essential to understanding the deep scars the nation still carries.

Armenia's north is home to **Dilijan National Park**, a wilderness criss-crossed with hiking trails through gorgeous forests and lakes, as well as the **Debed Canyon**, where you'll find an astonishing collection of beautiful medieval monasteries amid creaking abandoned Soviet industry – a perfect microcosm of the country's history. **Gyumri**, Armenia's second city, is also in the north, a friendly place with a smattering of interesting museums and yet more lovely monasteries in the nearby countryside.

South of Gyumri is Armenia's highest peak, **Mount Aragats**, which can be scaled in a day's trek. It's a lovely climb which requires no technical expertise. East from Aragats, you'll find **Garni Temple** – unique in the Caucasus as the only Graeco-Roman monument still standing – and the gorgeous rock-hewn **Geghard monastery**, which sports intricate and beautiful carvings. Garni and Geghard form one of the most popular day trips out from Yerevan.

Lake Sevan, just north of Garni and Geghard, is also a hugely popular day trip, but it can feel busy and overdeveloped, so it may be best to visit early or late to avoid the

crowds. Heading southeast from Yerevan, you'll come to the monastery of **Khor Virap**, which sits in a dramatic position in front of Mount Ararat and is the birthplace of Christianity in Armenia. Many of Armenia's vineyards are found here too, so a visit to **Areni** to sample some of the local wares is highly recommended.

Travel further southeast and you'll be able to explore Armenia's ancient history at the stone circle of **Zorats Karer** (billed as Armenia's Stonehenge) and the fantastic petroglyphs around **Ughtasar Lake**. Around the city of **Goris**, the cave city of **Khndzoresk** throws further light on the ancient peoples of Armenia, and this region is also home to the magnificent **Tatev** monastery, reached across a valley by one of the world's longest cable-car trips.

Visitors to Azerbaijan are almost certain to begin their trip in **Baku**, the country's capital and the largest city in the Caucasus. It's a modern, pulsing city on the shores of the Caspian Sea, alive with new and gleaming architecture – the Heydar Aliyev Centre, for example, may be one of the most innovative buildings you'll ever see. By contrast, in Baku's Old Town, history is still very much in evidence, and the Maiden Tower and the Palace of the Shirvanshahs are both essential to understanding Azerbaijan's history.

Around Baku, you'll learn why Azerbaijan is sometimes known as the Land of Fire. The **Ateshgah Fire Temple** on the Abseron Peninsula is a focal point for Zoroastrian worship, while at the remarkable **Yanar Dağ,** slightly further inland, you can see an entire hillside continually ablaze where natural gas emerges from the ground. Further geological oddities can be found south of Baku in the **Qobustan National Park**, where a field of cold mud volcanoes bubble away, resulting in an extremely odd and strangely enthralling sight. Qobustan is also home to a remarkable set of ancient petroglyphs, further evidence of the long history of this region.

Inland from Baku, fans of history or architecture will be fascinated with the town of **Shamakhi**, where one of the oldest mosques in the Caucasus can be found, as well as **Sheki**, which is home to an utterly remarkable pair of eighteenth-century khans' palaces. This region is also home to Azerbaijan's share of the Caucasus Mountains. Treks around **Xinaliq** village are beautiful, and the traditional village of **Lahıc** gives the chance to wander the cobbled streets and gain an insight into the traditions of local copperwork.

When to go

The Caucasus has a continental climate, resulting in very hot summers and very cold winters with temperatures dropping to -5° Celsius. In summer, Yerevan tends to be hottest, with July temperatures averaging around 35° Celsius, but Tbilisi and Baku aren't far behind with averages of 29° and 31° respectively. In winter, temperatures swing round to the opposite extreme, with Yerevan's January temperature averaging 2°, while Tbilisi and Baku are a little warmer at 5°.

This makes spring and autumn the ideal time to travel to the Caucasus. It's warm but not baking hot, and although you will probably get a couple of days of rain, by and large the weather will treat you well. Spring is particularly beautiful, with wildflowers in bloom across the region. If you're in the region in the autumn and planning to head up into mountainous regions such as Tusheti, note that routes tend to close by mid- to late-October.

High temperatures in the summer months of June to August can make travel at this time rather sticky and unpleasant, especially if you're in **Armenia's lowlands** around Yerevan and Ararat, or in Nakhchivan, where the still air and heat can be stultifying. The days tend to be very hot, until the weather breaks each evening in heavy rain and occasional dramatic lightning storms. It's difficult to recommend travelling in the region at this time of year, but if you're determined, then Azerbaijan is perhaps the easiest prospect as it's a little cooler than the other two countries thanks to the winds blowing in from the Caspian Sea. It's also a good time to head up into the **mountains**, which are at their most accessible in the summer.

Similarly, the winter is perhaps not the best time to travel unless you're hoping to indulge in winter sports. Heavy **snowfall** across Georgia makes many regions unreachable particularly Tusheti and Khevsureti, but getting to Svaneti and Kazbegi can also be difficult. Armenia gets heavy snowfall too, though Azerbaijan's winters tend to be a little milder.

AVERAGE DAILY MAXIMUM TEMPERATURES

	Jan	Feb	Mar	Apr	May	Jun	Jul	Aug	Sep	Oct	Nov	Dec
TBILISI												
Max/Min °C	5/-4	6/-3	10/-1	15/4	20/9	25/13	28/17	29/17	23/13	17/7	10/6	6/-3
Rain (mm)	7	7	10	13	16	20	21	21	18	14	11	8
YEREVAN												
Max/Min °C	1/-7	3/-5	9/-1	15/3	20/7	26/12	30/16	30/16	25/12	17/6	9/-1	3/-5
Rain (mm)	32	36	53	65	44	18	10	7	9	19	30	34
BAKU												
Max/Min °C	7/3	7/3	10/5	14/9	21/15	26/20	29/23	29/23	25/20	19/15	13/9	9/6
Rain (mm)	31	31	26	24	14	7	7	6	23	39	45	38

Author picks

Our authors have traversed every corner of Georgia, Armenia and Azerbaijan, from the Old Town of Baku and the monasteries of Armenia to the mountains of Svaneti. Here are some of their favourite experiences.

Hiking in the Caucasus Take a walk among Europe's highest peaks, and enjoy the unspoilt mountain scenery in the north of Georgia. Hikes can be anything from a few hours to several days.

Wine-tasting Georgia's Kakheti region is dotted with hundreds of vineyards, so take a day or two to explore them and discover the quality of the country's ancient winemaking tradition.

Get down underground There are several fantastic caves in the Caucasus. Try the archaeologically significant system at Areni, or the stalactite formations at Prometheus or Sataplia.

Sleep in a caravanserai Pretend you're a Silk Road merchant travelling with your wares, and break for the night at the well-preserved caravanserai in Sheki, now a smart hotel.

Geological wonders Azerbaijan is home to some of the oddest geology you'll ever see, from burning hills and flammable water to small volcanoes spurting cold mud.

A puppet show The performances at Tbilisi's Rezo Gabriadze Puppet Theatre are fantastically innovative and often deeply moving. The wonderful stories can be enjoyed by all and need no translation.

Gorgeous monasteries Church architects were at the top of their game in medieval Armenia, designing some immensely beautiful structures.

Caucasian cuisine Whether it's sampling the delights of the Georgian khachapuri or enjoying an Armenian khorovats barbecue, there are few cuisines to match the wonders of the Caucasus.

Innovative and bizarre architecture The Caucasus is a hotbed for architecture, from the Flame Towers of Baku to the Alphabet Tower in Batumi, via the National Bank of Georgia HQ and the replica of Tower Bridge in Xacmaz.

Our author recommendations don't end here. We've flagged up our favourite places – a perfectly sited hotel, an atmospheric café, a special restaurant – throughout the Guide, highlighted with the ★ symbol.

TBILISI'S PUPPET SHOWS

BANK OF GEORGIA HQ

25

things not to miss

It's not possible to see everything that Georgia, Armenia and Azerbaijan have to offer in a single trip – and we don't suggest you try. What follows is a selective taste of the countries' highlights, including magnificent hiking trails, historic monasteries, stark Soviet architecture and memorable beaches, not to mention hearty cuisine. All highlights are colour-coded by chapter and have a page reference to take you straight into the guide, where you can find out more.

1 NORAVANK MONASTERY

See page 228

A perfect medieval Armenian monastery, the orange stone of the church is particularly beautiful at sunset.

2 TBILISI'S OLD TOWN

See page 56

The bustling heart of Tbilisi, the Old Town is a warren of gorgeous, crumbling streets.

3 SHEKI KHAN'S PALACE

See page 298

The intricate interior decorations of this eighteenth-century palace perfectly complement the superb stained-glass windows.

4 USHGULI

See page 136

High in the Caucasus, this Svan village is packed to bursting with distinctive stone towers, built to protect blood feuding families.

5 WINE

See page 38

Eight thousand years of winemaking mean Georgia and Armenia know their way around a vine.

6 THE CASCADES

See page 159

Yerevan's centrepiece is this quirky collection of statues and fountains situated on a staircase stretching up the hill, with views of Mount Ararat on a clear day.

7 QOBUSTAN NATIONAL PARK

See page 281

Bubbling mud volcanoes and ancient petroglyphs make for a unique day trip from Baku.

8 THE DEBED CANYON

See page 209

Armenia in microcosm, this canyon hosts a wealth of magnificent monasteries amid the ruins of Soviet industry.

9 GERGETI TRINITY CHURCH

See page 92

Iconic and beautiful, the sight of the Gergeti Trinity Church framed beneath the mighty bulk of Mount Kazbek is simply breathtaking.

10 BAKU

See page 246

Azerbaijan's astonishing capital is home to an evocative Old Town alongside modern, innovative architecture.

11 SOVIET MONUMENTS

See page 69

Big and blocky relics of recent history, you'll find stark Soviet monuments dotting towns and countryside across the Caucasus.

12 VARDZIA

See page 104

Riddling a cliff face in the Mtkvari river gorge is this utterly remarkable cave monastery.

13 CLIMBING MOUNT ARAGATS

See page 189

Armenia's highest peak is an enjoyable and non-technical day climb.

14 YEREVAN HISTORY MUSEUM

See page 167

One of the best museums in the Caucasus, this is the place to come for an engaging walk through Armenia's fascinating history.

15 NAKHCHIVAN CITY

See page 314

The obsessively neat and tidy Nakhchivan City hosts a wealth of architectural monuments, including the Tomb of Noah.

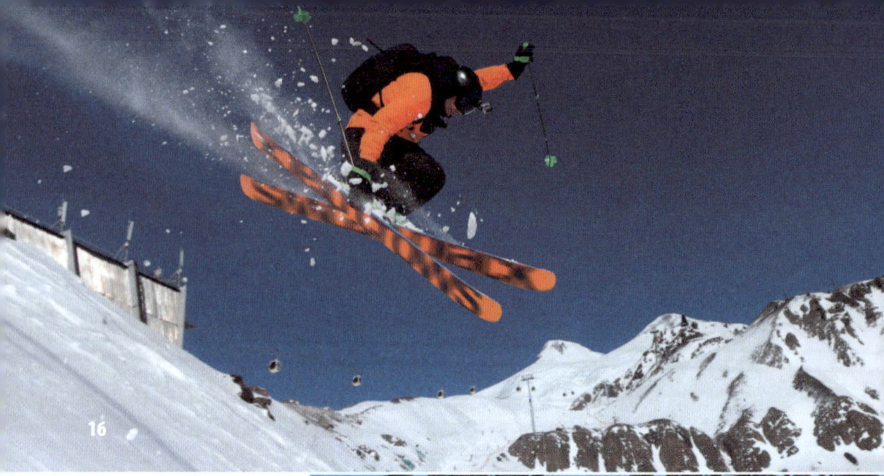

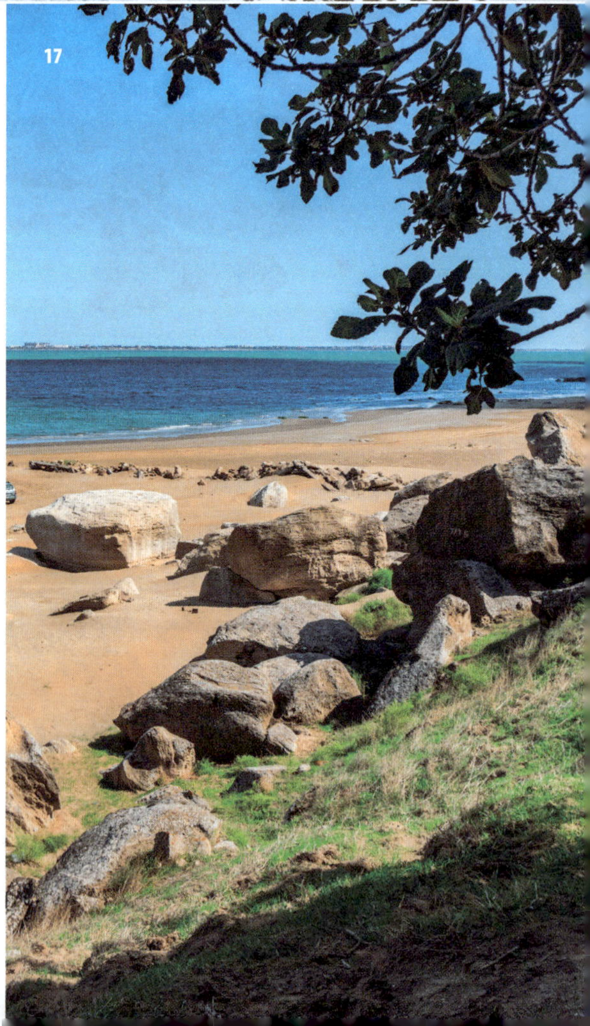

16 SKIING
See pages 91 and 295
The Caucasus mountains are home to several great ski resorts, including Georgia's Gudauri and Azerbaijan's Qabala.

17 CASPIAN BEACHES
See page 274
Overlooked by towering oil derricks, the Caspian Sea beaches may not be traditional sun, sand and surf, but they are unforgettable.

18 HOVHANNAVANK MONASTERY
See page 189
The zenith of medieval Armenian church architecture, Hovhannavank is intricate and beautiful.

19 KHACHAPURI
See page 37
All of Georgia's cuisine is sublime, but these dough-and-cheese concoctions are simply heavenly.

20 ABUDELAURI LAKES
See page 95
Trekking to these beautiful lakes high in the Caucasus is one of the region's best hikes.

18
19
20

21

22

23

24

21 ALINJA CASTLE
See page 323
Billed as Azerbaijan's 'Machu Picchu', this (heavily restored) medieval castle offers superb views.

22 TSKALTUBO
See page 118
A major holiday destination in Soviet times, Tskaltubo is now home to a vast number of derelict sanatoria slowly falling into beautiful decay.

23 TATEV MONASTERY
See page 236
Take one of the world's longest cable car rides to this perfect medieval Armenian church.

24 HIKING IN BORJOMI NATIONAL PARK
See page 100
Exploring the well-established hiking trails in this park offers one of the best opportunities to get up close with Georgia's varied wildlife.

25 YANAR DAĞ
See page 270
Learn why Azerbaijan styles itself the Land of Fire at this hill which has been continually aflame since the 1950s.

25

Itineraries

Georgia, Armenia and Azerbaijan may be small, but they're varied, so it would be a challenge to see everything in just one trip. Each of the following suggested routes makes for a great way to spend two or three weeks in the region.

CAUCASIAN CIRCUIT

This trip around the region's highlights, which gives a great feel for the essence of the Caucasus, should take approximately three weeks.

❶ **Yerevan** Begin your trip in Armenia's capital. Once you've explored the city's museums and street life, make a few day trips out to surrounding attractions such as the Khor Virap and Noravank monasteries. See page 156

❷ **Dilijan** Take a *marshrutka* up north to Armenia's outdoor capital and hike in the Dilijan National Park. See page 200

❸ **Tbilisi** Explore Georgia's capital, taking in its crumbling Old Town and the shiny new 21st-century architecture – and don't miss the fantastic restaurants and nightlife. See page 54

❹ **Stepantsminda** Journey up the Georgian Military Highway to Stepantsminda, from which you can undertake fantastic hiking in the mountains of the Caucasus. See page 92

❺ **Sighnaghi** Head east to Sighnaghi, in the heart of Georgia's wine region. Spend a couple of days relaxing in this pretty hilltop town and exploring the local vineyards. See page 149

❻ **Sheki** Cross the border into Azerbaijan and stop off in Sheki, the eighteenth-century capital of the Sheki Khanate, to visit the breathtakingly beautiful Khan's Palace. See page 298

❼ **Baku** Arrive in Baku, the capital of Azerbaijan, and check out the historic Old Town before wandering alongside the Caspian Sea. Make sure to take a day trip to the mud volcanoes and fascinating petroglyphs of Qobustan National Park or the varied sights of the Abşeron Peninsula. See page 249

❽ **Nakhchivan** If you have extra time, you could take a flight from Baku to Nakhchivan City and explore this culturally distinct enclave. See page 312

GEORGIAN JOURNEY

Explore Georgia in depth with this three-week trip to really get a handle on this fantastic and varied country.

❶ **Tbilisi** Start off with a couple of days in Tbilisi, checking out its gorgeous Old Town, exploring the wealth of museums, and enjoying delicious food and wine in one of the many excellent restaurants. See page 54

Create your own itinerary with Rough Guides. Whether you're after adventure or a family-friendly holiday, we have a trip for you, with all the activities you enjoy doing and the sights you want to see. All our trips are devised by local experts who get the most out of the destination. Visit **www.roughguides.com/trips** to chat with one of our travel agents.

❷ **Kutaisi** Take the train to Kutaisi and use this attractive, low-key city as a base to explore the Gelati Monastery, the Prometheus Cave, and the Soviet sanatoria in Tskaltubo. See page 108

❸ **Svaneti** A long marshrutka ride will bring you to Mestia, in the heart of Svaneti, for trekking with dramatic views. See page 131

❹ **Batumi** From the mountains to the sea – head south to Georgia's top beach resort and relax in the vibrant, pulsing city of Batumi. See page 125

❺ **Borjomi** This chilled-out town offers the chance for walking and horseriding in the Borjomi National Park. See page 96

❻ **Vardzia** A couple of hours south of Borjomi, wander around the intricate cave monastery of Vardzia. See page 104

❼ **Georgian Military Highway** Head north past Tbilisi and stop to visit Ananuri Fortress, ski at Gudauri, and see the beautiful Gergeti Trinity Church beneath Mount Kazbek. See page 90

❽ **Kakheti** After all that history and hiking, toast the end of your trip with a relaxing glass of red or white in Georgia's wine region. See page 140

ARMENIA THROUGH THE AGES

Step back through the relics of Armenia's rich and varied history on this two-week excursion round the country's highlights.

❶ **Yerevan** Kick off in the capital with a visit to the History Museum to give context to your trip, then check out the Soviet-era Cascades. Then head to Garni Temple. See page 167

❷ **Gyumri** Take a train to Armenia's second city, a laid-back place that maintains the air of an imperial Russian town. See page 215

❸ **Debed Canyon** Head east to Vanadzor and check out the Debed Canyon, where medieval monasteries sit side-by-side with the remnants of Soviet industry. See page 209

❹ **Amberd Fortress** Take the road south past Mount Aragats, pausing to visit hisory-rich Amberd castle. See page 189

❺ **Khor Virap** Hugely significant to Armenian history, this little monastery beneath Mount Ararat is where the country's Christian tradition started in AD 301. See page 226

❻ **Zorats Karer** Journey southeast to this windswept spot and its mysterious stone circle. While you're here, check out the fantastic petroglyphs of Lake Ughtasar. See page 235

❼ **Khndzoresk** Just east of Goris town lies the cave village of Khndzoresk. See page 239

❽ **Yerevan** Return to the capital and visit the ancient Erebuni fortress, before exploring Hovhannavank's medieval church architecture. See page 168

Sustainable travel

Despite a Soviet legacy of industry, the Caucasus countries are developing plenty of options for travellers wishing to minimize their footprint and travel more sustainably.

During the twentieth century, Georgia, Armenia and Azerbaijan were centres for industry under the USSR, and the scars of irresponsible development can still be clearly seen in across the region. There remain environmental concerns over industrial activity in all three countries, particularly Azerbaijan, which remains a major producer of oil, the driving force of its economic boom. Despite this, awareness of sustainable and ethical travel is on the rise and there are some great options to lessen your impact when you visit.

CHOOSE LOCALLY-OWNED ACCOMMODATION

You can try to ensure the money you spend benefits communities by staying in locally-owned guesthouses and hotels rather than international chains. This not only assists the local economy, but gives you a more authentic, memorable experience, with even the smallest villages offering welcoming guesthouses where you can eat and sleep in the family home. Smaller guesthouses tend to offer local produce for breakfast and dinner, which is both more sustainable and delicious.

CARRY A REFILLABLE WATER BOTTLE

Tap water is safe to drink in most places across the Caucasus, especially the larger towns and cities. It's worth exercising more caution in rural areas. Water fountains are common on city streets in Armenia (where they're known as pulpulaks, often boasting very elegant designs) and to a lesser extent in Georgia. Also note that it's not uncommon for complimentary bottled water to be presented as standard in restaurants and hotels: you can save on plastics by not using it. Instead, take a water container with you on your trip and refill at fountains or from the taps in your accommodation.

USE PUBLIC TRANSPORT

The public transport network in the Caucasus is reasonably well developed, particularly if you're travelling between the larger towns and cities. All three countries have a train network and although this rarely serves smaller, offbeat locations, you can easily nip by train between many of the top sights: Georgia's route from Tbilisi all the way to Batumi is particularly useful. Try to avoid local flights where possible, although with Azerbaijan's land borders closed at time of writing, planes are currently the only way to enter the country. Road travel between towns and cities is usually by marshrutka, which offers frequent and well-connected public transport, but do tend to be older minivans and quite pollution-heavy.

HEAD OFF-THE-BEATEN-TRACK

Although there are very few spots in the Caucasus that could be described as overtouristed, there are several destinations that tend to make it onto every traveller's itinerary. When planning yours, consider heading to less visited areas: you could explore the Tusheti region instead of the ever-popular Stepantsminda, for example, or seek out empty monasteries in the towns and villages south of Mt Aragats in Armenia. You'll be able to put money into the local economy by staying in guesthouses and eating in restaurants in areas that often don't see the tourist dollar.

GET INVOLVED

There are numerous opportunities for volunteering while in the Caucasus, allowing you to contribute to local development programmes. One of the best publicised is the Transcaucasian Trail, an initiative to create a hiking route through all three Caucasian republics and at the same time promote conservation- and nature-based tourism. There are annual calls for volunteers to help build the trail: check out the website (w transcaucasiantrail.org/en/volunteer) to sign up. You can also find plenty of local opportunities on w workaway.info, which offers free accommodation to volunteers in return for various types of work, ranging from teaching English to harvesting grapes, and everything in between.

BUY LOCALLY MADE PRODUCE

A great way to support the local economy is by purchasing locally made souvenirs.

WATER FOR HIKING

There are some particularly good options in Azerbaijan: visit Sheki or Basgal, for example, to pick up beautiful silk scarves, or head up to the mountain village of Lahıc to browse its outstanding copperwork. In Georgia and Armenia, meanwhile, locally produced wines make excellent, if short-term, souvenirs. Farmers often sell their produce by the roadside as well, so consider stopping to buy fruit for a delicious snack while travelling.

CASCADE COMPLEX IN YEREVAN

Basics

Getting there

All three Caucasian countries have one major airport (Tbilisi International Airport in Georgia, Yerevan's Zvartnots International Airport in Armenia, and Baku's Heydar Aliyev International Airport in Azerbaijan) and a couple of smaller airports, of which you're most likely to find Georgia's Kutaisi David the Builder Airport useful thanks to its budget connections to some European hubs.

The region is particularly well-served with flights from former Soviet countries, as well as regional destinations. There are few direct flights to anywhere further afield than western Europe. Each country has its own airline – Georgian Airways, Azerbaijan Airlines, and Armenia's Fly Arna – which offer a variety of routes, but you'll probably find it cheaper to take a connecting flight. There's little variation in cost year-round, and taking a flight here is likely to be the single most expensive outlay you'll make on your trip to the Caucasus.

Flights from the UK and Ireland

Pre-Covid, the cheapest option for a direct flight to the Caucasus was Wizz Air's (W wizzair.com/en-gb#) route from **London-Luton** to Kutaisi, but at time of writing, there was no indication of when or if this route might reopen. Similarly, Georgian Airways' flight connecting **London-Gatwick** and Tbilisi is no longer running. This means that the fairly pricey twice-weekly Azerbaijan Airlines (W azal.az/en) flight from **London-Heathrow** to Baku is currently the only direct flight from the UK into the Caucasus. The flight takes about five hours.

If you're not heading to Azerbaijan, the best connections are those offered by Turkish Airlines (W turkishairlines.com) and Pegasus (W flypgs.com/en), which between them serve all three major Caucasian airports, as well as Kutaisi. With a transfer at Istanbul or Antalya, UK travellers can reach the Caucasus in less than eight hours. This option often works out very cheaply: if you're on a budget, it's a much better choice than the direct flight with Azerbaijan Airlines.

The budget airline Wizz Air (W wizzair.com/en-gb#) flies into the region from various European destinations (Milan, Rome and Vienna to Yerevan, Budapest and Rome to Baku, and a whole host of places including Berlin, Budapest, Prague and Warsaw to Kutaisi) so it's possible to put together a connecting flight from the UK.

There are no direct flights from Ireland into the Caucasus. You could use the Turkish Airlines option from Dublin to Istanbul or Antalya, but if you're looking to keep things cheap, your best bet is to take a Ryanair (W ryanair.com/gb/en) flight from Dublin to Berlin or Budapest, and connect to a Wizz Air flight from there.

Flights from the US and Canada

There are currently no direct flights between the US or Canada and the Caucasus region., so your best bet for Tbilisi and Baku will be to fly with Turkish Airlines (W turkishairlines.com) to Istanbul and take a connecting flight. From **New York JFK** to Tbilisi, this will take about 15 hours, or from **New York JFK** to Baku it'll take somewhere between 13 and 20 hours. Turkish Airlines don't yet fly to Yerevan, though with the political rapprochement between Turkey and Armenia coming along apace, it's possible a route may open in the near future. In the meantime, though, your best option is the Brussels Airlines (W brusselsairlines.com) route from **New York JFK connecting in Brussels**, or the minutely cheaper Lufthansa (W lufthansa.com) route via **Frankfurt**. Either of these options will take between 16 and 20 hours.

Flights from Australia, New Zealand and South Africa

Not easy and not cheap. Emirates (W emirates.com) and Qatar Airways (W qatarairways.com) are probably the best option from Australia, offering return flights from **Sydney and Melbourne** to all three capital cities via Dubai, taking approximately 20 hours.

A BETTER KIND OF TRAVEL

At Rough Guides we are passionately committed to travel. We believe it helps us understand the world we live in and the people we share it with – and of course tourism is vital to many developing economies. But the scale of modern tourism has also damaged some places irreparably, and climate change is accelerated by most forms of transport, especially flying. We encourage all our authors to consider the carbon footprint of the journeys they make in the course of researching our guides.

From New Zealand, the Emirates option (Ⓦemirates. com) can get you from **Auckland** to Yerevan or Baku via Dubai, taking 22 hours. You can use the same Emirates route for Tbilisi, but the Qatar Airways (Ⓦqatarairways.com) flight from Auckland via Doha is a little cheaper, though thanks to an inconveniently long layover, the total time comes out at 29 hours, making it something of an endurance test.

Emirates (Ⓦemirates.com) and Qatar Airways (Ⓦqatarairways.com) are also the best choices from South Africa, with routes from **Cape Town** to Tbilisi, Yerevan or Baku via Dubai or Doha tending to take between 12 and 17 hours. Turkish Airlines (Ⓦturkishairlines.com) via Istanbul are a decent backup, but tend to take longer owing to extended layover times. Emirates, Qatar Airways and Turkish Airlines also operate out of **Johannesburg OR Tambo**, from which flights to the Caucasus tend to be slightly quicker and cheaper.

Trains

At time of writing, there were no active railway lines running into the Caucasus. Pre-pandemic, the only line was the connection from the north, via Russia's Dagestan region, into Azerbaijan along the Caspian coast, but with Azerbaijan's land borders currently closed, this service is not operating. Given travel in Russia is not advised due to the war in Ukraine – and the fact that even before the war, the UK FCDO advised against all travel to Dagestan – it seems unlikely that you'll make use of this route even if it resumes. If it does, though, it'll probably be a weekly service that takes two days, four hours to travel from Moscow to Baku.

The much-vaunted rail line linking Kars in Turkey to Tbilisi, and thus enabling a **sleeper service** all the way from Istanbul to Baku, was due to open in 2020, but as of early 2024 this service still has not materialised. There have also been noises made about the possibility of connecting Azerbaijan's rail network in the south to the Iranian one, but no serious effort appears to have been made in this direction.

Buses

If you're travelling overland, it's far more likely you'll enter the region via bus, and the likeliest route in is from **Turkey into Georgia**. There are two principal borders: at Sarpi, on the Black Sea, and at Türkgözü near Akhaltsikhe. Twice-daily buses operated by Metro Turizm (Ⓦmetroturizm.com.tr/en) ply the route from Trabzon in Turkey across the Sarpi border to Batumi, taking four hours. Tickets can be booked

---

BORDER CROSSINGS

You're far less likely to use other land borders into the region, which include the following. Note that at present, all borders entering Azerbaijan are closed, though you may be able to leave Azerbaijan overland.

- **Russia to Georgia**. The Kazbegi border crossing between Vladikavkaz and Stepantsminda is open to travellers. Buses and shared taxis leave from Vladikavkaz's bus station when full.
- **Russia to Azerbaijan**. The road from Dagestan into Azerbaijan crosses the border at Samur. You may be able to find a marshrutka heading across the border, otherwise it'll need to be a taxi, shared or otherwise.
- **Iran to Azerbaijan**. The Iranian town of Astara and the Azerbaijani town of the same name are separated by an easy to cross border. Buses heading between Tehran and Baku use this route, and if there are no direct buses, then shared taxis from Astara to Baku are easy to come by.
- **Iran to Armenia**. The border between Iran and Armenia is very small, but includes a crossing point at Norduz to Agarak. There are no scheduled buses, but you can cross on foot and easily pick up a taxi on the Armenian side to take you on to Kapan, Goris or Yerevan.
- **Iran to Nakhchivan**. Regular local buses crosses the Jolfa–Julfa border and although tourists are not commonly seen here, as long as your Azerbaijani visa is in order, you should have no problem crossing.
- **Turkey to Nakhchivan**. A tiny sliver of land connects Turkey and Nakhchivan, with a surprisingly regular bus service provided by a company named Igdir. Azerbaijan's border guards are polite and friendly but will want to check your passport and visa extensively. This border was once notorious for demanding bribes from travellers, but seems to have cleaned up its act considerably in recent times.

online, and in high season, you should do so as early as possible as this route does fill up.

In summer, there is a twice weekly coach service run by VIPTurizm that travels from Kars in Turkey to Tbilisi, taking eight to nine hours on a **scenic route**. Out of season, there are no regular buses crossing the Türkgözü border. The closest you'll get is the Turkish village of Posof, 15km southwest, which you can reach by minibus in a couple of hours from Kars. From Posof, you can take a taxi to the border, cross into Georgia, and then find a taxi to the nearest town of Akhaltsikhe.

Ferries

You can enter the Caucasus by sea along a couple of routes: on the Black Sea, UKR Ferry (ⓦukrferry.com/eng) runs a slower service between Constanta in Romania and Poti in Georgia, while on the Caspian Sea, ferries cross to Baku from Aktau in Kazakhstan and Ashgabat in Turkmenistan, but trying to arrange this can be a logistical nightmare: try online at ⓦasco.az/en or speak to the Aktau ferry office on ☏+7 777 4904663, but don't get your hopes up. Note that entering Azerbaijan by sea was not an option at time of writing, but once the land borders reopen, the ferry route should also be possible again.

Visas and entry requirements

Visa requirements for the three Caucasian nations are fairly straightforward. Many nationalities do not need visas at all for Georgia and Armenia, and although Azerbaijan has a slightly stricter regime, you're unlikely to have any problems with the **e-visa** system.

Georgia

Nationals of the UK, Ireland, EU countries, US, Canada, Australia, New Zealand and South Africa do not need a visa to visit Georgia. The country's visa require-ments can be found at ⓦgeoconsul.gov.ge/en/entering-georgia. **Passport stamps** entitle visitors to remain in Georgia for up to one year. Extensions are not possible. Your passport needs to be valid for the entire time you'll be staying in Georgia.

Georgia embassies and consulates

Armenia 2/10 General Babayan St, Yerevan, ☏+374 10 200742, ✉yerevan.emb@mfa.gov.ge
Australia 28 Kareelah Vista, O'Malley, Canberra, ☏+61 2 6162 0126, ✉canberra.emb@mfa.gov.ge
Azerbaijan 13–15 Yaşar Hüseynov küç, Baku, t+994 12 4974560, ✉bakucon@mfa.gov.ge
Canada 340 Albert St, Suite 940, Ottawa, ☏+1 613 421 0460, ✉ottawa.cons@mfa.gov.ge
Ireland 17 Morehampton Rd, Donnybrook, Dublin, ☏+353 1905 9191, ✉dublin.emb@mfa.gov.ge
South Africa 270 Carina St, Waterkloof Ridge, Pretoria, ☏+27 12 346 1831, ✉pretoria.emb@mfa.gov.ge
UK 20 St George's Sq, London, ☏+ 44 207 348 1942, ✉london.con@mfa.gov.ge
USA 1824 R St NW, Washington ☏+1 202 387 2390, ✉embgeo.usa@mfa.gov.ge

Armenia

Nationals of the UK, Ireland, EU countries, US, Australia and New Zealand do not need a **visa** to visit Armenia. Nationals of Canada and South Africa need a visa, which can be obtained on arrival or online using the e-visa system at ⓦevisa.mfa.am. You can check Armenia's current visa regime at ⓦmfa.am/en/visa. Passport stamps are issued entitling visitors to a stay of 120 days, and it's possible to extend this for a further 60 days by contacting the Ministry of Foreign Affairs (3 Vazgen Sargsyan St, Yerevan, ☏+374 60 620516, ✉visa@mfa.am).

Armenia embassies and consulates

Canada 7 Delaware Ave, Ottawa, ☏+1 613 234 3710, ⓦcanada.mfa.am/en
Georgia 4 Gia Tetelashvili St, Tbilisi, ☏+995 322 951723, ⓦgeorgia.mfa.am/en
UK 25A Cheniston Gardens, Kensington, London, ☏+44 207 938 5435, ⓦuk.mfa.am/en
USA 2225 R St NW, Washington, ☏+1 202 319 1976, ⓦusa.mfa.am/en

Azerbaijan

Nationals of the UK, Ireland, US, Canada, Australia, New Zealand and South Africa need a **visa** to visit Azerbaijan. Azerbaijan's visa policy can be found on the Ministry of Foreign Affairs website at ⓦmfa.gov.az/en/category/visa. The process for obtaining a visa is easy, thanks to the user-friendly e-visa system. You'll need to complete the online form at ⓦevisa.gov.az/en and pay US$25 and within three days you'll receive the visa via email, which you should print out and bring with you. The visa is valid for 30 days from date of entry and cannot be extended. On arrival, your passport will be checked, and if there is any evidence you visited **Nagorno-Karabakh** while it was under Armenian control, you may be permanently denied entry to Azerbaijan.

If you're staying in Azerbaijan for more than 15 days you'll need your passport to be registered with the State Migration Service. Most hotels or hostels will do this for you as a matter of course, but guesthouses probably won't. There's allegedly an online service if you need to do it yourself, but it never seems to work, so it's best to go in person. You can check where the nearest Migration Police outlet is at ⓦ migration.gov. az/en. Make sure you get proof of registration or you may be fined when leaving the country.

Azerbaijan embassies and consulates

Australia 5 Mialli Pl, O'Malley, Canberra, ☏ +61 2 6290 5600, ⓔ canberra_mission@mfa.gov.az
Canada 275 Slater St, Suite 1203, Ottawa, ☏ +1 613 288 0497, ⓦ ottawa.mfa.gov.az/en
Georgia 4 Vakhtang Gorgasali St, Tbilisi, ☏ +995 322 242220, ⓦ tbilisi.mfa.gov.az/en
South Africa 302 Albert St, Waterkloof, Pretoria, ☏ +27 12 346 1018, ⓦ pretoria.mfa.gov.az/en
UK 4, Kensington Court, London, ☏ +44 207 938 3412, ⓦ london.mfa.gov.az/en
USA 2741 34th St NW, Washington, ☏ +1 202 337 3500, ⓦ washington.mfa.gov.az/en

Nagorno-Karabakh

Following Azerbaijan's recovery of the territory of Nagorno-Karabakh, entry from the Armenian border is no longer possible, and the former visa process is no longer in operation. The Azerbaijani authorities occasionally run propaganda-heavy tours to the region, but otherwise travel to Nagorno-Karabakh is not currently possible. Remember that if your passport contains a Nagorno-Karabakh visa dating from the period of Armenian control, you are almost guaranteed to be **denied entry** to Azerbaijan.

Arrival

You're most likely to arrive in the region by plane and will find that the airports are well-connected to their respective cities. If you enter by bus or train, you'll almost certainly find yourself deposited in the centre of town.

By plane

Each of the main airports in the region has **good bus connections** into the capital city. In Tbilisi, it's bus number 337, which runs 24/7 every 20 minutes or so. In Yerevan, the airport bus runs between 7.30am and 10.30pm. Baku's bus is the H1, which runs every half hour in the day and every hour at night. In all three cases, it's easy and affordable to pick up taxis into the city from the airport.

By bus

If you're arriving overland, chances are you're coming into Batumi from Turkey. The bus station in Batumi is just to the southeast of the centre, and a taxi from there to your hotel should be easy to find. Alternatively, you may be bypassing Batumi and heading all the way to Tbilisi, and it's also technically possible to get a bus to Tbilisi from Vladikavkaz in Russia. If so, Tbilisi's main bus station is right in the centre of town and is on the metro line.

Azerbaijan's land borders are closed at time of writing, but when they reopen, it'll likely be possible to catch a bus from Iran or Russia's Dagestan region. If you arrive by either of these routes, you'll find yourself at Baku's big bus station, which is inconveniently a fair way out of the city centre. Fortunately, it's on the metro line, so you can get into the town centre with relative ease.

By train

With Azerbaijan's land borders closed and travel in Russia currently not advised, arrival overland by train is unlikely. If the situation changes, you may be able to reach Baku through Russia. Happily, Baku's main train station is in the centre of town, and it has a handy metro station to connect you to the rest of the city.

Getting around

Public transport in the Caucasus is cheap but can feel a little chaotic. While there are a couple of regional flights available, as well as a limited rail network, the main method of travel is by road. The system inherited from the Soviet era is the marshrutka, or minivan, which (sometimes) ostensibly runs to a timetable but more often than not simply departs when it's full. You'll rarely find yourself stranded – one of the joys of the Caucasus is that you can almost always find someone willing to take you where you want to go.

For Armenia, there's a useful (but unofficial) transport website at ⓦ t-armenia.com/en, which seeks to give accurate and up-to-date information about transport routes around Armenia. It doesn't cover everywhere, but it's an undeniably handy resource. In Georgia,

georgia.travel/regional-transport serves a similar purpose, though it isn't comprehensive.

By bus

The most common and cheapest mode of transport in all three countries is the bus. This rarely means a coach, though there are a few routes served by comfortable modern buses. It's more likely to be a **marshrutka**, a minivan designed to carry about 10 passengers but on some journeys may cram in several more.

Georgia's marshrutka system is probably the easiest to get your head around. There's usually a schedule to which they at least vaguely adhere, and tourist information centres are able to supply you with up-to-date timetables. Azerbaijan and Armenia stray a little further into the realms of organised chaos, but asking around at the bus station will usually get you the information you need. If nothing else, marshrutkas are inexpensive: the five- to six-hour journey between Tbilisi and Yerevan, for example, costs about US$13, while domestic services are even cheaper.

By taxi

If there's no marshrutka, you may be able to pick up a shared taxi, which tend to hover around bus stations collecting customers who want to make the journey a little faster and in a little more comfort, for only a little more money. It's also eminently affordable to take a taxi for a half- or full-day private hire if there's a clutch of specific sights you want to see that would be difficult or time-consuming on public transport: this is easy enough to do in any town by flagging down a taxi, but you could also use the **GoTrip** service (gotrip.ge/en), a handy website that allows you to book a driver and arrange a price in advance. GoTrip covers Georgia extensively and also serves plenty of Armenian destinations.

Picking up taxis for short hops within cities is easy and **inexpensive**, and in most cases you won't be paying more than the equivalent of US$5 for any trip. The exception to this is by and large to airports.

The app-based taxi service Uber does not operate in Georgia or Armenia, though it is available in Azerbaijan. Similar services are provided by Bolt and Yandex in Georgia and Azerbaijan, while in Armenia Yandex is the best choice. Coverage is not extensive outside the major cities.

By car

Hiring a car to drive yourself around the region is not particularly cheap, but it is by far the best way to ensure that you'll be able to take in everything you want to see. Be warned that the driving style of other road users can be **erratic**, though rarely aggressive, and road surfacing quality isn't all it could be: even on what seems like a perfect smooth tarmac surface, be prepared for sudden pot holes. The most confusing aspect of driving here is the approach to roundabouts. Technically, traffic joining the roundabout has the right of way, but this doesn't always seem to apply, and there's no apparent rhyme or reason to when it does.

Some roads in the region are only suitable for 4WDs, and at least one – the route from Telavi into Tusheti in Georgia – is considered among the world's most dangerous, so make sure you look up your route before setting off. Road quality to the places mentioned in this guide is noted. Georgian hire car companies will often specify places that it's not permitted to drive to: these are likely to include Tusheti, Khevsureti, Abkhazia and South Ossetia.

Note that technically UK drivers need a 1968 International Driving Permit to drive in the Caucasus. In practice, you're very unlikely to be asked to show this, but it's better to have one just in case you do need it. In the UK, you can easily get an International Driving Permit at the Post Office for a minimal fee, provided you have a driving license and are over 18 years old. In the US, you may need to allow a bit longer if applying via mail (the issuing authorities are either the American Automobile Association or the American Automobile Touring Alliance) but the process should still be straightforward.

Depending on the terms of your rental agreement, you may be able to take the car **across borders**, often subject to a surcharge. Don't try to take an Armenian car into Azerbaijan, or vice versa, nor should you attempt entry to Abkhazia or South Ossetia in a Georgian car.

The cost of **petrol** is low. Speed limits are usually well-signposted, but if not, as a general rule they are 60 km/h in towns, 90 km/h outside towns, and 110 km/h on highways. Fines for speeding can be high, especially in Azerbaijan. If an oncoming car flashes its headlights at you, it's most probably to alert you to police on the road ahead.

If you break down, call your hire car company, and if you're involved in an accident, you'll need to speak to the police (112 in Georgia, 102 in Armenia and Azerbaijan).

CAR RENTAL AGENCIES

International car rental agencies, including Hertz (hertz.com), Europcar (europcar.com) and Sixt (sixt.com) offer car hire across the region, from most major cities and airports.

By train

The Caucasian rail network isn't exactly extensive, but it can get you around to a **limited** extent. The west of Georgia is relatively well served, with routes from Tbilisi to Kutaisi, Batumi and Gori, but there's not much on offer in the north and east, other than the international route to Baku. You can browse the Georgian train timetable and book online at Ⓦ railway.ge/en. Prices are very reasonable.

Azerbaijan has a well-developed network of trains, with frequent and reliable services. Baku is the hub, with train routes heading out to Ganja, Lankaran, Astara, Sheki (though note that Sheki's train station is some 20km south of town), and north into Russia. Prices are generally fairly low. Azerbaijan's rail website is found at Ⓦ ticket.ady.az, but the formerly excellent English language option has been removed in an apparent effort to make things difficult.

Armenia's rail network is less extensive, not least because the train line to Baku was blown up in the 1990s during the Nagorno-Karabakh War. The only line now runs between Yerevan and Tbilisi, calling at Gyumri and Vanadzor – among other, smaller, destinations – en route. Prices are very affordable. You can look at the timetable and book tickets at Ⓦ railway.am.

By bike

The stunning scenery of the Caucasus makes this region a lovely one to bike, but it's certainly not flat, so be prepared for aching leg muscles. The usual caveats that apply to cycling anywhere apply: beware of other road users, who may not be as considerate as you'd like, and note that you're likely to attract the unwelcome attention of **dogs**, who often regard a bike as an unholy apparition that needs to be furiously pursued.

By plane

While you can fly between Tbilisi and Yerevan, or Tbilisi and Baku, it's not generally worth the effort and cost.

Distances are short enough that once you've factored in travel to the airport, check-in, etc, you're not saving much time. The one flight you will need, though, if you're thoroughly exploring the region, is from Baku to Nakhchivan. Nakhchivan is cut off from the rest of Azerbaijan by a corridor of Armenia and thus cannot easily be accessed overland. Fortunately, Azerbaijan Airlines run a frequent and cheap service (up to five flights a day) from Baku to Nakhchivan. This route does sell out, so you generally can't go on a whim – make sure you book at least a week in advance.

Accommodation

Accommodation across the region is generally good-value: a mid-range en-suite hotel room in the capital cities can go for the equivalent of about £35/US$45, and it's often even cheaper in the smaller towns.

The cheapest accommodation can be found in **hostels**, which are most common in Georgia, though there's a burgeoning scene in Armenia and a more nascent one in Azerbaijan. The next step up is the **guesthouse**, more prevalent outside the capital cities and often the best style of accommodation available due to the frequently excellent, friendly and attentive hosting. Most expensive are **hotels**, ranging from mid-range basics through lovely boutique options, all the way to the top-class internationals.

Air conditioning comes as standard in hotels but not necessarily in guesthouses. Wi-fi is always available, though signals are frequently a bit patchy in smaller places. You're unlikely to find **baby cots** anywhere except the top-end hotels. Breakfast is usually included in hotels but extra at guesthouses, and it tends to be worth paying for it as it commonly involves delicious homemade fare.

Even during peak season it would be surprising if you couldn't secure a room, as there are a great many options available. The most comprehensive range of accommodation to be found online is at Ⓦ booking.com, and you may also find Ⓦ agoda.com useful, particularly for Azerbaijan. Airbnb (Ⓦ airbnb.com) does operate in the region, but more often than not it's used as another online booking engine for guesthouses and small hotels that are also to be found on other hotel booking sites.

There's not a lot of seasonal variation, with prices tending to remain relatively **static year-round**. The price you see on booking websites includes tax, so that's the price you pay, unless you have extras such as breakfast.

ADDRESSES

Addresses in the Caucasus generally work much the way you'd expect them to – a number, street, town – but in smaller places, you'll often find that there are no street names or numbers at all. In this case, you may need to ask around, though online mapping apps are usually quite accurate.

Hotels

Hotels in the region range from relatively cheap to quite expensive. Note that, especially in Baku's Old Town, price isn't necessarily an indicator of quality.

The cheapies are basic, offering nondescript, usually en-suite rooms with air con, decent wi-fi, a TV and a desk. They're generally not bad, but they can be unexciting. This is particularly the case in the capital cities, where it pays to do your research if you're looking for somewhere more personal or boutique.

Mid-range hotels are often more interesting. There's a crop of places springing up which have made an effort with decoration and style, and the staff are often friendly and willing to help with your travel plans. You can usually book decent value tours through these hotels. Rooms are en suite, the beds are generally very comfortable, and wi-fi is available.

The top-end options, meanwhile, cater for the international business traveller and tend to involve the use of a gym, sauna, swimming pool, and other similar services. Rooms are always extremely comfortable, but often fall into the trap of being plain and unexciting. There's usually a very stylish bar on site, and frequently a restaurant too.

Breakfasts are usually included at both cheap and mid-range hotels and tend to be buffets, varying from basic to extensive. The high-end hotels, on the other hand, are likely to charge extra for breakfast, sometimes as much as 10 percent of the room cost, though it must be said that there's usually a huge spread on offer.

Guesthouses

Frequently the best accommodation in the Caucasus, stays in a guesthouse range from taking a spare room in a family home to slicker, more B&B-like operations. Whatever end of the scale your guesthouse is at, it will offer a fascinating look at the inside of local homes, and the hosts are usually the friendliest people you'll ever meet. Don't expect a lot of English to be spoken in these places, but you can count on being treated like an honoured guest.

Guesthouses, which are generally pretty **cheap**, are more prevalent in smaller towns and villages, having largely been edged out of the market in the capital cities by hotels. . Bathrooms may be en suite or shared. Breakfast is usually extra and tends to involve a veritable spread of home-made bread, honey, jam, yoghurt, and plenty of other delicious things. Guesthouse hosts will also sometimes offer dinner, which is a great opportunity to enjoy Caucasian home cooking, though note you'll not necessarily get a choice in what is served up.

Hostels

If you're doing the Caucasus on a **budget**, hostels are your best choice: it's possible to take a dorm bed for no more than £2/US$2.60. The Caucasian hostelling scene can be found primarily in Georgia. Tbilisi and Batumi both have a number of comparatively vibrant hostels, and the idea has begun to take root in Yerevan too, which has seen some new and funky places spring up in recent years. In Baku, hostels aimed at backpackers are a relatively new concept, and while there are several hostels in town, a lot of them are quite grotty.

TOP FIVE HOTELS

Rooms Hotel, Stepantsminda See page 94. A top-end hotel with beautiful furnishings, offering fantastic views from the rooms across the valley to the Caucasus mountains.

Karavansarai, Sheki See page 302. Live like a Silk Road trader in this genuine eighteenth-century caravanserai, now operating as a one-of-a-kind hotel.

Alexander, Yerevan See page 171. One of the swankiest hotels in the Caucasus, the Alexander in central Yerevan boasts gorgeous rooms, excellent facilities, and a great rooftop restaurant.

Shah Palace Hotel, Baku See page 263. An evocative place in the city of Baku's Old Town, the Shah Palace seeks to bring a touch of oriental luxury to your stay.

Alexandrapol, Gyumri See page 218. Thoroughly over-the-top, the Alexandrapol is a ridiculous shrine to glitz and shine which has to be seen to be believed.

TOP FIVE GUESTHOUSES

Hestia, Gori See page 88. An incredibly friendly and welcoming place with stylish décor, and home-made wine freely available in the evenings.

Old House Guesthouse, Sheki See page 303. Step back in time a couple of hundred years with a stay in this beautiful rambling Azeri guesthouse, which retains many fantastic period features.

Artsiv Guesthouse, Dilijan See page 202. The rooms are good, but it's the magnificent breakfast that makes Artsiv one of the best places to stay in Armenia.

Guest House Eko and Gia, Sighnaghi See page 151. Right in the centre of Sighnaghi, the friendly Eko and Gia have a lovely guesthouse with a beautiful, converted wine cellar.

Green Flower, Kutaisi See page 115. The lovely Green Flower is enormously welcoming and sitting out on the terrace with a glass of the home-made wine makes for a perfect evening.

Camping

Wild camping is permissible in most areas of the Caucasus, and if you're doing multi-day treks in the mountains then in most cases it's your only option. If you're camping but prefer to have bathroom facilities and other niceties, most guesthouses with gardens will be happy to let you camp for a reduced charge.

Food and drink

In the days of the Soviet Union, Georgia was renowned as having the best food in the entire USSR. Political entities may have changed but the quality of food hasn't, meaning visiting Georgia is still a culinary treat. Armenia and Azerbaijan aren't far behind, so in all three countries eating out can be one of the greatest pleasures of your trip.

The three capital cities are generally the best places to eat, with great local options and a wide range of international cuisines. Azerbaijan is a popular destination for Indian holidaymakers, which means that Baku has a great selection of restaurants offering food from the subcontinent.

Smaller towns, naturally enough, tend to have fewer eateries, but there's almost always somewhere that can be recommended. You should also strongly consider eating in your guesthouse if the option is there, as this will give you the chance of experiencing genuine home-cooked food and may well prove to be the best meals you have on your trip.

Eating places usually open about 9am and remain open until late. There is **no set time** at which people tend to eat. The main meal of the day is in the evening, but whether you interpret that as 6pm or 9pm is up to you.

Breakfast/lunch

If you're in a guesthouse you're likely to get a breakfast of freshly baked bread, honey, jam, yoghurt, cheese and eggs, along with generous salad sides of olives, cucumber and tomato, and maybe a couple of frankfurter sausages. It's often fantastic and a great way to set yourself up for the day. In hotels, you'll probably get the same sort of thing, though it'll be presented as a buffet so you can pick and choose for yourself.

Even if **breakfast** is included in the price of your accommodation, you may choose to go elsewhere. In larger towns you'll find **cafés** that do breakfast options – omelettes are pretty popular – but do bear in mind that they often don't open till 9am, so if you're hoping for an early start then taking your accommodation's breakfast is the better option. Also note that smaller towns are unlikely to offer much in the way of alternatives to the breakfast offered by your hotel or guesthouse.

Lunch can be found in cafés, where at the very least you ought to be able to get a *khachapuri*, a salad, soup or pizza. There are often plenty of other options too, such as Georgia's *khinkali* dumplings (traditionally stuffed with minced meat, but cheese or potatoes are often found too), the Armenian and Azerbaijani *lahmacun* (flatbread topped with mincemeat) or the

EATING OUT PRICE GUIDE

Two course meal for one person, including a glass of wine.

$\overline{\underline{\$\$\$\$}}$ = over US$35
$\overline{\underline{\$\$\$}}$ = US$25-35
$\overline{\underline{\$\$}}$ = US$5-25
$\overline{\underline{\$}}$ = under US$5

KHACHAPURI

Available in cafés and restaurants all over Georgia – and, to a lesser extent, in Armenia and Azerbaijan – *khachapuri* (cheese pies) have to be one of the best lunch options in the Caucasus. These dough and cheese concoctions – considered Georgia's national dish – are utterly sublime and come in several varieties.

Imeretian The entry level option, the Imeretian *khachapuri* is a round pastry containing cheese in the centre.

Megrelian The Megrelian takes things up a notch by being essentially the same as an Imeretian, but with a layer of melted cheese on top as well.

Achma An Abkhazian speciality, the achma is a crispier version of *khachapuri* with multiple layers of cheese.

Adjaran For serious *khachapuri* lovers, the Adjaran is the ultimate treat. It's boat-shaped with melted cheese on top accompanied by a runny egg and a generous dollop of melted butter. It's ridiculous, but amazing.

Caucasus-wide *dolma* (leaves stuffed with rice and meat or vegetables).

Dinner

All three capitals have a wealth of **restaurants** to choose from. In Tbilisi, in particular, the number of options can be quite overwhelming. Local cuisines are well represented, as are international options. Even in the more upmarket restaurants, you won't be spending a fortune: meals are pleasingly **affordable**.

The standard evening meal is barbecued meat, which is found all over the Caucasus under a number of names: *mtsvadi* in Georgia, *khoravats* in Armenia and *shashlik* in Azerbaijan. In Georgia and Armenia, it's most commonly pork, while in Azerbaijan you're more likely to find chicken or mutton. **Barbecues** are found in restaurants in cities, towns and villages, and as you travel the countryside you're likely to see roadside barbecue stalls too. You'll need to order sides separately – fried potatoes and salad tend to make a good accompaniment.

Other common dishes include the Georgian stews of *chakapuli* (lamb or beef and plum) and *chakhokhbili* (chicken and tomato), Armenian *dzhash* (another stew, containing meat, vegetables and spices, served with rice) and Azerbaijan's *plov* (rice, meat and chopped vegetables or herbs). Georgia's *chizhi-bizhi* dish – tomatoes baked with eggs and herbs, sometimes topped with cheese – is also not to be missed.

REGIONAL SPECIALITIES

You'll find that there's a huge range in the local cuisines, not just between the countries but within them as well. Here's a couple of the options you shouldn't miss if you're in the relevant region.

Kubdari Found in Georgia's Svaneti region, *kubdari* is similar to a *khachapuri*, but contains meat and spices instead of cheese.

Lavangi A speciality of southern Azerbaijan – particularly Lankaran – *lavangi* is a dish of baked chicken or fish stuffed with a mixture of walnuts, onions, raisins and pomegranate syrup, served with pilaf rice.

Lobio Found all over Georgia, but particularly renowned in Mtskheta, *lobio* is a dish of red kidney beans mashed with onions, garlic, black pepper, and plenty of herbs and spices, and served in a clay pot.

Piti A northern Azerbaijani dish, perhaps at its best in Sheki, *piti* is a stew/soup of mutton which is served with bread, onions and sumac, as well as a piece of lamb fat. To eat it, you first pour the broth over the bread and eat this mixture, then add more bread and sumac to the leftover meat and the lamb fat, and crush it all together.

Zhingyalov hats A Nagorno-Karabakh speciality but found across Armenia, these creations are flatbreads stuffed with greens (such as spinach, lettuce and herbs) and then fried. They're shaped like hats, hence the name.

Desserts

Azerbaijanis have a reputation for having a **sweet tooth**: the town of Sheki is famous for its production of *halva*, a type of bakhlava made of hazelnuts, cardamom and plenty of sugar. In Georgia and Armenia, you'll come across *churchkhela*, a candle-shaped treat made from dried grape juice, flour and walnuts. In all three republics, it's not uncommon to see roadside stalls selling dried fruit, rolled out and flattened into enormous thin colourful circles. If you're looking for something a little more familiar, ice cream parlours are very popular, especially in Georgia.

Drinks

Tap water in Georgia and Armenia is generally **safe** to drink, but other than in Baku, it's best avoided in Azerbaijan. In Armenia there are drinking fountains on the streets of most major cities, which are extremely welcome in the hot summers. Bottled water is readily available, and in Georgia you may wish to try the national favourite, Borjomi mineral water, which is sparkling and salty to taste. Jermuk mineral water is Armenia's equivalent. Both Borjomi and Jermuk can best be described as an acquired taste.

International branded soft drinks are to be found all over the region, and many cities have outdoor fresh juice bars, but for something more unusual you can try the local lemonades. Particularly prevalent in Georgia, these may be described as **lemonade** but they come in all flavours, including pear, grape, tarragon and vanilla. Some of them are delicious, others are vile, and at least one of them is a disconcerting shade of bright green.

Coffee is generally not a massive highlight, though you will find a few places – in Tbilisi, Yerevan and Baku, primarily – that can do a really good artisan coffee. Most of the time, it's run-of-the-mill and sometimes you'll get the dreaded 3-in-1 powdered sachets. Black and green **tea** is popular in Georgia, which was the world's fourth biggest tea exporter in the 1980s. In Azerbaijan, Turkish-style tea is the drink of choice.

Alcohol

The principal alcoholic drink in the region is **wine**. Both Georgia and Armenia claim to have been its birthplace, and they each have venerable wine-making traditions going back thousands of years. Georgia's approach is perhaps the more unusual: grapes are pressed in large troughs, and the resultant juice is poured – along with the grape skins, stalks and pips – into an earthenware vessel known as a *qvevri*, which is then sealed and buried so the wine ferments underground. This tends to give the product a unique flavour, and the process has been recognised on UNESCO's list of Humanity's Intangible Cultural Heritage.

Armenia's wine production methods are more traditional but the product is no less excellent: there are many Armenian vineyards which can be visited for tastings and several wines have won international awards. Azerbaijan, meanwhile, has a nascent wine industry which is attempting to rebuild itself after years of Soviet neglect: it would probably be fair to describe its wines as solid but unremarkable.

In terms of spirits, Armenia is probably the leader of the pack, with a **brandy** industry that was famous across the Soviet Union and was legendarily a big favourite of Winston Churchill's. Georgia's national offering is chacha, which some Georgians will describe as Georgian brandy and others will say is Georgian vodka. Feelings run high on the matter, particularly among the brandy crowd who may get quite offended if you refer to it as vodka. Whatever it is, you'll find it's a warming spirit with a seriously high alcohol content (up to 65 percent).

Each country has a small local **beer brewing industry**: Tbilisi has latched onto the notion of craft beers and you'll find a few bars in the city dedicated to the art. Armenia's main beer choices include the

---

TOP FIVE EATING SPOTS

Lushnu Qor, Mestia See page 135. A great place to get acquainted with the wide range of Svan dishes.

PhotoStory Mix Food Tour, Ijevan See page 207. So the name is a little off-beat, but this little place serves the best *khoravats* you'll find in the entire Caucasus.

Pheasant's Tears, Sighnaghi See page 152. One of the best places in Georgia to try traditional cuisine, expertly paired with fantastic Kakhetian wine.

Xezer Kafe, Baku See page 265. An underground spot in Baku's centre, this place feels authentically local and serves up great traditional Azerbaijani food.

Xan Lankaran, Lankaran See page 284. A rustic place on the outskirts of Lankaran town, it's the best spot to try the fantastic local *lavangi*.

WINE ON MARS?

Not content with its claim to having been the first country on Earth to make wine, in 2019 Georgia announced its intention to develop grapes that can be grown on Mars too. The idea is in response to NASA's call for ideas for a "sustained human presence" on Mars, and enthusiastic Georgian scientists have begun to develop the bacteria required to transform Mars' surface into fertile soil. There's even a simulated Martian environment being constructed in a Tbilisi scientific lab in order to test which grape variety would be best able to thrive on the red planet. We're not likely to be sipping Georgian-Martian wine for some time, though – manned missions to Mars aren't expected to be launched for at least 25 years, and even after that, the grapes will need to have time to grow.

bottled brands Kilikia, Gyumri and Kotayk, while Azerbaijan's flagship brand is Xirdalan. A few international options are also sometimes available.

The media

In 2023, Georgia and Armenia respectively were ranked 77th and 49th in the world by the Press Freedom Index. This represents something of a drop for Georgia, which had hovered around 60th for some years, while it's a big leap for Armenia, which has sprung up from its position as 80th in 2018.

It's perhaps unsurprising that Armenia's press freedom improved over this period, given the prime minister, Nikol Pashinyan, cut his teeth as a journalist railing against corrupt politicians. Nonetheless, there's some distance to go for both countries: owners of television channels frequently dictate editorial content and threats of violence against journalists are not unknown. Even so, Georgia and Armenia can be proud of the fact that – with the exception of the Baltic States – they have by some distance the freest press to be found in any of the former countries of the Soviet Union.

The situation is very different in Azerbaijan, which is more than seventy places behind its neighbours on the Press Freedom Index, with a score of 151 putting it amongst the most **press-restricted countries** on the planet. Journalists, bloggers and any other critics of the government are subject to blackmail, violence, intimidation and jail time, and there are very few print or broadcast media that are not state-owned or at least subsidised. Despite this, the Constitution of Azerbaijan – apparently without irony – guarantees freedom of speech.

If you're looking for news from home when travelling in any of the three Caucasian republics, your best source will be online. Access to the BBC and Voice of America, for example, is (perhaps surprisingly) not blocked. Print newspapers from home are not easy to come by.

Newspapers, magazines and online news

There are plenty of local newspapers in each country's national language, as well as a fair smattering of Russian-language publications, but not many in English. The following are all primarily web-based, but a number of them also have a print presence.

Georgia

Georgia Today Ⓦ georgiatoday.ge A twice-weekly newspaper, *Georgia Today* also maintains a (mostly politics-focussed) website which offers a good way to keep up to date with news from around the country.

The Financial Ⓦ finchannel.com *The Financial*'s reports revolve around Georgian business-related news. It's probably the only periodical you'll ever find that maintains a regular Khachapuri Index, which plots the month-on-month costs of making khachapuri on a graph.

OC Media Ⓦ oc-media.org Covering Georgia, Armenia and Azerbaijan, as well as Russia's North Caucasus, *OC Media* is based in Tbilisi and is one of the best outlets for independent regional news.

Caucasian Journal Ⓦ english.caucasianjournal.org An online-only periodical launched in 2019, it intends to eventually provide coverage on all the Caucasian states in English, Georgian, Armenian and Azerbaijani. For now it's only in Georgian, Armenian and English, and its material is currently Georgia-centric.

Armenia

Armenpress Ⓦ armenpress.am/eng The state news agency Armenpress has been in operation for more than 100 years. Its English-language website keeps a finger on the pulse of Armenia-related news from around the world as well as in the country itself.

Azerbaijan

Azernews ⓦazernews.az Azerbaijan's main English-language news source, *Azernews* has an online presence and publishes a weekly paper. It fawns over the government extensively. You'll find a lot of articles about the recent miraculous activities of President Aliyev.

Television and radio

There isn't an enormous range of television and radio channels in the Caucasus, so don't expect much in the way of English-language broadcasting.

Georgia

First Channel ⓦ1tv.ge/en Regular news bulletins, soap operas, and foreign imports (Midsomer Murders seems popular, so John Nettles enthusiasts can still get their fix) make up the programming of Georgia's oldest TV channel. The same company, Georgia Public Broadcasting, also runs **Second Channel**, which has considerably less distribution.

Rustavi 2 ⓦrustavi2.ge/en An independent channel established in the 1990s, Rustavi is considered to lean politically in favour of the United National Movement party. Its schedule consists of news reports, soaps and chat shows.

In terms of radio, Georgia's national broadcast stations – **Sakartvelos** and **Ori** – aren't enormously popular. There are a considerable number of regional stations offering news bulletins and music programming.

Armenia

Public Radio of Armenia ⓦen.armradio.am Armenia's national radio company has been operating since 1926, offering music, news and sport programmes. There's an online international branch of the station which has some English broadcasts.

Public Television of Armenia ⓦ1tv.am/en Otherwise known as 1TV or ArmTV, this station was Armenia's first TV station, established in 1956. You can watch online, even outside Armenia.

h2 ⓦtv.am/en Proudly billing itself as Armenia's second TV channel, h2 broadcasts news bulletins, films and general interest programmes.

Azerbaijan

ASANRadio ⓦasanradio.az You'll get music, news and chat on this state-sponsored station.

AzTV ⓦaztv.az/en The state-owned national TV channel, AzTV offers a heady brew of films, news bulletins and nice programmes extolling the virtues of military service. It's not independent, but it is pervasive.

The main independent TV channel in Azerbaijan – ANS TV – was closed down in 2016 after falling foul of the government by planning to air an interview with an anti-Turkish cleric. The closure came despite ANS having been reliably pro-government for the preceding 25 years of its existence. With the loss of ANS there is no broadcasting in Azerbaijan that even pretends to be non-partisan.

Festivals

The Caucasus is host to a number of festivals throughout the year, which tend to celebrate national events or religious holidays. Many towns have their own individual festival too, usually in the autumn, which mostly revolve around community traditions and offer an opportunity to sample local produce – particularly wine. They're generally low-key affairs, but some – such as Tbilisi's Tbilsoba – can be fantastically colourful and vibrant, featuring national dance displays, street performances, and endless food and drink stalls.

Some festivals are also public holidays, which may result in some tourist attractions closing, but by and large, festivals being underway shouldn't affect your itinerary.

Festivals and events calendar

Most festivals don't have specific dates. Where the date changes from year to year rough timings have been listed.

JANUARY/FEBRUARY/MARCH

Trndez (February 13) A festival of purification held across Armenia, you'll see bonfires being built, circled, and finally leapt over by celebrants.

Novruz (March 21) The Iranian New Year is celebrated in Azerbaijan with bonfires, national games, musical performances and a traditional meal.

APRIL/MAY/JUNE

Day of Victory (May 9) Celebrated throughout the former Soviet Union, May 9 is the anniversary of the surrender of Nazi Germany to the USSR in the Great Patriotic War. It's a public holiday in all three countries, usually a sombre occasion involving the laying of wreaths at war memorials.

Culture Week Tbilisi (May) A four-day festival celebrating art, theatre, music and dance, with participants from across Georgia and the whole Caucasus.

Yerevan Wine Days (June) Predictably enough this is a showcase for Armenia's wine industry: it's a two-day event featuring wine tasting from across the country, as well as local cheeses and other snacks, soundtracked by Armenian jazz performances.

Yerevan With Flair (June) Dedicated to Armenian cuisine, there's an argument that the Yerevan With Flair festival is just an excuse for a massive barbecue.

Batumi Summer Festival (June) Live music, sports contests, local produce and Georgian and international DJs entertain attendees at an action-packed beach festival, culminating in a fireworks display at 3am.

JULY/AUGUST

Art Gene (July) Held at Tbilisi's Open-Air Museum of Ethnography, the Art Gene festival is a popular event featuring concerts of folk music as well as demonstrations of traditional crafts.

Black Sea Jazz Festival (July) Launched in 2007 and no longer limited to just jazz, this major Batumi-based festival has attracted big-name international performers of many genres.

Watermelon Festival (July) The main draw here is seeing Yerevan-based artisans carve watermelons into elaborate designs in a way similar to Halloween pumpkins, but there are also games for visitors to try, and of course, plenty of watermelons to eat.

Vardavar (July) A major event on the Armenian calendar, the Vardavar festival is held 14 weeks after Easter. Intended as a symbolical cleansing, in practice the day begins with a church ceremony and quickly progresses to buckets of water being hurled around. It's a joyous occasion but be warned that tourists are not spared and you will get very wet very quickly!

Qabala International Music Festival (July) Featuring performances of classical music, this Qabala-based festival has attracted Azerbaijani and international talent since 2009.

Raspberry Festival (July) Ashtovan, in Armenia's Syunik Province, is the host for a pleasant little festival focused on the various ways to eat raspberries: in pies, as jam, as juice, and so on.

Summer Set (July) An electronic music festival featuring local and international talent, hosted in the ski resort of Gudauri.

One Caucasus (August) The One Caucasus festival, which takes place annually in the Georgian region of Kvemo Kartli near both the Armenian and Azerbaijani borders, aims to provide an event at which peoples from all over the Caucasus can meet in safety and enjoy music and art productions. It's a popular, well-attended event with a great ethos.

Beer Fest (August) Held in Yerevan, this one's a chance to try the products of the country's top brewers, as well as enjoy local music and dances. Once you're suitably uninhibited, there are games and competitions to enter.

SEPTEMBER/OCTOBER

Batumi Music Fest (September) A classical music festival, Batumi Music Fest features several days' worth of performances as well as music master classes.

Rural Life and Traditions Festival (September) This Yerevan-hosted festival focuses on agricultural produce and handicrafts.

Tbilsoba (October) Tbilisi's top festival celebrates the city's history, featuring folk song and dance displays, street food, and of course wine and chacha. If you have the chance to attend this fantastic and colourful event, don't miss it.

Mtskhetoba-Svetitskhovloba Festival (October) Held in Mtskheta, this festival involves traditional dance displays, folk music, and handicraft demonstrations.

Baku Jazz Festival (October) The biggest event of the year in Baku is the Jazz Festival, which lasts two weeks and attracts performances by big international names. Check out Ⓦ bakujazzfestival.com for details.

Gandagana Festival (October) This Batumi-based festival offers visitors a chance to experience Adjaran culture, including musical performances and participation in cookery classes.

Quba Apple Festival (Autumn) The Azerbaijani town of Quba is nationally famous for its apples, and at this annual festival you'll get a chance to try various products made from this versatile fruit, as well as watching national dance displays.

Sighnaghi Wine Festival (Autumn) Usually held in October, Sighnaghi's wine festival brings local producers in from all around Kakheti for you to try their wares.

NOVEMBER

Pomegranate Festival (November) The central Azerbaijani city of Goychay hosts an annual festival dedicated to the pomegranate, at which you'll learn about the different pomegranate varieties, enjoy fresh pomegranate juice, and perhaps participate in a pomegranate eating contest. There are also national music and dance displays.

Sports and outdoor activities

The gorgeous scenery of the Caucasus mountains makes Georgia, Armenia and Azerbaijan excellent venues for outdoor activities, the most popular being hiking, horseriding and skiing. In all three countries, you'll find perfect opportunities to get out of the towns and into the great outdoors.

If you intend to undertake any of these pursuits, it's best to confirm that you're covered by your insurance.

Hiking and trekking

Georgia, Armenia and Azerbaijan are all blessed with plenty of ideal opportunities for hikes. Of the three, Georgia has the best infrastructure for it, with a clear understanding of what hikers want, but Armenia is catching up rapidly, while Azerbaijan lags behind a little. In all three the default for hiking is that your trip is self-managed: you aren't required to take a guide and in many cases you may find it hard to arrange one.

Borjomi National Park, in Georgia, is perhaps the best organised hiking venue, with an utterly fantastic visitor information centre that can supply maps, recommend routes and rent out camping equipment, as well as offering guides on request. Armenia's Dilijan National Park is similarly well organised. In other venues around the Caucasus, you're left to your own devices a little more, but you should still be able to find a guide in Stepantsminda or Mestia if needed.

Hikes available range from short walks to multi-day treks. One of the most popular of the former is perhaps the walk up to Gergeti Trinity Church above Stepantsminda, while the four-day Mestia to Ushguli trek is probably the most common multi-day hike. The Transcaucasian Trail, an ambitious programme that aims to create a route right from Georgia's Svaneti region down to Armenia's border with Iran, is still in development, but sections of the Trail are now open for exploration.

Depending on where you're trekking, you'll find either that trails are frequently and clearly marked, or not marked at all. If you're doing the popular routes, there will usually be other hikers around that you can follow, but even so, it's best to have a **map** and **compass** and to know how to use them. Be careful trekking in some **border regions** such as Georgia's Tusheti – you don't want to accidentally cross into another country.

Trekking in the Caucasus is a very seasonal activity. From late September to mid-May many routes are impassable due to heavy snowfall. If you're planning a trek in the mountains make sure to check local weather conditions before setting out.

Very few published hiking books for the Caucasus region exist, though among them is *Hiking in the Caucasus*, a 2020 guide written by – among others – Tom Allen, one of the minds behind the *Transcaucasian Trail*. There's also a 2013 guide entitled *Walking in the Caucasus* by Peter Nasmyth, who has lived in Georgia for more than 30 years. Beyond books, you'll find a number of excellent online resources, of which Caucasian Trekking (Ⓦ caucasus-trekking. com) is particularly recommended, though it only covers hikes in Georgia. For Armenia, HikeArmenia (Ⓦ hikearmenia.org) is a handy resource allowing you to choose a trek and book a guide in advance. Several travel companies also offer dedicated walking holidays in the region, including Bookatrekking (Ⓦ bookatrekking.com/en) and Camp Caucasus (Ⓦ campcaucasus.com).

Horseriding

Popular and easy to arrange, horseriding is available in many locations across the Caucasus. Mestia, Borjomi and Dilijan are some of the easiest destinations, and it's also possible in Quba. Ask in your guesthouse,

CHECKLIST OF CAMPING AND TREKKING ESSENTIALS

In a few places across the Caucasus – Mestia, Borjomi and Dilijan particularly spring to mind – you'll be able to hire some of the equipment required for trekking, but in most cases it's up to you to bring along what you need. In particular, it's essential to bring a good pair of hiking boots, as getting hold of these in the Caucasus won't be easy.

ESSENTIALS

Backpack
Compass
First aid kit (basic)
Hiking boots
Lightweight, quick-drying trousers
Map
Rainproof coat
Sandals or rubber shoes (for wading through streams)
Sun block
Toilet paper
Torch
Water bottle

OTHER USEFUL ITEMS

Binoculars
Emergency snack food
Hat, with brim
Heavy-duty refuse bag (to rainproof your backpack)
Insulation mat
Lip balmPocket knife
Sewing kit
Sleeping bag
Sunglasses (UV protective)
Tent
Towel
Trekking poles

hotel or at the tourist information office, and they'll be able to put you in touch with a local outfit.

Rafting

Less widespread than some other outdoor activities, river rafting is increasing in popularity, primarily in Georgia. The company Rafting in Kutaisi (ⓦrafting-inkutaisi.com) get consistently good press for their rafting tours, which range from an afternoon trip on Kutaisi's Rioni River to a full 7-day adventure in various locations across the country. You'll also find plenty of operators in the village of Makhuntseti, on the road between Batumi and Akhaltsikhe; just stop in the village centre and you'll be approached by rafting company personnel within seconds. In Armenia, the Rafting in Armenia company (ⓦfacebook.com/raftingarmenia) offer rafting trips in the Lori region, including up the Debed Canyon.

Skiing

All three Caucasian republics have well-established ski resorts: Gudauri and Bakuriani in Georgia, Shahdag and Qabala in Azerbaijan, and Tsaghkadzor in Armenia. In all three countries, access to the ski runs is considerably cheaper than in many international destinations, and the runs are generally considered decent if not world beating. Ski equipment rental and purchase is available in all the ski resorts.

Watersports

Though there aren't loads of opportunities for watersports enthusiasts, a couple of options do present themselves: Azerbaijan's Blueplanet Kite Beach (ⓦkitesurfing.az) offers kite-surfing on a lagoon of the Caspian Sea just north of Baku, while there are a number of operators in Batumi who can set you up with paddleboarding, kayaking and windsurfing possibilities on the Black Sea. Ask at the tourist information centre for recommended companies.

Culture and etiquette

There are very few pitfalls to watch out for here. The Caucasus is generally a relaxed place where people don't mind too much what you do. Even if you do accidentally commit a faux pas, locals are unlikely to take enormous offence.

Body language

Body language in the Caucasus differs little from that in Western countries. For example, you should maintain eye contact when talking to people and shake hands when greeting them. Perhaps the greatest difference is that Caucasian people often do not smile as much as Westerners, but this does not mean that they are unfriendly.

There are a couple of hand gestures not necessarily offensive to Westerners, but which you should avoid: in Armenia, don't hold your palm outward, with fingers outstretched, towards somebody; in Azerbaijan, don't form a circle with the thumb and forefinger (the American 'OK' gesture), or point with one finger; and in Georgia, don't bend your arm in an L-shape with the fist upward, while holding your bicep with the other arm (the 'bras d'honneur' gesture). It's unlikely you'd accidentally make that last gesture, but the others are potential pitfalls.

Dress

Standards of dress are pretty liberal across the Caucasus. The only time you might encounter some disapproval for your choice of clothing is when visiting houses of worship such as active monasteries (Vardzia, for example) and mosques, where shorts and miniskirts should be avoided in favour of trousers or longer skirts. Otherwise, you're free to wear pretty much what you like, particularly in the cosmopolitan capitals.

Smoking

Smoking is very common in the Caucasian republics. It's technically banned in indoor spaces in all three countries, but enforcement is lax. Even so, you won't generally find people lighting up in restaurants or hotels, though you will in drinking establishments. Drivers booked through tour operators won't smoke in the car, but taxi drivers might.

Tipping

In Tbilisi, Yerevan and Baku, the previously unfamiliar practice of tipping is becoming much more commonplace, and especially in Baku you may find a service charge has already been added to your bill. Outside the busy capitals, tipping isn't generally expected, but it is always welcome. Tipping taxi drivers is not necessary, but you might want to round up to the nearest round figure if it seems sensible. If a tour guide has been particularly good, a tip will be appreciated.

Visiting places of worship

The churches, monasteries and mosques of the region are open to tourists (note See **Women Traveller's** below), in many cases right round the clock, but if there's a service going on in a church or it's prayer time in a mosque, it's probably best to come back later. Before entering mosques, of course, you'll need to remove your shoes, and in both churches and mosques you should dress conservatively. There are very few mosques with segregated entrances for men and women.

Photography in churches and mosques is almost always permitted in Armenia and Azerbaijan, but it's not always in Georgia: if photography is forbidden there's usually a sign to say so. If there's no sign but there is a guardian around, check with them before snapping away.

Women travellers

Historically, the traditional role of women in the Caucasian societies was to marry, bear children and stay at home. This is still a reasonably common perception, especially in less metropolitan areas, but you'll still find a considerable number of women in the workplace, particularly in tourism businesses like hotels and tour operators.

Women travellers are unlikely to run into any problems when travelling alone or with other women: local attitudes to foreign women are generally **respectful**. You should bear in mind that in Georgia's Tusheti region, it's not permitted for women to approach the animist shrines, and in Azerbaijan, it's not the done thing for solo women to go to tea houses.

Shopping

There are plenty of interesting and unique souvenirs you can pick up in Georgia, Armenia and Azerbaijan. Carpets, metalwork, woodcarvings, and Soviet memorabilia are among some of the most popular items for tourists to bring back home. Most visitor attractions will have at least one or two souvenir sellers hovering around with their wares, and there are also plenty of dedicated spots to shop. In many cases, bargaining is acceptable – especially with carpet sellers – but sometimes your savings will be in the form of a slight discount if you buy more than one item.

Carpets

All three Caucasian nations – but especially Azerbaijan – are skilled in carpet production. Woven with beautiful and intricate patterns, they make a lovely souvenir, and can be purchased in numerous shops in the region. Baku's Old Town is a particularly good place to shop, but the prices will be relatively inflated compared to buying in less touristy places. You could try in Quba if you're determined to find something a bit cheaper – but even here, you're not going to be getting anything at bargain basement prices, and the value for money is evident in the intricate work involved. If buying a carpet in Azerbaijan, you're best advised to get an **export certificate** from the seller. If you're buying in Armenia or Georgia, the situation is a bit less clear, but if the carpet is less than 50 years old, you should not need a certificate.

Handicrafts

Caucasian handicrafts range from small, crafted dolls to intricate woodcarvings, with much in between. Many tourist sites will have a souvenir stall selling such things, which is a nice opportunity to support the **local community**. One of the best places in the region to see a full range of high-quality offerings is the Vernissage open-air market in Yerevan, where you'll find woodcarvings, metalwork, local art, and much more besides, for reasonable prices. You could also head to Lahıc in Azerbaijan, where local handicrafts – particularly the copper work – are renowned.

Food and drink

One of the most obvious souvenirs to purchase in Georgia and Armenia is a bottle or two of the local tipples. Particularly in Georgia, there are **wine** shops everywhere in the big cities, most of which are happy to let you try before you buy. You'll also have the opportunity to make purchases if you're visiting Kakheti, particularly if you're doing a wine tour. Armenian wine is also a good choice, for sale in Yerevan shops or when visiting vineyards. As well as traditional whites and reds, Armenia has a flourishing line in fruit wines, such as pomegranate. Armenian brandy and Georgian *chacha* are also easy to find and make for a unique souvenir.

For something non-alcoholic, you could consider bringing home some local tea, or the sweetened strips of fruit and walnuts known as *churchkhela*.

Memorabilia

Tbilisi's Dry Bridge Market, Yerevan's Vernissage, and Baku's Asef Zeynally Street (near the Maiden Tower) are excellent spots to go looking for vintage Soviet memorabilia and other antiques at the local flea markets. You'll find badges, stamps, medals, and perhaps a nice clock sporting Stalin's face. There will also be old silverware, ancient cameras, ornate daggers and much more on sale in these places, so they're great for finding something unique.

Travelling with children

People across the Caucasus tend to love children, so you're likely to find that travelling with kids is a great way to break the ice with locals. However, it's not the easiest destination to travel with children. Facilities aren't extensive, public transport can be uncomfortable, and opportunities for child-friendly activities are few and far between. On the other hand, there's no problem bringing children anywhere. They're welcome in restaurants, at churches and monasteries and any tourist attraction you may choose to visit – which is just as well, because you're very unlikely to find any babysitting facilities, even at the top-end hotels.

Specific activities that children might enjoy include Tbilisi's Experimentorium (see page 66), a science museum aimed directly at kids. There are a number of **amusement parks** across the region which – while not state-of-the-art – may offer a couple of hours' entertainment. The Mtatsminda Park (see page 66) in Tbilisi is probably the best of these. Equally, many town squares have fairground rides. Older kids may also enjoy outdoor activities and watersports – minimum age for rafting, for example, is usually ten years old. Yell Extreme Park (see page 206), near Ijevan in Armenia, may also be a good choice for teenagers, with several zip wires and horseriding tours available.

All three capitals do maintain a **zoo**, but they are all a little dated and to Western sensibilities, the enclosures are likely to seem small. Baku's zoo, which enjoyed an extensive renovation and modernisation between 2019 and 2021, is probably the best. Tbilisi's zoo suffered the loss of almost half of its animals in the floods of 2015 and is yet to fully recover.

In terms of practicalities around **baby care**, there are a couple of things to bear in mind: obtaining disposable nappies is possible in the capitals and larger towns, but they are less available elsewhere. It's not difficult to find baby milk for sale and breastfeeding in public is fine so long as you are discreet. Highchairs and dedicated changing facilities are uncommon, though in more modern cafes/restaurants in the capitals and larger cities you may come across them. Baby **cots** are not commonly available in hotel rooms, though the more international options sometimes offer them.

Travel essentials

Accessible Travel

Georgia, Armenia and Azerbaijan are **not enormously accessible** destinations for travellers with disabilities. Pavements are often uneven, ramps are uncommon, and lifts are by no means ubiquitous. Staying in the more upmarket hotels will make things a bit easier, but using public transport is by no means easy, as most buses and metro systems offer no wheelchair-adapted access.

Georgia is slightly ahead of the other two countries in this respect, with attempts underway to adapt tourist sites for disabled visitors and making wheelchair-adapted taxis available. The public transport system, however, remains non wheelchair-accessible. A list of improvements that have been made can be found at Ⓦ georgia.travel/accessibility. Armenia and Azerbaijan are a little behind Georgia, though central Baku is quite wheelchair-friendly, and some buses now have low floors for disabled access.

In summary, the Caucasus is not a particularly easy destination for travellers with disabilities, but it's not a complete impossibility. The agencies listed below can help with forward planning.

AGENCIES

Araratour (Ⓦ araratour.com/holidays-armenia-people-disabilities) Armenian-based tour operator that can help design bespoke trips for travellers with disabilities.
Coalition for Independent Living (Ⓦ disability.ge/index.php/en) Georgia's largest disability organisation, with the aim of improving the country's inclusivity towards people with disabilities.
Disability Inclusive Development (Ⓦ didarmenia.am/en/home) Armenian NGO dedicated to safeguarding the rights of persons with disabilities.
Disabled Holidays (Ⓦ disabledholidays.com) Small list of disability-adapted accommodation in Tbilisi.

Costs

The Caucasus is not an expensive destination. It's possible to get by on no more than £20/US$25/EUR24 per day if you're staying in hostels, eating cheaply and travelling by marshrutka. Doubling that will open the doors to guesthouses and the occasional more expensive restaurant and tripling it will allow you to live very comfortably.

Better value living is found outside the capitals, in particular in Azerbaijan: accommodation and eating in Baku has quite a price-hike compared to the rest of the country. On balance, Armenia is the cheapest country, and Georgia is the most expensive, but there isn't a lot in it. The largest outlays you're likely to make are getting there in the first place and hiring a car, which can come in at about £50/US$64/EUR58 per day.

Crime and personal safety

In general the Caucasus is a very **safe** place to travel, but there's always the risk of casual pickpocketing, especially in busy spots like train and bus stations. Take sensible precautions, such as wearing a money belt, not carrying around large quantities of cash, and using the safety deposit box in your hotel. It's probably a good idea to take a photocopy of your passport, in case it's lost or stolen. If you need to report a crime, then get a copy of the police report for insurance purposes.

Violent crime is rare, though there's been more than one report of muggings in Abkhazia, especially in the region between Sukhumi and Zugdidi. If you're travelling in this area, make sure to do so in daylight and try to stay near other people.

You should steer clear of drugs while in the Caucasus. Possession, supply and smuggling carry penalties including heavy fines and prison terms. The one exception is Georgia, where in 2018 it became legal to possess and smoke **cannabis**, though

cultivation and selling remains illegal. If bringing personal medication into Georgia, you should also bring a letter from your doctor confirming what the medicine is, how much you take, and noting that it's for personal use.

In Azerbaijan there are a number of local laws that you should be aware of: **jaywalking** in Baku is subject to instantaneous fines, attempting to convert people to any religion is illegal, and the authorities regard having visited Nagorno-Karabakh while it was under Armenian control as illegal entry to Azerbaijan. At best, you'll be denied entry to the country if there's any evidence of you having visited, and there have been reports that travellers have been briefly imprisoned.

Georgia has a similar attitude to entering Abkhazia or South Ossetia from Russia: it's illegal entry to Georgia, and you could be subject to a **prison** sentence of up to four years. If you do visit either of these territories from Russia do not attempt to continue into Georgia proper.

Electricity

The mains voltage in the Caucasus is **220 volts**. The plug sockets are standard European, with the very occasional unexpected appearance of a British socket.

Health

Vaccinations

There are no required vaccinations for travellers visiting the Caucasus, though being up to date with your polio, tetanus, typhoid and hepatitis inoculations is recommended. It's also worth getting vaccinated for rabies if you're intending any contact with animals, or if you'll be hiking off-grid out of reach of immediate medical help.

Cuts, bites and stings

There's a very low risk of malaria in southeast Georgia (between June and October) and southern Azerbaijan, and mosquitoes can be a pain in all three countries, so you may want to bring some insect repellent with you. Venomous snakes are rare and will generally seek to avoid you, but if you are bitten you should minimise movement and call for an ambulance. If one of your limbs has been bitten, apply a pressure bandage, if possible, to slow the spread of any venom.

Altitude sickness

Altitude sickness (or acute mountain sickness) can occur if you ascend above around 3500m, which includes peaks such as Georgia's Mount Kazbek

---

EMERGENCY PHONE NUMBERS

GEORGIA
Fire service/police/ambulance ☎112

ARMENIA
Fire service ☎101
Police ☎102
Ambulance ☎103

AZERBAIJAN
Fire service ☎101
Police ☎102
Ambulance ☎103

THE FRONT LINES

Several internal borders in the Caucasus can be dangerous. The UK FCDO advises against travel within 5km of the border between Armenia and Azerbaijan, and it's also best to avoid getting near the South Ossetian and Abkhazian borders..

(5034m) or Armenia's Mount Aragats (4090m). Symptoms can include dizziness, headache, shortness of breath and nausea, and severe cases can be life threatening. Painkillers and other over-the-counter drugs can bring symptomatic relief, but the best response is to descend to a lower altitude.

Drinking water

Tap water in Georgia and Armenia is generally **safe to drink**, as are the drinking water fountains found on the streets in many cities across these two countries. Outside Baku, tap water in Azerbaijan is better avoided. Stick to bottled water.

Medical resources for travellers

To access emergency care, call ☎ 112 in Georgia and ☎ 103 in Armenia or Azerbaijan. Note that there are no reciprocal healthcare agreements between the UK and the Caucasian countries. There are hospitals and clinics in most of the major towns and cities in the region, but those in the capitals are generally the best equipped. Every town of any appreciable size will have at least one pharmacy.

Websites

Ⓦ travelhealthpro.org.uk and Ⓦ fitfortravel.nhs.uk are both helpful resources for travellers.

Insurance

You'll want to take out travel insurance before visiting the Caucasus. Policies usually cover the loss of bags, tickets and cash (to a point), as well as journey cancellations. Note that some policies may not cover extreme sports – even skiing – so do ensure you check carefully what's included.

Occasionally, travellers have been asked to supply evidence of their insurance on arrival in **Georgia**, and if you haven't got any this may cause problems.

Internet

All accommodation and most restaurants offer **wi-fi**, and the connection is usually pretty good. You'll also find free wi-fi hotspots in a few locations around the region, mostly in the capitals: Baku's Bulvar, for example, has several, as does Tbilisi's old town. Internet cafés have largely disappeared thanks to the proliferation of smartphones, and those that do remain have generally remodelled themselves as networked gaming shops.

Buying a **local SIM** card is a good way to stay online. Coverage when you're using roaming data is good. See page 49 for more information on phones.

Laundry

There are laundrettes in the bigger cities but hotels and guesthouses usually offer a laundry service too, which is generally easier. In guesthouses it's often offered at no extra charge, while hotels will ask a fee – the pricier the hotel, the pricier the laundry is likely to be.

LGBTQ+ travellers

Homosexuality is not illegal in any of the three Caucasus republics, but there's still a fair degree of

ROUGH GUIDES TRAVEL INSURANCE

Looking for travel insurance? Rough Guides partners with top providers worldwide to offer you the best coverage. Policies are available to residents of anywhere in the world, with a range of options whether you are looking for single-trip, multi-country or long-stay insurance. There's coverage for a wide range of adventure sports, 24-hour emergency assistance, high levels of medical and evacuation cover and a stream of travel safety information. Even better, Ⓦ roughguides.com users can take advantage of these policies online 24/7, from anywhere in the world – even if you're already travelling. To make the most of your travels and ensure a smoother experience, it's always good to be prepared for when things don't go according to plan. For more information go to Ⓦ roughguides.com/travel-insurance.

intolerance towards it. LGBTQ+ people in Georgia have experienced harassment throughout the twenty-first century: far-right protestors – and some of the country's clergy – instigated violence against the LGBTQ+ community in 2013 at a gay rights demonstration, while Tbilisi Pride events suffered violent counter-protests in 2021 and 2023. Furthermore, in 2019 protestors attacked cinema-goers who were attending the premiere of *And Then We Danced*, a Swedish film telling a love story of two male dancers in Georgia's national ballet ensemble. On the plus side, there is a growing movement in favour of tolerance: Tbilisi's big nightclubs, for example, enforce a zero-harassment policy.

Armenia, meanwhile, saw its first registered transgender woman make a speech in the National Assembly in April 2019, sparking a nationwide backlash and threats of violence against her. The situation is no better in Azerbaijan, which in 2023 was ranked the worst place in Europe to be LGBTQ+, according to the rights group ILGA-Europe.

Bearing all this in mind, LGBTQ+ travellers should be **discreet**. You're unlikely to encounter any particular problems, but there's no real LGBTQ+ scene to seek out, with the exception of Tbilisi's Bassiani nightclub, which is probably the most LGBTQ+-friendly place in the Caucasus.

Living in Georgia, Armenia and Azerbaijan

The Caucasus isn't the most obvious place to seek employment, but a few opportunities may present themselves, primarily working as a tour guide or as an English language teacher. It's also not impossible to secure work in the hospitality industry but many guesthouses are family-run and are unlikely to take on non-familial workers.

STUDY AND WORK PROGRAMMES

Armenian Volunteer Corps Ⓦ armenianvolunteer.org Opportunities to take part in a wide range of voluntary programmes in fields as diverse as education, environmental science, law, and much more. Placements are between one month and one year.

OneCaucasus Festival Ⓦ onecaucasus.org/about-onecaucasus Each year, this festival – which aims to bring people from all over the Caucasus together – requires volunteers to run events, educational programmes, and design and build the OneCaucasus village.

Teachaway Ⓦ teachaway.com Lists posts for teachers, including both TEFL (Teaching English as a Foreign Language) and specific school subjects. Formal qualifications are not always needed for TEFL work in the Caucasus.

Transcaucasian Trail Ⓦ transcaucasiantrail.org/en/volunteer The ambitious project to build a trail running the length of the Caucasus is always in need of volunteers.

Workaway Ⓦ workaway.info Offers voluntary work – such as teaching, gardening, even designing and marking hiking trails – in exchange for free or discounted board and lodging. Postings include options both in the cities and out in the countryside.

Mail

All three Caucasian countries have reasonably efficient postal services – in Georgia it's Georgian Post (Ⓦ gpost.ge), in Armenia it's HayPost (Ⓦ haypost.am/en) and in Azerbaijan it's Azerpost (Ⓦ azerpost.az/en/index). There's at least one post office in every town of any size, and information on postage costs, services, etc, can be found on their websites. Post sent from the Caucasus is likely to take one to two weeks to arrive at international destinations.

If you're buying large items – such as carpets, for example – many shops will offer a service to post your souvenir home for you, saving you the bother of carting it around.

Maps

Internet mapping apps are generally pretty accurate in the Caucasus, particularly in the bigger cities. If you're desperate for printed city maps, there are very few commercially available options, but pretty much every tourist information centre and hotel hands out free city maps as if they're going out of fashion. These are usually sufficiently accurate for tourist purposes.

There are a few options for road maps: Gizi Maps offer a 1:1,000,000 scale map that covers the entire Caucasus, but this is quite small scale and you'll probably find larger maps more useful, such as the Reise-Know-How 1:400,000 series which include one map for each country. ITMB's Georgia and Armenia 1:430,000 is also a decent combined option.

Money

Georgia's currency is the **lari** (abbreviated to GEL), and one lari is made up of 100 tetri. Banknote denominations run through 5, 10, 20, 50, 100 and 200 lari, while coins include 1 and 2 lari, and 5, 10, 20 and 50 tetri. At the time of research, the exchange rate was around 2.7 GEL to US$1 and 3.3 GEL to £1.

Armenia uses the **dram** (AMD) which technically can be divided into 100 luma but in reality you won't be interested in splitting dram. Banknotes start at 1000 dram and run through 2000, 5000, 10,000, 20,000, 50,000 and 100,000. There are some 50, 100 and 500 notes in circulation, but very few. Coins in circulation are 10, 20, 50, 100, 200 and 500 dram. At the time of research the exchange rate was around 405 AMD to US$1 and 510 AMD to £1.

Azerbaijan's currency is the **manat** (AZN), subdivided into 100 qapiks (the name of which is derived from the Russian kopek). You'll see banknotes of 1, 5, 10, 20, 50, 100 and 200 manat, and coins of 1, 3, 5, 10, 20 and 50 qapiks. At the time of research the exchange rate was around 1.7 AZN to US$1 and 2.1 AZN to £1.

If crossing between the Caucasian countries, you can always find **moneychangers** at the border, though your rates are likely to be better if you wait until you reach a town or city. You can't exchange Armenian AMD in Azerbaijan or Azeri AZN in Armenia, but Georgia will deal in either of these. If you're strapped for local currency **US dollars** or **Euros** will probably be accepted, especially for accommodation. Travellers' cheques are of no use whatsoever.

ATMs are ubiquitous in all but the very smallest places and accept both Visa and Mastercard. There's usually no fee for withdrawing cash, other than your bank's charges. You can exchange money in banks but there tend to be long queues, so unless you've got time to kill you'll be better off using a moneychanger, of which there are plenty in Tbilisi, Yerevan and Baku.

The only places you're likely to be able to pay by **credit** or **debit card** are in hotels (not guesthouses) and in some higher-end restaurants.

Opening hours and public holidays

Shops in the Caucasus often have **no set hours**, tending to open between 9am and 10am and staying open until after 11pm, especially in the capital cities. Banks are usually open from about 9.30am until about 5.30pm, but opening hours vary from branch to branch. At weekends, banks will be closed on Sundays and operate shorter hours on Saturdays. Restaurants tend to open from about 9am if they do breakfast, or from 11am otherwise, and stay open until about 11pm.

Most tourist attractions are open between 9am and 6pm. A good many of them close on Mondays, so if you're planning a deep trawl through a capital city's museums, schedule it for any other day. Monasteries and churches across Georgia and Armenia are often accessible at any time.

Phones

Roaming charges in Georgia, Armenia and Azerbaijan are liable to be pricey, so you might want to consider getting a local SIM card. This is easy, and the process is the same in all three countries: choose a local mobile phone company, go along to their shop with your phone and your passport, and make some choices about how much data you want. It's always easy to find a mobile phone shop–, which are pretty ubiquitous even in small places.

In Georgia, local companies include **MagtiCom**, **Geocell** and **Cellfie**, while in Armenia you can select from **Team Telecom**, **Viva Cell** and **Ucom**. In Azerbaijan, your choices are **Azercell**, **Bakcell** and **Nar**: the first two of these are by far more frequently seen. Data packages tend to be cheap and coverage is generally excellent, even in the more mountainous regions. Note that SIMs from any one country do not work in any of the other countries.

Photography

There's little need to be cautious about where you point your camera in the Caucasus. Up to the

---

PUBLIC HOLIDAYS

On most of the below dates you'll find business hours limited and museums closed in the relevant country.

January 1st New Years' Day (all)
January 6th Armenian Church Christmas (Armenia)
January 7th Orthodox Church Christmas (Georgia)
January 20th Martyrs' Day (Azerbaijan)
Late March Novruz (Azerbaijan)
Late March/early April Easter (Georgia, Armenia)
April 9th National Unity Day (Georgia)
April 24th Armenian Genocide Memorial Day (Armenia)
May 9th (Great Patriotic War) Victory Day (all)
May 26th Independence Day (Georgia)
May 28th Republic Day (Armenia, Azerbaijan)
June 15th National Salvation Day (Azerbaijan)
September 21st Independence Day (Armenia)
November 8th Victory Day (Azerbaijan)
November 9th State Flag Day (Azerbaijan)
December 31st International Solidarity Day of Azerbaijanis (Azerbaijan)

CALLING HOME FROM ABROAD

To make an international call dial the international access code (in Georgia it's ☎+995, in Armenia, ☎+374, and in Azerbaijan, ☎+994), then the destination's country code, before the rest of the number. Note that the initial zero is omitted from the area code when dialling the UK, Ireland, Australia and New Zealand from abroad.

Australia International access code ☎+61
New Zealand International access code ☎+64
UK International access code ☎+44
US and Canada International access code ☎+1
Ireland International access code ☎+353
South Africa International access code ☎+27

mid-2010s Azerbaijani police could be suspicious of travellers photographing border zones or government buildings, but they seem to have relaxed considerably. Even Nakhchivan, where once officials seemed paranoid, poses few problems – though it's still worth thinking twice before photographing anything military. It's also better if you don't take photos around the Iranian border zones in Azerbaijan and Armenia.

In Georgia, photography inside churches is sometimes not permitted. If this is the case, there's usually a sign to tell you. This is particularly likely in churches with frescoes, where it's generally better to assume photography is not permitted and to seek permission from the attendant before snapping away.

Etiquette-wise, people are often keen to be photographed, and it's a great way to make local friends – they'll often ask you to send them a copy. Always ask before taking pictures of people, of course.

Public toilets

Public toilets are **not common** and not always enormously pleasant when you do find them. Toilets in train stations can be particularly unappealing. Your best option is generally to have a drink in a café and use their facilities.

Time

Georgia, Armenia and Azerbaijan are all four hours ahead of Universal Time (GMT), and do not have daylight saving time systems. This puts them seven hours behind Sydney, nine hours ahead of US Eastern Standard Time and twelve hours ahead of US Pacific Standard Time. In summer, sunrise is about 5.30am and sunset about 8.30pm, while in winter sunrise is about 8.30am and sunset about 5.30pm.

Tourist information

Georgia leads the pack in terms of tourist information. You'll find a local office in pretty much every tourist destination, almost always staffed by friendly, helpful and knowledgeable people. In these offices, you'll find leaflets aplenty, some of which can be quite useful. The Georgian National Tourism Administration's website (Ⓦ georgia.travel) is also a good resource.

Armenia's tourist information network is a little more hit-and-miss. While most towns have a tourist information centre, they vary wildly in terms of how helpful they can be. Dilijan's is by far the pick of the bunch, with an excellent and professional team offering assistance on everything from local hiking to transport options. Sisian's branch is also fantastic. Others, such as Gyumri, are enthusiastic and friendly but not necessarily terribly knowledgeable. Each office tends to have its own individually-designed website, and the country-wide resource supplied by the Tourism Committee (Ⓦ armenia.travel/en) is a handy starting point.

Azerbaijan's tourist information centres – with the exception of the utterly fantastic Sheki office – are generally only useful for acquiring leaflets and booking tours. However, they are always friendly and will try their best to help with any query. For general information, try the Azerbaijan Travel website (Ⓦ azerbaijan.travel).

GOVERNMENT WEBSITES

Armenian Ministry of Foreign Affairs Ⓦ mfa.am/en
Australian Department of Foreign Affairs Ⓦ dfat.gov.au
Azerbaijani Ministry of Foreign Affairs Ⓦ mfa.gov.az/en
British Foreign & Commonwealth Office Ⓦ gov.uk
Canadian Department of Foreign Affairs Ⓦ international.gc.ca
Georgian Ministry of Foreign Affairs Ⓦ mfa.gov.ge
Irish Department of Foreign Affairs Ⓦ dfa.ie
New Zealand Ministry of Foreign Affairs Ⓦ mfat.govt.nz
US State Department Ⓦ state.gov
South African Department of Foreign Affairs Ⓦ dirco.gov.za

Tbilisi

NARIKALA FORTRESS AND TBILISI

Tbilisi

Georgia's vibrant capital, Tbilisi, almost manages to encapsulate the entire Caucasus experience within the city limits. Here you'll find ancient fortresses up against state-of-the-art modern architecture, Christian churches and Eastern bathhouses, and a Soviet legacy positioned against a forward-looking attitude. The fantastic eating and drinking scene, and above all the friendly welcoming people, make Tbilisi a city you'll be reluctant to leave.

Georgia's capital city sits in a wide valley carved out by the Kura river. Its name, Tbilisi, derives from Old Georgian, meaning "site of warm springs", and these springs have long been put to use in the **baths district** in the heart of the **Old Town**. The city bears signs of almost every era of its existence, from the ancient **Narikala Fortress** on the hill above the Old Town, through the medieval churches, eighteenth-century merchant houses, grandiose imperial Russian buildings and stolid Soviet concrete, all the way to today's shiny glass architecture. Just to walk the streets is to experience the flow of history.

Tbilisi impresses with a fine array of fascinating museums – the **National Museum** for history and the **Georgian Museum of Fine Arts** for modern art are particularly recommended – and a lively vibe from its fantastic café culture, excellent eateries, and the best nightlife the Caucasus has to offer. Expect to want to stay longer than you've planned: Tbilisi is a city that draws you in.

Brief history

Apocryphally founded by King Vakhtang Gorgasali in the fifth century (see page 67), the area around Tbilisi (originally known as Tiflis) has been sporadically inhabited since at least the Bronze Age. Vakhtang's successor, King Dachi, named Tbilisi as his capital and the city grew due to its position on trading routes. However, this favourable location also made the city a tempting target for **invaders**, and over the next few centuries Tbilisi was fought over by a revolving cast of Persians, Byzantines, Arabs and Seljuk Turks.

In 1122, however, King David the Builder – ruling from Kutaisi – was able to exploit the Turks' recent defeat in the First Crusade to attack their weakened position in Tbilisi. After a siege, his troops took the city and it became the capital of a unified Georgia, ushering in what is often known as **Georgia's Golden Age**. The torture and murder of many of Tbilisi's residents and the wanton destruction of much of the city casts a pall over this victory.

The invasion of the Mongols in 1226 brought the Golden Age to an early end. The Mongols eschewed direct rule, however, allowing the Georgian kings to remain in situ, but tributary to the **Mongol Khanate**. Despite frequent rebellions against the Mongols, Tbilisi remained under their dominion for a century until they retreated of their own volition.

The **Safavid Persian dynasty** took control of Tbilisi in the sixteenth century and the Georgian kings ruled under their authority until the first years of the nineteenth century, when the Russians arrived to annex Georgia. Western European style buildings sprang up and infrastructure within and around the city was modernised. However, a desire for **Georgian independence** was growing in Tbilisi, which was also a hotbed of Marxist revolutionary activity.

After a stint as the capital of the very short-lived **Transcaucasian Federation** in 1918 – the only time in history Georgia, Armenia and Azerbaijan have been united as one

Highlights

❶ Wandering the Old Town The streets of Tbilisi's Old Town are a living history museum, a fantastic labyrinthine survival from the eighteenth and nineteenth centuries. It's easy to spend hours exploring. See page 56

❷ National Museum Of the many excellent museums in the city, the National Museum is the best: a well-presented journey through Georgia's eventful history. See page 64

❸ Getting up high in the cable car A thrill ride from the riverside up to the ancient Narikala Fortress, Tbilisi's cable car is both a fun experience and a great way to save your legs from the climb. See page 67

❹ Innovative architecture Amongst the ancient churches and nineteenth-century residences you'll find shiny twenty-first-century edifices – the Bridge of Peace, now an iconic Tbilisi sight, is foremost among them. See page 68

❺ Open-Air Museum of Ethnography Escape the city hustle and bustle for a few hours in this lovely park full of traditional buildings from all over Georgia. See page 69

❻ Nightlife Whether you want to chill in an ancient wine cellar with a glass of Kakheti's finest or party till dawn in a pulsing techno club, Tbilisi covers all the bases. See page 75

HIGHLIGHTS ARE MARKED ON THE MAPS ON PAGES 56 AND 58

1

republic – Tbilisi became the capital of independent Georgia, but this lasted only a few years before the Red Army invaded in 1921, occupying Tbilisi and incorporating Georgia into the USSR.

Under **Soviet rule**, Tbilisi's population expanded and the city was industrialised. There were three major protests against the authorities during the Soviet period, the last of these, in 1989, led to violent suppression by the army, which in turn resulted in serious embarrassment for the USSR's leaders. Two years later, with the Soviet Union disintegrating, Georgia's independence was once again proclaimed in Tbilisi.

The 1990s were difficult years for Tbilisi, with a civil war in the earlier part of the decade and the city being under the domination of mafia gangs and corrupt authorities for much for the subsequent years. The election of Mikheil Saakashvili in 2004, following the **Rose Revolution**, brought stability and growth to the city, and in the years since it has quickly gained a reputation as a fascinating tourist destination, regularly being listed among Europe's most vibrant capitals.

Old Town

Tbilisi's Old Town, which tumbles down from Narikala Fortress to the banks of the Kura River, contains many of the city's most compelling sights, and is an ideal place to start your explorations. Wandering the attractive streets from the Rezo Gabriadze

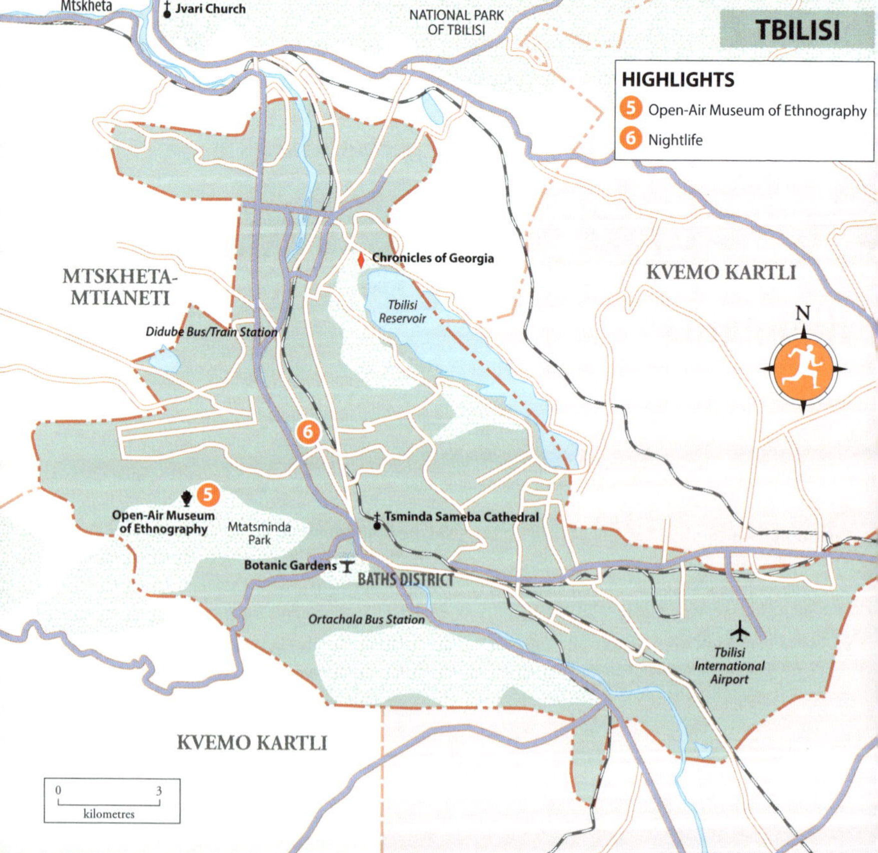

Clock Tower up to Narikala will take you through the heart of the city, taking in ancient churches, botanic gardens and the sulphur baths district, as well as offering plenty of enticing cafés should you need refreshment en route.

Clock Tower

13 Ioane Shavteli St • Free • Ⓜ Liberty Square

The whimsical **clock tower** attached to **Rezo Gabriadze's Puppet Theatre** is perhaps self-consciously ramshackle, but it's nonetheless very attractive and makes a great feature on this pedestrianised street. Designed by Rezo Gabriadze himself, the tower was added to the theatre in 2011. Make sure to see it on the hour, when an angel will emerge and strike the bell. There are often musical street performers to be found here.

Anchiskhati Basilica

11 Ioane Shavteli St • Free • Ⓦ anchiskhati.ge • Ⓜ Liberty Square

This yellow stone church in a small courtyard off Shavteli Street, accessed via an unusual brick portal, is Tbilisi's oldest – it has survived since its initial construction in the sixth century, though it has been modified several times. Originally known as the Church of St Mary, it was given its present name after an icon made in Anchi (now located in northern Turkey) was transferred here in 1675 to save it from an Ottoman invasion. The church has a few exterior carvings, while inside there are some faded but still very impressive frescoes, as well as a lovely pervasive smell of incense.

Residence of the Catholicos

1 Erekle II Sq • Free • Ⓜ Liberty Square

You can't see a lot here unless the ornate gates are opened, but this large building is where the patriarch of the Georgian church lives. It's opposite a small leafy park, home to some well-fed and friendly cats.

Sioni Cathedral

3 Sioni St • Free • ☎ 995 322 988953 • Ⓜ Liberty Square

Bedecked with bright – perhaps slightly over-restored – frescoes, the **Sioni Cathedral** houses the original cross of St Nino (the saint who brought Christianity to Georgia in the fourth century). The cross is not on show: what you see here is a replica. The church itself has gone through many incarnations of destruction and rebuilding since its initial construction by King Vakhtang Gorgasali in the fifth century. The current building dates from the thirteenth century and is of standard medieval Georgian design and proportion. In 1802, the Georgian nobility were forced to accept Russian sovereignty over Georgia here.

Tbilisi History Museum

8 Sioni St • Charge • Ⓦ museum.ge • Ⓜ Liberty Square

The pleasingly old-school **Tbilisi History Museum** is housed in an impressive old caravanserai building. It presents a variety of goodies from the city's past, including pottery, ornate daggers, and a fantastic charabanc. There are some great models of Tbilisi's traditional buildings too, and some interesting early twentieth-century photos. In the basement is the **Georgian Wine Museum**, which walks you through the country's unique wine production process.

1

EATING

Alubali	3
Badagoni Home	10
Café Dastarhan	8
Café Littera	11
Falafel Box	15
Keto & Kote	4
Khinkali House	7
Kiwi Vegan Café	14
Piano	12
Sabai Thai	5
Salobie Bia	13
Seoul	1
Shavi Lomi	2
Sushi Room	6
Tanini	9

DRINKING & NIGHTLIFE

41° Art of Drinks	7
Acid Bar	4
Bassiani	2
Black Dog	8
Chacha Corner	6
Khidi	1
Shavi Coffee Roasters	3
Woland's Speakeasy	5

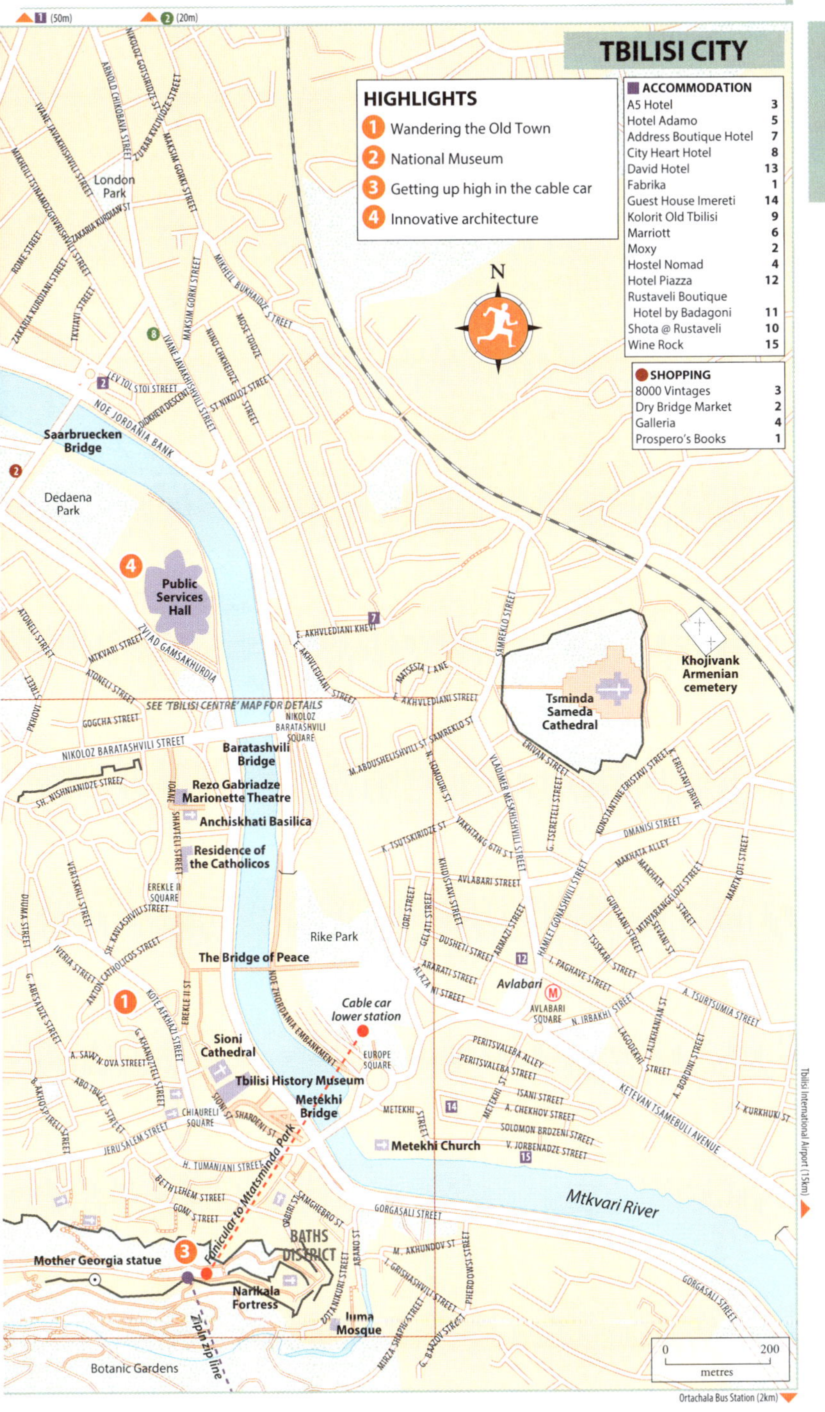
(50m)
(20m)

TBILISI CITY

HIGHLIGHTS
1 Wandering the Old Town
2 National Museum
3 Getting up high in the cable car
4 Innovative architecture

N

ACCOMMODATION
A5 Hotel 3
Hotel Adamo 5
Address Boutique Hotel 7
City Heart Hotel 8
David Hotel 13
Fabrika 1
Guest House Imereti 14
Kolorit Old Tbilisi 9
Marriott 6
Moxy 2
Hostel Nomad 4
Hotel Piazza 12
Rustaveli Boutique
 Hotel by Badagoni 11
Shota @ Rustaveli 10
Wine Rock 15

SHOPPING
8000 Vintages 3
Dry Bridge Market 2
Galleria 4
Prospero's Books 1

IVANE JAVAKHISHVILI STREET
MIKHEIL TSINAMDZGVRISHVILI STREET
ZAKARIA KURDIAN ST
ARNOLD CHIKOBAVA STREET
NIKOLOZ GOTSIRIDZE ST
ZURAB KVLIVIDZE STREET
MAKSIM GORKI STREET
MIKHEIL BUKHAIDZE STREET
MOSE TOIDZE
NINO CHKHEIDZE STREET
ST NIKOLOZ STREET

London Park

ROME STREET
TKVIAVI STREET
ZAKARIA KURDIANI STREET

LEV TOL STOI STREET
IVANE JAVAKHISHVILI STREET
DIOKHEVI DESCENT

8
2

NOE JORDANIA BANK

Saarbruecken Bridge

2

Dedaena Park

4
Public Services Hall

ZVIAD GAMSAKHURDIA
ATONELI STREET
MTKVARI STREET

ATONELI STREET

PKHOVI STREET

E. AKHVLEDIANI KHEVI
7
E. AKHVLEDIANI STREET
MATSESTA LANE
E. AKHVLEDIANI STREET
E. AKHVLEDIANI STREET

SAMREKLO STREET

Khojivank Armenian cemetery

Tsminda Sameda Cathedral

SEE 'TBILISI CENTRE' MAP FOR DETAILS
NIKOLOZ BARATASHVILI SQUARE

GOGCHA STREET

NIKOLOZ BARATASHVILI STREET

SH. NISHNIANIDZE STREET

Baratashvili Bridge

Rezo Gabriadze Marionette Theatre

Anchiskhati Basilica

Residence of the Catholicos

IOANE SHAVTELI STREET

EREKLE II SQUARE

VERISKHVILI STREET
SH. KAVLASHVILI STREET

DIUMA STREET

M. ABDUSHELISHVILI ST
SAMREKLO ST
M. IOMOURI ST
VLADIMER NESKHISHVILI STREET
ERIVAN STREET
G. TSERETELI STREET
KONSTANTINE ERISTAVI STREET
K. ERISTAVI DRIVE

DMANISI STREET
MAKHATA ALLEY
MAKHATA
MARTA QELI STREET

K. TSUTSKIRIDZE ST
YAKHTANG 6TH ST
KHIDISTAVI STREET
AVLABARI STREET

IORI STREET
GELATI STREET
ARMAZI STREET
HAMLET GONASHVILI STREET
GURIAANI STREET
MTAVARANGELOZI STREET
SEVANI ST
TSISKARI STREET

Rike Park

The Bridge of Peace

1

IVERIA STREET
ANTON KATHOLICOS STREET
KOTE AFKHAZI STREET
EREKLE II ST

G. ABESADZE STREET
A. SAMTS'NOVA STREET
G. KHANDZTELI STREET
ABO TBILELI STREET
B. AKHOSPIRELI STREET

Sioni Cathedral

Tbilisi History Museum

CHIAURELI SQUARE
SIONI ST
SHARDENI ST

Metekhi Bridge

DUSHETI STREET
ARARATI STREET
ALAZA NI STREET

Avlabari
M
AVLABARI SQUARE
N. IRBAKHI STREET
I. PAGHAVE STREET
A. TSURTSUMIA STREET
N. ALIKHANIAN ST
LAGODEKHI STREET
A. BORDINI STREET

Cable car lower station

NOE ZHORDANIA EMBANKMENT

EUROPE SQUARE

PERITSVALEBA ALLEY
PERITSVALEBA STREET

METEKHI STREET
ISANI STREET
A. CHEKHOV STREET
KETEVAN TSAMEBULI AVENUE
I. KURKHUKI ST

JERUSALEM STREET

H. TUMANIANI STREET

METEKHI
14
SOLOMON BRDZENI STREET
V. JORBENADZE STREET
15

Metekhi Church

BETHLEHEM STREET
GOMI STREET

Mother Georgia statue

3

Zipline zip line

Funicular to Mtatsminda Park

ORBIRI ST
SAMGHEBRO ST
BATHS DISTRICT
ZOTA NIKURI STREET
ABANO STREET
MIRZA SHAPHI STREET
G. BAAZOV STREET

Juma Mosque

Narikala Fortress

GORGASALI STREET
M. AKHUNDOV ST
I. GRISHASHVILI STREET
PHERDOWSI STREET

Mtkvari River

GORGASALI STREET

Botanic Gardens

0 200
metres

Tbilisi International Airport (15km)

Ortachala Bus Station (2km)

1

Jvaris Mama Church

41 Kote Afkhazi St • Free • Ⓜ Liberty Square

Brightly coloured frescoes – including an action-packed one depicting a Turkish invasion – adorn the interior of this small church. Outside, the church is of red brick and has an unusual mosaic-tiled alcove in the southern wall.

The larger church in the yard is the Norashen Armenian church, which has been the subject of disputes over jurisdiction between Armenian and Georgian clergies, and at

present stands closed and derelict. However, you can peer through the grilled window on the north side to catch a glimpse of the faded frescoes within.

Meidan Bazar

Vakhtang Gorgasali Sq • Free • ☎ 995 577 000705 • Ⓜ Liberty Square

The busy trafficky square by the Metekhi Bridge is lined with restaurants and cafés, but underneath the ground is the old market, a brick-lined passageway that feels like a Turkish or Moroccan souk – albeit a very quiet one. The present incarnation was restored and reopened in 2014, but a market is thought to have occupied this site for centuries. It's an attractive place to hunt for souvenirs.

Museum of Georgian Folk Songs and Musical Instruments

6 Samghebro St • Charge • ☎ 995 322 457721, ✉ sakravebismuzeumi@gmail.com • Ⓜ Liberty Square

This is a sweet little museum that does what it says on the tin. There's a large range of musical instruments here, as well as gramophones, an impressive "Kalliope" music box and a magnificent barrel organ. It's also probably the best place in the city to see a range of photographs of early twentieth-century Georgian choirs, if you happen to be that way inclined.

Armenian Church of St George

5 Samghebro St • Free • Ⓦ armenianchurch.ge/en • Ⓜ Liberty Square

Until the 1930s, the seat of the Armenian archbishop in Georgia was Pashavank church, the largest church in Tbilisi, but Pashavank was demolished by the Soviets and the Armenian archbishop's seat transferred to St George's. It's a very historic building, dating back to the 1250s, and Armenian historians insist that there has been an Armenian church on the site since at least the seventh century. Owing partly to major reconstruction in the early 2010s, though, it doesn't look terribly old. It's the final resting place of a number of notables, including the revered Armenian poet and musician Sayat Nova, who died here during a Turkish invasion in 1795.

Archaeological Museum

1 Abano St • Charge • Ⓜ Liberty Square

This museum houses a small and rather haphazard collection of artefacts from Tbilisi's history. Perhaps the most interesting item is the large wooden wine press, which you'll find in the attractive garden. The enthusiastic owner is likely to show you around the collection.

Baths district

Abano St • Free • Ⓜ Liberty Square

You can smell the sulphur in the air in the **baths district**, a part of town with a distinctly oriental feel. There are several bathhouses here offering spa experiences, saunas and massages. Among them are the Gulo Thermal Spa (Ioseb Grishashvili St, Ⓦ facebook.com/tbilisithermalspa), which is one of the traditional domed hamams, and the Orbeliani Baths (31 Abano St, Ⓦ chreli-abano.ge/?lan=en), with the look of a Central Asian mosque. There are often temporary photographic exhibitions along the outside walls of the baths.

Juma Mosque

32 Botanikuri St • Free • ☎ 995 577 623002 • Ⓜ Liberty Square

On the hill up to the Narikala Fortress is one of Tbilisi's few active mosques. Dating back to 1895, it's an attractive brick building that's more interesting from outside than within.

Botanic Gardens

1 Botanikuri St • Charge • Ⓦ nbgg.ge • Ⓜ Liberty Square

A peaceful and extensive area below the Narikala Fortress, the **Botanic Gardens** are a pleasant place to escape from the busy town centre for a while, though they could do with a bit of TLC. Paths lead you through trees and past small flower beds, and there's a waterfall at the park's western edge, which makes a good central feature. The gardens also offer good views of the Narikala Fortress, particularly on a sunny afternoon.

The **ZipIn** zip line (entry from the top of the cable car, Ⓦ facebook.com/Zipintbilisi, charge) makes for a fun and adrenaline-pumping method of entry to the Botanic Gardens.

Narikala Fortress and Mother Georgia

Orbiri St • Free • Ⓜ Liberty Square

There's been a castle on this rocky crag overlooking the city since at least the fourth century, though most of the current structure dates from the seventeenth and eighteenth centuries. Some of its strong walls remain, but it's mostly quite ruined now. It's still well worth a trip up the hill for the all-encompassing city views, but in all honesty the fortress is better viewed from the exterior. If you do enter the ruins, note that the paths are scrubby and not well-maintained, and you should be careful if you walk the walls – they're narrow and there are some steep drops.

The easiest way to get up to the fortress is by the cable car from Rike Park (see page 67): once at the top, the fortress can be accessed via a path to your left. If you head right instead, you'll find yourself at the base of **Mother Georgia** (Kartlis Deda), a twenty-metre-tall aluminium statue that's visible from much of the city centre. Dating from 1958, Mother Georgia holds a welcoming bowl of wine in one hand and a drawn sword in the other – a representation of Georgia's hearty hospitality to friends and ferocity to enemies.

Betlemi Churches

Betlemi Rise • Free • ☎ 995 599 153449 • Ⓜ Liberty Square

SOLALAKI DISTRICT MUSEUMS

The area at the base of the Betlemi Stairs is home to a few lower profile museums. First up is the **Museum of Repressed Writers**, housed in a magnificent Art Nouveau building, which is dedicted to writers who suffered under the Soviets, particularly during the Stalinist era. At time of research it was still awaiting opening, which has been delayed by modern-day political complications.

A few blocks away is the **Museum of Georgian Jews**, which covers the history of Jews in Georgia in a small but relatively engaging collection. Meanwhile, the **Yota Royal Gallery** (found underground on Shalva Dadini St, and quite easy to miss) is home to an enormous number of miniature models and dioramas.

The museums keep sporadic hours and are not always open when they should be, but wandering round the district is a pleasure in itself: many of Tbilisi's most attractive nineteenth and early twentieth century buildings can be found here on quiet and peaceful streets.

Take the stairs down from Mother Georgia and you'll reach the **Betlemi Churches**, a pair of eighteenth-century buildings on the site of much earlier churches. They are often locked and are in any case of limited interest inside, but the terrace outside the upper of the two churches offers sweeping city views and the attention of numerous extremely friendly cats. A small alley leading east from the terrace will lead you to the **Ateshgah**, a fifth century fire worship site originally built by the Persians.

Rustaveli Avenue and around

Rustaveli Avenue is the main artery of the new town, a busy wide road lined by enormous buildings, some of which are nineteenth century and others distinctly Soviet. It's here that you'll find Tbilisi's 'big three' museums: the **National Gallery**, the **National Museum** and the **Museum of Fine Arts**. Though Rustaveli itself feels pretty modern, venture just one block off the avenue in either direction and you'll find that the old Tbilisi isn't far away. Beautiful, crumbling buildings with collapsing, ornate balconies predominate here, just as in the Old Town. Fragments of the old city wall are visible along Baratashvili and Pushkin Streets, quite heavily restored in places. At the end near the bridge, Baratashvili Street is also home to some fun street sculpture.

Freedom Square

Freedom Sq • Free • Ⓜ Liberty Square

At the bottom of Rustaveli Avenue, **Freedom Square** (formerly Lenin Square) is a busy roundabout surrounded by grandiose buildings, with a garish statue of St George slaying the dragon atop a huge column in the centre. First built in the early nineteenth century, the square has been the site of several dramatic events, including a 1907 bank heist by Bolshevik revolutionaries and a 2004 attempted assassination of US President Bush. Assuming nothing so exciting happens on your visit, you'll probably consider the square to be little more than a useful but traffic-heavy road junction.

Art Museum of Georgia

2/4 Aleksandr Pushkin St • Charge • ☎ 995 322 999909 • Ⓜ Liberty Square metro

This museum may not look promising – and indeed its small collection of paintings is eminently missable – but the treasury section is a real highlight, housing some of Georgia's most impressive religious relics. The pride of the collection is the **golden cross of Queen Tamar**, a relic bearing jewels aplenty, and you can also see the Anchi icon here, after which the Anchiskhati Basilica is named. At time of writing, the museum was closed for refurbishment, with no set date for reopening; hopefully when it does, the requirement for visiting the treasury by an expensive guided tour only will be dropped.

TBILISI STREET ART

If you're a fan of **street art**, you'll find some very good examples across the city, usually in underpasses. The best places to seek it out are subject to change, given the city authorities undertake graffiti clean-ups on occasion, but the underpasses on either side of Baratashvili Bridge are quite consistently good places to look, as is the underpass on the corner of Baratashvili and Aleksandr Pushkin Sts. **Walking tours** can guide you around some of the city's best pieces: book online at Ⓦ tbilisifreewalkingtours.com/tbilisi-street-art-tour.

THE TIFLIS BANK ROBBERY

Requiring funds to purchase weaponry to carry out their revolutionary activities in the early years of the twentieth century, the 'Finance Group' of the Bolshevik Party frequently engaged in "expropriations" of governmental property. The **1907 Tiflis** (as Tbilisi was then known) **Bank Robbery** was one such expropriation. The robbery was arranged by Lenin and other high-ranking Bolsheviks, but the detailed planning was left to Joseph Stalin and one of his comrades, the Armenian Simon Ter-Petrossian, codenamed Kamo.

Thanks to friends working at the State Bank, Stalin was able to obtain inside information on the bank's operations, including the schedule giving the times at which large deliveries of cash would arrive. Thanks to this intel, Stalin and Kamo were able to arrange for twenty armed revolutionaries to take up position in the square at 10.30 in the morning of 26th June, 1907, when the bank's stagecoach arrived, filled with vast quantities of banknotes.

Immediately, the square was filled with the detonation of grenades, hurled by the robbers from all directions. The stagecoach was brought to a halt and Kamo snatched up sacks of money, assisted by another revolutionary named Kupriashvili. The two of them loaded the sacks into Kamo's own coach, and – disguised as a cavalry captain – he rode out of the square, brazenly ordering approaching police to hurry to the scene of the crime.

It's thought that up to forty people were killed in the raid. The State Bank could not even say for certain how much money was stolen, but losses were estimated at 340,000 roubles – approximately **US$3.4million** today. Kamo smuggled the money out of Georgia, eventually bringing it to Lenin in Finland, and using it to purchase weaponry in Belgium.

Kamo was arrested in Berlin, where he feigned insanity to avoid trial and escaped from the psychiatric ward after three years. Pushing his luck somewhat, he returned to Tbilisi and was subsequently arrested again while planning another armed robbery. On this occasion, he was sentenced to death, which was commuted to life imprisonment, and he was released following the Bolshevik October Revolution. He was killed in a road accident in 1922 – though some say that the accident was arranged by his former colleague, Stalin.

Garden of the First Republic of Georgia

6 Shota Rustaveli Ave • Free • Ⓜ Liberty Square

A pleasant garden close to Freedom Square, it was in the palace here that Georgia declared itself a republic in 1918, and where its constitution was adopted in 1921. At time of writing, the garden was closed, but the palace could still be seen through the railings.

Georgian National Museum

3 Shota Rustaveli Ave • Charge • Ⓦ museum.ge • Ⓜ Liberty Square

A modern and well-presented museum which covers Georgia's history from prehistoric times right through to the modern day. The ground floor is devoted to the prehistory section, which is excellent, particularly the hall of skulls tracing the long path of human evolution. There's also a **natural history exhibition** tucked away at the back, which features some not quite right taxidermy but is still a good place to learn about the biodiversity of the Caucasus.

Down in the basement, the **archaeological treasury** section displays astonishing pieces discovered in sites all over Georgia. The collection of jewellery, much of it nearly two thousand years old, contains many beautifully intricate items, including rings, brooches and earrings. Look out for the fourth century collection of rings with tiny engravings of animals on the gemstones, and the utterly remarkable fifth century BC gold necklace with 31 tortoise pendants. There are also gold and silver cups that date back more than 3500 years and are astonishing in their complexity. The treasury is usually the busiest part of the museum, so try to dodge the crowds by visiting early or late in the day.

The first floor is home to the finest collection of ancient artefacts in the country, accompanied by engaging and informative text panels, allowing you to get a good grip on Georgia's ancient history. The second hall on the first floor hosts temporary exhibits.

The top floor is excellent – an exhibition on Georgia's fortunes under the USSR, concentrating largely on the suppression of those actively pursuing Georgian independence. This is one of the few museums in the country that gives much of an airing to the Soviet era – most regional museums seem to regard history as ending in the late nineteenth century – and it's not to be missed.

Georgian Museum of Fine Arts

7 Shota Rustaveli Ave • Charge • Ⓦ finearts.ge/en • Ⓜ Liberty Square

A very stylish interior – glass floors and staircases and bare white walls – is the ideal décor for this exhibition of modern works (mostly late twentieth century) of Georgian artists. It's a great place to get an introduction to the many varying styles of **modern Georgian art**, which range from traditional oil watercolours by Mamuka Tsetskhladze and the brightly coloured abstract works of Uri Berishvili to the surreally stylised canvases of Temo Gotsadze.

Parliament Building

8 Rustaveli Ave • Free • Ⓦ parliament.ge/en • Ⓜ Liberty Square

Opposite the Georgian Museum of Fine Arts is the Soviet-era **Parliament Building**, now in use again following the transfer back from Kutaisi in January 2019. It's been the scene of many historic events, notably the violent dispersal of anti-Soviet protestors in 1989 (there's now a memorial to the tragedy in front of the building), and it sustained heavy damage in the military coup in 1992, before being repaired and used as the seat of government until 2012. Between 2012 and 2019, parliament was transferred to a new purpose-built structure in Kutaisi, but this proved an unpopular move, and the government soon returned to Tbilisi.

Tours, lasting about an hour, are usually available if you contact the parliament via email (Ⓔ contact@parliament.ge) or telephone (☎ 995 322 281693) at least three days in advance. Specify if you need an English-speaking guide.

National Gallery

11 Shota Rustaveli Ave • Charge • Ⓦ museum.ge • Ⓜ Liberty Square

Sometimes referred to as the **Dmitri Shevardnadze Museum**, the National Gallery houses a collection of artwork by Georgian artists of the nineteenth and twentieth centuries. The ground floor features a fair variation of styles but nothing to really get the blood pumping, so if you're short on time it's better to head upstairs, particularly to the rooms dedicated to Lado Gudiashvili and Georgia's most famous painter, Niko Pirosmani (see box, page 149).

Moma Tbilisi (Zurab Tsereteli Museum of Modern Art)

27 Shota Rustaveli Ave • Charge • Ⓦ tbilisimoma.ge/?lng=eng • Ⓜ Rustaveli

The impressive art and sculpture on show here is all the work of Zurab Tsereteli, a Georgian artist now living in Moscow, who has gifted many of his works to Tbilisi – the George and the Dragon statue in Freedom Square, for example. It's interesting enough – there seems to be an odd obsession with Charlie Chaplin – but there's little variation in style. It might be worth taking a look at examples of Tsereteli's work online in advance to see if it's for you.

Experimentorium

17 Pavle Ingorokva St · Charge · Ⓦ facebook.com/experimentorium.ge · Ⓜ Liberty Square

A great outing for parents and children alike, this science museum features eighty exhibits, most of which are interactive, giving fun and informative demonstrations of physics and chemistry. It's probably the only museum specifically aimed at children in the entire Caucasus.

National Book Museum

5 Gudiashvili St · Free · Ⓦ nplg.gov.ge/?m=165 · Ⓜ Liberty Square

You get the impression that the **National Book Museum** doesn't get many visitors. It's housed in a vaguely Gothic, early twentieth-century building, and the entrance hall is the very epitome of faded grandeur. It may be worth popping your head in just to see this, though the museum itself – the prize exhibit of which is a nineteenth century edition of *The Knight in the Panther's Skin* – isn't up to much.

Public Service Hall

2 Zviad Gamsakhurdia · Free · Ⓦ psh.gov.ge · Ⓜ Liberty Square

This shiny edifice, which looks a little like a cluster of giant mushrooms, sprang up in the Saakashvili era as part of the drive to reduce corruption in local government. You're unlikely to have any particular reason to go in. It is better admired from the outside: there's a good view of it from Baratashvili Bridge.

Mtatsminda Park

22 Daniel Chonqadze St (lower funicular station) · Free, charge for funicular · ☎ 995 322 492323 · Ⓜ Liberty Square

A couple of blocks to the west of Rustaveli Ave is a lovely funicular railway – first established in 1905 – that trolls its way up and down the hill to **Mtatsminda Park**, a funfair with some surprisingly decent rides at the base of the Soviet **TV tower**. As well as the **fairground**, there are several restaurants, a tent that hosts temporary art exhibitions, tremendous city views and the chance to look at the TV tower more closely.

For children, in addition to the funfair, there's a **petting zoo** (at which a Georgian translation of *Old McDonald Had A Farm* plays incessantly – pity the poor staff at the ticket office), and there are allegedly some dinosaurs up here too, though they're not exactly easy to find, so be prepared to spend some time searching for them. If the funfair and the TV tower don't appeal, you may prefer to get off the funicular at its first stop, halfway up the hill. Here you'll find the **Pantheon**, a graveyard containing the remains of many prominent Georgian figures, including the poet Nikolaz Baratashvili, the writer Ilia Chavchavadze, and the painter Niko Pirosmani.

The east bank

The east bank of the Kura is home to a couple of Tbilisi's highlights, which range from an ancient church to the innovative modern architecture which dots Rike Park. You'll also find a couple of interesting museums here, as well as Tbilisi's glitzy twenty-first century cathedral.

Metekhi Church

Metekhi St · Free · ☎ 995 322 228532 · Ⓜ Avlabari

Occupying a prime piece of real estate above the river, **Metekhi Church** is often claimed to sit on the site of a fifth century church built by King Vakhtang Gorgasali. However,

1

KING VAKHTANG GORGASALI

Tbilisi owes its existence to **King Vakhtang Gorgasali**. According to legend, this fifth-century ruler was out hunting, and saw his quarry fall into a hot spring. This prompted Vakhtang to order the construction of a city on the spot, to be called Tbilisi "site of hot springs". Whatever the truth of this story, he's now credited with founding **Tbilisi**, and is regarded by Georgians as the very epitome of a perfect medieval monarch: brave, strong and devout.

In real life, Vakhtang's career had varying success. At the age of seven he succeeded his father to the throne of Iberia (the name given at the time to the kingdom covering territory roughly equivalent to modern Georgia's east and southwest), and found the realm in a troubled state, being assaulted by Ossetians from the north and Persians from the south.

When he turned sixteen Vakhtang defeated the Ossetians – allegedly involving single combat against a giant – and in the following years he skilfully steered Iberia through wars and political manoeuvrings, which resulted in his acquisition of the territory of Colchis, thanks to an alliance with the Persians. He subsequently made common cause with the **Byzantine Empire** against Persia, an unpopular move resulting in his temporary unseating by his nobles.

Vakhtang's alliance with the Byzantines appears to have brought him little happiness: they offered him no assistance when the Persians invaded Iberia in the early sixth century. It's thought that Vakhtang was killed by a treacherous servant in this conflict. He's buried in Svetitskhoveli Cathedral in Mtskheta, which was the capital of Iberia at the time.

the first possible mentions of the church in written sources date from the twelfth century, so it's far from clear if he did in fact found the church. Whether he did or not, there is a cheery statue of Vakhtang here, though he appears to be waving at his associates across the river instead of displaying the imposing look they were presumably going for.

The present church dates from the thirteenth century, and has had a chequered history, including use as a prison, a theatre, a gunpowder store and an outlet of the **Museum of Art**. Towards the end of the Soviet period, in 1988, the church became a place of worship once again. It's a good place to come in the evening for a view of the city.

Rike Park

East bank • Free • Ⓜ Liberty Square

A pleasant grassy area on the east side of the river, **Rike Park** is home to several strange sculptures, but its central feature is the enormous glassy building somewhat resembling a disembodied pair of legs. A legacy of the Saakashvili years, it was intended as a concert hall but never opened. Appropriately, it forms a good foreground to Saakashvili's presidential palace, the glass-domed building on the hill above. Rike Park is also home to one of Tbilisi's newer tourist attractions, the **Air Balloon** (Ⓦ airballoontbilisi.ge) which operates every 20 minutes (when weather conditions permit) and rises to a height of 150 metres, affording great views of the city.

Cable Car

Rike Park • Charge, Tbilisi metro card required • ☎ 995 599 708722 • Ⓜ Liberty Square

For a white-knuckle ride above Tbilisi, the **cable car** travels at some speed from the south end of **Rike Park** up to Narikala. At the top, it's a short two-minute walk to the Soviet era **Mother Georgia** statue in one direction, and a slightly longer walk of ten minutes in the other direction to the **Narikala Fortress** (see page 62).

1

> ### CHILDREN'S RAILWAYS
>
> During the Soviet era, **Children's Railways** were built in many cities across the USSR. Usually using narrow-gauge stock, they were intended as a means of allowing children to learn how to operate trains and railways. The first example opened in Moscow's Gorky Park in 1932. In the Caucasus, Tbilisi, Yerevan and Baku all had Children's Railways; Baku's was dismantled in 2009, but those in Tbilisi and Yerevan remain.

The Bridge of Peace

Between Old Town and Rike Park • Free • Ⓜ Liberty Square

Dubbed the 'Always Bridge' owing to its resemblance to a sanitary towel, the **Bridge of Peace** is a glitzy glass and metal piece of work that is lit up at night. It was designed by the Italian architect Michelle De Lucchi and completed in 2010. At the bridge's opening, President Saakashvili grandly stated that it was a bridge between Georgia's past and its future. It's a great place for views down the river in both directions, and – less pleasingly – to be serenaded by enthusiastic buskers and harangued by boat trip sellers.

Tsminda Sameda Cathedral

Samreklo St • Free • ☏ 995 571 002942 • Ⓜ Avlabari

Visible from all over the city, this enormous yellow stone edifice was opened in 2004. It's an attractive enough building, constructed in the traditional Georgian church building style, but it somehow feels rather showy – the gold roof in particular is a little on the garish side. Inside, it's unexpectedly relatively plain – frescoes adorn the apse behind the altar and there are a few hanging icons here and there, but otherwise the walls are bare.

There's one icon that you won't spot: in January 2024, curious observers noted that it contained an image of Josef Stalin meeting St Matrona of Moscow. Donated by a populist right-wing political party, the icon had apparently been hanging in the cathedral for several months before anyone noticed. Once attention was drawn to it, it was swiftly removed.

Museum of Georgian Medicine

51 Dimitri Uznadze St • Charge • Ⓦ medeamuseum.gov.ge • Ⓜ Marjanishvili

This relatively small but extremely interesting museum offers an overview of the history of Georgian medicine, starting with Medea and the Argonauts in the Bronze Age, and working from there right up to the modern day. If the owner offers a guided tour, it's well worth taking him up on it.

Silk Museum

6 Giorgi Tsabadze St • Charge • Ⓦ silkmuseum.ge • Ⓜ Station Square

Although Georgia was not on the main branches of the famous Silk Road from China to Istanbul, the country was on the periphery of the silk trade, and this **museum** explores this heritage through exhibits on all stages of silk manufacture, from the worm to the dyeing process. One of the city's oldest museums, it was undergoing renovation in 2024, and has no expected reopening date.

Across the road is the **Mushtaid Park**, which has a number of low-key amusement park rides, but is more notable for the being the site of **Tbilisi's Children's Railway** (see box, page 68): a preserved locomotive from the system still stands near the park's entrance.

Further afield

1

Although most of Tbilisi's top attractions are found in the city centre, the outskirts contain a couple of interesting diversions, including an Open-Air Museum containing traditional houses from across Georgia, and a number of very fine Soviet-era buildings.

Open-Air Museum of Ethnography

Kus Tba St • Charge • Ⓦ museum.ge • Bus 345 from Ⓜ Rustaveli, then walk up Tus Kba St; best reached by taxi

This excellent and extensive **open-air museum** contains approximately seventy buildings, including examples of traditional homes from across Georgia. Not all of them will be open, but you can usually enter about ten of those nearest to the entrance. You'll see plenty of ethnographic items, including wine presses and bread ovens. Staff are on hand at many of the buildings and can lend context to what you're seeing and point out particular highlights, such as the baby walker on the veranda of the Atsana house.

   Though the site is well maintained, it's not always clear which houses are open, and there's no map. Open houses usually have a guide inside them who will give you information and then direct you to the next open house, but be prepared to wander. Guided tours are available, which will ensure you don't miss anything, but they are quite expensive, and – given the presence of the guides – they're a little unnecessary.

Turtle Lake

Kus Tba St • Free • Bus 345 from Ⓜ Rustaveli to Vake Park, then take the cable car

A few kilometres further up the hill from the Open-Air Museum is the small **Turtle Lake**, which is relatively unexciting but is popular for pedalo excursions and

---

TBILISI'S SOVIET ARCHITECTURE

Tbilisi is home to many excellent pieces of innovative Soviet architecture. If you're interested in this side of the city's heritage, consider seeking out the following:

The Palace of Rituals This swirling concrete monstrosity on the north bank of the river, along from the Metekhi Church, was built in the 1980s as a wedding venue. It's a little hard to get an unrestricted view of it: try from the small rise next to the Aragveli Bridge.

The Circus A squat circular building with occasional ornate flourishes, sat atop a small hill on the west side of the Queen Tamar Bridge. It was built in 1940 and was one of the USSR's largest circuses. It's still used for occasional performances.

The Bank of Georgia Headquarters Commonly considered one of the world's most impressive brutalist buildings, the Bank of Georgia HQ resembles a stack of interlocking Jenga blocks. It's best viewed from its car park, which can be accessed by driving south along the west bank of the river.

Terminal Business Centre The building itself would be unremarkable if it weren't for the enormous brightly coloured mosaic that adorns its frontage. Designed by Zurab Tsereteli in 1977, it's an abstract celebration of the sixtieth anniversary of the Bolshevik Revolution.

Sky Bridge Found in a western suburb, an experiment in brutalism resulted in three Soviet apartment blocks being connected by bridges on upper floors. It's possible to enter the buildings, use the public elevator, and cross the slightly rickety bridges.

The metro Built in the 1960s, Tbilisi's metro stations tend towards the grand, but there's nothing on the system to compare with the ostentatious stations in, for example, Moscow or Tashkent. Perhaps the most interesting station is Technical University, which has a fine bas-relief at its exit and a diamond patterned ceiling.

swimming in summer. There are a couple of decent cafés at its edge. The lake can also be reached by a fairly antiquated cable car from Vake Park (in summer only).

Expo of Georgia

118 Akaki Tsereteli Ave • Free • Ⓜ Gotsiridze

Built in the 1960s, the **Expo of Georgia** makes a great stop for anyone with an interest in Tbilisi's **Soviet heritage**. It consists of eleven separate halls set in a small park with pleasant paths which weave among the buildings and cross bridges over square ponds. Several of the buildings were decorated with marvellous Soviet imagery: particular highlights include the brilliantly blocky statue outside Hall 7 and the striking mosaic on the wall of Hall 8. A further mosaic can be seen on the wall of Hall 3, and there's also an outstanding statue at the expo's admin centre, of a stylised flying woman pointing toward the sky.

Chronicle of Georgia Monument

Off Unknown Heroes St • Free • Ⓜ Ghrmaghele, then bus number 60

Another donation to the city by Zurab Tsereteli, the **Chronicle of Georgia** is a monument out by the reservoir known as the Tbilisi Sea. Its enormous monolithic pillars are bedecked with carvings depicting momentous events from Georgia's history, as well as biblical stories: particular highlights are the fairly graphic Massacre of the Innocents and the imagery of hell, which seems to consist of the devil gesturing smugly at three snakes in a cauldron.

ARRIVAL AND DEPARTURE   **TBILISI**

By plane Tbilisi International Airport (☏ 995 32 2310421, ⓦ tbilisiairport.com), approximately 20km east of the city centre, is one of the main entry hubs to the Caucasus. The national airline, Georgian Airways, serves Western European destinations from here, including Berlin Brandenburg, Paris Charles de Gaulle and Amsterdam Schiphol. Turkish Airlines provide links to Istanbul and Ankara, and numerous airlines offer short-haul trips to Baku or Yerevan, or flights to Central Asian destinations.

The airport arrivals hall has a tourist information desk, car rental services, bureaux de change, ATMs and outlets to acquire a Georgian SIM card.

To/from Tbilisi International Airport The easiest way to get from the airport to the city centre is bus number 337 from the bus stop just outside the arrivals hall. It leaves every 20 minutes or so and takes about half an hour, bringing you to the Public Services Hall in the centre. The bus operates 24 hours a day.

There is a train that operates between Tbilisi's central train station and the ridiculously glitzy train station at the airport, but it only runs two services a day, so unless your flight arrives or leaves at a particularly opportune moment, it's unlikely to be of much use. It was announced in 2018 that a new metro line would soon begin construction linking the airport to the Samgori metro station, though there's precious little evidence of this as yet. Still, if and when, it's complete, it will offer an easy alternative route to the airport.

There's a desk by the airport exit offering fixed price taxi services to the centre. The pricing depends on exactly where within the city you're going, but in any case, the cost is reasonable.

By train The not enormously attractive central train station, which doubles as a shopping mall, is located in the north of the city. Reach it by travelling to Station Square on the metro line. Train tickets are sold on the top floor with a well-organised system involving taking a number and going to the relevant window when your number is called. At time of writing, the only international journey available was the overnight sleeper to Yerevan (every other day, 13 hours). Prior to the Covid-19 pandemic it was also possible to take an overnight sleeper to Baku (daily, 12 hours), but Azerbaijan has yet to reopen its land borders and the train service remains suspended. For any international journey you will need to go to the station and physically buy a ticket. Make sure you do so several days in advance as tickets sell out.

Domestic routes include Batumi (three daily, five hours), Zugdidi (daily, six hours), Kutaisi (daily, six hours), Gori (four daily, 1 hour), and Mtskheta (daily, 30 minutes). All domestic train trips can be purchased online at ⓦ railway. ge/en. You'll need to set up a profile before buying, but it's not a complicated process. Of course, you can also buy tickets at the station if you prefer.

By bus Naturally, Tbilisi is well connected, and it's not difficult to pick up a marshrutka to almost any Georgian destination. The most popular routes are listed below. It's recommended you arrive at the bus station approximately 30 minutes before departure time to negotiate the often chaotic situation. Payment for marshrutkas is cash only, direct to the driver, and bear in mind you will sometimes have to pay extra for your bags. There are two bus stations: Didube and Ortachala. Didube is reached on the metro line (at the Didube stop, predictably enough), while you can get to Ortachala on bus number 71 or 80.

The following services leave Tbilisi's central bus station at Didube (☎ 995 593 350519): Mtskheta (every 30 minutes from 8am, duration 20 minutes), Gori (every 30 minutes from 8am, duration one hour), Stepantsminda (every hour from 8am, duration three hours), Kutaisi (every hour from 8am, duration 3.5 hours), Zugdidi (every hour from 8.30am, duration five hours), Batumi (every hour from 7am, duration 5.5 hours), Borjomi (every hour from 8am, duration 2 hours), Akhaltsikhe (every hour from 8am, duration three hours).

For Telavi, marshrutkas leave every hour from 8am from Ortachala bus station (1 Dimitri Gulia St, ☎ 995 322 753433), with journey times of 3 hours. If you're heading for Tusheti you'll need to start by taking the marshrutka to Telavi. For Sighnaghi, you'll need to take the marshrutka that leaves every two hours from 9am from the Samgori metro station (Ketevan Tsamebuli Ave). The journey lasts 2 hours.

There are two marshrutkas per day to Mestia, both leaving at 7am, one from Didube bus station and the other from the Samgori metro station. The journey is 8 to 9 hours.

For those venturing to Khevsureti, a marshrutka departs to Shatili on Wednesdays and Saturdays at 9am from Didube bus station, and from Samgori metro station on Tuesdays and Fridays, also at 9am. The the duration is between 4 and 5 hours. This is seasonal, as the road is usually closed between the end of October and the middle of May.

Internationally, Yerevan, minibuses depart Ortachala bus station from 8.20am onwards, leaving when full. The journey lasts 5 to 6 hours. You can also pick up shared taxis to Yerevan at Didube and Avlabari metro stations, every two hours between 9am and 5pm. With Azerbaijan's land borders currently closed, the daily bus to Baku no longer runs, but as and when normal service resumes, it will likely depart Ortachala bus station. Some travel agents in the Old Town can sell you tickets to Yerevan (and will doubtless be able to do so for Baku when the borders reopen), but there's quite a mark-up.

All of this information is subject to change. Double-checking with the Tourist Information Centre is recommended.

By car Rental cars are available at the airport and from outlets in the city centre. Driving in Tbilisi centre can be busy and a bit chaotic, and not always easy to park. Note that there's little free parking in the city – you'll need to pay using the machines on the street, but charges aren't extortionate.

If you bring your car into the city you'll probably arrive either by the S5 road from the east or the E60 from the north and west. The S5 runs almost to the town centre; follow it to its end, then head down Queen Ketaveni Avenue until you reach Avlabari metro station. From here you can follow Wine Rise down to the Old Town. If coming by the E60, you can follow it for its entire distance into the town centre.

GETTING AROUND

Tbilisi's public transport system is composed of the metro and a series of bus networks: to use either, you'll need to get a reloadable Metromoney card. Cards are available at metro stations, and there are machines for topping up located at most bus stops.

By metro When it opened in 1966, Tbilisi's metro was the fourth in the USSR. It now extends to two lines, which intersect at Station Square. It's regrettably not as grand as many ex-Soviet metro systems, with most stations feeling rather drab. That aside, it's quick and efficient, the major downside being that there are quite long distances between stations, thus making it not particularly handy for getting around within the centre. Almost everything a tourist would want to visit is within range of Liberty Square station, and you'll probably find that you only use the system to take you up to the train and bus station.

By bus The bus network extends around much of the city, though it doesn't venture into the Old Town. Bus stops are usually equipped with information boards to let you know when the next bus will arrive. Information on the bus network – including a route map and a journey planner –

can be found at the Tbilisi Transport Company's website at ⊕ ttc.com.ge/en. The bus fare can be paid either with the Metromoney card or in cash.

By cable car A cable car runs between Rike Park and Narikala Fortress, payable only by the Metromoney card.

By taxi Taxis are plentiful in Tbilisi, and trips within the city are inexpensive. Some taxis are equipped with meters, but if you pick up one without, make sure to agree the price before getting in. Taxi app services such as Bolt are common and reliable.

By bike Tbilisi is not an ideal city for cyclists. The main thoroughfares are very busy and drivers are unforgiving and unpredictable. It's also a little on the hilly side so it won't be a leisurely way of getting around.

By foot The vast majority of Tbilisi's main tourist attractions are easily accessible on foot from the centre. You may get bored of plodding up and down Rustaveli Avenue; if so, try the streets just one block back in either direction for a bit of variation –they're filled with attractive old buildings along the route.

INFORMATION

Tourist Information Centre Pushkin Park, Freedom Sq, ☎ 995 322 158697, ✉ Tictbilisi@gmail.com Ⓦ georgia. travel, Ⓦ gnta.ge. In a small hut on Freedom Square, the Tbilisi tourist info centre is staffed by a friendly team who can give accurate, up-to-date information about transport and city activities. June–Sept 9am–9pm, Oct–May 10am–9pm.

Listings Ⓦ info-tbilisi.com/events/theatres and Ⓦ georgia. travel/en_US/events are good first ports of call to see what's going on in town. For live music, Ⓦ residentadvisor. net/events/ge/tbilisi is reliable and exhaustive.

Tours Free walking tours leave from in front of the tourist information centre at 11am. Double-check with staff in the info centre that the tours are running. There are also paid walking tours that focus on particular aspects of the city – for example, Soviet heritage or street art. Check out Ⓦ tbilisifreewalkingtours.com to see what's available. A hop-on-hop-off sightseeing bus tour is also available, tickets for which can be booked online at Ⓦ cstbilisi.com/ city-bus-tours/city-bus-24-hours.

ACCOMMODATION

Tbilisi has accommodation for every budget, from expensive palatial piles to backpacker digs. The Old Town area has some of the nicest places, often in converted old buildings, and there are some very good options in the area around Rustaveli Avenue too. Slightly further from the action, but still eminently walkable, you'll find a cluster of quieter places in the streets between the Metekhi Church and the Avlabari metro station.

OLD TOWN, SEE MAP PAGE 60

Babilina B&B 31 Shota Nishnianidze St ☎ 995 597 222512; Ⓜ Liberty Square. A friendly and welcoming little guest house with a great location in the Old Town, *Babilina* offers decent rooms and a good breakfast. There's a lovely terrace on the top floor with views across to Rike Park and Tsminda Sameda Cathedral. $$

Kalasi Hotel 25 Kote Afkhazi St ☎ 995 322 439600; Ⓜ Liberty Square. In a great spot just a few minutes' walk from Freedom Square, *Kalasi* is a solid choice that won't let you down, though the rooms are perhaps a little bland and corporate. Try to get a room at the back if you're a light sleeper. $$

Mariam R 20 Grigol Khandzteli St ☎ 995 322 988864; Ⓜ Liberty Square. In the heart of the Old Town, the twelve rooms at *Mariam R* are a good solid choice. The landings are painted in strong primary colours while the rooms are more relaxing pastel hues. Breakfast is included, there's a lovely terrace, and work is underway converting the old wine cellar for future use. $$

Mukhrantubani Boutique Hotel 23 Baratashvili St ☎ 995 322 997474; Ⓜ Liberty Square. This smart hotel incorporates part of the old city walls into its structure, and boasts a stunning interior atrium which successfully blends old and modern aesthetics. The rooms are large and comfy, and the breakfast is very good. It's well-located just round the corner from the clock tower. $$$

★ **No12 Boutique Hotel** 12 Vakhtang Beridze St Ⓦ no12hotel.com; Ⓜ Liberty Square. The pleasantly decorated rooms set around a little courtyard in this old town haunt make for a lovely Tbilisi stay. It's very central but also delightfully quiet, and the penthouse suite on the top floor is absolutely gorgeous. $$$

Silver 34 Boutique 34 Vertskhli St Ⓦ silver34bh.com; Ⓜ Liberty Square. *Silver 34*'s décor aim for 'kitsch' and overshoot massively. The basement breakfast room, with its faux gold stone pillars and ornate tiled fireplace, has to be seen to be believed. The fifteen rooms are slightly more toned down, achieving a certain early twentieth-century elegance. The staff are really friendly and it's on an attractive old town street. $$

Tbil Home Hostel 5 Irgvlivi Turn ☎ 995 551 422415; Ⓜ Liberty Square. Friendly hostel on a quiet street leading up to the Narikala Fortress, with mixed and female only dorms. There's an open common area but no kitchen facilities. $

RUSTAVELI AVENUE AREA, SEE MAP PAGE 58

A5 Hotel 33 Tabukashvili St ☎ 995 322 552255; Ⓜ Liberty Square. Close to the Opera House, the smart *A5 Hotel* has thirty rooms with attractive and stylish décor choices. Breakfast is served on the seventh floor in the piano bar with good city views. $$

Hotel Adamo 8 Polikarpe Kakabadze St Ⓦ hoteladamo. com; Ⓜ Rustaveli. A smart hotel in a distinctive building on the hill towards Mtatsminda Park. Staff are friendly, the rooms are quiet, comfortable and stylish, and there are good views over town from the fourth-floor restaurant. The small wine bar, decorated with a fun mountain diorama, is a great place to sample local vintages. Breakfast is decent but could be made better by turning the incessant ABBA playlist off. $$$

City Heart Hotel 13 Dzmebi Zubalashvilebi St ☎ 995 595 090409; Ⓜ Liberty Square. Housed in a lovely old building far enough off Rustaveli to be quiet, but close enough that you're still in the thick of things, the rooms at *City Heart Hotel* are clean and attractively decorated, and the breakfast is excellent. Maria, the owner, is very friendly and happy to help with any questions you may have about Tbilisi and Georgia in general. $$

★ **David Hotel** 16 Iashvili St Ⓦ facebook.com/ sultanhotel; Ⓜ Liberty Square. This fantastic little gem of a hotel may have the air of a junk shop, but you get the feeling the owners know exactly where everything is. The lobby and landings are decorated with antiques from televisions to typewriters, and there are traditional drinking horns affixed to the walls of the immaculate stylish bedrooms. The free glass of chacha on arrival is no bad thing either. $\overline{\underline{SS}}$

Kolorit Old Tbilisi 7 Kote Meskhi St ⓦ koloritoldtbilisi. business.site; ⓜ Liberty Square. Not far from the lower station of the Mtatsminda Park funicular, *Kolorit* is a great little guest house where you'll feel at home almost immediately. Breakfasts are excellent, the owners Manana and Davit are hugely welcoming, and the rooms are extremely comfy. The house was once the home of the Soviet Armenian film director Sergei Parajanov. $\overline{\underline{S}}$

Marriott 13 Rustaveli Ave ⓦ marriott.com/hotels/ travel/tbsmc-tbilisi-marriott-hotel; ⓜ Liberty Square. There are 127 international standard rooms in this hotel, as well as a sauna and small gym, but the calling card is the beautifully ornate lobby and bar, which are positively palatial. It's in a very good location on Rustaveli Avenue. $\overline{\underline{SSSS}}$

Hostel Nomad 21 Dzmebi Zubalashvilebi St ☎ 995 599 475474; ⓜ Rustaveli. A welcoming hostel in a quiet street a few blocks up from Rustaveli. There's a cosy common area and good kitchen facilities, twenty beds across three dorms (one female only), and one private room. $\overline{\underline{S}}$

Rustaveli Boutique Hotel by Badagoni 4 Freedom Sq ⓦ badagonihome.com/en; ⓜ Liberty Square. 15 smart and modern rooms, some decorated with scenes from *Rustaveli's The Knight in the Panther Skin*. There are several with balconies looking out over Freedom Square, though it's probably quieter to take a room facing the back. Breakfast at the excellent attached restaurant is included. $\overline{\underline{SSS}}$

Shota @ Rustaveli 1 Shevchenko St ⓦ shotahotels. com; ⓜ Liberty Square. If you're looking for a touch of luxury for your stay in Tbilisi, *Shota @ Rustaveli* should go to the top of your list. This lovely hotel offers fantastic hospitality across its stylish rooms, excellent restaurant and great bar. Try to snag one of the 'Relaxation' rooms if you're on a romantic getaway. There's a pool, sauna and gym here too, and the wine shop has a wide selection of very tempting goods. $\overline{\underline{SSS}}$

OVER THE RIVER, SEE MAPS PAGES 58 AND 60

Address Boutique Hotel 10 Elene Akhvlediani Khevi ☎ 995 551 200293; ⓜ Avlabari. This budget hotel won't be winning any awards, but it's certainly a good choice in its price range: clean, quiet and comfortable, and in a relatively convenient spot just over the Baratashvili Bridge. The unexciting breakfast is where it lets itself down a bit. $\overline{\underline{SS}}$

Fabrika 8 Egnate Ninoshvili St ⓦ hostelfabrika.com; ⓜ Marjanishvili. Who among us hasn't dreamed of sleeping in a converted former Soviet sewing factory? Well, now's your chance. There are six dorms at *Fabrika*, ranging between three and twelve beds, as well as a couple of private rooms. It's a great place to meet other travellers, and it's in a complex of designer shops and fancy bars, so you don't need to go far to find the nightlife. $\overline{\underline{S}}$

Guest House Imereti 4 Chekhov St ⓦ imereti. tripcombined.com; ⓜ Avlabari. *Imereti* offers spotless en-suite rooms in a family home on a quiet cul-de-sac. The owners are friendly and helpful, and it's a relaxing place to stay. There's no sign outside: it's the white house to the left of the street number, not the red house to the right. $\overline{\underline{S}}$

Hotel Nata 2 Dutu Megreli St, ☎ 995 322 772336; ⓜ Avlabari. This hotel doesn't look promising from the exterior, so it's a pleasant surprise to get inside and find that the rooms are set around a courtyard with a little fountain in a rambling old-fashioned place. Traditional wooden balconies offer great views across the river to the old town. $\overline{\underline{S}}$

Hotel Piazza 26 Dusheti St ⓦ hotel-piazza-tbilisi. business.site; ⓜ Avlabari. A good solid mid-range choice, the *Piazza* has fifteen rooms, some with city views, some with city views and balcony, and some with windows to the internal courtyard only. It's super convenient for Avlabali metro station but still very quiet. $\overline{\underline{SS}}$

Moxy Saarbrucken Sq ⓦ marriott.co.uk/hotels/travel/ TBSOX-moxy-tbilisi; ⓜ Marjanishvili. Part of the Marriott group, the *Moxy* is a trendy brick and plate-glass structure in an up-and-coming part of town. The rooms are a little bland and corporate, but the bar is fantastically quirky. $\overline{\underline{SS}}$

Wine Rock 17 Viktor Jorbenadze St ☎ 995 599 789618. Each of the clean and comfortable rooms here has its own small kitchen, so may be ideal if you're intending to self-cater. The rooms at the back directly overlook the river, with views across to the south bank. $\overline{\underline{SS}}$

EATING

SEE MAPS PAGES 58 AND 60

It's easy to eat with in Tbilisi — there are restaurants almost everywhere, and the vast majority of them are of a high standard. That being said, it's worth being careful when making a selection on Erekle II St around the Sioni Cathedral: there's a long line of places here, many of which are of lower quality than elsewhere.

Alubali 6 Giorgi Akhvlediani St ⓦ facebook.com/ alubalirestaurant; ⓜ Rustaveli. This fantastic restaurant is a perfect place to try a wide variety of Georgian cuisine, from *khachapuri* breads to *mtsvadi* kebabs, by way of *lobio* beans and *chakapuli* stew. Make sure to try the Adjaran baklava for dessert. $\overline{\underline{SS}}$

Badagoni Home 4 Freedom Sq ⓦ badagonihome. com; ⓜ Liberty Square. The cellar restaurant attached to the Rustaveli Boutique Hotel is a good place to splash out a little. The breakfast is regarded as one of the best in the

1

city, and the evening meals – innovative takes on classic Georgian dishes, with perfect wine choices – are excellent too. $\overline{\underline{\$\$\$}}$

Café Dastarhan 8 Ivane Javakhishvili St 995 579 139355; Marjanishvili. It's not fancy, but if you want to give Uzbek cuisine a go, this little place is an excellent spot. The *plov* (rice with lamb and vegetables) is fantastic, and the *manty* dumplings are delicious. $\overline{\underline{\$}}$

Café Littera 13 Ivane Machabeli St culinarium.ge/emenu/littera; Liberty Square. In the garden of the Tbilisi Writers' House, this place is highly recommended for innovative takes on classic Georgian dishes. It's a bit pricier than most restaurants in Tbilisi, but absolutely worth it, both for the great food and for the historical surrounds. $\overline{\underline{\$\$\$}}$

Entrée 47 Kote Afkhazi St entree.ge/en; Liberty Square. An excellent French-style café offering croissants, sandwiches, pastries and good coffee. There are multiple branches across the city. $\overline{\underline{\$}}$

Falafel Box 26 Shalva Dadiani St 995 555 598270; Liberty Square. Cosy little place serving up vegan and vegetarian Middle Eastern dishes – primarily falafel, but also shakshuka, fattoush and baba ganoush, among other options. Sometimes also offers vegetarian pizzas. $\overline{\underline{\$\$}}$

Keto & Kote 3 Mikheil Zandukeli Dead End facebook.com/ketodakote; Rustaveli. This Georgian restaurant, named after a popular opera, is set in a beautiful old traditional Tbilisi building. The food and service can be variable, but the setting is gorgeous. $\overline{\underline{\$\$}}$

Khinkali House 2 Vladimer Meskhishvili St facebook.com/khinkalihouseofficial; Avlabari. No messing about with this place: khinkali's the name and *khinkali is the game*. It's a great place to try the traditional Georgian dumplings, as well as plenty of other classic national dishes, while sitting on the terrace with city-wide views. $\overline{\underline{\$\$}}$

Kiwi Vegan Café 6 Ivane Machabeli St kiwivegancafe.com; Liberty Square. A place frequented by Tbilisi's young and left-leaning crowd, this minimalist café promotes respect and tolerance for all people and animals. The food – which includes soups, salads and burritos – is good, and there's an interesting soundtrack that veers wildly from Placebo to Boyzone. $\overline{\underline{\$\$}}$

Luca Polare 34 Kote Afkhazi St lucapolare.com/en/.html; Liberty Square. Just what you need on a hot Tbilisi day – an ice cream parlour with a great selection of flavours. They also do coffee, cakes and a small selection of lunch options, but the ice cream is what it's all about. There are several other branches of this popular chain across the city. $\overline{\underline{\$}}$

Odo's House 21 Samghebro St odoshouse.my.canva.site/oursite; Liberty Square. No idea who Odo is, but given his website rather boldly describes his restaurant as the eighth wonder of the world, it's worth giving him a go. Whether you agree with this claim or not, there's no arguing with the fact that he serves a mean khachapuri in his small and homely place just downhill from the Narikala Fortress. The menu also runs to a selection of other Georgian classics. $\overline{\underline{\$\$}}$

Organique Josper 12 Bambis Rigi St organique-josper-bar.business.site; Liberty Square. This upmarket place has been welcoming meat lovers for over a decade. Their signature steaks are excellent, and the pork ribs get rave reviews, but you should also consider other options, such as the divine Svan trout. $\overline{\underline{\$\$\$}}$

Piano 14 Galaktion Tabidze St 995 322 983008; Liberty Square. Great Italian food – mainly pizza and pasta – in a characterful and thoughtfully decorated restaurant, with books and ornaments set tastefully in alcoves, and the eponymous piano against the wall. Service is friendly, there's a good wine list, and the cocktails are top-notch. $\overline{\underline{\$\$\$}}$

Sabai Thai 96 Zakaria Paliashvili St facebook.com/sabaithairc; Rustaveli, then bus number 78. Out towards the residential Vake part of town, *Sabai Thai* has a reputation for offering some of the best Thai food in Tbilisi. $\overline{\underline{\$\$}}$

Salobie Bia 17 Rustaveli Ave facebook.com/salobiebia; Liberty Square. Ask any local where the best place to eat Georgian food is, and chances are they'll reply with this little spot. With a great menu, it's a wonderful place to introduce yourself to the wide range of options available in Georgian cuisine. $\overline{\underline{\$\$}}$

Seoul 7 Budapeshti St facebook.com/seoul.ge; Medical University. Highly recommended by Korean expats, the menu here is extensive and authentic, and it's a very welcoming spot. It's a fair way out of the town centre, but if you want Korean food this is the best choice in town. $\overline{\underline{\$\$}}$

Shavi Lomi 28 Zurab Kvlividze St facebook.com/BlackLionRestaurant; Marjanishvili. *Shavi Lomi* (Black Lion) is a lovely stylish Georgian restaurant, with a great garden and rustic atmosphere. The food is excellent, and the resident cats are very friendly. $\overline{\underline{\$\$}}$

Sofiko 8 Dzmebi Zdanevichebi St facebook.com/Sofikostan; Liberty Square. Elegant restaurant offering upmarket Georgian cuisine – it's a good place to sample some of the country's excellent meat and stew dishes. The pork belly with apricot is absolutely delicious. Get a table on the marvellous terrace to enjoy great views down to Rike Park. $\overline{\underline{\$\$\$}}$

Sushi Room 10/12 Irakli Abashidze St sushiroom.ge/en; Rustaveli. If you're a sushi fan, it's worth the trip out here towards the Vake area of town to sample what locals consider to be the best sushi in town. As well as the excellent fish dishes, there are plenty of good vegetarian options. $\overline{\underline{\$\$}}$

Taj Mahal 15 Ovanes Tumaniani St 995 598 900786; Liberty Square. This basement spot in the old town is one of Tbilisi's best Indian restaurants. It's short on atmosphere, regrettably, but the food is downright excellent, and it attracts a loyal crowd from the subcontinent. $\overline{\$\$}$

Tanini 14 Shota Rustaveli Ave Ⓦfacebook.com/ Tanini14restaurant; Ⓜ Liberty Square. This conveniently located cellar restaurant midway along Rustaveli makes a great lunch stop if you're doing a museum crawl. The food consists of Georgian standards – the *khinkali* in particular are very good – and the service is friendly, attentive and fast. $\overline{\$\$}$

DRINKING

SEE MAPS PAGES 58 AND 60

★41° Art of Drinks 19 Galaktion Tabidze St Ⓦfacebook.com/41gradus; Ⓜ Liberty Square. A funky little underground spot where the expert mixers can prepare from a list of ten house cocktails (all named after Georgian legends, such as the Golden Fleece), or from the weekly changing list of "experimental" cocktails. It's a friendly place with a great soundtrack. It is (perhaps purposefully) difficult to find – you need to slide open the black metal door in the archway by Number 19 and descend the stairs.

Acid Bar 9/1 Leonidze Street Ⓦfacebook.com/ acidbartbilisi; Ⓜ Liberty Square. Cosy and casual place, packed to the rafters with books. A good place to relax with a coffee. Food is served too, but it's nothing special.

Black Dog 33 Lado Asatiani St Ⓦfacebook.com/ blackdogbars.georgia; Ⓜ Liberty Square. A small and fun bar that's one of the best places to seek out craft beer in Tbilisi. There's a jukebox here too, so you can compose your own soundtrack to the night.

Chacha Corner 11 Giga Lortkifanidze St Ⓦfacebook. com/Chacha-Corner-172315056655614; Ⓜ Liberty Square. The friendly Vato really knows his chachas. The walls of this tiny shop/bar are lined with a huge variety of bottles of the Georgian spirit, and Vato can help you find the one perfect for you and explain the fermentation process.

Grafika 5 Mikheil Lermontovi St Ⓦgrafikatbilisi. business.site; Ⓜ Liberty Square. Friendly bar/restaurant in an artsy space, with a very fine range of cocktails and wines, as well as one of the best hot chocolates in Tbilisi. The menu also runs to decent international dishes, and should you find you can't tear yourself away, there's also a hotel upstairs.

Jazz Café Singer 8 Sioni St Ⓣ995 595 054025; Ⓜ Liberty Square. The name of this place should offer a clue as to what you're going to get. There are often live jazz performances here, and even if there's not one when you come by, it's a pleasant place on a pedestrianised street to sit for a drink.

Karalashvili Wine Cellar 19 Vertskhli St Ⓦkaralashvili. ge/en; Ⓜ Liberty Square. There are literally hundreds of wine cellars in Tbilisi, but this has to be one of the best. A relaxed brick-walled place with a wooden beamed ceiling and wooden furnishings, there are barrels in the corners and wine bottles popping out from every alcove. The guys here know their stuff too; all in all, it's a great place to sample Georgian wine.

★Linville 11 Kote Afkhazi St Ⓦfacebook.com/Linville. Cafe; Ⓜ Liberty Square. From the moment you begin to climb the jauntily angled stairs and hear the live piano playing inside you'll know you're onto something special. *Café Linville* oozes early twentieth century decadence: this is your chance to relax into the persona of a coffee shop intellectual amid the authentic period furnishings.

MacLaren's Irish Pub 5 Rkinis Rigi St Ⓦfacebook. com/MaclarensPubTbilisi; Ⓜ Liberty Square. Tbilisi has several Irish bars, of which this one is perhaps the best. It's very popular and is in a central area with many other bars nearby. It sometimes hosts live music performances.

Shavi Coffee Roasters 40 Mikheil Zandukeli St Ⓦshavi.coffee; Ⓜ Rustaveli. A great little place devoted to serving up truly excellent coffee, which can be something of a rarity in Georgia. Make your selection from the fine range of Ethiopian beans, and grab one of the excellent pastries while enjoying the chilled soundtrack.

Rewine 2 Metekhi Rise Ⓦtinyurl.com/4vfjxt2c; Ⓜ Avlabari. Just outside the Metekhi Church is this friendly little wine bar, where there's a great selection of Georgian vintages on offer. It's a chilled spot where you could easily while away the evening.

Social.Lab 17 Lado Asatiani St Ⓦfacebook.com/ SocialLab; Ⓜ Liberty Square. You'll find delicious cocktails mixed by the expert bartenders at this funky place with a vague chemical lab theme. Select from the carefully curated menu, or ask for an individual drink to be created just for you.

Woland's Speakeasy 2 Ivane Machabeli St Ⓦfacebook. com/wolandsspeakeasy; Ⓜ Liberty Square. Head to the back of this apparently derelict restaurant and descend the staircase into this secret brick cellar bar, where the mixologists prepare excellent cocktails – many of them named after characters from Mikhail Bulgakov's *The Master and Margarita*. There's a marvellous soundtrack that veers between 40s jazz and 50s rock'n'roll. *Woland's* also frequently hosts events, including pub quizzes and movie nights; check their Facebook page to see what's going on (and whether you'll need a password to get in!)

NIGHTLIFE

SEE MAP PAGE 58

Tbilisi is certainly the most happening place in the Caucasus at night, with plenty of techno clubs that keep the punters dancing till dawn.

Bassiani 2 Akaki Tsereteli Ave Ⓦbassiani.com; Ⓜ Tsereteli. This techno club in a former swimming pool is generally acknowledged to be Tbilisi's best spot for an all-night rave, due to its excellent sound system and lighting effects. The club is also the focal point of more progressive elements in the still sometimes conservative Georgia: it's defiantly pro-LBGTQ+, for example. The club is no secret, so expect a long queue to get in.

Khidi Vakhushti Bagrationi Bridge, Ⓦkhidi.ge; ⓂTsereteli. After Bassiani, *Khidi* is probably Tbilisi's hottest spot for all-night techno. Like Bassiani, it also has a zero-tolerance policy towards any form of harassment.

ENTERTAINMENT

Movement Theatre 182 Agmashenebeli St, Mushtaidi Garden Ⓦmovementtheatre.ge/en; ⓂTsereteli. Hosting a variety of eclectic performances – dance, opera, circus acts, live music, you name it – the *Movement Theatre* has been in operation since 2001. Check the website for what's on. Prices vary wildly.

★ **Rezo Gabriadze Marionette Theatre** 13 Ioane Shavteli St Ⓦgabriadze.com/en; ⓂLiberty Square. Put all thoughts of Punch and Judy out of your head – the puppet shows of the *Rezo Gabriadze Theatre* are some of the most fantastically innovative performances you'll ever see. The most famous of the plays is the beautiful *Stalingrad*, but for our money the achingly sad *Ramona* (a tale of two trains separated by World War II) is the best of the shows available. But whatever you can get tickets for, don't miss this remarkable experience.

Tbilisi Opera and Ballet Theatre 25 Rustaveli Ave Ⓦopera.ge/eng/home; ⓂRustaveli. The striking red and yellow striped opera house on Rustaveli Avenue puts on plenty of performances of both opera and ballet. Check the website to see what's on, but, despite indications to the contrary, you can't buy tickets through the website; you'll probably have to go to the box office.

Cinemas If you're looking for a cinema in Tbilisi to see the latest blockbusters, there are a couple of decent options. Probably the most convenient is **Cavea** (2/4 Rustaveli Ave, Ⓦcavea.ge) in the Galleria shopping mall.

Escape rooms The immersive game room craze has spread to Tbilisi, with a fair number of impressive options available. **TTE Rooms** (5 Andria Benashvili St, Ⓦfacebook.com/TTETBILISI) is a particularly recommended choice

SHOPPING SEE MAPS PAGES 58 AND 60

8000 Vintages 27 Revaz Tabukashvili St; ⓂRustaveli. There are enough bottles on the floor-to-ceiling shelves here that you can easily believe there are indeed eight thousand vintages, probably more. The staff know their wines and can help you choose.

Dry Bridge Market By Saarbruecken Bridge; ⓂLiberty Square. This long-established flea market is a great place to pick up an offbeat souvenir; stalls sell items as diverse as swords, drinking horns, ancient cameras and glassware. Particularly popular, of course, is the seemingly endless supply of Soviet memorabilia – stamps, lapel pins, large metal pictures of Stalin: if it has a hammer and sickle on it, they've probably got it.

Galleria 2/4 Rustaveli Ave Ⓦgalleria.ge/en; ⓂLiberty Square. This enormous modern shopping mall on Rustaveli Avenue hosts a vast array of all manner of shops. There's a food court and a cinema too, among other services.

Meidan Bazar Vakhtang Gorgasali Sq Ⓣ995 577 000705; ⓂLiberty Square. Here you can buy just about any souvenir you could dream of, including, but not limited to, wine, spices, cheese, honey, musical instruments, or the inevitable fridge magnets. It's usually quiet and there's no hassle to buy.

Prospero's Books 34 Rustaveli Ave Ⓦprosperosbookshop.com/en/home; ⓂRustaveli. A long-established bookshop Prospero's offers a good range of English-language local interest material, as well as a decent stash of novels and non-fiction. It also has a popular coffee shop attached.

DIRECTORY

Banks and exchanges The Old Town is awash with money changers, who can offer decent rates on US dollars, Euros and Russian roubles, and slightly less good rates on British pounds, Armenian dram and Azerbaijani manat. ATMs are found all over town; the most common banks are the TBC Bank and the Bank of Georgia.

Casinos You won't be hard-pressed to find a casino in Tbilisi. The most prominent is Shangri-La (by the Bridge of Peace, Ⓦshangrila.ge), but there's also the Iveria, in the Radisson Blu hotel (Rose Revolution Sq, Ⓦcasinoiveria.com) and the Ambassadori (17 Ioane Shavteli St, Ⓦambassadori.com/tbilisi/ambassadori-casino), among many others.

Embassies Armenia, 4 Gia Tetelashvili St (Ⓣ995 322 951723, Ⓦgeorgia.mfa.am/en); Azerbaijan, 4 Vakhtang Gorgasali St (Ⓣ995 322 242220, Ⓦtbilisi.mfa.gov.az/en); Canada, 70 Murab Kostava St (Ⓣ995 322 982072, Ⓦinternational.gc.ca/country-pays/georgia-georgie/tbilisi-tbilissi.aspx) France, 49 Krtsanisi St (Ⓣ995 322 721490, Ⓦge.ambafrance.org); Germany, 38 Nino Chkheidze St, (Ⓣ995 322 447300, Ⓦtiflis.diplo.de) Russia, 51 Ilia Chavchavadze Ave (Ⓣ995 322 912675, Ⓦgeorgia.mid.ru); UK, 51 Krtsanisi St (Ⓣ995 322 274747, Ⓦgov.uk/world/organisations/british-embassy-tbilisi); USA, 29 Georgian-American Friendship Ave (Ⓣ995 322 277000, Ⓦge.usembassy.gov).

There are no Australian, Irish, New Zealand or South African embassies in Georgia.

Emergencies Police, ambulance and fire, Ⓣ112.

Festivals Tbilisi's top festival is Tbilisoba, held in October, to celebrate Tbilisi's history. It features folk song and dance displays, street food, and of course wine and chacha. It's a fantastic and colourful event; if you have the chance to attend, don't miss it.

Hospitals American Medical Center Tbilisi (11 Dimitri Arakishvili St, ☎ 995 322 500020, ⓦ tbilisi.amcenters.com), Central Republican Hospital (25a Iona Vakeli St, ☎ 995 322 244033, ⓦ respublikuri.ge/ka).

Laundries Most hotels, guesthouses and hostels will offer a laundry service. There are also several branches of the Pressto chain around the city, though none are particularly central. The one on Iakob Nikoladze St (☎ 995 322 195020, ⓦ pressto.ge/eng/home) is probably the most convenient.

Pharmacies There's a little cluster of pharmacies around Freedom Square – try Aversi (11 Aleksandr Pushkin St, ☎ 995 322 922644) or Pharmadepot (4 Giorgi Leonidze St, ☎ 995 322 400004).

Post offices There are plenty of outlets of Georgian Post across the city, though very few of them are in the centre. The most convenient is at 3 Lesia Ukrainka St.

Central Georgia

MOUNT KAZBEK AND STEPANTSMINDA

Central Georgia

The area between Stepantsminda, right on the Russian border in the north, and Akhaltsike, bordering Turkey in the south, can be defined as Georgia's heartlands. The country's most important historical and religious sites are here, giving the nation much of its identity, right from the beginnings of Georgia's Christian tradition through to its most famous twentieth-century son, Josef Stalin. But it's not just history: the region's scenery is stunning and there are ample opportunities to get outdoors and explore. Central Georgia is compelling, and journeying around it will bring you an in-depth understanding of the country as a whole.

Central Georgia is home to a disproportionate number of the country's historical highlights. From the country's early Christian churches in the former capital of **Mtskheta** and the incredible twelfth-century cave monastery of **Vardzia** to the legacy of Russia and the USSR in towns such as **Akhaltsikhe** and **Gori**, this region punches considerably above its weight. And if that weren't enough, it's a paradise for nature-lovers, with fantastic opportunities for hiking around **Stepantsminda**, **Khevsureti** and **Borjomi**. All things considered, you're likely to spend a good chunk of your Georgian trip here, enjoying the remarkable sights as well as the famed Georgian hospitality.

Brief history

Known to the Ancient Greeks and Romans as Iberia, much of Central Georgia was once the kingdom of Kartli, centred around the capital of Mtskheta. It was here that St Nino converted Queen Nana and King Mirian to Christianity, ushering in the adoption of Christianity as the state religion. The capital was shifted to Tbilisi by King Dachi in the sixth century, but Mtskheta remained the spiritual centre of the country.

The Georgian Golden Age under Queen Tamar the Great and King David the Builder brought prosperity and unity to the kingdom, which expanded from this region to encompass much of the South Caucasus. The mid-fifteenth century saw the kingdom disintegrate, and the region became a Persian possession. A short spell of independence in the eighteenth century soon gave way to Russian annexation, and the 1800s found the Russians occupying the country, adding infrastructure such as today's Georgian Military Highway.

A second brief moment of independence following World War I was ended with Georgia's incorporation into the USSR, which was governed from the late 1920s until 1953 by Josef Stalin, a 'local boy done good' from the town of Gori, where his memory is still revered. In the post-Soviet era, the region has seen catastrophe with the declaration of independence by South Ossetia and two short but nasty wars, which have resolved nothing and if anything seem to have hardened positions. Outside South Ossetia, though, the region is now prosperous, with tourism making up a considerable portion of its economy.

Mtskheta

The small town of **Mtskheta** was the capital of the Kingdom of Iberia for 800 years until the early sixth century AD, when King Dachi moved the capital to Tbilisi, the city which his father King Vakhtang had founded. Mtskheta remained an important symbolic site, however: many subsequent Georgian kings were crowned here, and the town's churches and cathedrals are of huge significance to the Georgian Orthodox

Highlights

❶ **Svetitskhoveli Cathedral** Containing the relic of Christ's robe, Svetitskhoveli in Mtskheta is perhaps Georgia's most important church and is certainly one of the largest and most beautiful. See page 83

❷ **The Stalin Museum** A fascinating insight into personality cults, the Stalin Museum is a little chilling but gives a view of Georgia's troubled relationship with its most notorious son. See page 85

❸ **Stepantsminda** It may be one of Georgia's most familiar images, but there's a reason for that – the sight of the Gergeti Trinity Church perched before the immense bulk of Mount Kazbek is simply stunning. See page 92

❹ **Borjomi National Park** The well-marked trails in this lovely, forested wilderness make for easy and beautiful hiking trips. See page 100

❺ **Rabati Castle** Pristine and over-restored it may be, but Akhaltsikhe's Rabati Castle is a joy to explore. See page 101

❻ **Vardzia** Formed of an extensive warren of tunnels and caves, this twelfth-century religious complex is utterly remarkable. See page 104

HIGHLIGHTS ARE MARKED ON THE MAP ON PAGE 82

CENTRAL GEORGIA
N
Lentekhi
RUSSIA
Khvanchkara
Ambrolauri
Kvaisa
Mount Khalatsa (3,938 m)
Roki Tunnel
Mount Kazbek (5,047 m)
Dariali Gorge
Stepantsminda
Shatili
Archilo
RUSSIA
Gudauri
Mleta
SOUTH OSSETIA
LIKHI NATURE RESERVE
Tskhaltubo
Tkibuli
Chiatura
Kutaisi
Kurta
Pasanauri
Tskhinvali
Ananuri Fortress
Akhalgori
Dusheti
Akhmeta
Samtredia
Zestaponi
Chokhatauri
Khashuri
Mtkvari River
Gori
Uplistsikhe
Svetitskhoveli Cathedral
Mtskheta
NATIONAL PARK OF TBILISI
Telavi
Bakhmaro
BORJOMI NATIONAL PARK
Borjomi
Timotesubani Monastery
Bakuriani
TBILISI
Zarzma Monastery
Rabati Castle
Akhaltsikhe
Tabatskuri Lake
Akhalsopeli
Rustavi
Khulo
Sapara Monastery
Isalka
Khertvisi Fortress
Khertvisi
Paravani Lake
Marneuli
Akhalkalaki
Bolnisi
Vardzia
Kazreti
AZERBAIJAN
TURKEY
Ninotsminda
JAVAKHETI NATIONAL PARK
ARMENIA
0   20
kilometres
HIGHLIGHTS
1 Svetitskhoveli Cathedral
2 The Stalin Museum
3 Stepantsminda
4 Borjomi National Park
5 Rabati Castle
6 Vardzia

Church. Its proximity to Tbilisi and position on main roads mean that it is now usually visited either as a day trip or en route to other destinations.

Svetitskhoveli Cathedral

Arsukidze St • Free

Svetitskhoveli Cathedral, surrounded by a fortified wall, sits in the centre of Mtskheta town. The current building dates back to about 1020, though there's been a church on the site since the fourth century. It's a ridiculously beautiful building – elegant, perfectly proportioned, and with sparse but exquisite exterior carving, sometimes intricate interlocking patterns, sometimes figures of people and animals.

The first thing you'll notice when you enter is the pervasive smell of incense. The second is the enormous fresco of Christ at the far end. There are plenty more magnificent frescoes (including an excellent one depicting the Apocalypse) along the main aisle and on the right-hand wall, as well as on a stone pillar towards the front. Apparently, underneath this pillar is Christ's robe, brought here by a Georgian Jew named Elias who was in Jerusalem at the time of the Crucifixion. Elias' sister, Sidonia, took the robe and immediately died after being overwhelmed by the experience of touching this sacred object. A story of a subsequent miracle on the site of Sidonia's grave involves a levitating cedar tree with the power to heal. This tree was eventually made into a column to support the cathedral's foundations, giving rise to the name Svetitskhoveli, which means 'life-giving pillar'.

Walk around to the right and you'll find what appears to be a church within a church. This is a copy of Jerusalem's Church of the Holy Sepulchre which was built in the thirteenth century to indicate that Svetitskhoveli is the second holiest place in the world. Elsewhere in the cathedral the tombs of several of Georgia's kings, including Vakhtang Gorgasali and Erakle II, can be seen.

Samtavro Church

Mtkheta-Shiomghvime Monastery Rd • Free

The very attractive **Samtavro Church** – built on the spot where Georgia's first church once stood – houses the tombs of Georgia's early monarchs, King Mirian and Queen Nana, who established Christianity as Georgia's state religion in 326. Their sarcophagi are beautifully carved and surrounded by golden mosaics. The church also contains magnificent, though faded, frescoes, particularly in the dome.

The small, attached museum (charge) contains a collection of ethnographic exhibits, much of it connected with the church. There's no English labelling.

On your way up here from Svetitskhoveli, take a quick look at the former town cinema, which has been enjoying a long-running conversion into a museum – its colourful Soviet façade is well worth a glance.

Jvari Church

Jvari Monastery Rd • Free • ☏ 995 555 346438 • No public transport, best accessed by taxi

On the hill above Mtskheta, **Jvari Church** is visible from everywhere in town. It's an ancient church which is very important to Georgia's Christian tradition, as it's on the site where a wooden cross was first erected by King Mirian and St Nino. There's a wooden cross in the centre even now, supplying a central feature usually absent in Caucasian churches.

The present church dates to the late sixth century and is on the UNESCO World Heritage Sites list, being an almost perfect example of an early medieval church and a huge influence on the subsequent development of Georgian religious architecture.

The view from Jvari Church, across the meeting of the Mtkvari and Aragvi rivers, is spectacular and well worth the trip up here in itself.

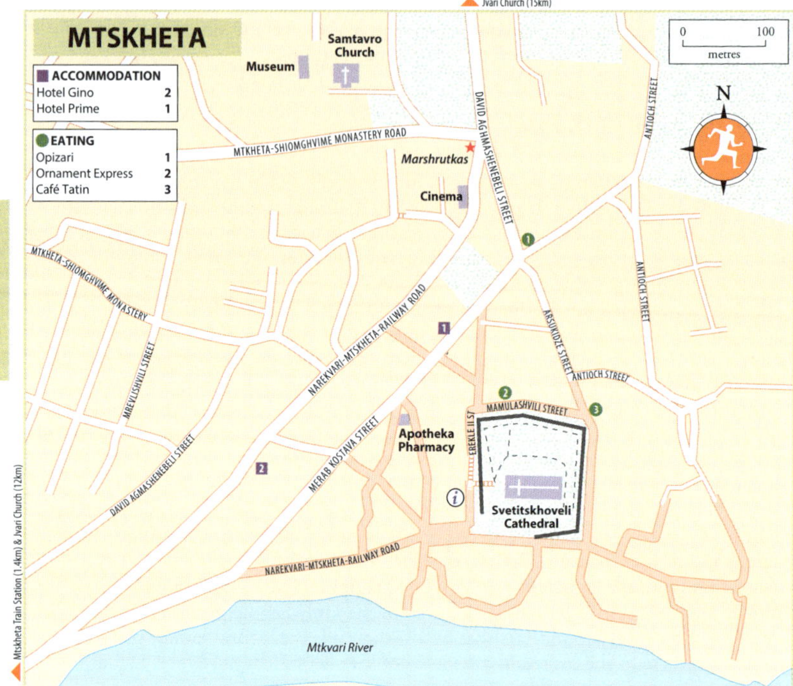

ARRIVAL AND DEPARTURE

MTSKHETA

By bus Marshrutkas to Tbilisi leave every 15 minutes from 6am to 8.30pm from the street below Samtavro Church.

By train Mtskheta's station is 2km west of Svetitskhoveli, where you can pick up a train to Kutaisi (9.10am, duration 5.5 hours) or to Tbilisi (4.50pm, duration 25 minutes).

By car Mtskheta has a quite elaborate one-way system, and you'll need to pay if you want to park in the centre, but otherwise it's easy enough driving here.

GETTING AROUND

Mtskheta's town centre is tiny, and much of it is pedestrianised. Walking is the best option, except to get up to Jvari church, which is best visited by taxi.

INFORMATION

Tourist Information Centre Erekle II St. The staff here are knowledgeable and can offer information on the town's sights, as well as transport options. Daily 10am to 6pm.

ACCOMMODATION

SEE MAP PAGE 84

Hotel Gino 37 David Aghmashenebeli St ⓦ ginohotel.com. For a bit of a treat, stay in one of the 22 rooms at this branch of the national spa chain. All rooms have a lovely old-fashioned vibe, with muted browns and greens making up the predominant colour scheme – it's nicer than it sounds. The terrace on the roof is a fantastic place for an evening drink, and use of the sauna, Jacuzzi and swimming pool is included. $$$

Hotel Prime 32 Kostava St ⓦ hotelprime.tripcombined.com. The centrally located Hotel Prime has large and comfortable, if somewhat spartan, rooms, some of which have fantastic views onto Svetitskhoveli Cathedral. Breakfast is excellent, and homemade wine is usually on offer. $

EATING

SEE MAP PAGE 84

Opizari 2 Mamulashvili St ☏ 995 322 513260. A swish, modern place aiming to look old – think solid oak tables and chairs, exposed brickwork, and a barn-like vibe. The menu of Georgian food is extensive but although the dishes are tasty enough, they're also a little overpriced. There is a very fine wine list though. $\overline{\underline{SS}}$

Ornament Express 14 Erekle II Street ⓦ facebook. com/ornamentexpress1. With a fantastic view of the Svetitskhoveli Cathedral from its garden and terrace, *Ornament Express* is ahead of the game from the start. The food measures up – there are great breakfast options and the main meals are good too. $\overline{\underline{SS}}$

★ **Café Tatin** 20 Mamulashvili St ⓦ facebook.com/ tatin.mtskheta. A charming little café that exudes a sense of nineteenth-century decadence. It's good for lunch – the lobio is excellent – or for a mid-afternoon coffee and slice of apple strudel. $\overline{\underline{S}}$

DIRECTORY

Banks Arsukidze St, running along south of Svetitskhoveli Cathedral, is home to a couple of banks with ATMs and there are also a few at the small square where the marshrutkas stop.

Pharmacies Less numerous than in many Georgian towns – one option is Apotheka on 17 Kostava St.

Mtskheta to Gori

If you're self-driving between Mtskheta and Gori, there are a couple of worthwhile diversions en route. First up is the **Shio-Mgvime Monastery**, which was established in the sixth century and quickly became one of the largest monastic complexes in Georgia. The exterior is attractive, while the inside is decorated with outstanding nineteenth-century frescoes.

Shio-Mgvime is at the end of a one-way canyon, so you'll need to return to Mtskheta before taking the E60 towards Gori. Castle enthusiasts may enjoy the scramble up to **Ksani Fortress**, which boasts a commanding position atop a hill, while wine lovers should make a point of stopping at **Château Mukhrani** (ⓦ facebook.com/ ChateauMukhrani). This nineteenth-century castle with extensive landscaped gardens featured in *World's Best Vineyards'* Top 50 list in 2023.

Gori

The area around Gori has been settled for thousands of years, and the city itself seems to date from at least the seventh century, but its main claim to fame is as the birthplace of Josef Stalin, an association of which many inhabitants are still proud. More recently, the city made headlines in 2008 when it was briefly occupied by Russia during the South Ossetian conflict, and it was rumoured it would be used as a base to attack Tbilisi. In the event, the Russians withdrew after nine days.

Stalin Museum

Stalin Park • Charge • ⓦ stalinmuseum.ge

More of a shrine than a museum, this large and grandiose complex takes hagiography to a whole new level. It's packed with photos, artwork, busts and even Iranian carpets of Josef Stalin, from his youth through to his many years as General Secretary of the Communist Party and leader of the USSR. Emphasis is placed, of course, on Stalin's revolutionary credentials and activities. Lenin merits an appearance or two, but opponents such as Trotsky, Bukharin and so forth naturally have a very low profile. Similarly conspicuous by its absence is much in the way of discussion – or even acknowledgement – of the enormity of the crimes committed by the man. There is a small, and rather unadvertised, room on the ground floor that gives some attention to the Gulag system and the Stalinist repression, but it feels extremely perfunctory, especially since it's lumped in with a small and quite graphic wall display about the Abkhazian War. After the rooms dedicated to his early career and his drive to modernise the USSR in the 1930s, you'll come to the room that deals with the Great Patriotic War, in which Stalin is bigged up at the expense of individuals such as Marshal Zhukov. Famous photos of Stalin with

2

Churchill and Roosevelt at Yalta are on display here, as well as possibly the most hideous table lamp you'll ever see.

You'll then have the pleasure of a ridiculously reverential room including Stalin's death mask on a plinth. Pictures of his funeral in Moscow are on the wall in the corner, showing thousands of mourners lining the streets. Finally, there's a room of jolly memorabilia, including vases, plates and ivory caskets all inscribed with Stalin's face, as well as gifts to him from foreign governments. In the gift shop you can buy similar items, including t-shirts, tote bags, wine and reusable coffee cups.

Free guided tours in English run regularly, and – dependent on which guide you get – there's a chance of getting a considerably more balanced perspective than that offered by the museum's exhibits.

Stalin's birthplace

Stalin Park • Free

The house where Stalin was born sits in front of the Stalin Museum, enclosed in a building designed to look like a classical temple – note the hammer and sickles installed on the ceiling. You can't enter the house, but it's interesting for a quick look from the outside. Not far away stands Stalin's personal railway carriage, on which he travelled to Yalta, entry to which is included with a museum ticket.

Gori Fortress

Erekle Tatishvili St • Free

Thanks to an earthquake in 1920, the castle overlooking Gori is now little more than a ring of walls atop a hillock, but in its day it was a powerful fortress used to control this strategic city and the surrounding trade routes. It's a good place for getting views of the town – and beyond, including to the separatist state of South Ossetia to the north. At the time of research, the castle was undergoing renovations, which will hopefully tidy it up a little, as it seems dishevelled and unloved.

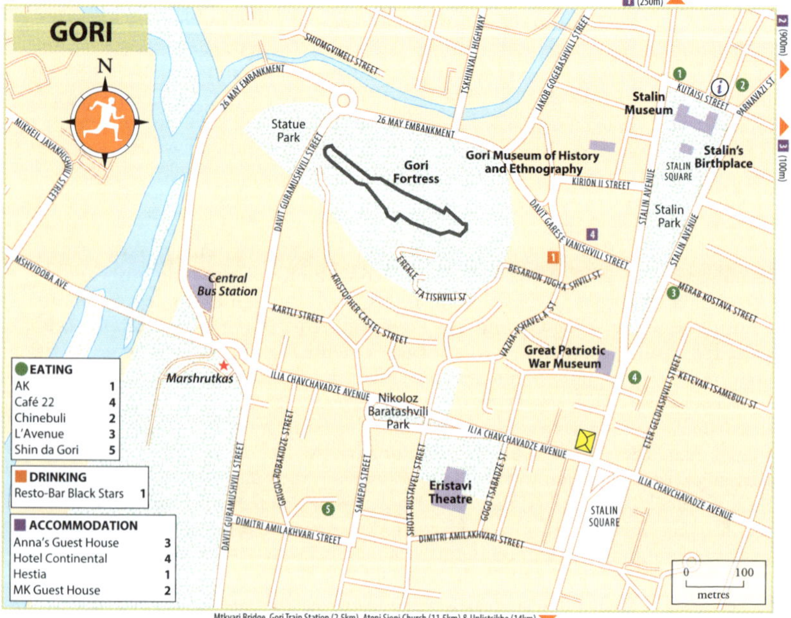

JOSEF STALIN

Josef Djugashvili, born in 1878 in Gori, was initially intended for the priesthood after excelling at school, but his interest in his studies at the Tbilisi Spiritual Seminary declined as he reached his mid-20s. Instead, he found himself influenced by the works of Karl Marx, and was inducted into social revolutionary groups, adopting the code name of **Stalin** ("Man of Steel") from 1912 onwards. After the split in the Russian Social Democratic Labour Party, he sided with **Lenin's Bolshevik faction**.

Along with Leon Trotsky, he became one of Lenin's closest advisors following the **October Revolution** and was appointed to the position of General Secretary of the Communist Party. In the early 1920s, however, Lenin became increasingly concerned about Stalin, and in his Testament he recommended that Stalin be removed from power. Following Lenin's death, however, Stalin moved decisively, allying himself first with one faction and then another, until he had eliminated all his rivals and was firmly established as the USSR's supreme leader.

The 1930s saw Stalin unleashing a **wave of terror** across the USSR. Following the assassination of Party member Kirov in 1934, Stalin became increasingly paranoid. Former rivals such as Bukharin, Kamenev and Zinoviev were denounced and executed as counter-revolutionaries; Stalin's old personal enemy Trotsky fled to Mexico, where he was murdered by Stalin's agents in 1940. All told, it's thought that up to 20 million people died as a result of Stalin's repressive regime.

During World War II Stalin was initially taken disastrously by surprise when Hitler attacked the USSR, but according to one of his chief generals, Zhukov, Stalin directed the war effort effectively. He was acclaimed in the West and affectionately referred to as '**Uncle Joe**'. Following the war, he became less popular as the USSR spread communism across Eastern Europe and the **Cold War** began.

Stalin **died in 1953** and his funeral in Red Square was attended by hundreds of thousands of mourners. After a brief power struggle – hilariously depicted in Armando Iannucci's 2017 black comedy film *The Death of Stalin* – Nikita Khrushchev emerged as Stalin's successor and embarked on a period of '**de-Stalinisation**', which involved the dismantling of the personality cult that had arisen and the removal of the hundreds of statues in cities across the USSR. Gori, however, would have none of this denigration of its famous native son and has stubbornly clung on to Stalin ever since.

Beneath the castle is a sculpture of a group of knights sitting in a circle, missing various body parts. It's in memorial of the lives lost in the 2008 Six Day War. Another memorial – a little further round, at the junction of 26 May Embankment and Tskhinvali Highway – has a hint of the space age about it with its clean sleek lines and smooth curves.

Gori Museum of History and Ethnography

12 Kirion II St • Charge • ☎ 995 370 272867

You'll likely visit many similar museums across Georgia, but this is definitely one of the best. It's well presented, well labelled and extensive, with friendly staff who speak great English, making it a perfect place to learn about the regional history beyond Stalin. In pride of place is a magnificent pottery drinking vessel, nearly three thousand years old, in the shape of a moose.

Great Patriotic War Museum

19 Stalin Ave • Charge • ☎ 995 370 272712

Largely consisting of photos and other Great Patriotic War memorabilia, this small museum also briefly covers Georgia's Abkhazian and South Ossetian conflicts, including Russian weaponry that fell on Gori in 2008. If you haven't seen enough of Stalin yet, there's another statue of him in here too. You'll need to speak Georgian or Russian to get much out of a visit.

Stalin Square

After visiting the Stalin Museum, you might enjoy a quick wander down the very wide Stalin Avenue to the even wider **Stalin Square**, where stands the centre of local government – an enormous neoclassical Soviet building that was once fronted by a statue of… Trotsky. Just kidding – it was of course a statue of Stalin, and it was only removed in 2010, under cover of night to try to avoid a mass outcry of outraged local Stalinists.

ARRIVAL AND DEPARTURE
GORI

By bus Gori's bus station is inconveniently sited about 2km north of the centre, on Tskhinvali Highway. There are marshrutka departures to Borjomi (12.40pm and 4.10pm), Akhaltsikhe (8.30am and 2pm) and the Batumi (9am and 12noon). For Kutaisi you need to go to the main highway and pick up a marshrutka from Tbilisi – taxis can take you to the best marshrutka pick up spot.

Those heading to Tbilisi have it easier: marshrutkas depart from the old, much more central, bus station on Chavchavadze Ave every 15 minutes between 7am to 7pm. There are no marshrutkas to Mstkheta, but one heading to Tbilisi may drop you en route.

By shared taxi If you don't want a marshrutka to Tbilisi, you can also take a shared taxi. These go regularly from outside the theatre (24 Chavchadze Ave).

By train Gori's smart, Soviet train station is 2.5km south of the town centre along Stalin Ave and over the Mtkvari Bridge. Three trains a day run to Tbilisi, the most conveniently timed ones leaving at 11.50pm and 4pm (duration one hour). The 4pm train also calls at Mtskheta (duration 50 min), and there's also one to Kutaisi at 10am (duration 4.5 hours).

By car Situated on the main road between Tbilisi and Kutaisi, Gori is easily accessible by car. The city presents no particular driving challenges, and there's plenty of parking available.

GETTING AROUND

By foot The sights in Gori are all centred around Stalin Park. Walking is the most sensible way to get between them.

By taxi You might want to take a taxi to the bus or train station; it's not far and shouldn't cost much.

INFORMATION

Tourist Information Centre 23a Kutaisi St, ☎ 995 370 270776, ✉ ticgori@gmail.com. The tourist information centre, opposite the Stalin Museum, is staffed by a friendly team who can tell you about the attractions in town and in the surrounding area, including giving out very handy and comprehensive leaflets about walking and hiking in the region. Free wi-fi is available here too. Daily 10am to 6pm.

ACCOMMODATION
SEE MAP PAGE 86

Anna's Guest House 60 Kutaisi St ☎ 995 577 091463. You have the entire ground floor to yourself at this friendly guesthouse, including a bedroom with 4 beds, a lounge area, and a bathroom. Breakfast is included, and the host family are lovely. $

Hotel Continental 6 Garsevanishvili St ☎ 995 598 150018. The *Continental* has nine shiny, clean and modern rooms on a reasonably quiet street near the main square, though for maximum quietness request a room at the back. The breakfast is good, and the hostess, Mega, is quite possibly the friendliest person you'll meet in all of Georgia. $$

★ **Hestia** 24 Ekaterine Jughashvili St ☎ 995 598 275522. One of Georgia's best guesthouses, Hestia is on a quiet street a few blocks north of the Stalin Museum. The rooms and common areas have all been decorated stylishly and to a high standard, the breakfast is outstanding, and there's free wine for guests in the evening. A lot of thought has clearly been given here to making a stay comfortable and relaxing, and the effort has paid off handsomely. $$

MK Guest House 1 Iliko Sukhishvili St ☎ 995 595 908691. About a kilometre northeast of the town centre, *MK Guest House* has three rooms: two double and one quad. Those upstairs are clean and nice enough, but the double downstairs is a beautiful rustic little den and a lovely place to spend the night. All rooms are en suite and breakfast is included. $

EATING AND DRINKING
SEE MAP PAGE 86

AK 4 Kutaisi St ☎ 995 555 932093. A little coffee shop on the main square, which – as well as a decent coffee – can supply you with pretty good freshly squeezed juices, baked goods, and ice cream. $

★ **Café 22** 22 Stalin Ave 🌐 facebook.com/cafe22gori. Funky, friendly and central, this little coffee shop serves decent coffee and incredible cakes. Snacky food such as pizza is available too, and takeaway baked goods are on offer, so all in all it's a good lunch option. $

Chinebuli 3 Kutaisi St ☎ 995 370 270602. A café-

SOUTH OSSETIA

The separatist republic of **South Ossetia** sits just to the north of Gori. Under the Soviet Union it was an autonomous *oblast* (province) within the Georgian Soviet Socialist Republic, but during the collapse of the USSR, it declared **independence from Georgia**. A short and bloody war ensued, ending in 1992 when Georgia's president Shevardnadze agreed that the majority of South Ossetia would remain under the control of its internationally unrecognised government.

The Saakashvili government, which came to power in 2003, was less tolerant of breakaway regions within Georgia. It was successful in bringing Adjara back under Tbilisi's control, but an attempt in 2008 to recover South Ossetia led to the disastrous **Six Day War**, when Russia temporarily occupied Gori. It's been theorised that had the West intervened on Georgia's behalf in this conflict, Russia may not have had the subsequent confidence to annex the Crimea in 2014. Since the Six Day War, Russia has adopted a "creeping border" strategy, gradually moving the South Ossetian border southward in extremely small increments, expanding its territory at the expense of Georgia.

South Ossetia is now administered entirely independently of Tbilisi, and its government is unrecognised internationally except by a handful of states, including Russia. Georgia maintains that it's illegally occupied territory, and it's not possible to visit this region from the Georgian side, nor is it advisable to get close to its borders. From Russia, access is only via the Roki Tunnel and will require a double-entry Russian visa and permission to travel from South Ossetia's Ministry of Foreign Affairs, which is not easy to obtain. Rough Guides does not condone this as it is regarded as illegal entry into Georgian territory. The UK's FCDO **advises against all travel to South Ossetia**.

restaurant with a long menu of Georgian classics, including khinkali, khachapuri, lobio and meat dishes, this is a good choice for lunch or dinner. It's quite spartan though, with less style than some other options in town, and its position opposite the Stalin Museum makes it an obvious place for tour groups. $\overline{\underline{\$\$}}$

L'Avenue 24 Stalin Ave ☎ 995 598 353949. The nice and central *L'Avenue* is friendly and stylish, with exposed brickwork walls and a slinky soundtrack. It does Georgian food, but is probably stronger on the pizza/pasta/burgers/etc options. $\overline{\underline{\$\$}}$

Resto-Bar Black Stars 13 Besarion Jughashvili St ☎ 995 591 153332. Just below the castle, this mostly outdoor bar is a pleasant place to while away a summer's evening with a tipple or two. Food is available too but it's better to stick to the drinks. A couple of gorgeous and friendly cats live here and may adopt you for the evening! $\overline{\underline{\$}}$

Shin da Gori 1 Rusudan Kurdadze St ⓦ shindagori.ge. Tucked away in a quiet courtyard to the south of the town centre, Shin da Gori is an unexpectedly large and popular spot serving up excellent Georgian dishes – the lobio and the ojakhuri are both particularly recommended – with a smattering of other options such as pizzas. On a warm evening the outside courtyard is perfect, and if it's colder, the upstairs indoor terrace is lovely. The downside – and it is quite a downside – is the positively glacial service. $\overline{\underline{\$\$}}$

ENTERTAINMENT

Eristavi Theatre 24 Chavchavadze Ave ⓦ facebook.com/goristeatri. There are occasionally dramatic or musical performances on at this theatre.

DIRECTORY

Banks Banks and ATMs can be found mostly along Chavchavadze Ave, but there is a branch of Liberty Bank at 26 Stalin Ave, which is slightly more convenient.

Pharmacies Chavchavadze Ave is Gori Pharmacy Central. You'll find a cluster of them here just south of the castle.

Post office The central post office can be found at 15 Stalin Ave. It's open 10am–5pm Mon–Fri.

Around Gori

There are a couple of interesting sites in Gori's immediate environs, both achievable with public transport and a bit of patience.

Uplistsikhe

Uplistsikhe Complex Rd • Charge • ☎ 995 595 520778 • Marshrutka to Kvakhvreli

Just outside Gori, the remarkable cave city of **Uplistsikhe** is one of the more unusual sights in Georgia. It's thought to date back perhaps as far as 1000 BC, though it was perhaps at its most prosperous between 300 BC and 300 AD. It lost its pre-eminence after Georgia's Christianisation, and terminal decline set in during the Mongol period, but it was only finally abandoned at the beginning of the nineteenth century. From the mid-twentieth century onward, there have been considerable archaeological explorations of the site, yielding many fascinating finds.

It's an extensive place which rewards full exploration. In particular, look out for the amazing carved ceilings in several rooms, including the Throne Hall and the arch above the Hall with Cascade. The only non-cave structure here is the ninth century church, which was built on top of a pagan temple. From the top of the complex there are lovely views across the river valley.

The modern and well-labelled museum – easy to miss down a staircase behind the café near the entrance – provides a good overview of the site's history, as well as displaying an interesting selection of archaeological finds from the site. It's easy to hire a guide in the car park to show you around, or you can pick up an audio tour from the ticket office. Note that guides may try to induce you to pay for the more expensive ticket, saying it allows entry to more caves, as well as including wine tasting and a guided tour. While it certainly includes the latter two, the claim around the extra caves is not true: the standard ticket allows entry to all.

To get here on public transport, you'll need the marshrutka from Gori to Kvakhvreli village – these run every 20 minutes, between 6.30am and 6pm. Once in Kvakhvreli, it's a 2km walk to the site. Alternatively, it's easy to arrange a taxi round trip from Gori, including waiting time.

Ateni Sioni Monastery

Khidistavi-Ateni Rd • Free, donations appreciated • ☎ 995 551 111482 • Marshrutka to Ateni

The lovely seventh century **Ateni Sioni** is one of Georgia's most beautiful monasteries, with a fabulous setting in a forested canyon surrounded by vineyards. The church itself is built of orange stone. Don't miss the relief carvings on the outside, including the one of deer running away from hunters. Inside, the church walls are covered with incredible medieval frescoes. The church is sometimes locked, but the caretaker can usually be found in the wooden kiosk by gate.

The road to get there is full of potholes but it's navigable with a bit of patience. If you're interested in doing a wine tour, there are plenty of vineyards dotted along this stretch of road. Marshrutkas from Gori's central bus station leave when full between 7am to 6pm.

Georgian Military Highway

The **Georgian Military Highway** – or, if you want to be a bit less romantic about it, the E117 – runs from Mtskheta to Vladikavkaz in Russia. Being one of the few routes through the Caucasus mountains, it's an ancient road, though its current form is largely due to Russian works undertaken throughout the nineteenth century which were deemed essential for Russia to maintain control of its new Georgian protectorate.

It's a very scenic road, and is well surfaced too, making it a pleasure to travel. The end destination of most travellers is the town of Stepantsminda, but there are several worthwhile stops en route. It's recommended that you either self-drive, or take a shared taxi up the Highway – allowing you to visit the various sights – and get a marshrutka back.

Ananuri Fortress

Ananuri village • Free

The picturesque monastery-fortress of Ananuri is one of Georgia's most iconic sights — a stunning, classically Georgian church nestled in wooded hills above a gorgeous blue reservoir, formed by the Zhindali Dam to the south. Stop in the car park and walk back along the bridge a little way to get a particularly good view of the complex.

There are two churches on the site: the more interesting is the **Church of the Mother of God**, which boasts beautiful exterior carvings, particularly around the doorway and on the wall to the right. The interior is mostly whitewashed, but where frescoes do remain, they are very impressive. On the wall to the left of the entrance door is a depiction of hell which is unsettlingly nasty, involving people being tormented by demons and, er, being eaten by horses.

The other church is usually locked. However, it's worth heading to the back of the complex so you can climb the castle tower (access via the wall and staircase to the left of its main door, which is also kept locked). From the top, you'll get a great view of the monastery complex and the reservoir beyond. Careful on the third floor, as the wood beams that make up the floor are a little widely spaced.

About 4km past Ananuri, in the village of Tsikhisdziri, keep your eyes peeled on the right side of the road for an excellent bus stop. Yes, a bus stop. It's richly decorated with bright yellow and orange tiles depicting Georgian legends, and it's great.

Gudauri

Georgia's premier **ski resort** (ⓦgudauri.info) is a straggly town of hotels and restaurants stretching up the switchbacking road. There's 64km worth of ski runs (including black, red, blue and green), which are consistently praised by skiing aficionados, and it's incredibly affordable compared with Western Europe. The resort suffered a setback in 2018 when a chair lift went into reverse, but this hasn't deterred skiers and snowboarders from visiting and enjoying the great pistes here. It's also the venue for the **Summer Set electronic music festival** (ⓦsummerset.ge/summerset) in July, previous headliners of which have included *Faithless* and *Cigarettes After Sex*, as well as local talent. If you're not visiting Georgia for winter sports, though, you'll probably want to pass on by.

ACCOMMODATION	GUDAURI

There are any number of hotels, guesthouses and apartments in Gudauri. Picking one near the ski lifts may be advisable if you don't want to lug equipment about, though plenty of places do offer a ski-to-door service.

Edelweiss Hotel Upper Gudauri ⓦedelweisshotel. tripcombined.com. Close to the chair lifts, the *Edelweiss* is a popular hotel with comfortable (if fairly corporate) rooms, good food, lovely staff, and a great bar with a log fire. A shuttle service to and from Tbilisi can be arranged. $$$

Gudauri Loft Gudauri St ⓦgudauriloft.ge. One of Gudauri's best choices, the *Loft* is a pleasant and stylish hotel with great facilities including equipment rental, a heated rooftop pool, a fantastic shabby-chic industrial bar, and a spa and sauna. $$$

Georgian-Russian Friendship Monument

Georgian Military Highway • Free

An enormous circular Soviet concrete delight, this monument was erected in 1983 to celebrate 200 years since the Treaty of Georgievsk between Russia and Georgia, which established Georgia as a protectorate of Russia. Whether the Georgians would consider this treaty, and the ensuing events, as worthy of celebration is perhaps debatable.

The monument stands on a bluff above the **Devil's Valley**. If the clouds lift from around it, you'll get beautiful views of the nearby mountains. If not, you can feast your eyes on the remarkable mural that extends around the entire internal length of the monument.

Travertines

Georgian Military Highway • Free

About 6km on from the Friendship Monument, you'll find this unusual geological formation: a large yellow-orange expanse of limestone, formed by millennia of reaction between water and calcium carbonate. There's a car park opposite, complete with souvenir stalls.

Stepantsminda

For most travellers, **Stepantsminda** is the final stop on the Georgian Military Highway. Known as Kazbegi during Soviet times – in honour of Kazi-Beg, an eighteenth-century local ruler who adopted the surname Kazbegi – the town is now a major tourist destination for visitors who come to hike in the surrounding majestic mountains. It's overlooked by the towering 5,054m-tall Mount Kazbek – thought to be the mountain to which Prometheus was chained in Greek mythology – which can be seen above the town on a clear day, but otherwise gives only ominous hints of its presence through the low swirling clouds.

Gergeti Trinity Church

Stepantsminda-Sameba Rd • Free • ☎ 995 598 978998

This small but iconic church is one of Georgia's best recognised sights, perched on a ridge high above Stepantsminda but still a considerable distance below Mount Kazbek's towering summit. It's a gorgeous church, with beautiful and intricate carvings on the exterior, including some very strange figures on the bell tower. You may find it difficult to get much of a sense of the inside as it's usually crammed with tourists.

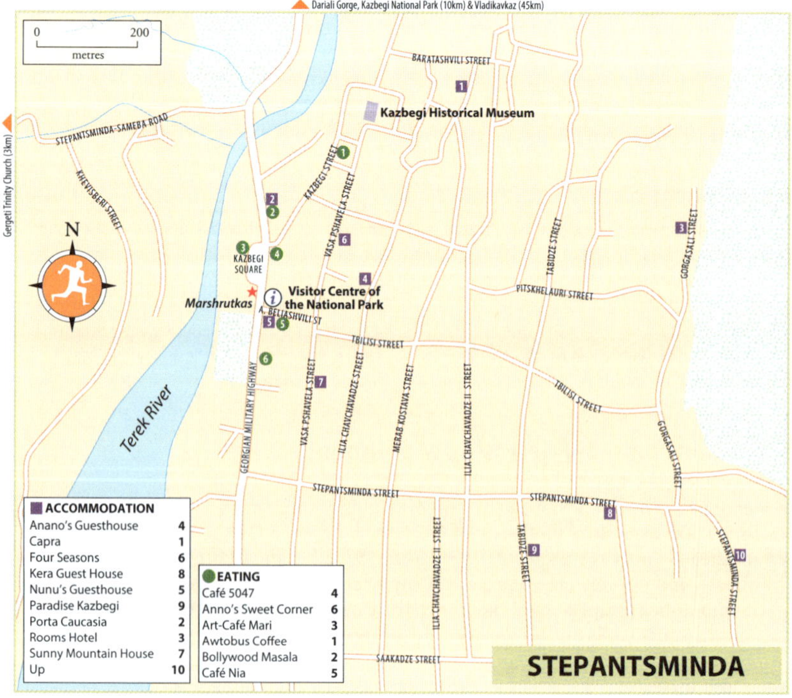

ACCOMMODATION	
Anano's Guesthouse	4
Capra	1
Four Seasons	6
Kera Guest House	8
Nunu's Guesthouse	5
Paradise Kazbegi	9
Porta Caucasia	2
Rooms Hotel	3
Sunny Mountain House	7
Up	10

EATING	
Café 5047	4
Anno's Sweet Corner	6
Art-Café Mari	3
Awtobus Coffee	1
Bollywood Masala	2
Café Nia	5

A new asphalted road up to the church has made driving up here considerably easier – though there's a strong argument that this road has seriously diminished the beauty of the spot – and you'll have no trouble getting a taxi up here from town. The best approach, of course, is the short but invigorating hike (see page 93).

Kazbegi Historical Museum

2 Kazbegi St • Free

The town's museum – housed in a building that was once the home of Alexander Kazbegi, a famous Georgian novelist – has been closed since the mid-2010s and there are no apparent plans to reopen it. It's still worth a quick glance if you're passing by, as it's a solid example of an old-fashioned Kazbegi house, and there's an attractive church next door, but it's not worth a special trip.

2

ARRIVAL AND DEPARTURE — STEPANTSMINDA

By bus Marshrutkas to Tbilisi run roughly hourly from 7am until 6pm in summer; in winter there are 5 marshrutkas a day, departing between 9am and 5pm, and taking 2.5 hours.

By taxi You can pick up shared taxis to Tbilisi from the main square. There's no public transport across the border to Russia but you can usually find a taxi willing to take you to Vladikavkaz. The journey should take one hour, assuming there's no delay at the border (which is admittedly quite an assumption, especially given the current at time of writing governmental advice against travelling to Russia).

By car The Georgian Military Highway up to Stepantsminda is, for the most part, a well-paved road and is an excellent drive, so long as you're confident with switchbacking mountain roads. Roads in the lower part of Stepantsminda itself are good, but several of the streets up behind the main square quickly become unpaved and bumpy. Parking is easy and free.

GETTING AROUND

Stepantsminda is a small place, in which your feet can take you everywhere you need to go. If you want a taxi up to the Gergeti Trinity Church, they're easy to find in the main square.

INFORMATION

Visitor Centre of the National Park Kazbegi Sq, ☎ 995 591 963335. The staff are knowledgeable and helpful, but can be a little pushy about tours. Daily 9am to 6pm.

WALK UP TO THE CHURCH

From Stepantsminda's main square, follow the main road to the north. Cross the bridge and then take Gergeti Street uphill past the *Panorama Restaurant*. When the asphalt ends, after about half a kilometre, turn left through the attractive stone village. You'll see a ruined tower on the hillock ahead, and the **church** still high above you on the right.

Pass *Café Gergeti* and take the right-hand route where the path forks – heading straight up towards the tower. (Alternatively, you can take the left fork, which meanders beneath the tower along a stream and rejoins the main path shortly afterwards with a bit of a steep slog uphill.) Follow the **white-red-white route markers**, pass between the tower and the hut and continue along the clear path clinging to the hillside.

This is a strenuous uphill heft for a while, but eventually the path levels out, at which point you should be able to see the church again, a little above you to the right. The path then splits again. Take the right-hand route continuing to follow the white-red-white markers on a slightly gentler ascent. You'll soon reach the plateau below the church. Turn right and head up to it.

Return by the same route, or you can extend your walk by heading over to the large square car park opposite the church, then taking the rough track up the hill. This will lead to a succession of church viewpoints, before bending around a corner and heading up to Mount Kazbek's summit. It's a good **day's walk** to the church, and then beyond, on this route, depending on how far you want to go – bear in mind that you also have to come back.

ACCOMMODATION

There are an awful lot of guesthouses in Stepantsminda, so it shouldn't be troublesome finding somewhere to stay. Other good options include the perennial favourites Anano's Guesthouse (40A V. Pashavela St, ☎ 995 595 099449) and Nunu's Guesthouse (2/6 Akaki Beliashvili St, ☎ 995 599 570915).

Capra 1 Merab Kostava Street ⓦ capra.tripcombined.com. A smart hotel that manages to combine modern and rustic aesthetics, Capra offers cosy rooms and a fantastic terrace for views across to Mount Kazbek. The breakfast is great, and extremely tasty evening meals are also available. All in all, a very good choice. ₷₷

Four Seasons 18 V. Pshavela St ☎ 995 591 710766. A pleasant guesthouse in a convenient spot just a block away from the main square, Four Seasons has cheap and comfortable rooms and good views. No breakfast though. ₷₷

Kera Guest House 16 Stepantsminda St ☎ 995 579 031708. Towards the top of the town, the en-suite rooms at *Guest House Kera* are cosy and snug, and the windows face Mount Kazbek, so good views are assured. The breakfast is a veritable feast. ₷

Paradise Kazbegi 74 Tabidze St ☎ 995 595 306725. Paradise has a lovely terrace overlooking town, clean stylish rooms and very friendly hosts. The walls are quite thin though – you might need earplugs. ₷

Porta Caucasia 2 Tergdaleulebi St ⓦ portacaucasia.com. A relatively recent challenger to Rooms' monopoly on Stepantsminda's luxury hotel scene, *Porta Caucasia* has the advantage of being nice and central, sitting just by the bridge to Gergeti Trinity Church. It has 33 rooms (even-numbered ones have views of Mount Kazbek) across three floors, as well as the requisite gym and sauna. There are two restaurants on site – Georgian and European – and breakfast is included. If all that's not enough, the owners also have a winery and sell the produce from the attached shop. ₷₷₷

★ **Rooms Hotel** 1 Gorgasali St ⓦ roomshotels.com/kazbegi. Occupying a prime position at the top of town, *Rooms* is a beautifully smart hotel with a gorgeous sense of style. The lobby has the feel of a cosy library – albeit one with full length windows affording marvellous views of the Gergeti Trinity Church and Mount Kazbek beyond. Half of the 155 rooms share this iconic view, and those that

---

RUSSIAN NORTH CAUCASUS

Passing through the Georgian-Russian border here – which is open to foreigners with appropriate visas – will bring you into the region of **North Ossetia**. Even before Russia's war with Ukraine, the British FCDO advised against visiting here, as well as the neighbouring provinces of Ingushetia, Kabardino-Balkaria and Chechnya, owing to security concerns. If and when the situation changes, travellers in this part of Russia will be able to see some fascinating, beautiful and rarely visited sights.

One of the most interesting lies not far from the Georgian border: the **Dargavs Necropolis**. Dargavs is thought to be a cemetery of plague victims, and it consists of many little stone buildings with beehive-like roofs, standing alone on a hillside above the Midagrabindon River. Old coins can be found here, owing to a local tradition involving a coin being thrown from the hillside to the cemetery. If it struck rock, the soul of the dead person had got to heaven. The site can be reached from Vladikavkaz, the capital of North Ossetia, after about an hour's drive.

Vladikavkaz itself is not an enormously exciting place, though it has one claim to fame: in 2016, Jamie Lafferty of *The Independent* newspaper proclaimed it to be the least friendly city in the world, which inspired a subsequent ambitious municipal campaign to "change the view of Jamie Lafferty". From Vladikavkaz, it's possible to visit the memorial to the tragic Beslan school siege, which claimed the lives of more than 380 people in 2004.

After years of unrest, the nearby **Republic of Chechnya** still makes occasional headlines owing to the actions of its autocratic ruler, Ramzan Kadyrov, a close Putin ally. The capital, Grozny, is a shining showpiece city, with wide avenues, enormous hotels, and one of the largest mosques in Russia. Elsewhere, the mountain scenery in Chechnya is stunning – but it all comes with a dark side: reports of human rights violations are common.

It's not easy travelling here – English is not widely spoken, police are best avoided, and if you get into trouble you'll most likely be on your own. However, owing to the war with Ukraine, visiting Russia – particularly this largely untouristed region – is currently **not advisable**.

don't have great vistas of other mountains instead. There's a huge terrace to sit on in good weather, and the in-house restaurant and bar are top-notch too. In addition, there's a spa, swimming pool and gym. If you're debating where to splash out on your Georgia trip, you could do much worse than choosing here. $$$$

Sunny Mountain House 56 V. Pshavela St ☎ 995 599 802099. Seven attractive, clean rooms all with modern private bathrooms, in a centrally located family home with a gorgeous dining room. Not all rooms have views, but there is a shared garden and terrace. Kitchen available for guests' use. $

Up 27 Stepantsminda St ☎ 995 591 816912. Appropriately named, being at the very top of the town, *Up* has four rooms, each with en-suite bathroom, and a stylish shared lounge and kitchen. Try to get one of the two upstairs rooms with balcony and fantastic views. Breakfast is included. The only downside is that it is quite a hike from the centre, but if you're looking for a quiet place then that could be an advantage. $

EATING SEE MAP PAGE 92

Although Stepantsminda has hundreds of hotels and guesthouses, places to eat are rather thinner on the ground. Many guesthouses will also offer evening meals, but you'll need to give them advance notice.

Café 5047 Kazbegi Sq ☎ 995 599 969114. In a fashionably dishevelled room featuring some beautiful antique furniture and some not particularly beautiful artworks, the rustic *Café 5047* is one of the liveliest options in town in the evening. The food – Georgian and international standards – is all very good, especially the Megrelian khachapuri, and it has a decent drinks menu. Best of all, there's a stove that keeps you lovely and cosy on cold evenings. $$

Anno's Sweet Corner Georgian Military Highway ☎ 995 514 007070. Primarily a little place for coffee and ice cream, *Anno's* also offers a short menu of snacky options. It's largely a fair weather only place, with little indoor seating. Ice cream from 3 GEL. 10am–7pm.

Art-Café Mari Kazbegi Sq ⊛ tinyurl.com/5n8mp422. Occupying a great spot on the main square, you're likely to find yourself gravitating towards *Art-Café Mari* at some point during your stay. With a menu covering plenty of Georgian classics, as well as pizzas, it's a good filling station, and the great view means you'll be more than happy to stay for a drink or two. $$

Awtobus Coffee Kazbegi St ☎ 995 599 47 10 55. Yes, it's a bit gimmicky, but who can resist having a cup of coffee on a grounded bus? The bus in question appears to have come from La Coruña in Spain; answers on a postcard please as to what it's doing here. As well as coffee and tea, there's a small selection of good cakes. Coffee from 3 GEL. 9am–9pm.

Bollywood Masala Tergdaleulebi St ☎ 995 592 900002. It comes as a bit of a surprise to find an Indian restaurant here in Stepantsminda. Although the food is a bit variable, it's definitely a good choice if you're looking for a break from Georgian dishes. $$

Café Nia Kazbegi Sq. It doesn't look promising, but the Georgian dishes on offer at this little restaurant on the square are among the best in town. If it's a nice day, it's more pleasant to sit at an outdoor table than in the spartan dining room. $$

Around Stepantsminda

Valleys to the south of Stepantsminda, including **Sno Valley** and **Truso Valley**, are beautiful spots for hiking trips. The Truso Valley, as well as being gorgeous walking country with some unusual limestone travertines, has a few points of minor historical interest, including the dramatically sited ruins of Zakagori Fortress. From the village of Juta, in the Sno Valley, you can make a two-day trip over the Chaukhi Pass to Roshka in Khevsureti, a lovely route that takes you past the beautiful Abudelauri Lakes. Detailed trekking routes can be found on the excellent Caucasus Trekking website (⊛ caucasus-trekking.com/regions/kazbegi).

Dariali Gorge

The road continues from Stepantsminda up to the Russian border. Before long it enters the **Dariali Gorge**, which is one of the very few passes through the Caucasus and has thus been of strategic importance throughout history – it was long believed that Alexander the Great set up huge gates here to keep out the uncivilised hordes in the north. The border is less impenetrable these days, and a steady stream of Georgian, Armenian, Iranian and Russian lorries ply the route. Even if you're not crossing, if you have your own transport it's an interesting and scenic drive up to the border. You'll know when you've reached it: there's an enormous and reasonably attractive new Georgian church just to the right of the road.

Khevsureti

High in the Caucasus mountains between Kazbegi and Tusheti lies **Khevsureti**, an isolated and beautiful part of Georgia which is only accessible during the summer months, and even then only with suitable vehicles. It's an ideal destination for trekking amid the unspoiled and beautiful hills. It's possible to trek between the Khevsureti village of Roshka and the Sno Valley in Kazbegi via the Abudelauri Lakes.

Shatili

The main village of Khevsureti, right up near the Chechnyan border, is **Shatili**. Composed of many defensive towers, all built together into one remarkable fortified settlement, it's one of the most striking villages in Georgia. The surrounding scenery is magnificent too, and venturing up here will provide ample opportunity for outdoor exploration.

ARRIVAL AND DEPARTURE   SHATILI

By bus Marshrutkas leave Tbilisi's Samgori metro station at 10am on Tuesdays and Fridays, or the Didube bus station at 9am on Wednesdays and Saturdays. They make the respective return trip on Wednesdays and Sundays at 10am, or Thursdays and Sundays at noon. It's only possible to make this trip in the summer months, usually between mid-May and the end of October.

ACCOMMODATION

Ethnic Hotel Shatili-Mutso Rd ☎ 995 595 503622, ✉ shatilihostel@gmail.com. In a converted tower, the *Ethnic Hotel* is a friendly and welcoming spot in the centre of the village. They're able to help arrange treks in the surrounding area, and serve fantastic food as well. June to October. $$

Shatili Guest House Twins Shatili-Mutso Rd Ⓦ tinyurl. com/3eh77j55. A pair of cosy guesthouses by the river, *Guest House Twins* is a good place to base yourself on a visit to Shatili. They offer very good food and home-made wine. June to October. $

Borjomi

A comparatively new town, **Borjomi** came to prominence in the nineteenth century with the Russian annexation of Georgia. Tsarist troops commanded by Colonel Popev were heading south for a campaign against the Ottomans when they came across a mineral spring here, which Popov sampled and concluded it had healing properties. The water's fame spread across Russia, and members of the Russian elite – including Tchaikovsky, Chekhov, and the royal family – journeyed here to bathe in the springs. A water bottling plant was built in the 1890s, and Borjomi water became hugely popular all over the USSR.

There's not much evidence of the nineteenth century in Borjomi's architecture today. In fact, it has a much more Soviet feel about it than many Georgian towns, with scrappy blocks of flats still rising in prime positions. On the plus side, there are some fantastic bas-reliefs on the sides of prominent concrete buildings, with a particularly fine example in the main square. However, on Baratashvili St and 9 April St, which lead up to Borjomi's Central Park, there are still some examples of beautiful older buildings, including the outstanding blue-timbered HQ of JSC Borjomi Waters.

Borjomi Central Park

50 9 Aprili St • Charge • Ⓦ facebook.com/borjomipark

Borjomi's Central Park, which has to be one of Georgia's loveliest parks, is home to a couple of interesting historical and cultural sights. The building on your left as you enter is the original bottling plant for Borjomi's famous mineral water, and shortly afterward you'll find a glass pavilion, underneath which you can taste the water straight from the source.

These two sights aside, the park may not seem that appealing at first – packed as it is with souvenir stalls, amusement park rides and enigmatic enticements such as "the funny room" – but walk past all that and you'll soon find yourself on a quiet path through trees, alongside the river; a perfect place for a stroll. After 2km or so, you'll reach the outdoor **Tsar Sulphur Baths** (☎995 322 221221, charge) – very popular among locals.

Cable car

50 9 Aprili St • Charge

Starting beside the park entrance, a disconcertingly creaky **cable car** clanks its way up and down the hill above the park, providing an easy way to get some excellent views over the town. At the top, there's an equally creaky **Ferris wheel** for those who just can't get high enough. Alternatively, you can pick up some pleasant forest walking trails here, with route waymarkers clearly marked.

Firuze Palace

48 9 Aprili St • Free • ⓦ borjomi.goldentulip.com

Now a hotel operated by the Tulip Group (see page 99), this palace was built in 1892 by Mirza Reza Khan, a politician under the Iranian Qajar shahs who was appointed First Consul of Iran in Tbilisi. It's a beautiful palace, which effectively combines Persian, Georgian and European influences into one of the most distinctive buildings in Borjomi and the whole of Georgia. The staff don't seem to mind you

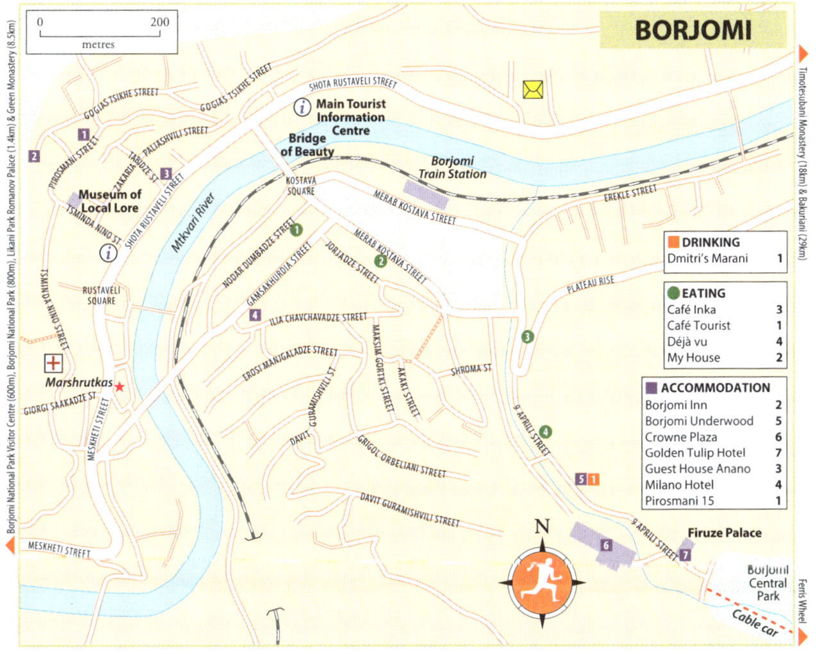

poking your nose in to have a quick look around the lobby and inner courtyard, but the frontage is the most impressive part.

Museum of Local Lore

5 Tsminda Nino St • Charge • ☎ 995 367 222362

The three floors of the **Museum of Local Lore** house an engaging mishmash of exhibits, from archaeology and ethnography to natural history. There's decent English language labelling on the ground floor, and an attempt has been made to modernise, with the museum getting more and more Soviet as you venture further upstairs, culminating in a marvellous natural history section that would have looked outdated in the 1970s. The building itself is a museum piece, with ornate ceilings, tiled floors, crumbling stairways, and display cabinets that seem as though they've slipped through a time warp.

The middle floor is perhaps the most interesting, housing oddities such as the first bottle of Borjomi water, 300-year-old bottles of wine, and some utterly repulsive pottery that once belonged to the Romanovs.

Likani Park Romanov Palace

Meskheti St • Charge • ⓦ borjomilikaniresort.com

The **Likani Palace** was built in the nineteenth century for Grand Duke Nicholas, the cousin of Tsar Alexander III. Now on the grounds of the Borjomi Likani Hotel, the impressive fairytale-like palace is roped off, but you can get reasonably close to it if you walk southwest from the hotel – assuming the hotel guards will let you onto the premises, which is likely but by no means a given. It is anticipated that the palace will be renovated and turned into a museum one day, but no-one knows when. The Tourist Information Centre suggested, without apparent confidence, that it might be by late 2024.

ARRIVAL AND DEPARTURE

By bus Borjomi's bus station is centrally located at 8 Meskheti St. Marshrutkas head hourly to Tbilisi (two hours), and to Akhaltsikhe (one hour). There are two marshrutkas a day to Gori (7.30am and 10.45am, 1.5 hours), two to Kutaisi (11.30am and 2.15pm, three hours) and one to Batumi (9am, five hours). For Bakuriani, seven marshrutkas a day leave between 9am and 5pm (45 minutes).

By train The twice-daily train from Borjomi to Tbilisi is slow (five hours); it leaves at 7am and the slightly less antisocial 4.40pm. More appealing is the narrow gauge railway trip to Bakuriani, an enjoyable Soviet relic which has unfortunately not operated since 2022. There's no anticipated reopening date.

By car Borjomi is on the main southern road that runs from Tbilisi to the Turkish border at Vale. At time of writing much of the road between Khashuri and Borjomi was under heavy reconstruction which meant that traffic could be slow. Driving in Borjomi itself presents no particular issues, but it's subject to short traffic jams at busy times.

GETTING AROUND

Borjomi's centre isn't large. You'll likely be staying in walking distance of the main sights.

INFORMATION

Tourist Information Centre 16 Shota Rustaveli St. Borjomi's tourist information centre is a glass-panelled building near the suspension bridge. The staff will answer any question you have, and can be quite informative if pushed, but the conversation may feel a bit like talking to a recalcitrant teenager. Daily 10am to 6pm.

There's also a small tourist information kiosk on the corner of Tsminda Nino St, next to the statue of Tchaikovsky, but it's no more helpful than the main office and its hours are irregular.

Borjomi National Park Visitor Centre 23 Meskheti St, ⓦ nationalparks.ge/en/site/borjomi-kharagaulinp. The staff at the National Park Visitor Centre are far more forthcoming than their counterparts in town, and are genuinely helpful and knowledgeable. Mon–Fri 9am–6pm, Sat–Sun 9am–4pm.

ACCOMMODATION SEE MAP PAGE 97

Borjomi Inn 4 Gogias Tsikhe St ☎ 995 577 481112. The four rooms in the *Borjomi Inn* are clean, plainly decorated, and en suite. Where this place really scores over its rivals is with its fantastic terrace, which is a great place to chill with a glass of wine while taking in the view right across town. $

Borjomi Underwood 40 9 Aprili St Ⓦ borjomiunderwood.ge. The smart *Borjomi Underwood* has 14 stylish rooms, designed and built by the friendly Dmitri and his family. All rooms have their own balcony, some are bordering on palatially sized, and some have Jacuzzis, so you may want to see a few before deciding what's best for you. Dmitri has great English and spent some years working in the national park, so is a good person to consult for tips on the best hikes. $$

Crowne Plaza 9 Baratashvili St Ⓦ tinyurl.com/et5ye5t4. Beautifully maintained and occupying a lovely position by the river, the *Crowne Plaza* certainly vies for the position of Borjomi's smartest and most exclusive choice. The 101 rooms are stylish and modern, the lobby is a relaxing place to hang out, and the bar has a touch of decadence about it. And naturally for a spa town, the spa, swimming pool and sauna are very good. $$$

★ **Golden Tulip Hotel** 48 9 Aprili St Ⓦ borjomi.goldentulip.com. Even if you don't stay here it's worth popping your head round the door of this palatial building dating from 1892. The rooms – set around an inner courtyard – are small but maintain a late nineteenth-century charm, and the restaurant is beautifully elegant. There's also a spa, a gym and – this has to be a first – a backgammon room. $$$

Guest House Anano 143 Rustaveli St Ⓦ anano.tripcombined.com. Nice and central yet extremely quiet – on an alley just off the main road – *Guest House Anano* has two rooms on the lower floor of a family home. Both are en suite, a rarity in Georgia in this price range, and the bathrooms are sparkling clean and modern. The rooms themselves are good too, and there are kitchen facilities. $

Milano Hotel 14 Gamsakhurdia St Ⓦ milanohotel.tripcombined.com. A good midrange place with a reasonably central location, this hotel offers clean and spacious rooms, most of which have great mountain views. The excellent breakfast is served on a lovely terrace. Rooms on the ground floor can be noisy, so try to score an upstairs one instead. $$

Pirosmani 15 15 Pirosmani St ☎ 995 568 761741. Friendly owners, super affordable prices, clean rooms and fantastic views over town from the balcony all combine to make Pirosmani 15 an excellent choice of guest house. Breakfast is very good, and there's often homemade chacha to sample. $

EATING SEE MAP PAGE 97

Café Inka 2 9 Aprili St ☎ 995 595 302077. A reliable restaurant serving the usual array of Georgian and international dishes. It's also good for coffee and cakes, with particularly good raspberry tarts. $$

Café Tourist 3 Nodar Dumbadze St. Back in the days of the USSR, customers in restaurants were treated as an unnecessary inconvenience and were served grudgingly at best. The incredible little *Café Tourist* singlehandedly keeps that honourable tradition alive with outstandingly surly service – and just to ensure you can't miss that this is a Soviet Union throwback, there's a lovely portrait of Stalin on the wall. The food isn't bad at all, but it's the experience you're here for. $$

Déjà vu 28 9 Aprili St Ⓦ tinyurl.com/mrysc7d5. Perhaps the best of the cafes along the street leading to Central Park, Déjà vu is a friendly place offering a good range of snacky lunches, with both Georgian and international options. On a warm day, its outside seating area is a lovely spot for watching the world go by.

My House 1200 Kostava St Ⓦ facebook.com/MYHOUSE55. The friendly staff in this sleek modern restaurant serve up good Georgian food (the ajapsandali aubergine stew is highly recommended, particularly paired with the khinkali), as well as plenty of international options available, including pizza, pasta and burgers. There's also a well-stocked bar here, so you can settle in for the evening.

DRINKING SEE MAP PAGE 97

★ **Dmitri's Marani** 40 9 April St Ⓦ tinyurl.com/2kv3zkae. The friendly and welcoming Dmitri (owner of the Borjomi Underwood hotel) makes his own Saparavi variety of wines and serves them up at his outdoor bar, along with wine-matured sulguni cheese. He's always up for a chat about wines, a subject on which he has considerable knowledge.

DIRECTORY

Banks There are banks intermittently along Rustaveli St for much of its length, with a particular concentration around the main square.

Hospitals Geo Hospital, 3 Giorgi Saakadze St, ☎ 995 322 505222, Ⓦ gh.ge/en.

Pharmacies The usual suspects, PSP Pharmacy and Aversi, have outlets on Rustaveli St.

Post office Borjomi's post office is a little way out of the centre, at 103 Rustaveli St. It's open 9am–5pm weekdays and 10am–2pm on Saturdays.

Around Borjomi

The area around Borjomi offers plenty of distractions, much of them outdoor activities: hiking in the nearby national park is hugely enjoyable, and there's also a decent enough ski resort, as well as the usual smattering of monasteries and castles.

Timotesubani

Tsaghveri-Timotesubani-Tadzari Rd • Free • Timotesubani marshrutka

The **Timotesubani Monastery** was built between the eleventh and eighteenth centuries. It consists of several churches, but the principal reason to visit is to view the outstanding frescoes inside the central Church of the Virgin Mary, which are thought to be contemporaneous with the reign of Queen Tamar the Great in the early 1200s. As well as more usual religious scenes, you'll find impressive frescoes of animals – including an elephant, a lion, a cheetah and a whole host of birds – on the arch on your right as you enter the church.

The grounds are beautifully maintained, and the complex is in a lovely quiet spot in the hills. The little shop opposite sells icons, candles, and local produce such as wine, chacha and honey. There are three marshrutkas a day here from Borjomi, leaving at 10.30am, 1.30pm and 5pm.

Bakuriani Ski Resort

Bakuriani village • Charge • ⓦ bakuriani.ski

Bakuriani is home to a **ski resort** with 29km of ski runs (the majority of which are black or red), and 20 lifts. It's not considered one of the world's greatest, but it's not bad. In summer, you can use the ski lifts as a good starting point for walking in the surrounding hills.

Until 2022, and hopefully again in the future, the best way to get to Bakuriani was on the very slow but very pretty narrow-gauge railway from Borjomi. Until the train service resumes, you'll need to go by car, so make sure you leave Borjomi via Tori St: as you head out of town, you'll see an old steam engine on a plinth, against a backdrop of a crumbling concrete monstrosity. On a grey day, it's somehow the most Soviet thing in the world.

Borjomi National Park

Visitor Centre: 23 Meskheti St • Free • ⓦ nationalparks.ge/en/site/borjomi-kharagaulinp

Borjomi National Park was founded in 1995 with the support of the WWF and the German government, and consists of 1,700 hectares of wild forest, through which thread 250km of marked trails, ranging in duration from two hours to five days (80km). From the park's highest points – for example, the summit of Mount Lomismta – views can extend to Turkey in one direction and all the way to Russia's Mount Elbrus in the other.

Activity options include hiking, horseriding, snowshoeing and mountain biking, all of which can be arranged through the visitor centre. There are shelters in the park for overnight stays, which consist of basic cabins with attached campsites. Wild camping is not permitted. You can rent all camping equipment from the visitor centre, as well as arrange hiking and horseriding guides, who can speak English, Georgian and Russian. Maps of hiking trails are also available from the visitor centre.

Visitors to the Park need to register. It's free, but you'll need to pay at the registration stage if you are planning to stay in the Park overnight. After being registered, you will be issued a permit, which may be checked by rangers, so don't lose it.

Green Monastery

Off Borjomi-Akhaltsikhe Highway • Free • Akhaltsikhe-bound marshrutka

Roughly 7km south of Borjomi on the Akhaltsikhe road, a rough track leads 1km up through a tree-lined canyon to the **Green Monastery**, so called because of the greenish tinge to the church's stones. The history of its foundation is unknown, but it's thought to date from around the ninth century, and is a beautiful tranquil spot. It's possible to drive up to the monastery, but parking on the main road and walking is far more enjoyable.

The Akhaltsikhe road

About 25km from Borjomi you'll see the very photogenic ruined fortresses of **Slesa and Moktseva** above the road. There's a place to park just beneath them, from which it's possible to scramble up to the fortresses for great views across the valley in both directions.

Continue 5km further on to reach Atskuri village, where you can't miss **Atskuri Castle** – possibly the most dramatically sited castle in the region. It's best admired from the road, or the bridge beneath it, as although it is possible to climb up to it (turn right after you cross the bridge and at the corner you'll find an arched staircase), it's very rough going and pretty unrewarding from the top, as the castle is full of scaffolding.

Akhaltsikhe

Akhaltsikhe (Georgian for "new castle") is a small city close to the Turkish border, making it a good entry point to the country for those travelling from Kars or Doğubeyazıt. It's a little further from the Armenian border, near Gyumri, but still close enough to be a sensible travel option between the two countries. Even if you're not heading out of Georgia, though, it's still worth making the trip down to Akhaltsikhe, as it's home to an enormous castle complex and is also a sensible base from which to visit one of Georgia's undisputed highlights, the remarkable cave monastery of Vardzia.

Rabati Castle

Kazbegi St • Charge • Ⓦ rabati.ge

This enormous rambling structure, which dominates Akhaltsikhe town, incorporates Byzantine, medieval, Italian Renaissance and Islamic styles. Initially constructed in the ninth century, most of the buildings here date from the eighteenth century or later. The most significant point in the castle's history came in 1828 with the Battle of

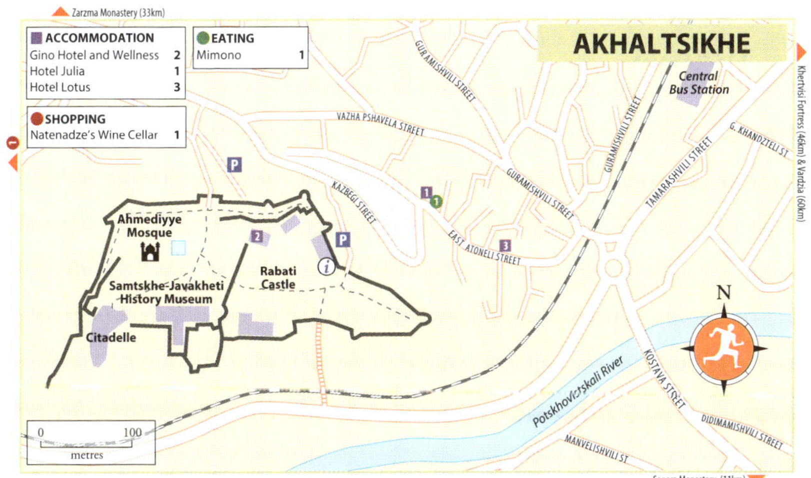

INTERNATIONAL CONNECTIONS FROM AKHALTSIKHE

If you're heading for the Turkish border you'll need to take the **marshrutka** to Vale, which runs roughly every hour between 8.30am and 6pm, but there's no public transport that actually crosses the border. You'll need to walk over and then find a taxi to take you to the small town of Posof, where you can pick up a minibus to Kars or Ardahan.

Travellers to Armenia have it easier. There are direct marshrutkas running to Gyumri (7am) and Yerevan (7.20am). As the border between Turkey and Armenia is currently closed, coming via Akhaltsikhe is the easiest way to travel overland between these two countries.

Akhaltsikhe, a major engagement during the Turkish-Russian War. The Turks lost, and the Russians advanced from here all the way to Kars in Turkey, which they held until after World War I.

The castle is now gorgeously maintained, but it must be admitted that it's a bit difficult to tell what's authentic after the extensive reconstruction works undertaken here in 2012. Even so, you'll be able to spend a happy two hours or so wandering the immaculate grounds, eventually making your way to the topmost tower for a fantastic view over the entire complex.

Also on site is the **Samtskhe-Javakheti History Museum** (charge, ☎995 322 997176), which offers an interesting overview of regional history and culture.

The outer courtyard of the castle – containing the café, restaurant, the Tourist Information Centre and the Gino Hotel, as well as a fair portion of the castle walls and several towers that are worth climbing – is open 24 hours and access is free.

ARRIVAL AND DEPARTURE   AKHALTSIKHE

By bus The central bus station is on the main square (Tamarashvili St), just below the castle. Marshrutkas run to Tbilisi every hour between 8am and 7pm. Two marshrutkas per day head to Batumi (8.30am and 10.30am), two to Kutaisi (8.30am and 1pm), and two to Vardzia (12.20pm and 5.30pm). The Tbilisi marshrutkas pass through Borjomi, and there are also half-hourly dedicated Borjomi services starting from 9am.

By car Reaching Akhaltsikhe by car doesn't present any issues if you're coming on the well-maintained road from Borjomi. It's rather more difficult if you want to come from Batumi, as the tempting road you'll see on maps linking the two is for the most part unpaved and is suitable only for hardy vehicles. At time of writing, however, the road was under reconstruction, funded by the Kuwaiti government, though it's not certain when the works will be completed. Check with the tourist information centre in Akhaltsikhe or Batumi before setting out, and if the road remains unfinished, you'll probably need to take the longer but easier route via Kutaisi.

GETTING AROUND

Akhaltsikhe isn't a large place. Most of the hotels and the few restaurants are within 5 minutes' walk of the castle.

INFORMATION

Tourist Information Centre Rabati Castle courtyard, ☎995 365 225028. The friendly tourist information centre can help with booking hotels, offering restaurant recommendations, and arranging taxis to take you to Vardzia or Sapara. They also have a handy marshrutka timetable. April–Oct 9am–8pm, Nov–March to 6pm.

ACCOMMODATION   SEE MAP PAGE 101

Gino Hotel and Wellness 1 Kharischirashvili St ⓦgino. ge. This international standard hotel – which boasts it was voted 32nd best hotel in the world in 2015, though it doesn't mention who was voting – is set in the castle grounds. The facilities are of course excellent (spa, sauna, hot tub, restaurant etc) and the rooms are very nice, but it's perhaps a little bland. ₾₾₾

Hotel Julia 66 E Atoneli St ☎995 579 777289. There's little English spoken at this small, family-run hotel very close to the castle, but the enormously friendly welcome transcends language barriers. Coffee, biscuits and chocolates are on tap in the lobby. ₾

Hotel Lotus 90 E Atoneli St ☎995 568 000095. A good and central choice with five double or twin rooms, all with private bathroom, as well as a kitchen available for use. Decoration approaches the boutique end of the scale. ₾

EATING

SEE MAP PAGE 101

Akhaltsikhe does not have a particularly lively nightlife. Restaurants tend to double as drinking holes, and the wine is usually good, but don't go looking for any hipster bars here.

Mimono 108 E Atoneli St ☎ 995 568 004440. Friendly, English-speaking restaurant with the full array of usual Georgian suspects on the menu, including a particularly good barbecue section. You may well get a free snifter of home-made vodka to follow your dinner. ⑤

SHOPPING

SEE MAP PAGE 101

Natenadze's Wine Cellar 13 Kharischirashvili St ⓦ natenadze.company. When the Turks invaded this region in the sixteenth century, they destroyed the vineyards and ended wine production here. Giorgi Natenadze has made it his life's work to explore the forests in the surrounding mountains to rediscover lost varieties of grape, and as a result the limited number of bottles he produces here are entirely unique. Giorgi also runs the excellent *Natenadze Wine Restaurant* in the castle courtyard.

DIRECTORY

Banks There's an ATM at Liberty Bank opposite the bus station; otherwise, ATMs are mostly to be found by crossing the river and walking up Kostava St.

Pharmacies Kostava St is the best place to find a pharmacy, with several outlets of PSP and Pharmadepot, among others.

Post office The central post office can be found on Tamar Mepe St. It's open 9am–5pm, weekdays only.

Around Akhaltsikhe

With your own transport, there's plenty to explore near Akhaltsikhe: close by, and reachable by taxi, is the peaceful Sapara Monastery, while further afield in opposite directions lie Zarzma Monastery and Khertvisi Fortress, the latter a worthwhile stop if you're headed to Vardzia.

Sapara Monastery

Sapara Monastery Rd • Free • No public transport

Hidden away along a well-paved road in the forested hills southeast of Akhaltsikhe, the perfect collection of churches that makes up **Sapara Monastery** is a beautiful, tranquil spot. The churches are often locked and there's not always anyone around, but if you can get in there are lovely frescoes inside. Otherwise, there's also a ruined castle above the monastery, which you can scramble up to by one of several paths for a great view over the monastery.

Zarzma Monastery

Zarzma Monastery Rd • Free • ⓦ zarzma.ge/home/0/eng • No public transport

The very bad road to Batumi heads west from Akhaltsikhe. It's possible to get as far as **Zarzma Monastery** in a normal car rather than an 4WD, and it's worth the trip, as the colourful sixteenth century frescoes inside are superb.

Khertvisi Fortress

Khertvisi-Vardzia Highway • Free • Vardzia-bound marshrutka

A good path saves you a steep scramble up to this fantastically positioned castle. It is strategically sited at the meeting point of two valleys where it could act as a lookout point and guard the important roadways that passed by it en route to what is modern-day Turkey. It's thought to be ancient – with potential links to Alexander the Great – but the current construction dates back only to the fourteenth century. Exploring the castle won't detain you long, but it's a worthwhile scenic stop on the way to or from Vardzia.

There's also a rickety suspension bridge slung across the river below the fortress, which is great fun to cross and affords decent views of the castle and surrounding hills.

Vardzia

An intermittently rough road from the Khertvisi turnoff will bring you to **Vardzia**, one of Georgia's most impressive and unique sights. The landscape here is more barren, and there's a feeling of isolation in this remote valley. Most visitors come as a day trip from Akhaltsikhe, but if you stay the night you'll enjoy a real sense of getting away from it all.

Vardzia Monastery

Khertvisi-Vardzia Highway • Charge • Marshrutka from Akhaltsikhe

The enormous and genuinely incredible cave **monastery** of Vardzia is a warren of tunnels and caves, with pathways on the outside of the cliff connecting them. Most of the rooms are plain, but the Church of the Assumption has beautiful frescoes both inside and out. A particularly fine tunnel leads from behind the Church of the Assumption to a great lookout point, though it's perhaps not recommended if you don't like slightly tight spaces.

Though the area has been inhabited for thousands of years, it seems that work on the monastery began in the mid-twelfth century and was largely completed by about 1203, but a major earthquake 80 years later damaged the complex and resulted in a further phase of building works. It's believed that Queen Tamar the Great visited Vardzia in the early thirteenth century and sallied forth from the monastery to a great victory over the Turks. Nearly four hundred years later, the Turkish occupation of the region led to Vardzia's abandonment.

It's easy to spend a happy hour or two wandering the complex. Try visiting earlier or later in the day to avoid large tour groups, who can clog up the narrow passageways. Also note that photography is forbidden in the church, and you should wear appropriate clothing when visiting the monastery (no shorts or miniskirts).

There are two marshrutkas a day from Akhaltsikhe, but they're not at very convenient times. A taxi round trip, which can also allow you to visit Khertvisi Fortress en route, can easily be arranged in Akhaltsikhe. This will also afford you the chance to stop at the viewpoint opposite Vardzia, which gives a great panorama of the entire complex.

Zeda Vardzia

Off Vardzia-Mirashkhani Highway • Free

A short hop of 3.5km further up the road from Vardzia, this small eleventh century church is a lovely additional stop if you have time. Set in beautiful grounds with colourful flowers and decent views down the valley, the church itself boasts some fantastic exterior and interior stone carving. It pre-dates the Vardzia complex – monks from here established Vardzia in the twelfth century – and was abandoned at the same time when the Turks invaded.

ACCOMMODATION   **VARDZIA**

Sada Guesthouse Vardzia-Mirashkhani Highway ☎ 995 577 527292. The friendly stone-built *Sada Guesthouse*, just to the left as you cross the bridge to the monastery, has one en-suite room with three beds. Camping on site is also possible. It's in a lovely spot by the river. There's a restaurant attached too offering good Georgian staples. $$

Vardzia Resort Akhalkalaki-Kartsakhi Highway ☎ 995 591 321515. A very upmarket option opposite the monastery – many of the 32 rooms have a view of the caves, and the others have a view of the hotel's lovely gardens. There are two outdoor swimming pools and a fantastic terrace where you can either simply chill out or challenge your nemesis to a table football match. The hotel can also arrange cookery classes if you want to master Meskhetian cuisine. The attached restaurant is good but expensive by Georgian standards. $$$

West Georgia

USHGULI VILLAGE

West Georgia

Georgia's west contains the most varied sights in the entire country, from the stunning and unspoilt Caucasus mountains in the north to the Gulf State-like architecture of the beach city of Batumi, via fantastic medieval monasteries and remarkable karst caverns. But more than sights, it's one of the best parts of the country to come to understand the huge variety in the peoples and cultures of Georgia. It's not a region that you can afford to miss if you want to experience the full diversity of this fascinating country.

The west of Georgia – including the regions of Imereti, Samegrelo, Svaneti, Guria and Adjara, as well as the separatist republic of Abkhazia – contains some of the country's most fascinating sights. Those here for natural splendour will be enchanted with the beautiful Caucasus mountains in **Svaneti** and the remarkable limestone cave systems around **Kutaisi**. If you're into history, the fantastic medieval monastery of **Gelati** and the Soviet holiday resort of **Tskaltubo** will provide two distinct counterpoints, and hedonists will adore the flashy beach city of **Batumi** and its outstanding **cuisine**. This region contains so many of Georgia's highlights that it's almost impossible to contemplate a visit to the country that doesn't involve coming here.

Brief history

As long ago as 1300 BC, much of this area was a prosperous nation-state, known to the Ancient Greeks as **Colchis**, the home of the Golden Fleece to which Jason and the Argonauts sailed. The Colchians were skilled in agriculture and metal-working, and their kingdom is considered the first proto-Georgian state. Colchis came under the domination of the Persians in the sixth century BC, which was followed by rule by the Romans and then the Byzantine Empire.

The region was an important part of the united Georgia during the medieval **Golden Age**. The tomb of the revered King David the Builder can be found at the monastery of Gelati, and it's thought that Queen Tamar is buried there too, though rival claims put her grave in Svaneti. Following the collapse of the kingdom, Georgia's west was conquered by the Turks, Persians and Russians – though up in the mountains, the Svan and Abkhaz peoples retained their independence longer than most.

Russian rule in the nineteenth century brought modernisation and prosperity to the big city of Batumi, and after a brief period of independence, the region was incorporated into the USSR in the 1920s. Post-independence, Georgia's west suffered considerable upheaval. Adjara found itself under a corrupt autocratic ruler, Kutaisi underwent significant economic depression, and, worst of all, a short but disastrous war in 1992 to 1993 followed Abkhazia's declaration of independence.

Prosperity returned to the region following the **Rose Revolution** in 2003. The Saakashvili government recovered control of Adjara and revitalised Kutaisi, even moving the country's parliament there for a period. The tourism industry has brought further recovery. Abkhazia, however, remains as far out of reach as ever, and there seems no resolution to this long-running dispute in sight.

Kutaisi

Georgia's third-biggest city, after Tbilisi and Batumi, **Kutaisi** is the capital of the Imereti region. In antiquity, it's thought to have been the capital of Colchis, to which Jason and the Argonauts voyaged in search of the Golden Fleece. It later became part of the

Highlights

❶ **Gelati Monastery** A survivor from Georgia's Golden Age, Gelati is home to some of the best medieval religious frescoes you'll ever see. See page 116

❷ **Prometheus Cave** Carved out of limestone over hundreds of years, this enormous cave system is packed with outstanding stalactites and rock formations. See page 118

❸ **Tskaltubo** A less obvious tourist destination than most, Tskaltubo is probably the best place in the Caucasus to see remarkable Soviet era buildings. See page 118

❹ **Batumi Bulvar** The ambitious architecture of Batumi's seafront is the face of Georgia looking to the future, and yet nodding to its past with the beautifully elegant Ali & Nino sculpture. See page 126

❺ **Adjaran cuisine** Georgian food is almost always amazing, but even amid stiff competition, the majestic *Adjaran khachapuri* stands out. See page 129

❻ **Ushguli** Nestling in a valley high in the Caucasus, Ushguli combines stunning natural beauty with fascinating Svan culture, exemplified in its magnificent towers. See page 136

HIGHLIGHTS ARE MARKED ON THE MAP ON PAGE 110

WEST GEORGIA
N
RUSSIA
SOUTH OSSETIA
Roki Tunnel
Mount Khalatsa (3,938 m)
Kvaisa
Tskhinvali
Gori
Mtkvari River
Uplistsikhe
Isalka
25
kilometres
0
Khashuri
Borjomi
BORJOMI NATIONAL PARK
Timotesubani Monastery
Bakuriani
Tabatskuri Lake
Akhalkalaki
Chiatura
Zestaponi
Tkibuli
Katskhi Pillar
Ambrolauri
Khvanchkara
Gelati Monastery
1
Prometheus Cave
2
Sataplia Nature Reserve
Kutaisi
Rabati Castle
Akhaltsikhe
Khertvisi
Khertvisi Fortress
Sapara Monastery
Ushguli
6
Mestia
Lentekhi
Okatse Canyon
Tskhaltubo
3
Samtredia
Zarzma Monastery
Chokhatauri
Bakhmaro
Khaishi
Enguri Dam
Jvari
Tsalenjhikha
Martvili Canyon
Zugdidi
Senaki
Khobi
KOLKHETI NATIONAL PARK
Lanchkhuti
Ozurgeti
Khulo
MTIRALA NATIONAL PARK
Makhuntseti
TURKEY
Tvarcheli
Gali
Poti
Batumi Botanic Gardens
Batumi
4 5
Gonio Fortress
Pichori
Anaklia
Ochamchira
ABKHAZIA
Sokhumi
Gulripshi
Sochi

HIGHLIGHTS
1 Gelati Monastery
2 Prometheus Cave
3 Tskaltubo
4 Batumi Bulvar
5 Adjaran cuisine
6 Ushguli

Ottoman Empire for seven hundred years, and after a brief spell of independence in the late eighteenth century, was annexed by Russia. During the Soviet era, Kutaisi's economy was heavily industrial – and organised crime was also big business. Post-independence, the Saakashvili government attempted to boost Kutaisi's declining fortunes by moving Georgia's parliament to a modern building on the edge of the city, but it didn't take off and by 2019 all functions had been transferred back to Tbilisi.

The majority of Kutaisi's relatively low-key sights are in an easily walkable area in the centre of town and can be visited in the course of a day or less.

Historical Museum

Alexander Pushkin St • Charge • ⓦ facebook.com/kutaisimuseum

A reasonably diverting mishmash of exhibits – from fossils and Bronze Age statuettes to charabancs and telephones – are exhibited in this attractive building, though the impressive ceiling and vaguely Baroque interior design in the main hall upstairs are possibly more interesting than some of the displays. The pride of the collection is the numerous examples of medieval Georgian goldsmith work and the religious icons.

Colchis Fountain

Shota Rustaveli Ave • Free

The town's centrepiece, this fountain recalls Kutaisi's ancient glory days as Colchis, with two golden ram-like animals atop a pyramid of bronze creatures surrounded by splashing water. The statues are based on examples of ancient jewellery found at Vani. The grand nineteenth-century **Meskhishvili Theatre** provides an impressive backdrop.

JASON AND THE ARGONAUTS

The tale of **Jason and the Argonauts** is one of the most popular in Greek myth, retold over the centuries in countless books and films. It concerns Jason, rightful king of the Greek kingdom of Iolcus, who was usurped by his uncle Pelias and despatched on a quest to acquire the Golden Fleece of Colchis, a quest from which he was not expected to return.

Jason gathered together many other **Greek heroes**, including Heracles and Theseus, and they voyaged across the Black Sea in their ship, the *Argo*, facing many dangers and ridding the lands of monsters, until they sailed up the River Phasis to Colchis – now thought to be the River Rioni and Kutaisi. Here they met King Aeetes, who agreed to give up the Golden Fleece if Jason would perform several difficult – some might say impossible – tasks.

Aeetes' daughter, Medea, took a liking to Jason, and being skilled in the art of sorcery, she was able to help Jason fulfil his tasks and claim the Fleece, but his prize brought him nothing but misery and ill fortune. When Jason returned to Iolcus with the Fleece, the people refused to accept him as king in Pelias' place, so Medea murdered Pelias. She and Jason were driven from the kingdom, and Jason died a lonely death many years later. Medea perhaps fared even worse: over the centuries of the myth's retelling, she gained a reputation as an evil witch, though some modern interpretations of the story see her as a feminist icon.

It's likely that the **Golden Fleece** in the story was a representation of the perception of the wealth of the Colchian kingdom, rather than a literal sheepskin made of gold – though it has been pointed out that the Greek philosopher and historian Strabo refers to sheepskins being used in ancient times to 'pan' for gold in the rivers of the Caucasus, in which case a fleece might appear golden. Other interpretations include the Argonauts' quest being a mythologised representation of the notion of sheep husbandry travelling from Georgia to Greece.

Whatever the truth, Georgians are proud of the myth and see it as evidence that Georgia is a western country, associated with the traditions of Europe rather than those of Asia.

Kutaisi Park

Shota Rustaveli Ave • Free

This shady park in the city centre is popular with locals who gather here to play and spectate games of backgammon. There's a statue of the Georgian composer and founder of the Georgian Philharmonic Society, Zakaria Paliashvili, at one end, and a set of imitation classical columns at the other, with pleasant fountains and sculptures dotted in between.

Just outside the park on the south side of Shota Rustaveli Ave, you'll find a small collection of Soviet-era sculptures which are worth a quick stop. Fans of Soviet architecture will also enjoy the magnificent relief, entitled Colchis, found on the frontage of Kutaisi's **Green Market**, a couple of blocks' walk west of the park.

Sports Museum

5 Paliashvili Alley • Free • ☎ 995 431 242817

You'll have very little hope of understanding what's going on in here unless you speak Russian or Georgian, or have an intricate knowledge of the history of Georgian/Soviet sport, but the collection is fascinating for its sheer scope. USSR football shirts sit alongside enormous pairs of antlers, with trophies, mascots, bikes and chess boards

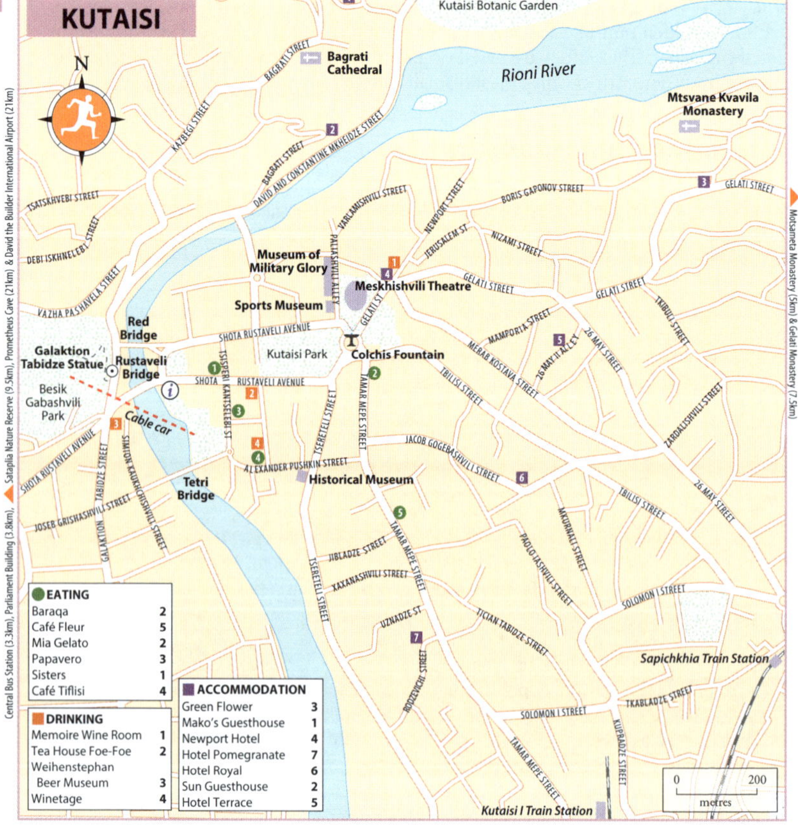

filling in the gaps between the multitudes of photos. There's even a whole cabinet dedicated to the Rhymney Rugby Club's tour of the USSR in 1977 – which must have been of only niche interest even at the time. Well worth a quick wander round. It's free, but the owner is a keen coin collector and will welcome a donation from your home country.

Museum of Military Glory

1 Paliashvili Alley • Free • ☎ 995 431 240935

An extensive collection of reproduced photos (and not a lot else) covering World War II as well as more recent conflicts, including the 2008 South Ossetia war and the Abkhazia separatism in the early 1990s. English language is limited, but the curator is friendly and will do his best if you want to know more.

Bagrati Cathedral

Bagrati St • Free • ☎ 995 591 616936

Overlooking the town at the top of a hill is **Bagrati**, a medieval cathedral dating back to 1003. It's had an eventful history, culminating in its collapse in 1692 during an Ottoman attack. It was added to the UNESCO World Heritage Sites list in 1994, but subsequently removed again in 2017 due to the heavy restorations that took place during the Saakashvili era, which almost entirely rebuilt the cathedral and which UNESCO considers "detrimental to its integrity and authenticity".

It has to be agreed that some of the restorations are entirely unsympathetic, not least the metal and glass balcony inside, but plenty of original stonework – including some particularly intricate and beautiful carvings around the entranceway – remains and it is certainly worth a visit. Also in the grounds are the remnants of walls and towers that were once Kutaisi's castle, and there are often musicians in traditional dress here performing to tourists.

Kutaisi Botanic Garden

David and Constantine Mkheidze St • Charge

Half well-tended and half not, the **Botanic Gardens** are a pleasant oasis of greenery on the edge of the river beneath the cathedral hill. There are a few odd sculptures to liven things up, and the beginnings of a small aviary. It's worth a wander if you have a bit of spare time: see if you can find the cute little chapel inside a hollow tree.

Mtsvane Kvavila Monastery

Gelati St • Free

This set of medieval churches – on the hill above the river – are a worthy target if you want an excuse to explore the attractive residential streets to the east of the centre. Your reward will be views across to the Bagrati Cathedral and over town, but the churches themselves will most likely be locked.

Cable car

Off Tsisperi Kantselebi St • Charge

A rickety **cable car** runs every 10 minutes from behind the tourist information centre up to a small amusement park on the hill. Here you can have a go on the merry-go-round or the big wheel, or try your hand at the accurately but alarmingly named dodgems equivalent, "Car Fight". It's probably most fun in the early evening, when the garish neon lights come into their own, but before it's too dark to admire the views down to the city.

> ### GALAKTION TABIDZE
>
> The tragic figure of **Galaktion Tabidze**, born near Kutaisi in 1892, was one of Georgia's greatest twentieth-century **poets**. Already in his early works, he was attracted to themes of isolation and despair, but this was compounded when, during the Stalinist purges of the 1930s, his wife was arrested and sentenced to a Siberian exile which claimed her life, while he himself suffered a brutal interrogation. He continued to write, but his later years were characterised by deep depression, and he eventually killed himself in a psychiatric hospital in Tbilisi. His works remain enormously popular across Georgia.

Tetri Bridge

Tetri Bridge • Free

The best way to cross the river, this funky **metal and glass bridge** is disturbingly transparent on the glass sections and rattly on the metal sections. Once on the west bank, walk north for 10 minutes or so to reach the beautiful and evocative statue of Galaktion Tabidze, on David and Constantine Street, in between Red and Rustaveli bridges.

Parliament Building

Irakli Abashidze St • Free • Bus number 1

The big bubble of a **Parliament Building** sits in a field by the river a couple of kilometres to the west of the town centre. There's a small park surrounding it, but it looks forlorn and neglected, which is unsurprising as it was never a popular decision to move the seat of government here. In January 2019, all parliamentary function was moved back to Tbilisi, and the future of this Saakashvili legacy is uncertain, though noises have been made about converting it into an IT hub. It was once possible to tour the parliament, but you now will have to settle for taking a look from the outside.

ARRIVAL AND DEPARTURE   KUTAISI

By plane Kutaisi is a low-budget entry point to Georgia, with Wizz Air flights from Berlin, Brussels, Paris, Rome and several other European cities, arriving at the David the Builder International Airport, about 15km out of town. The airport facilities include car hire companies, a couple of cafés, an information desk, and a stand to get a Georgian SIM card. Marshrutkas to Kutaisi are on hand after plane arrivals, and you'll also find a waiting crowd of taxi drivers, who will be happy to take you to Kutaisi, Tbilisi or even Mestia. There's also a train station 2km from the airport, to which there are free shuttle buses, but it has no train connection to the city, though it's handy if you're intending to move on immediately to Tbilisi, Zugdidi or Batumi.

By train Kutaisi has two train stations; the more useful one for tourists is Kutaisi 1, found on Tamar Mepe St, just over a kilometre south of the town centre. Here, you can catch the daily train to Tbilisi (departs 12pm, arrives 17.45), which also calls at Gori. If you're heading west, you'll need to head out of town to the Kutaisi International Airport station, from which five trains a day leave for Zugdidi and Batumi. pm Tickets can be purchased online at Ⓦ railway.ge.

By bus The main bus station is found 4km southwest of the town centre; from here you'll be able to pick up marshrutkas to Tbilisi (hourly from 8am to 6pm), Zugdidi (roughly every hour from 7am to 5.30pm), Batumi (hourly from 8am to 6pm), Mestia (between 8am and 10am, departing when full), and Akhaltsikhe via Borjomi (four daily between 8.20am and 1pm).

By car Kutaisi is well-connected by road and is an easy drive to or from Tbilisi, Borjomi, Zugdidi, Mestia and Batumi.

GETTING AROUND

By bus Bus number 1 is the most useful route. It runs in a circle from the city centre to Kutaisi 1 train station and then to the main bus station.

By taxi Local taxis are honest, efficient, and inexpensive. Meters are uncommon, so agree a price before setting off.

By car Driving within Kutaisi is easy enough, but the authorities do have a habit of digging up roads and not repaving them particularly quickly, so routes in the outskirts can be unpaved and quite rough. Rustaveli Ave, which heads out to the airport, can get busy, but is rarely stationary. If you're driving up to Bagrati Cathedral, note that Petre Iberi I Alley is very steep – it's better to go up Bagrati St.

By foot The majority of Kutaisi's sights can be reached on foot, and the city centre is a nice place to walk.

INFORMATION

Tourist information centre 9a Rustaveli Ave, ☎ 995 322 370000. Kutaisi's tourist information centre is staffed by a very friendly and helpful team who can assist with onward travel and arrange tours. There's also a small souvenir shop here. Daily 9am–6pm.

Listings They're not fully comprehensive, but both ⓦ georgia.travel/en_US/events and ⓦ dodago.ge/ru/events/kutaisi are decent places to start for checking what's on in town.

The **website** ⓦ kutaisi.travel/en, run by the tourist info centre, is helpful in helping you to contact a local guide or tour agency, if you need one.

ACCOMMODATION   **SEE MAP PAGE 112**

In 1868, the John Murray Handbook for Travellers in Russia stated that "there are two hotels at Kutaisi: the proprietor of one is a Hungarian, and of the other a Russian; but no comforts will be found at either of them". Happily, the situation has improved somewhat: Kutaisi is now full of hotels and guesthouses. The area around the Mtsvane Kvevila Monastery contains some of the best, and although these may be a little further out of town, it's where you're more likely to experience fantastic Georgian hospitality.

★ **Green Flower** 101 Gelati St ☎ 995 574 468282. Family-run property with 14 rooms across two houses, all en suite and tastefully decorated. There are marvellous views from the terrace, and the family room on the lower floor of the older house is home to an eclectic museum of family treasures. The excellent home-made wine flows like water. $̲$̲

Mako's Guesthouse 19 Petre Iberi I Alley ⓦ makos-guest-house.business.site. There are four clean rooms (3 double and 1 twin), some with shared bathroom, at this welcoming place on a steep hill by the Bagrati Cathedral. Price includes attention from the friendly resident Labrador. $̲

Newport Hotel 1 Newport Street ⓦ nhkutaisi.com/en. Housed in the town's early twentieth century grand former courthouse, the smart Newport Hotel is a strong choice. Rooms are international standard and extremely comfy, the location is perfect, and the attached restaurant is excellent. $̲$̲$̲

Hotel Pomegranate 54 Tamar Mepe St ☎ 995 551 020236. Pomegranate is great for its central location and bargainous pricing, but it's otherwise rather forgettable. Rooms are very bland and functional, and it can be noisy. Staff are variable too – some are very friendly, while others are very much not. $̲

Hotel Royal 27 Jacob Gogebashvili St ☎ 995 593 795240. Featuring some quite ridiculously flamboyant décor, the Hotel Royal is a great choice if you're looking for a place with a bit of character. The owner, Giorgi, is lovely, and justly proud of his hotel. It's on a quiet street about 10 minutes walk from the town centre. $̲

Sun Guesthouse 2 Bagrati St ☎ 995 595 237236, ⓦ facebook.com/hostelsun. Converted old house with fantastic views from the terrace. Four rooms for between one and four persons, all with shared bathroom and kitchen facilities. Breakfast available, as is good home-made wine. $̲

Hotel Terrace 10 26 May II Alley ⓦ hotel-terrace-kutaisi.business.site. A relative newcomer on Kutaisi's hotel scene, the *Terrace* offers rooms that are clean and smart, if a little bland. The calling card is, of course, the eponymous terrace – a lovely bar area on the roof where you'll get excellent city views. $̲$̲

EATING   **SEE MAP PAGE 112**

Baraqa 7 Tamar Mepe St ⓦ facebook.com/BaraqaKutaisi. A consistently popular place which serves up a wide range of good Georgian food – including a tomato/egg dish with the excellent name of chizhi-bizhi – as well as a few international options like pizzas. The menu does a good job of explaining the various dishes, and the friendly staff will explain further if needed. $̲$̲

Café Fleur 26 Tamar Mepe St ⓦ facebook.com/cafefleurofficial. Popular place just south of the central square offering food throughout the day, though it's particularly recommended for breakfast – the shakshuka (baked tomato and eggs) is very good. If the weather is good enough, take a seat outside as the interior is a bit characterless and will treat you to very loud music. $̲

Mio Gelato 7 Tamar Mepe St ⓦ facebook.com/miogelato8. Central and friendly ice cream parlour with a decent range of flavours and fun, if slightly twee, décor. The coffee is good too. $̲

Papavero 5 Tsisperi Kantselebi St ⓦ restaurantpapavero.ge. Lovely and very popular restaurant specialising in Italian food, with a good selection of Georgian options too. Service is friendly (if a tad slow), the food is great, and there's a very good wine and cocktail list. $̲$̲

Sisters 33 Paliashvili St ⓦ facebook.com/Debiishxnelebidan. Popular and highly rated, *Sisters* offers a decent menu of Georgian classics in shabby chic premises. Don't be surprised if an impromptu jazz concert begins while you're eating. Booking advised. $̲$̲

Café Tiflisi 1 Tsminda Nino St ⓦ facebook.com/cafetiflisi. A pleasant and central option specialising in Georgian food. The khachapuri is excellent, and the trout also comes highly recommended. $̲

DRINKING
SEE MAP PAGE 112

Memoire Wine Room 5 Newport St ☎ 995 598 404051. Hidden away in the basement of the Hotel Memoire, this wine cellar has style in spades, with red and black tiled tables, exposed brick walls, artfully hung velvet curtains, and – best of all – a whole wall of wine bottles to choose from. The only problem is that you can often only buy by the bottle, not the glass.

Tea House Foe-Foe 5 Shota Rustaveli Ave ⓦ facebook.com/tearoomfoefoe. You'll find a very extensive tea menu in this café, which is decorated with something of a superhero theme. If it's not tea you're after, the food menu of Georgian and a few international standards is good too. ⑤

Weihanstephan Beer Museum 9 Galaktion Tabidze St ☎ 995 591 123456. If you're thirsting for something other than wine, this spot dedicated to craft beer and done out like a German beer hall will probably hit the spot. Food is available too, but it's a little hit and miss.

★ **Winetage** 2 Tsminda Nino St ☎ 995 598 807063. You'll receive a warm welcome from the hugely friendly owner Irakli at this wine bar and shop. Irakli really knows his wines, offering a marvellous selection from all over Georgia, and can find a perfect choice for you. There are outdoor and indoor tables, making it a lovely place to relax for the evening.

ENTERTAINMENT

Theatres The Meskhishvili Theatre (Gelati St, ☎ 995 555 770083, ⓦ meskhishvili-theatre.ge) is your best bet for catching a performance; the website is kept up to date with upcoming productions.

DIRECTORY

Banks and exchanges Banks, ATMs and exchange offices are clustered around the Colchis Fountain roundabout and down Tsereteli St.

Hospital Kutaisi's central hospital (Kupradze St, ☎ 995 431 246322) is about 1km southeast of the centre.

Laundry Your guesthouse should be able to arrange laundry for you, but if you prefer to go it alone, you could try Benvenuto, 12 Nikea St, ☎ 995 591 205203, ⓦ facebook.com/KutaisiBenvenutoKutaisi.

Pharmacies There's no shortage of the usual Georgian pharmacy chains (primarily Aversi and PSP) in the town centre; try along Tsminda Nino St.

Post office The central post office (Tsminda Nino St, ☎ 995 322 240909) is open Monday to Friday 9am–5pm and Saturday 9am–2pm.

Around Kutaisi

Kutaisi is a good base for exploring the surrounding area, which boasts a wide variety of interesting diversions, from medieval monasteries to enormous cave systems. It's easiest with your own vehicle, but some of these sights can be visited with public transport.

Motsameta monastery

Motsameta St • Free, parking charge • Gelati Marshrutka

Motsameta is a gorgeous little monastery in an utterly spectacular setting on the edge of a cliff above the gorge. According to legend, it's the site of the martyrdom of a pair of brothers who attempted a rebellion against the Arabs in the eighth century. Inside, the church walls are decorated with modern frescoes. Note that wearing shorts inside the monastery is not permitted.

If you're coming by public transport, take the marshrutka to Gelati and ask to be let off at the Motsameta junction. It's a 2km walk from there, sometimes uphill, and it's not shaded so can get sweaty in summer.

Gelati monastery

Gelati Monastery Rd • Free • ☎ 995 598 678076 • Gelati Marshrutka

The complex of **Gelati** is a large and attractive monastery, first established in 1106 during Georgia's Golden Age by King David the Builder, who is buried here. It was long famous as a centre of learning, and the interiors of the churches have been decorated with magnificent frescoes. The hugely colourful examples in the small Church of St George, on your left after you come through the entrance gate, are particularly impressive, and make sure you don't miss the beautiful carvings around its entrance.

The central Cathedral of the Nativity of the Virgin is bedecked with marvellous frescoes too, though many have been subjected to recent enthusiastic restoration and as a result seem a bit too clear and distinct. Check out the side chambers for some that remain in their original state, especially the room containing pictures of hermits with long white beards. At time of writing, the cathedral was undergoing further restoration and was covered with scaffolding both inside and out, but several frescoes, including that of Christ in the central dome, were still visible.

Gelati is also home to the Gates of Ganja, a superb piece of craftsmanship from the city of Ganja in Azerbaijan, which were captured by King Demetrius I in 1139 and brought here as a prize of war. The surviving door is now on display near David the Builder's tomb.

Marshrutkas labelled 'Gelati' leave Kutaisi for Gelati from the Meskhishvili Theatre five times a day, starting at 7.30am. It's possible to walk between Gelati and Motsameta, and even back to Kutaisi. Alternatively, it's very affordable to arrange a taxi to take you to both.

Geguti Palace

Off Geguti-Kutaisi highway • Free • Marshrutka 211

Just off the highway about 15km south of Kutaisi is the mildly diverting **Geguti Palace**, a ruined residence of the medieval Georgian monarchs. There are English language information boards on site, and the friendly guardian will give you a tour in Georgian, whether you understand or not. It's not signposted from the road. If you're coming by marshrutka, ask to be let off just before the motorway junction opposite the Syngenta shop, then walk up the minor road to the east and turn right when it becomes a gravel track.

Vani

About 30km southwest of the Geguti Palace is the town of Vani, a small place with a long history, dating back at least as far as the Colchian period in the eighth century BC. The main reason to visit today is the excellent **Archaeological Museum** (charge, ☎ 995 322 998022), which offers an imaginatively presented exhibition of Colchian remains, including jewellery, vases, and some very impressive bronze sculptures.

Sataplia Nature Reserve

M111 road • Charge • Ⓦ apa.gov.ge/en/eco-tourism/servisebi-da-tarifebi/sataflia • Best reached by taxi

Sataplia is a small nature reserve about 10km to the northwest of Kutaisi, which packs a wide variety of attractions into its diminutive size, including a limestone cave, dinosaur footprints, and a pleasant panoramic viewpoint. The downside is that you're required to join a tour to look around, so on busy occasions it can be difficult to actually see what you've come to see.

The well-organised excursion takes you to the dinosaur footprints, which are between 60 and 100 million years old and are enclosed in a large hangar-like structure with walkways built above them. The footprints themselves are impressive, but it's easy to be distracted by the images on the walls, which include a photo-shopped picture depicting a pair of T-Rexes happily frolicking on a beach.

The rest of the park involves a pleasant walk through shady trees to a panoramic viewpoint from which you can see all the way to Kutaisi's Parliament Building and the Gelati Monastery. At the bottom of the park is a 300-metre-long cave packed with fantastic stalagmites and stalactites, with a well-maintained walkway to take you through.

LENIN AND THE FIRES OF HELL

About halfway along the main road between Kutaisi and Zugdidi is the small town of Abasha, from which it's a short 5km diversion to the village of Sujana. Here you'll find the **Church of St George**, decorated with attractive but initially unremarkable frescoes. Look a little closer, though, and you'll spot the unmistakeable visage of **Lenin**, burning in the **fires of hell**. The fresco was painted in the 1990s, shortly after Georgia's independence from the USSR, and is a vivid illustration of the Orthodox Church's feelings towards the years of Soviet rule.

Prometheus Cave

Kumistavi village • Charge (boat ride through latter portion of cave additional) • Ⓦ apa.gov.ge/en/eco-tourism/servisebi-da-tarifebi/ Prometheuscave • Best reached by taxi

The 11km long **Prometheus Cave** – named after the Titan who in Greek myth brought fire to mankind and was chained to Mount Kazbek in the Caucasus by Zeus as punishment – is a further 25km from Sataplia. Your visit will involve a 1.2km walk inside the cave, which is hugely impressive and packed with stalactites and other formations. For an extra fee, you can enjoy an underground boat ride too.

The cave can only be visited on a guided excursion, which goes roughly every half hour. There's a mildly diverting visitor centre to entertain you while you wait. The excursion begins with a ridiculously lengthy speech delivered in three languages (Georgian, Russian and English) in an echoey room, but once that's over you are able to enter the cave. Even so, you may find that being ushered around like a school crocodile becomes grating.

If you don't feel you want to bother with both Sataplia and Prometheus – which are expensive by Georgian tourist attraction standards – then Prometheus is the more impressive cave, but Sataplia counters this by offering more variety. They're not easy to achieve by public transport, so you'll probably want to arrange a taxi round-trip from Kutaisi to take in both of them Alternatively, it's easy to drive to them yourself: they're well-signposted and the roads are good.

Tskaltubo

Tskaltubo, a small town which you'll pass through on the way to Prometheus Cave, was an major tourist destination in the days of the USSR, when its mineral water cemented its popularity as a spa town. During the Soviet era, around twenty spa resorts were built here, most of which have long since been abandoned. These grand buildings, their exquisite decorations now decaying and slowly being reclaimed by nature, are still beautiful in their own right and make Tskaltubo probably Georgia's ultimate destination for urban explorers. Particularly worthy of a look is the **Medea Sanatorium**, which is one of the grandest such buildings, with its magnificent colonnade of pillars; the **Sanatorium Metalurgist**, with its beautiful entrance hall, is another fine example.

Note that some of the sanatoria are now occupied by displaced persons who lost their homes in the Abkhazia war. Although they are by and large happy for visitors to take a look around, and may even offer unofficial tours for a small price, make sure to show respect and ask permission to enter a building if you meet people as you approach. Also be aware that the sanatoria may be unsafe: there's often broken glass on the floor, stairs may be unstable, and holes in the floor are not uncommon. The Medea Sanatorium is among the most accessible in town: it's been cleaned up considerably, though it's still worth exercising caution as you explore.

East of Kutaisi

The main road between Kutaisi and Gori is home to relatively few distractions, though if you've got time and your own transport, it's well worth a visit to **Ubisi church** to see its outstanding frescoes. Alternatively, it may be worth diverting onto the northern loop that takes you via Chiatura and the Katskhi Pillar.

Katskhi Pillar

Off Gomi-Zestaponi Highway • Free

If you're a group of monks looking to isolate yourself from the world so you can contemplate eternal questions in peace, then where could be better than the top of a 40-metre-tall limestone column? This was certainly the approach taken by an ambitious but sadly unknown monastic fellowship in the fifth century, who somehow scaled this huge rock pillar and erected a church.

The hermitage is accessed by a steep metal ladder, but it's forbidden for tourists to climb up, which will come as a relief to those who suffer from vertigo. Instead, you can stand at the bottom and admire the singular determination it must have taken to scale this pillar in the first place. There's also a small museum on site, with a mildly diverting collection of liturgical and archaeological exhibits from the surrounding area.

There's an access road that runs almost to the pillar's base, which is punctuated by a rather excessive number of car parks: it's best to ignore these until you reach a 12 percent downhill slope, at the bottom of which is the largest and most sensible/convenient place to park.

It's also possible to rock-climb in the surrounding canyon. To arrange this, you could contact Ilia Berulava, a professional mountaineer who runs a three-day climbing

---

OKATSE AND MARTVILI CANYONS

The attractive green landscape to Kutaisi's west is criss-crossed with deep canyons and gorges, which make for good walking country. This has not escaped the notice of the Georgian Agency of Protected Areas, which has developed Okatse and Martvili Canyons into premier attractions. The result is that they feel a little heavily touristed, but there's a reason for that: they are both very impressive.

Neither are particularly easy to reach on public transport, though it's possible if you're willing to spend a fair bit of time on it. It's simpler to take a taxi from Kutaisi, which should cost between 50 and 100 GEL, depending on which canyons you want to visit and whether you also want to include Prometheus or Sataplia on your trip.

Okatse Canyon (Gordi village; Charge; Ⓦ apa.gov.ge/en/eco-tourism/servisebi-da-tarifebi/CanyonofOkatse) consists of a pleasant paved path through wooded parkland – inhabited by pigs, horses and cows – which eventually descends into the gorge, at which point you can try your nerves on a vertigo-inducing metal walkway attached to the cliff edge. This culminates in a lovely viewpoint/gangplank over the gorge. Note that the charge is for access to the walkway only; the rest of the path is free.

Martvili Canyon (Martvili village; Charge; Ⓦ apa.gov.ge/en/eco-tourism/servisebi-da-tarifebi/martvilis-kanioni) involves a pretty river walk across bridges to see waterfalls, and the option of a boat ride for an additional charge (which is worth it – it takes you along a stunning part of the river that you can't otherwise access).

If you want to stay in the region, **Karma Hostel** (Chikvanaia St; Ⓦ karmahostelmartvili.com), which has a rustic feel and fun and friendly hosts, comes recommended.

programme, which can be booked at ⓦexplore-share.com/trip/3-day-rock-climbing-in-chiatura-and-katskhi-georgia.

Chiatura

Grit, metal, industry. And concrete. Lots of concrete. **Chiatura** made its fortune on the mining of manganese deposits, and it remains a heavily industrial town. It's worth a quick stop to see a town that retains a distinct Soviet aesthetic – concrete piles amid the beautiful setting of the Kvirila river gorge, a combination which proves surprisingly attractive.

The town's real draw, though, are the **cable cars**. These relics of the Soviet age look like rusty tin Tardises, and they once plied the many lines from the town centre to the cliffs above. The original cars are no longer in service, but some of the cable car stations were renovated and reopened in 2021 with shiny modern cars, and taking a ride on one is a great way to get a bird's eye view of town: the Sanatorium line probably offers the best trip.

Even without riding the cars, it's great fun wandering the river's length taking in the derelict machinery and checking out the once grand cable car stations. A particularly fine example stands on a corner by a bridge across the river at the Tbilisi road end of town, opposite a prominent bas-relief on a roundabout: it's fenced off, but you can still admire its grandiose architecture, and see if you can spot Lenin and Stalin depicted on the facade.

Heading out of town towards Tbilisi the road is lined with further astonishing examples of decaying concrete buildings and rusting industry. It's not pretty in the conventional sense, but it's unquestionably eye-catching.

Zugdidi

You'll probably find yourself passing through **Zugdidi** if you're travelling in the west of Georgia. It's at the crossroads of the routes to Mestia, Batumi and Kutaisi, as well as being the gateway to Abkhazia. With Abkhazia's border currently closed, however, tourists tend to pass on by, which is a bit of a shame. Although its attractions won't be making Top 10 lists, Zugdidi is a very pleasant place to stop for the night and explore its handful of low-key sights.

The main street, Rustaveli Avenue, is home to a fantastic Soviet bas-relief on the side of the PSP Pharmacy building, and you could briefly imagine yourself somewhere tropical given all the palm trees. One block up, on Gamsakhurdia Avenue, fans of straight lines will rejoice in the magnificently clean blockiness of the **Public Services Hall** – though be discreet in taking photos of it, as this is for some reason unpopular with the local police.

The bustling **market** – on Rustaveli Avenue, just before the river bridge – is also worth a quick look, with spices, fruit and honey all contributing to a heady and inviting aroma.

Dadiani Palace

116 Merab Kostava St • Charge • ☎ 995 415 251695

Resembling an English stately home, and set in beautifully maintained gardens, the palace of the noble Dadiani family makes for an excellent visit. Note the fine parquet floors throughout and admire the magnificent wooden dressers incorporating carved animals, the splendid mother-of-pearl and ivory inlaid table, and, a little unexpectedly, Napoleon's bronze death mask. English labelling is sporadic, but you're still able to get a real sense of the family's history.

3

There's also a separately charged exhibition of **religious icons**, including some marvellous tenth century triptychs and an outstanding 1619 bronze icon from Tsaishi Church, which depicts the life of Christ in twelve images.

Botanic gardens

Merab Kostava St • Free

Zugdidi's botanic garden, just behind the Dadiani Palace, is a pleasant and well-maintained **leafy retreat** from the busy town featuring a lake as the centrepiece: buy some fish food at the entrance and feed the hungry carp. The park also contains the ruins of a number of palaces, including the unfortunate Mtsutri Palace which burned down no less than three times in the space of thirty years in the mid-1800s. After the final conflagration, it was evidently decided it was not worth rebuilding yet again.

ARRIVAL AND DEPARTURE
ZUGDIDI

By train From Zugdidi's train station, just off Rustaveli Ave in the west of town, you can pick up the daily train Tbilisi (5.45pm, 6 hours); this train also calls at Kutaisi International Airport (2 hours).

By bus Up to twenty buses or marshrutkas per day leave from the train station for Tbilisi between 7am and midnight. There are half-hourly departures for Kutaisi (from 7.15am), eight per day for Batumi (from 6.50am), and one for Borjomi (10am). For Mestia, marshrutkas depart when full from either the train station or St Nikoladze St, 50 metres to

WHAT'S NAPOLEON DOING IN ZUGDIDI?

There are four copies of **Napoleon's death mask** in existence. They can be found in London, Paris, Havana, and **Zugdidi**. Zugdidi's inclusion on this list seems a little strange, and it's not entirely clear why the mask is here, but the most plausible explanation is that the mask found its way here when Napoleon's nephew, Achille Murat, married Salome Dadiani and moved to the Palace, bringing his family heirlooms along with him.

3

ABKHAZIA

In the wake of the collapse of the Soviet Union, the region of Abkhazia (which makes up roughly an eighth of Georgia's total area) declared its independence from Georgia. A short war in the early 1990s resulted in the loss of Georgia's control of the region, a situation exacerbated by the 2008 Six Day War. Since then, the political situation has remained tense. Most nations continue to regard Abkhazia as part of Georgia, but Russia recognises Abkhazia's independence. For their part, the Georgians consider that Abkhazia is illegally occupied by Russia.

Between 2008 and 2019, it was usually possible to visit Abkhazia from Georgia, crossing the Enguri Bridge border near Zugdidi. However, apparently due to increased tensions between Georgia and Russia, as well as the Covid-19 pandemic and the Russian invasion of Ukraine in February 2022, this checkpoint has closed and there is no indication of when it might reopen.

Abkhazia also borders Russia, and that border is still open. As such it is possible to enter Abkhazia from Russia (most commonly via Sochi), but you should bear in mind that Georgia considers this a violation of its borders and if you are found to have entered Abkhazia via this route, you will be subject to a fine or possibly imprisonment. If you do enter Abkhazia from Russia, you should not attempt to continue your journey into Georgia proper and instead will need to go back to Russia – thus necessitating a double-entry Russian visa. **Rough Guides does not condone entering Abkhazia from Russia.**

If you want to visit Abkhazia, you will need to first apply for a visa from the Abkhazian Ministry of Foreign Affairs (ⓦmfaapsny.org/en/consular-service/permission). Responses are received quickly and the staff are relatively helpful. The visa costs 350 Russian roubles for a month's entry, payable only if the visa is granted.

If the Georgian border reopens and you are approved to visit, you will be emailed a security clearance document. You'll need to show this at the border, then go through several

---

the right after crossing Rustaveli Ave's bridge heading west. If/when the Abkhazian border reopens, you'll need the bus to Rukhi Bridge, which currently goes four times a day between 8am and 5pm. There are any number of buses and marshrutkas to Anaklia.

By car Zugdidi is easily reachable by car and poses no particular difficulties, other than finding the road out to Mestia, which is not as well-trafficked as you'd expect and thus leaves you with a faint sense of unease that you're going the wrong way. Parking in the city centre is easy, especially at the entrance to the Dadiani Palace.

GETTING AROUND AND INFORMATION

By foot Zugdidi isn't large; it will probably take no more than 30 minutes for you to walk between any two spots in town.

Tourist Information Centre 79 Rustaveli St, ☏ 995 591 445345, ⓔticzugdidi@gmail.com. Helpful and friendly, the tourist information office can tell you a little about the sights in town and provide bus and train timetables for onward travel plans. Daily 10am–6pm.

ACCOMMODATION

SEE MAP PAGE 121

Green Garden 8 Ninoshvili St ☏ 995 571 223868. In a good location just a short walk from the Dadiani Palace, Green Garden has three clean rooms, with a shared bathroom. Breakfast is not included, but it's worth paying the extra charge for it, as it's very good. ⑤

Leto Hotel 31 Gamsakhurdia St ⓦfacebook.com/ LETOZugdidi. One of the city's smarter hotels, the centrally-located *Leto* is expensive by Zugdidi's standards, but this is explained by the excellent facilities including a spa, gym, and a beautiful infinity pool on the rooftop, all included in the price. Note that there is little difference between standard and superior rooms, but the suites are considerably larger. ⑤⑤⑤

Hotel River S 55 Bako St ⓦrivers.ge. It's a little out of the way, on the other side of the river from the town centre, but the *River S* is a good, upmarket choice. There are some interesting stylistic choices on the landing – a seven-piece suite sits alone in the middle of a vast open space – but the rooms are clean and decked out in pastel colours. It's quiet at night, the staff are friendly, and the breakfast is very good. ⑤⑤

Shorena's House 119 Stalin St ☏ 995 577 720082. A good choice for those on a tight budget, Shorena's House is a welcoming guesthouse about a kilometre south of the town centre. There are four rooms, two of which have private bathrooms, and good homemade breakfasts are available. ⑤

checkpoints (manned by Georgian, Abkhazian and Russian border officials), and once you get to the republic's capital, Sukhumi, you will need to go to the Ministry of Foreign Affairs (21 Lakoba St, Sukhumi, ☎ 7 840 226 70 69) and collect the visa. This is when you will pay the visa fee.

Once you've fulfilled all these formalities, you're free to explore. You'll likely begin with **Sukhumi**, which in the days of the USSR was a prime Black Sea beach resort and is still popular with Russian tourists. There's an attractive promenade along the beachfront, as well as a botanical garden, and, for those that way inclined, plenty of crumbling Soviet architecture to enjoy.

It's also worth a trip to the town of **New Athos**, where you can visit a beautiful orthodox monastery, built in 1874, which is in an impossibly picturesque location on the seafront. While in town, you can also visit the ruins of a fifth-century Greek fortress, or take a train ride through **New Athos Cave**, one of the world's largest caves. (Veryovkina and Krubera – which extend more than 2000 metres underground and are the world's two deepest caves – are also to be found in Abkhazia, but aren't open to visitors.)

Abkhazia's other main draw is **Lake Ritsa**, a beautiful – and very cold – lake up in the Caucasus mountains. It's possible to hike in the area around the lake and also visit Stalin's dacha, where he spent numerous summer holidays.

Note that Georgian GEL is not accepted in Abkhazia., so you'll need to get your hands on some Russian roubles. Exchange kiosks in Zugdidi can supply these, which is preferable to changing money at the border.

Also be aware that while Abkhazia's more touristy sites are generally safe there have been multiple reports of robberies in the southern region between Sukhumi and the Georgian border. If you are travelling in this area, it's advisable to do so in the morning instead of the afternoon, and certainly not after dark. Finally, remember that consular assistance is not available in Abkhazia, so if you run into trouble, you'll most likely be on your own.

EATING AND DRINKING
SEE MAP PAGE 121

You wouldn't necessarily describe Zugdidi's wining and dining scene as "vibrant", but there are a couple of decent places around.

Diaroni 9 Meunargia St ⓦ diaroni.ge. You'll find a very extensive menu of Georgian and international dishes at this smart restaurant, which brings a touch of palatial elegance to Zugdidi's dining scene – that is, until the disco of Songs You Never Wanted To Hear Again kicks in at about 9pm and the party starts. ₷₷

Garden Palace Hotel 1 Teatri St ☎ 995 557 323028. The terrace on the top floor of this smart hotel is probably the most happening place in town in the evening, with a well-stocked bar and occasional impromptu dancing. ₷₷

Pancake House 58 Kostava St ⓦ facebook.com/PancakeHouseZugdidi. If you're craving something a little different, try the great pancakes here – there are both sweet and savoury options available, but you probably can't beat the classic pancake with ice cream and seasonal fruits. ₷

Tamtini 87a Rustaveli St ☎ 995 595 014069. Pleasant little café with outdoor seating offering delicious cakes and very good coffee. A great place to relax for a little while in between sightseeing. ₷

DIRECTORY

Banks Banks with ATMs can be found along the length of Rustaveli and Gamsakhurdia avenues.

Pharmacies Zugdidi is very well supplied with pharmacies. You should be able to find what you're looking for on Gamsakhurdia Ave.

Post office Zugdidi's central post office is at 92 Rustaveli Ave, ☎ 995 322 240909. Mon-Fri 9am-5pm, Sat 9am-2pm.

The Black Sea Coast

From Zugdidi, it's just a short hop to the Black Sea coast and its array of both sandy and pebble beaches, many of which are home to popular beach resorts. In the north, and closest to Zugdidi, is Anaklia, while further south along the road to Batumi, you'll find Shekvetili and Kobuleti. In between is the port city of Poti, which is home to a smattering of low-key cultural attractions.

Anaklia

A brainchild of the Saakashvili government, **Anaklia** was intended to be a major Black Sea resort, and while these plans didn't exactly fail, it would be hard to call the scheme an unmitigated success. Anaklia is now a surreal little place with a few enormous hotels and casinos, the Black Sea's biggest water park (**Aquapark**, Anaklia beach, charge), and a very smart bridge over a lagoon, which claims to be the longest pedestrian bridge in Europe. The sandy beach attracts bathers primarily from Georgia and Russia and is a pleasantly calm and quieter alternative to Batumi.

Poti

If you're travelling from Zugdidi to Batumi you might want to consider breaking your journey in **Poti**, which – while not offering any world-beating sights – has a couple of attractions that will divert you for an hour or two.

Poti is an unexpected entry point to Georgia should you be coming by boat: ferries operate to and from Constanța in Romania. Book online at ⓦukrferry.com/en.

Museum of Colchian Culture

9 26 Mai Street • Charge • ☏ 995 493 23502

In a grand nineteenth-century mansion house, this museum exhibits a wealth of archaeological finds from Bronze Age Colchis, as well as a room upstairs of model ships reflecting Poti's maritime tradition. The museum is determinedly old-school – it could do with a bit more English labelling and you may have to use all your charm to persuade the staff to turn the lights on so you can actually see the exhibits – but for all that it's definitely worth a visit.

Other sights

While in town, you might also want to take a quick look at the ornate **St Virgin Cathedral** in the centre of what has to be the world's most unnecessarily large roundabout, as well as checking out the candy-cane striped **lighthouse** on the front, which you can climb for great views – though unfortunately you can't go out on the balcony at the top. Twitchers will be rewarded by a visit to the **Kolkheti National Park**, an important wetlands area which offers good birdwatching opportunities. The **World War II Memorial** on the road down to Batumi is also worth a stop, being more imaginative and less concretey than most.

Poti to Batumi

The road heading south from Poti to Batumi for the most part hugs the coast, passing through the popular beach resorts of **Shekvetili** and **Kobuleti**. If you're looking to relax on the Black Sea, there are plenty of resort hotels here to choose from, as well as a couple of mildly diverting attractions.

Miniature Georgia Park

E70, Kobuleti-Shekvetili Highway • Charge • ⓦ tinyurl.com/3ww46m7z • Shekvetili-bound marshrutka from Batumi

If you were hoping to visit everywhere in Georgia but just don't have time, the Miniature Georgia Park might be the ideal destination: here you'll find models of the country's top tourist sites, all designed with an impressive attention to detail. The model of Tbilisi's old town is particularly well done.

Petra Castle

E70, Batumi-Kobuleti Highway • Charge • ☏ 995 422 225603 • Kobuleti- or Shekvetili-bound marshrutka from Batumi

On a hill on the main road leading north sits this small castle, which reopened in 2021 after extensive archaeological digs and renovations. It's an early medieval fortress built by the Byzantine emperor Justinian, and offers great views over the Black Sea as you stroll around the ruins.

Batumi

Big brash Batumi, Georgia's **second biggest city** and the capital of the autonomous region of Adjara, is the country's party and beach capital, a crazy, pulsing city of Gulf State-esque architecture mixed with a very European party spirit. If you're entering Georgia overland from Turkey it's probably the first place you'll reach, and it's hardly representative of the rest of the country. Indeed, Batumi is unlike anywhere else in the Caucasus, and it attracts fewer Westerners than it does Russian holidaymakers, who come to the city to make the most of the **beach** and revel in the lively **nightlife** and **casinos**.

It wasn't always thus. Batumi began life as a Greek colony, and then passed successively into the Roman and Byzantine empires before becoming part of the unified Georgia in the medieval period. Taken by the Turks and recaptured by the Georgians multiple times over the sixteenth and seventeenth centuries, Batumi was annexed by Russia in 1878, and was swiftly developed as a major Black Sea port: railway links were built, the city became the end of the Baku-Tbilisi-Batumi oil line, and the population and economy boomed.

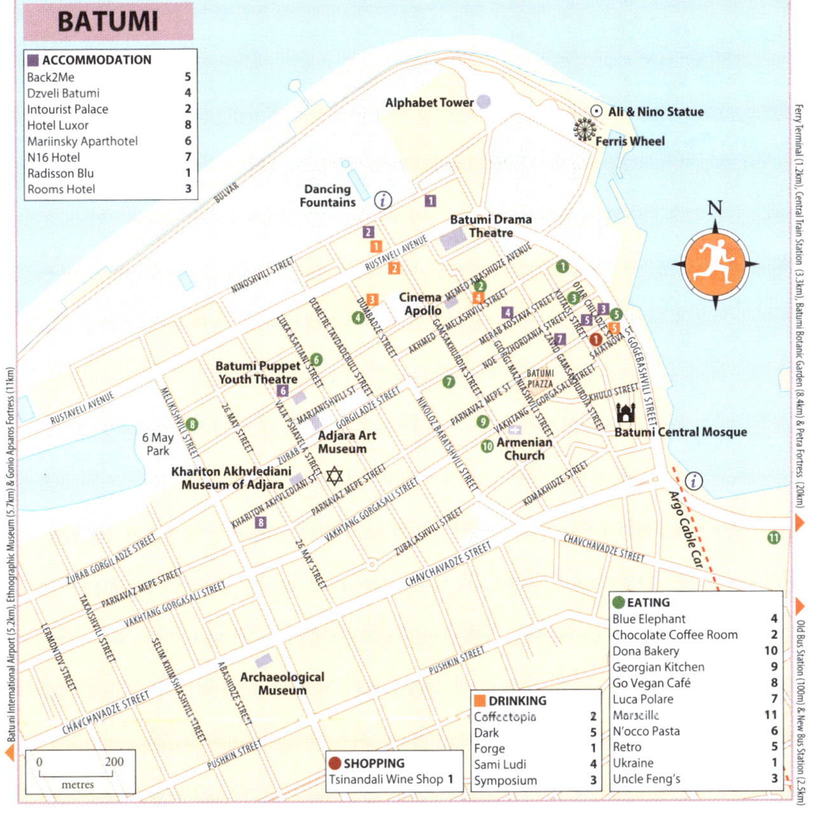

ALI & NINO

Set during World War I in various locations across the Caucasus, the novel *Ali & Nino* offers a fascinating insight into the many different cultures, traditions and peoples in the region. The characters **Ali and Nino** live in Baku: Ali is a member of a noble Azeri family, in love with the Georgian princess Nino, and the novel explores the difficulties inherent in such a relationship, at a time of enormous upheaval. It's a must-read for anyone hoping to get under the skin of the Caucasus.

It's credited to Kurban Said, but no such individual seems to have ever existed, and the authorship of the **novel** is unknown. The Ukrainian Jewish novelist Lev Nussimbaum seems the most likely candidate, but Azerbaijani writer Yusif Vazir Chamanzaminli is a potential rival to the author claim. The truth is likely to remain unknown forever.

Under the **Treaty of Brest-Litovsk** in 1918, Batumi was returned to Turkish rule, but handed back to the Soviet Union in 1920 by Atatürk. During the Soviet period, the city was a popular holiday destination, but afterwards the region of Adjara was subject to the autocratic and corrupt rule of Aslan Abashidze. Eventually tensions rose in 2004 when the new Saakashvili government sought to reassert Tbilisi's control over Adjara, resulting in Abashidze's deposition. Ever since, tourism and real estate have brought the city a vibrant economy. At one point there was even a plan to put up a Trump Tower here, though this was cancelled in January 2017.

Bulvar

The **seafront boulevard** (Bulvar) is Batumi's centre of activity, and it's a fantastic place for a stroll, especially at twilight when the garish neon lights are in full contrast with the golden sunset. If you fancy a boat ride around the bay (including for fishing or diving), you should be able to arrange it here.

Attractions include the enormous **Ferris Wheel** (charge) which affords a fine view of town. At the foot of the wheel is the **Ali & Nino sculpture** (free), a fantastically innovative piece of work, featuring two figures who dance around one another, their bodies eventually intermingling before separating and starting again. It's inspired by the classic novel of the same name.

Alphabet Tower

Bulvar • Charge • ☎ 995 514 152255

A lift whisks you up this impressive tower, which looks like a double helix and has the thirty-three letters of the Georgian alphabet inscribed on the side. At the top, there's a café and a slowly revolving restaurant, with nightly jazz concerts livening things up from 9pm.

Beach

Bulvar • Free

The stony **beach** is enormously popular for both swimming and sunbathing, and the promenade behind is lined with a string of pleasant, lively bars and restaurants. Come by the nearby park in the evening, around sunset, to watch the **Dancing Fountains** show, when the fountains are synchronised with a light show and a pop/rock soundtrack.

Town centre

The **town centre** is likeable and well-signposted, and there are frequent photographs on boards showing scenes of Batumi from a hundred years ago. The epicentre is **Europe Square**, an attractive open space with architecture reminiscent of a Central European city such as Prague (there's even an astronomical clock here), though the centrepiece

– a 2007 concrete monolith, topped with a statue of Medea of Argonauts fame – feels very Caucasian.

Adjara Art Museum

8 Zurab Gorgiladze St • Charge • Ⓦ ajaramuseums.ge/en/museums/art

A small but well-curated collection of works from both Georgian and international artists, this museum is unlikely to detain you for very long but it's still worthy of a quick visit. Pieces by one of Georgia's most famous artists, Pirosmani, can be found upstairs.

Khariton Akhvlediani Museum of Adjara

Jincharadze St • Charge • Ⓦ ajaramuseums.ge/en/museums/khariton

In this well-presented museum covering regional topics including natural history, archaeology and ethnography, you'll see fossils, ancient pottery, models of traditional houses, and a fair whack of stuffed wildlife, not all of it expertly done. The collection of eighteenth-century doors is gorgeous, but the pride of the museum is a large fifth-century BC Greek vase. Don't miss the amazing Soviet tractor and the whale skeleton in the back yard.

6 May Park

Rustaveli Ave • Free

These low-key gardens surrounding a large lake, on which you can rent a pedalo, aren't the most exciting you'll ever see – though the love-heart shaped floral display is quite fun, as is the fountain which appears to be propelling a huge rock into the air – but as a place to stretch your legs, it's nice. The park also contains a small zoo with monkeys and lemurs, as well as a dolphinarium and a little fairground.

Archaeological Museum

77 Chavchavadze St • Charge • Ⓦ ajaramuseums.ge/en/museums/arch

The **Archaeological Museum** hosts a fair collection of local artefacts, beginning with the Stone Age, explained by good English labelling. There are some particularly beautiful fifth-century BC glass perfume vessels, and some impressive examples of decorated Greek pottery. The museum is at pains to demonstrate Ancient Georgia's links with the Greek world.

Armenian Church

Gamsakhurdia St • Free

Used as a planetarium during Soviet times, this attractive 1885 **church** is now an active place of worship again. The interior is relatively plain: it's better admired from outside.

Batumi Piazza

Parnavaz Mepe St • Free

Flanked by pseudo-Venetian architecture and lined with enticing cafés and restaurants, this attractive square's centrepiece is an impressive, somewhat abstract mosaic, inspired by the relationship between sea and town. To the piazza's northeast is the orthodox, red- and white-striped **St Nicholas Church**.

Mosque

Kutaisi St • Free

Batumi's small **mosque** is Turkish in appearance and style, reflecting the influence of the many years of Ottoman rule here. It isn't enormously noteworthy, but mosques are something of a rarity in Georgia so it may be worth a quick look if you happen to be passing by.

Argo Cable Car

Gogebashvili St • Charge • Ⓦ argo-batumi.ge/en/home

The **cable car** starts at the harbour and heads up to the top of the hill behind the city. The views as you travel up are fantastic, but there isn't really a lot to do once you get to the observation deck at the top.

Ethnographic Museum

14 Mikheil Sharashidze St • Charge • ☎ 995 514 330101 • Bus number 12

In the suburbs on the southern side of town, the **Ethnographic Museum** is a labour of love for its owner and curator, Kemal Turmanidze. Many of the artefacts on display here were handmade by him, and he's certainly a very talented woodcarver. While this may raise a few questions around authenticity, the informative guided tours use these items as a jumping-off point to discuss and demonstrate traditional ways of life.

ARRIVAL AND DEPARTURE   BATUMI

By train Batumi's Central Station is not central at all: in fact, it's a rather unhelpful 4km around the bay from the town centre. Bus numbers 3 and 10 go to and from the station. Four trains a day leave for Tbilisi, at 0.45am, 8.10am, 5.15pm and 6.20pm; the journey takes about five hours.

By bus Batumi is blessed with two bus stations. The new is at 1 Gogol Street and the old is at 1 Mayakovsky Street. Services include marshrutkas to Tbilisi, which leave hourly from the old bus station, or from the new bus station there are larger buses every hour. To Zugdidi, there are marshrutkas eight times a day from the old bus station and twice a day from the new, as well as hourly from the train station. Marshrutkas run to Akhaltsikhe at 8.30am and 10.30am from the old bus station, and there's one marshrutka a day to Borjomi, at 10am from the old bus station. In summer, you can get a marshrutka to Mestia from the Argo cable car at 3pm, or from the new bus station at 2.30pm.

If you're heading to Turkey, the Metro Georgia bus company is a professionally run outfit. Tickets from Batumi to Trabzon, leaving the new bus station at 3.30pm and 10.30pm, and taking between 4 and 6 hours, can be booked online at Ⓦ metrogeorgia.ge.

By car The road from Zugdidi, via Shekvetili and Kobuleti, is a good and easy drive. By contrast, the road from Akhaltsikhe is in large part entirely unsuitable for all but the hardiest vehicles, though at time of writing construction works were ongoing, after which this convenient route should be achievable. Batumi itself is a busy place to drive in and you're likely to get caught in traffic, but it's not difficult. It's one of a very few places in Georgia where you may have to pay to park in the city centre, but it won't break the bank. You can pay at parking meters, or online at Ⓦ tbcpay.ge/en/services/transporti/batumis-parking.

By plane Batumi's international airport, 2km south of town, offers flights to Tbilisi, Yerevan, Baku, Istanbul, Moscow, Tehran, Riga and Dubai, among other destinations.

By boat Prior to the Russian invasion of Ukraine, UKR Ferry operated weekly ferries across the Black Sea to Ukraine's Chornomorsk port. If this service restarts, look for online bookings at Ⓦ ukrferry.com/en.

A hydrofoil operated by Batumi Express (☎ 995 593 333966, Ⓔ expressbatumi@mail.ru) sometimes zips along to Sochi in Russia in five hours, if weather conditions permit, though at time of writing this service was suspended. If it resumes, tickets can be reserved by calling or emailing in advance.

GETTING AROUND

By bus Batumi has a decent network of public buses; the most useful for tourists are likely to be the numbers 3 and 10 to the train station. An incomplete list of routes can be found at Ⓦ wikiroutes.info/en/batumi/catalog. You can also ask at the tourist information centres if you have any specific queries. Travelling by bus requires a reloadable Batumi card, which you can acquire at the airport, tourist information centres, or the Metro Service Plus office at 55 Gorgasali St.

By taxi Taxis are reasonably plentiful and cheap enough.

Some have meters, but if the one you pick up doesn't, agree prices before setting off.

By bike Batumi's bulvar is ideal for cycling. There are bikes for hire along the front, though to avail yourself of these, you'll need a BatumVelo card, available from the tourist office.

By foot Batumi is a relatively big city, but most places of interest to tourists are within an easily walkable radius so you'd never need to go more than about 2km.

INFORMATION

Tourist Information Centre There are two tourist information centres in central Batumi: one by the cable car (Gogebashvili St, ☎ 995 577 909093, 24 hours in summer, 9am–11pm in winter) and the other by the Bulvar (2 Ninoshvili St, ☎ 995 577 909091, Summer 9am–10pm; winter 9am–9pm). They are staffed by a friendly team who can supply town maps and advise on local activities, transport and accommodation, as well as selling Batumi cards for bus travel.

Listings Anything happening in Batumi will be listed on the tourist information centre's website, at ⓦgobatumi.com/en/events, or on the Batumi Events website at ⓦbatumievents.com.

Websites The official tourist information centre website ⓦgobatumi.com/en, is an extremely useful resource for travellers seeking to plan visits to Batumi and the surrounding area.

ACCOMMODATION SEE MAP PAGE 125

Batumi is well served with hotels, from big glitzy international standard towers to small guesthouses. If you're a light sleeper, do bear in mind that Batumi is a city that is lively for much of the night. You may want to request a room at the back.

Back2Me 4 Otar Chiladze St ⓦba2me.ge. A popular and well-regarded place, *Back2Me* is a sleek and modern hostel with 40 beds across five dorms, some mixed. The restaurant is accessed by a vaguely submarine-like ladder. Each bed has curtains, but there are no curtains over the dorm's windows, which feels a little strange. $

Dzveli Batumi 24 Merab Kostava St ☏995 422 277157. This is a friendly rambling B&B on a quiet street near the centre. All rooms are individually decorated and there's plenty of artwork in the lobby/family living room. Room three, on the second floor, has a large terrace and is probably the best choice, but you can't go wrong with any of the rooms here. $$

Intourist Palace 11 Ninoshvili St ⓦintouristpalace.com. If you always wanted to stay in a Stalinist Intourist hotel but missed your chance in the Soviet era, here's your opportunity. This magnificently blocky building has been fully modernised and is now a top-class hotel, but still retains a great 1930s ambience, and many of the staff have that fabled Soviet (lack of) charm. It's even got a model in the lobby of the beautiful church that was knocked down to build this monstrosity. $$$

★ **Hotel Luxor** 13 Jincharadze St ⓦluxor. tripcombined.com. The *Luxor* is a friendly, quiet and eclectically decorated hotel a little way from the town's main action. It's housed in an older building, and rooms all have individual touches: some are a little, or a lot, over the top. $$

★ **Mariinsky Aparthotel** 50 Memed Abashidze Ave, ⓦfacebook.com/MariinskyApartHotel. The rooms in this centrally located apartment block are delightfully spacious and airy, and despite being in the city centre it's very quiet. The whole place is very well maintained, and there's a pleasant roof terrace which is a lovely place to relax on a warm day. $$

N16 Hotel 16 Parnavaz Mepe St ☏995 571 489090. The stylish, comfortable and clean *N16 Hotel* is a good choice. It's in a great location near Batumi Piazza, with great views from its terrace, and the breakfast is very good. $$

Radisson Blu 1 Ninoshvili St ⓦradissonhotels.com/en-us/hotels/radisson-blu-batumi. A shiny modern wavy glass building, the *Radisson* occupies a good position on the Bulvar. It has a spa and pool, and the rooms are to the international standard that you'd expect. Service is well-meaning but can be quite inefficient. $$$$

Rooms Hotel 10 Gogebashvili St ⓦroomshotels.com/hotel/batumi. A branch of the upmarket Georgian chain, Rooms is a very stylish hotel occupying a grand building on the front. Somehow managing to look both nautical and space-age, the bedrooms are extremely comfortable, while the restaurant and bar offer great food and cocktails. $$$

EATING SEE MAP PAGE 125

Batumi offers perhaps the most cosmopolitan dining choices in Georgia outside Tbilisi, so if you're keen for a change from the standards, this is your chance. On the other hand, you won't want to miss the opportunity to try the incredible Adjaran khachapuri – a big boat-shaped piece of dough, full of cheese, melted butter and an egg – here in its hometown. There are also a great many Turkish and Indian fast food places on Kutaisi Street by the mosque.

Blue Elephant 8 Dumbadze St ⓦblueelephant.ge. A great café catering to Batumi's hipsters with upmarket breakfast options, including pink eggs toast (eggs marinated in beetroot and served with avocado) and truffle scrambled egg toast with salmon. The sandwiches and salads make it a good shout for lunch too, and there's a very fine range of desserts and cakes. $$

Chocolatte Coffee Room 13 Memed Abashidze Ave ☏995 558 176991. Intimate and friendly little café with a short but well-considered menu, including a rotating daily special. It's a good place for a quick breakfast. $

Dona Bakery 41 Vakhtang Gorgasali St ☏995 422 275814. Remarkable range of brightly coloured cakes, all freshly made and very good. Coffee and tea are also available. The concept of queuing seems to evade most customers here, so get your elbows in. There's a second branch at 121 Parnavaz Mepe St. $

Georgian Kitchen Gamsakhurdia St. There's plenty of Georgian fare on offer here, so you'll be spoilt for choice, but it's one of the best places to get one of Batumi's famous super-unhealthy but incredibly delicious Adjaran khachapuri. $

Go Vegan Café 23 Melikishvili St ⓦfacebook.com/vegancafebatumi. It can be difficult finding vegetarian and vegan options in Georgia, which makes this place all the more welcome. There are plenty of dishes on offer here, with the falafel being one of the best choices. $

Luca Polare 3 Irakli Abashidze St Ⓦ lucapolare.com. Very popular among locals, Luca Polare is considered the home of Batumi's best gelato. There are numerous smaller branches along the beachfront. $

Marseille 32 Gogebashvili St Ⓣ 995 422 272849. A local place which feels oddly like an English pub, *Marseille* is well-positioned by the harbour and is thus very good for fish. Staff can be a little surly, but the food makes up for it. $$

N'occo Pasta 13 Luka Asatiani St Ⓦ facebook.com/NoccoPasta. Build your ideal meal at this tiny Italian joint – first choose your pasta, then your sauce, then your meat. It's very tasty. $

★ **Retro** 12 Gogebashvili St Ⓣ 995 599 511722. The

Adjaran khachapuris here are known for their high quality, and it's also sometimes possible to undertake a cooking course with the owner to learn how to make one. The menu is limited here, but what it does, it does very well. $

Ukraine 1 Akhmed Melashvili St Ⓦ tinyurl.com/hbueva4m. Great Ukrainian food in an attractive restaurant: pretty much everything on the menu is delicious, but it's particularly worth trying the draniki (potato pancakes) or the varenyki (dumplings) in cherry sauce. $$

★ **Uncle Feng's** 3 Noe Zhordania St Ⓦ facebook.com/unclefengs. A small, authentic, and downright excellent Chinese place, not far from the Bulvar. The salt and pepper chicken is fantastic, and it is recommended you say yes when they ask if you want your rice spicy. The TV appears to be stuck on late 1990s MTV, which is also very pleasing. $$

DRINKING   SEE MAP PAGE 125

Coffeetopia 6 Konstantine Gamsakhurdia St Ⓦ coffeetopia.ge. Funky and fashionable place with a lengthy menu of coffees, a great chilled playlist, a few board games to play, and several models of koalas randomly dotted around the place. It's a strong contender for the best coffee in Batumi.

Dark 6 Saiatnova St Ⓦ linktr.ee/darkbarbatumi. Friendly little drinking spot with a gothic theme. The staff whip up tasty cocktails, and trying on the scary masks that adorn the walls is not just allowed but actively encouraged.

Forge 16 Rustaveli Ave Ⓣ 995 568 977637. An underground lair for music lovers – there's usually someone playing here, but if not, the playlist is reliably excellent, and the surprisingly tuneful regulars will likely be singing

along anyway. The bar is well stocked too, offering beers and spirits.

Sami Ludi 5 Giorgi Mazniashvili St Ⓦ tinyurl.com/3nkxwb67. This nice and central little spot with an industrial feel is one of Batumi's best spots for craft beer. There's usually a good number of Georgian beers on tap, and the bartenders are great for recommending one to your taste. Decent food also served.

Symposium 6 Nikoloz Baratashvili St Ⓣ 995 558 504044. This very well-stocked wine bar just off Europe Square is a great place to idle away an evening over a glass or two of Georgia's finest, especially if you get yourself one of the cheese and charcuterie plates to nibble on as you go. They also offer tastings.

ENTERTAINMENT

Batumi Drama Theatre 1 Rustaveli Ave Ⓦ batumitheatre.ge. There are occasional performances at Batumi's central theatre. Check the website to see what's on.

Batumi Puppet Youth Theatre 49 Memed Abashidze Ave Ⓣ 995 276 270593. While perhaps not in the same league as Tbilisi's puppet theatre, there are fun

performances here, particularly for children.

Cinema Apollo 17 Abashidze St Ⓦ kinoafisha.ge. Batumi's main cinema is central and housed in a fantastic Art Nouveau building. There's one screen, usually with three to four showings per day, including latest blockbusters shown in their original language.

SHOPPING   SEE MAP PAGE 125

Batumi is a very good place to buy Georgian wine and chacha. There are many shops which will allow you to try before you buy.

Tsinandali Wine Shop 5 Parnavaz Mepe St, Ⓣ 995 577

383720. is one such place, but you'll find many more as you wander the streets, particularly in the area southeast of Europe Square.

DIRECTORY

Banks There's no shortage of banks and ATMs in Batumi; try along Rustaveli Avenue and around Europe Square.

Hospital Batumi International University Hospital (237 Fridon Khalvashi St, Ⓣ 995 422 213333, Ⓦ bih.ge).

Laundry VipServ (Griboedov St, Ⓦ facebook.com/viplaundryge, 10am–7pm) is a cheap and high-quality self-

service laundry spot.

Pharmacies Outlets of PSP, Aversi and Pharmadepot are plentiful in the town centre, particularly along Gamsakhurdia Street.

Post offices The most convenient post office is at 4 Melashvili Street, open Mon–Fri 9am–7pm, Sat 9am–5pm.

Around Batumi

The outskirts of Batumi offer a few pleasant diversions, all accessible by public transport.

Botanic garden

Mtsvane Kontskhi Rd • Charge • Ⓦ bbg.ge/en/home • City bus 15, marshrutka 31 or 40

A large area of parkland just above the beach attractively set out with paths amid the trees offering frequent Black Sea views. It's a lovely place for a walk away from the busy city. The garden consists mainly of trees rather than flowers, though the New Zealand floristic display is excellent. There's also an electric train that will ferry you from one end of the gardens to another (charge).

Gonio Apsaros Fortress

E70, Batumi-Sarpi Highway • Charge • ☏ 995 595 352120 • Bus number 16

A square of well-preserved crenellated walls dating back to the Roman and Byzantine eras, **Gonio** contains very well-tended gardens and occasional ongoing archaeological excavations. By the southern wall you can see a baths complex, as well as water system pipes from Roman, Byzantine and Ottoman periods. In the centre is a shrine to St Matthew, one of Jesus's apostles, who may have been martyred here.

Batumi to Akhaltsikhe

The road between **Batumi** and **Akhaltsikhe** is currently paved only as far as Khulo and then again from Zarzma, leaving a 50km stretch in the middle which is virtually impassable without a 4WD. Fortunately, a project funded by the Kuwaiti government to seal the road began in 2019, though no completion date is yet in sight. When this work is finally finished, the travelling time will be reduced by several hours.

In the meantime, it's possible to travel as far as Khulo in a smaller car, and the road is very pretty, following a river valley through wooded hills for much of the way. About 30km from Batumi you'll reach the settlement of **Makhuntseti**, which sports a medieval arch bridge and a reasonably attractive waterfall, beneath which is a popular swimming pool. You can also easily arrange river rafting trips from here.

The road continues for some time, passing another, more impressive, arch bridge at Dandalo, and eventually reaching Khulo, where a cable car (charge) – built in 1985 and seemingly untouched since – offers a ride of almost 2km, very high above the valley floor, with splendid views.

Svaneti

The region of **Svaneti**, in Georgia's northwest, is commonly regarded as one of the most beautiful corners of the country. It's a gorgeous area, in the heart of the stunning Caucasus mountains, and is perfect for hiking, horseriding, skiing, and other outdoor activities. On top of that, the area's relative isolation – which, in some cases, lasted until the Soviet era – led to the development of a culture which produced a distinctive style of architecture. The villages in the region are all populated by a plethora of defensive stone towers, which complement the surrounding scenery beautifully. If you only have time to visit one mountain area in Georgia, Svaneti should definitely be it.

Zugdidi to Mestia

The road to Svaneti is utterly spectacular. Mountain vistas await with every twist and turn, and you'll forever be stopping to drink in the views. Specific sights – other than the tremendous scenery – along the way are few, the most obvious being the **Enguri Dam** (Ⓦenguridam.ge, charge). When it was completed in 1978 it was the tallest in the world, and although it has now been relegated to eighth place, it's still a rather impressive sight: a huge wall of concrete holding back an expanse of turquoise water, with a fine backdrop of wooded mountains. The visitor centre here offers three tours – long, short and walking. Unless you're a particular dam enthusiast, the walking option should be sufficient – it offers a great viewpoint over the dam, with a couple of info boards detailing a brief history of the dam and comparing it to other sizeable dams worldwide. You'll also get access to a small cinema which plays a short film about the dam and whets your appetite for the longer tours. The walking tour is available at all times, but if you want either the long or short tour it's worth calling ahead to arrange. Note that it's not possible to leave the tour early once you've begun.

Mestia

The town of **Mestia** is Svaneti's capital, a friendly and well-touristed place with a good number of traditional Svan towers, surrounded by the kind of mountains you drew as a child: conical, snow-topped, and utterly beautiful. A particularly fine example is Mount Tetnuldi, a great view of which can be had from the bridge just down from Liberty Bank. Sunset is the best time, as the sky turns purple and the clouds clear from around the summit.

Mestia's town centre, in particular the area around Seti Square, is a slightly odd place, having been done up like a Swiss village with cobbled streets and chalet-like buildings. That being said, it's not unpleasant, but it does feel a little unreal and twee. The streets to the north, which are winding and narrow, give a more realistic sense of the town's former character.

Svaneti Museum

7 A Ioseliani St • Charge • ☏ 995 322 997176, Ⓦ museum.ge/index.php

This fascinating and well-presented museum exhibits a huge range of artefacts from throughout Svan history. The religious icons are remarkable, and there are some

OUTDOOR ACTIVITIES

The main street has a number of establishments to buy or hire **ski equipment**, and **horse rental** is easy to come by too. Oddly, **guided walks** are harder to arrange. You could try the Tourist Information Centre, but don't be surprised if your enquiries are met with shrugging and an insistence that guides are not necessary. Your guesthouse might be a better place to organise guided trips. Most taxi drivers know the start point of popular walks and tend to congregate around Seti Square in the morning to pick up hikers.

beautiful liturgical books, some dating as far back as the ninth century. You also can't miss the enormous ritual cauldron. The central hall hosts temporary exhibitions.

Mikhail Khergiani House Museum

35 M Khergiani St • Charge • ☎ 995 591 051163

The famous Svaneti mountaineer Mikhail Khergiani grew up here, and the house is now home to an exhibition of very interesting mid-twentieth-century mountaineering paraphernalia, as well as objects specific to Khergiani himself. English language labelling is sporadic, though there is a fascinating readable copy of the Scottish Daily Express dating from Khergiani's 1960s visit to Glencoe. The museum also has a typical Svan tower, which you can climb for great views.

Margiani House Museum

Lanchvali St • Free

This small ethnographic museum offers another great opportunity to climb a Svan tower and the views from the top are excellent, though bear in mind that the tower's roof is enclosed so you'll be looking through arched windows. Also note that while getting up the steep ladders presents little problem, getting the right angle to come back down can be more challenging!

St Nicholas Church

Avtandil Khergiani St • Free

Not really a highlight of Georgia's Christian tradition, **St Nicholas** sits on a small rise slightly to the south of town. Inside it features modern frescoes, but unless you're a dedicated student of these you'll probably be more interested in visiting to get a decent view over the river back to the Svan towers on the north side of town.

For a quick diversion if you're heading to the ski lift from here, cross the bridge and turn left down the track (instead of right up to the ski lift). In about five minutes, you'll come to a small spring dispensing salty and fizzy water similar to that found in Borjomi, which locals prize for its health benefits.

Hatsvali Ski Lift

Zugdidi-Jvari-Mestia-Lasdili Highway • Charge

Whizzing you to the top of Mt Zuruldi, the **Hatsvali Ski Lift** is a great way to get some fantastic views with very little effort. There are two lifts, and it's a short walk to transfer between them halfway up. At the top of the second, there's a slightly lacklustre restaurant, from which you can enjoy beautiful views over town the surrounding mountains. Hikers may want to consider turning left at the top of the ski lift and head along the ridge for an excellent out-and-back walk – a 6km round-trip will get you up to the viewpoint at Mentashi Hill.

ARRIVAL AND DEPARTURE — MESTIA

By plane Mestia is reachable via a bumpy plane ride operated by Vanilla Sky (ⓦ ticket.vanillasky.ge/en) from Naktakhtari airport (about 30km north of Tbilisi; the ticket usually includes a transfer from Tbilisi), which takes an hour. This service runs every day except Saturdays, with two flights on Tuesdays and Thursdays. Vanilla Sky also operate a 40-minute flight from Kutaisi to Mestia on Mondays and Wednesdays. Mestia's airfield is only 2.5km from the town centre.

The flights are on very small propeller planes and they do get booked up, so if you're intending to get to Mestia this way then book as far in advance as you can. There's no allocated seating on the plane, so if you want a window seat (and you DO want a window seat!) then try to be among the first to board.

By marshrutka The main destination from Mestia is Zugdidi; there are five marshrutka departures a day from the main square, the first at 8am and the last at 6pm, taking four hours. There are also once daily departures to Batumi (8am, six hours), Tbilisi (8am, eight hours) and Kutaisi (8am, five hours). You can also take the 10am marshrutka to Ushguli (two hours), but depending on your group size you may find it better value to take a shared taxi.

By car The 140km road between Zugdidi and Mestia is generally good, though there are a few unpaved patches. It's a winding road that ascends and descends a fair bit, but it's never hairy, and is in fact a lovely drive. Note that there are no petrol stations anywhere between Jvari (30km north of Zugdidi) and Mestia, so ensure you have a full tank preferably before leaving Zugdidi. There are several petrol stations in Mestia, so again, make sure you fill up before leaving town.

INFORMATION

Tourist Information Centre Seti Sq ☎ 995 551 080894. It would be a stretch to say that the Tourist Information Centre is enormously helpful, but they do have maps (which you can photograph but not take) of hikes around Mestia, as well as information on public transport/taxis and appropriate prices. Daily 10am–6pm.

Websites The excellent Caucasus Trekking (ⓦ caucasus-trekking.com/regions/svaneti) lists a great range of hikes you can do in the area, from day trips to multi-day treks.

ACCOMMODATION

SEE MAP PAGE 132

It can feel as though every other property in Mestia is a guesthouse or hotel, so you shouldn't have trouble finding a room here even at the height of the season. It should be noted that price is not necessarily an indicator of quality.

Chalet Mestia 47 Bethlemi St ⓦ facebook.com/ ChaletMestia. You can't miss the *Chalet Mestia*, which looms up on the road just before you reach the main square. The interior décor is vaguely inspired by Swiss chalets but is mainly bland, international standard accommodation. Rooms at the back are recommended to avoid traffic noise. §§

House Mon Amie 2 Nugzar Dzhaparidze St ⓦ facebook. com/housemonamie. *Mon Amie* sports six pleasantly decorated rooms, all sharing one bathroom. Breakfast is included, and there's a well-tended garden to relax in. The main disadvantage is that it's some way (about 15 minutes' walk) from the centre, but if you're after peace and quiet, it might suit you. §

Inga Jafaridze Guesthouse Pele 21 Guladi Jafaridze St ☎ 995 599 192944. It doesn't look like much outside, but the interior of this welcoming guesthouse is warm and cosy. The breakfast is very good, and home-cooked meals

---

WALK TO CHALAADI GLACIER

One of the easiest and most attractive walks in Mestia's vicinity is the route to **Chalaadi Glacier**. While it can be entirely walked from the centre of Mestia (just follow the airport road for about 10km), this is a little tedious so it's more rewarding to drive or take a taxi to the small car park at the glacier's base. From here, cross the suspension bridge, turn right, and follow the well-marked (with white-yellow-white symbols) path uphill through the forest. It's initially a little steep but quickly levels out, and you'll soon find yourself hugging the bank of the river, which is often milky and torrential with glacial meltwater.

The **path** eventually emerges from the forest, though at the top of a small rocky rise it veers left into another small patch of trees; briefly divert to the right here and you'll get a fine view of the glacier ahead. Return to the main path and walk through small fields alive with wildflowers, with the glacier in your sights, until you reach the boulder field at its base. Return by the same route; allow 2.5 to 3 hours (or all day if you're walking all the way from Mestia).

At the suspension bridge, there are two **cafés** with erratic opening hours, both offering cold drinks and snacky food. Arguably the better of the two is the one to the south of the suspension bridge, slightly further from the trail.

DEDE

The 2017 film **Dede** was filmed in **Ushguli**, all with local actors, and is an interesting snapshot into the traditions, ways of life and challenges of being a woman in this region. The plot concerns the struggle of a young woman called Dina who is promised in marriage to David, but loves David's comrade Gegi. The film was shown at several festivals when it first came out and won several international awards, including **Best Film** at the Eurasian International Film Festival and **Best Cinematography** at the Beijing International Film Festival.

are often available in the evening. $

Guesthouse Khergiani 9 M Khergiani St ☎ 995 595 054939. In a quiet street at the east end of town, the friendly Khergiani has eight clean en-suite rooms and a veranda with a marvellous view. Breakfast is provided and the kitchen is available for self-catering. $

Guesthouse Oribeli 6 Givi Japaridze St ⓦ oribeli. business.site. This guesthouse on a quiet street just north of the main square has a couple of rooms, all with private bathroom. There's a lovely terrace with views over the mountains and Svan towers. The breakfast is excellent, and the owners can help arrange trips to Ushguli. $

★ **Hotel Panorama Svaneti** 11 Avtandil Ioseliani St ☎ 995 551 041144. Occupying a lovely quiet spot between the Svaneti Museum and the cable car, Hotel Panorama has 12 clean and comfortable en-suite rooms — make sure to get one on the upper floor facing town so you can enjoy the fantastic views from the balcony. The breakfast is plentiful and extremely tasty, especially the pancakes. $

Posta Hotel Seti Sq ⓦ facebook.com/hotelpostamestia. Mestia's smartest — and correspondingly most expensive — option, *Posta* sits in the heart of town. The 28 rooms are clean and modern, and are also very stylish, especially the deluxes. Service isn't all it could be, being honest. $$$

EATING   SEE MAP PAGE 132

Blue Mountains 20 Tamar Mepe St ☎ 995 550 000741. A friendly café-restaurant on the main road running through Mestia, Blue Mountains has a lovely terrace overlooking the river, on which you can enjoy khachapuri, lobio or mtsvadi. Friendly if occasionally slow service. $$

Erti Kava 5 Seti Sq ☎ 995 568 809420. A small place that approaches hipster, *Erti Kava* serves up good coffee as well as other hot drinks. Most seating is on bean bags, there are board games to play, and the soundtrack consists of chilled beats. $

Café Laila 7 Seti Sq ⓦ facebook.com/cafebarLaila. official. Right on the central square, it's hard to miss Café Laila: it's always busy with punters keen to sample its tasty Georgian meals. There's sometimes live music. $$

Lanchvali Café Lanchvali St ⓦ facebook.com/ cafelanchvali. At the top of town by the Margiani House Museum, the Lanchvali Café is a great place to enjoy well-prepared and tasty Georgian and Svan classics. The khachapuri and kubdari are both particularly

recommended. $

Lile Seti Sq ☎ 995511290770. The centrally located Lile has an extensive menu of excellent Georgian meals, with the cheesy mashed potato a particular highlight. A good selection of wines and cocktails make it a pleasant place to while away an evening. $$

★ **Lushnu Qor** 44 Tamar Mepe St ☎ 995 591 043395. An excellent choice in Mestia's centre, the friendly staff at the rustic *Lushnu Qor* serve up lovely food: the lamb with cheesy mashed potato is fantastic, and it's also a great place to try the traditional Svan kubdari. There's free table football and a pool table upstairs. $$

Posta Seti Sq ☎ 995 595 337345. The bar and restaurant of Mestia's smartest hotel has a small but good menu of Georgian food, and it's also undoubtedly the best place in town for a cocktail. Service for food can be unforgivably slow, though, and the Georgian folk music that kicks off around 8pm is loud and, regrettably, not very good. $$

ENTERTAINMENT

Dede Pub Cinema 38 Tamar Mepe St ☎ 995 595 089508. Small place on the main road which offers drinks,

but whose raison d'être is to show the acclaimed film *Dede* several times a day.

SHOPPING

There are several souvenir shops along Mestia's main street, though not as many as you might expect in such a touristy place. They mainly sell fridge magnets, snowglobes, postcards and the like, but usually also stock a fair range of

local wines, chacha and honey.

In the back streets you'll often see signs advertising the sale of Svan salt, a spice mix involving salt, pepper, coriander and chilli, among other ingredients.

DIRECTORY

Banks You'll find ATMs and banks around Seti Square.
Hospitals Mestia's small hospital, at the end of Gabliani Street, is only open weekdays 9.30am–7pm.

Pharmacies There aren't many pharmacies in town but one option is the Pharmadepot at 13 Gabliani St, by the hospital.

Mestia to Ushguli

It's about 50km from Mestia to Ushguli, and there are two ways of getting there: by car, or on foot. If you choose to walk, you won't be alone – it's one of Svaneti's most popular multi-day treks. It takes four days and the route is well marked with red-and-white stripes, starting from Seti Square in Mestia. There are plenty of guesthouses in the villages along the way, and it's a beautiful walk which isn't technically difficult. Due to heavy snow in winter the trek is usually only possible between May and September.

If you're coming by car, you'll find that the first 30km or so of the road, as far as the village of Kala, is (mostly) paved. Don't get any funny ideas about driving it yourself, though, unless you've got a 4WD or a desire to destroy your car, as the remaining 20km is very tough, involving single-track bumpiness and the occasional stream to ford. You can pick up shared taxis or marshrutkas in Mestia's Seti Square or along Queen Tamar Street.

It's an incredibly scenic drive, following the Enguri river valley for much of the way and periodically climbing to fantastic viewpoints. There are plenty of Svan towers to look out for too, most notably the **Tower of Love**, just beyond the village of Ipari, which is the subject of a folk story concerning two lovers whose families forbade their marriage. You can climb it for a small charge, but there are limited views from the top and it's probably better admired from outside.

It's also worth a quick stop at **St Barbara's Church of Khe**, about 10 minutes on from the Tower of Love, which contains some beautiful, if faded, frescoes and a number of icons dating back as far as the sixth century.

Ushguli

Ushguli, one of the highest villages in Europe at 2100 metres, is a conglomeration of four hamlets: Chvibiani, Chazhashi, Zhibiani and Murqmeli. Chvibiani has much of the tourist infrastructure – guesthouses, cafés, etc – and Chazhashi is perhaps the most atmospheric, with narrow unpaved streets winding between Svan towers.

It's easy in Ushguli to find a place offering horseriding, and most guesthouses can arrange guided hikes. For other pursuits, such as skiing or rafting, you may have to bring along equipment yourself.

Ushguli is short on specific sights: it's all about wandering the narrow streets of the village (dodging the pigs that also wander at will), admiring the sheer number of Svan towers and the gorgeous setting.

TOWERS AND BLOOD FEUDS

The **medieval towers** that dot the villages and landscape are one of Svaneti's most distinctive features. Their function was defensive, and contributed to Svaneti's successful resistance to all invaders until the mid-nineteenth century arrival of the Russians. However, it has been theorised that the towers were not only for defence against outsiders, but also for internal disputes.

Blood feuds between Svan families have a long history. According to ancient Svan tradition, blood must be paid for with blood, and even as late as 2002 the UK's *Guardian* newspaper reported on a dispute that had been running for a hundred years. The practice survived through Soviet times into the post-independence era, but has – according to National Geographic – virtually disappeared since 2004.

MOVING ON FROM USHGULI

The **mountains** around **Ushguli** offer unparalleled opportunities for trekking, mountain biking and horseriding. One particularly recommended trip is the five-hour walking route from Ushguli to Tsana over the Zagar mountain pass, which offers spectacular mountain views amid untouched nature, as well as passing the abandoned village of Koraldashi. If you're biking, you could head from Tsana down towards Letekhi along a horrendous potholed road with a steep cliff down to the river below, crossing mountain streams and passing under small waterfalls – but the absolutely stunning scenery makes it more than worth it.

Queen Tamar's Tower

Off Zugdidi Jvari Mestia Lasdili Highway • Free

Referred to as **Queen Tamar's Winter Palace**, this tower provides a great vantage point for views down the valley in both directions, offering stunning vistas of the towers and the village. On the mountain ridge to the south, you can see another tower known as Queen Tamar's Summer Palace.

Ethnographic Museum

Chvibiani • Charge • ☎ 995 577 962847

Based in a 900-year-old house, still furnished in the traditional fashion, the museum exhibits a plethora of Svan artefacts – mostly beautifully carved wood – as well as the skins of three unfortunate foxes. The friendly curator can explain in good English the purpose of the items and give a brief précis of the Svan way of life.

Lamaria Church

Chvibiani • Free

This small ninth-century church sits on the hill at the northeast end of the village and is worth a visit for its fading frescoes as well as the spectacular views up the valley.

ACCOMMODATION　　　　　　　　　　　　　　　　　USHGULI

Guesthouse Qaldea 21 Jibiani St ☎ 995 599 385398. Just behind the Ethnographic Museum, *Qaldea* is a friendly place with six rooms and one shared bathroom. The owners can help arrange guided hikes from Ushguli, or transport back to Mestia or beyond. $

Hotel Koshki Chvibiani ⓦ facebook.com/hotelkoshkiushguli. This central place offers 13 rooms, all with private bathroom and some with balcony. Try to get a top floor wooden chalet-style room, as the standard rooms on the middle floor look a little tired. There's a good café on site too. Breakfast not included. $$

Nizharadze's Tower Chazhashi ⓦ nizharadze. tripcombined.com. A guesthouse in the quieter Chazhashi part of town, in an area where there's a high concentration of picturesque towers, *Nizharadze's Tower* has six rooms with shared bathroom. The décor is magnificently unfashionable. Closed Oct–Apr. $

Ushguli Cabins Zhibiani ☎ 995 598 760630. In the centre of the village, the Ushguli Cabins offer a number of lovely self-contained chalets which sleep between two and four people each. The owners are fantastic and proactive in arranging hiking or horse-riding trips in the surrounding area. $$

EATING AND DRINKING

Café Bar Enguri Zugdidi Jvari Mestia Lasdili Highway ⓦ facebook.com/EnguriBar. A large wooden chalet-like structure at the river bridge, *Enguri* is a busy and popular place for food and drinks, including Ushguli's best coffee. The outdoor seats by the river are a relaxing place to chill. As with most places in Svaneti, service can be unaccountably slow. $

Old Tower Café Chvibiani ⓦ oldtower.tripcombined. com. Offering the expected Georgian staples, the *Old Tower* is – true to its name – based out of a Svan tower. The food is good, if unremarkable, and service is friendly. There are a couple of rooms available here too. $

Kakheti

HORSES GRAZING ON TUSHETI'S MEADOWLAND

Kakheti

The province of Kakheti forms the entirety of Georgia east of Tbilisi. It's one of the most popular touristic areas of Georgia, due to the twin attractions of remarkable history and excellent wine. But if that's not enough to tempt you into a visit, it's also home to the outstandingly beautiful Tusheti, a mountainous region offering pristine hiking opportunities for those who feel Svaneti and Kazbegi are getting too crowded. To top it off, it's a hugely relaxing area: Kakheti goes at a much more sedate pace than much of the rest of Georgia. It's a great place to slow down and take it easy.

Kakheti is the epicentre of Georgia's wine industry, with vineyards virtually everywhere you look in the northern half of the region, and they're almost always happy to welcome tourists for **wine tasting** sessions. The lovely hilltop town of **Sighnaghi** is a great place to base yourself for a couple of days, enjoying the great local food and wine before getting involved in more active pursuits. For the real hardcore, the fantastic mountain scenery of **Tusheti** is the ideal spot for hiking or horseriding, but if you don't fancy a journey along one of Europe's most dangerous roads, the slightly easier **Lagodekhi National Park** is no slouch in the hiking stakes. And for the historian, there are countless monasteries and cathedrals in the region. The majestic **Alaverdi cathedral** sits in lush fields beneath the Caucasus mountains, while **Davit Gareja**, one of Georgia's greatest treasures, can be found in a unique semi-desert landscape.

Brief history

Kakheti was an independent kingdom for much of its early history, though it was occasionally brought under Georgia's rule when particularly ambitious and powerful monarchs, such as David the Builder, were on the throne. In the eighteenth century, however, it was unified with the neighbouring kingdom of Kartli by Erakle II, who was born in Telavi and is held in high regard by Kakhetians. Erakle's rule, however, was characterised by attempting to defend his kingdom against the encroaching Persian Empire, and in doing so, he agreed to make Kakheti a **Russian protectorate**. Within three years of Erakle's death, Russia had annexed Kakheti, ushering in nearly two centuries of Russian rule.

During the Soviet period, when wine was regarded as a Georgian speciality, its production was encouraged here, using the traditional *qvevri* method. Since independence, the region has seen an upturn in tourism, to the extent that it is now regarded as the area's principal economic activity other than agriculture and viticulture.

Tbilisi to Telavi

There are a couple of interesting historical sites between Tbilisi and Telavi, but owing to the relative lack of public transport, they're probably best visited with your own vehicle or by hiring a driver.

Ninotsminda Cathedral

Ninotsminda town • Free • Telavi or Sighnaghi marshrutka from Tbilisi

The ruined cathedral of **Ninotsminda** is one of Georgia's most often overlooked highlights. Seriously damaged by nineteenth-century earthquakes, the church – dating

Highlights

❶ **Alaverdi** A beautiful cathedral set in rolling vineyards, Alaverdi is one of Georgia's most elegant and evocative churches. See page 145

❷ **Wine tasting** A visit to Kakheti wouldn't be complete without sampling several products of the excellent local vineyards. See page 146

❸ **Tusheti** Accessible only via a long and sometimes scary mountain road, this isolated corner of the Caucasus is ideal for truly adventurous hikers. See page 148

❹ **Sighnaghi** The region's jewel in the crown is the Italianate town of Sighnaghi, where you'll relax into living with Kakheti's slower pace. See page 149

❺ **Lagodekhi protected areas** Near the Azeri border, Georgia's first national park is a haven for animals and is criss-crossed with beautiful hiking trails. See page 152

❻ **Davit Gareja** Away in Kakheti's south, the cave monastery of Davit Gareja is home to magnificent medieval frescoes. See page 153

HIGHLIGHTS ARE MARKED ON THE MAP ON PAGE 142

back to the year 575, when it was hugely influential in the development of Georgian religious architecture – is now rarely visited. That's a shame, because the ruins are gorgeous and there's enough left to give you a good impression of what the church was like in its heyday.

It's surrounded by defensive walls, erected in the seventeenth century, and the gardens are beautifully tended and full of flowers. The remains of frescoes can be seen on the apse wall, with those on the arch particularly well preserved. There's also a very unusual brick-patterned bell tower, which – as part of the still-functioning monastery – you can look at but not enter.

Marshrutkas heading from Tbilisi to Telavi or Sighnaghi can drop you off on the main road that passes Ninotsminda to the south. From here, it's no more than a 10-minute walk to the cathedral. Be prepared, however, that you may have difficulty picking up onward transport as passing marshrutkas are most likely to be already full so it will be a bit of a waiting game.

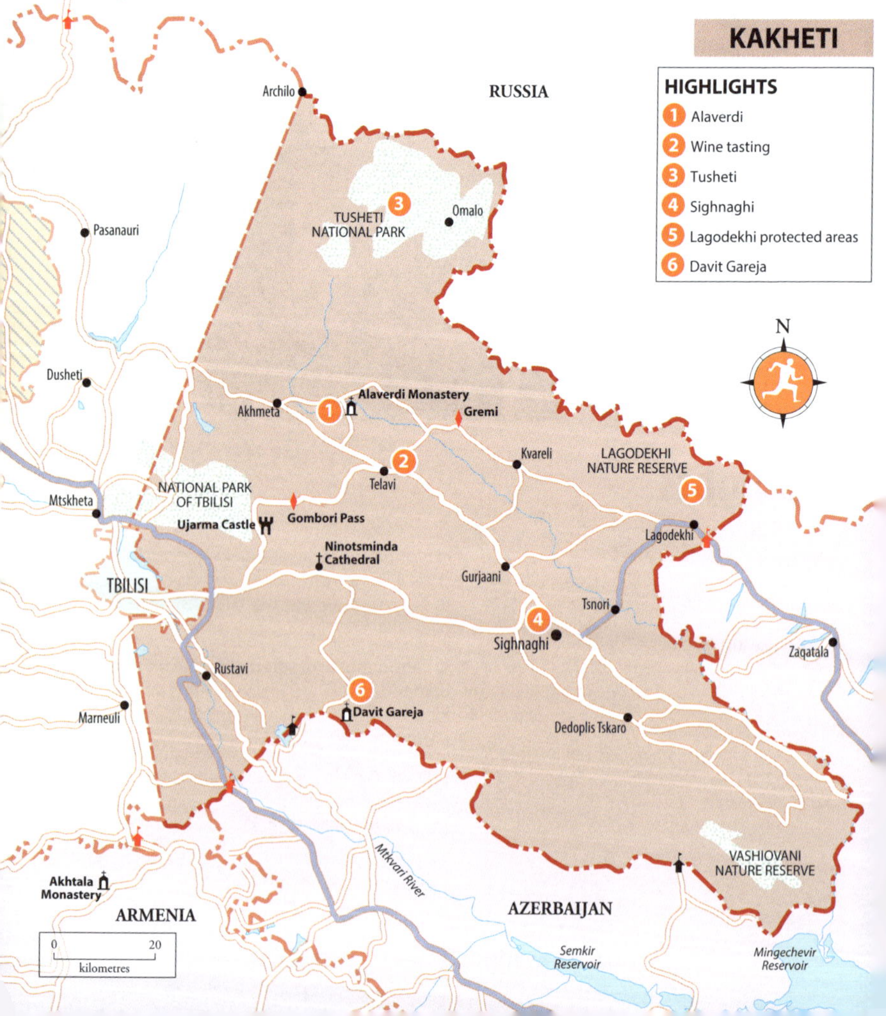

Ujarma Castle

Ujarma highway • Charge • No public transport

The partially ruined **Ujarma Castle** stands on a knoll beside the Tbilisi-Otaraani road. Built by the pleasingly named King Asparagut in the third century, it was an important strategic stronghold for many rulers, including Tbilisi's founder, Vakhtang Gorgasali. It's a picturesque site, high above the Iori river, and infrequently visited. Renovation work is unobtrusively underway and viewing platforms have been positioned around the walls. There's also a two-floor chapel in the castle grounds, the upper floor of which is only accessible via a bridge.

There's **no public transport** to Ujarma. If you're driving, it's a good stop between Tbilisi and Telavi if you're going via the Gombori Pass: the road is switchbacky and sometimes not well paved, but manageable even in a non-4WD and extremely beautiful.

Telavi

Telavi is both the largest city in, and the capital of, Kakheti. It's been a settlement for at least two thousand years, but its zenith came in the eighteenth century when, under King Erakle II, it became a centre of strategic importance for trade. This of course transformed it into the second most important city in Georgia. Today, it's still a prosperous little city, which serves as a great base to visit the large number of beautiful monasteries in the surrounding countryside, as well as for vineyard visits to sample the local wines.

Sights in the town itself are relatively minor, but they're worth a morning's exploration. There's some impressively grandiose architecture on its main street, Erakle II, and on the smaller streets in the town centre you'll find some beautiful brick-built houses in a style quite unlike elsewhere in Georgia.

Batonis-Tsikhe Fortress

Erakle II St (entrance on Teimuraz II St) • Charge • Ⓦ telavisistoriulimuzeumi.ge/home

The town's centrepiece is the large castle, guarded by a big statue of Erakle II on horseback. It's a square of defensive walls, which are not enormously interesting in themselves, but they contain two attractions which you visit on the same ticket.

Firstly, there's the **History Museum**, which is in a striking modern structure in the centre of the castle grounds. It contains a very well-presented exhibition on the region's history and ethnography, as well as a temporary exhibitions hall usually used for artwork.

Secondly, towards the rear of the complex is the seventeenth-century **palace**, which – although built by the Christian kings of Georgia – is clearly influenced by the Persian architecture of the time and bears some resemblance to the palaces in Sheki in Azerbaijan. It's thought that the town's favourite son, King Erakle II, was born in this palace.

The plane tree

Chess St • Free

Telavi is very proud of its enormous nine hundred-year-old **plane tree**, which is the sole survivor of what was once a full grove of these trees. It's hollow and quite fun for a brief look, especially since it allegedly has the power to make wishes come true.

Just down from the tree is a steampunk sculpture of three snails made of cogs, metal and wheels. It's a nice little feature to stop and admire if you're having a slow day.

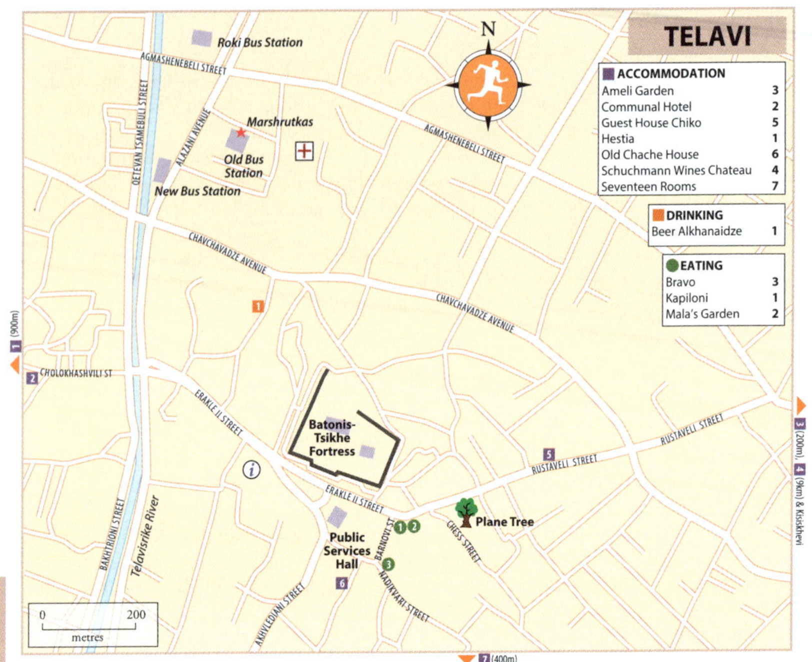

Elsewhere in town

On the main square, the striking modern **Public Services Hall** (Erakle II St, ☎995 322 405405) is worth a quick look. Otherwise, having a wander in the attractive old streets just up the hill from the castle is a pleasant way to spend a lazy morning.

ARRIVAL AND DEPARTURE   TELAVI

By bus There are three bus stations in Telavi, which seems a bit excessive, but fear not, they're all very close to each other, on Alazani Avenue. Buses to Tbilisi go from the new bus station (☎995 350 274390); there are up to 20 departures a day. The new bus station is also the place to be if you're heading to Lagodekhi; there are five buses a day, starting at 7.30am. For Sighnaghi, you'll need the marshrutka departure from the old bus station (☎995 350 271619) at 3.15pm on weekdays only. The tourist office can supply a timetable for all the local buses (for Alaverdi, Gremi, etc) and the corresponding bus station.

By car There are two routes to Telavi by car; the main highway, which is a longer route that passes close to Sighnaghi, and the shorter journey over the Gombari Pass on a smaller road. Both are easy to drive, though the Gombari Pass probably has the edge as it's a very pretty route. Once in Telavi, there's nothing difficult to negotiate, and parking is easy.

GETTING AROUND

By foot Telavi's sights are all within about five minutes' walk of each other, as are the various bus stations. Some guesthouses are about 15 minutes' walk from the town centre. If you want a taxi, they're plentiful and cheap.

INFORMATION

Tourist Information Centre Erakle II St, ☎995 350 275317. The tourist information office is on the main square, in a traditional building with a pleasant balcony. The staff can help with onward travel information, give suggestions on local wineries to visit, and arrange trips to Tusheti. Mon–Fri 9am–6pm, Sat–Sun 10am–5pm.

ACCOMMODATION   SEE MAP PAGE 144

★ **Ameli Garden** 8 Rustaveli St (Second Lane) ⓦfacebook.com/AMELITELAVI. A top-notch guesthouse,

Ameli Garden has a choice of huge rooms – some with en-suite bathrooms – all decorated in homely style. This, combined with the friendliness of hostess Khatuna, means that you'll feel like you've come to stay with a kindly relative. It doesn't hurt, of course, that the breakfast (extra charge) is excellent and that there's free home-made wine available – all you need do is ask! $

Communal Hotel 11 Cholokashvili St w communalhotels.com/home/telavi-2. One of a small Georgian chain, the Communal Hotel offers beautifully elegant rooms and great service. Breakfast is very good, it's in a great central location, and there's an outdoor pool on-site. It's a good choice if you're looking to splash out a bit. $$$

Guest House Chiko 23 Rustaveli St ☏ 995 551 648443, w tinyurl.com/mbthnmc2. Four sleek modern rooms – a double, a single, and two triples – all with private bathroom, in a converted old house owned by a friendly family. There's a terrace for breakfast and a lovely garden to relax in, as well as a fun wine cellar. $

Hestia 109 Kvirike Didi St ☏ 995595072507. On a quiet street a little way out of the centre, Hestia is a great hotel with stylishly minimalist décor. An excellent breakfast is available, and there's a lovely terrace with city views. You're also likely to be offered some very good home-made wine. $

Old Chache House 2 9 April St ☏ 7 777 0431133 w old-chache-house-hotel.business.site. In an attractive old house right in the centre of town, the *Old Chache House* has three rooms which are clean and modern, as well as a beautiful shared lounge with exposed brickwork. The Kazakh hostess, Yevgeniya, is very friendly and speaks very good English. $

Schuchmann Wines Chateau Kisiskhevi village w schuchmann-wines.com/hotel. Schuchmann is an upmarket and popular hotel in an attractive stone building with its own restaurant and vineyard. The wine tours are very good, but service at the hotel and restaurant isn't what it should be, and some of the rooms are past their best. $$$

Seventeen Rooms 3 Giorgi Leonidze St w facebook.com/Hotelseventeenrooms. Smart and upmarket hotel on the edge of the city centre. The lobby and bar are very stylish, while the rooms are a little blander but extremely comfortable. Breakfast is excellent too. $$

EATING AND DRINKING SEE MAP PAGE 144

A little oddly, given the area around Telavi is known for wine, there are very few wine bars in town. Luckily, all restaurants have a good selection of local wine choices available, and calling in at vineyards (see box, page 146) is also an option.

Beer Alkhanaidze 26 Bagrationi St ☏ 995 598 538400. Just what you expect to find in the heart of Georgia's wine country – a brewery. It's a very good one, with an excellent range of local craft beers on tap; perfect if you want a break from the grape.

Bravo 11 Nadikvari St ☏ 995 593 152713. An extremely extensive and reasonably priced menu makes *Bravo* an excellent choice for lunch or dinner, especially if it's warm enough to sit out on the terrace. $

Kapiloni 10 Barnovi St ☏ 995 350 278767. Locals cite this central spot as the best place to eat in town. Staff are friendly and the food is certainly very good, but perhaps a little pricey by Georgian standards. $$

Mala's Garden Erakle II St ☏ 995 592 030131. A good central choice, *Mala's Garden* does standard Georgian dishes and it does them well – but often half of the menu options seem to be unavailable, which can be frustrating. The interior can be a little stuffy so best to visit at a time of year when you can sit in the eponymous garden. $

DIRECTORY

Banks There are no shortage of banks and ATMs on Erakle II St.

Hospitals Telavi Referral Hospital (Sekhniashvili St, ☏ 995 32 2550505)

Pharmacies There's a cluster of pharmacies around the bus stations on Alazani Ave, including PSP Pharmacy and Aversi.

Around Telavi

There's a wealth of great day trips to be taken from Telavi. Using public transport you'll struggle to fit more than one or two of them in, but you should be able to visit most, if not all, with your own car or by hiring a driver for the day. If you go for the latter option, Mamuka Jangualashvili (☏ 995 555 156715) is a highly recommended driver.

Alaverdi Cathedral

Ikalto-Alvani Rd • Free • Marshrutka from Telavi's old bus station every 20 minutes

KAKHETIAN WINE TOURS

One of the main draws for tourists visiting Kakheti is its seemingly endless number of excellent wineries. Much wine in the region is made in the traditional method – in the large earthenware jars known as *qvevris,* which are buried in the ground, allowing wine to ferment and mature. Almost every guesthouse in the region will offer you a sample of their home-made wine, but you can also visit local vineyards for wine tasting sessions. Many are well-marked with brown touristic signs on any road you happen to be travelling, but obviously you'll need a driver for the day if you're planning on heading out of Telavi for this activity.

Telavi's tourist information centre has very extensive information available about the local vineyards and can arrange tours for you. Some suggested wineries include:

Vaziani Winery 42 Mshvidoba St, Telavi, ⓦ vaziani.ge/?lng=eng. Offers a free tour around the factory including information about the wine-making process and tastings of four of the varieties available here.

Rostomaant Marani 9 Rcheulishvili St, Telavi, ⓦ rostomaantmarani.ge. Tastings here involve four wines, a sample of chacha, accompanied by excellent bread and cheese.

Shumi Winery Tsinandali village ⓦ facebook.com/SHUMIWINERY. Reds, whites, sparkling, rose and chacha are all available to sample at Shumi, which also has a small museum on site.

Zurab Kviriashvili Vineyards 39 26 May St, Telavi ⓦ zkvineyards.com. Zurab offers friendly and enganging wine tastings at this well-hidden spot in Telavi town.

Mosmieri Kisiskhevi village ⓦ mosmieri.ge. A very professionally run winery with great tours. Prices vary depending on how many wines you want to try. Bread, cheese and chacha are also involved.

This is just a very small sample of the many options available. You could spend weeks touring the Kakheti's many excellent vineyards. It's best to call the vineyards before visiting or check your plans with the tourist information centre.

Even if you've seen hundreds of churches by this point in your trip, do not miss **Alaverdi**. A hugely atmospheric place, set beneath rolling hills amid fields and orchards, this vast eleventh-century cathedral is surrounded by fortified walls and contains a still active monastery and vineyard, which grows 104 varieties of Georgian grape, including 82 from Kakheti. Until the construction of Tsminda Sameba in Tbilisi in 2004, this was the tallest church in Georgia.

The interior of the church retains a fair few frescoes, especially on the right (apse), but it's mostly plain. It's the sheer scale of the place that will impress the most. Try to visit about half an hour before closing time, when the tour groups have gone and the monks begin evening prayers, the perfect acoustics of the cathedral amplifying the beautiful chanting.

Ikalto Monastery

Ikalto Academy Rd • Free • ☎ 995 571 306120 • Marshrutka from Telavi's old bus station every 20 minutes

The **Ikalto Monastery** complex is a beautiful place, set in a grove of cypress trees atop a hill several kilometres west of Telavi. The central Transfiguration Church dates from the seventh century, though it has been extensively modified over the years. Even older are the Chapels of the Trinity and of the Birth of the Holy Mother, which were built in the sixth century. Around the northern side of the complex are the ruins of the academy that once stood here, where the poet Rustaveli is thought to have studied.

It's a lovely peaceful spot, especially in the early evening. It's clearly signposted from the main road and the road leading up to it is tarmac all the way. If using public transport, you'll need to take the marshrutka heading to Akhmeta and get off in Ikalto village, then walk the 2km up to the monastery.

Shuamta Monastery

Old Shuamta Monastery Rd • Free • No reliable public transport

There are actually two monastery complexes along the same road bearing the name of **Shuamta** – Dzheli (Old) Shuamta and Akhal (New) Shuamta. Despite the name, Akhal Shuamta was actually built in the sixteenth century. It was closed for renovation at the time of research but should be open again by time of publication.

Dzheli Shuamta, meanwhile, is a beautiful complex consisting of three small churches, dating back at least 1300 years. The largest, a seventh-century church reminiscent of that at Jvari (Mtskheta), still retains very faint fresco traces inside. The church on the right, with its conical roof and perfect symmetry, is an utterly perfect example of church architecture.

These monasteries are a challenge to reach by public transport, as though some marshrutkas to Tbilisi may come this way, most will go via the main highway. Ask in the tourist office in Telavi if you're determined to get here, or take a taxi.

Gremi

Telavi–Kvareli road • Free • ☎ 995 599 132532 • Marshrutka from Telavi's old bus station every 40 minutes

Gremi was once the capital of the Kakheti region, but this magnificent cathedral-fortress is all that remains of its glory days. Imposingly positioned on a knoll above the road, the cathedral contains some of Georgia's most impressive religious frescoes. The complex also contains a winery and a very disappointing museum (charge).

Once you've visited the complex and come back down the stairs, follow the cobbled path to your right. This will bring you past a pair of ancient small churches to the much better **Gremi Museum** (charge), which is relatively short on exhibits but gives a great history of the area. If you continue to walk the cobbled path, you'll reach some ruined buildings, an old baths complex and a small Armenian church.

From Telavi, the Kvareli-bound marshrutka will bring you here. It's obvious where to get off – you can't miss Gremi when it comes into view.

Nekrisi Monastery

Nekrisi Monastery Rd • Free • Marshrutka from Telavi's old bus station every 40 minutes

Perched high on a hill, with sweeping views across the fields of Kakheti, **Nekrisi Monastery** was once an important religious centre for a thriving town that flourished from about 100 BC until the early medieval period, when it suffered earthquakes and Arab invasions, resulting in its almost total abandonment by the late Middle Ages.

The monastery is now a charming, slightly ramshackle complex that is a delight to wander round. Don't miss the wine cellar in the bishop's palace, where you can still see the press and the holes in the ground for the *qveri*.

If you're coming by public transport you'll need the marshrutka from Telavi to Kvareli, but you'll have to get off at the junction to the monastery and walk the remaining 3km to the car park. From there, it's either a stiff 1.5km trek uphill, or for a small fee you can take the shuttle bus which departs every 30 minutes or when full.

Alexander Chavchavadze House Museum

Tsinandali village • Charge • ⓦ tsinandali.ge/en • Marshrutka from Telavi's old bus station every 30 minutes

A nineteenth-century Georgian noble with a European outlook, Alexander Chavchavadze's estate in this village just outside Telavi makes for a lovely visit. The park, designed by European landscape architects, is attractively laid out and perfect for a walk, while the house museum itself is a fascinating insight into Chavchavadze's times. There's a winery here as well, and the park often hosts events such as musical performances. Check the website to see what's on.

ALEXANDER CHAVCHAVADZE

Son of Erakle II's ambassador to Russia, **Alexander Chavchavadze** was a member of the Georgian nobility but born and raised at the Russian court in St Petersburg until he was 13. It's a measure of the favour his family was held in that the Russian Empress Catherine the Great acted as his godmother. He lived something of a charmed life, managing to combine a career of decorated military service in the Russian army with occasional nationalistic rebellions against Russia on behalf of his native Georgia.

Despite participating in the failed 1804 anti-Russian uprising, Chavchavadze served with distinction in the **Napoleonic Wars**, after which he spent two years in Paris where he absorbed French culture, which had a vast influence on his own writings and in turn the writings of his protégés. Much of Chavchavadze's work focused on the romanticism of Georgia's past, contrasted with its then current position under Russian rule.

With such leanings, it's perhaps not surprising that he involved himself in the 1832 plot to restore Georgia's monarchy, which ended in disaster. Chavchavadze was spared punishment on the condition that he lead a military expedition against the **Dagestani tribes** that were in rebellion against the Russian authority. Much of the rest of his military career was spent in the North Caucasus. He died in 1846 after losing control of his horse, in an incident officially deemed an accident, but was, according to some, the work of Russian assassins.

4 Tusheti

This northeastern region of Georgia is one of its most isolated and yet most popular corners. There's only one road in and it's only passable in summer – usually mid-May to mid-October – and even then it's a long and disconcerting ride over the Abano Pass, which at 2990 metres is the highest road in the entire Caucasus, to the village of Omalo.

Once you get there, though, you'll know why you've made the journey. The region is utterly stunning, the beautiful mountain scenery being perfect territory for hiking. It's also a fascinating cultural experience. There are defensive towers aplenty, as in Svaneti, and you'll see evidence of **Tusheti**'s religion, though nominally Christian, retaining considerable influence of pagan and animist tradition.

Apart from visiting the defensive towers in the villages, the principal activity in Tusheti is hiking or horseriding. If you're based in the main village, Omalo, there are several opportunities for day hikes or multi-day treks, including the eight-hour round trip to Diklo Fort, the five-day one-way trek to Shatili in Khevsureti, or the four-day loop up to the Nakaicho Pass and back. Some multi-day treks will require camping – which is possible almost anywhere in the region – but the Nakaicho route can involve homestays in villages along the route, if you choose.

There are excellent hiking guides online at ⓦcaucasus-trekking.com/regions/tusheti#treks and ⓦtravelsauro.com/travel-hiking-tusheti. It's always possible to arrange guides through your homestay, or you can contact the very helpful and friendly Giorgi Bakuridze on ⓔgio.bakuridze@gmail.com. Horseriding trips are also best arranged locally on arrival.

It should be noted that Tusheti's sheepdogs are not keen on strangers. If you encounter a dog when out walking, avoid getting anywhere near the flock. The shepherd ought to be close by to restrain the dog, but you must exercise caution as they can be nasty.

ARRIVAL AND DEPARTURE   TUSHETI

By car The road from Alvani to Omalo is unsuitable for anything other than 4WDs. It's a very difficult and dangerous drive, so it is strongly recommend you leave it to drivers who are familiar with it. If you do tackle it yourself, Telavi's tourist office recommends against driving it in bad weather or after 5pm. Note also that many hire car companies expressly forbid driving to Tusheti in their vehicles.

You can pick up minibuses to Alvani from Telavi's old bus station; at Alvani you'll transfer into a shared taxi for the ride to Omalo. The tourist information centre in Telavi can advise on and arrange transport for you.

ACCOMMODATION

There's no shortage of guesthouses in Tusheti, though they do get booked up in summer. Prices vary wildly. Places with private bathrooms tend to demand the highest prices. Camping is also possible throughout the region.

Guesthouse Lasharai Upper Omalo Ⓦfacebook.com/guesthouselasharai. Probably the closest thing to an international standard hotel in Tusheti, *Lasharai* offers clean, en-suite rooms in a stylish place which was built in 2013, though it has made a worthy effort to appear traditional. The breakfast and dinners are excellent and the view is magnificent. They can also arrange transport direct from Tbilisi airport to Tusheti for a very reasonable price. §§

Guesthouse Nazo Kvemo Omalo Ⓦfacebook.com/nkhvedaguridze. This lovely guesthouse has comfortable rooms with shared bathrooms. The owners are enormously friendly and the food – and homemade wine – is excellent. §§

A North Home Upper Omalo ☏995 598 337627. Formerly called Dark Towers – which was a strong contender for most ominously named guesthouse in Georgia, if not the world – this place has renamed itself perhaps in the hope of not bringing Sauron to mind. Luckily, nothing else has changed: it still has cosy rooms with private bathrooms, a bar and a lovely terrace overlooking Omalo's defensive towers. §§

Hotel Tevdore Kvemo Omalo ☏995 555 183090. The rooms are perhaps the definition of no frills, but *Tevdore* makes the cut due to its hugely welcoming owners and the fantastic food, which is included in the price. §§

EATING

You're likely to take most meals in Tusheti at your guesthouse, but if you fancy a trip out there are a couple of decent options.

Odila Tusheti Upper Omalo ☏995 599 267517. The friendly and welcoming *Odila* is an arty spot offering good Georgian food and great Kakhetian wine. It's a lovely place to while away an evening. §

Sighnaghi

The lovely hilltop town of **Sighnaghi** dates back to the eighteenth century, when it was founded by Erakle II. It's got an Italian feel to it, with beautiful cobbled streets running between houses with elegant wooden balconies, and a church that looks like it's been transplanted straight from the Adriatic. While short on must-see "sights", it's a very popular tourist destination, and no wonder: it's a great place to relax for a couple of days and sample the excellent local food and wine.

Sighnaghi Museum

8 Rustaveli Alley • Charge • ☏995 322 232448

NIKO PIROSMANI

Now one of Georgia's most famous painters, **Niko Pirosmani** was born in the nearby village of **Mirzaani** in 1862. A self-taught artist who painted in the naïve style, he was never able to support himself through his artwork and spent time in various other employment, including as a railway conductor and a dairy farmer. His talents largely went unrecognised in his lifetime, and it was only after his death in the 1918 flu pandemic that he gained a greater reputation, particularly in Paris in the 1920s and in the USSR in the 1950s. Approximately two hundred of his works survive, most of which are in **Tbilisi's National Gallery**, though a good number can be seen in **Sighnaghi's History Museum**.

Sighnaghi's museum takes the visitor through Kakheti's history, from ancient times to the medieval period, in a well-presented exhibition with some fascinating items and good English labelling. After the Middle Ages, though, it seems to lose interest and rushes through a lacklustre ethnographic section. The second floor, though, is better: it's home to a good showcase of works by the local artist Pirosmani, as well as hosting temporary exhibitions.

The little park outside the museum usually hosts a small souvenir market, and you'll also find here a statue of Kakhetian philosopher Solomon Dodashvili.

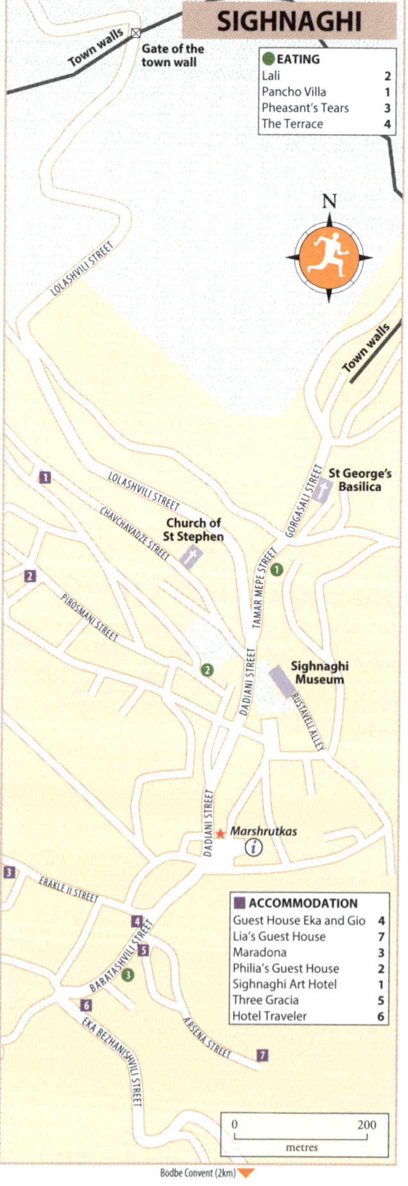

St George's Basilica

Gorgasali St • Free

The conical bell tower of this church, which would not look out of place in Venice, is Sighnaghi's most iconic sight. Built in the eighteenth century, the church is of more interest from outside than within.

Town walls

Gorgasali St • Free

Follow the road down to the left of St George's Basilica and take a cobbled path labelled "Tourist Track". This will bring you to a tower, which you can climb – though a torch will be handy since the stairs are dark and uneven. From this tower you can access a stretch of the **town walls** and lovely views across the plains to the Caucasus.

Church of St Stephen

Chavchavadze St • Free

This small church, built partly within a tower on the town walls, is probably Sighnaghi's highest point, and as such affords a magnificent view over the town and beyond.

Bodbe Convent

St Nino Monastery Rd • Free

The burial place of St Nino is set in beautiful grounds with immaculate lawns and flower beds, just a few kilometres out of Sighnaghi on the Tbilisi road. There are a couple of churches here, as well as an Italianate

ST NINO

There's a special place in Georgians' hearts for **St Nino**, who is considered responsible for bringing **Christianity** to the country in the early fourth century. She is thought to be one of the few survivors of the Armenian King Tiridates' slaughter of the community of nuns of Sts Gayane and Hrispane.

Following this incident, Nino seems to have travelled from Armenia, preaching along the way, and reached Mtskheta in the 320s, where she cured Queen Nana of an unspecified disease. Nana converted to Christianity, and before long her husband, King Mirian, followed in her footsteps. Nino baptised him in 326, after which he pronounced Christianity to be Georgia's state religion.

Nino and Mirian planted a wooden cross in a pagan temple, where Jvari Church in Mtskheta now stands. Mirian set about converting Georgia to the new religion, while Nino travelled to Bodbe, where she died. The **monastery** was established shortly after in honour of her memory.

bell tower. The first church, St George's, is on the site of St Nino's grave and dates back to the fourth century. Its interior is covered in attractive frescoes, as well as a remarkable decorative screen. In complete contrast, the other church – which is much larger and only consecrated in 2019 – is entirely white inside. There are beautiful views to the mountains from here on clear days.

ARRIVAL AND DEPARTURE   SIGHNAGHI

By bus Marshrutkas run to Tbilisi at 7am, 9am, 11am, 4pm and 6pm, and to Telavi at 9am. They depart from the square just in front of the tourist office.

By car Driving to Sighnaghi is easy enough – though it's a very winding ascent if you're coming from Telavi – and the only real difficulty you'll face is having to drive slowly on the cobbled streets. There's plenty of parking available.

INFORMATION

Tourist Information Centre Baratashvili St, ☏ 995 355 232414. The staff at the Sighnaghi tourist office will begrudgingly offer information on the town's attractions and onward travel, but are unlikely to help you arrange a tour of any wineries. and You'll be better off asking in your guesthouse or hotel. Daily 10am–6pm.

ACCOMMODATION   SEE MAP PAGE 150

★ **Guest House Eka and Gio** 3 Baratashvili St ☏ 995 555 230254. The three rooms in this guesthouse are homely and welcoming, all with private bathrooms and breakfast available. The ace in the pack, though, is the ancient wine cellar, which Gio has lovingly restored and now uses to make his own qvevri wines. Entrance is through a small shop, also run by the family; there's a neon sign outside. ₷

Lia's Guest House 16 Arsena St ⓦ lias-guest-house. business.site. A lovely choice, *Lia's Guest House* is at the end of a road that leads to a hill edge and, as such, has amazing views from the balcony. The staff speak good English, the breakfast is fantastic, the beds are comfy, and it's really quiet without being too far from the town centre. ₷

Maradona 42 Erakle II St ☏ 995 591 242111. This place does seem to have been touched by the Hand of God. The four en-suite rooms are clean, quiet, newly decorated and spacious, and there's a lovely terrace. The family couldn't be more welcoming and friendly. It's close to the town centre, but quite well hidden so it's worth asking for directions. ₷

Philia's Guest House 45 Pirosmani St ⓦ philia. tripcombined.com. A delightful little place, *Philia's Guest House* has three en-suite rooms, all with lovely homely touches. There's a fantastic terrace and a remarkable wine cellar too. Philia herself is very friendly, though no English is spoken. It's a little way out of the town centre. ₷

Sighnaghi Art Hotel 44 Chavchavadze St ⓦ facebook. com/arthotelsighnaghi. A little boutique hotel, full of antiques, the *Art Hotel* has six rooms, including two that incorporate part of the town walls. The lounge is a lovely place to relax, with a wood fire when it's cold, and there's a pleasant terrace for when it's sunny. There is also a beautiful resident cat. ₷

Three Gracia 8 Baratashvili St ⓦ tinyurl.com/599sw8rh. Friendly guesthouse on the main street, with a terrace that has good views over town and is available for barbecues. The three rustic rooms contain wooden furniture made by the owner. ₷

Hotel Traveler 26 Nikoloz Baratashvili St ⓦ tinyurl.

com/3yw77486. Clean and smart rooms, a great central location, and excellent food in the attached restaurant all combine to make Hotel Traveler a very good choice. The owners are friendly and can help arrange local transport and excursions. $\overline{\$\$}$

EATING

SEE MAP PAGE 150

Lali 5 Pirosmani St ☎995 599 320368. Pleasant restaurant just off the main drag, which does the usual range of Georgian favourites and also offers wine tasting, of course. When it's cold, the indoor exposed-brick restaurant with beamed ceiling is lovely and cosy, and when it's warm the garden is very relaxing. Rooms are available, too. $\overline{\$\$}$

Pancho Villa 9 Tamar Mepe St ⓦ facebook.com/mexfood. Well, this is a surprise – a Mexican restaurant in Sighnaghi. Even more surprisingly, it's very authentic and rather good, especially the excellent margaritas. It's especially welcome if you've been travelling in regional Georgia for a while and fancy a change from the usual options. $\overline{\$\$}$

★ **Pheasant's Tears** 18 Baratashvili St ⓦ pheasantstears.com. A Sighnaghi institution, *Pheasant's Tears* has long been regarded as the best place in town for food and wine. The reputation is well-deserved. The wine-tasting sessions are great fun, the food is excellent, the atmosphere is lovely, and the staff are friendly and knowledgeable. Booking ahead is advised as this place isn't exactly a secret. $\overline{\$\$}$

The Terrace 10 Baratashvili St ⓦ facebook.com/theterrace.sighnaghi. A great restaurant at the top of town, offering tasty Georgian dishes and, naturally, great wines. Best of all is the eponymous terrace: come for lunch and enjoy sweeping views across town to the mountains beyond. $\overline{\$\$}$

DIRECTORY

Banks A couple of banks with ATMs can be found on the square near the tourist information centre.

Pharmacies An outlet of the Aversi pharmacy chain is on the square near the tourist office.

Lagodekhi Protected Areas

On the route towards Azerbaijan is the town of **Lagodekhi**, which lends its name to a pleasant national park. Established in 1912, it was the first nature reserve in Georgia. It's home to a variety of animals, including the East Caucasian tur, a goat-like creature only found in Eastern Georgia and Dagestan, as well as predators such as bears, wolves and lynx.

If you want to visit, you'll need to start at the excellent **Visitor Centre** (197 Vashlovani St, Lagodekhi, ☎995 577 101834), where you will be asked to register before entering the park. The helpful staff can recommend hikes, which range from the five- hour round trip to Ninoskhevi Waterfall to the three-day trek to Black Rock Lake, and supply maps, as well as renting out equipment. Routes are well marked, but you can hire a guide at the Visitor Centre if needed (best arranged in advance).

ARRIVAL AND DEPARTURE

LAGODEKHI PROTECTED AREAS

By bus The bus station is on the main S5 road that heads through town towards Azerbaijan. There's no shortage of marshrutkas to Tbilisi; these depart approximately every 45 minutes between 6.45am and 5.30pm. Otherwise, you could head to Telavi on one of the five daily marshrutkas that leave between 8am and 2pm.

By car Driving to Lagodekhi poses no problems; it's a well-travelled route. Parking in town is easy too.

ACCOMMODATION

Guest House Gardenia and Wine Cellar 127 Vashlovani St ☎995 599 457500. A lovely guesthouse with fantastically friendly owners and tremendous food – make sure you take them up on the dinner option. There's also a wine cellar on site; you'll certainly be invited to try some of the excellent product! Some rooms have shared bathrooms. $\overline{\$}$

Royal Palace Hotel 191 Vashlovani St ⓦ facebook.com/ROYALPALACELAGODEKHI. Right at the park's entrance, the *Royal Palace* offers rooms in the hotel or in cottages set the garden. The onsite restaurant is very good, and there are facilities such as table tennis and a swimming pool. The hotel is not very well soundproofed, so if you're a light sleeper, you'll probably want to score one of the cottages. $\overline{\$\$\$}$

Southern Kakheti

The southern half of Kakheti is far less visited by tourists than the northern, largely because it's mostly a barren semi-desert area that lacks any particular sights. Most visitors who do head out this way are here for the culturally significant monastery of Davit Gareja, which is the best-known and most developed of numerous cave monasteries in the region.

Davit Gareja

Davit Gareja Monastery Rd • Free

Davit Gareja monastery, the main attraction in southern Kakheti, is an impressive religious complex in the steppe lands on the Georgian-Azeri border. Unfortunately, the border is yet another of those post-Soviet dispute zones in which the Caucasus excels. Both nations claim the complex as being an integral part of their heritage, with Azerbaijan maintaining that Davit Gareja was built by the Caucasian Albanians (see page 329), though it seems clear the monastery was a sixth-century Georgian construction. While in the past, the disputed territory was fairly cordial, things have become a little more tense in recent years, and Azeri soldiers now frequently patrol the ridge above the monastery, refusing access to half of the complex.

The lower part of the complex feels like a combination of a church and a ramshackle fairytale castle. This is **Lavra Monastery**, where most of the monks now live. You can explore the courtyard, the church, and the upper balcony, but cannot go any further. A path leads up from behind the monastery to a small caged-off cave where Davit's Spring resides behind a mesh screen. It was reputedly the only source of water at the monastery when it was built. Now there are water channels in the rocks around the monastery, most likely carved by the early monks to bring water from the spring to their dwellings.

If the political situation defuses you should be able to climb the ridge and visit the cave monastery of Udabno on the other side, where there are some magnificent frescoes, dating back as far as the tenth century. For now, you'll probably be stopped by the Georgian military if you get too close to the disputed area.

The History Museum in Sighnaghi (see page 149) has some very detailed information on the Davit Gareja complex, which is handy, as there's little to no information here.

ARRIVAL AND DEPARTURE DAVIT GAREJA

By bus The easiest way to reach Davit Gareja is to pick up the very affordable daily marshrutka service from Pushkin Square (near the tourist information centre) in Tbilisi at 11am, which will bring you here, give you a couple of hours at the complex, then take you to Udabno village for dinner and return you to Tbilisi at 8pm. This service runs from April to October only; there is no public transport to Davit Gareja in the winter months.

By car The road to Davit Gareja is well-paved and can be driven with ease. Whether coming from Tbilisi or Telavi, head to the town of Sagareto and then take the 172 road south.

ACCOMMODATION AND EATING

Oasis Klub Udabno village ⓦ oasisclubudabno.com. Similar to an arty, hippy commune, it seems a little unlikely to find a place like the *Oasis Klub* in quiet Udabno village. You can stay in one of the six wooden cabins with private bathroom, or in the hostel. Decent food is available too, and they run horseriding and canoeing trips, as well as offering wine-tasting. $

Yerevan

CAFESJIAN CENTER FOR THE ARTS

Yerevan

Armenia's capital is a beguiling city. At first glance, it seems to be heavily Soviet and over-trafficked, but look twice and you'll find a fascinating place with a long history. The celebrations for Yerevan's 2800th anniversary in 2018 showcased the pride Armenians have in their city's status as one of the oldest continuously inhabited settlements on Earth, and though many of the buildings here only date from the days of the USSR, there's a degree of innovation on show even in the architecture of the mid-twentieth century. Add to that the huge range of excellent museums, a vibrant artistic scene, and the best restaurants and nightlife to be found in Armenia, and it all adds up to a city that you simply can't miss.

Sitting stolidly on the plains beneath Mount Ararat, Yerevan is likely to be your entry point to Armenia and possibly the entire Caucasus. It's a good introduction: the city is friendly, easy to navigate – thanks to its unusual circular grid layout – and blessed with a huge number of fascinating things to do. Get your bearings by climbing the **Cascades** where you'll be able to see the city stretched out with Ararat behind. Next get stuck into visiting the museums, whether it be the outstanding **History Museum of Armenia**, exploring the excellent collection of ancient texts at the **Matenadaran**, or the introduction to Armenia's artistic heritage with the **house museums** of its notables. A sobering trip up to the **Tsiternakaberd Genocide Memorial** is essential if you're to understand the terrible wrongs that have been done to the Armenian people, and to see Yerevan's beginnings you should visit the ancient **Erebuni Fortress**. At the end of the day, you can relax in the excellent restaurants and enjoy the city's low-key but excellent **nightlife**.

Brief history

Though the area around Yerevan has been inhabited for thousands of years, the city dates its foundation to 782 BC, when King Argishti I of the Urartian Kingdom ordered the construction of the **Erebuni Fortress** on a hill which is now a few kilometres east of the centre. Erebuni was soon conquered by the Achaemenids, but following Alexander the Great's campaigns, it was able to achieve independence and became part of the newly formed Kingdom of Armenia, though not as the capital.

Christianity was introduced to Erebuni in the early fourth century by King Tiridates III, influenced by St Gregory the Illuminator. Over the following centuries, the city was subject to invasions by Persians, Arabs, Turks and Mongols, somewhere along the way acquiring the new name of Yerevan. By the fourteenth century, it was arguably the most important cultural and economic city in the region and was fought over by the Persian and Ottoman Empires, only to eventually be ceded to the Russians following the 1828 Russo-Persian War.

The Imperial Russian period saw Yerevan expand considerably, becoming famous for its production of brandy, a distinction which it stills holds today. After the Russian Revolution, Yerevan became the capital of the newly independent Republic of Armenia in 1918, but two years later it was once again invaded, this time by the Soviet Union's Red Army. Under Soviet rule, Yerevan was rapidly developed into an industrial centre, as well as being remodelled into its current circular grid plan and undergoing enormous and sometimes grandiose building projects. The popular demonstrations in 1965, on the fiftieth anniversary of the Armenian Genocide, led to the construction of the Tsitsernakaberd memorial, a striking example of expressive architecture.

Highlights

❶ **The Cascades** A white marble staircase stretches up the shallow hillside with exhibitions of fantastically avant-garde sculpture, and at the top a magnificent view to drink in. See page 159

❷ **Matenadaran** Home to a huge collection of medieval Armenian texts, you'll be astounded by the beauty and intricacy of the remarkable manuscripts on display here. See page 160

❸ **House museums** Yerevan is dotted with house museums of notable literary and artistic figures, which are a great entry point to learning about the country's intellectual heroes. See page 164

❹ **History Museum of Armenia** Quite possibly the best museum in the Caucasus, the History Museum of Armenia has an embarrassing wealth of fascinating exhibits. See page 165

❺ **Tsitsernakaberd** Pay your respects to the victims of the Armenian Genocide at this sombre 1960s memorial. See page 167

❻ **Nightlife** Evenings in Yerevan offer something for everyone: hipster cocktail hangouts, relaxed wine bars, jazz clubs, or opera performances – take your pick. See page 173

HIGHLIGHTS ARE MARKED ON THE MAPS ON PAGES 158 AND 162

5

Post-independence, Yerevan has taken its place as the **capital of the Republic of Armenia**. A further building boom has seen work continue on the stalled Soviet Cascades project and extensive remodelling of the city centre, including the installation of 2800 (small) fountains in 2018, the 2800th anniversary of the city's foundation. Politically, independent Yerevan has seen numerous periods of unrest, including 2018's Velvet Revolution, a civil disobedience campaign which led to the peaceful toppling of Serzh Sargysan's government and the installation of Nikol Pashinyan as prime minister, and protests following Armenia's losses in its engagements with Azerbaijan over Nagorno-Karabakh.

The Centre

The vast majority of Yerevan's sights are found in the city centre, and can be explored on a roughly north to south walking itinerary, starting at the city's centrepiece, the impressive Soviet-era **Cascades**.

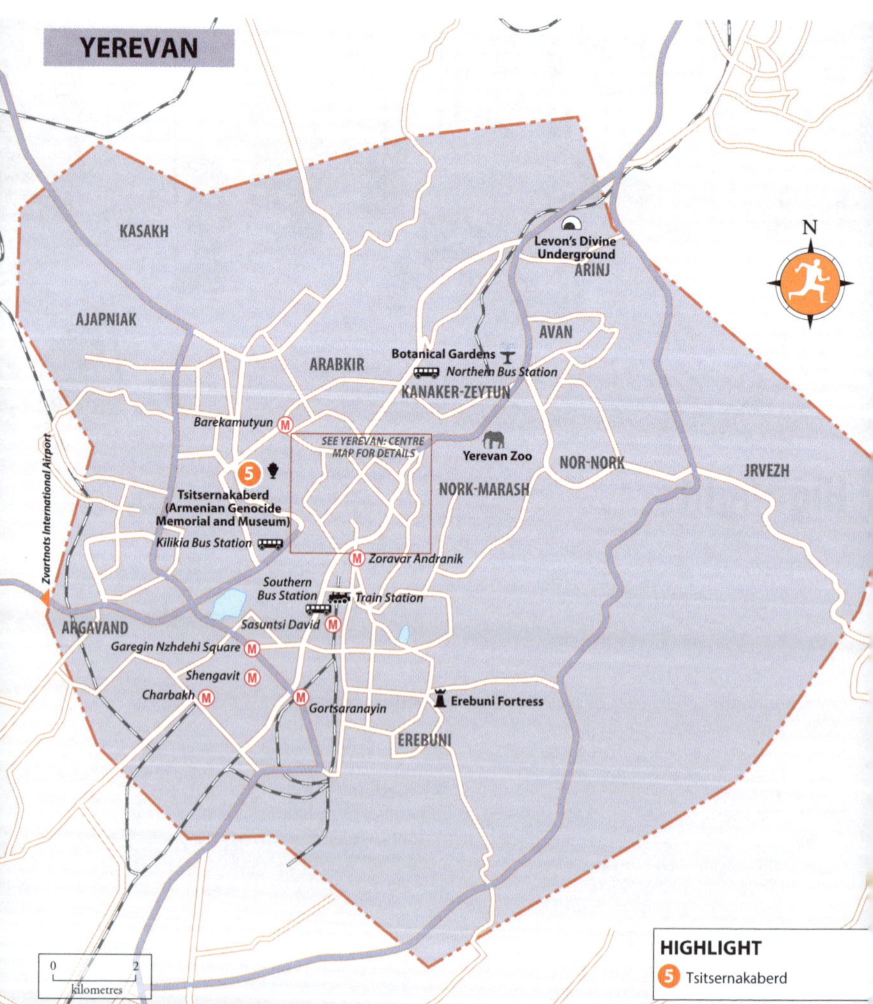

Cascades

Tamanyan St • Free • Ⓦ cmf.am • Bus numbers 5, 26, 35, 54

One of Yerevan's most unique features, the **Cascades** (also known as the Cafesjian
Centre for the Arts) is an enormous white marble staircase, leading from the central
Tamanyan Street up to the northern neighbourhoods of the city. Originally conceived
in the 1930s as the brainchild of local architect Alexander Tamanyan, construction of
the Cascades began in 1971 and has proceeded in fits and starts ever since, its most
recent phase thanks to the patronage of the American-Armenian philanthropist Gerard
Cafesjian. It's still a work in progress – the top of the staircase does not yet reach the
top of the hill – but it's undeniably an impressive piece of architecture and an iconic
Yerevan sight.

You can climb all the way up the exterior stairs, viewing the various open-air
sculptures along the way, and occasionally turning around to see the city unfolding
behind you, possibly with views of Mount Ararat beyond if it's a clear day.
Alternatively, there's an escalator inside – head for the doorway labelled Cafesjian
Centre for the Arts. The escalator is free and provides easy (and, crucially in summer,
shaded) access to every level, with sculptures for you to view as you travel. There are
also several internal galleries here of further artworks.

On the third level, on the opposite side from the escalator, there's an easily overlooked
door which gives access to the **Eagle Garden Gallery**. This small room contains a
collection of eclectic items gathered by Cafesjian himself, including an enormous
model of a ship called the Corsair, which was constructed by an Englishman from
Leyland and shipped to Yerevan with considerable difficulty: just getting it out of the
house in Leyland required the demolition of one of the house's walls.

Once you reach the upper limit of the escalator, you can continue your journey to the
top outside. The attractive marble stairs quickly end and a disused building site takes
over where work on the Cascades may one day continue. For now there's a path that
leads around the building site and to the platform at the top. This platform is home
to the Monument to 50 Years of Soviet Armenia, a tall thin stela erected in the 1970s.
Behind this sombre monument is a more entertaining park, which houses sculptures
with a loose Noah's Ark theme – a very cartoonish ark stands in the centre, surrounded
by animals in a variety of styles and a silver statue of a pirate captain, who may or may
not be a replica of Noah himself.

Military Museum of Mother Armenia

Victory Park • Free • ☎ 374 10 201400 • Bus number 14

Surrounded by tanks, planes and missiles, and housed in the Mother Armenia statue
base, the patriotic outlook of the **Military Museum** isn't exactly well concealed. There
are models of important World War II battles, but the main focus of the museum
are the Karabakh Wars and hagiographic biographies of Armenian heroes of those
conflicts. English labelling is scant.

The Mother Armenia statue itself was erected in 1962, after the removal of a statue
of Stalin that once occupied the spot. She directly faces Mount Ararat, in recognition
of the mountain's special symbolism to Armenians. The museum and statue are set in a
rather dishevelled amusement park.

Yervand Kochar Museum

39/12 Mesrop Mashtots Ave • Charge • Ⓦ kochar.am • Bus numbers 5, 26, 35, 54

The avant-garde artist and sculptor **Yervand Kochar** was a prominent figure in
Armenian art in the 1920s and 30s, during which time he was based in Paris. He
returned to Armenia in 1936 and was imprisoned during the early years of World War
II. He was eventually released and continued to produce works until his death in 1979.

This museum dedicated to him exhibits a large number of his works, so it's a great place to get an introduction to his style.

Matenadaran

53 Mesrop Mashtots Ave • Charge • Ⓦ matenadaran.am/en/matenadaran/home • Ⓜ Yeritasardakan

Containing over twenty three thousand manuscripts and more than five hundred thousand documents, the **Matenadaran** (literally "book repository") is the world's largest collection of medieval Armenian writings. A stark, grey basalt building, the Matenadaran is fronted by a stylised statue of Mesrop Mashtots – the creator of the Armenian alphabet – and flanked by statues of other prominent ancient and medieval Armenian scholars.

Constructed in the 1940s and 50s to house the thousands of Armenian manuscripts that had until that point been stored in the National Library, the Matenadaran has been added to UNESCO's Memory of the World Register as a collection of vast importance to the world's documentary heritage. It was considered one of the most important cultural sites in the USSR, even placed by Pravda in 1989 alongside St Petersburg's Hermitage and Moscow's Tretyakov Gallery. It's still a centre of study and learning, and there are ongoing efforts underway to digitise the collection to ensure permanent preservation.

Inside, you'll be astounded by the colourful beauty of the manuscripts on display and will quickly realise that medieval Armenian illuminators were true masters of their craft. Looking around the collection is likely to divert you for a couple of hours. Look out in particular for the utterly magnificent eleventh-century Mugni Gospel and the fabulous seventeenth-century illustrated History of Alexander the Great.

Folk Art Museum

64 Abovyan St • Charge • ☎ 374 10 569383 • Bus number 63

At the northeastern end of Abovyan St, this fascinating museum contains exhibits of folk art from across Armenia, including carpets, embroidery, metalwork, and plenty more besides. It's in a lovely building, and it's easy to spend longer than you

MESROP MASHTOTS

One of the most revered figures in Armenian history, **Mesrop Mashtots** was born in the mid-fourth century in the Taron province of Greater Armenia. He received a good education – as befitted his noble status – and found a job as the king's secretary. However, after some time in this role he made the choice to withdraw from the world and enter a monastery.

By the year 394, he had emerged from his monastic studies and taken up an active life as a missionary, converting the people in the area that is now the southeast of Azerbaijan's Nakhchivan region. He found that a major barrier to his activities was the lack of an Armenian written language. Considering the standard Greek or Persian scripts to be unsuitable for the Armenian tongue, Mashtots set himself the task of creating an Armenian alphabet.

Assisted by the Armenian Patriarch, Isaac, **Mashtots' alphabet** – consisting of 36 letters – had been devised by the year 405, and he began to disseminate it by establishing and teaching in schools across the country. His disciples began work on translating major spiritual works into the new written Armenian language. By the time Mashtots died in 440, Armenian literature was well established. One of the first original compositions in the alphabet was Koryun's 'The Life of Mesrop Mashtots', which makes the unsubstantiated claim that Mashtots invented the Georgian alphabet as well.

planned here checking out the many displays of beautiful ethnographic items. The museum was formerly called the Centre of Popular Creation, and you may find it still known by that name.

Freedom Square

Tumanyan St • Free • Bus numbers 5, 26, 35, 54

Dominated by the solid bulk of the enormous 1930s **Opera House**, this square is a pleasant traffic-free oasis. It's very popular with local parents, who bring their children here to ride bikes and toy cars in the vast open space. In 2015, the square hosted a free Kanye West concert, which ended abruptly and rather ignominiously when he leapt into the adjoining **Swan Lake** after proclaiming he was "going to do something different".

You can follow the pedestrianised Northern Avenue south from here down towards Republic Square. It's a pleasant avenue packed with upmarket shops, restaurants and hotels. Beneath the pavement, running parallel underground, is the Tashir Street shopping gallery, an extensive mall catering for the moneyed of Yerevan.

Katoghike Church

17 Abovyan St • Free • ☎ 374 55 913545 • Ⓜ Yeritsardakan

The tiny medieval **Katoghike Church** – which sits on a small square on the corner of Abovyan and Sayat Nova streets – dates from the thirteenth century. It was entirely surrounded by the structure of a seventeenth-century church and its existence was unknown until the 1930s, when the Soviet authorities began to demolish the newer church to make way for residential buildings. When it was discovered, archaeologists prevailed upon the Soviets to spare the ancient church, which is still used for prayers. Other religious services are held in the much larger and more modern St Anna Church, just next to the Katoghike.

Avetik Isahakyan Museum

20 Zarobyan St • Charge • Ⓦ isahakyanmuseum.am/index_eng.html • Bus numbers 1, 35, 45

A member of Tumanyan's Vernatun literary circle and a friend of the writer Yegishe Charents, Avetik Isahakyan was a talented Armenian writer and a dedicated traveller. He spent several years in Leipzig and Venice, but his heart belonged to the ruined Armenian city of Ani. The museum contains copies of his works – including his 1909 masterpiece, Abou-lala Mahari – as well as photographs of him and his family. Downstairs the house is set up just as it was when he lived here in the 1950s. Look out for the amazing television; Isahakyan was one of the first people in Yerevan to own one. The staff at the museum are lovely and will happily guide you around.

Hovhannes Tumanyan Museum

40 Moskovyan St • Charge • Ⓦ toumanian.am/en • Bus numbers 1, 35, 45

Hovhannes Tumanyan, the founder of the early twentieth-century Vernatun literary circle, is one of Armenia's most celebrated writers and poets. As well as producing a considerable number of poems and novels – many of which were adapted into films during the Soviet era – Tumanyan was a humanitarian who expended considerable effort in assisting refugees fleeing the Armenian Genocide. He died in 1923, at the age of 54.

The ground floor of the museum dedicated to him features four rooms containing photographs, models of the writer's childhood home, and the occasional high-tech gimmick, including a hologram of Tumanyan strutting around. Upstairs, you'll find

ACCOMMODATION
Alexander Hotel 9
Apricot 12
Arm Hostel 3
Avenue Hostel 7
City Centre Hotel by Picnic 10
Daniel Boutique Hotel 13
Grand Hotel 6
Highland Hostel 11
Hin Yerevantsi Hotel 2
Hotel Boulevard 8
Imperial Palace Hotel 1
Kantar Hotel & Hostel 16
Marriott 14
Median Hotel 5
Mia Casa 15
Seven Visions 4
Tatev Hotel 17

SHOPPING
GUM Market 4
Tufenkian Carpets 2
Vernissage Market 3
Vino & Vino 1

GYULBENKYAN STREET
KYUPENKLAN ST
JAMES BRYCE ST
SOSE STREET
LER KAMSAR STREET
LER KAMSAR ST
ANTARAIN STREET
SARMEN STREET
ANTARAIN STREET
VERIN ANTARAIN
ZAROBYAN STREET
MARSHAL BAGHRANYAN AVENUE
MARSHAL BAGHRANYAN AVENUE
Marshal Baghramyan M
DERENIK DEMIRTCHYAN STREET
AYGEDZOR STREET
1ST LINE OF THE AYGEDZOR STREET
1ST LINE OF THE AYGEDZOR STREET
PROSHYAN 1ST LANE
PROSHYAN STREET
DZORAPI STREET
HRAZDAN GORGE
DZORAPI STREET
DZORAPI STREET
Hrazdan River
DZORAPI STREET
PARONYAN STREET
KOZERN STREET
FRIK STREET
DERENIK DEMIRTCHYAN
Hovhannes Tumanyan Museum
RAFAEL LEMKIN STREET
MARTIROS SARYAN STREET
Martiros Saryan Museum
TUMANYAN STREET
ARAM BACK STREET
PUSHKIN STREET
GHAZAR PARPETSI STREET
MESROP MASHTOTS AVENUE
PUSHKIN STREET
PAVSTOS BUZAND STREET
ARAM STREET
Diana Abgar Park
Yeghishe Charents House Museum
YEZNIK KOGHBATSI STREET
TERYAN STREET
Children's Railway
RUSTAVELI STREET
KOND ST
KOND ST
PARONYAN STREET
MARTIROS SARYAN STREET
AMIRYAN STREET
Missak Manouchian Park
LEO STREET
Modern Art Museum
MESROP MASHTOTS AVENUE
AMIRYAN STREET
History Museum of Armenia
ARAM STREET
ABOVYAN STREET
ATHENS STREET
Sergei Parajanov Museum
ISKAVE LYAN STREET
PARONTAN STREET
MOVSES KHORENATSI STREET
Blue Mosque
ZAKYAN STREET
REPUBLIC SQUARE
Ararat Brandy Factory
ADMIRAL ISAKOV AVENUE
VICTORY BRIDGE
MESRO P MASHTOTS AVENUE
GRIGOR LUSAVORICH STREET
Yerevan History Museum
ZAKYAN STREET
Children's Park
BEIRUT STREET
VAZGEN SARGSYAN STREET
VAZGEN SARGSYAN STREET
Shahumyan Park
PETROS
TAIROV STREET
ARGISHTI STREET
Yerevan 2800th Anniversary Park
ITALY STREET
English Park
DIGRAHYAN STREET
MHER MKRTCHYAN STREET
ADAMYAN ST
TAIROV STREET
TEMIKLSON FORMER HIGHWAY
KHORBRDARAN STREET
Sundukyan State Academic Theatre
MOVSES KHORENTSI STREET
AGATANGEGHOS STREET
Rossia Mall
Zoravar Andranik M

YEREVAN: CENTRE

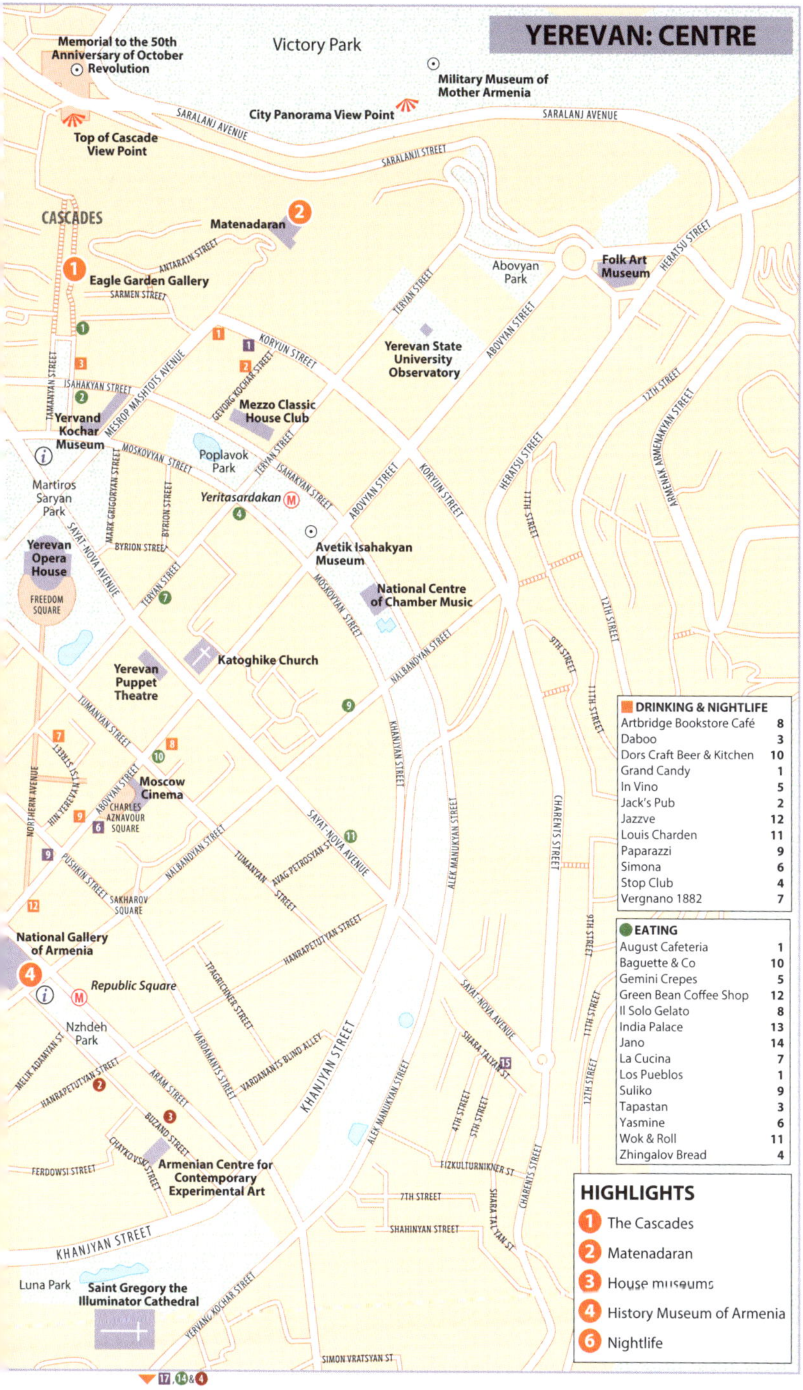

Victory Park

Memorial to the 50th Anniversary of October Revolution

Military Museum of Mother Armenia

City Panorama View Point

SARALANJ AVENUE

SARALANJ AVENUE

Top of Cascade View Point

SARALANJI STREET

CASCADES

Matenadaran **2**

HERATSU STREET

Abovyan Park

Folk Art Museum

ANTARAIN STREET

Eagle Garden Gallery **1**

SARMEN STREET

TERYAN STREET

ABOVYAN STREET

ARMENAK ARMENAKYAN STREET

12TH STREET

KORYUN STREET

Yerevan State University Observatory

ISAHAKYAN STREET

GEVORG KOCHAR STREET

MESROP MASHTOTS AVENUE

Mezzo Classic House Club

Yervand Kochar Museum

MOSKOVYAN STREET

MARK GRIGORYAN STREET

BYRION STREET

TERYAN STREET

Poplavok Park

Martiros Saryan Park

ISAHAKYAN STREET

ABOVYAN STREET

KORYUN STREET

HERATSU STREET

HERSS HILL

BYRION STREET

Yeritasardakan (M)

Avetik Isahakyan Museum

National Centre of Chamber Music

MOSKOVYAN STREET

12TH STREET

Yerevan Opera House

SAYAT-NOVA AVENUE

FREEDOM SQUARE

TERYAN STREET

9TH STREET

Yerevan Puppet Theatre

Katoghike Church

NALBANDYAN STREET

TUMANYAN STREET

11TH STREET

Moscow Cinema

ABOVYAN STREET

CHARLES AZNAVOUR SQUARE

HIN YEREVAN

1ST STREET

NORTHERN AVENUE

KHANJYAN STREET

CHARENTS STREET

PUSHKIN STREET

SAKHAROV SQUARE

NALBANDYAN STREET

TUMANYAN STREET

AVAG PETROSYAN STREET

SAYAT-NOVA AVENUE

National Gallery of Armenia

Republic Square (M)

TPAGRICHNER STREET

HANRAPETUTYAN STREET

ALEK MANUKYAN STREET

Nzhdeh Park

MELIK ADAMYAN ST

HANRAPETUTYAN STREET

ARAM STREET

VARDANANTS STREET

VARDANANTS BLIND ALLEY

KHANJYAN STREET

SAYAT-NOVA AVENUE

SHARA TALYAN ST

15

BUZAND STREET

CHAYKOVSKY STREET

Armenian Centre for Contemporary Experimental Art

FERDOWSI STREET

ALEK MANUKYAN STREET

4TH STREET

5TH STREET

SHARA TAL YAN ST

CHARENTS STREET

12TH STREET

11TH STREET

9TH STREET

FIZKULTURNIKNER ST

KHANJYAN STREET

7TH STREET

SHAHINYAN STREET

Luna Park

Saint Gregory the Illuminator Cathedral

YERVAND KOCHAR STREET

SIMON VRATSYAN ST

17 14 & 4

DRINKING & NIGHTLIFE

Artbridge Bookstore Café	8
Daboo	3
Dors Craft Beer & Kitchen	10
Grand Candy	1
In Vino	5
Jack's Pub	2
Jazzve	12
Louis Charden	11
Paparazzi	9
Simona	6
Stop Club	4
Vergnano 1882	7

EATING

August Cafeteria	1
Baguette & Co	10
Gemini Crepes	5
Green Bean Coffee Shop	12
Il Solo Gelato	8
India Palace	13
Jano	14
La Cucina	7
Los Pueblos	1
Suliko	9
Tapastan	3
Yasmine	6
Wok & Roll	11
Zhingalov Bread	4

HIGHLIGHTS

1 The Cascades

2 Matenadaran

3 House museums

4 History Museum of Armenia

6 Nightlife

5

further photographs and a recreation of the house in which Tumanyan lived in Tbilisi, punctuated by informative labels.

Martiros Saryan Museum

3 Martiros Saryan St • Charge • Ⓦ sarian.am/index_eng.html • Bus numbers 1, 35, 45

Mostly a gallery of his work, the **Saryan Museum** is an excellent introduction to Martiros Saryan, arguably Armenia's most famous painter. His work is mostly brightly coloured and very stylised rather than realistic, and was inspired by oriental themes, as well as influences of French painters such as Matisse. The lower floor is set up as the house was when Saryan lived here, but it's considerably less interesting than the artwork.

Yeghishe Charents House Museum

17 Mesrop Mashtots Ave • Charge • ☎ 374 10 531412 • Bus numbers 1, 23, 26, 44

Yeghishe Charents, who features on the older thousand-AMD note, was a prominent poet during the early years of the twentieth century, before falling victim to the Stalinist purges of the 1930s. The museum is a well-presented exhibition of his life and belongings, including the flat on the third floor where he lived for the last few years of his life, still set up and furnished in the style of a 1930s Yerevani apartment. Particularly poignant is the chess set that he used to play with his friend Arghasi Khanjyan, the First Secretary of the Armenian SSR, and also a victim of the Stalinist purges. Charents was rehabilitated following Stalin's death and the ban on his works was lifted.

Diana Abgar Park

Mesrop Mashtots Ave, between Aram St and Pavstos Buzand St • Free

A pleasant open space with illuminated fountains running down the centre, and decorated with an occasional topiary elephant or two, this square is very busy on summer evenings and is a great place for people-watching. The park is named after the first female Armenian diplomat, Diana Abgar, through whose efforts in 1920 Japan became the first nation to recognise the independence of Republic of Armenia.

Modern Art Museum

7 Mesrop Mashtots Ave • Charge • Ⓦ en.mamy.am • Bus numbers 23, 26

A collection of works dating from between the 1960s and contemporary, the **Modern Art Museum** houses some extraordinary pieces in a wide range of styles – mostly pictures, but occasional sculptures too. It's a fascinating look at how the boundaries of art could be pushed in the Soviet era, especially as the museum was given no governmental backing in its early years and relied on artists donating their works. Photography in the museum costs extra.

Blue Mosque

12 Mesrop Mashtots Ave • Free • ☎ 374 10 522193 • Bus numbers 23, 26

The only working mosque in Armenia, dating from the eighteenth century, the **Blue Mosque** was used as a museum during the Soviet period. Following independence, the Iranian government has assisted with the building's restoration. It's an attractive mosque, with a patterned façade, a blue tiled dome, and an elegant, red-carpeted interior. The well-tended gardens make it an oasis of calm in the city.

Sergei Parajanov Museum

Dzoragyugh 1st St • Charge • Ⓦ parajanov.com • Bus numbers 5, 23, 47

Sergei Parajanov was a film director, active from the mid-1950s onwards, whose works and style repeatedly brought him into conflict with the Soviet authorities. Suspecting him of subversion of the socialist norm, they sentenced him in 1973 to five years in Siberia on charges of rape and production of pornography. Parajanov was released in 1977 but did not resume directing until the more relaxed years of the following decade. He died in 1990.

The **museum** dedicated to his works was opened in 1991, and it's well worth a trip. As well as props and screenplays from his films, the exhibits include artistic works he created during the years when he stopped directing: photographs, collages, paintings, even the dolls he made while in prison. The museum staff's enthusiasm and passion for Parajanov is infectious.

Republic Square

Republic Sq • Free • Ⓜ Republic Square

This site has been a public square for centuries, but its current incarnation dates from 1924, when it was extensively remodelled by the prominent Armenian town planner Alexander Tamanian. During the Soviet period, the square was called Lenin Square and was, predictably enough, presided over by a Lenin statue, which was removed after Armenia's declaration of independence from the USSR. Renamed **Republic Square** in 1990, it remains a focal point of Yerevan, recently coming to prominence during 2018's Velvet Revolution and in the wake of the Nagorno-Karabakh conflicts in the 2020s as the main site for anti-government demonstrations.

It's an attractive square, surrounded by grand buildings constructed from orangey-pink tuff stone, so it's a bit of a shame that it's such a busy traffic junction. Every evening, there's a sound-and-light show, with the central fountains dancing to the sound of overblown orchestral music.

History Museum of Armenia

4 Republic Sq • Charge • Ⓦ historymuseum.am/en • Ⓜ Republic Square

Armenia's **History Museum**, housed in a grand building on Republic Square, is a fascinating place, taking the visitor though the nation's history from its earliest beginnings to the modern day. The exhibits on the third floor – which cover the Stone Age through to the sixteenth century – are particularly interesting, with highlights including 3,500-year-old chariots and the world's oldest shoe, while the twentieth-century-centric sections on the second floor present an essential if harrowing account of the Armenian Genocide. The ground floor is perhaps the least vital, dedicated primarily to carpets. Guided tours are available in English and various other languages on request for an extra charge. Photography not allowed.

National Gallery of Armenia

4 Republic Sq (upper floors) • Charge, guided tour extra • Ⓦ gallery.am/en • Ⓜ Republic Square

Armenia's principal **art gallery** begins on the seventh floor, in the same building as the History Museum, and works its way down to the third, where temporary exhibitions are hosted. The seventh floor, home to European and American art, is very much of minor interest only, and the Russian section on the sixth floor isn't much better. The fifth and fourth floors though, with their excellent exhibitions of influential Armenian artists such as Edgar Chahine, Hovahannes Aivazovsky and Yeghishe Tadevossian – as well as Armenia's most famous painter, Martiros Saryan – are well worth the entrance fee.

5

If nothing else, it's fun to visit to experience the marvellous Soviet-era elevator and enjoy the attentions of the fierce attendants, who insist on you visiting the museum's rooms in a very specific order and will not tolerate any deviation.

Nzhdeh Park

Nalbandyan St, between Aram St and Pavstos Buzand St • Free • Ⓜ Republic Square

This open space on the other side of Nalbandyan Street from Republic Square hosts a permanent exhibition of khachkars, which serves as a good introduction to the concept, with plenty of examples of different types. It also hosts a good souvenir market, where you can buy items ranging from ceramics and small wooden khachkars to musical instruments, paintings, brandy, wine, swords and carpets, as well as genuine Soviet memorabilia such as stamps, medals and pin badges.

Armenian Centre for Contemporary Experimental Art

1/3 Buzand St • Free • Ⓦ accea.info • Ⓜ Republic Square

Established in 1992, the **Armenian Centre for Contemporary Experimental Art** aims to discover and showcase new and innovative local artists, and as such it hosts a regularly changing programme of temporary exhibitions. It also stages plays in the centre's theatre, and has a small cinema for the screening of short films.

Shahumyan Park

Sargsyan St • Free • Ⓜ Republic Square

Walking southwest from Republic Square, the wide, tree-lined pedestrian walkway leads to a 1931 monument to Stepan Shahumyan, the leader of the ill-fated Baku Commune (see page 248). It's a typically 1930s Soviet blocky monument, which probably won't detain you too long.

Yerevan 2800th Anniversary Park

Between Beirut and Italy Sts • Free • Ⓜ Republic Square

Constructed in 2018–19 to commemorate the 2800th anniversary of the founding of Yerevan, this lovely park is filled with thousands of tiny fountains. At the end is a monument to Alexander Myasnikyan, Armenia's first Communist president, which is diverting enough, but the real treasures here are the delightful water-themed bronze statues, including one of a girl under a raincloud and a boy playing with a paper boat. The park is very busy on summer Sunday mornings with children (and some adults) playing in the many fountains, especially the water tunnel.

KHACHKARS

An art form unique to Armenia, **khachkars** are stone stelae carved with the Christian cross, amid other symbolism. They are often extremely intricate and beautiful, and each one is entirely individual. Sometimes used as memorials and sometimes as focal points for worship, the artistic high point of khachkar-carving is considered to be the twelfth and thirteenth centuries.

Khachkars were inscribed on UNESCO's list of Intangible Cultural Heritage of Humanity in 2010. You'll see them at most monasteries you visit in Armenia, but particularly fine examples can be found at Noravank (see page 228), Hovhannavank (see page 189) and Goshavank (see page 204). It's also worth a stop at the Noratus cemetery (see page 199), which contains the largest collection of khachkars in the world.

Yerevan History Museum

1 Argishti St • Charge • Ⓦ yhm.am/?lang=en • Bus numbers 5, 23

Housed in a huge and grand building, the **Yerevan History Museum**'s exhibition aims to take visitors through the history of the capital, but it's sadly not very engaging – though the enormous model/map of the city is fun enough. If you've got plenty of time in Yerevan then it's worth a trip, but if you're on a tight schedule skipping this one won't hurt.

Ararat Brandy Factory

2 Admiral Isakov Ave • Charge • Ⓦ en.araratbrandy.com • Bus numbers 5, 23

Ararat brandy is a Yerevan institution. Dating from 1887, the factory's product attained international prominence when it was served up at the Yalta conference towards the end of World War II. There's a myth – unsubstantiated but perpetuated by this factory, among others – that Churchill loved the brandy so much that Stalin sent him 300 bottles per year every year thereafter.

You'll hear this, and other interesting stories, on the engaging tours around the factory, which give a history of the company and a brief rundown of the manufacture process. It's a slick operation, with the tour focussed more on quirky facts than on details about the distilling. If you want to know more about the actual manufacturing process, and see the type of machinery used, then the factory tour in Ijevan (see page 204) may be more to your liking.

Displays include a reconstruction of the office of the factory's founder, examples of brandy bottles from 1902 to the present day, and barrels of brandy that have been presented to foreign presidents who have visited the factory. The pride and joy of the museum, though, is the Nagorno-Karabakh Peace Barrel, which will only be opened when peace is established between Armenia and Azerbaijan. It's surrounded by signatures of visitors wishing a speedy resolution to the conflict. The tour concludes with a tasting of between two and four brandies.

You need to book in advance to attend a tour. It's easiest to do so online, but bookings are also accepted in person or over the phone.

Saint Gregory the Illuminator Cathedral

Yervand Kochar St • Free • ☎ 374 10 543332 • Ⓜ Zoravar Andranik

Just south of the city centre, Armenia's largest cathedral – named after the saint who brought Christianity to the country in the early fourth century – was built in the late 1990s. It's a huge and fairly spartan building which, although impressive in scale, lacks the charm of many of the country's older churches and monasteries.

Outside the centre

Outside Yerevan's centre are a couple of sights, of which the Armenian Genocide Memorial is the most essential, if sobering. Elsewhere, explore the city's origins at the hilltop Erebuni Fortress, or check out quirkier attractions like the Children's Railway and Levon's Divine Underground.

Tsitsernakaberd (Armenian Genocide Memorial and Museum)

Tsitsernakaberd Highway • Free • Ⓦ genocide-museum.am/eng/index.php • Bus number 26

On the hill to the west of the city centre stands the **Armenian Genocide Memorial**, a sleek concrete structure composed of a tall tapering tower and a circle of inward sloping concrete walls surrounding an eternal flame. Construction began in 1966, a year after the 50th anniversary of the massacres when demonstrators across Armenia demanded the Soviet authorities recognise the killings as genocide.

The memorial is simple and affecting, with considerable layers of meaning – the gap that runs down the length of the tower symbolises the separation of Eastern and Western Armenians, while the 12 concrete walls represent the 12 provinces of Western Armenia that were ceded to Turkey by Lenin in the 1920s. In the grounds leading up to the memorial, there's a wall inscribed with the names of villages where massacres took place, and gardens where fir trees have been planted by individuals and organisations who have expressed solidarity with the Armenian people and acknowledged the genocide.

The museum (free entry, guided tour by appointment, charge) was opened in 1995, on the 80th anniversary of the genocide, and it aims to convey the horror of the massacres through contemporary documents and photographs. A visit here is not easy, but it is utterly essential in gaining an understanding of the history of the Armenian people.

Children's Railway

Dzorapi St • Free • Bus number 11

During the Soviet era, a narrow-gauge railway was built on the outskirts of the city centre which was used as a real-life learning centre for children to learn how to work on the railways. Although no longer in use, the steam locomotives and carriages are still here, as is the grandiose old station, set amidst trees and an abandoned amusement park. It's a slightly haunting place that's perfect for a spot of Soviet-era urban exploration.

Erebuni Fortress

38 Erebuni St • Charge • ☎ 374 10 432661 • Bus numbers 1, 18, 58

THE ARMENIAN GENOCIDE

Much of the eastern half of Turkey was once part of the nation of **Greater Armenia**. However, from the sixteenth century onwards this territory was definitively part of the **Ottoman Empire**, under which the rights of Armenians and other Christian minorities were curtailed. The latter years of the nineteenth century saw massacres of Armenians across the empire, seemingly with tacit official approval. During World War I, the Ottomans ramped up propaganda against the Armenian minority, insisting that they were in league with the Russians and would betray the empire.

Against this background, on 23rd April 1915, 250 Armenian intellectuals from Constantinople were rounded up and deported, in what is considered the first act of the Genocide. A month later, the **Tehcir Law** was introduced, under which the Ottomans declared that they had the authority to deport anyone who was a threat to the empire, and this was immediately used against the Armenian community.

Victims were marched out into the Syrian desert and denied food, water or shelter from the blazing sun. Concentration camps were established, and victims were subjected to burnings, drownings, and horrific medical experimentation. In total, it is thought that up to 1.5 million Armenians died as a direct result of Ottoman policy, and many fled the region, resulting in today's Armenian Diaspora: less than a third of Armenians worldwide live in Armenia.

Many nations – including the USA, Canada, France, Germany and Russia – have formally acknowledged the killings as **genocide**, but Turkey has yet to do so. In 2019 the Turkish president Recep Erdoğan even referred to the deportations as having been "appropriate at the time", despite having described them as "inhumane" in 2015. The issue remains a major stumbling block in Turkish-Armenian relations..

A YEREVAN WALKING TOUR

Start at Republic Square and admire the fountains and striking pink buildings, then head southwest through the shady park down the centre of Vazgen Sargsyan Street to the Shahumyan monument. Cross Movses Khorenatsi Street to continue through the Yerevan 2800th Anniversary Park, taking in the attractive fountains and water features.

Take a right onto Grigor Lusavich Street; this road is busy and uninteresting, so you could walk through the **Children's Park** instead, where you'll find a bust of Nelson Stepanyan, a pilot twice awarded the title of Hero of the Soviet Union for his remarkable performance in the Great Patriotic War.

Once out of the park, cross Zakyan Street and turn right onto Yerevan's main thoroughfare, Mesrop Mashtots Street. Admire the grandiose entrance to **Pak Shuka** on the opposite side of the road, which was once a colourful central market but is now a shopping mall. It's not particularly worth looking in, but the golden patterned arch is remarkable. Call in at the Blue Mosque, then cross Khoranatsi Street and turn right onto Amyran Street where you can stop for coffee and cake at Louis Charden before continuing back to Republic Square.

Turn left up Abovyan Street, then half left up the pedestrianised Northern Avenue, where you can see the Opera House at the end and the Memorial to **50 Years of Soviet Armenia** beyond it in the distance. Proceed until you reach Freedom Square. Once you've taken in this attractive plaza, head out of the square to your right and take Sayat Nova heading southeast.

Pass the **Puppet Theatre** stopping to admire the little Katoghike Church on the corner, before turning left up Abovyan Street, checking out the statue of Alexander Mantashyants en route. Mantashyants was a nineteenth-century oil magnate, who moved to Manchester in his youth and learned the fundamentals of the textile industry. On his return to the Caucasus, he and his father made a fortune from the cotton trade. After his father's death, Mantashyants began investing in oil, enabling him to fund the Baku-Batumi oil pipeline, and making him even wealthier. He reinvested vast quantities of his wealth to put up public buildings in Tbilisi and Yerevan, and is fondly remembered for his charitable nature.

Cross Moskowvyan – for ease, head down into the underground shopping mall – and turn left to walk through the park between Moskowvyan and Isahakyan streets, passing the blocky metro station on your right and various statues and sculptures. Skirt round to the right to avoid Zazaland funfair and emerge onto Isahakyan.

Follow Isahakyan Street for two blocks, crossing Mashtots, and turn right onto the **Cascades square**. Admire the various sculptures, then either take the escalator or climb the steps. Turn around and look back for a fantastic view over the city, hopefully including Mount Ararat beyond. If you have more energy, continue to the plaza at the top to see the 50 Years of Soviet Armenia and take the underpass beneath Azatutyan Avenue to visit Mother Armenia.

The walk is roughly 5km in total. Allow two to three hours, including stops.

Yerevan dates its existence from 782 BC, when the Urartian King Argishti I established the **fortress of Erebuni** on a hill which is now in Yerevan's eastern suburbs. It's worth making the trip out here to explore the remains of the fortress, which are not enormously extensive but still offer a good idea of the scale of the fortifications. Erebuni also offers good views over Yerevan, and there's also a museum here– opened in 1968 on the 2,750th anniversary of the fortress' foundation – which exhibits finds from both Erebuni and other local Urartian sites, with a particular interest in cuneiform inscriptions which tell the story of the city's foundation.

Levon's Divine Underground

Arinj • Charge • ☎ 374 96 800366 • Bus number 47

In the northern suburb of Arinj is one of Yerevan's more offbeat visitor attractions: a huge **network of caves** dug out over the course of 23 years by Levon Arakelyan, who in

5

1985 was initially asked by his wife to dig a potato cellar beneath their house. Once he began work, he found he couldn't stop, eventually producing the labyrinth of rooms and passageways that today makes up the Divine Underground. After exploring the intricately decorated caves, check out the small museum which tells the story of Levon's inspiration and how he undertook the work.

ARRIVAL AND DEPARTURE

By plane Yerevan's Zvartnots Airport is about 15km west of the city centre; there are no direct flights to the UK, but connecting services are available via Istanbul. Air France operates a service to Paris, and WizzAir offer routes to various European cities including Milan, Rome and Vienna. Eurowings connects Yerevan and Berlin, and the Armenian budget airline FlyOne offers a few useful routes, including to Düsseldorf, Lyons and Paris. As a demonstration of the gradual thaw in relations between Armenia and Turkey, passenger flights to Istanbul with Pegasus began in 2021.

The airport terminal is a shiny modern building which opened in 2011, and hosts all the amenities you'd expect – a tourist information desk, car hire, duty free shops, and a few cafés. You can also buy Armenian SIM cards here on arrival. The old terminal – a masterpiece of blocky concrete Soviet Armenian architecture – now sits forlorn and unloved next to the modern terminal. If you have the time or inclination, you can get a good look at it from the outside balcony by the departures hall: with your back to the entrance, turn left and walk to the corner.

A bus runs between the airport and Republic Square between 7am and 10.30pm. Taxis are easy to pick up at the airport and the journey into town takes 20 minutes. Most hotels will arrange an airport transfer for you, though the price is likely to be double that of the taxi fare.

By bus Unhelpfully, Yerevan has a selection of bus stations to choose from. The central Kilikia bus station lies about 2.5km southwest of the town centre; you can reach it from the town centre with bus numbers 5, 23, 47 and 259. International routes from Kilikia include to Tbilisi (hourly 8am–11am, six hours), to Akhaltsikhe (8.30am, seven hours), and to Batumi (Mon, Tues, Thurs, Sat 7am, 11 hours). There's also two daily buses to Tehran via Tabriz (11am and 12.30pm, 25 hours).

Domestic services from Kilikia include to Echmiadzin (from 7am, departing when full, 30 minutes), Ashtarak (six daily between 9am and 5pm, 30 minutes), Sisian (9am, four

hours) and Jermuk (1pm and 4pm, three hours).

The Southern Bus Station is behind the train station, easily reachable on the metro – get off at the Sasuntsi David stop. Domestic services from here include to Goris (7am and 3pm, four hours) and Gyumri (four daily between 10am and 1.30pm, 2.5 hours).

Finally, the Northern Bus Station – which is a hefty 10km northeast of the centre; take bus number 46 to get here – offers services to Dilijan (from 9am, departing when full, 1.5 hours). You can also use the Dilijan-bound bus to get to Sevan (45 minutes).

By train Yerevan has two train stations, but despite this, there are very few passenger services. The central station in the south of the city (take the metro to Sasuntsi David) is slightly more useful, with a train to Tbilisi every other day at 9.30pm (10 hours). The Tbilisi train also calls at Gyumri (three hours) and Vanadzor (4.5 hours). In addition, there are also four daily trains to Gyumri (7.55am, 9.15am, 2.25pm and 6.25pm, three hours). If you're looking for something to distract yourself while you wait for your train, there's a small railway museum (free) here with train models and a slightly unexpected number of antique telephones.

Almast Station, in the north of the city, runs trains to Sevan in summer at 8.30am. Information about Armenia's train network can be found on the official website at ⓦ railway. am, and if you set up a user account, you can book tickets online.

By car The main roads into the city are the M1 from Ashtarak, the M4 from Sevan, and the H8 from the south. All are well paved and generally easy to navigate. Avoid driving into Yerevan in the evening, between 4pm and 7pm, as the roads tend to get very busy and traffic slows to a snail's pace. Otherwise, driving here is manageable, if a bit hectic. Parking isn't always free but it won't break the bank. Finding a space might prove more troublesome.

GETTING AROUND

By metro The Yerevan metro system is a cheap, speedy and efficient way of getting around the city, but those hoping for a grand Soviet underground system akin to Moscow's will be disappointed, as the stations are mostly relatively unadorned. The only particular exception is the Republic Square station, though even this isn't worth a special trip to see it.

The metro consists of a single line that runs through the city roughly north to south. Tourists will probably primarily use Yeritasardakan and Republic Square stations for the north and south of the city centre respectively, and Sasuntsi David for the train station and southern bus station.

By bus Yerevan is riddled with bus and marshrutka routes, which make for the city's most extensive internal transport network. They can be challenging to work out, though. The most useful lines are probably numbers 5, 23 and 47, which run from Kilikia bus station along Mesrop Mashtots Avenue to the Cascades.

By taxi Taxis in Yerevan are plentiful. They tend to congregate around Republic Square, but you should be able to flag one down wherever you are. A trip anywhere within the town centre should cost no more than 1000 AMD. If you're going to Erebuni or Tsitsernakaberd you can expect to pay up to 2500 AMD.

By bike Cycling in Yerevan is not a particularly pleasant experience. The roads are mostly wide but busy, and traffic is unlikely to be enormously considerate of cyclists.

By foot It's very enjoyable to walk around Yerevan's centre, but it's quite large and you're likely to get tired, especially in the heat of summer. Fortunately, there are plenty of museums and/or cafés to rest at.

INFORMATION

Tourist Information Centre Yerevan's tourist information needs are served by two kiosks, one near the Cascades (France Sq, ☎374 11 514230, 10am–9pm, to 7pm in winter) and the other in the southwest corner of Nzhdeh Park, just across the road from the History Museum (Nalbandyan Street, 10.30am–6.30pm). Both have well-informed staff, who can help with questions about the city's sights and public transport.

Listings You can find out what's on and what's upcoming in Yerevan with ⓦvisityerevan.am/browse/things-to-do-events/en. If you can read Armenian or have infinite patience with a translation app, then ⓦyerevanevents.am is also a useful resource.

Websites Yerevan's official webpage is ⓦvisityerevan.am/en. The site gives detailed information on the city's sights, museums and theatres, as well as recommending restaurants and bars. You can also book walking or bus tours of the city through the site.

ACCOMMODATION

SEE MAP PAGE 162

Alexander Hotel 3/4 Abovyan St ⓦtinyurl.com/b3xyfwax; ⓜRepublic Square. The *Alexander* opened in 2018 and clearly seeks to be Yerevan's most exclusive address, its drive to impress being apparent the moment you step into its borderline over-the-top lobby. Equipped with swimming pool, gym, sauna, conference facilities, a cigar bar and a rooftop restaurant – all of which are open to non-residents – it also boasts 114 rooms across 10 floors, which range from the merely very smart superior guest rooms to the insanely opulent presidential suite. $$$$

Apricot 15/3 Paronyan St ⓦyerevan.apricothotels.am/eng; bus number 20. Non-smoking throughout, the *Apricot* features sleek, rustic-effect rooms (think wooden walls, floors and furniture in the bedrooms and exposed-brickwork in the bathrooms), with large, comfortable beds. Breakfast is served on the roof terrace with fantastic views of Mount Ararat. The staff are friendly and there are pleasant touches, such as umbrellas to borrow when necessary. It is, however, on a busy road, so ask for a room at the back if you're a light sleeper. $$$

Arm Hostel 29 Mesrop Mashtots Ave ☎374 77 161169; bus numbers 5, 23, 47. The *Arm* has two mixed dorms of eight beds and one female-only four-bed dorm, as well as three private rooms. There's a kitchen and laundry service, and they do tours too, including specialised hiking trips. It could be a bit more welcoming though, and it's not easy to find, as there are three doors for Number 29 and there's no sign – you need to dial 11 on the intercom on the left-most door, next to the Vorsord shop. $

Avenue Hostel 8 Teryan St ☎374 77 600332; ⓜRepublic Square. Cheap, cheerful and central, you can't go too far wrong with the Avenue Hostel if you're looking for a good budget place to bed down for the night. There are three dorms, some mixed and some female only. $

City Centre Hotel by Picnic 20 Yeznik Koghbatsi St ⓦpicnichotels.com; ⓜRepublic Square. They weren't lying when they called it "city centre hotel": it's only about 10 minutes' walk from both Republic and Opera House squares, and thus is within walking distance of almost everywhere. The rooms are clean but small, and they can be quite noisy, both from interior and exterior sources. The wi-fi is very patchy. $$

Daniel Boutique Hotel 4/3 Movses Khorenatsi St ⓦdanielhotel.am; bus numbers 5, 23, 47. In a quiet courtyard off Khorenatsi Street, the Daniel has eight rooms, all slightly different and decorated with attractive art works. The courtyard is shady and cool with a swinging chair, making it a great place to chill. Also provides lunch and dinner and can arrange tours of the country. $$

Grand Hotel 14 Abovyan St ⓦgrandhotelyerevan.com; ⓜRepublic Square. Opened in 1926, this is the oldest hotel in Yerevan, and as such has gone through numerous changes in ownership, from the state-run hotel of the Armenian SSR to its current incarnation as part of the Small Luxury Hotels of the World group. With pretensions of Graeco-Roman grandeur in the lobby and staircases, and regular live piano music in the atrium, it makes a good first impression, though the standard rooms are perhaps a little nondescript and corporate. The grand suites with views over the Charles Aznavour Square are tempting, though. $$$

Highland Hostel 18 Mesrop Mashtots Ave ☎374 94 520567; ⓜRepublic Square. This small top-floor hostel has just one eight-bed dorm and one private room, as well as kitchen facilities and a lounge. It's friendly and squeaky clean, and the owners can also arrange tours of Yerevan and beyond. $

5

Hin Yerevantsi Hotel 31/6 Mesrop Mashtots Ave ⓦ hinyerevantsihotel.yerevanhotelapartment.com; bus numbers 5, 23, 47. There are three spacious and light rooms in this hotel, which has been converted from an old family home, retaining some very attractive furniture including a particularly magnificent fireplace. It's a little tricky to find – come through the arch on Mashtots Street to the right of Number 31, then you'll find it on the left at the end of the yard, and reception is through the garden rather than in the immediately obvious doorway. $$

Hotel Boulevard 37 Pavstos Buzand St ⓣ 374 12 700007; ⓜ Republic Square. Slick and attractive hotel with business standard rooms in a good location in the heart of town. Unfortunately the windows are paper-thin and you can hear the (luckily not terribly busy) street outside perfectly, so earplugs are advised if you want a good night's sleep. $$

Imperial Palace Hotel 23 Koryun St ⓣ 374 10 588040; ⓜ Yeritasardakan. There's a hint of Tsarist era decadence at this larger hotel near the Matenadaran. The rooms are spacious and plush, the staff are friendly, and the breakfast buffet – served in the shiny well-lit basement – is excellent. Cleaning standards can be hit-and-miss, though, and it's arguably a little expensive for the quality. $$$

Kantar Hotel & Hostel 10 Deghatan St ⓦ staykantar. com; ⓜ Republic Square. The *Kantar*, convenient for Republic Square, is a clean and welcoming place with both hostel dorms and hotel rooms. The breakfast is very good, and it's a good place to meet fellow travellers. $

Marriott Republic Sq ⓦ tinyurl.com/53v8vyp4; ⓜ Republic Square. The Marriott on Republic Square is something of a Yerevan institution. It was built in the 1950s and opened as Intourist's Hotel Armenia, the largest and grandest hotel in Soviet Armenia. Post-independence, it was acquired by the Marriott group and reopened to Marriott's usual international standards in 1998. Its perfect location is its main draw, though its spa and pool are also excellent. $$$

Median Hotel 75 Yeznik Koghbatsi St ⓦ medianhotel. am; bus numbers 5, 26, 35, 54. The 17 rooms at this very central hotel are smart and comfortable. The staff are very friendly and welcoming and will help arrange tours of Armenia on request. $$

Mia Casa 13 Shara Talyan St, ⓦ miacasa.am; bus number 38. A short walk outside the centre, *Mia Casa* is a friendly and quiet place. There's a common area with some deep red leather sofas and a bling chandelier, seemingly just to offset the 10 clean and well-maintained, if not enormously exciting, rooms. $$

Seven Visions 40 Paronyan St, ⓦ 7visionshotels.com; bus number 11. A short walk from the hustle and bustle of the centre is this remarkably stylish upmarket hotel, which – in addition to the lovely plush rooms, some with great city views and balconies – has a gorgeous restaurant, an outdoor swimming pool, a state-of-the-art spa and gym, and even its own theatre – which stages regular acrobatic shows – and a high-end nightclub. This latter can mean that the hotel is noisy at weekends. $$$$

Tatev Hotel 2 Yervand Kochar St ⓣ 374 96 246655; ⓜ Zoravar Andranik. Not the most centrally located place, perhaps, but it's clean, comfortable and welcoming, and the cost is very reasonable. The breakfasts are very good. $$

EATING

SEE MAP PAGE 162

There's a clutch of Chinese and Japanese restaurants in the east of the city centre, on Sayat Nova and Tumanyan streets. Without much to choose between them, *Wok & Roll* is recommended (33 Sayat Nova, ⓣ 374 11 525200) just to reward the pun.

August Cafeteria 2 Tamanyan St ⓦ facebook.com/augustcafeyerevan. This place at the foot of the Cascades offers a range of standard issue options, including soups, salads, sandwiches, pizzas and pastas. It's a good place for people-watching from the outdoor seating, or you can retreat to the rustic, air-conditioned interior if the heat gets a bit much. $$

Baguette & Co 20 Abovyan St ⓦ facebook.com/baguetteandco. A busy yet relaxed café with a very European feel. It's particularly good for breakfasts, with its great selection of croissants, sandwiches and that all-important first coffee of the day. $

Gemini Crepes 31 Tumanyan St ⓦ tinyurl.com/yc4vux9e. A small cafeteria popular with French expats. As well as good coffee, they serve up both sweet and savoury crepes. $

Green Bean Coffee Shop 38 Isahakyan St ⓦ facebook. com/thegreenbeancascade. There's not only a huge range of coffees available (not all of which sound like a good idea – coffee infused with Snickers and Twix?), but also an extensive breakfast menu, and pastries and sandwiches available throughout the day. Their green ethos and dedication to biodegradable packaging puts them ahead of the pack in Armenia. $

Il Solo Gelato Hin Yerevantsi St ⓣ 374 55 268070. A small ice cream parlour with a row of outdoor tables on a quiet street. Also serves cakes, but the excellent ice cream is what you're really here for. $

India Palace 3 Amiryan St ⓦ indiapalacearmenia.com. A stylish subterranean restaurant near Republic Square, the very good *India Palace* will satisfy all your spice cravings with its hugely extensive menu, which includes all the old favourites and some dishes that may be less familiar. It dabbles in a few Chinese options as well. $$

Jano 59 Tigran Mets Ave ⓦ jano.am. A little out of the way down by the train station, *Jano* is a pleasant little place serving some of the best Middle Eastern food to be found in the Caucasus. The owner's family, originally from Aleppo, have been in the restaurant business since 1946, so they know what they're doing. The mouttabal is divine. $\overline{\underline{SS}}$

La Cucina 52 Teryan St ⓦfacebook.com/lacucinayerevan. It could probably stand to work on its décor, which is a little bit IKEA, but the pizza and pasta at this centrally located Italian spot can't be argued with. They offer a decent range of Armenian and international wines too. $\overline{\underline{SS}}$

Los Pueblos Cascades, 6 Tamanyan St ⓦlospueblos. am. One of Yerevan's surprisingly numerous Mexican restaurants, *Los Pueblos* has great ambience and a good location, with a well-decorated courtyard just off the Cascades stairway. The service is fast – perhaps a little too fast – and the food is reasonable if not world changing. The cocktails are very good. $\overline{\underline{SS}}$

Suliko 37 Nalbandyan St ☎374 10 580286. Georgian restaurant offering a good introduction to the classic cuisine of Armenia's northern neighbour. The khachapuri is particularly good. If you order the Georgian lemonade, be aware that it's bright green and looks distressingly like mouthwash, though it does taste good. $\overline{\underline{S}}$

Tapastan 6 Martiros Saryan St ⓦfacebook.com/Tapastan. Good for a bit of a splurge, this upmarket, attractively decorated and friendly restaurant serves delicious Caucasian dishes as small plates with exciting names such as "slices of beefy joy". It's got a great selection of wines too. $\overline{\underline{SSS}}$

Yasmine 26 Ghazar Parpetsi St ⓦyasmine.am. Good selection of well-made Middle Eastern dishes, served in a relatively plain but attractive room. The staff are friendly and attentive. $\overline{\underline{SS}}$

Zhingalov Bread 62 Teryan St. A cheap and cheerful spot which is one of the best places in town to try the Nagorno-Karabakh speciality of zhingalov hats – a delicious flatbread stuffed with greens and herbs. $\overline{\underline{S}}$

DRINKING SEE MAP PAGE 162

Artbridge Bookstore Café 20 Abovyan St ⓦartbridge. am. As the name suggests, it's both a bookshop and a café, with a good range of new and second-hand English-language fiction. The coffee is nice and strong, and the outside seating is a great place to watch shoppers go by.

Daboo 38 Isahakyan St ⓦdaboobar.com. Underground cocktail bar, with friendly and expert staff creating concoctions from the extensive menu. It's not a happening place early in the evening but gets busier later. Entrance is via an easy-to-miss staircase, just to the right of the Café de France.

Dors Craft Beer & Kitchen 4/6 Amiryan St ⓦfacebook. com/dors.craftbeerandkitchen. One of only a few places in Armenia serving craft beers, this friendly bar with industrial décor offers up a number of choices including a good Bavarian Weizen and some flavoured options such as cherry. There's a decent cider available too, and a reasonable bar menu.

Grand Candy 54 Mesrop Mashtots Ave ☎374 10 565686. This brightly coloured temple to sugary overdrive is likely to be a big favourite if you have kids with you. Otherwise, it may be best to avoid visiting the café, which looks a bit like it's escaped from a dystopian version of the *Barbie* movie. The attached shop, selling a huge array of pick and mix sweets and chocolates, is another matter.

In Vino 6 Martiros Saryan St ⓦfacebook.com/InVinoEVN. A good place to introduce yourself to Armenia's excellent wines, In Vino has a vast selection of vintages to try, and also hosts regular wine tasting evenings. On warmer evenings it's very relaxing to sit at the outside tables and watch the world go by.

Jack's Pub 21 Gevorg Kochar St ⓦfacebook.com/p/Jacks-Pub-Yerevan-100075708018691. It's not an enormously inspiring name, and nor is it particularly accurate, as Jack's is rather less of a pub and more of a slinky cocktail bar, with an extensive menu mixed by expert bartenders. Pictures of various famous Jacks adorn the walls.

Jazzve 2 Abovyan St ⓦjazzve.am. There are outlets of the *Jazzve* chain all over the city, offering good coffee and cakes, but the branch on Abovyan St is nice and central and does a truly excellent cherry pastry.

Louis Charden 11 Amiryan St ⓦfacebook.com/louischarden.mbg. An upmarket café-bakery with a slight touch of the French about it, this pleasant place with a soft-jazz soundtrack offers coffee, fresh juice, alcoholic drinks, and a range of delicious pastries. Service can be a little slow.

Simona 80 Aram St ⓦfacebook.com/simonabarhome. Friendly underground cocktail bar with subdued lighting and a great soundtrack. Staff are expert cocktail makers, who can either make standards or individual cocktails to specification based on your preferences.

Vergnano 1882 9 Hin Yerevantsi St ⓦfacebook.com/CaffeVergnanoArmenia. This branch of the worldwide Italian-based chain is a very centrally located place for coffee and cake. It may not be very imaginative, but it's friendly and reliable.

NIGHTLIFE SEE MAP PAGE 162

Yerevan, unlike its fellow Caucasian capital Tbilisi, is not known as a place for dancing in cool electronic or techno clubs. Here, 'night clubs' are usually strip clubs.

Paparazzi 3 Abovyan St, ⓦfacebook.com/PaparazziclubYerevan. is an exception, playing house, techno and hip-hop music till late.

5

Stop Club 37 Moskovyan St, ⓦfacebook.com/ stopmusicclub. is a reasonable choice if you're into rock music.

ENTERTAINMENT

Mezzo Classic House Club 28 Isahakyan St ⓦmezzo. am; ⓜYeritasardakan. For jazz lovers, there's nowhere better in Yerevan. This stylish place with unique interior design hosts regular performances every Saturday and Sunday, as well as impromptu concerts during the week. The food and drinks are excellent too.

Moscow Cinema 18 Abovyan St ⓦmoscowcinema. com/en; ⓜYeritasardakan. This classic Soviet building has been a cinema since it opened in 1936. It now shows the latest Hollywood offerings (though usually dubbed into Russian or Armenian), as well as current Russian films.

Yerevan Opera House Opera House Sq ⓦopera.am/ en; bus numbers 5, 26, 35, 54. The 1930s *Yerevan Opera House* frequently hosts opera and ballet performances from both Armenian and international companies. If you can, catch a production of *Anoush* – an Armenian opera by Armen Tigranian, based on a work by Hovhannes Tumanyan – which is often performed here.

Yerevan State Puppet Theatre 4 Sayat-Nova Ave ☏374 10 520254, ⓦarmpuppet.am/en; bus numbers 5, 26, 35, 54. Aimed primarily at children, and performed mostly in Armenian or Russian, the puppetry on display here is impressive and inventive nonetheless.

SHOPPING
SEE MAP PAGE 162

GUM Market 35 Movses Khorenatsi St ☏374 10 578441; ⓜZoravar Andranik. South of the city centre, *GUM* is a covered market which is worth a visit to browse the colourful food stalls, where fresh fruit and vegetables sit alongside lavash bread, nuts, spices and dried fruits.

Tufenkian Carpets Hanrapetutyan St ☏374 98 559959, ⓦtufenkiancarpets.am/en; ⓜRepublic Square. There are plenty of places to buy carpets in Yerevan, but this friendly shop is one of the best. It has a great range of modern and traditional style rugs, including one must-buy design that appears to depict Cringer from He-Man.

Vernissage Market Buzand St; ⓜRepublic Square. Just southeast of Republic Square, you'll find this open-air market selling a wide range of souvenirs, from Armenian handicrafts to Soviet memorabilia.

Vino & Vino 28/1 Paronyan St ☏374 10 500028, ⓦvinovino.am; bus number 20. With a huge range of Armenian wines, *Vino & Vino* is a great place to pick up a local vintage, or a bottle of Ararat brandy.

DIRECTORY

Banks and exchanges Banks and ATMs are ubiquitous through Yerevan – try along the pedestrianised Northern Ave, around the Cascades or Republic Sq. Exchange offices aren't quite as common but banks will exchange money for you. Best rates are for US dollars, Euros and Russian roubles; British pounds attract slightly poorer rates.

Casinos Yerevan's – and Armenia's – top casino is the 24 hour Shangri-La (Yerevan-Sevan Highway, ⓦshangrila. am), found just outside the city limits on the Sevan road.

Embassies Canada, 10 Vazgen Sargsyan St (☏374 10 583786, ⓦvisa.vfsglobal.com/arm/en/can); France, 8 Grigor Lusavorich St (☏374 60 651950, ⓦam.ambafrance. org); Georgia, 10 General Babayan St (☏374 10 200738, ⓦarmenia.mfa.gov.ge); Germany, 29 Charents St (☏374 10 523279, ⓦeriwan.diplo.de); Russia, 13a Grigor Lusavorich St (☏374 10 567427, ⓦembassyru.am); UK, 8th floor, 2 Vazgen Sargsyan St (☏374 10 264301, ⓦgov. uk/world/organisations/british-embassy-yerevan); USA, 1 American Ave (☏374 10 464700, ⓦam.usembassy.gov). There is no Australian, Irish, New Zealand or South African embassy in Armenia.

Emergencies Call ☏102 for police, or ☏103 for ambulance.

Hospitals Muratsan Hospital Complex (114 Muratsan St, ☏374 10 450230, ⓦmuratsan.am/en).

Laundries There are a couple of options in central Yerevan, including 5asec (4 Vardanants St, ☏374 10 580033) and Selena Service (4 Zakyan St, ☏374 99 310310, ⓦfacebook. com/SelenaServiceArmenia).

Pharmacies There's no shortage of pharmacies here: Mesrop Mashtots Ave seems to have a particular concentration of them, including a couple of branches of the Natali Pharm chain.

Post office Yerevan's main post office is on Saryan St, at the top of the Aram St park; possibly more convenient are the smaller post offices at 21 Nalbanyan St and on Republic Sq.

5

Around Yerevan

HOVHANNAVANK MONASTERY

Around Yerevan and Mt Aragats

If you're looking for an easy day trip from Yerevan, you've got plenty of choice – the regions surrounding Armenia's capital offer an enormously varied selection of sights, from the country's only Graeco-Roman temple to its highest mountain, via a staggering number of beautiful monasteries and a quirky monument to the Armenian alphabet. Public transport is well developed here, and the roads are good, making travelling in this area easy and endlessly rewarding.

Armenia's not a big country, but even so it's incredible how many top-notch sights can be found within easy striking distance of Yerevan. You don't have to travel more than half an hour to reach the religious epicentre and former capital of **Echmiadzin** or the fantastic medieval monastery **Hovhanavank**. The iconic Soviet-era memorial **Sardarapat** and the astonishing rock-hewn **Geghard** monastery (where you can also see **Garni Temple** – unique in being the only Graeco-Roman monument in the Caucasus) are also less than an hour away. Taking a longer day out will give you the opportunity to visit the beautiful but relatively unexplored **monasteries** to Yerevan's west, or for walkers, there's a relatively easy hike up Armenia's highest mountain, **Mount Aragats**. With all this on the doorstep, basing yourself in Yerevan and taking a succession of day trips out is a great way to gain a feel for the country.

Brief history

The area around Yerevan has been inhabited for thousands of years, with many settlements pre-dating Yerevan itself. Incorporated into the Kingdom of Armenia in the fourth century BC, several of the region's cities – including Echmiadzin and Armavir – became the kingdom's capital for a number of years. It was during the life of the Kingdom of Armenia that the temple of Garni was constructed.

After Armenia's Christianisation starting in 301 AD, Echmiadzin became the centre of religious life until the seat of the Catholicos (the head of the Armenian Church) was transferred to Dvin 150 years later. Throughout the medieval period, the region passed back and forth between Persians, Byzantines, Turks and Armenians, and was on the front line of the Russo-Turkish War in the early nineteenth century, by which time Echmiadzin was once again Armenia's religious capital.

Relations with Turkey deteriorated considerably in World War I, when victims of the Armenian Genocide flooded across the border seeking refuge. In the wake of the collapse of Tsarist power in the region, this area became part of the newly declared Republic of Armenia, but had to quickly mount a defence against an invading Turkish army, which was roundly defeated at Sardarapat, in a victory that saved the entire country and is still celebrated today.

Under Soviet rule, the region enjoyed peace and relative prosperity, especially after Stalin's era when the laws against religion were relaxed and Echmiadzin regained a degree of its old importance. Since independence, the region's economy – already well-served by agriculture and viticulture – has received a considerable boost from an increase in tourism.

Garni and Geghard

The gorge carved by the Azat river is the setting for two excellent sights, which can be combined into an easy half-day trip from Yerevan. Note that both Garni and Geghard are enormously popular at weekends – so if you want a bit more seclusion, visit on a weekday.

Highlights

❶ Geghard Half-carved out of rock, the splendid monastery of Geghard is as unique as it is stunning. See page 181

❷ Echmiadzin The centre of the country's religious life, Echmiadzin is an essential stop if you want to understand the importance of the role of the church in Armenia. See page 182

❸ Sardarapat Memorial Soviet and Armenian sensibilities combine in this enormous, blocky monument to the Armenian victory at the Battle of Sardarapat. See page 186

❹ Hovhanavank Monastery Unquestionably one of Armenia's most beautiful monasteries, Hovhanavank sits on the edge of the Kasagh Gorge and is home to remarkable intricate carvings. See page 189

❺ Climbing Mount Aragats Mount Aragats is Armenia's highest mountain. Climbing to one of its four peaks and gazing into the volcanic crater is exhilarating. See page 189

❻ Anipemza One of Armenia's oldest surviving churches, the beautiful Anipemza Basilica sits on the Turkish border, flanked by relics of the Iron Curtain. See page 191

HIGHLIGHTS ARE MARKED ON THE MAP ON PAGE 180

Garni Temple

Marzpetuni St, Garni village • Charge • ☎ 374 94 001138 • Bus number 284 from Yerevan

The Graeco-Roman temple of **Garni** is the only such monument you'll find in the Caucasus. Dated to the first century AD, it seems to have been built by King Tiridates I, who had recently visited Rome to be crowned by Emperor Nero and embarked on a building spree when he returned to his kingdom. Most scholars consider that the temple was dedicated to the sun god Mithras, but some – curious as to why a pagan temple would survive when all such others were destroyed in the early Christian era – have theorised that Garni is not a temple at all, but the tomb of an early Armenian king.

Whatever its intended purpose, Garni stood until 1679 when it collapsed in a severe earthquake that also wrought serious damage to Yerevan, Khor Virap and Hovhannavank. There were no surviving images of it prior to its destruction, but after archaeological excavations and in-depth study, the architectural historian Alexander Sahinian proposed a reconstruction project, which was approved by the Soviet authorities and completed in 1968.

Other buildings on the site have been left unreconstructed but can still be explored. Most notably, next to the temple lay the ruins of the Sion Church, which was constructed on the circular Zvartnots model in the seventh century and destroyed during the Arab period. Also on site are ruins of secular buildings, including a well-preserved bath complex where remains of hypocausts and mosaics can be seen. While in Garni village, it's also worth a quick look at the attractive **Mashtots Hayrapet church**, a twelfth-century classically Armenian structure, built of grey-black stone with a pink dome, decorated with beautiful carvings inside and out.

Symphony of the Stones

Unnamed Road, beneath Garni village • Charge • Bus number 284 from Yerevan

The gorge beneath the village is home to a set of fantastic Giant's Causeway-esque basalt columns, known locally as the **Symphony of the Stones**. It's a very popular spot, and a wide paved path has been built beside the river for ease of access.

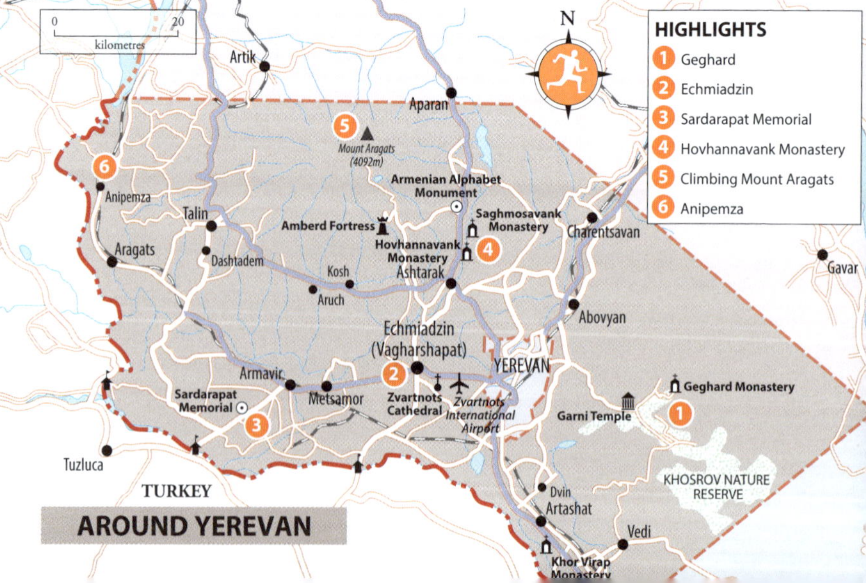

PIGEON FANCYING

At Geghard – and many other churches and monasteries across Armenia – you're likely to see people selling pigeons and doves in cages. Thanks to the story of Noah's Ark, when Noah released a dove to ascertain if the flood waters had receded enough to safely disembark, Armenians hold a special place in their hearts for these birds, and the releasing of a pigeon is an integral part of a wedding celebration – hence their availability at churches.

The **pigeons** sold for this purpose will usually return to the seller after release, making it a sustainable business. The pigeon sellers often become very attached to their birds. Prices can vary too. Usually, a pigeon costs a mere 3000 AMD, but there are stories of particularly valuable ones selling for thousands of US dollars.

The most exciting event in the pigeon seller's year comes in spring, when the birds are released in a high-stakes competition to see which can remain airborne the longest. Winners get a cash prize, but it's been said the respect afforded to a good pigeon is the main incentive. The winning pigeons are likely to be exempt from the other side of Armenia's pigeon-based traditions: in Gyumri, pigeons are sacrificed and eaten on special occasions…

Geghard

Geghard Monastery Rd • Free • ☏ 374 95 371367 • Bus number 284 from Yerevan

You will have realised by now that Armenia has a lot of monasteries, almost all of them beautiful, but even among this exalted company, you shouldn't miss **Geghard**. It's utterly splendid: constructed mostly of black stone, it also features chambers carved out of the rock of the gorge itself, making it part church and part cave monastery. As well as being beautiful, Geghard is also one of Armenia's holiest spots, once housing the Spear of Longinus, which wounded Christ during the Crucifixion. Geghard translates as 'the Monastery of the Spear', though you won't see this holy relic here, as it's been moved to Echmiadzin.

At the gate you'll see people throwing pebbles into high alcoves on the wall – it's thought that if the stone lands in the alcove, wishes will come true. Once through the gate, you'll find yourself in the monastery's courtyard with the principal church – St Astvatsatsin – ahead and slightly to your left. It's a beautiful church from outside, especially the fantastic carved portal, but it's utterly remarkable inside.

The first room into which you'll step is the gavit, a wide, open space supported by four rock columns, with a magnificent carved interior dome. From the gavit, you can access the side chapel which houses the tomb of the Proshyan princes, who patronised the monastery. There's a great carving here of a pair of chained lions flanking an eagle clutching a ram, which is likely to be the family symbol of the Proshyans. Elsewhere in this chapel, the meticulous intricacy of the stone carving is astonishing, including khachkars and further heraldic devices.

In the cliff above St Astvatsatsin, there are magnificent rock-hewn churches and chapels. You'll need to climb a staircase and follow a ten-metre passageway to reach the most impressive, a second Proshyan tomb with absolutely fantastic acoustics. Dotted around the whole complex are some of Armenia's best khachkars. Exploring here will occupy you for a good hour or more.

Khosrov Forest State Reserve

Visitor Centre, Havuts Tar Trail, Garni • Charge • ☏ 374 23 421352 • Bus number 284 from Yerevan

The **Khosrov Forest State Reserve**, which is actually in Ararat Province but best accessed from Garni, is a state-protected area which is home to some of Armenia's most endangered wildlife, including the very rare Persian leopard, though you'll have to be extremely lucky to catch sight of one. The reserve is riddled with hiking trails. One of the easiest and most popular is the 30-minute walk from the Visitor

Centre up to the eleventh-century Havuts Tar monastery, which was ruined in the 1679 earthquake.

The Havuts Tar Trail can be accessed under your own steam but venturing deeper into the Reserve will likely require the services of a guide as the tracks are very rough and not suitable for all vehicles. Other sites of interest within the reserve include the imposing Kakavaberd Fortress and the attractive Vahagn and Astghik waterfalls.

ARRIVAL AND DEPARTURE

GARNI AND GEGHARD

It's easiest to visit by self-driving or hiring a taxi to take you to both Garni and Geghard, but public transport is possible. Take bus number 22 or 63 to Gai Avenue, then pick up a marshrutka from the small bus station opposite the Mercedes-Benz dealership. These marshrutkas run as far as Goght village, which is fine for Garni but falls about 4km short of Geghard, for which you'll have to walk, hitch or taxi the rest of the way.

INFORMATION

Tourist Information Centre End of Alekyan Street, ☎ 374 93 099039. Garni's tourist information centre will offer help with the surrounding attractions, including booking accommodation in the area. Daily 10am–6pm.
Khosrov Forest Visitor Centre Havuts Tar Trail, Garni, ☎ 374 23 421352, ✉ khosrovreserve@gmail.com. Contacting the visitor centre for the Khosrov Forest State Reserve in advance is advised if you're planning a trip. The helpful staff will be able to help you plan your visit, including arranging a guide if necessary. Daily 8.30am–6pm.

ACCOMMODATION

Given the proximity of Garni and Geghard to Yerevan, it's not likely you'll see the need to stay here, but Garni village does have a couple of options. Possibly the best is:
Garni Hinyard 1/7 Azatamartikner St ✺ garnihinyard.am. Garni Hinyard is a lovely rustic hotel, with charmingly decorated rooms, a delightful garden, and a fantastic terrace, from which there are marvellous views across the gorge. The breakfast and dinner on offer here are absolutely outstanding. $$

EATING

Merojakh Off Marzpetuni St ☎ 374 91 195932. Close to the entrance of the temple complex, Merojakh is a convenient tavern-like place that serves up traditional and tasty Armenian food. $$

DIRECTORY

Banks There are few banks and ATMs in Garni: those there are can be found on Alekyan St, but it may be prudent to ensure you've got all the cash you need before arrival.
Hospital Garni Medical Centre (Alekyan St, ☎ 374 22 272710)
Post office There's a branch of Armenia's HayPost on Alekyan St, Mon–Fri 9am–5pm.

Echmiadzin

Technically, Armavir Province's largest city is called Vagharshapat, but it's commonly known as **Echmiadzin**, the name of Armenia's mother cathedral which is in the centre of town. It's an ancient place, dating back at least to the fifth century BC, and for a 200 year period, until 330 AD, it was the capital of Greater Armenia. It declined in importance during the Middle Ages, owing to its being conquered by Mongols, Turks, Byzantines and Persians – among others – but enjoyed a wave of expansion in the Soviet period. It's now the fourth largest city in Armenia and can easily be reached by marshrutka from Yerevan's Kilikia bus station.

Mother See of Holy Echmiadzin

Main entrance on Araratyan St, Echmiadzin • Free entry to complex; charge for some individual sites • ✺ armenianchurch.org

The **Mother Holy See of Echmiadzin** is Armenia's holiest site. It was built in the early fourth century on the spot where St Gregory the Illuminator saw a vision of Christ descending to Earth on a beam of light and indicating with a golden hammer where the church should be built: Echmiadzin literally translates as "Christ came down". Until the year 484 or 485, Echmiadzin was the seat of the Catholicos – the head of Armenia's church – but the seat then transferred through numerous other locations before eventually settling back at Echmiadzin in 1441, where it has remained since.

The UNESCO-listed complex boasts an extensive – almost baffling – array of churches and administrative buildings, and it's one of the most visited places in the country. For all the reverence Armenians feel towards it, though, it's not an easy place to love, with some areas of the grounds messy and untended, and seemingly permanent building works in progress. Information boards are also frustratingly absent.

That being said, it's worth visiting to gain an insight into Armenia's religious life and tradition, and the best way to get information is to ask around. All the staff are friendly and very happy to explain the history and purpose of the buildings.

Gate of St Gregory and Open Air Altar
Free

The **Gate of St Gregory and Open Air Altar** form the main entrance to the monastic complex. Built in 2001 to commemorate 1700 years of Christianity in Armenia, it's a striking, if rather brutalist, structure which feels somewhat at odds with the sense of history it was presumably hoping to convey.

To your left, after you pass through the gate into the complex, is the **Vatche and Tamar Manoukian Library**, which holds approximately 80,000 books, including rarities such as the earliest printed Armenian Bible, which dates from 1666. Its holdings are not limited to theology, and in particular, its ancient and medieval Middle Eastern history section is substantial. It is not open to general tourists, but if you are a scholar wishing to conduct research you can register with the staff for access.

On your right is the **Gevorgian Seminary**, established by Catholicos Gevorg IV in 1874 and now considered to be Armenia's oldest university. Naturally enough, its principal focus is theology. It's an attractive enough domed building, but you can't explore inside.

Church of the Holy Archangels
Free

Built and consecrated between 2007 and 2011, the **Church of the Holy Archangels** is a tall church that consists of a single tower, which is plain and undecorated inside and out. It's used mainly by the staff and students of the Gevorgian Seminary. Visitors will find their attention drawn to the two huge pillars with stone snakes carved at the top, which relate to Jesus' instruction of his followers to be as wise as snakes (Matthew 10:16).

Echmiadzin Cathedral
Free

The most important church in the entire Mother See complex, the original **Echmiadzin Cathedral** was first built by St Gregory the Illuminator, shortly after his release from the pit at Khor Virap (see page 226). This initial cathedral lasted only half a century before being destroyed in the invasion of the Persian King Shapur. Reconstructions and renovations followed, and the current structure mostly dates from approximately 484 AD.

After the seat of the Catholicos was transferred to Dvin – and subsequently various other locations around Greater Armenia – Echmiadzin remained a significant site for Armenian Christianity but fell into neglect as a result of Mongol and Turkish invasions. In 1441, a council of prominent churchmen voted to return the seat to Echmiadzin.

The cathedral suffered further when Shah Abbas I of Persia determined to move the centre of Armenian religion to Isfahan. Important relics, including the right arm of St Gregory the Illuminator, were moved to the newly established Armenian quarter in New Jolfa. The cathedral survived, despite the interruptions of wars with the Ottomans and the Russians, and the complex became a place of sanctuary for refugees following the Armenian Genocide.

In the early Soviet period, despite the atheist policy of the government, the cathedral continued to operate with a skeleton staff. Following 1945, the cathedral gradually regained its prominence, especially during the Khrushchev years, when a major renovation took place. Following independence, the cathedral was assigned UNESCO World Heritage Site status in 2000.

The cathedral has been closed for renovations for some years, but will hopefully have reopened by the time this book is published. When it does, visitors will be able to admire the remarkable frescoes on the interior dome and the reliefs on the exterior walls – thought to be among the oldest examples of Armenian sculpture.

Alex and Marie Manoogian Treasury Museum

Charge • ☎ 374 10 517110

At the back of the complex you'll find the **Treasury Museum**, accessible by guided tour only. Tours are available in Armenian, Russian and English. The treasures consist of decorated liturgical robes, wooden icons, and holy relics (including, but not limited to, the tooth of St Stephen, a fragment of Noah's Ark, several pieces of the True Cross, and the Spear of Longinus). There are some fantastically beautiful items here.

The Treasury Museum also hosts a replica of the office of Alex Manoogian, the Armenian-American inventor of the one-handed faucet tap, which seems slightly incongruous until it's explained that Manoogian donated the funds for the construction of the Treasury Museum. He and his wife Marie are now buried in the grounds.

Rouban Sevak Museum

Charge • ☎ 374 10 517110

The **Rouban Sevak Museum**, to the south of the cathedral, houses four rooms of art, including works by Sevak himself, who was a victim of the Armenian Genocide. Unless you're an enormous fan of Sevak, it's safe to skip this one.

Agape Refectory

Free • ☎ 374 91 433495

The second oldest building in the complex, having been built in the seventeenth century, this splendid vaulted hall has not always been a refectory. In its colourful history it has been an overnight rest stop for Silk Road merchants, a sanctuary for victims fleeing the Armenian Genocide, and – according to the staff – a black market goods hall during Soviet times. Even if you're not eating here it's worth popping your head inside to take a look.

Elsewhere in the complex

There are also a number of other minor sites in the complex, including a graveyard with both old and new khachkars to the south and a memorial to the Armenian Genocide.

Elsewhere in Echmiadzin

Most visitors to **Echmiadzin** take in the cathedral complex only, but there are a couple of other sites which are worth a quick glance.

First up, as you enter the city from Yerevan, you'll see a blocky pillar with a sculpture of a hand atop it – this is a monument to the **Right Hand of Gregory the Illuminator**. About half a kilometre past this, on the street's right, is the church of **St Hripsime** (Mesrop Mashtots St, free), which dates from the seventh century. The church contains the tomb of Hripsime, an early Christian martyr who was tortured and killed by King Tiridates III for refusing to submit to his advances. The story goes that Tiridates was driven mad as divine punishment for his treatment of Hripsime, and was later cured by Gregory the Illuminator.

In a fairly despondent square off Mashtots Street, you'll find the remnants of the church of **St Mariane** (Mesrop Mashtots St, ☎374 231 53696, free), one of the nuns of the Hripsime's community who suffered a similar fate. Despite a sign trying to summon up enthusiasm for the ruins, there's not a lot to see.

The nearby twin-turreted church of **Shoghakat** (Petrozavodsk St, ☎374 231 55593, free) is a much more pleasing proposition, positioned in shady, but untended, grounds. The name means "drop of light" and refers to a beam which descended from heaven to illuminate Hripsime's martyred nuns. The current structure dates from the late seventeenth century, built on the site of previous churches. There's fantastic carving on the ornate entranceway, and the smell of incense inside is intoxicating.

Zvartnots Cathedral

Yerevan-Echmiadzin Highway • Charge

On the outskirts of Echmiadzin, the ruins of **Zvartnots Cathedral** date from the mid-seventh century. Built on the spot where St Gregory the Illuminator met King Tiridates III and named after a group of angels known as zuartounks, the cathedral was hailed by contemporary historians as "astonishingly beautiful", "marvellous" and "radiant", amongst other extravagant praise. Despite the fact the cathedral collapsed in the tenth century due to either an earthquake or deliberate destruction by Arab invaders, it's easy to see from the elegant ruins that these compliments weren't far off the mark.

The remains consist of a large polygonal platform with an incomplete circle of columns surrounding the centre of what was once the cathedral's ground floor. In the centre is a small pit where St Gregory's relics were once housed, and a larger semi-circular pit. Excavators of the site believe that the cathedral had a further two levels on top, each a smaller size than the one below, so that the church may have vaguely resembled a wedding cake.

Behind the ruins of the cathedral itself are the remains of the adjoining palace of Nerses III, the Catholicos of the Armenian Church, who, as well as his religious office, had considerable political power and was a close ally of the Byzantine Emperor Constans II. Nerses was responsible for the construction of Zvartnots, and the ruins of his palace suggest that it was once a luxurious elegant building.

Towards the back of the site there's a very good on-site museum containing extracts from historical texts concerning the cathedral, an extensive exhibit about the various archaeologists who excavated Zvartnots, architectural information on other similar sites (most of which are in Eastern Turkey), a model of how the cathedral is thought to have looked, and a room of various finds such as pots and tools. There is also sometimes a distracting live musical performance. The site is quieter in the morning as tour groups tend to visit in the afternoon on their return from Echmiadzin.

ARRIVAL AND DEPARTURE   ECHMIADZIN

By bus Buses and marshrutkas travel between Yerevan and Echmiadzin regularly. They leave, when full, from Yerevan's Kilikia bus station and Echmiadzin's Komitas Square. If you want to visit both Echmiadzin and Zvartnots it makes most sense to see Echmiadzin first, then ask the bus to drop you at Zvartnots on the way back. Make sure the driver knows you want Zvartnots cathedral, not Zvartnots airport. There are also marshrutkas than run roughly hourly to Ashtarak (30 minutes) between 10.15am and 5.30pm.

By taxi Taxis will take you from central Yerevan to Echmiadzin. It's a bit harder to pick up a return taxi in Echmiadzin, so it may be worth negotiating an hour or two of waiting time with the taxi driver on the way out. This can work nicely, incorporating a stop at Zvartnots on the way back too.

By car Echmiadzin is an easy drive along the main highway from Yerevan, and it's a small enough place that you'll have no trouble finding your way around and getting a parking spot.

INFORMATION

Tourist information centre There's no tourist information centre in Echmiadzin or Zvartnots, but the staff in Agape Refectory are very friendly and knowledgeable about the Echmiadzin site. If you need practical information, you'll probably want to consult one of the Yerevan tourist information kiosks before your visit.

GETTING AROUND

Echmiadzin is a small place and it won't take you more than 20 minutes to walk wherever you want in the centre. If you want to get from Echmiadzin to Zvartnots you'll need a Yerevan-bound marshrutka.

ACCOMMODATION

Echmiadzin's proximity to Yerevan means that it tends to attract day-trippers rather than overnight tourists, and due to the absence of any particularly inspiring hotels in town, it's advised you follow the crowd and base yourself in Yerevan too. If you're completely committed to staying in Echmiadzin, you could try the below:

Artson B&B 55 Petrozavodsk St ☎ 37477990710. On the outskirts of town, the Artson B&B has five rooms, some with private bathrooms. The host family are very friendly, and are able to rustle up an excellent dinner. $

EATING AND DRINKING

You're unlikely to consider Echmiadzin a gourmet destination, as most visitors come only for the sights and eat back in Yerevan. There are a clutch of workmanlike cafés which serve food around the Komitas Square roundabout, but be aware that while the food is acceptable it's thoroughly unremarkable, and service can be very slow.

Agape Refectory Mother See of Holy Echmiadzin Complex ☎ 374 91 433495. The best option in town, the Agape refectory serves good Armenian food at reasonable prices. Choose between eating in its vaulted hall or outside on the pleasant terrace. The staff are very friendly and keen to tell you about the refectory's history. $$

Tashir Pizza Mesrop Mashtots St ☎ 374 94 504151. A branch of the reliable, if unexciting, Armenia-wide chain, Tashir Pizza will fill you up with quick and cheap doughy goodness. $$

SHOPPING

Echmiadzin Bookstore Mother See of Holy Echmiadzin Complex ☎ 374 10 517110. The cathedral complex has a decent bookshop containing plenty of texts on Armenian history and architecture, as well as more devotional material. It's oddly light on information about Echmiadzin. Also sells souvenirs.

DIRECTORY

Banks You'll find plenty of banks and ATMs along Mesrop Mashtots St, which leads northeast from Komitas Sq.

Hospital Vagharshapat Hospital (Spandaryan St, ☎ 374 60 704656)

Pharmacies Natali Pharm, on Mesrop Mashtots St, is the most central of a number of pharmacies around town.

Post office There are several post offices in town. The most convenient is the one on Mesrop Mashtots St (Mon–Sat 9am–6pm), next to the Hotel Richmind.

West of Echmiadzin

Few visitors venture past Echmiadzin into **Armavir Province**, primarily because it is not blessed with many interesting sites and it's a bit of a hassle getting public transport here. However, there are a couple of spots worth a visit if you're self-driving.

Metsamor Castle

Taronik village • Charge • ☎ 374 10 545570 • Armavir-bound marshrutka from Yerevan

The remains of this Iron Age stronghold and astronomical observatory aren't much to look at – consisting largely of some ruined walls and a line of standing stones – but there's a good museum on site which houses archaeological finds from the excavations.

Sardarapat Memorial

M5 highway, Araks village • Free • ⓦ facebook.com/Sardarapat • Marshrutka to Armavir

This enormous complex was constructed in 1968 to commemorate the 50th anniversary of the **Battle of Sardarapat**, a decisive encounter when the Armenian

THE WORLD'S LARGEST YAZIDI TEMPLE

The **Yazidis** – a Middle Eastern ethnic group with their own monotheistic religion – form a sizeable minority population in Armenia. Their presence in the country seems to date back to the nineteenth century, when they came seeking refuge from persecution in Turkey, and arrivals increased in the early twentieth century when they were also targeted during the Armenian Genocide. More recently, they were subject to attempted genocide by the Isis terrorist group, which has resulted in further Yazidi immigration to Armenia.

In the town of **Aknalich**, about 13km from Echmiadzin, stands the world's largest Yazidi temple. Completed in 2019, it's also one of the first Yazidi temples to be built outside Iraq. Constructed of white stone, it bears some resemblance to Armenian church architecture, but clearly has a heritage of its own. One large dome is surrounded by seven smaller ones with imagery of peacocks – the central figure of Yazidi religion – everywhere.

On the grounds, there's also a monument memorialising the Isis-led genocide, and one commemorating Armenian-Yazidi friendship. It's a fascinating place to visit, offering another perspective on Armenia and its population.

army achieved an unexpected victory over an invading Turkish force, preserving the newly independent country's integrity and preventing it being subsumed into Turkey. The principal sight is a grandiose pair of red stone bulls which frame a tall thin bell tower at the top of an austere staircase. From here, follow the formal gardens to the Victory Wall, on which you'll see bas-reliefs of winged horses and snakes, representing the Armenian and Turkish forces respectively. It's not exactly subtle, but it gets the point across.

There's also an onsite museum explaining more about the battle, and if you're hungry you can get a decent lunch at the refectory. The memorial complex is not normally busy, but between 21st and 29th May (the dates of the battle), there can be large crowds. It's not an easy site to visit via public transport; you can take a marshrutka from Yerevan to Armavir but then you will need a taxi. If you're self-driving it's an easy 20-minute drive from Echmiadzin, except for a slightly confusing road system around Armavir. The memorial of the Battle of Sardarapat is rather cleverly not in Sardarapat village, so make sure your sat nav is programmed accordingly.

Ashtarak

An obvious stop on the road if you're heading north from Yerevan, **Ashtarak** has been settled since the Bronze Age, if not before, and is considered one of the oldest towns in Armenia. Located by the Kasagh Gorge, it's a relatively quiet place, which makes for a good place to base yourself for visiting the surrounding cultural sites or for climbing Mount Aragats.

Start a tour of Ashtarak's low-key attractions with the medieval arched and cobbled **bridge** over the Kasagh river, which is overlooked by the nineteenth-century **Saint Sargis church**. There are also three ruined early medieval **churches** to visit on the other side of the canyon, subject of a slightly silly legend about three sisters. Of these churches, **Karmrovar** is small but the best preserved, and also features the added bonus of a life-size model of a stork perched on a nearby telegraph pole.

Perch Proshyan House Museum

10 Perch Proshyan St • Charge • ⓦ gatmuseum.am/en/branches/proshyan

This museum is mostly of interest if you're a Proshyan fan, which is unlikely as there are no English translations of his novels, which focused on social inequalities in nineteenth-century Ashtarak. As well as a writer, he was an accomplished translator, photographer and teacher. The staff will happily explain the museum's exhibits for you, but you'll probably be more interested by the ethnographic items in the nineteenth-century building, including a tonir oven for lavash baking, among other antique cooking equipment.

ARRIVAL AND DEPARTURE
ASHTARAK

By bus Ashtarak's main bus station is on the outskirts of town, on Yerevanyan St. From here, you can pick up marshrutkas to Yerevan (approximately 15 daily between 7.30am and 7.30pm, duration 35 minutes) and Echmiadzin (hourly between 10.15am and 5.30pm, duration 30 minutes).

By car It can be surprisingly busy driving into Ashtarak, and off the main highways some of the roads are quite narrow. It's mostly well-paved and you shouldn't have any trouble parking.

GETTING AROUND AND INFORMATION

Slightly too spread out for walking, but not really big enough to warrant a taxi, the question of how to get around Ashtarak can be a bit of a conundrum. One option for exploring the town would be to take a taxi from your guesthouse down to the old bridge and to walk back from there, visiting the minor sites as you do so.

Tourist information centre Ashtarak doesn't have a tourist info centre. If you need local information ask in your guesthouse.

ACCOMMODATION

Ashtarak Garden 15 Mayisyan St ⓦtinyurl.com/y8m2z9sr. One of the few accommodation options in town, *Ashtarak Garden* offers fairly small and plain rooms. On the plus side, it's comfy, the breakfast is good, and there's a fun little ethnographic setup in the garden in which the owners will photograph you. $̄

Yeganyans Guest House and Wine Yard 8 Smbat Shahaziz St ⓦtinyurl.com/3r5r7mfw. A fantastic guesthouse run by the friendly Set, Nelly and family. The rooms here are relatively simple but clean and comfortable. There's a lovely garden to relax in, home-made wine is freely available, and the evening meals (extra cost) are sublime. Set and Nelly are very knowledgeable about the local area and can help you plan your onward travel. $̄$̄

EATING

If you're staying in Ashtarak, it is highly recommend that you have dinner in your guesthouse. The home-cooked meals here are generally excellent. If you're just passing through, there are a few good restaurants, mostly around Petrosyan Street.

Old House 51 Petrosyan St ⓦtinyurl.com/yp87ps7w. In a 100-year-old building – hence the name – the *Old House* is a family-run place serving the usual Armenian suspects at a very high standard. The pork khoravets is particularly recommended. The main entranceway doesn't look enticing, but once inside you'll find the dining room decorated as a traditional tavern, or if it's summer, you can eat in the attractive garden. $̄$̄

DIRECTORY

Banks There's a little concentration of banks and ATMs at the junction of Nerses Ashtaraketsi and Norayr Sisakyan sts; you'll also find a branch of VTB Bank on Vardges Petrosyan St.

Hospital Ashtarak Medical Centre (61 Grigor Narekatsi St, ☎ 374 23 231949)

Pharmacies They're not exactly plentiful here, but you'll find a few pharmacies on Norayr Sisakyan St.

Post office The central post office is at 1 Norayr Sisakyan St, open Mon–Fri 9am–6pm.

North of Ashtarak

The area around Ashtarak is home to a good variety of sights, including two lovely monasteries, an ancient fortress, the country's highest mountain, and a quirky little monument to the country's unique alphabet. Visiting these isn't easy on public transport, but they make a very nice circuit if you hire a taxi from Ashtarak or Yerevan for half a day. If you're under your own steam, note that neither Hovhannavank nor Saghmosavank are particularly well signposted from the main road, so you'll probably need to use a mapping app to guide you.

Hovhannavank

Ohanavan village • Free

In a beautiful setting on the edge of the Kasagh Gorge, **Hovhannavank** is one of Armenia's big-hitters. The oldest part of the current church dates back to the fifth century, but it's thought that there may even have been an earlier structure, built by St Gregory the Illuminator, to house the relics of John the Baptist. The majority of the complex, however, was built in the thirteenth century, in the magnificent and confident style of church architecture that predominated at the time.

The exterior, built of orange and black stone, is beautiful, but it's as nothing compared to the interior. The intricate carvings in the gavit are absolutely spectacular. Look out for the magnificent khachkars, as well as a carved scene from the Parable of the Wise and Foolish Virgins above the portal. As you'll have realised by now, Armenia is home to many gorgeous monasteries, but Hovhannavank is one that should not be missed.

Saghmosavank

Saghmosavan village • Free • Ⓦ facebook.com/Saghmosavan

About 6km north of Hovhannavank, **Saghmosavank**'s location on the edge of the Kasagh gorge is similarly stunning. On a clear day, there are views all the way to Ararat. Saghmosavank also dates to the thirteenth century, and there are lovely carvings both outside and on the ceiling of the cool interior, but it's perhaps a less essential stop than Hovhannavank. It's a popular picnic spot with locals.

Armenian Alphabet Monument

Artashavan village • Free

One of the odder sights in the country, this **monument** consists of large stone sculptures of every letter in the Armenian alphabet, surrounded by statues of the monks who invented it, including Mesrop Mashtots (see box, page 160). It's not worth a special trip, but it's a fun 5-minute stop if you're nearby.

If you drive from here to Amberd Fortress and Byurakan, don't be deterred by the poor state of the road. While it's initially appalling, it improves considerably after three or four kilometres and is only occasionally awful thereafter. Be careful: after all the letters at the Alphabet Monument, it would be a shame if you came to a full stop.

Mount Aragats

At more than 4000m tall, **Mount Aragats** is the highest mountain in Armenia. It stands to the north-west of Ashtarak, and along with Ararat, it's held sacred by Armenians, featuring in a great deal of national poetry and literature. Compared to Ararat, though, it can be climbed in one day with relative ease – if you start early enough, you can even manage to reach all four of its summits. It's best to go with a guide, which can either be arranged through tourist agencies in Yerevan, or by contacting your guesthouse in Ashtarak.

Amberd Fortress

Amberd Rd, Aragats • Free, parking charge • ☎ 374 77 317395 • No public transport

Perched precariously on a promontory on the lower slopes of Aragats, **Amberd** is one of Armenia's best-preserved medieval forts. Initially built in the seventh century, the present construction mostly dates from the tenth century. It was taken and ruined during the Mongol incursion of 1236 and abandoned until reconstruction works began in the twentieth century. The site is encircled with excellent footpaths, and is particularly beautiful in spring, when purple, red and yellow flowers are in full bloom around the castle.

Also on site is the attractive black stone **church of St Astvatsatsin**, which holds no great architectural surprises but it does offer rather sensational views from in front of its door.

You can hike from Amberd to the **Byurakan observatory**, with a clear footpath beginning on the left off the path heading down from the fortress to the church. Byurakan – once one of the USSR's premier astronomical sites – is still in use, and it's possible to visit and use the telescopes to view the night sky (Ⓦbao.am).

West of Ashtarak

Heading west from Ashtarak along the M1 road, skirting the southern slopes of Mount Aragats, you'll find a line-up of impressive and rarely-visited churches, monasteries and castles, many of which are set in gorgeous scenery. Following this road to Gyumri makes a worthwhile alternative to the more well-trodden route around the east and north of Aragats.

Kosh

The first stop on the road is the village of **Kosh**, from which you can visit a gorge containing the **Church of St Stephanos**. This pretty church sits rather precariously on the edge of the gorge's left cliff. You can either drive up to the church along a dirt road, or walk up from the village's cemetery – there's no clear path, but it's easy to see which direction to take.

Aruch

7km on from Kosh is **Aruch**, home to the large and semi-ruined **Church of St Grigor**. Dating back to 666, it's built of attractive red-orange stone and is missing its cupola, meaning the interior is open to the elements. Just outside the village to the north is another impressive site: the remains of a thirteenth-century **caravanserai**, once a place for merchants to make an overnight stop as they travelled the Silk Road.

Talin

Another 20km brings you to **Talin**, in which you'll find the seventh-century **Talin Cathedral**. This large church is similar to but larger than that at Aruch, and though it too has lost its cupola, more of the dome's drum remains, meaning it appears rather less squat. Inside, fresco traces can be seen.

Dashtadem

The M1 road heads north from Talin to Gyumri, but if you have time, it's worth diverting south to **Dashtadem** instead: this village offers two sites of interest. First up is the village's tenth-century **castle**: one of the largest medieval fortresses in the Caucasus, it boasts extensive outer walls (onto which you can climb, but take care on the steep staircase) and a well-preserved inner keep, where you'll find a beautiful Arabic inscription, seemingly carved in 1174 when this area was under the rule of the Shaddadid emirs. Inside, a metal staircase leads up onto the keep's roof, which offers fantastic views but has no safety rails and is perhaps not a great choice if you suffer from vertigo. There's a lovely garden café just outside the walls, which is ideal for a drink on a warm sunny day.

Further from the village centre, **St Christopher's church** sits on a cliff edge with spectacular views of Mount Ararat. It's especially beautiful at sunset.

ANI

Standing on the cliffs above the gorge carved by the Akhuryan river, the now desolate ruined town of **Ani** was, in the tenth and eleventh centuries, the capital of the then-powerful Armenian kingdom and one of the largest cities in the world. However, in 1064 the city fell to the Seljuks, who sacked the town, and further damage was dealt by a Mongol incursion in 1236 and a devastating earthquake in 1319. Although the town remained a small settlement until the 1700s, it never regained its political importance.

Thanks to the **Treaty of Kars** signed by Turkey and the USSR in 1921, this important site of Armenian history found itself located in Turkey, a situation that rankles with Armenia, especially since for much of the twentieth century Turkey made very little effort to safeguard the ruins. Fortunately, matters have improved from the 2000s onwards, with the beginning of conservation and restoration programmes and the addition of Ani to UNESCO's World Heritage Sites list.

A visit to Ani is a ghostly experience. The ruins of the site lie scattered across the bleak landscape, and despite it being a popular excursion from Kars, it's a disconcertingly quiet place. The buildings that remain are primarily churches, some of which are unique and intriguing examples of medieval Armenian architecture, and there are utterly magnificent frescoes in the church of **St Gregory of Tigran Honents**.

Despite encouraging signs of rapprochement, the border between Armenia and Turkey is currently closed, so getting to Ani isn't a simple matter of popping between the two countries. You'll need to transit via Akhaltsikhe in Georgia if you want to visit. It's worth it, though: these are the most extensive medieval Armenian ruins to be found anywhere, and they offer an evocative glimpse into a once-powerful kingdom.

Anipemza

From Dashtadem, it's 40km or so to Armenia's border with Turkey, which follows the line of the Akhouryan River. This part of the country sees few visitors, but it's well worth heading out here to the small settlement of **Anipemza**, where you can explore ruins from two very different eras of Armenian history. For the medievalists, there's the extremely impressive orange stone **Yereruyk basilica**, which dates from the fifth century and is one of Armenia's oldest extant churches. Students of more modern history will likely be fascinated by the rusting **pylon** just north of the village: this relic of the Soviet era is decorated with a hammer and sickle and other such similar USSR imagery, serving as a reminder that this remote landscape was once a frontline of the Iron Curtain.

Viewpoints over Ani

From Anipemza, the H17 road runs north to Gyumri hugging the Turkish border. It's a pleasant route with views across the rolling grass steppe-like landscape of eastern Turkey to the left, but you'll probably need to keep your eyes ahead: this is one of the worst surfaced roads in Armenia.

Just across the border here is the ancient Armenian capital of **Ani**, but it's frustratingly difficult to see it. In the village of **Kharkov**, there's a good viewpoint, but it's administered by Russian soldiers who guard the sensitive border between Armenia and Turkey. It's possible to arrange access by visiting the Ministry of Foreign Affairs in Yerevan to get a permit. Some tour agencies can also arrange a trip. Either way, you'll need to give at least a week's notice.

Far easier to reach is the viewpoint in **Haykadzor** village. From the village centre, tempting though it looks, don't take the track leading up to the war memorial; instead head diagonally left and follow the further signs to a huge map of the Ani site. Ani itself is, however, quite a long way away, so unless you have binoculars and/or a very good zoom lens you'll barely be able to see it.

North Armenia

CHURCH OF THE HOLY SAVIOUR

North Armenia

Armenia's northern regions are home to a fantastic variety of sights, with an irresistible combination of gorgeous natural scenery, stunning medieval monasteries, and modern cosmopolitan towns. It's here that you'll find the best hiking country in Armenia, with trails that cross mountain ranges and pass beautiful churches, while the cities are friendly, welcoming and perfect for exploration. With some of the country's undisputed cultural highlights and arguably its most beautiful landscapes, the north is an essential part of any Armenian itinerary.

North of Yerevan is **Lake Sevan**, Armenia's largest lake, which is popular with local holidaymakers enjoying the beach life, though it's perhaps more notable for the brooding silence of the **Noratus cemetery**, found on the lake's southern shore. Further north, the landscape is either lush and forested or bleak and steppe-like, but always beautiful. The marvellous natural scenery is best explored around **Dilijan National Park**, which is a treat for outdoorsy types with its many hiking trails, but a trip up the **Debed Canyon** will also have you admiring the magnificent vistas, when you're not too busy exploring the fantastic monasteries which hug the canyon walls. Monastery-lovers should also find space on their agenda for **Harichavank** and **Marmashen**, a pair of lovely medieval church complexes within easy reach of Gyumri.

Gyumri and **Vanadzor**, Armenia's second and third towns respectively, also reward exploration. Gyumri's architecture features a good deal of lovely black tuff stone, giving it an unusual style, and the town is a friendly place with plenty of museums and restaurants, as well as an excellent open-air market. Vanadzor, meanwhile, is home to some of Armenia's best Soviet architecture, including the railway station and numerous factories. Speaking of factories, the **Ijevan Wine-Brandy Factory** is not to be missed, with its excellent tours walking you through the full process of wine and brandy manufacture, and rounding off with some fantastic product sampling. Cheers!

Brief history

The history of Armenia's northern regions dates back many thousands of years, with evidence of human habitation at least as long ago as 9000 BC. The area seems to have been part of the Urartian Kingdom – based at Van, now in Eastern Turkey – from the ninth century BC, but was conquered by the Cimmerians in 720 BC, who established the modern city of **Gyumri**.

Rule by the ancient Kingdom of Armenia followed, after which came Achaemenids, Byzantines and Persians, before the area entered a period of prosperity from 885 AD under the medieval Bagratid Armenian Kingdom, which was ruled from Ani, just across the border in Turkey. In this time, a large number of monasteries were established in the region, becoming important and celebrated centres of learning.

The Bagratids lasted less than two hundred years before their kingdom fell to the Byzantines in 1045, who were in turn supplanted by the Seljuk Turks only 25 years later. The region became the front line for invading forces, including the Mongols, Turks and Persians for several hundred years, until the Russians arrived in the early nineteenth century and annexed the area, which was then developed and industrialised.

Under Soviet rule, the region experienced further industrialisation, though it was also regarded as a holiday destination. Unfortunately, the 1988 earthquake, with its epicentre at Spitak, caused thousands of deaths and brought much of the region's prosperity to an abrupt end. The effects are still felt decades later, with the area around Spitak and Gyumri continuing to undergo restoration work, and unemployment

IJEVAN WINE-BRANDY FACTORY

Highlights

❶ Noratus Cemetery The largest collection of Armenian gravestones in the world, Noratus is an enormous cemetery set in a bleak landscape beneath towering mountains. See page 199

❷ Hiking in the Dilijan National Park Criss-crossed with trails, the idyllic Dilijan National Park is perfect for hiking trips. See page 204

❸ Ijevan Wine-Brandy Factory Want to know how all that wine and brandy you've been sampling is made? The Ijevan Wine-Brandy Factory offers a fascinating tour through the process – and then gives you a tasting session. See page 205

❹ The Debed Canyon The sheer concentration of beautiful medieval monasteries up this river gorge makes a trip up the Debed Canyon essential for any visit to Armenia. See page 209

❺ Gyumri Armenia's second city, Gyumri is a friendly and attractive place, packed with charming little house-museums. See page 215

❻ Harichavank Monastery On the lower slopes of Mount Aragats, Harichavank monastery features some of the most intricate and exquisite stone-carved decoration you'll see in Armenia. See page 220

HIGHLIGHTS ARE MARKED ON THE MAP ON PAGE 196

remaining high. Meanwhile, Dilijan and Vanadzor, the other main towns in the area, have positioned themselves as leading tourist hotspots, with Dilijan in particular earning frequent accolades as an up-and-coming destination.

Tsaghkadzor

Armenia doesn't tend to instantly spring to mind when considering destinations for a skiing holiday, but the slopes accessible from the resort town of Tsaghkadzor are a decent choice if you're into winter sports. Even if skiing doesn't appeal, the town is a pleasant place for a relaxing break, boasting a smattering of interesting sights and some of the country's top hotels.

Ropeway

Tandzaghbyur St • Charge • ⓦ ropeway.am

Most visitors to Tsaghkadzor are here for the skiing: there's a **ropeway**, which will whisk you up into the mountains to access the 27km worth of runs, and it's possible to hire equipment from the rental service at the ropeway's lower station. If you're not skiing, it's fun to ride the ropeway up into the mountains, though there's little to do at the top.

Orbeli Brothers Museum

Orbeli Brothers St • Charge • ⓦ orbelimuseum.am

Tsaghkadzor's local **museum** focuses on the Orbeli brothers, a high-achieving family who worked in fields as diverse as marine archaeology and physiology. There's a room dedicated to each of the brothers, with a potted history of each and a selection of their belongings, including passports, a doctoral cap, and a somewhat inexplicable model of a collection of rabbits in a boat.

Kecharis Monastery

Khachatur Kecharetsi St • Free • ☎ 374 93 966059

Uphill from the Orbeli Brothers Museum is the **Kecharis Monastery**, on which work began in the early eleventh century. It consists of three churches, of which the gavit of the St Gregory the Illuminator Church (to the left as you enter the churchyard) is the most interesting, with attractive carvings around and above the door.

ARRIVAL AND DEPARTURE — TSAGHKADZOR

By bus Twice daily buses leave Tsaghkadzor for Yerevan's northern bus station, taking one hour 15 minutes. You may also be able to pick up a marshrutka from Sevan.

By car The road to Tsaghkadzor is pretty rough, owing to seemingly endless resurfacing works, which also extend to quite a few of the roads in the town centre. It's easy finding a place to park once you're in town.

ACCOMMODATION

Teghenis Holiday Home 31 Tandzaghbyur St ⓦteghenis.am/en. Up at the top of town near the ropeway, Teghenis offers a small number of clean and comfortable rooms and villas, all set within a pleasant little estate. There's a pool, sauna and gym, as well as a decent restaurant and bar. The breakfast is delicious and quite ridiculously plentiful. $$$

Tsaghkadzor Marriott 2 Tandzaghpyur St ⓦtinyurl. com/4whjh35j. Big and corporate, perhaps, but the Marriott is a great choice if you're looking for a relaxing break in an international class hotel. The rooms are cosy and comfortable, the pool and spa facilities are top notch, and the restaurant is pretty good too. $$$

Writers' House 4 Charents Lane ⓦwritershotel.am/new. A marvellous relic of the USSR years, the Writers' House was once a spa facility for – yes – writers. The interior retains the Soviet-era bas-reliefs and mosaics in the corridors, ensuring the place feels like a real time capsule. The rooms could do with a bit of updating, but that might result in it losing its fantastic ambience, so perhaps it's better they don't risk it. $

EATING

Ji.Ser 10 Orbeli Brothers St ⓦtinyurl.com/msbvs9jj. The menu at Ji.Ser is unabashedly international, focusing on burgers, pizzas and pastas. There's a solid cocktail menu, and the waiters know their stuff when it comes to the short but well-curated wine list. $$

Pur 16 Orbeli Brothers St ⓦfacebook.com/purtrestaurant. A central, attractively decorated, and welcoming restaurant offering a good menu which includes many Armenian barbecue classics, as well as a smattering of Georgian options and a fine selection of cakes. The apple strudel is particularly recommended. There's a small souvenir shop downstairs. $$

Yasaman 8 Orbeli Brothers St ⓦyasaman.am/en/tsaghkadzor. A centrally located place, Yasaman offers up good quality Armenian fare. There's a lovely terrace to sit on in summer, or if it's winter you'll be sure to keep warm and cosy by the log fire. $$

DIRECTORY

Banks There are a couple of ATMs in Tsaghkadzor – try around Tsaghkunyats Sq and along Orbeli Brothers St.

Post office The post office (Mon–Fri 9am–5pm) is found on Grigor Magistros St.

Lake Sevan

Since Armenia lacks a coastline, the large freshwater **Lake Sevan** in the northeast serves as the country's primary beach resort. It's hugely popular with weekending Yerevanis and vacationing Russians, and while it's undeniably a pretty spot, you may well find that the over-development on the lake's shores makes a visit to the famous Sevanavank Monastery feel frenetic rather than relaxing. It's certainly worth stopping by to see the sights around the lake, but you're unlikely to want to spend too long here.

Sevan

Sevan town is not a must-see destination, though you'll no doubt be travelling through on your way to Sevanavank and beyond. As you do it's worth taking a look at the shockingly red-orange **Sevan Church**, which provides an astonishing contrast to the grey apartment blocks that surround it. This will, however, only detain you for a minute or two.

Sevanavank village

The **Sevanavank** peninsula was once an island, but the lake's exploitation in the Soviet era for hydro-electric power and irrigation led to a 20 percent drop in the water level, which left Sevanavank attached to the mainland. The monastery here – which was of course isolated on the island and operated a strict and unworldly regime – is an iconic Armenian sight and appears on tourist posters all over the country.

Unfortunately, its popularity means the peninsula is usually packed with a heaving mass of tourists slogging up the stairs to the monastery, visiting tacky souvenir stalls and afterwards dining in uninspired restaurants. The tranquility that must have once existed here is also now frequently disturbed by regular tourist helicopter flights over the lake and peninsula, and jet-skiing tourists zipping across the water. It's not a relaxing place, and is best visited early in the morning to see the monastery at its quietest.

Sevanavank Monastery

Sevanavank • Free

The **monastery** complex itself, consisting of the churches of the Holy Apostles and St Astvatsatsin, sits on a spectacular bluff overlooking the lake. The site is thought to have been a pagan place of worship before the advent of Christianity, and in the fourth century the ever-present St Gregory the Illuminator established a pair of churches here. However, much of the current complex dates from the ninth century, when, according to legend, Princess Mariam had a dream the twelve apostles flew over the lake to show her where to build.

There's a short walk from the path behind the monastery up to a viewpoint at the end of the peninsula, which offers fine vistas of the lake and surrounding mountains (slightly spoiled by the fence in the foreground, which protects a residence of the Armenian president).

After descending from the monastery, fans of Soviet architecture should take a quick walk along the peninsula's southern shore. About 5 minutes from the central car park, look up towards the monastery and you'll see the superb Sevan Writers' House, a gloriously space-age structure built in the 1960s, jutting out confidently towards the lake. It is still, sporadically, open as a café if you want to pop inside.

The northern shore

To see a more serene side of Lake Sevan, you could try travelling the **northern shore** round from Sevanavank to **Shorzha**. Shorzha is not, in itself, a place of any particular interest, being a sleepy little village which tends to have more geese than people wandering the streets, but it is the terminus of the train line from Yerevan. The road to get there is a very pleasant and peaceful drive with great lake views.

Hayravank Monastery

Hayravank village • Free

In a fantastic location by the lake's edge about 25km southeast of Sevan, the 9th monastery of **Hayravank** is short and squat from the outside, but the interior is gorgeous. There are hundreds of crosses and Armenian script carved in the black stone walls and pillars, and the tessellating diamond shapes in the dome are beautiful. The faint smell of incense that lingers inside only adds to the mystical feel.

Noratus cemetery

Noratus village • Free

Following the destruction of the khachkars at Jolfa in Nakhchivan (see page 312), the **Noratus cemetery** is now home to the greatest concentration of Armenian khachkars in the world. There's even a legend that Tamerlane's invading army mistook the gravestones for enemy soldiers and retreated due to the sheer number of them. It's a beautiful site, full of butterflies and birdsong in summer, and is a tranquil antidote to the hustle and bustle elsewhere around Lake Sevan.

Wandering around, you'll begin to see the evolution of Armenian grave styles, from intricately carved medieval khachkars through to the simpler coffin style of the nineteenth and early twentieth centuries, to the ornate marble or granite modern, which sometimes comes with a sculpture or picture of the deceased.

If you're self-driving, note that it's not massively well signposted from the main lakeside road. Whichever way you're coming, you'll be able to see a flyover approaching, at which you should take the exit and head in the opposite direction from Gavar. As you arrive in Noratus village, you should follow the (semi-) regular blue signs to the cemetery, and do not trust mapping apps, which have some peculiar ideas about the best route there.

The southern shore

If you're heading across the Selim Pass to Yeghegnadzor, you'll pass through the small towns of Nerkin Getashen and Martuni, and then begin to climb towards the mountains and Geghovit town. None of them have much to interest tourists, with the minor exception of Nerkin's **Kotavank** church, which sits on a small hill overlooking the town with beautiful khachkars dotting its grounds.

ARRIVAL AND DEPARTURE   SEVAN

By bus From Sevan's central bus station, at the junction of Nairyan and Sayat Nova streets, marshrutkas leave hourly between 9am and 5pm to Yerevan's inconvenient northern bus station (one hour). Marshrutkas to Dilijan coming from Yerevan stop in Sevan, though not to any regular timetable (35 minutes).

By train The rail line between Sevan and Yerevan operates only in summer (and some years not even then). If it is running, there's usually a connection to Yerevan daily, and to Shorzha on the lake's northern shore at weekends.

By car Driving the lake's coastal road is easy; figuring out how to get into Sevan town is slightly less easy, given the confusing junctions on the main road. Once you're in town, there are no problems parking or finding your way around.

GETTING AROUND

By car If you're wanting to thoroughly explore the lakeside's various attractions, you're going to need to go by car. Self-driving is easy, despite the lack of signposting which makes Noratus a little tricky to find, and at busy times you may have difficulty finding a parking spot in Sevanavank. It's also easy to arrange a taxi for the day from Sevan, Tsaghkadzor or Yerevan to take you on an excursion to Sevanavank, Hayravank and Noratus.

ACCOMMODATION

Lake Sevan's accommodation scene is largely made up of beach resorts, which don't really cater to the independent traveller. It's recommended that you visit in a day and return to Yerevan or continue to Dilijan, but if you do find yourself wanting to spend the night in the lake's environs, you could try one of the following.

Lake Sevan Hostel 17 Sargis Sevanatsi St, Sevan ⓦ lakesevan.business.site. Despite the name, this hostel is in Sevan town, not on the lake. If you do want to stay in the town, though, it's a very good choice: the dorms are clean and comfy, the owners are friendly, and there's a nice communal area for relaxing. Evening meals may be available. $̄

Noy Land Sevan-Gavar Highway ⓦ noylandresort.am. On the road between Martuni and Sevan, *Noy Land* is a typical example of the Lake Sevan resort genre. It has a hotel with twelve rooms (six with balcony and lakeside view) and 31 wood-framed cottages for four people. The restaurant is an extravagant silver-domed affair, and facilities include a spa and sauna, as well as the inevitable private beach, outdoor swimming pool and water sports. Horseriding is also available on request. Slightly more surprising is the light aircraft on the grounds, explanation for which seems to elude the staff. $̄$̄$̄

Tufenkian Avan Marak Tsapatagh Tsapatagh village ⓦ avan-marak-tsapatagh.tufenkianheritage.com. Found on the quiet northeast shore of Lake Sevan, this resort – part of the upmarket Tufenkian chain – is one of the best places to stay in the environs of the lake if you're looking for a place to get away from it all. There are lovely lake views, wonderfully comfy bedrooms and excellent spa facilities, and the restaurant is top notch too. $̄$̄$̄

EATING

There are plenty of roadside restaurants along the Sevan highway offering freshly caught fish from the lake.

★ **Bohem Studio Teahouse** Sayat Nova St ⓦ facebook.com/bohemsevan. This is precisely the sort of hipster establishment you'd never expect to find in Sevan. Shelves groan with books, board games and random statuettes ranging from Mother Mary to Super Mario. Artists spend their days here painting, and talented local musicians accompany the blues guitar soundtrack with improvisation on the piano in the corner. The menu is limited – though the Armenian pancakes are very good – but the real treat is experiencing the ambience and meeting the extremely friendly and welcoming locals. $̄

Gata Boulangerie Sevanavank. At the foot of the staircase up to the monastery, this bakery is a good place to grab a tasty pastry. There's no seating though; takeaway only. $̄

Yasaman M4 road, between Sevan and Tsovagyugh ⓦ yasaman.am/en/sevan. A very popular lakeside restaurant, especially recommended for its barbecued fish. It's particularly worth a visit on a sunny day to sit on the terrace and enjoy views across Sevan. $̄$̄

DIRECTORY

Banks ATMs can be found along Nairyan Street in Sevan. There's nowhere to get cash in Sevanavank.

Pharmacies Not exactly plentiful round here. Try Ararat Apteka at 151 Nairyan St, Sevan.

Post office The central post office is at 171 Nairyan St, Sevan. Mon–Fri 9am–6pm, Sat 9am–3pm.

Dilijan

Slap bang in the centre of the Dilijan National Park, a 240km² area of pristine forest and gorgeous mountains, riddled with hiking trails – including a considerable length of the ambitious new Transcaucasian Trail – it's no surprise that **Dilijan** is swiftly becoming the outdoors capital of Armenia. The town itself dates back to the medieval period when it was used as a base for noble hunting parties. Today, it is a welcoming place confident in its future as a touristic centre – though this has led to the construction of some Swiss-style chalet cottages, which border on twee but just about get away with it.

Dilijan is best regarded as an excellent base for hikes, but a wander around town will reveal a few sites of minor interest. Starting at the roundabout in the centre of town by the small lake, you'll find a couple of items of Soviet memorabilia. It's hard to miss the fantastically space-age white **Monument** erected to celebrate 50 years of Soviet Armenia, while on the other side of the roundabout there's a statue of three characters from the film **Mimino**, which contained a line praising the quality of Dilijan's tap water. Accordingly, there's a drinking water fountain in between the characters.

Dilijan Local Lore Museum & Art Gallery

28 Myasnikyan St • Charge • ☎ 374 268 24451

Featuring a collection of Armenian and European paintings, archaeological finds and ethnographic exhibits, this museum – sometimes confusingly referred to as the **Geological Museum** – is nothing if not eclectic. The art gallery, found on the upper and ground floors, is home to a collection of artworks of varying style and quality: the best are upstairs, where you'll find a couple of works by Martiros Saryan, one of the country's most celebrated painters, as well as a series of lively modern works by Garnik Zouloumyan (also known as Garzou) and Khachatur Jeranyan.

On the ground floor is an exhibition of increasingly silly chairs, including one made from cutlery and another from a piano. The oddest of all is the Meat Mincing Chair, which is very much not something on which you'd want to sit. The galleries around the centre feature communist-era sculpture and artworks, while in the basement is the Local Lore Museum, which boasts the array of ethnographic goods that's typical of Armenian museums, with ancient pots, 19th century kitchen and farming goods, and attractive carpets taking centre stage. Information about the exhibits is sadly lacking.

Yesayan Museum

Old Dilijan Complex, Sharambeyan St • Free

On the Tufenkian Complex grounds, this small museum contains nineteenth- and twentieth-century artefacts of local life. The Tufenkian Complex in general is an installation of 'old' traditional houses and artisan workshops, which feels a bit like a Hollywood film set of an Armenian village rather than something real.

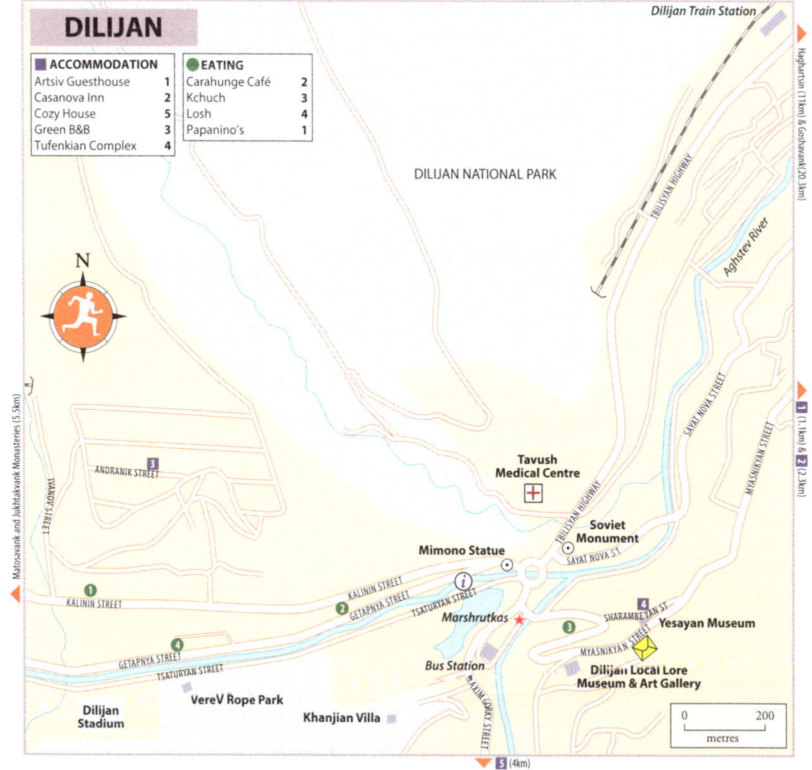

Khanjian Villa

Off Maxim Gorky St • Free

Fans of grandiose Soviet-era architecture should make a quick stop at the **Khanjian Villa**, a vast circular mansion built for the politician Aghasi Khanjian in the 1930s. Unfortunately, Khanjian fell victim to the Stalinist purges before he could enjoy living in his new home, which has now fallen into picturesque disrepair.

VeraV Rope Park

City Park, 1 Getapnya St • Charge • ⓦ facebook.com/VereVRopePark

Thrill seekers will get immense enjoyment from a trip to Dilijan's adventure park, which features a small but entertaining network of ropewalks dangling between the park's trees. It's particularly fun if you go as part of a group, as the staff can organise competitive games for you.

Matosavank and Jukhtakvank Monasteries

Off Abovyan St • Free

This evocative pair of ruined monasteries nestled in the woods at Dilijan's western end are home to some beautifully carved khachkars. They're best accessed on foot, as the road is truly awful and finishes before you reach either church. It is a relatively steep walk, though, and some hikers have reported troublesome dogs on the route.

ARRIVAL AND DEPARTURE   DILIJAN

By bus Dilijan's bus station is on the central roundabout at the bottom of Myasnikyan Street. Buses to Yerevan go every hour between 8am and 4pm (duration 1.5 hours). You will need to book a ticket in advance, which you can do at either the bus station or the tourist info centre. Buses to Ijevan (duration 50 minutes) leave twice daily at 9.15am and 10.15am, or you can pick up the Yerevan to Ijevan service, which stops by every hour until 7pm. Marshrutkas ply the routes to local villages from the CPS petrol station on the roundabout, but they don't have any set hours, just leaving when they are full. There are five buses a day to Vanadzor, between 8.30am and 6pm (duration 45 minutes).

By car Dilijan sits at a convenient junction of roads between Vanadzor and Sevan. Driving here presents no problems. In town, some roads are narrow and a few are unpaved, but the main roads are easily navigable.

GETTING AROUND AND INFORMATION

Dilijan is quite spread out, so be prepared to walk 20 minutes or so to the centre. Taxis are reasonably cheap and easy to come by.

Tourist information centre Tsaturyan St, ☎ 374 94 399336, ⓦ facebook.com/DilijanTIC. Dilijan's outstanding tourist information centre is a short walk from the central roundabout. The friendly and extremely helpful staff can arrange all manner of activities, including cookery classes, bike rental, and wine tours, and are enormously informative on local hiking opportunities. They also rent out camping and walking equipment including tents, sleeping bags, mattresses, trekking poles, snowshoes, and torches. April–Nov 9am–8pm, Dec–Mar to 6pm.

ACCOMMODATION   SEE MAP PAGE 201

★ **Artsiv Guesthouse** 19 Usanogakana St ⓦ facebook. com/artsivguesthousedilijan. Plain but clean and spacious en-suite rooms on the ground floor of a friendly family home. Beds are comfortable and there's a rustic feel to the wood and stone rooms. The generous breakfast – including pastries, fried eggy bread, homemade jam, and succulent cherries – is one of the best in Armenia. $$

Casanova Inn 63 Hovsepyan St ⓦ facebook.com/ Casanovainnboutiquehotel. The Casanova is towards the top of the town with great views down to the valley, which can be enjoyed from the swinging chairs on the balcony. The common area is large and is decorated with a mural of Venice, while well-chosen art hangs in the spacious en-suite rooms. The breakfast is extensive and tasty, and there's also a good restaurant with a fine selection of Armenian wines for the evening. $$

Cozy House 126 Kamo St ⓦ cozy.am. Indulge your Middle Earth fantasies with a stay at this great little place, which looks for all the world like a little hobbit village: there are thirteen separate cabins, all with little round wooden doors and turfed roofs. Inside, they're stylish and – as advertised – cozy. Just watch out for a wizard popping by to send you off on a quest to nick some gold from a dragon. $$$

Green B&B 13 Andranik St 374 41 367778. An excellent budget option, *Green B&B* offers four double rooms with a shared bathroom on the upper floor of a family home. The balcony and shared lounge is a nice place to meet other travellers. No English spoken. . Wi-fi is a bit patchy, but at this price who's complaining about that? $

Tufenkian Complex Sharambeyan St tufenkianheritage.com/en/accommodation/old-dilijan-complex. In the centre of town, the Tufenkian Complex is a little Swiss-style village, incorporating a restaurant and various craft shops as well as the luxury Ananov Hotel, which has 18 rooms designed to give the air of a traditional Dilijan home. Six rooms face the road, so avoid these if you are a light sleeper. $$

EATING SEE MAP PAGE 201

Carahunge Café Kalinin St 374 43 220003. Named after the stone circle near Sisian (see page 232), this trendy café-bar offers a wide-ranging menu, and is also well stocked with a remarkable number of wines, which you can enjoy in the atmospheric wine cellar bar. On top of this, it doubles as a wine and brandy shop, and if that's not enough, upstairs there's a great bookshop with plenty of titles in English. $

Kchuch 37 Myasnikyan St facebook.com/KchuchDilijan. This friendly place prides itself on cooking all its food in the wood-fired brick oven, resulting in fantastic clay pot dishes, great barbecued meats, and the most authentically Italian (and most interesting topping combinations) pizzas you're likely to find in Armenia. Even the desserts are cooked in the brick oven – except the ice cream, as the menu is careful to point out. $$

Losh 6a Getapnya St 374 95 886003. A trendy café-restaurant with eclectic decoration and a vaguely rustic feel. The food tends to stick to Armenian standards, with decent pizzas thrown in for good measure. $

Papanino's 104 Kalinin St 374 95 734500. You get a two-for-one here: downstairs is a café where you'll find good coffee and excellent cakes and pastries, while upstairs is a great restaurant serving lovingly prepared Armenian classic dishes. There are 150 wines available, and the staff will be able to select the perfect one to accompany your meal. $$

DIRECTORY

Banks There are plenty of banks with ATMs about. Try along Myasnikyan St from the Local Lore Museum up to the town hall.

Hospital Dilijan Medical Centre (7/3 Sayat Nova St, 374 268 22999).

Pharmacies Among others, Doc Pharmacy along Kalinin St is a well-stocked option.

Post office Dilijan's central post office is on Myasnikyan St, close to the town hall. It's open Mon–Sat 9am–6pm.

Around Dilijan

The immediate environs of Dilijan are home to two impressive medieval monastery complexes in the forested hills nearby. Neither is accessible via public transport, but you could take a taxi on a half-day trip from Dilijan to visit them both. If you're self-driving, the roads to them are winding but well-maintained.

Haghartsin Monastery

Haghartsin Rd • Free • spiritofhaghartsin.weebly.com

Perched on the edge of a wooded valley, **Haghartsin Monastery** is an attractive set of churches in a glorious location. Its history is unknown, but its earliest church – dedicated to St Gregory the Illuminator – dates from the tenth century. In 2011, it enjoyed an alaborate restoration financed by the UAE's Sheikh of Sharjah.

The largest church in the complex is the eleventh-century St Astvatsatsin, and the smallest is the neighbouring St Stephanos, which dates from the thirteenth century. Walk to the right of St Stephanos to see an ornate sundial and beautiful Armenian script carved on the wall. You'll also find a small chapel here, built in 2002, where you can see the tombs of the tenth-century kings Smbat and Gagik. The thirteenth-century refectory is worth stopping in to admire its beautiful vaulted ceiling.

> ### HIKING IN THE DILIJAN NATIONAL PARK
>
> Exploring the beautiful scenery of the **Dilijan National Park** is likely to be your number one reason for visiting this part of the country. It has some of the best walking infrastructure in Armenia, with a network of well-established trails – some of which are well signposted, while others will require a bit of self-sufficiency and even guesswork. They range from short out-and-back or loop walks to multi-day hikes. One of the latter is a lengthy stretch of the Transcaucasian Trail, an ambitious project which aims ultimately to link Mestia in Georgia's Svaneti region with Agarak right down on Armenia's Iranian border. For more information, check out the website at ⊕ transcaucasiantrail.org/en/home.
>
> Fortunately, to help you make sense of the many hiking options, the staff at Dilijan's tourist information centre are knowledgeable and can supply leaflets and trail plans. From Dilijan centre, they particularly recommend a short 3.5km walk through woodland to the King of the Forest – a tree carved into the figure of a stern looking man, found near the Khanjian Villa. For a longer hike, the 9km trek, starting from the amphitheatre on Myasnikyan Street to the attractive **Parz Lake**, is a good option; once there, you can either return the same way, or take a taxi back to town.

Once you've finished exploring the churches, wander over to the well-tended garden with nice views looking up at the complex and over the valley. There's a small outdoor café here serving coffee, fresh lemonade, and *gata*, a cheese and tarragon pastry which is outstanding: don't leave the monastery without trying it.

If you walk back down the road from the monastery about 200 metres, you'll find a small hillock with a number of impressive khachkars. It's also possible to pick up the 3.5km **Hidden Waterfall** hiking trail from here, just to the right of a wooden hut. Alternatively, if you're a real Haghartsin completist and/or a fan of rusting machinery, you might fancy a stop at the abandoned Soviet cable car station on the way down. It's quite interesting for a very quick snout about.

Goshavank Monastery

Gosh Rd • Free

Built in 1188 by Mkhitar Gosh, a prominent Armenian scholar and priest, **Goshavank** is a pleasant monastery, consisting of two churches and numerous other buildings, including two chapels and a bell tower which also acted as a scriptorium. The complex is best known, however, for the utterly magnificent late-thirteenth-century khachkars, created by a master carver by the name of Poghos, which are regarded as some of the best examples of the craft to be found anywhere in Armenia.

The central church – dedicated to St Astvatsatsin – has its original stone dome, while the bell tower and the church of St Gregory the Illuminator have new glass domes, installed during recent renovations, which give the complex a not unattractive modern veneer. A short walk up to St Gevorg Church, on the small rise opposite the monastery, affords a good view of the complex.

The Transcaucasian Trail passes the monastery. It's clearly marked where to pick it up if you want to hike along it to Gosh Lake, or keep going further on to the village of Khachardzan.

Ijevan

Ijevan – the Armenian word for "caravanserai" – has been a stop on historic trading routes for hundreds of years, but it only coalesced into a town in the early 1800s. The Soviet period saw it becoming an industrial centre, with two major factories for the production of carpets and brandy. The carpet factory closed post-independence, but the brandy factory continues to go strong and is now the main reason tourists visit the town.

Ijevan's town centre features a small sculpture park, which contains blocky statues with paths among shady pine trees. With a little more maintenance it would be a pleasant place to wander, but at present it feels scrappy and uncared for. There are further sculptures on Valansi Street along the riverbank.

Ijevan Wine-Brandy Factory

9 Yerevanian St • Charge • Ⓦ facebook.com/IjevanWineArmenia

Ijevan's main tourist draw, a visit to the **factory** is a fascinating insight into Armenia's wine and brandy industry. Employing 100 to 150 people, depending on the season, the factory produces 1.5 million bottles of brandy and 3 million bottles of wine annually. Tours take approximately 45 minutes and have no set times – the staff will happily show you round whenever you are ready. It's not a slick touristy operation like Yerevan's Ararat Company: here, you'll be looking round the machinery and learning about the manufacture processes, which is genuinely informative and interesting. The price varies depending on how many different drinks you'd like to sample at the end of the tour.

NIKOL PASHINYAN

Ijevan's most famous native son, **Nikol Pashinyan** became prime minister of Armenia on May 8th 2018, after leading the **Velvet Revolution**, sparked when the outgoing president, Serzh Sargsyan, was elected prime minister. Pashinyan's early career as a journalist in the mid- to late-1990s saw him founding the *Oragir* newspaper, which was aligned with the opposition in the 1999 parliamentary elections. The highly critical nature of his articles led to him being prosecuted for defamation in a trial which was considered politically motivated and was widely criticised by human rights groups.

Entering the political arena in the mid-2000s, Pashinyan worked with other liberal Armenian politicians in an effort to tackle corruption and oust President Kocharyan and Sargsyan (prime minister at the time). The 2008 election took Sargsyan to the position of president, but the result was disputed. The opposition candidate, Ter-Petrosyan, claimed to have won. Pashinyan sided with Ter-Petrosyan and helped organise major protests in Yerevan's Republic Square, which were ultimately dispersed by force.

Arrested following the protests, Pashinyan spent the next few years in prison. He was released in 2011 and resumed his political activities, with the goal of removing Sargsyan from office. After the 2013 election, when Sargsyan won again, Pashinyan denounced the vote as rigged. When Sargsyan stepped down as president in 2018 and was elected prime minister several days later, Pashinyan instigated a campaign of civil disobedience which led to Sargsyan's resignation on April 23rd 2018.

Pashinyan was elected **prime minister** on May 8th 2018, and rode the wave of popular support, making efforts to improve conditions for small business owners by lowering taxes, reducing corruption and also to make foreign investment in Armenia attractive. His popularity suffered a downturn following Armenia's defeat in the Second Karabakh War in 2020, particularly due to his Pashinyan's agreement of terms with Azerbaijan in the conflict's aftermath. After political paralysis and frequent street protests, some of which Pashinyan described as a coup attempt, he called a snap election in summer 2021, which he won by a comfortable margin. Azerbaijan's subsequent capture of the remainder of Nagorno-Karabakh in September 2023 led to further protests, but there were no serious attempts to remove Pashinyan, and his position appears secure.

Ijevan History Museum

Yerevanian St • Free

Ijevan Museum, found in a not particularly convenient spot on the main highway between the brandy factory and the town centre, contains an eclectic collection of local archaeological finds and ethnographic exhibits. It's worth a quick stop if you have time to kill.

ARRIVAL AND DEPARTURE

IJEVAN

By bus From the bus stop on Yerevanian Street by the central market, four marshrutkas a day depart to Dilijan, between 8.30am and 5pm, taking 55 minutes. There's also a marshrutka to Yerevan, which leaves at 8.30am (duration 2.5 hours).

By car The road from Dilijan to Ijevan is well-paved and easy to drive, and it's easy to park in the centre of town.

GETTING AROUND AND INFORMATION

Ijevan is quite small, so getting around the centre on foot presents no problems. The Wine-Brandy Factory, however, is about 2km south of the centre along a busy road, so you may want to pick up a taxi for the trip.

There's no tourist information centre in Ijevan. The Dilijan tourist info centre may be able to help with any questions about the area.

ACCOMMODATION

It's probably a better choice to stay over in Dilijan and visit Ijevan from there, but if you do want to overnight here, there are a few places in town, including:

Kamar Hotel 2 Nalbandyan St ☏ 374 93 191200 ⓦ kamar.business.site. The clean and modern rooms are a plus point here; the hugely welcoming hospitality from the owners is another, and the excellent breakfast makes the experience just about perfect. It's about a kilometre north of the centre. ⑤

EATING

★ **PhotoStory Mix Food Tour** May 28 St ⓦ facebook.com/artur.altun.37. Listed online with the unwieldy name of Prestige M Chef Eco Fresh Food, there's nothing awkward about the excellent barbecued meat dishes served up by the friendly owner, Artur. Don't be put off by the uninspiring exterior and the café-like interior: the food is mouth-wateringly good, especially the barbecue chilli pork skewer. ⑤

DIRECTORY

Banks There are plenty of banks with ATMs along Melikbekyan St, and a couple on Valansi St.
Pharmacies You'll find a few pharmacies on Ankakhutian St, as well as one next to the central market.
Post office The post office is at 10 Yerevanian St. It's open Mon–Sat 9am–6pm.

Around Ijevan

The road heading north from Ijevan would be a tempting route to Tbilisi in Georgia, but after the small town of Krivoy Most it passes very close to the Azerbaijani border and at present is best avoided. Before Krivoy Most, though, there are a couple of minor attractions which are worth an explore.

Yell Extreme Park

61 Arajin St, Yenokavan village • Charge • ⓦ yellextremepark.com • No public transport

Roughly 12km out of Ijevan into the Yenoqavan mountains, **Yell Extreme Park** is a great spot for adrenaline junkies: the park contains five zip lines, some of them up to 300 metres above the ground, as well as a rock-climbing route, ropeways, off-road trucking and paintball. For those wanting a slightly less terrifying experience, horseriding trips are also available. Each activity is costed separately, or there's a one day pass available, which includes all activities except paragliding.

Makaravank

Unnamed road, 13km north of Ijevan • Charge • ☎ 374 93 966059 • No public transport

Accessed by a long and beautiful road from the small town of Krivoy Most, **Makaravank Monastery** is a peaceful complex set in attractive woodland with good views over the surrounding countryside. The monastery itself is gorgeous, with fine carvings of animals and birds decorating its exterior walls and above the doorways. In particular, check out the spectacular carvings inside the **Mother of God Church**, which is the building on the right of the complex as you enter the monastery through the main gate.

There are many other extremely pretty monasteries in the hills in this part of the country, but due to the proximity of the Azerbaijan border, it's not recommended to travel north past Makaravank.

Vanadzor

Armenia's third largest city, **Vanadzor** was founded in 1826 by Russian troops needing a base for operations in the Russo-Turkish War. It expanded when the train line between Yerevan and Tbilisi was built in the 1890s, and it was the site of the 1918 Battle of Karakalisa, when Garegin Nzhdeh's Armenian troops defeated a larger Turkish army. This, along with the contemporaneous Battle of Sardarapat (see page 342), preserved the Republic of Armenia's existence.

Today, the centre of Vanadzor has a pleasant, prosperous air, with busy, shop-lined streets. There are no must-see sights in town itself, but it's a nice place to base yourself for trips up the Debed Canyon.

It's worth taking a walk along Grigor Lusavorich Street between Myasnikyan and Mkhitar Gosh Streets, as this is where market stalls are set up with spices and coffee beans; the smell is marvellous.

Vanadzor Fine Arts Museum

52 Tigran Mets Ave • Charge • Ⓦ vanart.org/eng

This curved building in the town centre is home to three floors of works, most of which are by local artists. Modernist works tend to predominate, including some interesting portraits, and there's a range of sculptures on the ground floor.

Chemical Factory Workers' Park

Tigran Mets Ave • Free

In this enticingly named green space you'll find the very grand but now decaying Palace of Culture, an atmospherically derelict amusement park, and also a monument to the Great Patriotic War. None of these are worth a special trip, but if you have time to kill you could do worse.

ARRIVAL AND DEPARTURE

The bus and train stations are next to each other on Kayarani Street. If you're looking for something to do while waiting for transport, you could take a quick walk around the park opposite, which contains a small Russian orthodox church.

By bus Between 8.45am and 7.30pm there are two marshrutkas an hour to Yerevan, taking 2.5 hours. There are also five marshrutkas per day to Dilijan (between 8.30am and 2.30pm, 50 minutes), two to Alaverdi (1.30pm and 3pm, 1.5 hours), one to Stepanavan (1pm, one hour), and four to Gyumri (between 9.30am and 4.30pm, 1.5 hours). There's also a once-daily marshrutka to Tbilisi, leaving at 8.30am and arriving four hours later.

By train Trains running between Yerevan and Tbilisi rumble through every other day. If you're heading to Yerevan it leaves on odd days of the month at 2.25am and takes 4.5 hours; for Tbilisi, it leaves on even days at 1.50am and arrives in Tbilisi at 7.50am. The Yerevan-bound line also calls at Gyumri, arriving at 3.50am.

Even if you're not travelling by train, it's worth looking inside the station to take a look at its magnificent map of the entire USSR's rail network, which occupies an entire wall in all its blocky Soviet glory.

By car At a junction of main roads, Vanadzor is easily accessible by car from Gyumri, Dilijan or Stepanavan. The road from Stepanavan crosses the Bazum mountain range and is quite switchbacky, but it's well-paved and is a great drive. Driving in Vanadzor itself is perhaps a little busier than you may be accustomed to in the rest of Armenia, but it presents no real difficulties.

GETTING AROUND AND INFORMATION

Exploring on foot is the best option within Vanadzor, but taxis are easy to find if you need a trip around town.

Regrettably, Vanadzor's hugely helpful tourist information centre has closed. The official website Ⓦ travellori.am helps to fill the void.

ACCOMMODATION

SEE MAP PAGE 207

Lori Guest House 10 Batumi St Ⓦ facebook.com/LoriGuestHouse2021. A great budget option, Lori Guest House is centrally located and offers accommodation either in private rooms or in dorms. Breakfast is very good, and there's also a restaurant serving decent meals. $$

MagHay B&B 21 Azatamartikner St ☎ 374 91 380305, Ⓔ maghaybb@gmail.com. Centrally located, very clean, with a lovely relaxed garden and wooden veranda to sit on, and offering a fantastic breakfast, *MagHay* is a solid choice. The walls between rooms, however, aren't quite so solid, so light sleepers might want to consider other options. $$

EATING

SEE MAP PAGE 207

Izagri 86 Vardanants St ☎ 374 55 042218. Well-decorated as a traditional tavern, *Izagri* offers a huge range of options, including pizzas, pastas, salads, barbecued meat and Armenian and Georgian standards. The grilled khachapuri is a novel take on the classic Georgian snack, and the pork ojakhuri (stew) is tasty. It's a shame the staff aren't a little friendlier, though. Note that the name is not displayed outside; there's just a sign saying 'kafe'. $$

★ **Sajj Terouh Setté** 24 Tigran Mets Ave ☎ 374 77 249543. Here's a welcome surprise: a super-authentic Lebanese restaurant, run by the lovely Kiki and Natalie, who emigrated to Armenia in 2021. The food, flavoured with proper Lebanese za'atar, is delicious. Whether you go for the fattoush, the chicken taouk wrap, the cheese sambousek pastries, or indeed anything else, you're sure to love it. $$

Tashir Pizza 44 Tigran Mets Ave ☎ 374 32 244401. The Vanadzor branch of this national chain is very popular with locals (and guidebook writers) for its wide-ranging and tasty selection of pizzas (and other options like pasta, burgers, etc, but really, it's all about the pizzas). 𝔰

DIRECTORY

Banks You'll find plenty of banks and ATMs along Tigran Mets Ave and Grigor Lusavorich St.

Hospital Vanadzor Medical Centre (Garegin Nzhdeh St, ☎ 374 322 23658).

Pharmacies There are several pharmacies in town; try Alfa Pharm at 26 Tigran Mets Ave.

Post offices Vanadzor offers a choice of post offices – one on the corner of Tigran Mets Ave and Teryan St, and the other on the corner of Grigor Lusavorich and Mkhitar Gosh sts. They're both open daily 9am–6pm.

Debed Canyon

A trip up the **Debed Canyon** is unquestionably one of Armenia's highlights. This beautiful gorge is home to a wealth of stunning monasteries and churches amid magnificent scenery, as well as the gritty Soviet legacy of derelict factories and machinery lining the riverside, some of which – particularly in the town of Alaverdi – manage to pass right through ugly into mesmerizing. The road leading up the canyon begins to get interesting from the village of Tumanyan, where you'll find the pretty church of Kobayr and see the first examples of the Soviet industrial legacy, and continues with worthy stops for nearly 40km up to the fantastic frescoes in the Akhtala church.

The road along the Debed Canyon is the main route between Yerevan and Tbilisi, so if you're under your own steam travelling between the two countries, it can make a perfect introduction to or farewell from Armenia.

Hovhannes Tumanyan House Museum

Dsegh village • Charge • ⓦ house-museum-of-hovhannes-tumanyan.business.site

One of Armenia's most famed writers, Hovhannes Tumanyan grew up in this building, which now houses a great deal of Tumanyan memorabilia, as well as a selection of ethnographic exhibits. The friendly staff will be able to talk you through the museum.

Kobayr

Kobayr village • Free

The next stop along the canyon is the half-ruined eleventh-century monastery of **Kobayr**. There's a car park (which is signposted with very little notice, so keep your eyes peeled) next to the railway line. From here it's a steep 10 to 15-minute walk up a reasonably well-marked path. Once you reach the top, the church is peaceful and atmospheric, with a fantastic view from the smaller chapel back towards Tumanyan. There are beautiful frescoes in the main chapel, but at time of writing these were partially obscured by scaffolding to aid the ongoing restoration.

You can pick up a short 5km path to **Horomayri Monastery** – which clings dramatically to the canyon walls – from a junction in the path leading up to Kobayr.

Odzun church

Odzun village • Free

A turn-off from the main valley road, about 10km on from Kobayr, will see you ascending the canyon's walls on a good road. Once you've reached the top, the views are beautiful. Keep your eyes open for eagles here – it's a great spot to see them wheeling and swooping over the gorge.

Drive on about 5km and you'll reach the village of Odzun, the centrepiece of which is a pleasing **church** set in peaceful grounds, with views of the beautiful surrounding hills in all directions. The churchyard is full of grave markers and khachkars carved in dark black stone, which provide an attractive contrast to the pink-orange hue of the church.

The church bears the signs of recent restoration, which has been undertaken reasonably sympathetically and will soon fade to a more natural weathered look. The cool light interior has a very tall ceiling, which seems higher than the church appears from outside. There's a large fresco of Mary and Jesus on the wall behind the altar.

The only other structure in the churchyard is a strange edifice reminiscent of the mysterious sixth-century "memorial" in Aghitu near Sisian. The origins of the Odzun memorial are unknown.

Ardvi

Ardvi village • Free

A few kilometres south of Odzun, the village of **Ardvi** is off the main road in a picturesque valley along a 2km dirt road. It's perhaps best suited to Debed Canyon completists, but if you do fancy the trip, the village's pair of tiny churches stand atop a pretty hillock with a small khachkar field opposite. It's particularly gorgeous in spring when the site erupts with wildflowers.

There's an immediately noticeable stratum of dark rock in the valley wall opposite. A local legend has it that this is the petrified remains of an enormous snake that attacked the village and was defeated by St Hohannes.

Alaverdi

Back on the main road, the town of **Alaverdi** was a centre of industry in the Soviet period, and while the principal reason to visit the canyon is of course to see the monasteries, it's also worth a quick stop on one of the town's river bridges to see the incredible – and rather sobering – decaying factories, and spare a thought for the devastating rampant industrialisation wrought here.

At one time the town's old industrial cable cars were available for tourists to ride up to Sanahin Monastery, but at time of writing they were no longer running. There are plans underway to redevelop and reopen them, but there's no projected timescale for this. In the meantime, Alaverdi is the canyon's main town, though it's fairly scrappy. You'll probably only want to stop briefly at one of the cafés to find yourself a snacky lunch.

Sanahin Monastery

Off Mikoyan St, Sanahin • Free

High above town on the edge of the canyon, **Sanahin** is a 15-minute drive from Alaverdi. It was once accessible by cable car, but for now you'll need to go by road. It's worth the drive, though: the monastery is a UNESCO World Heritage Site and is a beautiful, peaceful place with a collection of many attractive churches in close proximity to each other, surrounded by trees in attractive grounds.

Originally established by the ever-busy St Gregory the Illuminator, the current buildings at Sanahin were built under the patronage of Queen Khosrovanush in 966. During the tenth and eleventh centuries, it was an important centre of learning, its school and library being famous across Armenia. The St Astvatsatsin church has a unique rectangular three-nave narthex, and the complex is also renowned for the stunning khachkars on the grounds.

Mikoyan Museum

Mikoyan St, Sanahin • Charge • ☎ 374 25 332574

Local brothers Artem and Anastas Mikoyan achieved considerable success in the mid-twentieth century: Artem was a celebrated aircraft designer, while Anastas was the only Soviet politician who managed to remain in the Politburo from Lenin's administration all the way through to that of Brezhnev. This genuinely interesting museum is dedicated to the lives of the talented pair, featuring exhibits from the lives of the brothers. The section on Anastas' stint as Commissar for Food, and the ongoing impact he had on the USSR's cuisine, is particularly fascinating – he was responsible for the introduction of ice cream and mayonnaise, among much else. Outside, you'll find a Mig-21 plane designed by Artem on display.

You can walk from Sanahin to Haghpat along a 12km hiking trail which comes highly recommended.

Haghpat

Haghpat village • Free

Founded in 976 by Queen Khosrovanush, **Haghpat** is a magnificent set of churches built of black stone atop the canyon walls. The complex includes the St Nshan cathedral, thought to have been built by Tiridates, the Armenian architect who repaired the Hagia Sophia in Constantinople after its dome collapsed in an earthquake in 989. Nshan's gavit is enormous and hugely ornate inside, with beautiful carvings on the walls and at the tops of pillars.

Elsewhere on site, you'll find the small and attractive churches of St Astvatsatsin and St Grigor, and the thirteenth-century Hamazasp chapel – make sure to check out its hugely atmospheric cavernous black stone interior – as well as beautiful intricate khachkars. Like Sanahin, it was a major centre of learning during the medieval period.

Akhtala

Akhtala village • Free

Akhtala appears to be a short squat church of relatively little interest from the outside, though its fortified walls hint at its troubled past. Once inside, however, any thoughts you may have of it being ordinary will soon disappear. The walls are covered in magnificent frescoes which date from around the year 1205 and are justly renowned as Armenia's finest. Even if you're getting monastery fatigue by this stage, don't skip this hugely significant site.

The grass in the churchyard is roped off for safety as there are hidden dangerous drops down into the fortifications below. Outside the complex you'll find a shop selling souvenirs made by disabled and disadvantaged women. Down at the bottom of the village, by the river, is yet more derelict industrial infrastructure, which makes for some fantastic dystopian views.

GETTING AROUND AND INFORMATION | DEBED CANYON

By car If you want to explore the Debed Canyon thoroughly, you're going to need either your own wheels or a hired taxi from Vanadzor for the day; if you want to use a taxi, your accommodation can probably help to arrange this.

By bus Two buses run daily (at 1.30pm and 3pm) from Vanadzor up the canyon. They take 1.5 hours to reach Alaverdi. You could use these to access the sights in the gorge, but it wouldn't be enormously convenient.

Two marshrutkas per day leave Alaverdi for Yerevan, one in the morning (when full) and the other at 1pm.

There's no tourist information centre in the Debed Canyon. Some info can be found on the official website ⓦ travellori.am.

ACCOMMODATION

Accommodation options in the canyon aren't exactly plentiful – though one of Armenia's most upmarket hotels can be found here – so chances are you'll want to visit as a day trip from Vanadzor, or en route to/from Tbilisi.

ApartHotel in Alaverdi 73 Jravazani St ☎374 91 661044. It's nothing fancy, but if you're wanting a convenient and comfortable place to lay down your head in Alaverdi, you could do a lot worse. There's a full range of accommodation on offer here, including single rooms, suites, apartments and mixed dorms. $̲

Avan Dzoraget Hotel M6 from Dzoraget village ⓦ tufenkianheritage.com/en/accommodation/avan-dzoraget-hotel. Part of the Tufenkian chain, this large hotel seeks to impress with its 54 rooms, all sleekly furnished and equipped with lovely Armenian carpets. Those at the front of the hotel have shared balconies with a river view, and there's a good restaurant on the ground floor. Facilities include swimming pool, sauna, massages, and a billiards table. $̲$̲$̲

DIRECTORY

Banks Alaverdi is home to a couple of banks with ATMs - try along Sayat Nova St or Jravazani St.

Hospital Alaverdi Medical Centre (20 Sayat Nova St, ☎374 253 23312).

Pharmacies There's just one pharmacy in Alaverdi, on the corner of Yeritasardakan and Jravazani sts.

Post office Alaverdi's post office is at 2 Khudyakov St, Mon–Sat 9am–6pm.

7 Stepanavan

Initially called Jalaloghli from its foundation in 1810, **Stepanavan** received its new name in 1923 in honour of the Bolshevik revolutionary Stepan Shahumyan. Though Shahumyan himself was born in Tbilisi, his wife came from Stepanavan, and it was here that Shahumyan founded Armenia's first revolutionary Marxist group. The town was a popular tourist destination during the Soviet era, but the 1988 Spitak earthquake did some major damage, from which Stepanavan is only now recovering. It makes for an interesting, if not essential, stop along the road.

Stepan Shahumyan House Museum

4 Nzhdeh St • Charge • ☎374 25 622191

On the central square, you can't miss the bizarre orange building encasing Shahumyan's father-in-law's house like a shell. Ostensibly dedicated to Stepan Shahumyan, the museum takes a wider approach to Stepanavan's history, starting with artefacts such as swords and pots found at Lori Berd, then moving through the founding of the town in the nineteenth century, after which it reaches Shahumyan's activities when he established the first Marxist circle in Armenia. The house – in the centre of the museum – has been preserved as it may have looked in the early twentieth century.

Elsewhere in the museum are photos of Stepanavan in the 1920s, 1960s, 1970s and 1980s, and an area detailing the effects of the 1988 Spitak earthquake on the town, and the subsequent restoration. Upstairs you'll find art of variable quality depicting Shahumyan and his Communist cronies, including a certain Mr V.I. Lenin.

There's a blocky statue of the man himself at the bottom of the main square by the roundabout, flanked by two equally blocky orange stone abstract-shaped columns. On the other side of the river bridge from here is a 2015 monument commemorating the Armenian genocide.

ARRIVAL AND DEPARTURE   STEPANAVAN

By bus From the bus stop by the Shahumyan statue, you can pick up a marshrutka to Yerevan (five daily between 8.30 and 1.30pm), to Gyumri (one daily, 2pm), and to Vanadzor (one daily, 4pm).

By car Stepanavan is at the junction of well-paved roads heading to Dilijan, Vanadzor and Georgia. Driving into town is easy, and there's plenty of parking.

GETTING AROUND AND INFORMATION

The town centre is very small and can be walked in about 10 minutes. If you're based here to visit surrounding attractions, taxis to Lori Berd or the Dendropark can be easily arranged.

Tourist information There's no tourist information centre in town. The staff at the Shahumyan Museum can usually help with minor queries.

Websites ⓦ stepanavan.net is a helpful, if rarely updated, resource if you're looking for accommodation options and information on local attractions. For the wider region, including Stepanavan, ⓦ travellori.am is useful.

ACCOMMODATION

There isn't any particularly compelling reason to stay in Stepanavan since it isn't all that far from the better options available in Vanadzor, Gyumri or Dilijan. However, if you do want to stay the night there are a few options:

Ruzanna's Bed & Breakfast 9 Milion St ☎ 374 93 230320. Ruzanna's Bed & Breakfast offers a couple of rooms with shared bathroom in a cosy family home. The hosts are lovely and friendly, and the breakfast is excellent. $

There are also some 'resort' hotels just out of town on Spandaryan Street, which are quite unappealing due to their out-of-the-way location and oddly ambitious pricing, but they might do at a pinch. *Hotel Nectar* is probably the best of the bunch.

EATING

Carahunge Café 48 Milion St ⓦ facebook.com/ CarahungeStepanavan. Another outlet of the quirky chain also found in Dilijan, this branch has the same rustic wooden charm and wide range of menu options. Thanks to the decent selection of wines and other alcoholic drinks, it's also probably the most happening place in town of an evening. $

Slobodka 44 Milion St ☎ 374 25 621772. This traditional Armenian restaurant comes recommended for its fine barbecued meats, which make up in quality what the place lacks in ambience. $

DIRECTORY

Banks There are a few banks in town, including Ardshinbank and Agricole. They're to be found on the main square.

Around Stepanavan

Stepanavan's immediate environs are home to a few moderately interesting sites, easily visited as a day trip from Stepanavan or as stops en route between Vanadzor and Gyumri.

Lori Berd Fortress

Lori Berd village • Free • No public transport

First built in 1005 by the Armenian Bagratid king David Anhoghin, this **fortress** sits on a promontory of land between two gorges, making it a remarkably defensible position. Perhaps the most important moment in its history came in 1177, when it was a base of operations for Prince Demna and Ivane Orbeli, who were rebelling against Georgia's King George III. It didn't end well – abandoned by their allies, Demna and Orbeli were defeated. In the aftermath Orbeli was executed, and Demna probably wished he was too, instead suffering blinding and castration.

The fortress is beautiful in spring, when it's alive with wildflowers, and it's sweltering hot in summer. The castle retains an impressive length of wall and the views down into the gorges on either side are spectacular. Make sure to explore the site beyond the walls – initially on arrival, it appears there is nothing more, but there are several other ruins, including an orange stone church, as you walk further in.

The road from the village of the same name is rough, but there's a smooth tarmacked car park on arrival, which hopefully signals an intent to asphalt the whole road in future.

If you have your own transport you can take a beautiful (and, crucially, well-paved) road along the Dzoraget river gorge from here to Ardvi and Odzun, and then down into the Debed Canyon, which is a much more enjoyable route than the H24 road via Kurtan, or the long way round via Vanadzor.

Church of St Nicholas Wonder-Worker

Amrakits village • Free • No public transport

The small nineteenth century Russian Orthodox church of St Nicholas Wonder-Worker could be mistaken for a Bavarian fairy-tale cottage, if it weren't for the small but distinctive onion domes on the building's roof. It's an attractive little place that's worth a quick stop if you're self-driving.

Stepanavan Dendropark

Gyulagarak village • Charge • ☎ 374 10 253141 • No public transport

Established in 1931, this arboretum contains pleasantly cool paths to wander, surrounded by evergreen trees and the occasional flower bed. It's not a huge or enormously exciting place but if you want a relaxing venue for an amble away from the hustle and bustle of the cities, it's a good option.

En route you'll see a couple of **ruined churches**. The one in Gyulagarak dates from the nineteenth century. It was used as a grain store in Soviet times and collapsed during the Spitak earthquake, while the one on the road to the Dendropark was constructed in the fifth century and destroyed at an unknown date.

Spitak

Spitak, mid-way between Vanadzor and Gyumri, was founded by the Persians in the sixteenth century and was a prosperous industrial centre under the USSR, but that came to an abrupt end when it found itself at the epicentre of 1988's devastating earthquake. The only particular reason to visit the now largely rebuilt town is to see the **monument**, erected by the Soviets a year or two later, which was clearly once grand but is now showing serious signs of neglect. The staircase up has all but disappeared, with the stone crumbled away and what's left covered in wildflowers and weeds. The monument itself has fared a little better, but this impressive example of Soviet

THE SPITAK EARTHQUAKE

Measuring 6.8 in magnitude, the **earthquake** that hit Spitak on 7th December 1988 was utterly disastrous for the town, which was entirely destroyed, resulting in more than 25,000 lost lives. Other towns, including Gyumri and Stepanavan, also suffered **devastating damage**: Gyumri is still undergoing repair work more than 35 years later.

International aid was immediately offered, including official help from the USA, France, West Germany and Japan, and private donations from the Armenian diaspora all over the world. There were also contributions from non-governmental organisations, such as the British music industry, which produced a Rock Aid Armenia single and album. In all, 113 countries contributed up to $500 million in aid.

In the immediate aftermath, a lack of medical expertise and an abundance of red tape led to a bungled response - for example, one American health care company was delayed in starting their assistance programme for four days while they awaited visas. The USSR's leader, Mikhail Gorbachev, cut short a visit to the USA to go to Armenia and set aside 5 billion roubles for the recovery effort. His trip – the only one he made to the Caucasus during his premiership – was somewhat marred when he got into a verbal spat over the brewing Nagorno-Karabakh issue during his visit to Yerevan.

The collapse of the Soviet Union, and the outbreak of the Karabakh war, hardly helped the reconstruction process, but Spitak has now been rebuilt. However, it took nearly 27 years for everyone made homeless by the earthquakes to be rehoused, and the town's economy remains stagnant, with high unemployment, due to the loss of much of its industry.

architecture remains unvisited and unloved by locals, whose advice is often that you should visit the memorial in Yerevan instead.

Note that it's not easy to find the start of the staircase to the monument. From the centre of town, head up Avetisyan Street for about 1.5 kilometres, and when you see a small red petrol garage called A&V, take the next right. Walk around a red prefab structure and you'll see the remains of the beginning of the staircase.

Gyumri

Armenia's second largest city, **Gyumri** has enjoyed a variety of different names since its establishment as Kumayri, possibly as long ago as the eighth century BC. Conquered by the Arabs in the mid-seventh century, it became a centre of Armenian resistance and, after independence, enjoyed the fruits of its proximity to the capital of Ani. However, this period didn't last long, and Kumayri was conquered by a bewildering succession of Byzantines, Turks, Mongols, Persians and finally Russians, under whom its name was changed to Alexandropol. Subsequently, it became Leninakan during the Soviet era, during which it was a major industrial centre before being hit heavily by the Spitak earthquake in 1988. Post-independence, it was renamed Gyumri, a modernized version of its original name.

Visiting this pleasant city today, you'll find that reconstruction following the earthquake is still ongoing. The centre is now mostly very smart, but just a few blocks away in any direction you'll find uneven and unpaved roads. Abovyan Street is a good

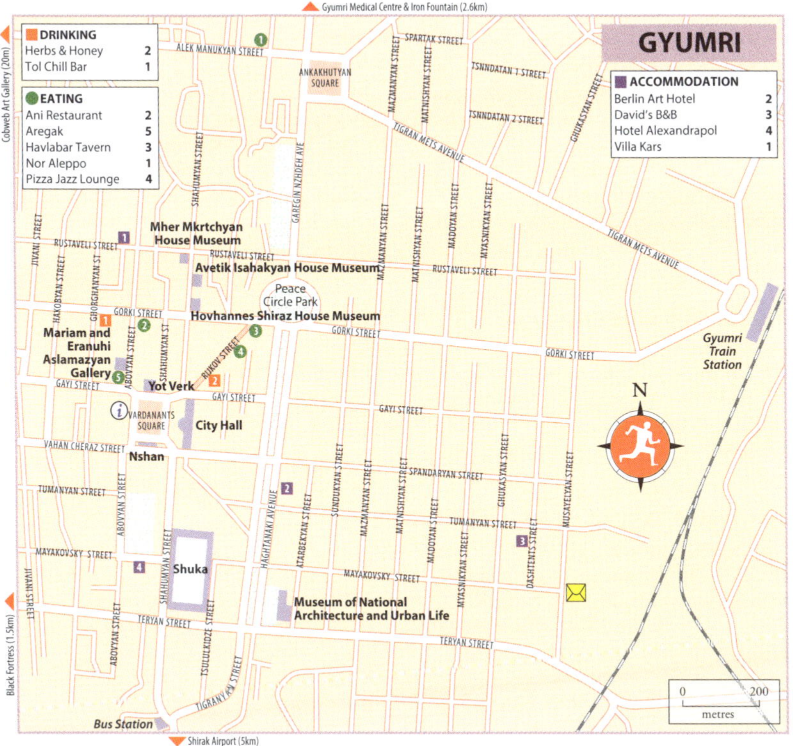

place to see the effects of the earthquake: plenty of original stone houses still stand, but there are large gaps and obvious reconstruction work in progress.

Gyumri is home to a number of interesting museums, but before visiting them, it's worth taking a wander around the small and friendly centre. Start in the **Peace Circle Park**, which hosts a small amusement park and is busy with families on summer evenings, then head southwest down **Rijkov Street**, a pedestrianized avenue lined with small cafés and shops. There are no sights in particular – unless taking a look at the outside of the home of Armenia's first prime minister, Hovhannes Kajaznuni, floats your boat – but it's a pleasant street which leads down to **Vardanants Square**.

Here you'll find attractive fountains and a **memorial statue** to the Battle of Avarayr, a conflict fought between Armenian and Persian armies in the year 451, considered one of the first battles in defence of the Christian faith. The grand **City Hall**, on the square's east side, dates from 1933. You'll also see a pair of churches on opposite sides of the square. To the north, **Yot Verk** is a large black stone building dating from 1873, with a modern interior featuring a sweeping wooden balcony at the back and a bright blue iconostasis at the front. On the south side, meanwhile, is **Nshan**, a striking red edifice, which has been reconstructed following its collapse in the earthquake. The original dome sits in the square south of the church, along with a **memorial** to the earthquake's victims.

You should also make a point of wandering through the **Shuka** (open air food market) on Mayakovsky and Tsululkidze streets, which is a treat for the senses, the vast array of fruit, spices and coffee beans creating an intoxicating cocktail of scents. It feels less Caucasian and more like a Middle Eastern souk.

Mariam and Eranuhi Aslamazyan Gallery

242 Abovyan St • Charge • ☎ 374 31 248205

Sisters **Mariam and Eranuhi Aslamazyan** were artists in the Soviet period who travelled extensively, and their work reflects their experiences in places as diverse as Japan and Cameroon. Generally speaking, the upstairs gallery of Mariam's work is more colourful with tangible enthusiasm for the outside world, while the gallery downstairs, featuring mostly Erahuni's art, suggests a more introspective outlook, with muted colours predominating. Also on display here is a terracotta warrior presented by the city of Xian.

Hovhannes Shiraz House Museum

Gorki St • Charge • ☎ 374 31 255142

This **museum** is dedicated to the Gyumri-born Hovhannes Karapetyan, who used the pen name Shiraz for his patriotic poetry. It's a decent enough place to see some traditional furniture and photos of old Gyumri, but it's of limited interest if you're not a Shiraz fan.

Avetik Isahakyan House Museum

91 Shahumyan St • Charge • ☎ 374 98 300482

Avetik Isahakyan was an Armenian patriot, writer and intellectual who was profoundly affected by the Armenian Genocide. His works reflect his experiences, and he was connected with the 1921 assassination of Talaat Pasha, one of the principal architects of the massacres. The **museum** is a great place to learn about him, as well as to see a traditional house and furnishings. The staff are extremely enthusiastic and knowledgeable on all things Isahakyan.

Mher Mkrtchyan House Museum

30 Rustaveli St • Charge • ☎ 374 31 255174

In the third in Gyumri's little collection of house museums, you'll find memorabilia from the career of Mher Mkrtchyan, one of Armenia's most successful comedic film actors during the Soviet years. Even if you're not familiar with his filmography, the enthusiasm of the staff is infectious.

Cobweb Art Gallery

97 10 26 Komisarner St • Free • Ⓦ cobweb-art-gallery.business.site

Here's a unique place – in this small **art gallery**, all the works are created from cobwebs. The award-winning pieces are extremely impressive, and the artist – Andranik Avetisyan – is often on hand to tell you about his fascinating process. The only problem is that it's a little hard to shake the disturbing thought that there must be an awful lot of spiders around somewhere.

Museum of National Architecture and Urban Life

47 Haghtanaki Ave • Charge • ☎ 374 31 253600

The best exhibit in this not enormously enthralling museum is an impressively detailed model of Gyumri as it was in 1910. Otherwise, you'll find old photos and plans of the town, as well as the tools of various trades such as blacksmith, copper workers and hat makers. The second building is a little more interesting than the first, with its rooms dressed up in the traditional style of both local craftsmen and more moneyed townspeople. There's also a small section devoted to local sculptor Sergey Merkurov, who found fame in the USSR years and produced death masks for many of the period's prominent figures, including Lenin, Tolstoy and Tumanyan.

Black Fortress

Off Kars Highway • Free

On the western edge of town is a slightly scrappy park, the centrepiece of which is a staircase leading up the hill to a monolithic **Mother Armenia statue**. At the top, turn right and follow the ridge along to the imposing circular **Black Fortress**, which was built by the Russians in the nineteenth century. It's now sometimes used to host events, but when it's not in use you can have a wander inside, though it's more impressive from the outside.

The Iron Fountain

Manushyan St • Free

Fans of Soviet avant-garde sculpture shouldn't miss this fantastic beast, which resembles nothing quite so much as a spiky UFO descending to Earth. Stood in a scrubby and slightly derelict park about 4km north of Vardanants Square, it's a perfect place to shoot the cover art for your next dystopian death metal concept album.

ARRIVAL AND DEPARTURE   GYUMRI

By bus The bus station is to the south of town, at the lower end of Shahumyan Street, and it's a bit of a chaotic place. Marshrutkas leave regularly to Yerevan (from 8.30am, departing when full, duration 2.5 hours); there are five daily departures to Vanadzor between 10am and 4pm (one hour). Shared taxis also hover around the bus station, costing much the same as marshrutkas but offering a higher degree of comfort.

Gyumri is relatively close to the Georgian border, and you can pick up marshrutkas from here to Tbilisi (one daily, 10.30am, five hours) or Akhaltsikhe (one daily, 10.30am, four hours). Even closer is the Turkish border, which has been closed since the 1990s. In 2022, reports began to surface suggesting the crossing would be reopened for third-party nationals; if this comes to pass, Gyumri will be a very convenient entry/exit point to Armenia, being just over an hour's drive from the city of Kars.

By train Gyumri's train station can be found east of the centre, at the end of Tigran Mets Avenue. If you're a Soviet architecture fan, it's almost worth a visit in itself: it's a very fine monolithic building. There are three daily departures to Yerevan (three hours) with an additional faster service at weekends (two hours), as well as the Yerevan-Tbilisi service that goes through on even days of the month, departing at 12.25am and arriving in Tbilisi at 7.50am. You could also take the Tbilisi-bound service to reach Vanadzor, though you'll be arriving at the inconvenient time of 1.50am.

By car Driving into Gyumri is easy enough – all roads in this part of the country lead here – but be aware there are a lot of unpaved roads here, a legacy of the 1988 earthquake, and are often closed for upgrading. Parking is easy, and finding your way around isn't a major challenge.

By plane Gyumri's Shirak Airport is the second largest airport in the country, but that doesn't mean there are lots of flights: at time of writing, it only offers flights to Moscow with the Russian airline Pobeda. Pre-pandemic, Ryanair briefly operated routes to Gyumri from Athens and Memmingen, but these show no signs of resuming.
The airport is about 5km south of the town centre; take bus number 1 from the corner of Tigranyan and Teryan streets.

INFORMATION

Tourist Information Centre 1 Vardanants Sq, ☎ 374 55 591553. The staff here are very enthusiastic and keen to help, but not always enormously knowledgeable. They can, however, give advice on the various museums in town and arrange tours, both of the city and the surrounding area, including a cycling trip to the Trchkan Falls. Daily 10am–7pm.

Websites Gyumri's official tourism website, ⓦ travelgyumri.com, is a handy guide to the city, with information on its various attractions.

Listings There's usually something going on in Gyumri, but frustratingly there's no dedicated website to tell you what (except the Events section on the tourist site at ⓦ travelgyumri.com/meet-gyumri/news-and-events, which isn't kept up to date). The best way to get a view on upcoming events is to Google "Gyumri events", which will bring up a list of possibilities.

GETTING AROUND

By bus Gyumri has a decent local bus network. You'll probably find number 1 the most useful, which plies the city from the airport in the south all the way through the centre to the Ani district in the north.

By taxi There are plenty of taxis in Gyumri, should you need one; trips round town are affordable.

By foot Gyumri is small enough to explore thoroughly on foot; you're likely to be sticking in the city centre around Vardanants Square for the most part. There are several pedestrianised streets in the centre which make wandering pleasant.

ACCOMMODATION　　　　　　　　　　　　　SEE MAP PAGE 215

Berlin Art Hotel 25 Haghtanaki Ave ⓦ berlinarthotel. am. Housed in a wing of a hospital built by German aid workers for earthquake relief, the *Art Hotel* has 20 clean en-suite rooms, each of which lives up to the 'art' part of the name by featuring paintings by Gyumri-based artists. The staff can help arrange tours of the surrounding region. $$

David's B&B 94 Dashtents St ☎ 374 98 647053, ⓔ davitkyasinyan@mail.ru. They're not flashy, but the rooms at *David's B&B* are clean and comfortable, and the hospitality of David and his wife Arusik is a step above. The breakfast is excellent too, and if they're doing evening meals it's worth taking them up on it. To top it off, it's not at all far from the centre, making this by far the best budget option in town. $

Hotel Alexandrapol 70 Mayakovsky St ☎ 374 31 250051. Leave your sense of subtlety at the door and prepare to live it up like an oligarch at the excessively bling *Alexandrapol*. Just walking into the entrance lobby is an affront to good taste. There are 20 rooms, including a presidential suite; it's hard to imagine what this might look like given the ridiculous opulence of the standard rooms. $$

Villa Kars Corner of Rustaveli and Abovyan Sts ⓦ armenianvillas.com/en/hotels/villa-kars.html. This beautifully converted old mansion, built of classic black Gyumri stone, is home to an impressive boutique hotel. The room evokes the early twentieth century, and are decorated with gorgeous antique furniture. The only downside is it can be a little noisy. $$$

EATING　　　　　　　　　　　　　　　　　SEE MAP PAGE 215

Ani Restaurant 133 Abovyan St ⓦ facebook.com/ ani.restaurant.gyumri. Probably the best place in town for traditional Armenian dishes, *Ani* is all wood and rustic charm inside. The English menu is well translated except for the rather ominous dish called 'surprise' and offers no further clues. $$

Aregak 242 Abovyan St ⓦ aregakbakeryandcafe. weebly.com. This bakery and café, opened in 2018, prides itself on being a disability-inclusive employer. What's more, the coffee and pastries are very good, and the café itself is very welcoming. $

Havlabar Tavern 58 Gorki St ☎374 93 901133. *Havlabar* is one of the best places in Armenia to get properly authentic Georgian cuisine. All the highlights of Georgia's menus are here – khachapuri, khinkali, chakhobili, lobio, and much more – and there's also a good number of Georgian wines available. $$

★ **Nor Aleppo** 1 Alek Manukyan St ⓦfacebook. com/noralepporestaurant. *Nor Aleppo* is an absolutely outstanding Syrian restaurant run by the friendly and welcoming Shant. The menu is well stocked with Levantine dishes and mezzes, many of which are close to Armenian cuisine but different enough to make a welcome change. The borek, the hummus with sujuk, and the barbecued chicken are particularly recommended. $$

Pizza Jazz Lounge 3 Rijkov St ⓦtinyurl.com/2bnpprup. It won't be winning any Michelin stars, but this chilled place with red sofas and, predictably, a jazz soundtrack outside on the pedestrianised Rijkov Street serves decent pizzas and is a good spot to watch the world – or at least Gyumri – go by. $$

DRINKING
SEE MAP PAGE 215

Herbs & Honey 5 Rijkov St ⓦfacebook.com/herbsandhoney.am. One of Gyumri's more hipster spots, *Herbs & Honey* is a friendly café offering a wide selection of teas, good coffee, and tasty cakes. Pancakes are sometimes on the menu too.

Tol Chill Bar 22 Shiraz St ☎374 77 350130. A very small bar in a lovely atmospheric Gyumri black stone cellar, *Tol Chill* is a welcoming spot for a beer or great cocktails, and meeting locals. The soundtrack appears to have got stuck on early 2000s nu-metal, but that somehow adds to the charm.

DIRECTORY

Banks It's not hard to find an ATM in Gyumri. Vardanants Square is a good place to look, but there are plenty of others around town.

Hospital Gyumri Medical Centre (3 Garegin Nzhdeh Avenue, ☎374 312 30311, ⓦgyumrimc.am/eng/index.html).

Pharmacies Outlets of Natali Pharm and Alfa Pharm can be found all over town; try on Rijkov St or along Sayat Nova Ave.

Post office Gyumri's main post office is at 4 Rijkov Street, open Mon–Fri 9am–6pm, Sat to 3pm.

Around Gyumri

If you've got time to spare, consider basing yourself in Gyumri and taking a few outings: the trip to the Trchkan waterfall is enjoyable, and the nearby Marmashen and Harichavank monasteries are both beautiful.

Marmashen Monastery

Marmashen Monastery Rd, Vahramaberd village • Free • No public transport

An attractive monastery in a pleasant setting by the Akhuryan river near the Turkish border, **Marmashen** is only about 12km from Gyumri. The five red-orange coloured churches here (three of which are mostly in ruins) date back to the tenth century and have suffered destruction or damage a number of times during Turkish and Mongol incursions. It's a peaceful place, well worth a visit from Gyumri. If you're driving, pass through the village of Marmashen and take the signposted turn-off at Vahramaberd. From here it's an unpaved, but manageable, drive downhill.

Trchkan waterfall

From Dzorashen village • Free • No public transport

About midway between Gyumri and Spitak, **Trchkan** – which translates as "jumping", after the trout that apparently jump the falls as they make their way upstream to spawn – is the tallest waterfall in Armenia, at 23 metres. In 2011, a proposed hydroelectric plant put the falls at risk, but coordinated environmental protesters saved the site, and it's now a designated protected place. It's not easy to reach though: the road is very bad, and you'll need a 4WD if you're self-driving. You can also arrange an organised trip through the Gyumri tourist office.

Harichavank Monastery

Harich village • Free • Marshrutka from Gyumri

Some 30km south of Gyumri, the red orange stone monastery of **Harichavank** is in a fantastic setting, on the edge of a small canyon surrounded by rolling green hills, and the peaks of Mount Aragats just peeping out behind. It's an utterly gorgeous complex, boasting some magnificent intricate carving.

A particularly noteworthy feature is the small carved church perched on top of the roof of the main monastery, and don't miss the outstanding stonework on the ceiling of the gavit of the St Astvatsatsin church. If you arrive in mid-afternoon on a sunny day, the St Astvatsatsin chapel is beautifully illuminated by a shaft of sunlight shining through the window. The complex was an important medieval centre of learning, experiencing its heyday in the thirteenth century but enjoying a revival in the nineteenth century. It's still an active monastery today.

It's not the easiest place in the world to get to on public transport, but there are marshrutkas from Gyumri that come through the nearby town of Artik. If you're self-driving, it's an easy and pleasant trip.

7

South Armenia

ORBELIAN'S CARAVANSERAI

South Armenia

The three provinces of Ararat, Vayots Dzor and Syunik, covering the mountainous regions to the east and south of Yerevan, are home to some of Armenia's top sights. Many of the country's most important historical sites can be found here, from beautiful monasteries to mysterious ancient petroglyphs, and the area is also Armenia's wine-making heartland. If all that isn't enough, the scenery is often spectacular. Add friendly and welcoming people to the mix, and it's easy to see that this corner of the country shouldn't be missed.

The H8 highway runs from Yerevan through **Ararat**, **Vayots Dzor** and **Syunik** provinces down to the Iranian border at Meghri, offering easy access to many of Armenia's top cultural sights. First of these – an easy day-trip from Yerevan – is the important monastery of **Khor Virap**, overlooked by the mighty Mount Ararat just across the border in Turkey.

The road then heads through the wine country of **Areni**, after which the scenery becomes more rugged as it crosses mountain passes to the regional hubs of **Yeghegnadzor** and **Sisian**. Neither of these are must-see locations but both are sensible bases for several top sights, including **Shaki waterfall**, the seven thousand year-old **petroglyphs at Ughtasar** and the mysterious stone circle of **Zorets Karer**, which has been compared – perhaps extravagantly – to Stonehenge.

Further along the road, the small town of **Goris** is a pleasant place to stop for a night or two, with the magnificent monastery of **Tatev** in easy reach to the west, and the troglodyte city of **Khndzoresk** to the east. You'll probably only venture to **Kapan** and the deep south if you're journeying to Iran, but it's not an unpleasant town to spend time in.

It's easiest to explore the area with your own transport, and harder with public transport, but if you do get your head around the marshrutkas this will give you a good opportunity to interact with locals. Alternatively, as it's probably Armenia's most visited region, you'll find plenty of tour companies operating out of Yerevan offering trips to the area. Many of these will be day trips, but these can feel rushed, and you'll get more out of your visit if you can spend longer. However you get around, you're likely to find this area to be a highlight of your trip to the Caucasus.

Ararat Province

Despite the evocative biblical name, **Ararat Province** has few specific sights to attract the visitor – with the sole exception of one of Armenia's big hitters, the monastery of Khor Virap – but the province is hugely important to the Armenian sense of self. Mount Ararat itself may be across the border in Turkey, but it is regarded by Armenians as a crucial piece of their identity: it's at the heart of the longed-for historical territory of Greater Armenia, and is at the centre of Armenia's coat of arms.

Artashat

Artashat is the principal town of Ararat Province, but was only founded in 1945 and offers little to distract the visitor. If you're under your own steam, you could check out the scant remains of the nearby ancient cities of **Dvin** and **Artaxata** (both of which are former Armenian capitals). Given Artashat's proximity to Yerevan and Yeghegnadzor there seems little reason to stay here overnight, especially given the rather limited accommodation available in town.

Highlights

❶ **Noravank** A stunningly beautiful medieval monastery in a red rock canyon, particularly gorgeous at sunset. See page 228

❷ **Orbelian caravanserai** One of the best-preserved Silk Road overnight stops to be found anywhere, it's almost possible to imagine medieval merchants still frequenting this atmospheric caravanserai. See page 230

❸ **Jermuk** A Soviet spa resort, Jermuk is blessed with a beautiful waterfall. While you're in town make sure to sample the bizarre warm, salty mineral water. See page 231

❹ **Zorets Karer** The 'Stonehenge of Armenia', this stone circle sits on a high plateau above Sisian town. See page 235

❺ **Ughtasar petroglyphs** Almost seven thousand years ago, ancient people recorded their lives on the rocks around this lonely lake. See page 235

❻ **Wings of Tatev** Armenia has many magnificent monasteries, but no others can be approached on a 5.5km cable car across an enormous valley. See page 236

HIGHLIGHTS ARE MARKED ON THE MAP ON PAGE 226

Khor Virap

H11 road, Pokr Vedi village • Free entry, parking charge • ☎ 374 93 533685 • Bus 467

About 10 kilometres from Artashat, perched on a small rocky outcrop in a largely barren landscape, **Khor Virap** – meaning "deep pit" – is not only one of the most important monasteries in Armenia, but a hugely significant site to the entire history of Christianity. If you're lucky enough to be there on a clear day, seeing the monastery with the enormous Mount Ararat as the backdrop will take your breath away.

St Gregory the Illuminator was imprisoned here in the eponymous deep pit for thirteen years by King Tiridates III for his efforts in preaching Christianity. He was only released after curing Tiridates of a bout of divine-inflicted insanity, which inspired Tiridates to adopt Christianity as the Armenian state religion in the year 301 AD – the first country in the world to do so.

The monastery now consists of a walled complex, including the central St Astvatsatsin church and the Nerses chapel, where you can descend by a devilishly steep ladder into Gregory's 6-metre-deep pit. The pit contains an icon of Gregory himself and is an important pilgrimage site. The initial few steps down the ladder are very narrow but it soon widens out.

For an overview of the monastery, before entering by the main gate, follow the walls around the complex to your right and take the short route up to the crosses on the

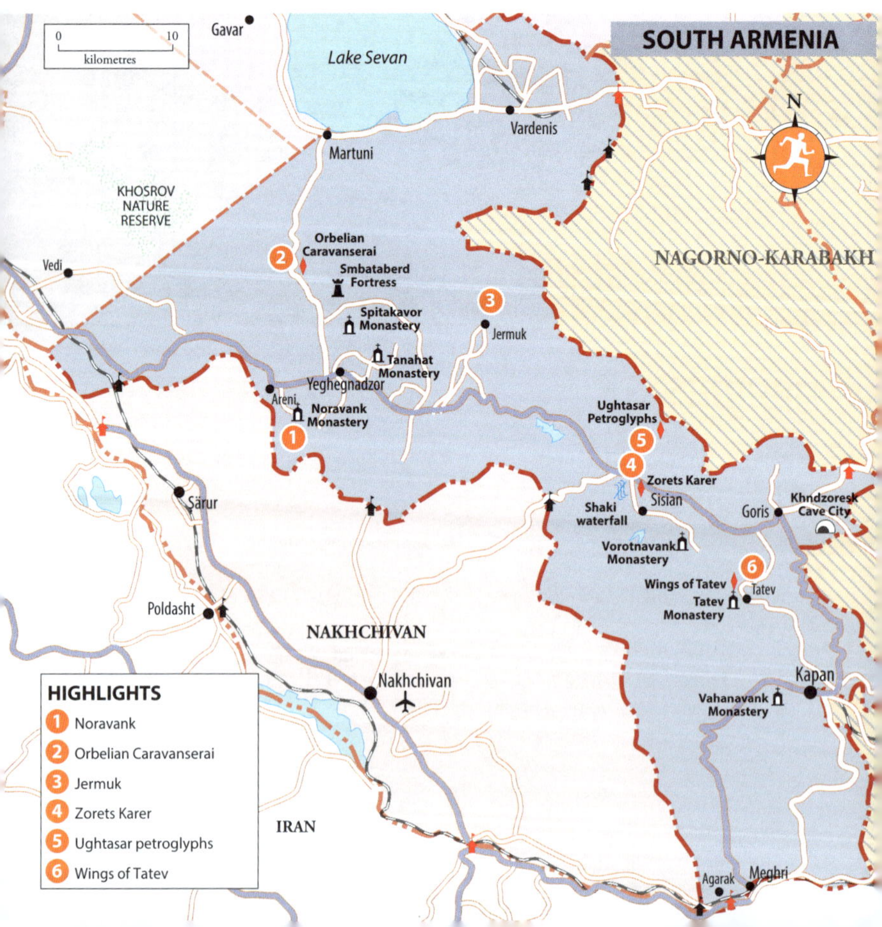

> ## MOUNT ARARAT
>
> *"No one can take Ararat from us – we keep it in our hearts."*
> The twin-peaked **Mount Ararat** is a truly iconic sight. Standing alone in the flat plains surrounded by Armenia, Turkey and Iran, the taller peak, at 5,896 metres, is the highest mountain in Turkey, and arguably the third highest in Europe. Both peaks are covered year-round in snow, and the mountain towers over Yerevan and can be seen along much of Armenia's southern road – when the summit isn't draped in clouds.
>
> That it's steeped in biblical associations as well as being gorgeous simply adds to its appeal. It's long been associated with the point at which Noah's Ark landed when the flood waters began to recede, and many expeditions to find the Ark's remains have taken place – all without success. Even if you're not looking for the Ark, it's still possible to climb it from Doğubayazıt in Turkey, though it's not an easy ascent.
>
> For Armenians, the mountain – though now outside the country's borders following the Turko-Armenian War of 1920 – is considered the national symbol. It sat at the centre of the ancient kingdom of Greater Armenia, and many Armenians dream of recovering the lands around the mountain in Turkey, which were home to sizeable ethnic Armenian populations prior to the 1915 Genocide. For now, Armenians must satisfy themselves by visiting Turkey to climb Ararat, and planting their flag on the summit.

small hill. The path starts well but becomes a bit of a scramble. If you're lucky and Ararat is visible, the best spot for photos is from the road before you reach the car park. The best time to visit is about 8am: Ararat is more likely to be visible, and there will be fewer tourists.

Bus number 467 from Yerevan will bring you within walking distance of Khor Virap. Take the metro down to Gortsaranayin station and pick up the bus from the nearby Labour Square roundabout. The journey takes approximately 45 minutes. Let the driver know where you want to get off and you'll be alerted at the right spot. Alternatively, it's easy to arrange a taxi from Yerevan, and you can request they wait for you while you visit.

Vayots Dzor Province

Vayots Dzor is home to much of Armenia's wine industry, as well as some of its most impressive and varied historical sites, including the Silk Road caravanserai in the Vardenis mountains and the beautiful Noravank monastery.

Areni and around

The village of **Areni** is known for two things – archaeology and wine. These two subjects run close together – there's an ancient winery that was discovered in the Areni-1 cave, but you'll probably prefer to sample the vintages available in the more modern wineries in the area.

Areni Wine Factory

Areni village • Charge • 374 94 424427

The **Wine Factory** offers tasting tours, involving explanations of the wine-making process, followed by a sampling of three wines. Inevitably, you then get the opportunity to buy, but since the wines are very good, this isn't too much of a hardship.

Areni-1 cave

Areni village • Charge • arenicave.am/en

Archaeologists exploring in this unassuming cave have found two extraordinary things – the world's oldest winery (consisting of a press, fermentation vats, and storage jars dating to 4000 BC) and the world's oldest shoe (dating to 3500 BC). The shoe is now on display at Yerevan's History Museum, but the winery is still in situ inside the cave: join a guided tour to see it, and various other fascinating remains.

Noravank

Noravank Monastery Road • Free entry, parking charge, museum charge

Founded in 1105 by Bishop Hovhannes of Syunik, **Noravank** is one of Armenia's most beautiful monasteries. Set in a red rock gorge, the churches of the complex are built of pink-orange stone which glows golden at sunset. There are two main churches on site, both of which merit exploration.

The St Astvatsatsin church – also known as the Burtelshen church after Prince Burtel who dedicated it in 1339 – in the centre of the courtyard is a beautifully elegant construction, which is undoubtedly one of the most attractive churches in the country. A very narrow exterior staircase leads to the upper floor, but access to this is now restricted. This church is more impressive from the outside, the interior on both floors being quite bare.

At the rear of the complex, the St John the Baptist church and attached gavit are bedecked inside and out with outstandingly beautiful khachkars and other carvings. The images above the gavit's door, depicting God giving life to Adam, are remarkable. Inside, look out for the image of an Orbelian prince having a difference of opinion with a lion on the wall, and the elongated and simpering lion on the floor.

For dedicated holy pit enthusiasts there's another example of the genre here, but if you've already visited Gregory's dungeon at Khor Virap, you'll probably want to skip this one, as it offers little more than the chance to climb down a ladder into a dank cave.

There's a museum on site, which isn't of much interest other than to check out the photos of the extremely ruined monastery complex pre-restoration. You'll also find a souvenir shop and a decent restaurant which offers good local wine alongside the Armenian cuisine. It's pleasingly quiet in the evenings (from 6pm onwards) as most tourists are on their way back to Yerevan by this time.

The road through the canyon to Noravank, as well as being a very scenic drive, is recognised as being an Important Bird Area, home to endangered birds, a huge colony of bats, and – allegedly – a Caucasian leopard.

ARRIVAL AND DEPARTURE

By bus To get to Areni on public transport pick up a Vayk-bound marshrutka from Yerevan's Labour Square and ask to be let off at Areni. The journey should take about 2 hours 15 minutes. Note that it's harder to pick up a marshrutka from here as they're usually already full.

By car Taking a taxi from Yeghegnadzor to cover visits to Areni's sights is easy to organise. Self-driving poses no problems.

ACCOMMODATION

ARENI AND AROUND

Areni has a smattering of good guesthouses, which are ideal places to stay if you wish to visit Noravank monastery late in the day, or enjoy the possibilities presented by being in the heart of the wine country.

LiViTi Areni Village ☎ 374 93 491999. Very welcoming guesthouse with a couple of rooms, all with private bathroom. The evening meals are excellent, as are the homemade wines and vodka. $$

Yeghegnadzor

Yeghegnadzor is the main town of Vayots Dzor province, and while it's not a must-see destination, it's a good place to base yourself for a day or two to explore the surrounding area. There are a couple of sights in town, however, which it's worth taking the time to investigate.

Vayots Dzor Museum

4 Shahumyan St • Charge • Ⓦ yeghegnadzor-regional-museum.business.site

This well-maintained little museum contains three rooms, covering archaeological finds from local sites and ethnographic exhibits from the nineteenth and early twentieth centuries. The archaeology room is particularly fascinating, the highlights being a thirteenth-century stone model of Tanahat church and a small Roman altar.

Old Bridge Winery

1 Yerevanyan Highway, Yeghegnadzor • Charge • Ⓦ oldbridgewinery.com • No public transport, best reached by taxi from Yeghegnadzor

Named after, well, the old bridge in the valley below Yeghegnadzor – which Marco Polo is alleged to have used on his epic travels – this pleasant **winery** offers two packages of wine tasting: standard and deluxe. The difference comes in the food served with the wine. Standard has cheese, olives and tomatoes, while deluxe has all this and three types of sausage too. But really, it's all about the wine tasting, which involves three dry reds and one dry white. The Old Bridge wines have won Europe-wide awards, and the tasting session is a great introduction to Armenia's excellent wine industry.

ARRIVAL AND DEPARTURE
YEGHEGNADZOR

By bus Marshrutkas to Yerevan leave roughly every hour between 9.30am and 6pm; the journey takes 2.5 hours. Other services include to Goris (one daily, 11.35am), Jermuk (twice daily, 3.35pm and 6.35pm). If you're going to Sisian, take the Goris marshrutka and ask the driver to let you off at Sisian.

By car Yeghegnadzor is on the main Yerevan-Goris road, which is generally well-surfaced and easy to drive. If coming from Yerevan, the turn to the town centre is to your left just as you come up a slight hill and may take you by surprise.

ACCOMMODATION
SEE MAP PAGE 229

B&B Hasmik 28 Spandaryan St ☎ 374 77 979707. *Hasmik* is a very good choice of guesthouse: the hosts are welcoming, the garden is beautiful and the rooms are small but homely. It's also possible to get an excellent evening meal here. There's no sign outside, just open the garage door and head through to the garden. $$

Nataly Guest House 3 Israyel Ori Alley Ⓦ nataly-guest-house.business.site. This lovely guesthouse on the edge of town boasts homely rooms, a pretty garden and friendly hosts who can help to arrange sightseeing in the area. Make sure to have dinner here: it's delicious. $$

Old Bridge B&B 16 Levonyan St

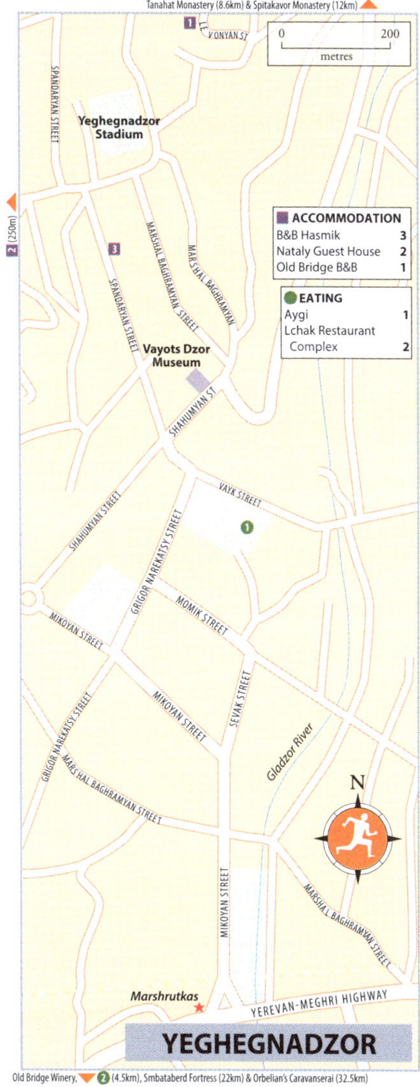

8

ⓦoldbridgewinery.com. The *Old Bridge* gets rave reviews from travellers who love the great views from its top-of-the-town location, the welcoming atmosphere and of course the dinner, which comes with wine from the associated winery. They also arrange wine tastings (see page 229). $\overline{\$\$}$

EATING

SEE MAP PAGE 229

You won't exactly be spoiled for choice when it comes to eating in Yeghegnadzor. If you're staying at a guesthouse, your host will almost certainly offer dinner – it's recommended you take this opportunity, as the home-cooked food is likely to be delicious.

Aygi 1 Momik St ⓦtinyurl.com/yc4dfcum. The best – and pretty much only – place to eat out in Yeghegnadzor town centre, Aygi is a simple and popular place offering decent pizzas. Nothing special, but reliable and reasonably priced. $\overline{\$\$}$

Lchak Restaurant Complex Yerevan Highway, 5km west of Yeghegnadzor ☎374 94 998355. A pleasant lakeside venue with private huts built into the water for groups of up to six to dine in. The menu is very extensive and barbecue-focussed, and the food is tasty and arrives in good time. Do note that on summer evenings the mosquitoes may get as much of a meal as you do. You'll need a taxi from the centre. $\overline{\$\$}$

Around Yeghegnadzor

A clutch of fascinating sights can be found on or near the M10 road, which heads north from **Yeghegnadzor** to cross the Vardanyets mountain pass heading towards Lake Sevan. The main road is bendy but well-paved and easy to drive. Bear in mind that it is only possible to cross the pass in summer months due to snowfall in winter.

Tanahat Monastery

H47 • Free • No public transport

Head out of Yeghegnadzor on the H47 road and you'll find **Tanahat Monastery**, a black stone monastery on a pretty, if rugged, mountain slope. It's not enormously noteworthy but is potentially the site of the famous Gladzor University, which – along with Tatev – was one of Armenia's principal medieval centres of learning. The monastery is now rarely visited so you'll probably have the place to yourself.

Spitakavor Monastery

Spitakavor Monastery Rd • Free • No public transport

About 10km north of the village of Vernashen – on a very difficult road – is the beautiful little monastery of **Spitakavor**. Set amid rolling green hills, this peaceful spot hosts the grave of Garegin Nzhdeh, an architect of Armenia's brief independence after World War I. It is challenging to get to by road, so hiking to it is probably the best option.

Smbataberd Fortress

Above Artabuynk village • Free • No public transport

Only accessible by 4WD or a one-hour hike up from the village of Artabuynk, **Smbataberd** is an impressive mountaintop fortress. Little is known of its history: seemingly occupied during the tenth and eleventh centuries, it is thought that it was abandoned following its capture by either Mongol or Seljuk invaders. The ramparts are still walkable and there are fantastic views across the mountains from here.

Orbelian's Caravanserai

Yerevanyan Hwy • Free • No public transport, best reached by taxi from Yeghegnadzor

Built in 1332 for the use of Silk Road merchants travelling through the Vardenis Mountains, this structure (also known as the Selim caravanserai) was later abandoned and fell into disrepair, but was restored in the 1950s and is now one of the finest examples of a caravanserai to be found anywhere in the world. Enter by the doorway into the first small chamber and check out the inscription in Armenian on the right wall. It explains that Prince Chesar Orbelian built the caravanserai for the salvation of his soul and the souls of his family. The second chamber, lit by an open shaft leading outside, is separated into three aisles by arches and pillars, and was where travellers and animals spent the night.

Jermuk

Meaning "warm spring", the town of **Jermuk** has been settled since at least the eighth century, and the town passed frequently between ownership of Armenia, the Nakhchivan Khanate, Persia and Russia. In the twentieth century, Jermuk achieved fame throughout the Soviet Union as a spa town and became a centre of tourism. Following the USSR's collapse, Jermuk went through hard times, but is now recovering with a revitalisation of the medical tourism industry.

It's still perhaps more popular with tourists from the ex-Soviet states, who come and stay here for up to three weeks to enjoy the treatments available, but it's certainly worth a visit to see another side to Armenia and get a glimpse of USSR-style holidaymaking, as well as checking out its beautiful waterfall.

Mineral Water Gallery

Off Shahumyan St • Free

The **Mineral Water Gallery** is a pink stone colonnaded hall of Graeco-Roman inspiration, full of pipes dispensing warm salty water into urns. You'll find cups for sale here, and visitors buy a cup, fill it up from the pipes and drink the mineral water. The taste can best be described as 'unusual', but it is thought to confer various health benefits, and should be tried, if only once.

If you have kids – or perhaps are a big kid yourself – there's a small lake in front of the gallery where you can hire pedalos. If you prefer something less energetic, you'll find market stands on the path up to the lake selling home produce such as jam, honey and dried fruit, and also art of dubious quality.

Jermuk Waterfall

Off Charents St, Jermuk • Free, parking charge

Jermuk's **waterfall** is below the town in the gorge, accessible by a short and well-maintained path which you can reach via a switchback road from the Israel Ori roundabout, or alternatively down a steep and disconcertingly rackety metal staircase

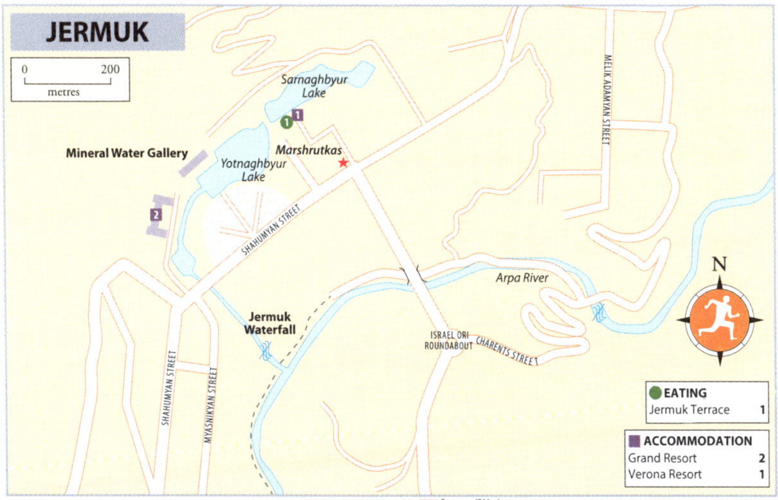

from behind the Jermuk Hotel on Myasnikyan St. The waterfall is a spectacular cascade, which at 64 metres high is the tallest in Armenia. It is referred to locally as the Mermaid's Hair, due to a local legend concerning a beautiful princess who became a mermaid as a result of her father forbidding her to marry her true love.

Ropeway

Yerevan-Jermuk Highway • Charge

This chairlift heads up to a height of 2500 metres and operates year-round, offering the opportunity to indulge in skiing and snowboarding in the winter months or simply enjoying spectacular views over the town and surrounding countryside in summer.

ARRIVAL AND DEPARTURE   JERMUK

By bus Jermuk is some 20 kilometres off the main Yerevan-Meghri highway, so there's no chance of getting off a marshrutka passing through; you'll need to take one specifically heading here. These leave from Yerevan's Kilikia bus station twice daily at 1pm and 4pm.

Marshrutkas from Jermuk include the daily departure to Yerevan at 11am, which also calls at Yeghegnadzor. If you're heading east, you'll need to take the 8am marshrutka to Vayk and hope you arrive in time to pick up the 11.55am to Goris.

By car The H42 road leads from the highway to Jermuk; when you arrive at the Israel Ori roundabout, take the second exit and head across the bridge, then turn left at the T-junction to find yourself in the centre of town. Parking is easy and free.

GETTING AROUND

The majority of Jermuk's sights are clustered around the Mineral Water Gallery on Shahumyan Street, but if you're heading down to the waterfall, it's probably best to take a taxi as it's either a fairly lengthy walk down a switchback road or a stiff climb down a very old metal staircase.

ACCOMMODATION   SEE MAP PAGE 231

Grand Resort 5–7 Shahumyan St ⓦ grandresortjermuk. com/en. This huge pink building next to the Mineral Water Gallery is a very smart modern place, having opened in 2015. It offers a huge range of spa treatments (from a bewildering array of massages to alarmingly vague propositions such as "recover your firmness" and "AHA's body peeling"), as well as a selection of medical therapies. If you'd prefer to have a room, luckily that's an option too: there are 92 standard king and queen rooms, five king suites, and one enormous presidential suite. Smoking and non-smoking rooms are available, and of course there's a swimming pool, jacuzzi, sauna, and gym. $$$

Verona Resort 9/1 Shahumyan St ⓦ jermukverona. am/en. In a pleasant spot on the edge of the lake, with a view across to the colonnade, Verona is a friendly and reasonably central choice. The rooms are comfy and well-appointed, breakfast is tasty and plentiful, and it's in very close proximity to the Terrace restaurant, as well as the marvellous derelict Soviet-era Palace of Culture. $$

EATING   SEE MAP PAGE 231

Jermuk Terrace 9/1 Shahumyan St ⓦ facebook.com/ JermukTerraceRestaurant. In an enviable position on the lakeside close to Verona Resort, Terrace offers a wide variety of meals, from Armenian barbecue favourites and Georgian khachapuri to international standards. A very solid choice. $$

Syunik Province

Armenia's deep south is bordered by mountains on almost every side. The main highway continues from Yerevan, heading down ultimately to Iran, running between the mountains of Nagorno-Karabakh to the east and those of Azerbaijan's Nakhchivan enclave to the west. En route, there's plenty to see, with many of Armenia's top sights found in this area.

Sisian

One of the largest towns in Syunik province, **Sisian** has existed since at least the eighth century BC. Its history includes the usual parade of conquerors: the Turks, Mongols,

Persians and Russians, and under the Soviets it was an industrial centre, with factories producing everything from concrete to textiles. Following the USSR's collapse, much of Sisian's industry ground to a halt.

It's now hard to escape the conclusion that Sisian is a once-successful town a little down on its luck. The beautifully ornate wrought-iron lampposts hint at its more prosperous past, but the central pedestrianised avenue between Sisakan and Israelyan Sts feels scrappy, and there are derelict buildings and industrial machinery all around, and areas of scrubby grass where you might expect to find shops or houses. For all that, it's got a friendly air, and there are a couple of decent places to stay, making it a good place to base yourself to visit the surrounding sights.

History Museum of Sisian

6a Adonts St • Charge • W sisianmuseum.am

Sisian's **museum** is in a small park which contains khachkars and ram carvings from the Middle Ages, as well as some petroglyphs which have been lifted from Ughtasar (see page 235), so if you're in town out of season and can't visit the actual site, you'll be able to get a preview of these ancient carvings. Inside, the museum features archaeological finds from Zorets Karer, an ethnographic section including traditional national costumes and some well-presented rooms focusing on Armenia's recent history, in particular on the Genocide, the Great Patriotic War, and the Nagorno-Karabakh War. English labelling is limited so a guided tour (extra charge) is definitely worthwhile.

There's little else of note in the town to see, but it's worth a brief stop at the **large Soviet monolithic memorial** to the heroes of the Great Patriotic War on the hill above the town. As you approach on the Zorets Karer road, you'll see a cross on a small hillock on your right. Leave the road here and take the well-paved track about 400 metres to the monument – or, even easier, park on the road and walk along the track. If you climb the mound nearby, you'll be rewarded with a good view of the monument, with Sisian in the valley below and the mountains of Nakhchivan looming in the distance beyond.

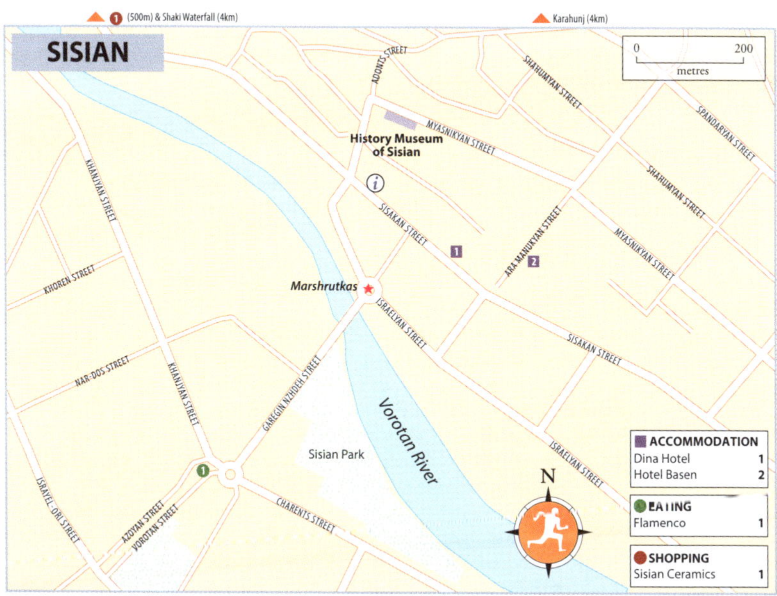

ARRIVAL AND DEPARTURE   SISIAN

By bus Marshrutkas pass from Yerevan and Goris, arriving and departing from the roundabout at the junction of Israelyan and Garegin Nzhdeh streets. Marshrutkas to Yerevan leave at 9am daily and to Goris at 9.30am daily. Marshrutkas also depart when full to neighbouring villages.

By car The main road into Sisian is the H44, which passes by the Shaki Waterfall (see page 234). There's also a minor road leading out to the north via Zorets Karer (see page 235). Parking in town is easy and free.

GETTING AROUND AND INFORMATION

Sisian is small enough that it can easily be navigated on foot. Should you need a taxi, they are plentiful and cheap. **Tourist Information Centre** 38 Sisakan St, ☎ 374 93 262533, ✉ sisiandevelopment@gmail.com. Extremely well-informed, friendly and helpful staff at this office will help you with arranging tours to the surrounding attractions or advise on how best to do it under your own steam. They also sell and rent outdoor equipment including tents, bikes, walking poles, etc. Mon–Fri, 10am–5pm.

ACCOMMODATION   SEE MAP PAGE 233

Dina Hotel 35 Sisakan St ⓦ dinahotel.am. Built in 1936, this is one of the most authentically Soviet places to stay in Armenia. The 31 rooms are all en suite and come with stone balconies, and while some effort has been made to modernise (there's wi-fi throughout, for example), ultimately the hotel feels as though it's stuck in the early 1980s. The small grounds at the front are a pleasant place to sit beneath the apple, apricot and cherry trees, especially if the fruit is in season and you can sample it. $$

Hotel Basen Ara Manukyan St ☎ 374 93 434727. The Basen was constructed in 1984 and certainly retains a Soviet aura, but the rooms inside are pleasant enough, though some are plagued with noisy plumbing. What sets it apart are the immensely friendly and helpful staff, who speak excellent English and will be able to assist you with your plans for the area, including arranging tours. $$

EATING   SEE MAP PAGE 233

There isn't a particularly lively dining scene in Sisian. Hotels and guesthouses usually offer dinner, which is worth taking up. Otherwise, there are a few fast-food places around the centre.

Flamenco Khanjyan St ☎ 374 28 325505. There's no particular indication anywhere outside that this place is actually called *Flamenco* – on the door it says "hotel pizza". Inside, follow the stairs to the first floor where you'll find a café that looks vaguely like a US diner, with bas-relief flamenco dancers carved on the walls. $

SHOPPING   SEE MAP PAGE 233

Sisian Ceramics 42 Grigor Lusavorich St ☎ 374 93 615661. Visitors to *Sisian Ceramics* can enjoy a ceramic-making experience, under the expert guidance of the friendly staff. Good fun with kids.

Around Sisian

Although Sisian itself is perhaps not an essential stop, there are several sights in its immediate surroundings that are real highlights, including the ancient stone circle of Zorets Karer, the even more ancient petroglyphs in the nearby mountains, and Shaki, one of Armenia's most beautiful waterfalls.

Shaki waterfalls

Off the H44 road from Shaki to Sisian • Free • No public transport, best reached by taxi from Sisian

The magnificent 18-metre-high **Shaki falls** are a 5- to 10-minute walk along an obvious path through a beautiful valley from the car park. The best view is, as expected, from directly in front of the cascade, but if you don't mind getting wet, you can take the path up to the right for a closer look. Bear in mind that the water flow is used for hydroelectric power and consequently the waterfall does not always have water. Luckily, there's a set timetable – 11am–6pm – when the water will be on.

If driving, you'll most likely be coming from the Yerevan–Meghri highway down to Sisian. If so, don't follow the first signs you see for Shaki. Instead, continue down the road for another kilometre and take the gravel track signposted for Shaki waterfalls for approximately 1.5km to the car park. At one point you'll come to an official-looking gateway but you can just drive through. It's quite a rough drive and by the end you're likely to feel fairly shaki yourself.

Zorats Karer
Off the unnamed road from Sisian to M13 road • Charge • No public transport, best reached by taxi from Sisian

Also known as Karahunj, this windswept site is considered Armenia's answer to Stonehenge, though it bears more resemblance to Avebury Ring and other similar stone circles. It has been dated to approximately 5500 years ago, though this has been disputed in a subsequent study which considers it to date from 2000 BC or thereabouts.

Theories also abound as to the site's purpose. The suggestion that has most caught public attention is that it was an ancient stargazing observatory, which is certainly more exciting than a previous theory suggesting it was an animal holding pen. Besides anything else, it was certainly a necropolis, as burial chambers excavated here, dating from the Early and Middle Bronze Ages, have yielded rich archaeological finds.

Whatever its intended function, **Zorats Karer** is a fascinating location and an essential stop on any tour of southern Armenia. The stones, some of them nearly 3 metres high, form a circle around the Early Bronze Age site, as well as rows of them tailing off in other directions. You'll notice some stones have round holes bored through them, an unusual feature that is part of the evidence leading to the observatory theory.

Note that there is an imitation stone circle just by the site's car park – don't mistake this for the real thing! Installed in 2013, it's a work by a local artist.

Ughtasar
Off the Yerevan-Meghri highway • Free • No public transport, best visited by guided tour from Sisian (charge)

High in the mountains above Sisian, right on the border with Nagorno-Karabakh, are the remarkable relics of an ancient people. As far back as the 5th millennium BC, the inhabitants of this region decorated the rocks surrounding Ughtasar Lake with petroglyphs depicting humanoid figures as well as animals – including bulls, stags and leopards, but with goats massively predominating. It has been theorised that goats acted as 'spirit guardians' hence their appearance on two-thirds of the petroglyphs.

As well as the obvious attraction of the outstanding petroglyphs, it's a great place to see mountain scenery and an attractive lake. In addition, it's not unlikely that you'll see eagles up here between June and August, so bring binoculars.

Ughtasar is at a height of 3300 metres, and consequently is inaccessible due to snow for a good proportion of the year, you'll be lucky if you can visit outside late June to mid-September. Other petroglyphs, on the same theme of goats, people, etc, can be seen in a neighbouring valley even if Ughtasar itself is still unreachable due to snow. They are perhaps less impressive but still worth a trip, especially since it involves a degree of hiking amid these beautiful mountains.

Don't even think about trying to get up here by yourself, unless you have a serious 4WD and an equally serious desire to get lost among the countless tracks. Even if you do have an appropriate vehicle, it's extremely unlikely you'd be able to locate any petroglyphs without knowing where to look. You will need a guide, and these can be arranged by the tourist information centre in Sisian or by your hotel. One recommended guide is Sasun Baghdasryan, ☎ 374 93 821472, a knowledgeable chap who's passionate about the Sisian area and also very proud of his 1984 Soviet Jeep, which seems utterly indestructible.

Vorotnovank Monastery
Vaghatin village • Free • No public transport, best reached by taxi from Sisian

About 20 minutes' drive along the beautiful road leading south from Sisian, this monastery sits on a bluff above the Vorotan river gorge. One of Armenia's most picturesque, yet largely unvisited, monasteries, it was founded in the fourth century by the ubiquitous St Gregory the Illuminator. The current structure dates from the early eleventh century, when it was built under the patronage of Syunik's Queen Shahandukht, who is buried here. The monastery was damaged in an earthquake in 1931 but has been subsequently restored: look out for the remains of a small fourteenth century fresco depicting two angels amongst the stars.

If you continue down the road from the monastery you'll find the remains of **Vorotnaberd Fortress**. This consists solely of a wall built into the cliff so is unlikely to take up too much of your time. If you're looking for a more interesting approach to the monastery, you can consider hiking from the village of Aghitu to Vorotnovank. Aghitu itself is worth a stop as it is home to a 1,500-year-old structure known as the **memorial**, though its precise function is unknown.

Sisian to Goris

From Sisian, the road continues east to the town of Goris, but before you get there, it's worth taking a diversion to the south to visit the beautiful Tatev monastery, accessed by the impressive Wings of Tatev cable car.

Wings of Tatev

H45 road, Halidzor village • Charge • Ⓦ tatever.am/en • No public transport, best reached by taxi from Goris

The **Wings of Tatev**, built in 2010, holds the world record for "longest non-stop double-track cable car", which sounds awfully specific. The upshot is that there are some longer cable car rides in the world, but not many, and even fewer that whisk you across a deep valley to a beautifully sited Armenian monastery saving you the trouble of a long switchback road.

Buy your ticket at the visitor centre, then walk up – via the vista point – to the departure station. Note that you have to specify when you buy your ticket what time you want to come back. The cars run every half hour so you'll have the choice of spending 40 minutes, 1 hr 10, etc – 40 minutes is too short, so go for at least 1 hr 10. If you miss your designated cable car, you'll be charged an additional 2000 AMD. Bear in mind that if there is a queue for the cable car, people may not be waiting for the same one as you, so listen carefully to the staff and make sure you don't miss your car by standing behind people who are waiting for the next one.

The extremely scenic ride takes 12 minutes to travel nearly 3.5 miles, saving you a very long trip down into the valley and back up the other side. There's a very jaunty – sometimes a bit frantic – medieval music soundtrack as you go, as well as a recorded audio information track in a variety of languages explaining the sights visible from the cable car.

Tatev Monastery

Tatev village • Free • Best accessed via Wings of Tatev cable car

The beautifully situated monastery of **Tatev**, perched on the edge of a precipitous cliff, was founded in the fourth century and became the seat of the Syunik bishopric and a major cultural and educational centre during the medieval period. It suffered numerous calamities throughout its history, including several earthquakes – most recently in 1931 – and lootings by Seljuk Turks, Persians and Tamerlane's forces. In 1920, the short-lived Republic of Mountainous Armenia was declared at Tatev, covering much of Syunik Province until its absorption into the USSR in July 1921.

The principal church in the complex, completed in the early tenth century, is dedicated to Saints Peter and Paul and once featured frescoes by French, Byzantine and Armenian artists, though little of these works remain today. Adjacent to the Saints Peter and Paul Church is the 1295 Church of St Gregory the Illuminator. Here you will find the magnificently carved tomb of St Grigor Tatevatsi, a prominent medieval philosopher based at Tatev monastery.

The monastery grounds are also home to a third church – the Holy Mother of God, up a staircase just to the left of the gatehouse – and a curious tenth-century "pendulous column", which at 8-metres tall will apparently wobble and give advance warning of earthquakes.

Just outside the monastery grounds is a seventeenth-century mill which was once used for the manufacture of olive oil. It now houses a well-presented and surprisingly interesting exhibition about the process.

After your visit to the monastery, follow the unpaved road to the right of the entrance for about 10 or 15 minutes to reach a vista point, where you'll get the 'classic' view of Tatev seen in tourist offices all over Armenia. The walk is an unshaded slog in summer, but a great way to warm up in autumn or winter.

ARRIVAL AND DEPARTURE TATEV

There is no public transport to Tatev, though marshrutkas en route between Sisian and Goris will stop at the junction of the M12 and H45 for you – you'd then need to hitch the remaining 10 kilometres to the Wings of Tatev Halidzor station. Taxis from Goris are thus the best way of visiting – drivers will be willing to drop you and later come back to pick you up at a set time.

INFORMATION

Tatev Info Centre & Café Tatev village ☎ 374 94 414272, ⓦ tatevinfo.com. Outdoor activities such as hiking and horseriding can be arranged through the helpful info centre, which is not far from the Wings of Tatev station. Daily 10am–10pm.

ACCOMMODATION

Tatev is close enough to both Goris and Sisian that there's no particular need to stay the night, but staying in the village is possible, with a few options available.

Saro's B&B 6 13 St Tatev ☎ 374 77 755417. Saro and his sister Maro run a very friendly guesthouse, with 16 rooms (with shared bathrooms) across two buildings. You'll be plied with home-made wine from arrival, and the simple but very tasty evening meals come highly recommended. $

EATING

If you're staying in Tatev village your guesthouse will be able to provide a good evening meal.

Tatevatun Wings of Tatev (Halidzor station) ☎ 374 60 463373. A stylish and modern café can be found at the cable car station on the Halidzor side. It's certainly a great location, with beautiful views across the valley from the terrace, but the food is more expensive than it should be and is perhaps a little underwhelming, so it's probably more advisable to stick to drinks here. $$

Goris

The town of **Goris** sits at the road junction between Yerevan, Meghri and Stepanakert. It's a pleasant place, with nineteenth-century stone houses lining the three long main roads that lead down from the highway to the centre of the action, Grigor Tatevatsi Square and Parc Vienne. There isn't much to see in town, but it's a decent spot to stay for a few days while you take in the surrounding area.

Thought to have been continuously inhabited since the Stone Age, it was under the Tsarist Russian administration that Goris came into its own, being one of four places in Armenia to be designated a city. At that time, it was a hotspot for crafts as diverse as carpet-making, metallurgy and brewing. In September 2023, it became the principal destination for the approximately 100,000 refugees from Nagorno-Karabakh, fleeing Azerbaijan's recapture of the breakaway region.

Aksel Bakunts House Museum

41 Mashtots St • Charge • ⓜ gatmuseum.am/en/branches/bakunc

The early twentieth-century writer Aksel Bakunts lived in Goris in this house. The museum has preserved a couple of rooms as they might have been in his lifetime and

put up a well-presented exhibition including photos of him and his family in the central room. Unless you're a massive Bakunts fan, though, you'll probably be most interested in the ethnographic side to the museum: the kitchen is fascinating, with a magnificently ornate iron oven in the wall, bronze water pitchers, and a massive wooden butter churn – just watch out for the lavash hole in the floor. There is little to no English labelling but the staff are enormously friendly and will happily walk you round, offering explanations.

Local Lore Museum

5 Mashtots St • Free • ☎ 374 77 111245

The **museum** – which originally opened in 1948 in an abandoned church, but was relocated to its present site following the 1990s Nagorno-Karabakh war – covers a wide range of exhibits spanning a vast time period, from 2nd millennium BC arrow heads, through ancient fire and water worship vessels, to Russian coins and banknotes from the nineteenth century. The pride of the collection is a second millennium BC five-faced stone idol, found during archaeological digs in Hagzhis near Goris, which bears similarities to artefacts from sites as wide-spread as Egypt and India. Labelling in the museum is erratic but exists almost everywhere you'd want it to.

ARRIVAL AND DEPARTURE
GORIS

Marshrutkas depart from different locations in town depending on where you're going. The twice daily to Yerevan (at 9am and 4pm) and the twice daily to Kapan (at noon and 3pm) leave from the tourist office, while the 1.30pm to Sisian leaves from Viva Cell on Mashtots St. Note that these timings should be taken with a pinch of salt; the marshrutkas will leave when they are full.

INFORMATION

Goris Tourist Information Centre 7 Komitas St, ☎ 374 28 422690, ✉ goristourism@gmail.com. The tourist information office is by Parc Vienne. Inside you'll find reasonably helpful staff who will offer information about marshrutka and shared taxi departures to various onward destinations, and supply a leaflet covering sights in the area. Mon–Fri 9.30am–5.30pm, Sat–Sun 10am–5pm.

GETTING AROUND

Goris is not a large place and the majority of places you're likely to want to visit within it are clustered around Parc Vienne, making walking the best option. If you do need a taxi, it's not hard to find one, and prices are low for a trip within town.

ACCOMMODATION
SEE MAP PAGE 238

Hotel Christy 9 Mashtots St ☎ 374 77 000047. This guesthouse offers seven rooms, each with a different colour scheme – pinks, greens and purples predominate. They are all different sizes too, so you may want to ask to see a couple before choosing. For light sleepers, rooms one and seven face the courtyard at the back instead of the road, so may be preferable. Breakfast is good, and they also offer an excellent dinner. $$

Hotel Goris 53 Khorenatsi St ☎374 41 330003. The garish orange and green façade, which looks like it's escaped from an unusually colourful version of 1970s Russia, suggests a decaying Soviet monolith, but actually this large hotel has been thoroughly renovated inside. The decent restaurant is an open-kitchen affair decorated in a rustic old Armenian style. $$

Mirhav Hotel 100 Mashtots St ⓦ hotelmirhav.am/en. The rooms in this boutique hotel are very stylish, with exposed stonework and traditional carpets. There's a lovely garden to relax in, and breakfast is delicious, as are the evening meals served in the attached restaurant. $$$

Popock 92/1 Movses Khorenatsi St ⓦ facebook.com/gorispopock. This modern hotel just a short walk from the centre is a great find, with comfortable rooms – some with lovely views – and friendly staff. There's a good restaurant here too, serving up classic Armenian fare. $$

EATING
SEE MAP PAGE 238

Most hotels and guesthouses offer evening meals, but if you would like to eat out, there are a couple of decent options in Goris.

De Luxe Lounge Café Parc Vienne ☎374 91 224477. In the Parc Vienne, opposite a children's playground, you'll find this smart and glitzy establishment. It offers indoor and outdoor seating and food and drinks, but isn't particularly friendly. $

Takarik Tavern 25 Syunik St ☎374 43 666222. A lively restaurant with a focus on Armenian food, as well as options from across the former Soviet Union such as Russian borsch, Uzbek pilaf and Georgian chakhokhbili stew. The downstairs room has a fantastic beamed ceiling, and stone walls with old black and white photos of Goris and surrounds on display. The house wine is not enormously good; it's worth stretching your budget slightly to try something better. $$

DIRECTORY

Banks Banks and ATMs can be found primarily around Grigor Tatevatsi Sq.

Hospital Goris Medical Centre (31 Grigor Tatevatsi St, ☎374 28 422152).

Pharmacies Goris Pharmacy is on Syunik St, between Komitas and Grigor Tatevatsi sts.

Post office The post office is opposite Hotel Zangezur on Ankakhutyan St.

Around Goris

Heading east from Goris, you'll enter mountainous territory as you travel the road that heads to Nagorno-Karabakh: in 2023, this road was travelled by the vast majority of the more than 100,000 refugees fleeing the territory in the wake of Azerbaijan's offensive. Now that Nagorno-Karabakh cannot be accessed, the main reason to head out this way is to visit the intriguing cave city of Khndzoresk.

Khndzoresk Cave City

Khndzoresk village • Free, donations welcome (in the box by the suspension bridge) • No public transport, best reached by taxi from Goris

It has been claimed that until the twentieth century, the **caves** in the hillside below Khndzoresk village formed the biggest village in eastern Armenia. They have now been uninhabited since the 1950s, except for occasional use as animal shelters, and it's fascinating to explore the paths between them. To allow easier access, a suspension bridge has been built spanning the valley – though it does sway unsettlingly as you cross.

The site is well maintained with clear footpaths and signage discouraging littering. There are rickety ladders in some of the cave chambers so you can crawl into narrow tunnels if the fancy takes you, but you'll probably prefer to walk the paths in this tranquil, beautiful site. Routes lead both left and right from the end of the bridge: it's advised that you take the time to explore thoroughly, but if you're pressed for time then the left path is marginally more interesting as it will lead you eventually to a still-functioning church. Some care is advisable as there are open shafts that could lead to a nasty fall into caves below.

If you have your own car to reach the caves be aware that it's a rough 3.5-kilometre track from the main road – turn right shortly before you reach the modern Khndzoresk village. Standard cars can manage, but 4WD are best. Once at the car park, descend the well-maintained wooden staircase to the suspension bridge.

The café at the car park sells welcome ice cream and cold drinks, as well as more substantial Armenian fare.

En route to Khndzoresk, you'll pass a set of five peculiar stone pyramids atop a hill: this is the Goris Town Viewpoint, constructed in 2018, which offers reasonable, if unspectacular, views into the valley.

Kapan

The capital of Syunik Province, about midway between Goris and the Iranian border at Meghri, **Kapan** makes a good staging post and introduction to Armenia for travellers arriving from Iran, or a sensible final stop for those leaving the country at the southern border. While not blessed with show-stopping sights, Kapan is a pleasant, typical Armenian town. Variously ruled as part of the medieval Kingdom of Armenia, the Persian Empire, the Russian Empire, and the USSR, it is now the administrative capital of Syunik Province and is principally a mining town. Most foreign visitors you meet are likely to be investors rather than tourists, and you may attract some curiosity.

In the Central Park you'll find the **Singing Fountains**, a small water display which is lit up at night. Following Melik Stepanyan Street uphill from the square will take you past the newly built **Surb Mesrop Mashtots church** to the **Garegin Nzhdeh Monument**, a concrete angular structure built in 2003 featuring a head-and-shoulders bust of Nzhdeh surrounded by four eagles.

Kapan History Museum

37 Shahumyan St · Charge · ☎ 374 28 528333

The **Kapan History Museum** is a small centre giving an interesting and well-presented background to the town, with a focus on the First Karabakh War, but with exhibits stretching back throughout Kapan's history.

Vahanavank Monastery

M2 · Free · No public transport, best reached by taxi from Kapan

Ten kilometres or so out of town on the road leading towards Meghri, **Vahanavank Monastery** is a typical Armenian church complex which dates back to the tenth and

---

GAREGIN NZHDEH

Born in 1886 in the village of Kznut (now in Azerbaijan's Nakhchivan province), Garegin Ter-Harutyunyan adopted the name of Nzhdeh (meaning 'pilgrim') in his struggle against the various great powers of the time. In the years prior to World War I, he fought for the independence of Balkan states against the Ottoman Empire, and despite differences with Tsarist Russia, he assisted the Russian army against Turkey during the war.

Following the Russian Revolution, **Nzhdeh** defended the newly established First Republic of Armenia from invading Turkish forces at the Battle of Karakilisa, and then became active in the **doomed attempts** to prevent Armenia's absorption into the USSR. When the Bolsheviks invaded northern Armenia, Nzhdeh established the Republic of Mountainous Armenia from Tatev monastery.

The Republic of Mountainous Armenia lasted a mere six months, and Nzhdeh retreated to Persia and then Bulgaria. During World War II he lent his support to the Wehrmacht in the hope that the Axis powers could restore Armenia's independence. On Nazi Germany's defeat, Nzhdeh was arrested and sentenced to prison for counter-revolutionary activity. He died in prison in 1953. His remains have been divided between **Spitakavor Monastery** near Yeghegnadzor and the slopes of **Mount Khustup** near his monument.

eleventh centuries. It's a quiet place which seems rarely visited and is pleasant to wander for half an hour or so.

Halidzor Fortress

M2 • Free • No public transport, best reached by taxi from Kapan

Also on the Meghri road is the **Halidzor Fortress**, an easily defensible position atop a hill which was the site of a celebrated defeat of the Ottoman army by the Armenian national hero David Bek. It is now a peaceful, ruined, but still largely intact, site. Halidzor can be reached by an approximately one hour unsignposted uphill hike starting about 8 km from the centre of Kapan – it's probably best to take a local guide, and it's not advisable in winter.

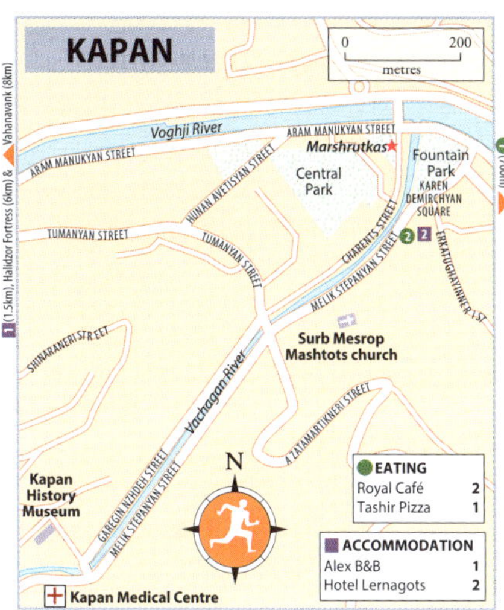

ARRIVAL AND DEPARTURE
KAPAN

The main road from Goris to Kapan winds along, and sometimes straddles, the border with Azeri-controlled Nagorno-Karabakh, and Azerbaijani soldiers refuse to allow traffic to pass. If heading this way, you will need to come by an alternative route from Tatev.

By bus A marshrutka heads to Yerevan daily at 8am (six hours), calling at various stops along the way, including Goris (1.5 hours) and Yeghegnadzor (four hours). To Meghri, there's one marshrutka a day at 3pm (two hours).

By car It's a winding mountainous road to Kapan, but it's decent enough. Parking in town is easy.

INFORMATION

There is no tourist information office in Kapan, but staff at your hotel or guesthouse should be able to help arrange tours or onward transport.

GETTING AROUND

Kapan is eminently walkable; even on foot, it won't take you long to explore.

ACCOMMODATION
SEE MAP PAGE 241

Alex B&B 13 G Arzumanyan St w alexbb.business.site. This friendly guesthouse is probably the best place to stay in Kapan: the rooms are comfy, the breakfasts are good, and the hosts will help to arrange your sightseeing in the region. Note that it's shared bathroom only, and it's not enormously central (though that does mean it's nice and quiet). $$

Hotel Lernagots 2 Karen Demirchyan Sq w lernagotshotel.am. *Lernagots* is centrally located, very cheap and it offers an authentic Soviet experience. On the other hand, it's looking ever more decrepit and it's quite noisy, especially if you get a room looking out on the square. $

EATING AND DRINKING
SEE MAP PAGE 241

Royal Café 2 Karen Demirchyan Sq t 374 98 624006. Tucked away around the corner to the right of Hotel Lernagots, *Royal Café* is a well-heeled modern café, serving snacky food such as Georgian khachapuri and pizzas. It becomes a reasonably happening bar at night and is almost certainly the trendiest place in town. $

Tashir Pizza 32 Shahumyan St t 374 55 032333. This branch of the popular Armenian pizza chain offers no-nonsense pizzas in a smart and modern restaurant. $$

DIRECTORY

Banks The Agricole bank sits on the central square, and Unibank is a short walk away down Tumanyan St. There's

> ## THE ARMENIA–IRAN BORDER
>
> So long as you have appropriate visas, the **crossing between Armenia and Iran** at Agarak to Norduz is simple enough. Assuming you're travelling into Iran, you'll be stamped out of Armenia, then walk across the short bridge over the Aras river and head for the building directly opposite to enter Iran. Don't try to bring in any alcohol, drugs, pork or pornographic material, and if you're female, make sure you're dressed appropriately (headscarf, trousers, loose fitting dress).

also a Moneygram outlet opposite Unibank. All these will be able to change money for you. Your hotel may also offer this service.

Hospital The Kapan Medical Centre is on Melik Stepanyan St.
Pharmacies There are several pharmacy stores in town, including Nor Dexatun on Melik Stepanyan St.

Meghri

Armenia's main road from Yerevan eventually winds its way down through the mountains to **Meghri**, right on the border with Iran. You're unlikely to want to linger here, but if you need to cross the border – in either direction – you may find yourself needing to spend a night.

If you're at a loose end while in town, the now mostly ruined eleventh-century **fortress** offers good views over both Meghri and into Iran. It's quite a hot and sticky climb up in summer months. **St Sargis church** is also worth a quick look for the frescoes inside.

ARRIVAL AND DEPARTURE

By bus It's a long eight or nine hours in the once-daily marshrutka from Yerevan to Meghri. You can also pick up marshrutkas or shared taxis from Kapan, taking about one hour. Travellers coming from Iran will find it easy to pick up a taxi at the border crossing; if you have no Armenian dram yet, payment in US dollars will most likely be accepted.

ACCOMMODATION

Haer B&B 14 Qarakert ☎ 374 93 545414. Run by the welcoming Erik, *Haer B&B* is probably Meghri's best option for accommodation. The cosy rooms are comfortable, the shared bathroom is clean, and the breakfast is excellent. 💲

EATING

Eating in your B&B is most likely the best option, but there are also a number of places along Adelyan Street.
Imper Adelyan St ☎ 374 77 997907. Offering fast food such as burgers and barbecued meat, *Imper* is also popular as a last stop for beer before heading into dry Iran. 💲

8

Baku

MAIDEN TOWER

9 Baku

Azerbaijan's capital Baku is the largest city in the Caucasus and has oriented itself as a forward-looking metropolis, attracting famous architects to erect incredibly innovative buildings across the city. The bustling modern town is packed with designer shops and spotless streets. It would be easy to forget that this is an ancient settlement if it weren't for the perfectly preserved Old Town, a bubble of medieval life surrounded by fortress-like walls packed with yellow sandstone buildings and narrow alleys. This delicate balance between past and present attracts visitors to Baku. Between the city's attractions and the day trips available you may find this often chaotic city charms you into a lengthy stay.

A metropolis of approximately 2.5 million people, Baku spreads out from its seafront location around the Bay of Baku on the Caspian Sea. It's the lowest capital in the world, at 28 metres below sea level – which may sound disconcerting, but don't worry, the Caspian Sea is even further below sea level. Baku's climate is mild year-round, but it's subject to fierce winds from the Caspian, which can make winters particularly cold.

It's a large city, but tourists are unlikely to want to venture particularly far from the centre, which is home to the Old Town – characterised by narrow winding streets and containing the UNESCO World Heritage Sites of the **Shirvanshahs Palace** and the **Maiden Tower** – and the adjacent modern town, where you'll find most of the city's excellent restaurants and bars. Close by is the **Bulvar**, a 4km long promenade along the Caspian seafront and home to the **Carpet Museum**, just one of Baku's excellent museums.

Above the Old Town, you can't help but spot the **Flame Towers**, a set of three iconic skyscrapers that evoke Azerbaijan's reputation as the Land of Fire. It's worth a trip up the funicular to get a closer look at the towers, as well as to visit **Martyrs' Lane**, a graveyard of the victims of Soviet repression, as well as Azerbaijan's late twentieth-century conflicts.

Brief history

The date of Baku's founding is unknown. Some sources suggest that Baku is in fact the city of Albanopolis, the site of the Apostle Bartholomew's martyrdom, and that Bartholomew met his end beneath the **Maiden Tower**. There's no particularly strong evidence to support this theory, however, and though it's known that there was a centre of Zoroastrianism in the locality from the fifth century onwards, the existence of Baku itself cannot be verified until the ninth century, when it was mentioned by Arabic geographers as being a small feudal town.

Following a major earthquake, the **Shirvanshah dynasty** moved their capital from Shamakhi to Baku in 1191, at which point the city began a rapid expansion. Baku survived and even prospered during the period of Mongol invasions, and under the Shirvanshahs in the fifteenth century the beautiful palace, now in the Old Town, was built. However, the Shirvanshahs' rule was ended in 1540 after an invasion by Safavid Persia, under whose authority the city remained for the next two centuries.

Following the collapse of the **Safavid Empire** in the eighteenth century, Baku managed to establish itself as an independent khanate but swiftly came under the dominion of the northern Quba khanate, which was at its zenith at this time. Even this state of semi-independence didn't last long, with the arrival of the Russians in the early 1800s, who were keen to exploit the region's plentiful oil.

Highlights

❶ Maiden Tower Arguably Baku's most iconic sight, this unusual medieval tower is associated with many mysterious legends. See page 249

❷ Palace of the Shirvanshahs The jewel of the Old Town, this palace complex gives a sense of the splendour of Baku's medieval court. See page 251

❸ The Bulvar Strolling along Baku's seafront is one of the city's great pleasures. See page 256

❹ Carpet Museum You may not think a museum dedicated to carpets could ever be that interesting, but this engaging exhibition seeks to persuade you otherwise. Its trump card: it's in a building shaped like a carpet. See page 256

❺ Heydar Aliyev Centre Strikingly original, the Heydar Aliyev Centre is one of the world's most innovative pieces of architecture. See page 259

❻ Shikhov Beach So ugly it's compelling – it's safe to say you'll never see another beach quite like this windswept expanse of sand and murky waters overshadowed by an enormous oil platform. See page 260

HIGHLIGHTS ARE MARKED ON THE MAP ON PAGE 248

9

Reports had circulated for centuries about the oil wealth in and around Baku: in the thirteenth century, Marco Polo wrote of "a spring from which gushes a stream of oil, in such abundance that a hundred ships may load there at once", and it seems that the first oil well was established in 1594 by a local craftsman. However, it was in the latter half of the nineteenth century that Baku fully experienced an oil boom, with production reaching seven million tons per year by World War I.

After the collapse of Tsarist authority in 1917, the city came under the control of Bolshevik forces, under whom **massacres** of the Muslim populace took place in late March 1918. The Bolsheviks established a government known as the Baku Commune, led by the Armenian Stepan Shahumyan, but this was short-lived. The Baku Commissars were ejected from power, imprisoned, and eventually executed as they attempted to escape across the Caspian Sea. They were regarded as martyrs by the fledgling USSR, which blamed British influence for the deaths of the Commissars.

Meanwhile, the city's enormous **oil** output had by now made Baku a tempting target in the war effort. It became the end point of a race between German, British and Turkish armies in the latter half of 1918 to take control of the oilfields. The British arrived first, but were ejected by the Turks the following day, who instigated a massacre of the local Armenian population in retaliation for the events of March. The British regained control of Baku briefly, but retreated in the face of the advancing Red Army.

Under the Soviets, Baku was further industrialised and valued for its oil wealth, with the German traveller Joseph Roth writing evocatively of the city's dedication to "Saint

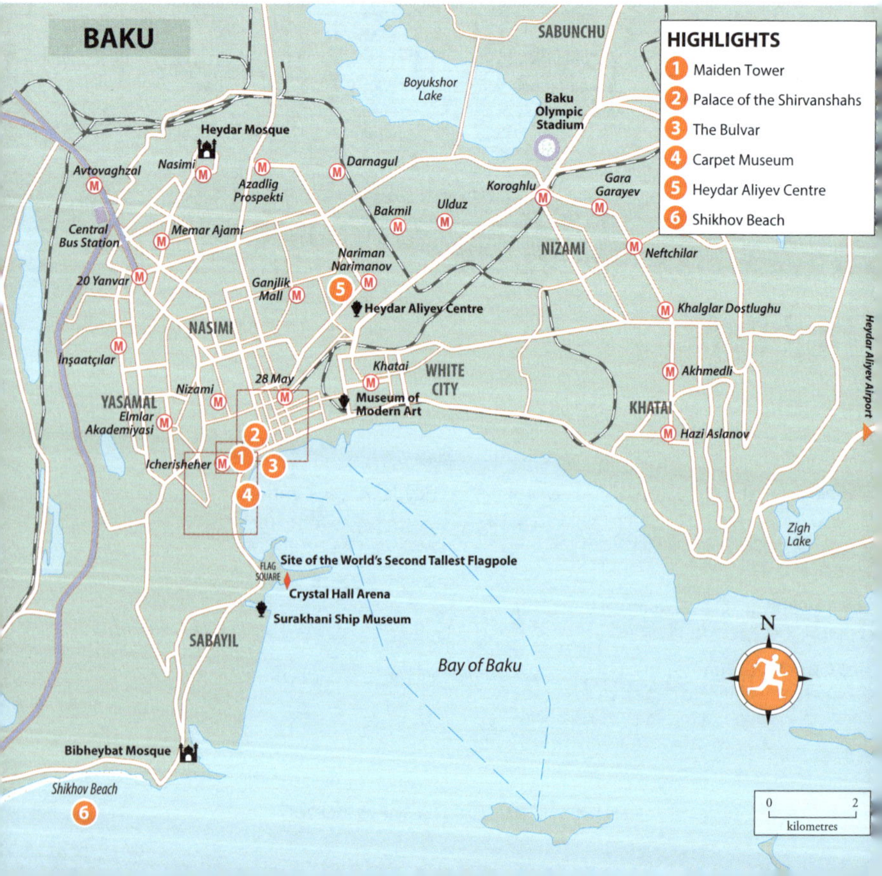

Petroleum". It was a major target of Nazi Germany in World War II, but despite a heavy offensive known as Operation Edelweiss, German troops never reached the city, stalling in the Caucasus mountains and eventually needing to divert to Stalingrad.

In January 1990, civil unrest resulting from tensions over Nagorno-Karabakh turned violent with anti-Armenian pogroms. Gorbachev attempted to restore order by sending in the army, but this proved an unwise move, with troops firing into crowds of protestors and killing up to three hundred people. The event – known as **Black January** – led to Azerbaijan's declaration of independence the following year and is memorialised at Martyrs' Lane.

Since **independence**, Baku has confidently entered the twenty first century, with prosperity from the still rich oilfields leading to the construction of modern, innovative architecture across the city, though controversy surrounds some such projects – the Crystal Hall, for example, was built on land forcibly taken from its owners without compensation. The city is now home to sizeable expat communities, and regularly hosts major international events such as the 2012 Eurovision Song Contest, an annual European Formula 1 Grand Prix, and the 2019 Europe League final. Baku also hosted the 2024 United Nations Climate Change Conference (COP29).

Old Town

Baku's **Old Town** dates back to at least the twelfth century, and possibly earlier, though the vast majority of buildings contained within its impressive sandstone walls are considerably newer. Much of the fun in this area is simply strolling around its bewildering alleyways, soaking up the ambience and exploring. If you're not minded towards random wandering, there's an audio-guide available from the tourist information office that will give you a bit more structure and ensure you don't miss anything.

For detailed information on the various sights in the Old Town, the official governmental website, ⓦ icherisheher.gov.az/en, offers a rundown of the major points of interest.

Maiden Tower

Neftchilar Prospect • Charge • ☎ 994 12 4923261 • Ⓜ Icharishahar

One of the two jewels of the **Old Town**, this 30-metre tall tower stands at the southern edge of the area. Architecturally, it's striking: the main tower is cylindrical, but there's an unusual protruding wall that juts out towards the Caspian Sea. The purpose of this projection is not certain. Suggestions range from an astronomical observations aid through to a breakwater for a time when the Caspian Sea extended further towards the city.

The tower's history is similarly unclear, though it's generally accepted that it was first constructed in the fifth or sixth century on the site of a much older fire worship temple, and extended to its present form in the twelfth century. Even the origin of the name Maiden Tower is unknown, though inside you'll find an interactive book of mutually contradictory legends explaining the name (spoiler alert: they all end with a maiden killing herself, usually by jumping from the tower).

Each of the seven floors contains a small exhibition, some of which are extremely silly, though others are informative (if less entertaining). Topics covered include the tower's dating, its potential function, its architecture and its water supply. There are also a few interactive exhibits, including a fun model of the tower's position within the Old Town with overlaid video and a table of other prominent fortresses in the region, as well as the aforementioned book of legends.

9

The view from the top is pretty good, but transparent plastic panels have been erected so you can't get as close to the edge as you might like, making photography tricky.

Open Air Museum

Kichik Qala • Free • Ⓜ Icharishahar

This twelfth-century courtyard, discovered during archaeological excavations in the 1960s, houses a small collection of **sarcophagi** (some with beautifully intricate carvings) and statues. You'll also see painted models of the Maiden Tower exhibited here. They were previously on display in the square in front of the tower itself.

Medieval archaeological sites

Qulla • Free • Ⓜ Icharishahar

In a courtyard just behind the Maiden Tower, you'll find three sunken areas, which were archaeological sites excavated in the 1980s, yielding finds from the Middle Ages. One of these sites has now been converted into the Qadim Beg restaurant, so if you've always wanted to have lunch in an archaeological pit, this is your chance.

QGallery

Qulla • Free • Ⓦ qgallery.net • Ⓜ Icharishahar

An excellent art gallery which is home to works by several of Azerbaijan's leading modern artists and sculptors. There are regular temporary exhibitions here too.

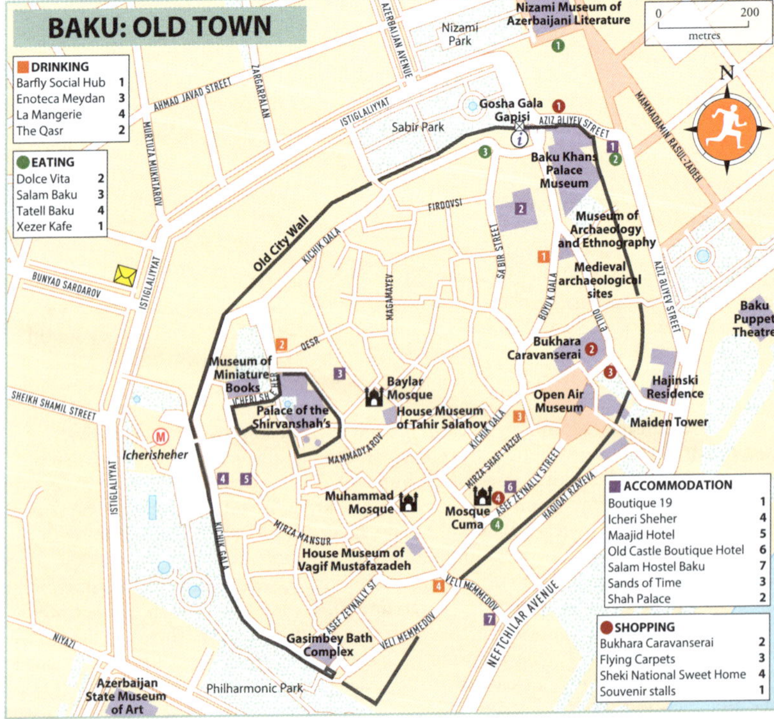

> **TAHIR SALAHOV**
>
> **Salahov** was a Baku-born **artist** who found success in the 1960s with his innovative "severe style" of Soviet art. While his work has roots in the prevailing socialist-realist style of the day, the drab colours and harsh or depressing subject matter – particularly in pictures such as *Morning Train* and *The Shift is Over* – give a clear impression of a lack of perfection in the USSR's world. Luckily for Salahov, his innovation did not result in censure – quite the opposite, in the 1970s, he became the First Secretary of the Union of Artists of the USSR, a position he retained until the Soviet Union's collapse. He died in May 2021.

Mosque Cuma

Asef Zeynally St • Free • Ⓜ Icharishahar

Originally built on the remains of a Zoroastrian fire temple, the current incarnation of this working mosque dates from 1899. It was used as a carpet museum throughout the Soviet era but has now returned to religious service. It has an elaborate sandstone carved doorway and an attractive minaret with further carvings at the top, and inside there's impressive pattern-work on the pillars and interior of the dome.

Muhammad Mosque

Kichik Qala • Free • Ⓜ Icharishahar

This mosque, which dates from 1078, is also known as the Siniggala (Damaged Tower) Mosque, as a result of being hit by Russian artillery in 1723 during the Russian-Persian war. It is usually closed.

Gasimbey Bath Complex

Kichik Qala • Free • Ⓜ Icharishahar

Count the domes on the roof of this attractive seventeenth-century **hammam** – apparently its owner had as many wives as there are domes. The baths are sadly no longer in operation, but they do host a **museum of pharmacy** with sporadic opening hours.

House Museum of Tahir Salahov

55 Ilyas Efandiyev St • Charge • ☎ 994 12 4921080 • Ⓜ Icharishahar

This museum is a good opportunity to view plenty of the works of one of Azerbaijan's most famous painters, as well as awards he's won and photos of the man himself meeting various politicians. The museum does a good job of pretending it's closed even when it's open – just ring the bell if the door is locked.

Palace of the Shirvanshahs

Kichik Qala • Charge • ☎ 994 12 4921073 • Ⓜ Icharishahar

A UNESCO World Heritage Site, the Palace of the Shirvanshahs is an impressive sandstone complex that forms the **Old Town's centrepiece**. Some of the buildings on site date as far back as the twelfth century, but most of the ensemble as seen today dates from the fifteenth century, when the Shirvanshahs were at the height of their power and influence. It's particularly associated with the three successive shahs, Ibrahim I, Khalilullah I and Farrukh Yasar, who ruled from 1382 to 1500.

The highlight is perhaps the **divankhana**, an octagonal platform in a small walled-off courtyard. This beautifully carved structure is thought to be where the Shahs convened

0   200
metres

SALATIN ASGAROVA STREET
SALATIN ASGAROVA STREET
SAMAD VURGUN STREET
SHAMIL AZIZBEYOV STREET
RASID BEHBUDOV STREET
SULEYMAN RUSTAM STREET
AZADLIQ AVENUE
MARDANOV GARDASHLARY STREET
RASUL RZA STREET
SHAMIL AZIZBEYOV STREET
SULEYMAN RAGIMOV STREET
BULBUL AVENUE
Salaam Cinema
Cinema Plus
FUZULI STREET
SULEYMAN RAGIMOV STREET
FUZULI STREET
Heydar əliyev Park
SHAMSI BADALBEYLI STREET
SULEYMAN RUSTAM STREET
FUZULI STREET
Fuzuli Park
SAMAD VURGUN STREET
DILARA ALIYEVA STREET
Winter Park
MIRZAGHA ALIYEV STREET
DILARA ALIYEVA STREET
KICHIK DANIZ STREET
RASID BEHBUDOV STREET
28TH MAY STREET
CHINGIZ MUSTAFAYEV STREET
MOLLA VALI VIDADI ST
BULBUL AVENUE
Hop On Hop Off Bus
ALIMARDAN TOPCHUBASHOV STREET
CHINGIZ MUSTAFAYEV STREET
MOLLA VALI VIDADI ST
BASHIR SAFAR-OGHLU STREET
ALOVSAT GULIYEV STREET
28TH MAY STREET
Azerbaijan State Academic Opera and Ballet Theatre
HAZI ASLANOV STREET
NIZAMI STREET
RASUL RZA STREET
LEV TOLSTOY STREET
KHAGANI STREET
ALOVSAT GULIYEV STREET
HAZI ASLANOV STREET
QOQOL STREET
NIZAMI STREET
NIZAMI STREET
UZEYIR HAJIBEYOV STREET
LEV TOLSTOY STREET
RASUL RZA STREET
NIZAMI STREET
KHAGANI STREET
BULBUL AVENUE
Sahil
NIZAMI STREET
FOUNTAINS SQUARE
YUSIF MAMMADALIYEV STREET
UZEYIR HAJIBEYOV STREET
SAMAD VURGUN STREET
HAJI ZEYNALABDIN TAGHIYEV STREET
ZƏRIFƏ ƏLIYEVA STREET
Museum Center
NEFTCHILAR AVENUE
Nizami Park
SEE BAKU: OLD TOWN MAP FOR DETAILS
Nizami Museum of Azerbaijani Literature
TARLAN ALIYARBEYOV STREET
National Museum of History of Azerbaijan
MAMMADAMIN RASULZADEH
AZIZ ƏLIYEV STREET
NEFTCHILAR AVENUE
Baku Khans Palace Museum
AZIZ ƏLIYEV STREET
ZƏRIFƏ ƏLIYEVA STREET
BOYUK QALA
SABIR STREET
Museum of Archaeology and Ethnography
Baku Puppet Theatre
Bukhara Caravanserai
Hajinski Residence
NEFTCHILAR AVENUE

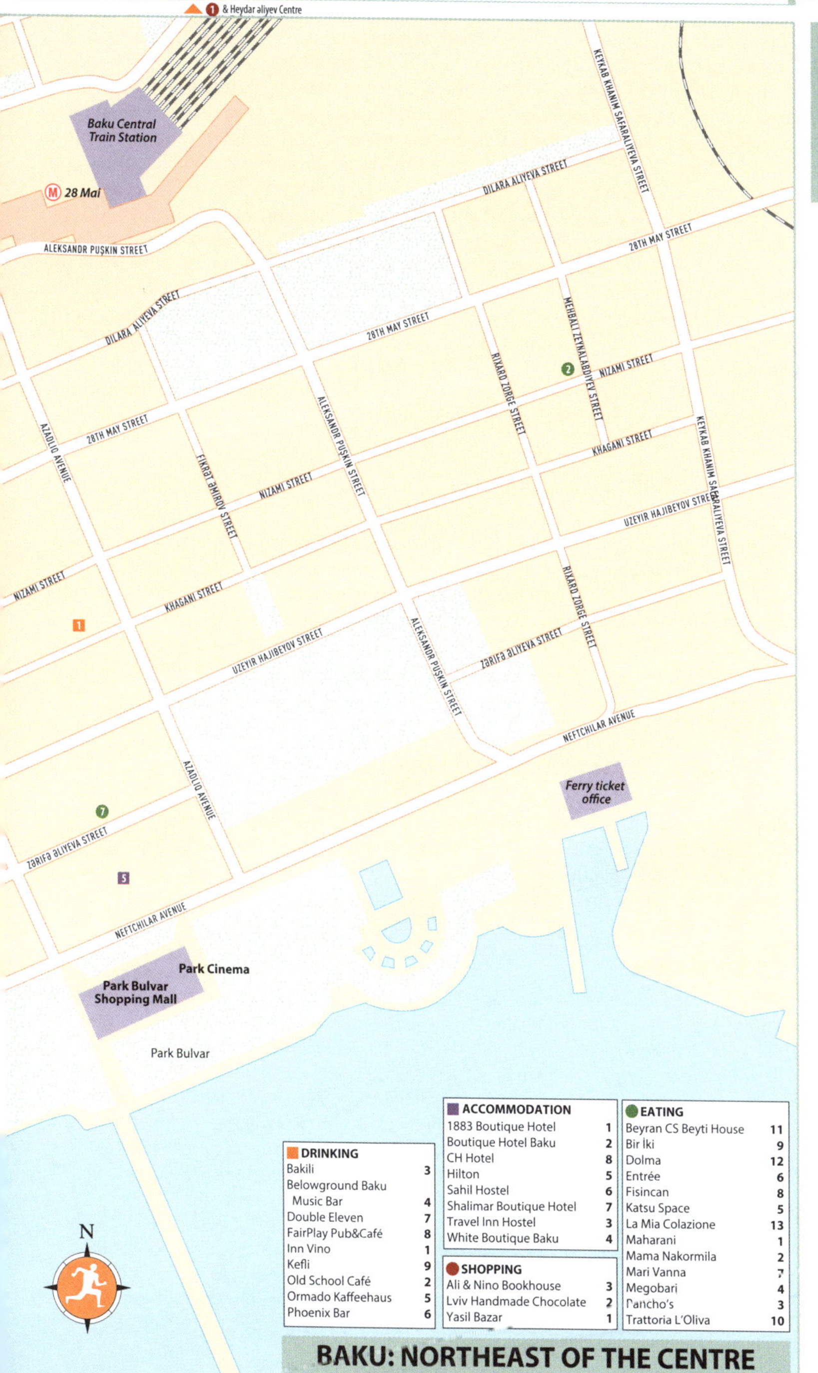

DRINKING

Bakili	3
Belowground Baku Music Bar	4
Double Eleven	7
FairPlay Pub&Café	8
Inn Vino	1
Kefli	9
Old School Café	2
Ormado Kaffeehaus	5
Phoenix Bar	6

ACCOMMODATION

1883 Boutique Hotel	1
Boutique Hotel Baku	2
CH Hotel	8
Hilton	5
Sahil Hostel	6
Shalimar Boutique Hotel	7
Travel Inn Hostel	3
White Boutique Baku	4

SHOPPING

Ali & Nino Bookhouse	3
Lviv Handmade Chocolate	2
Yasil Bazar	1

EATING

Beyran CS Beyti House	11
Bir İki	9
Dolma	12
Entrée	6
Fisincan	8
Katsu Space	5
La Mia Colazione	13
Maharani	1
Mama Nakormila	2
Mari Vanna	7
Megobari	4
Pancho's	3
Trattoria L'Oliva	10

BAKU: NORTHEAST OF THE CENTRE

their court. It's easy to miss the entrance to the divankhana's courtyard: turn left after buying your ticket and step through the gap in the wall.

The main palace building hosts an informative museum, exhibiting a variety of artefacts including weapons, musical instruments, copper dishes and ceramic tiles. As is standard practice in Azerbaijani museums, there are some silly multimedia exhibits, but here these are less intrusive than they usually are and consist generally of random inexplicable clunking noises emerging from holes in the ground.

After visiting the divankhana and palace building, head down the staircase under the arch to the remainder of the palace grounds. Don't miss the family tomb (dating from the 1430s) with the magnificent ornate carving on its entrance, or the view from above of the ruined but fascinating bathhouse. Finally, at the back of the complex, you'll find the small but distinctive **Key Gubad Mosque**, which was built in the early fourteenth century and thus pre-dates much of the complex. It was partly destroyed in 1918 during the inter-ethnic violence of the March Days.

Guided tours and audio-guides are available and, depending on the quality of the guide, these can be excellent or uniquely tedious.

Museum of Miniature Books

67 Icheri Sheher • Free • Ⓦ minibooks.az/en • Ⓜ Icharishahar

The quirky **Museum of Miniature Books** does what it says on the tin: it houses a huge collection of tiny books, with titles ranging from the Qu'ran to *The Tale of Peter Rabbit*. Books are organised by country of origin (to some extent) and there is also a delightful children's section. As of 2014, the collection was recognised by the Guinness Book of Records as being the largest collection of small books in the world, though this claim does rather raise the question of how many other collections of small books there are in the world.

Museum of Archaeology and Ethnography

Boyuk Qala • ☎ 994 12 4925236 • Ⓜ Icharishahar

Closed for renovation at the time of research but promising to reopen soon, the museum's exhibits cover Azerbaijan's history from the Stone Age to the medieval era, as well as an extensive ethnographic section largely focused on the eighteenth and nineteenth centuries.

MARCH DAYS

The chaos that followed the collapse of Tsarist power in the Caucasus broke out into **violence** in late March 1918, when Soviet authorities – led by **Stepan Shahumyan** (see page 212) – considered themselves under threat from the 'Savage Division', a former Imperial Russian cavalry unit composed of Caucasian soldiers, primarily Muslims from Azerbaijan, Dagestan and Chechnya. Ignoring Lenin's advice to practice diplomacy, Shahumyan arrested the Division's commander, igniting a spark that led to a short but bloody **civil war** between the Soviets and Armenian Dashnaks on one side, and the Azerbaijani Musavat party on the other. This quickly descended into indiscriminate ethnic violence, resulting in the deaths of up to ten thousand Azerbaijanis and 2,500 Armenians.

The conflict officially ended after five days, but killings continued for weeks afterwards. The immediate political result was the end of Musavat influence in the Baku area, allowing the Soviets to establish the Baku Commune. The Soviet authorities tried to suppress the incident, and omitted mention of it in historical texts. Azeris now regard the **March Days** as an act of genocide, and there are monuments in remembrance across the country, most notably the **Genocide Complex at Quba**.

Baku Khan's Palace Museum

Kichik Qala • Ⓜ Icharishahar

This eighteenth-century palace was home of the Baku khans following the collapse of the Shirvanshah state. It has enjoyed substantial renovations, and is now a clean and tidy pedestrianised area with a couple of cafés, as well as a glass floor through which you can admire the palace's bathhouse.

Fountains Square and around

Less than a five-minute walk from the old town's northern gate is Fountains Square, a modern city centre square which contains, among other things, the world's largest KFC. In the immediate vicinity are a couple of museums of varying interest, but the main attraction of this area is the impressive early twentieth century architecture and the many enticing eating, drinking and shopping outlets.

Fountains Square

Fountains Sq • Free • Ⓜ Sahil

Fountains Square is an attractive large plaza with small, well-tended, mildly exotic gardens in the centre, flanked by sculptures and statues that range from the treasured to the tacky. At one end of the scale the replica moai heads are utterly unnecessary, at the other, the bronze statue of a Baku girl sitting on a bench applying her make-up seems to sum up the whole city somehow.

There's also a cluster of large, mirrored spheres which offer interestingly angled reflections of the square and a number of fountains, though these don't always have water in them and can be thus a bit underwhelming. The best time of day to catch them with water is the early evening, when local families tend to visit the square to see and be seen.

Nizami Museum of Azerbaijani Literature

53 Istiglaliyyat • Charge • Ⓦ nizamimuseum.az/en • Ⓜ Sahil

This museum, though not exclusively limited to literature, focuses on the great historical writers who hailed from Azerbaijan, most notably Nizami Ganjevi. It frequently seems to be closed for "clean up", but even if the museum isn't open, the exterior is worth a look, with a beautiful Central Asian-style door and statues of prominent Azerbaijani writers in alcoves along the west side.

National Museum of History of Azerbaijan

4 Haji Zeynalabdin Taghiyev St • Ⓦ azhistorymuseum.gov.az/en/ • Ⓜ Sahil

The building is the former home of a nineteenth-century oil magnate and the museum interior is decorated with all the opulence that you'd expect. The exhibits, which range from ancient coins to Soviet carpets, will give you an overview of Azerbaijan's history from the Neolithic period to the present day. Look out for the beautifully decorated **eighteenth century cradle** of Muhammad Husayn, the khan of Sheki.

Museum Center

123a Neftchilar Prospect • Tues–Sun 10am–6pm • Charge • Ⓦ museumcenter.az/en • Ⓜ Sahil

This grand Neoclassical building on a traffic island in the middle of Neftchilar Prospect is more interesting from the outside than in. Once the Lenin Museum, it still has the carved hammer and sickle above the door. The building contains two permanent exhibitions. One is a display of musical instruments, which is exactly what it sounds like it is, while the other offers a display on the independence of Azerbaijan, which is very partisan on the issue of Nagorno-Karabakh and is also an excellent demonstration of the personality cult around Aliyev Sr and Jr.

You can pay an additional charge for an English guide, which will certainly give you a thorough understanding of the exhibits, but it's only recommended if you have time on your hands as the tours are very in depth.

Bulvar

Visitors to Baku will inevitably soon find themselves on the Bulvar, a large pedestrianised area that stretches along the Caspian seafront which is ideal for strolling. Along its length are several attractions, of which the one must-see is the outstanding Carpet Museum.

Carpet Museum

28 Mikayıl Hüseynov Prospekt • Charge • Ⓦ azcarpetmuseum.az/front/en • Ⓜ Icharishahar

A **striking building** that resembles a rolled-up carpet, the **Carpet Museum** walks the visitor through the history of Azerbaijani carpets, detailing which plants are used for dyeing particular colours and exhibits instruments used in carpet making. You're then teased with goods like saddlebags and cushions made in the same way as carpets. All that's well enough, but the real draw here are the carpets themselves, of which there are a lot, some of them remarkably beautiful.

On the first floor, there are plenty of rugs, interspersed with detailed information about the various carpet styles to be found around Azerbaijan. If that's not enough carpet for you, then the second floor has an exhibit about Azeri carpet-making in the twentieth century, some of which attempted – for better or worse – to bring a socialist realism aesthetic to the carpet designs. More modern design efforts offer striking departures from traditional patterns, with one 2012 example featuring an oil rig.

There's an additional fee if you want to take photos on your camera, but there's no charge for smartphone photography.

Little Venice

73 Neftchilar Prospect • Charge • Ⓜ Icharishahar

This is a very silly area near the Carpet Museum where it is possible to hire a gondola and punt around a short series of artificial waterways. No one ever seems to actually do this, so it's probably best reserved for those wishing to make a show of themselves.

Baku Eye

Bulvar • Charge • Ⓜ Icharishahar

For a good view over the city and the Caspian, take a ride on Baku's big wheel, just along the Bulvar from the Carpet Museum and the Sydney-Opera-House-aping **Caspian Waterfront Mall**. Note that if it's windy the **Baku Eye** will not be operating.

Flag Square

Bulvar • Free • Bus 125

At one time this square hosted the world's tallest flagpole, but it was soon outdone by a contender from Tajikistan. Perhaps in a fit of pique, the Azerbaijani government removed the flagpole for renovation in 2017 and it hasn't been seen since. There was a flurry of excitement in early 2022, when it was announced that a new flagpole would be soon erected here which would reclaim the title of World's Tallest Flagpole. No further progress seems to have been made.

Nearby is the **Crystal Hall**, a striking if not particularly attractive building constructed for Baku's hosting of the 2012 Eurovision Song Contest. It's subsequently hosted concerts by international artists such as Rihanna, and it is the fifth largest concert hall in the world by capacity, if that's the sort of statistic that excites you. Also in the vicinity is a steam engine sitting proudly, if incongruously, on the seafront.

Surakhani Ship Museum

Gulla • Charge • Ⓦ surakhanishipmuseum.az/en • Bus 125

This **former oil tanker** has been converted into an interesting museum which explores the history of the oil and shipping industry of Azerbaijan and the Caspian Sea. It's a well laid out place, with plenty of information and interactive exhibits. The guided tours are excellent.

Central Baku

The area between the Old Town and the funicular is compact but hosts a couple of sights, as well as some immaculate gardens running parallel to the Old Town walls southeast from Ⓜ Icharishahar to the Bulvar, which make a very pleasant location for a stroll.

Azerbaijan State Museum of Art

9/11 Nizayi St • Charge • Ⓦ nationalartmuseum.az • Ⓜ Icharishahar

This large museum is housed in a grand nineteenth-century edifice that was once a girls' school. Inside, you'll find collections of both Azerbaijani and European art. The European section, in the magnificent de Boer mansion, cleverly begins with works from Iran and China, before moving on to displays of Russian, French, German and Dutch art, none of which are particularly noteworthy.

The Azerbaijani side, meanwhile, is a showcase for the **nation's most famous painters**, including the brightly coloured canvases of Sattar Bahlulzadeh and modernist works by Asaf Jafarov. There are some interesting works here – including Tahir Salahov's reframing of the Eiffel Tower as a red-eyed demon and Rasim Babeyev's monochrome, almost comic-book-esque picture of Xinaliq.

The second floor houses an engaging exhibition on Azerbaijani art through the ages, including archaeological finds, ethnographic exhibits and some fantastically beautiful carpets, as well as pictures, while the top floor is home to modern Azerbaijani art as well as a hall for temporary exhibitions.

Taze Bey Hamam

Abdullah Shaig St • Free • Ⓦ tazebey.az • Ⓜ Icharishahar

For an astonishing insight into utter madness, stick your nose into this hamam. It's crazy enough on the outside, with gold statues of people and animals adorning the street, but inside this is taken to a whole new level of ridiculousness. Every wall in the vast labyrinthine place is coated with a demented mishmash of random things – pictures, toys, lamps, you name it. It is a working hamam, but the staff have no problem with you simply wandering around if you don't want to be scrubbed and buffed.

9

Flame Towers area

The Flame Towers can be seen from pretty much anywhere in the city, but close up their size is truly impressive. Nearby, you'll find the Martyrs' Lane, which commemorates the victims of recent conflicts and Soviet repression.

Funicular

Shovkat Alakbarova • Charge • Ⓜ Icharishahar

The easiest way between the Bulvar and the Flame Towers is via the **funicular** railway, which takes four minutes to trundle up or down the hill. It's soundtracked by minor pop hits of the late 90s which you've probably forgotten about and had no great desire to remember. You will probably need to queue at the Bulvar end but coming back down you can usually get straight on.

At the top of the funicular are a couple of monuments of minor interest: a sculpture of the Azerbaijani Great Patriotic War hero **Hazi Aslanov** (see page 283), and a **monument to the Turkish forces** killed fighting against the Bolsheviks in 1918. There's

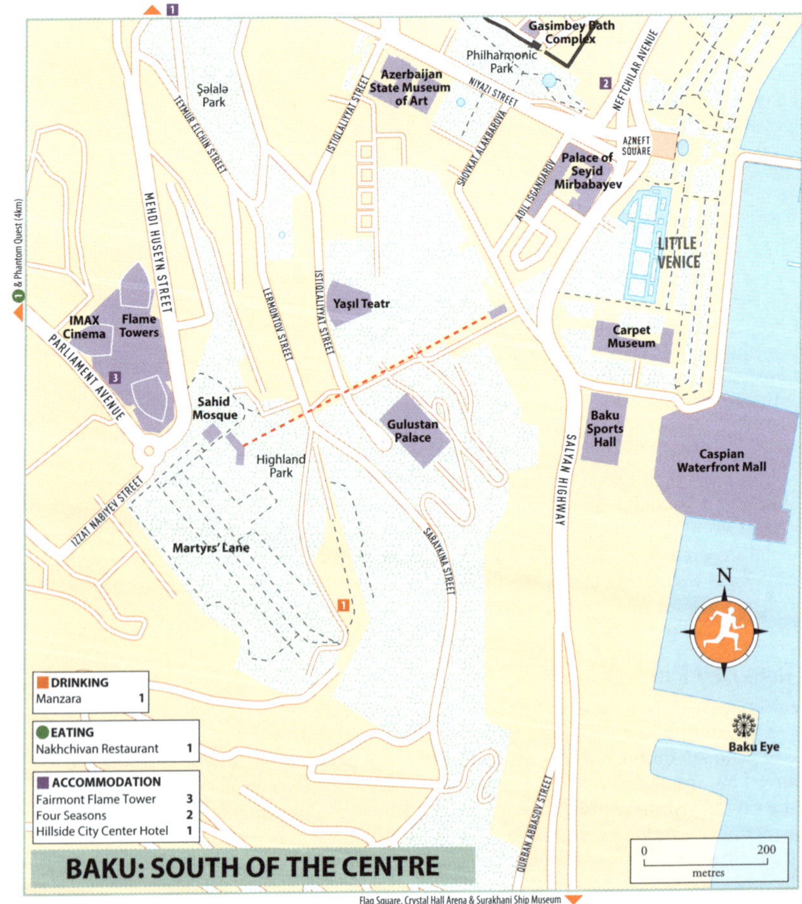

also the **Sahid Mosque**, an elegant little mosque with beautiful tiles and stained glass inside.

Flame Towers

Parliament Ave • Free • Funicular

Visible from all over Baku, the **Flame Towers** are a set of three plate-glass skyscrapers designed to look like tongues of fire. At night, they're lit up with LED screens for an ever-changing display of colours and effects, and form an impressive backdrop to the city. The towers are home to apartments, offices, and the luxury Fairmont Hotel (see page 263).

Martyrs' Lane

Mehdi Huseyn St • Free • Funicular

This site was initially used as a cemetery for the Muslim victims of the **March Days**, but under Soviet rule the area was swiftly remodelled to suppress any memory of these events. Following independence, the park became a memorial ground once again. There are now three pine-tree-lined avenues of black marble graves of the victims of the 1990 Soviet crackdown and the Nagorno-Karabakh Wars. At the southern end is the **Shahidlar (Eternal Flame) Monument**, an elegant octagonal structure.

Follow the path down to the left of the Shahidlar Monument and you'll come to a large paved platform where you'll get a great view of the sweep of the Bay of Baku and the city's innovative architecture – you can easily spot the Carpet Museum, Crystal Hall and the waterfront mall from here. It's also a great place from which you can admire the Flame Towers.

East of centre

Although most of Baku's sights are handily located in its centre, it's well worth taking the time to make a trip out to the east of the city to see one of its architectural masterpieces: the sleek and sparkling white Heydar Aliyev Centre. Also found to the centre's east is the often overlooked but immensely enjoyable and Museum of Modern Art.

Heydar Aliyev Centre

1 Heydar Aliyev prospekt • Charge • Ⓦ heydaraliyevcenter.az • Ⓜ Nariman Narimanov

The **Heydar Aliyev Centre** is a truly remarkable building. Designed by the late Iraqi-British, award-winning architect Zaha Hadid, it seems to flow with endless curves rather than restricting itself to the tyranny of angles. The building is bright white and on a sunny day it reflects the light in the most mesmerising way, and you'll enjoy walking around it, viewing its fabulousness from all perspectives. There's a sculpted grassy park leading up to it, populated by colourful statues of rabbits and snails.

The Centre contains an exhibition about the life of – who else? – Heydar Aliyev, which is interesting enough in its own hagiographic way. There's also a classic cars exhibition, ticketed separately.

Next door, the Baku Convention Centre is striking in its own right but pales in comparison to the Heydar Aliyev Centre. Apparently the Convention Centre is "not for civil people", so you'll have to be content with admiring it from the outside only anyway.

THE "WAR CRIMES THEME PARK"

To the east of the Museum of Modern Art is the distasteful **Military Trophy Park**, which was established in 2021 after Azerbaijan's victory in the Nagorno-Karabakh conflict the previous year. As well as displaying military hardware, the park contained hundreds of helmets belonging to dead Armenian soldiers, and waxwork dummies of Armenian soldiers with exaggerated features. The park drew international condemnation, with the European Parliament describing it as a "glorification of violence" and many independent observers branding it racist and ghoulish. The helmets and waxworks were subsequently removed, but the park remains open, despite calls for its immediate closure.

Museum of Modern Art

5 Yusuph Safarov • Charge • Ⓦ moma.az/en • Ⓜ Khatai

A little out on a limb at a less-visited end of the Bulvar is Baku's **Museum of Modern Art**, which is well worth a visit to view its fine – if eccentrically arranged – collection of contemporary works by Azerbaijani artists, which are complemented by pieces by European painters including Dali and Picasso. The museum guides are knowledgeable and can offer interesting tours.

Outskirts

If you have time to spare, there are a couple of minor attractions on the seafront road heading out of town to the west. If you have your own transport, or an accommodating taxi driver, they make a decent quick stop on a trip to Qobustan (see page 281).

Shikhov Beach

Salyan Highway • Free • Bus 125

If Mordor from *The Lord of the Rings* book trilogy had a beach, it would not be dissimilar to this. The sand is gritty and at times more akin to mud. The water is murky. Dust from the adjoining building site whips into your eyes. It's strewn with litter and glass. And there's an imposing oil platform just offshore. It's almost mersmerisingly ugly, yet strangely compelling.

  It takes about half an hour to get there on bus number 125 from outside the Unique shop on the seafront, opposite Little Venice. Get off by the customs building when the oil platform comes into view, then cross the dual carriageway – carefully! – and take the dirt track opposite down to the beach.

Bibiheybat Mosque

Bibiheybat Road • Free • Bus 125

Built on the site of the grave of Okuma Khanim, sister of the eighth Imam of the Shiite branch of Islam, the **Bibiheybat Mosque** was constructed in the thirteenth century and destroyed in the Soviet anti-religious campaign of the 1930s. Following the independence of Azerbaijan, it was decided to reconstruct the mosque based on photographs and written records of the original. It's an attractive yellow stone building, with beautiful carving around its portal, and is well worth a stop if you're heading out along the road to the south.

ARRIVAL AND DEPARTURE   BAKU

By plane There are regular flights to Baku's Heydar Aliyev Airport from worldwide airports, including London, Moscow, Beijing and Delhi, as well as from more local cities such as Istanbul and Tbilisi. Your flight will most likely arrive at the clean, shiny and modern Terminal 1. The more dated Terminal 2 is primarily for internal flights, including those to Nakhchivan.

Getting through the border is quick and easy so long as your documents are in order. Luggage reclaim shouldn't keep you waiting too long either, and there's a currency exchange booth and a cash machine in the baggage hall. Once through customs, you'll find a variety of services such as car rental and SIM card vendors: don't exit the airport until you're sure you've got all you want from these services, as you'll have to join a queue to have your bag X-rayed if you want to re-enter.

To/from the airport The Airport Express to town goes every half hour in the daytime, and hourly at night. You can buy a single ticket or purchase a BakuKart for a small additional cost, which will allow you to travel elsewhere on the city's public transport. Either way, you buy tickets from the machines which are surreptitiously placed on either side of the airport's exit.

Bear in mind that the machines don't give change so if you only have large denomination notes then buy a coffee from the friendly stand on the right side of the exit (as you look at it from outside). The owner of this stand is a chatty fellow who'll wax on about the origin of Americano coffee and – perhaps more relevantly – can explain how the BakuKart works.

There are plenty of police hovering around to 'help' but they are prone to telling you that the bus doesn't go to your intended destination and may try to hustle you into a taxi – just remain friendly but firm in your intention to buy a bus ticket.

The road to/from the airport is a good multi-lane highway and along the way you'll see plenty of Baku's extravagant, ambitious and – some might say – slightly silly modern architecture. The bus terminates at 28 Mai Square, where you can transfer onto the red line on the metro if you're heading to the Old Town.

Alternatively, a taxi to or from the town centre is about 40 manat. Be aware that occasionally you will be quoted "25" – you're not getting a bargain, the driver is simply quoting you in US dollars.

By train Baku's central train station is at 28 Mai Square, a convenient location but still probably too far to walk from or to your hotel; use the red line on the metro from the Old Town or the Fountains Square area. You can buy tickets at the station, or in advance online at ⓦ ticket.ady.az, though at time of writing this once-helpful website had removed all its English language information.

Domestic services include Ganja (three daily, four to six hours), Sheki (daily, overnight sleeper, eight hours), Lankaran (daily, overnight sleeper, seven hours) and, for the Iranian border, Astara (daily, overnight sleeper, eight hours). International routes from Baku were suspended during the Covid-19 pandemic and at time of writing have yet to resume. Assuming the same services are on offer when the borders reopen, there will be a daily train to Tbilisi, taking 12 hours, and a more irregular service to Derbent in Russia running roughly every two to three days and taking about seven hours. There may also be a weekly service to Moscow, taking two days. There have long been plans to link Azerbaijan's rail network with Iran's, but no progress on this project has been made for several years.

By bus Baku's main bus station (Sumqayit Highway, ☏ 994 12 4997038) is not particularly conveniently positioned. It's about 10km north of town, on a separate branch of the metro line (at the station Autovozgul), meaning you'll have to change trains twice (once at 28 Mai and once at Memar Ajami) to get there. Alternatively, you can get bus number 37 from the centre or take a taxi.

Domestic buses go to pretty much everywhere in Azerbaijan from here; destinations include Sheki (approximately every hour from 8am, five hours), Qabala (four daily, hourly from 1pm, four hours), Ismailli (every hour from 9am, 2.5 hours), Ganja (every half hour from 7am, five hours), Lankaran (every hour from 8.15am, 2.5 hours), Astara (every hour from 7.30am, three hours), and Quba (every hour from 7.30am, 2.5 hours).

Azerbaijan's road borders with its neighbours are closed to incoming travellers, but may be open for those leaving the country. If they are running, international destinations include Tbilisi (twice daily, 9pm and 11pm, nine hours), Machakhala (Thurs 2pm, seven hours), Moscow (Sat, 2pm, 32 hours), Tehran (Fri–Sun, 9am, eleven hours) and Istanbul (daily, 11am, 32 hours).

Buses to Nakhchivan are also available here, but they go via Iran, so unless you've got a double-entry Azeri visa and an Iranian visa this service will be of little use to you.

Domestic bus tickets can be booked online at ⓦ avtovagzal. az – note that this website can only be used to book buses from Baku.

By car Car hire is possible from the airport and the centre of town. Driving in the centre is not particularly recommended, as the traffic is heavy, the driving style can be aggressive, and it's not easy to find a place to park – and even if you do, the chances of being boxed in by someone parking around you are pretty high. Taking a car from the airport to travel round the rest of the country, however, is a good option, allowing you to see Azerbaijan on your own terms. Traffic is much lighter outside Baku.

By ferry The idea of taking a ferry across the Caspian Sea (to Aktau in Kazakhstan or Turkmenbashi in Turkmenistan) is a romantic one, but the reality is rather different. The services are not luxury passenger liners, but cargo ships which are willing to sell you a berth. These ships depart from the large port of Alat some 70km south of Baku rather than the capital itself, and although there's technically a schedule, you can't expect the services to stick to it. You may find yourself aboard ship for hours or even days waiting to depart, or waiting to disembark at the other end. At time of writing, it was not possible to enter Azerbaijan by this route, but leaving is permitted. When Azerbaijan reopens its land borders, it should once again be possible to arrive by ferry. Tickets for the service can be purchased online at ⓦ asco.az/en, where you'll also find information about the upcoming schedule. You could also try going to, the ticket office on the Bulvar near the Marriott Hotel, but there's very rarely anyone there. Calling the office on ☎ 994 559 999124 (for the Aktau route) or ☎ 994 559 999061 (for Turkmenbashi) may yield results.

INFORMATION

Tourist information Baku's tourist info centre is found on Boyuk Qala, just inside the main gates to the Old Town. It contains a couple of interactive maps of the Old Town showing sights, restaurants, hotels and more. The staff can arrange walking tours of the Old Town for you, and they do offer tours outside the city to Qobustan, Abseron and so forth, but oddly they try to discourage you from taking these tours. They can also offer advice on onward transport by bus or train but cannot arrange it for you. Mon–Fri 9am–6pm.

Maps Free maps of Baku's centre are available at the tourist information centre, as well as in most hotels.

Listings ⓦ azerbaijan.travel/new-event-calendar will tell you what the big upcoming events are in Baku, such as international football matches and major concerts. For more detailed listings, try ⓦ 10times.com/baku-az or ⓦ iticket.az/en/events. ⓦ azerbaijan.travel/entertainment-with-kids will give those travelling with children a few ideas.

Tour operators You can barely move in the Old Town without being offered a walking tour or a day trip, so it's not hard to find someone willing to take you wherever you want to go.

TES Tours 25 Sabir St, ☎ 994 55 6991040, ⓦ testour.az; ⓜ Icharishahar. Slicker than most, this helpful agency run tours to national destinations both near and far – it's even possible to visit Xinaliq or Qabala from Baku using their services, though it is a long day. Their easy-to-use website allows online booking, and they employ knowledgeable guides with excellent language skills.

GETTING AROUND

Baku has a good public transport network, consisting primarily of buses and the metro. Trips on both are very cheap and need to be paid for with a reloadable BakuKart, which can be purchased from all metro stations, and several bus stops.

By metro The metro system is fast and efficient, with three lines: red, green and purple. LED displays on station platforms give the name of the next train's destination in the appropriate colour for its line, so you'll always be sure you're on the correct train. The red and green lines run parallel for much of their length and you're likely to only use the purple line for getting to the bus station. On arrival, stations are announced in Azeri and English in a rather smug tone, with some calming musical accompaniment. Photography in the stations is not permitted, which is a shame as some of them have a degree of Soviet grandeur.

By bus The bus network is extensive, but it's not easy to find reliable information on the schedule. The user-maintained website Wikiroutes (ⓦ wikiroutes.info/en/baku/catalog) offers some hints, but things change frequently and it's best to ask at your hotel or in the tourist information centres. Helpfully, many bus stops (in the centre at least) have an electronic display telling you what services are coming and how soon they are expected.

You could also make use of the Hop-On-Hop-Off tourist bus, which will take you on a one-hour 30-minute circuit round the city's top sights, including the Maiden Tower, the Heydar Aliyev Centre and the Flame Towers. You can pick it up from Azadlag Square from 10am. It's not the cheapest option, though.

By funicular The funicular chugs up and down the hill to the Flame Towers every 15 minutes or so.

By taxi There are plenty of reliable taxis roaming the streets in Baku; particularly handy spots to pick them up are from outside the Old Town gates, from the Bulvar by the Four Seasons Hotel, and in 28 Mai Square. Some taxis are older Ladas, while others are smart purple London-style cabs, but there's no difference in price between them.

By bike Cycling along the Bulvar is pleasant, but elsewhere the busy roads and excitable driving styles make getting around by bike a not particularly recommended experience.

On foot The Old Town, Bulvar and Fountains Square district are walkable – it should take you no longer than 30 minutes to get wherever you need to be within this area. The Old Town is mostly pedestrianised, and there are large areas of pedestrianised streets around Fountains Square too. You can also walk up to the Flame Towers via a staircase next to the funicular in about 10 to 15 minutes.

Note that Baku's roads are busy and its drivers take no prisoners. Be extra careful when crossing roads, and be aware that some roads – notably Neftchilar Prospect along the Bulvar – have underpasses for pedestrians. It's illegal to cross the actual road, and there are plenty of police around at all times to extract fines if you do so.

ACCOMMODATION

Baku has accommodation in abundance. It can feel like every other building in the Old Town is a hotel, and it's not always easy to identify the good ones. You often get what you pay for when it comes to hotels; bargains – and even midrange prices – in the Old Town and around Fountains Square quite often indicate noisy or tired rooms.

The concept of hostels has been slow arriving in Baku. A couple of decent ones are beginning to spring up around Ⓜ Sahil. Many of those near the Ⓜ 28 Mai can't be recommended as they feel grubby and unfriendly.

OLD TOWN, SEE MAP PAGE 250

★ **Maajid Hotel** 58/ 1 Gasr ☎ 994 12 4922101; Ⓜ Icharishahar. In a converted old building just down the road from Shirvanshahs Palace, the *Maajid Hotel* has stylishly left much of the stonework exposed. The beds are comfortable, the staff are friendly and the location is great. Quite probably the best option in this price range in the Old Town. $$

Old Street Boutique Hotel 12 Sabir St Ⓦ oldstreethotel.com. A solid old town choice, the Old Street Boutique Hotel offers pleasant and spacious rooms, but perhaps the real draw is the excellent buffet breakfast served on the fantastic roof terrace. Some rooms suffer from a drainy smell, so ask to see a few. $$

Sands of Time 30 Kichik Qala ☎ 994 50 6808077; Ⓜ Icharishahar. A bit more effort has gone into the decoration here than in many other Old Town hotels in this price range. Also in its favour is its location on a quiet, yet central, street. On the downside it is plagued by internal noise – try to get a room on the top floor to minimise this. $$

Seven Rooms Boutique Hotel 27 Boyuk Qala Ⓦ sevenrooms.az/en; Ⓜ Icharishahar. This one does what it says on the tin: there are indeed seven rooms, all of which are clean and nicely decorated. Some rooms also have balconies which look out over this quiet street in the old town. The staff can also arrange drivers for excursions. $$

★ **Shah Palace Hotel** 47 Kichik Qala Ⓦ shahpalacehotel.com; Ⓜ Icharishahar. By far the most luxurious choice in the Old Town, the *Shah Palace* boasts beautiful rooms set around a sympathetically updated caravanserai dating from the eighteenth century. In the central courtyard you'll find various archaeological exhibits on display in glass cases set into the floor. $$$

EAST OF THE CENTRE, SEE MAP PAGE 252

1883 Boutique Hotel 37C Bulbul Ave Ⓦ 1883boutiquehotel.com; Ⓜ Sahil. With décor recalling the early twentieth century, this small hotel is friendly and comfy, and does a decent breakfast. It's not hugely central, and you'll want a room at the back if you're a light sleeper. $$

Boutique Hotel Baku 136 Alovsat Guliyev St Ⓦ boutiquehotelbaku.com; Ⓜ Sahil. The word 'boutique' is bandied about quite a lot in Baku's hotel scene, but this place perhaps deserves it more than most. The decoration

is attractive with flashes of decadence, the staff are friendly, and the breakfast – which is served on the top floor, from which you'll get great views – is very good. $$

CH Hotel 2 Tarlan Aliyarbeyov St ☎ 994 50 2555121; Ⓜ Sahil. In a good location not far from the Old Town and the Bulvar, the CH Hotel is clean and comfortable. It's a little lacking in character but at this price in this part of town, that's not a deal-breaker. $$

Hillside City Center Hotel 13 Jafarov Gardashlari St ☎ 994 50 2447095; Ⓜ Icharishahar. A short walk from the Old Town (calling itself 'city center' is pushing it a little), this friendly place offers snug and comfortable rooms at very reasonable prices. $

Hilton 1B Azadlig Ave Ⓦ hilton.com/en/hotels/ gydhbhi-hilton-baku; Ⓜ 28 Mai. Occupying a spot along the Bulvar not particularly close to the main sights, the Hilton offers 309 international standard rooms, but the jewel in its crown is the 360-degree rotating restaurant and bar (open 5pm–1am) which provides sensational views across the city and sea. It also has the gym, spa, and swimming pool that you expect in a hotel of this calibre. $$$$

Sahil Hostel 27 Zarifa Aliyeva St ☎ 994 50 8882101 Ⓦ sahilhostel.com. A strong contender for Baku's best hostel, the centrally located Sahil offers both dorms and private rooms, as well as a common area and kitchen facilities. It's a popular backpacker haunt, so is a great place to meet fellow travellers. $

Travel Inn Hostel 3rd floor, 16 Khagani St ☎ 994 70 4981008; Ⓜ Sahil. One of the better hostels in Baku, this clean and well-run place has several dorms, one of which is female only. It's in a very convenient location, and there's a balcony offering great views over the street below. $

White Boutique Baku 2nd floor, 49 Nigar Rafibayli ☎ 994 99 8151410; Ⓜ Sahil. White is definitely the word: these six rooms are all decorated in very pastel colours, mainly white. All rooms are slightly different, the best catch being the one with the balcony overlooking Nizami Street. Note that it's on the second floor, so when you enter the building don't be put off by the slightly grotty hall. $$

SOUTH OF THE CENTRE, SEE MAP PAGE 258

Fairmont Flame Tower Flame Towers, 1A Mehdi Huseyn St Ⓦ fairmont.com/baku; Ⓜ Icharishahar, then funicular. The arty lobby makes a good first impression, and the 312 rooms in the iconic Flame Tower hotel are all very classy, but feel somehow a bit sterile. Obviously there are fantastic views, the best is from the viewing gallery on Floor 28. The hotel also features a gym and spa (offering a range of treatments including the surprising "caviar and algae massage"), and there's an indoor and an outdoor pool. $$$$

Four Seasons 1 Neftchilar Prospect Ⓦ fourseasons. com/baku; Ⓜ Icharishahar. From the moment you enter the opulent and elegant lobby you know you're in for a classy experience. Even the standard rooms are luxurious, and all have a balcony with a view of the Old Town or the Caspian seafront; those facing the Old Town are generally better both view- and noise-wise. There are Italian and Azeri restaurants onsite, as well as a well-regarded whisky and cigar bar, and the requisite gym, pool, and spa. Staff are very proud of the TVs installed in the bathroom mirrors. ₷₷₷₷

EATING

You'll find a large number of places serving traditional Azerbaijani food in the Old Town, mostly along the northern wall. All offer the same cuisine and are nice enough but be aware that they are there for the tourist market and the prices reflect this. *Salam Baku* is our pick of these.

There are also loads of restaurants around Fountains Square, but exercise caution as many are overpriced and underwhelming. If you crave fast food, this is also where you'll find outlets of *McDonalds*, *Pizza Hut* and *KFC* – specifically, the largest *KFC* in the world.

OLD TOWN, SEE MAP PAGE 250

★ **Dolce Vita** 19 Aziz Aliyev St ☎ 994 50 2739919; Ⓜ Icharishahar. With a real Italian chef this classy restaurant is a step ahead of other Italian options in Baku. The pasta, pizzas and meaty main courses all taste authentic, the décor has a touch of the Sicilian about it and it's fun to watch the cooks at work in the open kitchen. There's a good wine list too. ₷₷

Salam Baku Kichik Qala ☎ 994 50 2021166; Ⓜ Icharishahar. One of many restaurants just inside the old city gates serving typical Azeri food, *Salam* has a pleasant outdoor terrace and an upstairs indoor room that feels a little decadent with velvet chairs and sofas, and an enormous bookshelf. It's good for breakfast (though watch out for the extravagantly priced orange juice) and evening meals – the lamb and apricot stew comes highly recommended. ₷₷

Pancho's 154 Lev Tolstoy St ☎ 994 55 6048023; Ⓜ Sahil. This relatively spartanly decorated restaurant serves up Baku's best Mexican food – burritos, tacos and nachos – as well as mixing very fine margaritas. The staff are extremely friendly, too, making it well worth a stop. ₷₷

★ **Xezer Kafe** 61a Istiglaliyat St; Ⓜ Icharishahar. The staircase down may look unassuming but once you're underground you'll find an evocative, traditionally decorated restaurant with an arched roof. This is one of the best central places for inexpensive and tasty local fare: in particular, the pilaf is great and the kebabs are excellent. ₷

EAST OF THE CENTRE, SEE MAP PAGE 252

Beyran CS Beyti House Fountains Square Ⓦ beyrancs. az; Ⓜ Sahil. You'll find excellent Turkish food at this popular place on Fountains Square: if it's lunchtime, go for one of the delicious pides, or in the evening try a perfectly grilled kebab or a warming güveç stew. ₷₷₷

Bir İki 27 Yusif MammadAliyev St, Ⓦ bir-iki.az/en; Ⓜ Sahil. If it's a quick and easy kebab you're after you won't find better than this convenient and cheap place just off Fountains Square. ₷

Dolma 53 Istigali St ☎ 994 12 4981938; Ⓜ Icharishahar. A vast cavernous place that seems to stretch right under Fountains Square, *Dolma*'s menu is as extensive as its floor space. The range of food covers Caucasian and Turkish cuisine, as well as a gesture towards Italian. The saj is good, as are the Georgian options, and the eponymous dolma are tasty too. ₷₷

Entrée 26G Nigar Rafibeyli St ☎ 994 55 5059592; Ⓜ Sahil. Great French-style bakery with a particularly good-value breakfast deal which includes a croissant, a sandwich, a glass of juice and a hot drink. There are several other branches around the city. ₷₷

Fisincan 63 Nizami St ☎ 994 12 5949990; Ⓜ Sahil. Conveniently located restaurant just off Fountains Square serving up tasty Azerbaijani fare: think pilaf, kebabs and dolma. There's a decent selection of local wines available to accompany your meal. ₷₷

Katsu Space 25C Khagani St ☎ 994 50 8007771; Ⓜ Sahil. Locals and tourists alike rave about the excellent Japanese food available at this place, a short walk from Molokan Gardens. The katsu curry comes particularly recommended. ₷₷

La Mia Colazione 8 Zarifa Aliyeva St ☎ 994 50 2328823; Ⓜ Sahil. If your hotel doesn't include breakfast, fear not – La Mia Colazione is here to save the day. Options include pancakes, scrambled eggs and avocado toast, accompanied by excellent coffee. Later in the day, it's a good choice for a waffle with fruit. ₷

Maharani off Dilara Aliyeva St Ⓦ maharani.az; Ⓜ 28 Mai. Smart and glossy Indian restaurant with plenty of staff and clientele hailing from the subcontinent. The spicy potato lollipops are innovative and excellent, the rice is fresh and fragrant, and the Lamb Kadai is delicious. ₷₷₷

Mama Nakormila 123 Khagani St ☎ 994 70 4931521; Ⓜ 28 Mai. This excellent and eclectically decorated Ukrainian restaurant is a great place to enjoy some hearty eastern European fare: highlights of the menu include goulash, varaniki dumplings and borsch. Finish up with a lipsmacking liqueur. ₷₷₷

Mari Vanna 93 Zarifa Aliyeva St ☎ 994 12 4049595; Ⓜ 28 Mai. The astonishing décor in this Russian restaurant genuinely feels as though you've stepped back in time to the Tsarist era. You'll find the Russian classics on the menu: stroganoff, borsch, syrniki pancakes, and plenty of vodka. In all honesty, the food can be hit and miss, but it's worth a visit to enjoy the old-time atmosphere. $$$

Megobari 19 Khagani St ☎994 55 2670501; Ⓜ Sahil. If you're hankering for Georgian food, this spot will do the trick. Khinkali and khachapuri are on the menu for lunch, and for more substantial fare, the lamb chakapuli is very tasty. There is sometimes live music in the evenings. $$

Trattoria L'Oliva 18 Haji Zeynalabdin Taghiyev St Ⓦ facebook.com/trattorialoliva; Ⓜ Sahil. Upmarket Italian restaurant serving decent pizzas, pastas and meat dishes. It's a little dark, which is nice and atmospheric in the evenings but can seem dingy in the daytime – try to get the table by the window. $$

SOUTH OF THE CENTRE, SEE MAP PAGE 258

★ **Nakhchivan** 8 Parliament Ave ☎994 12 4808585; Ⓜ Icharishahar, then funicular. Part of the Beat Group which operates several upmarket restaurants across Baku, this elegant place specialises in cuisine native to the Nakhchivan region, which generally means a greater emphasis on fruit and nuts. The sweet and sour pomegranate chicken is an excellent choice. It's decorated in an interesting style – modern, but with a hint of nineteenth-century decadence. $$$

DRINKING

There aren't as many cafés along the Bulvar as you might expect – instead, it's mostly just takeaway coffee and ice cream stands. However, the ice cream stands seem to specialise in goats' milk ice cream, which is something interesting to try. There are a few cafés located in other areas as well as tea houses and plenty of wine bars.

OLD TOWN, SEE MAP PAGE 250

Barfly Social Hub 41 Boyuk Qala Ⓦ facebook.com/barfly.baku; Ⓜ Icharishahar. DJs spin funky grooves and bar staff theatrically mix superb cocktails for you at this hip local hangout in the Old Town. Sometimes closed for private parties, and sometimes not closed for private parties, but they tell you it is if they don't like the look of you. They also offer local wine-tasting most afternoons.

Book and Coffee 8 Qulla ☎994 12 4977777; Ⓜ Icharishahar. Long-established café in the Old Town, decorated with bookshelves and serving up excellent coffee and cakes. Come the evening it turns into a relaxed spot for a glass or two of wine.

Çay Bağı 145 3 Kichik Qala ☎994 50 6000145; Ⓜ Icharishahar. This teahouse in the courtyard opposite the Maiden Tower may be a bit of a tourist trap, but in honesty, there isn't anywhere in the Old Town that offers a better view with your glass of çay.

Merci 16 Asef Zeynally St Ⓦ mercibaku.co; Ⓜ Icharishahar. Attractive café-bar opposite the Imam Ali mosque, bedecked with plants and fresh white furniture. There's a pleasant outdoor terrace too. You pay a little extra for location compared to options outside the Old Town.

EAST OF THE CENTRE, SEE MAP PAGE 252

Bakili 160 Lev Tolstoy St ☎994 50 9634214; Ⓜ Sahil. This stylish bar with a vaguely industrial feel has a a friendly vibe and great cocktails – either choose from the menu or ask the bar staff to mix something specially for you.

Belowground Baku Music Bar 121 Suleyman Tagizade St Ⓦ facebook.com/Belowgroundbaku; Ⓜ Sahil. This rather grungy underground nightspot is a great hangout, offering cheap beer, regular live music, and a friendly crowd. They also do food, though it's nothing special. It also sometimes goes by the name of Le Chateau.

Double Eleven 6C Haji Zeynalabdin Taghiyev St ☎994 50 2092611; Ⓜ Sahil. Cosy and centrally located bar with an excellent cocktail menu, a very fine wine list and a chilled soundtrack. You could do worse than settling in here for the evening.

Fairplay Pub&Café 8a Yusif MammadAliyev St Ⓦ facebook.com/FairPlayPubCafe; Ⓜ Sahil. Small and friendly pub offering local Xirdalen beer on tap, as well as plenty of bottled international beers. There's also a nice range of bar snacks including olives, deep-fried cheese and fried dushbara (mini-dumplings).

Inn Vino 73a Khagani St ☎994 55 3246383; Ⓜ Sahil. So many wine bottles… There's an amazing selection here, and the staff really know their stuff: they'll be able to recommend you a perfect wine, whatever your taste. The excellent cheese and meat plates make a delicious accompaniment.

★ **Kefli** 4a Tarlan Aliyarbeyov St Ⓦ facebook.com/kefliwinebar; Ⓜ Sahil. Swish and modern wine bar with an impressive selection of Azerbaijani wines. There is a weekly rotation of wines available by the glass, friendly staff and a chilled crowd, making this a good spot to while away the evening.

★ **Old School Café** 23 Alimardan Topchubashov St Ⓦ facebook.com/oldschool.cafeandshop; Ⓜ Sahil. Very heavy on the nostalgia – full of relics from the Russian and Soviet eras – and with a fantastic jazzy soundtrack, the *Old School Café* is an atmospheric place for a coffee by day or a beer by night. Limited food menu available.

Ormado Kaffeehaus 23b Yusif MammadAliyev St ☎994 50 2535563 Ⓦ ormado.de; Ⓜ Sahil. The frontage makes this place look a bit dingy but once you enter you'll find a sleek, modern, friendly coffee house. The owner is (with good reason) very proud of the Kenyan coffee which is imported here via Germany.

Phoenix Bar Yusif MammadAliyev St ☎994 12

3059090; Ⓜ Sahil. A spit-and-sawdust place for a couple of beers, the *Phoenix* feels like a British pub, though admittedly not a particularly good one. There's a pool table and good Xirdalen on tap.

SOUTH OF THE CENTRE, SEE MAP PAGE 258

Manzara Panoramic viewpoint, off Lermontov St ☎ 994 10 3160001; Ⓜ Icharishahar then funicular. Great for a coffee, tea or soft drink after yomping your way up the stairs to the panoramic viewpoint, *Manzara* is an obvious tourist spot but a very pleasant one. Sit and enjoy the views over the city and sea. Make sure to study the bill carefully as sudden rampant hyperinflation has been known to strike.

ENTERTAINMENT

Planet Hollywood has a wide range of activities for you to try, including karaoke, a private cinema and a PlayStation room.

CINEMAS

It's not too hard to find a spot for the latest blockbusters, though they're sometimes dubbed into Russian, so do check before buying tickets. Options include the Park Cinema on the Bulvar (ⓦ parkcinema.az) and Cinema Plus in the 28 May mall (ⓦ mall28.az/brands/cinema-plus). The Salaam Cinema (10 Süleyman Rüstam Street, ⓦ facebook.com/salaamcinemabaku) is probably the best place to see indie films in Baku. There's also the IMAX cinema in the Flame Towers (ⓦ imax.com/en/gb/theatre/azercell-imax).

THEATRES

Azerbaijan State Academic Opera and Ballet Theatre 95 Nizami St ⓦ iticket.az/en/venue/azerbaijan-state-academic-opera-and-ballet-theatre; Ⓜ Sahil. Regular performances of opera and ballet in a grand rococo theatre, which could do with a bit of TLC. Ticket prices are reasonable.

Baku Puppet Theatre 77 Neftchilar Ave ⓦ kuklateatri.az; Ⓜ Sahil. Built in 1910 as a cinema, this neoclassical building has been operating as a puppet theatre since the 1930s. Performances are for both adults and children.

SHOPPING

The Old Town is awash with souvenir stalls and shops. The stand opposite Rast Café just to the west of the Maiden's Tower is a good place to find Soviet memorabilia. Carpet shops are ubiquitous – Flying Carpets next to the Maiden's Tower is one of many.

Outside the Old Town there are several glitzy shopping malls (including 28 May Mall (ⓦ mall28.az) and Port Baku Mall (ⓦ portbakumall.az), and along the pedestrianised Nizami Street you'll find plenty of shops.

Ali & Nino Bookhouse 19 Haji Zeynalabdin Taghiyev St ⓦ alinino.az/?lang=en; Ⓜ Sahil; see map page 252. Named after the famous Azeri/Georgian novel, *Ali & Nino* has a great selection of English language fiction and non-fiction books for adults and children. They also sell stamps and postcards. There's a second branch in the 28 May Mall.

Bukhara Caravansarai Quilla; Ⓜ icharishahar; see map page 250. Located in the Old Town, this is an evocative setting for souvenir shopping – an actual old caravanserai. Most of the goods on offer are the same as anywhere else in the Old Town.

Lviv Chocolate House 24 Yusif MammadAliyev St ☎ 994 50 5550170; Ⓜ Sahil; see map page 252. Baku is perhaps not the most immediately obvious place to go to buy Ukrainian chocolate, but don't let that put you off – it's excellent! There's also a café attached, so if you're not in a rush, stop for a hot chocolate.

Sheki Sweet Home 11 Aziz Aliyev St ☎ 994 77 7221122; Ⓜ Icharishahar; see map page 250. Great shop selling all manner of Azerbaijani treats, including baklava, boiled sweets, honey and tea.

Yaşil Bazaar Khatai Ave ☎ 994 50 7514141; Ⓜ 28 Mai; see map page 252. This large and friendly fruit and vegetable market near the central train station is a great place for a quick wander. It smells fantastic and the produce is lovely and fresh. You can also buy spices, tea and sweets (including excellent Turkish Delight).

DIRECTORY

Banks and exchanges You can exchange money in plenty of spots around the Old Town and Fountains Square area; the best rates are for US dollars and Euros. It's easy to find ATMs too, except in the Old Town.

Embassies France, 9 Rasul Rza St (☎ 994 12 4908100, ⓦ az.ambafrance.org), Georgia, 13–15 Yashar Huseynov St (☎ 994 12 4974560, ⓦ azerbaijan.mfa.gov.ge), Germany, 69 Nizami St (☎ 994 12 4654100, ⓦ baku.diplo.de), Russia, 17 Bakikhanov St (☎ 994 12 5970870, ⓦ azerbaijan.mid.ru), Turkey, 94 Samad Vurgun St (☎ 994 12 4447320, ⓦ baku.emb.mfa.gov.tr/Mission), UK, 45 Khagani St (☎ 994 12 4377878, ⓦ gov.uk/world/organisations/british-embassy-baku), USA, 111 Azadliq Ave (☎ 994 12 4883300, ⓦ az.usembassy.gov)

There are no Australian, Canadian, Irish, New Zealand or South African embassies in Azerbaijan.

Emergencies For police ☎ 102; Ambulance ☎ 103; Fire ☎ 101.

Hospital Central Clinic Hospital (76 Parliament Ave, ☎ 994 12 4921092, ⓦ merkeziklinika.az/index)

Laundries It's easiest to ask your hotel, guesthouse or hostel about laundry, but if you're determined to go it alone, you could try Passage Laundry (80 Suleyman Taghi-Zadeh St, ⓦ passagelaundry.az) or Flavie (95 Azadliq Av, ⓦ flavie. boutique).

Mobile phones Acquiring a local SIM card is easy. Azerbaijan's major networks are AzerCell and BakCell, and there are outlets of both all around town, most prominently on Fountains Sq opposite the silver balls sculpture. The AzerCell shop at 83 Nizami St is quick and friendly. You'll need your passport, and you should be in and out in about 10 minutes.

Pharmacies Pharmacies are abundant in Baku. Try Avis Pharmacy (Fountains Sq, ☎ 994 12 4989322) or Zeytun Aptik (91 Nizami St, ☎ 994 12 4987875).

Post offices The central post office is conveniently located at 72 Uzeyir Hajibeyov St (☎ 994 12 4988000, ⓦ azerpost. az/en/index).

Coastal Azerbaijan

XINALIQ

Coastal Azerbaijan

Azerbaijan's coastal regions vary geographically, with a trip along the Caspian Sea taking you from beautiful Caucasus mountains to arid desert, via desolate post-apocalyptic landscapes, marshy wetlands and lush wooded hills. The coastal strip contains many of the country's most impressive – and bizarre – sights, the majority of which can easily be reached as day trips from Baku. Any visit to Azerbaijan is incomplete without venturing out of the capital city to visit some of these utterly unique locations.

The area adjoining the Caspian Sea is Azerbaijan's prime real estate, particularly around the Abşeron Peninsula, whose vast reserves of oil and gas are the foundation for the country's booming economy. The exploitation of this resource, however, has left the Peninsula scarred by industry and many people bitter that much of the fuel was extracted during Soviet times to benefit the entire USSR, rather than Azerbaijan itself.

To the north and south, independent khanates dominated small territories for much of recorded history. Perhaps the most successful of these was Quba under Fatali Khan, but even this proved no match for the Russians when they took control of the region in the late eighteenth century. Post-independence, the area has worked to put itself on the tourist map, with varying degrees of success.

Visitors will be drawn to the eye-catching and bizarre natural wonders such as Qobustan's **mud volcanoes** and the **burning hillside of Yanar Dağ**, both of which can be visited as day trips from Baku. If you're exploring at a slower pace, you'll find towns such as **Lankaran** and Quba are relaxed and friendly places, and the most laid-back of all is the high mountain-top village of **Xinaliq**. Travellers in this region will experience the full variety of everything Azerbaijan has to offer: history, natural wonders, and a fascinating culture.

North of Baku

Baku sprawls northward, with much of the Abşeron Peninsula and the ostensibly separate city of Sumqayit now feeling almost like suburbs. Easily visited on a day trip from the capital, this area is host to some interesting stops, including a fire temple, a castle, and a geologically odd burning hillside.

Abşeron Peninsula

The Bay of Baku, around which Azerbaijan's capital is nestled, sits on the south side of the **Abşeron Peninsula**, a fascinatingly ugly place which you'll find oddly captivating. A perfect location for filming a post-apocalyptic movie, the bleached, dusty industrial wasteland hosts a couple of Azerbaijan's big tourism hitters – both natural wonders and historical sites. It's also got a beach or two, if you're not too picky. Best of all, it's easily reached in a day from Baku, especially if you have your own vehicle – you'll be able to visit the top sights and be back in the big city in time for tea.

Yanar Dağ

Binagadi-Balakhany Highway •Charge • ⓦ yanardag.az/en • (From Baku) take the metro to Koruglu station, then take bus 217

One of the oddest sights in Azerbaijan – and possibly the world – is this bleak brown hillside north of Baku, with a fire burning ferociously at its base. There's no obvious

Highlights

❶ Yanar Dağ A desolate hill with a ten-metre stretch of flame burning along its base, this is a perfect place to see Azerbaijan's natural gas reserves in action. See page 270

❷ Ateshgah This fire temple was established in the eighteenth century by Indian pilgrims plying the Silk Road. See page 273

❸ Xinaliq By some definitions Europe's highest village, it's certainly one of the remotest and most beautiful. See page 278

❹ Hit the slopes 17km of ski runs await at Shahdag Mountain Resort, high in the stunning Caucasus mountains. See page 280

❺ Qobustan mud volcanoes Natural wonders don't come weirder than this: six-foot tall mounds of mud deposits, bubbling away atop a barren hillside. To top this, there are remarkable ancient petroglyphs close by. See page 281

❻ Lankaran town Lankaran is a perfect place to get a sense of small-town Azerbaijan, particularly at the bustling and friendly bazaar. See page 282

HIGHLIGHTS ARE MARKED ON THE MAP ON PAGE 272

COASTAL AZERBAIJAN
N
RUSSIA
Xacmaz
Quba
Shahdag Ski Resort
Xinaliq
SHAHDAG NATIONAL PARK
Sijazan
Lahıc
Five Finger Rock
Khizi
Shamakhi Observatory
Ismayıllı
Shamakhi
Ağsu
Sumqayit
Yanar Dağ
Qala
Mərdəkan Fortress
BAKU
Ateshgah Fire Temple
Sahil
Khazar Islands
Qobustan Petroglyphs
Qobustan
Sabirabad
Qobustan Mud Volcanoes
Shirvan
Imishli
SHIRVAN NATIONAL PARK
CASPIAN SEA
Bilasuvar
Neftçala
Cəlilabad
GIZIL-AGACH NATURE RESERVE
IRAN
Masalli
Germi
Lerik
Lankaran
HIRKAN NATIONAL PARK
Yanar Bulag
Astara
0   20
kilometres
Aktau (Kazakhstan)
Turkmenbashi (Turkmenistan)
HIGHLIGHTS
1 Yanar Dağ
2 Ateshgah
3 Xinaliq
4 Hit the slopes
5 Qobustan mud volcanoes
6 Lankaran town

fuel, but in fact the flames are fed by natural gas seeping through from beneath the surface of the hill. The official website claims that the fire has been continuously burning for 20,000 years, although other sources suggest that it was actually first ignited in the 1950s. Either way, the phenomenon – if not this specific site – has been known for centuries: in the thirteenth century, Marco Polo made reference to a legend of an ever-burning fire in this region.

A shiny new visitor centre was built in 2018, with wooden amphitheatre benches providing a comfortable place to watch the fire, and there's an interesting museum, as well as a café and souvenir shop. The great big Instagram-ready #YanarDag sign was perhaps a step too far though. Staff at the visitor centre can also arrange a guide to take you on a tour of nearby sights including a mud volcano, sulphur springs and an ancient kurgan (grassy mound) tomb.

Ateshgah Fire Temple

Balandin St, Surakhani • Charge • Ⓦ ateshgahtemple.az/en • (From Baku) take the metro to Hazi Aslanov station, then take bus 104

A fascinating and easy half-day trip from Baku, the **Ateshgah Fire Temple** is located in the suburb of Surukhani. It's thought that fire has been worshipped on this site for centuries, but the temple here dates from the eighteenth century and is thought to have been built by Indian Hindus or Sikhs – or possibly Zoroastrians, depending on which source you consult.

It's in a yellow caravanserai-like complex, with the numerous rooms in the outer walls housing museum exhibits of varying quality. The information boards about the temple and the oil fields are engaging, while the model people and sound effects are somewhat distracting. What you're here for, though, is the central altar, with its continually burning flame and four surrounding pedestals, also holding bowls of fire. The fire was once fed by natural gas from under the ground, but the gas ran out in the 1960s and now has to be piped in.

In the larger courtyard around the temple is a decent restaurant and plenty of gift shops, including one with the enigmatic suggestion that you can "touch carpets with your own hands".

Mardakan Fortress

Off Sergey Yesinin St, Mardakan • Charge • (From Baku) take the metro to Hazi Aslanov station, then take bus 136

In the small and otherwise uninteresting town of Mardakan is this medieval castle with impressive two-metre thick walls, dating from 1187. It was built by Akhsitan I, the Shirvan ruler responsible for moving the capital from Shamakhi to Baku. Start by exploring the grounds around the tower's base, where you'll see archaeological remains including a wine press, several bread ovens and a very deep well.

The friendly caretakers can explain the site to you in reasonable English, and will show you a tunnel which they claim runs all the way to the Caspian Sea. They'll also take you on a climb to the top of the tower up a very steep and unlit staircase: once you get there, unfortunately, the views are not enormously inspiring.

Qala Museum Complex

Mira St, Qala • Charge, Waste to Art free • ☎ 994 12 4595158 • (From Baku) take the metro to Ulduz station, then take bus 101

Qala is a compact settlement towards the eastern end of the Abşeron Peninsula, with a small **museum complex** that's home to four separate museums of varying quality. They're each charged separately, though it's debatable whether any of them are worth the entry fee. They're distracting enough if you have your own transport, but it's probably not worth the effort of getting out here by public transport.

Ethnographic Outdoor Museum

A mildly diverting collection of buildings – or foundations thereof – including a potter's yard, a blacksmith, and so on. The area also contains a number of stone idols, petroglyphs (some original, some reproductions) and ancient glasswork and pottery, all laid out in a small park that's enjoyable for a short wander. Perhaps the most unusual exhibit is the "tambourine stone", a rock that produces a strange metallic sound when hit with another rock. There's nothing must-see about any of it, but it's all reasonably interesting.

Museum of Antique Items

This museum contains a variety of mostly metal exhibits dating from around the eighteenth century, including belts, lamps, jugs and plates, but is especially obsessed with samovars.

Castle Museum

Surrounded by further examples of rock art similar to those in the outdoor museum, the heavily reconstructed fourteenth-century castle is the most visually striking of the museum ensemble, especially given the stylised statue of a Turkic warrior outside. You can't climb the walls, which is a pity, but you can go up the round tower for views over town. Inside another room in the castle there's a good collection of pottery on display.

From Waste to Art

In this quirky museum you'll find old glass, metal, plastic and so on, having been re-purposed into objets d'art. There's a boat made out of CDs and origami T-shirts made from Soviet banknotes. It may not all be beautiful, but it's got great style.

Sumqayit

It may not be to your taste – in fact, let's be fair, it's almost certainly not to your taste – but Azerbaijan's second largest city is a good place to see the Caspian Sea beach culture. The seafront road is lit with gaudy neon lights and lined with hotels and restaurants. The beaches are strewn with shells, which is quite nice, though the dead fish are less so. It doesn't put off the beach tourists, though, who are here in their hundreds. If you want to stay, you could do worse than the **Hotel Regnum** (Samad Vurghun St, ⓦ facebook.com/regnumbaku, $$), which has its own (slightly cleaner) beach and also a decent restaurant attached.

North Azerbaijan

Heading north from Baku towards Russia, you'll find yourself sandwiched between the Caspian Sea to the east and the Caucasus mountains to the west. It's from this road that some of Azerbaijan's best mountain scenery can be accessed, via the interesting town of Quba.

The Northern Road

There's not a lot to interest the traveller between the Abşeron Peninsula and Quba, but if you're under your own steam you could do worse than take a quick diversion along the road towards the settlement of Xizi for a view of the **Candy Cane Mountains**, which, as the name suggests, are hills of red and white striped rock. Xizi itself is not very exciting but can act as a springboard for hikes in the local **Altiaghaj National Park**.

If you're into water sports, the nearby **Blueplanet Kite Beach** (ⓦ kitesurfing.az) in Şuraabad offers a great opportunity for kite-surfing on a lagoon, with instructors available for beginners. It's also a beach resort and hotel.

North of the Xizi turnoff there's very little to look out for on the road until the Quba turnoff, except for **Five Finger Rock**, a spiky rock formation which dominates the hillside and is considered a minor religious site with a reputation for granting wishes. It can be admired from below, but if you want to get up to it, there's a track (best suited to 4WDs) up to a car park, from which you can ascend on foot to the top in about half an hour.

Quba

10

If you're heading north from Baku, you're almost certainly going to stop at **Quba**, the largest city at this end of the country. It's a likeable town, easily explored in a day, and small enough that you could be forgiven for overlooking the fact that it was once the centre of the most powerful khanate in Azerbaijan. Under the leadership of Fatali Khan in the eighteenth century, Quba conquered Derbent (now in Dagestan, Russia), as well as the Baku and Shirvan khanates, and spent much of the remaining years of the century wrangling with Georgia, Russia and Persia. After Fatali's death in 1789, the Quba khanate was soon incorporated into the Russian Empire.

Meydani Park

Mammad Amin Rasulzade St • Free

This central park area, with a small amusement park, comes alive towards the evening and is a nice place for people-watching. Some buildings surrounding the park – such as the Jala Salonu wedding dress shop – are beautiful examples of old Quba architecture with overhanging balconies.

Juma mosque

Fatali Khan St • Free

A striking red nineteenth-century mosque with separate beige sandstone minaret, **Juma** was undergoing reconstruction work at time of research and entry was not possible. You can still admire it from the outside.

There's also a further pair of mosques in the town centre: **Ardabil Mosque** and **Haji Jafar Mosque**. They're both brown and mint green on the outside and also date from the nineteenth century.

Chukhur hamam

Ardabil St • Charge

The principal claim to fame of this high-domed bathhouse, built in the nineteenth century, is that the French novelist Alexandre Dumas, author of *The Three Musketeers*, bathed here on his visit to Quba in the 1850s. It was restored between 2015 and 2018 and is now open as a museum for visitors to explore the impressive chambers, which have been decorated with floral baskets and photos of the restoration process.

Nizami Park

Qasim Ismailyov St • Free

A smart, white arch welcomes visitors to this small park, which houses the **History Museum**. At the other end, a staircase furnished with statues of sportsmen and women offers a shortcut down to the Genocide Memorial and across the bridge to Qirmizi Qasaba.

Museum of History and Ethnography

Nizami Park • Charge • ☎ 994 23 335 25 54

Occupying two floors in the castle-like structure in Nizami Park, the museum takes you through Quba's history with particular reference to Fatali Khan. On the upper floor there's also an exhibit about the local writer Abbasqulu Bakixanov – who was a

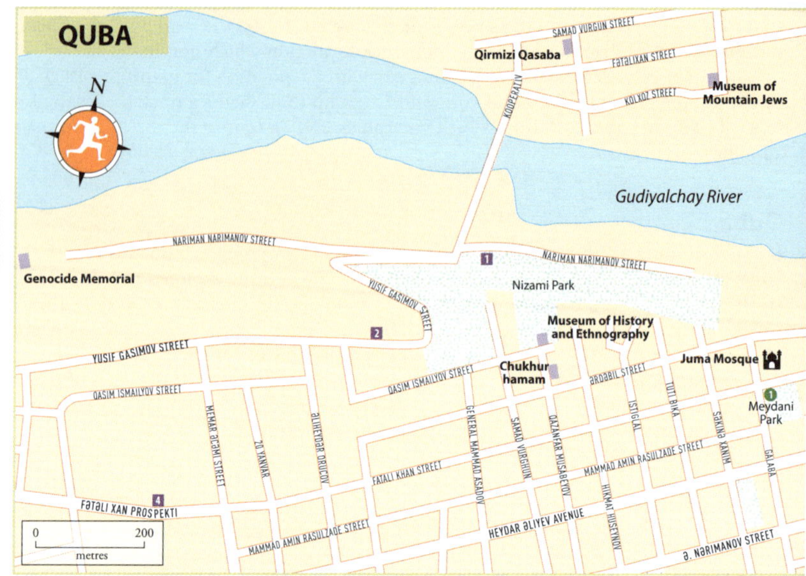

friend of Pushkin – and a display of local carpets. There's very little English labelling but you will get a guided tour.

Genocide Memorial

Nariman Narimanov St • Free • ⓦ soyqirim.az/en

Stark white pyramidal shapes and an enormous Azerbaijani flag greet you on the approach to this sombre memorial to the victims of the massacres of ethnic Azeris that occurred in March 1918 across Azerbaijan. The complex is built on the site of a mass grave of local victims and includes a subterranean museum. It's a very affecting visit and the obvious raw feelings on display serve as a reminder of the importance of history and the seemingly insoluble inter-ethnic hatred in this region.

To reach the memorial from the centre of town, walk down the staircase from Nizami Park and take the residential road to the left before reaching the bridge.

Qirmizi Qasaba

Samad Vurgun St and around • Free

Believed to be the only wholly Jewish town outside Israel and the US, **Qirmizi Qasaba** (also known as Red Town) dates from the eighteenth century and is particularly associated with the enlightened rule of Fatali Khan. It's an interesting district for a walk, especially to check out the ostentatious mansions along Samad Vurgun Street. To explore the history of the area, pop into the **Museum of Mountain Jews** (7 Rashbil Zakharyayev St, ⓦ jewish-museum.az/en, charge), a well-presented exhibition housed in a former synagogue.

ARRIVAL AND DEPARTURE   QUBA

By bus The only public transport options serving Quba are buses and marshrutkas. The shiny cylindrical bus station (on Molla Panah Vaqif Street) is about 3km outside the town centre and thus not the most convenient spot, but you can pick up bus number 1 or a taxi to get you there. Buses to Baku leave hourly 9am–5pm, taking two hours.

By car Driving in Quba is easy enough; the roads are mostly well paved and there's plenty of parking. Note the town is a grid pattern and there is a one-way system to negotiate, but it's well-designed and signposted.

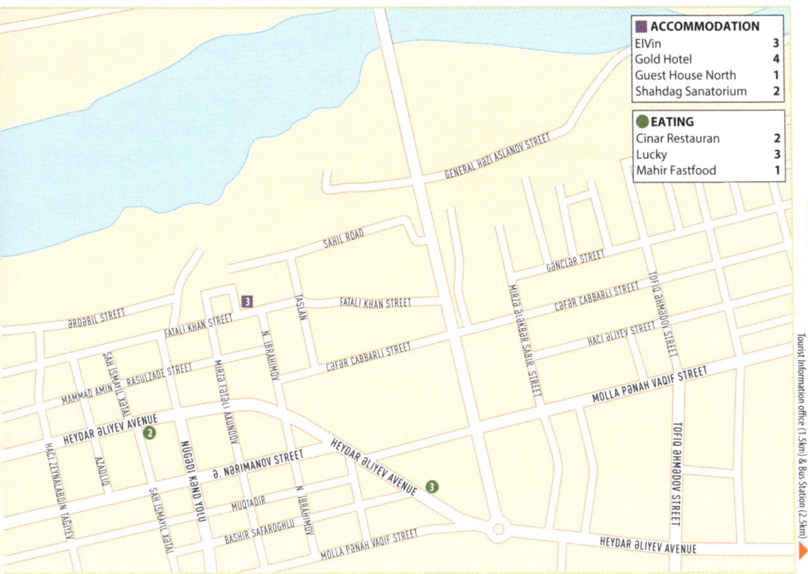

Tourist Information office (1.5km) & Bus Station (2.5km)

INFORMATION

Tourist Information Centre 3rd floor, Heydar Aliyev Centre, Heydar Aliyev St, ☎ 994 23 3356465, ✉ guba@tourism.gov.az. The helpful tourist information office can recommend hotels, drivers for visiting the surrounding area and give info about onward travel. The only downside is their location, which is near the bus station some distance out of the town centre. Mon–Fri 9am–1pm and 2–6pm.

GETTING AROUND

Other than to and from the bus station (bus number 1), you shouldn't need more than your feet to get you around Quba. Most of the town's attractions are in the old part of town surrounding Nizami Park. It will take about 25 minutes to walk from the park to Qirmizi Qasaba – the furthest point you might wish to visit.

ACCOMMODATION SEE MAP PAGE 276

ElVin 133 Fatali Khan St ☎ 994 55 7411155. A great budget choice, the *ElVin* hostel offers good rooms with shared bathrooms, and it's in a conveniently central location. The friendly owners can arrange trips to Xinaliq for you – and sometimes will even drive you there themselves. Breakfasts are very good and evening meals are available. ⑤

Gold Hotel 9 Fatali Khan St ☎ 994 51 6352753. The Gold Hotel won't be winning any awards, but it's a perfectly decent place to get a bed for the night. It's reasonably central and the rooms are unfussy, though the breakfast leaves a little to be desired. ⑤⑤

Guest House North 64b Nariman Narimanov St ☎ 994 50 2072520. Run by the friendly Rauf, who has a number of guesthouses around the area and can also arrange hiking, *Guest House North* offers three rooms with shared bathroom. It's a short walk up to the Nizami Park. ⑤

Shahdag Sanatorium 66 Yusif Gasimov St ⊕ qubasanatorium.az. The smartest option in central Quba, though that's not saying a lot, the *Shahdag* makes a fair stab at international standard rooms. Bedrooms are large and decorated with a touch of oriental charm, and there's a decent rooftop restaurant too, as well as the usual range of gym, sauna and spa options. It's in a central location by Nizami Park. ⑤⑤⑤

EATING SEE MAP PAGE 276

Cinar Restauran Heydar Aliyev St ☎ 994 21 5104126. This central spot just down from Meydani Park comes recommended by locals for its good Azerbaijani fare. Watch the bill though – prices can be variable and sometimes rather extravagant. ⑤

Lucky Heydar Aliyev St ⊕ facebook.com/luckyquba. The sleekly decorated *Lucky* is probably the best option in town. The food is the standard Azerbaijani options – kebabs,

10

FATALI KHAN

Considered a clever, wise and far-sighted ruler, **Fatali Khan** inherited the khanate of Quba in 1758, at the age of 22, and immediately set about fulfilling his big ambitions to expand his territory. Beginning with the khanate of Derbent, he conquered this northern territory and blinded its ruler after inviting him to negotiations. He used less violence to exert his authority over the Baku khanate, instead marrying his sister off to Baku's khan, Melik Muhammed, and then moving in to help 'protect' Baku.

Making common cause with the Sheki khanate against that of Shamakhi, Fatali Khan took control of Shamakhi too, but the khan of Sheki seems to have concluded after the fact that this had resulted in **Quba** becoming too powerful. Allied with Dagestani forces, the khan of Sheki defeated Fatali in 1774, forcing him to retreat to Derbent, where he sought the aid of Tsarist Russia, which restored him to his former position. The following years saw him attempting, unsuccessfully, to subordinate the Karabakh khanate to Quba and eventually giving up, instead allying himself with the Georgian King Erakle II and conquering the Sheki and Ganja khanates. He was gearing up for a campaign to Azerbaijan's southern regions when he died in 1789.

Quba under Fatali was undoubtedly a force to be reckoned with, but it's debatable whether his rule had any real lasting benefits. Much of the period was spent engaged in local wars: the intention seems to have been to unify Azerbaijani territory under one ruler, and while there was a fair degree of success during Fatali's lifetime, the results fell away almost immediately after his death, with the troops of Russia's Catherine the Great occupying Quba by 1796. On the positive side, Fatali had a reputation for religious tolerance, leading to the establishment of a sizeable **Jewish community** in Quba, which still prospers today.

dolma, and so forth – and it's not at all bad. The staff are very proud of the internal water feature. \$\$
Mahir Fastfood Meydani Park ☏ 994 70 3649413. In the Meydani Park, Mahir serves up reliable fast food classics such as pizzas, burgers, etc, though it's probably better as a drinks and people-watching spot than a dining venue. \$

DIRECTORY

Banks Banks and ATMs aren't in short supply; try on Heydar Aliyev Ave just south of Meydani Park.
Pharmacies There aren't any pharmacies in the centre, but you'll find a few near the roundabout by the *Lucky* restaurant.

Quba to Xinaliq

The road from **Quba to Xinaliq** is quite possibly the most beautiful in all of Azerbaijan. Shortly after leaving Quba, you'll enter a forest with plenty of cool tea houses and fruit sellers under the trees. As you continue, the road climbs and emerges from the trees into rolling green hills, where you'll see locals riding horses and possibly practicing chovgan, a polo-related sport.

The landscape soon changes again, becoming craggy as the road hugs the mountainside above the river. You'll soon reach the Qudiyalcay canyon, a beautiful rocky gorge through which the road briefly winds before climbing again to emerge into green windswept mountains. There are plenty of stopping spots for photos, including one at a decrepit eagle statue. If you're lucky, you'll see the real thing circling in this valley.

Xinaliq

Eventually the road arrives at **Xinaliq** village itself, which at 2200 metres above sea level can be considered – under some definitions – Europe's highest village. Its setting is spectacular, surrounded by huge rolling green mountains, recalling Iceland or the Yorkshire Dales, with clouds often sitting ominously around the summits.

Xinaliq was one of the 29 provinces of Caucasian Albania (see box, page 297), and the inhabitants still speak a separate language called Ketch which is a descendant of the Caucasian Albanian language. Islam did not reach Xinaliq until the twelfth century, before which the villagers were fire worshippers. As a further demonstration of the village's isolation, the first car did not reach Xinaliq until 1960.

The village was a candidate for UNESCO World Heritage status but modern additions to buildings made in the early 2000s unfortunately made it ineligible. The government has since outlawed making modernisations to the village's buildings.

You'll see bricks of animal manure around the village, stacked up into walls. As well as a building material when mixed with clay, these bricks are an excellent and sustainable fuel source for the winter.

History-Ethnography Museum of Xinaliq

Xinaliq Yolu • Free, donation expected

Housed in a fake castle building, the museum showcases various archaeological finds, beautiful books from the village mosque and ethnographic exhibits, as well as some unexpectedly heavy meteorite fragments.

Abu Muslim Mosque

Xinaliq Yolu • Free

An attractive stone building with wooden pillars and beams both inside and out, on which you'll see carvings that look almost Scandinavian. Some of the stones in the wall around the door bear inscriptions that locals will tell you are Caucasian Albanian. Inside the mosque is a disassembled fourteenth-century Qu'ran kept in a wooden box, and if the imam is there he will show this to you. The flat roof of the mosque is the highest point in the village and offers great views.

ARRIVAL AND DEPARTURE | XINALIQ

Xinaliq is only reachable on the road from Quba, which is well-paved (if narrow) for most of its length, but becomes a gravel track as it approaches the village. It's served by shared taxis from Quba, and can also be reached on an organised day trip from Baku. If you're driving yourself, you should be a confident driver, preferably with a 4WD.

ACCOMMODATION

Overnighting in Xinaliq is not luxurious, but it is very authentic. The homestays here are welcoming and provide an unparalleled opportunity to experience life in one of Europe's remotest corners. If you're prepared to rough it a little bit – toilets are usually outhouses – then you'll enjoy getting away from the city with a stay here. There are no restaurants in Xinaliq – you'll most likely have a meal at your guesthouse.

Ecomama ⓦ ecomamainkhinalig-guest-house. business.site. Rahma and his family run a fantastic guesthouse and can also arrange horseriding trips. The traditional food is top-notch as well and they can even accommodate vegetarians. $

Xinaliq Qonaq Evi ☎ 994 50 9654926. Friendly hosts and great food are the main draw for a stay at *Qonaq Evi*. If you contact them in advance they will help you arrange transport to Xinaliq. Note that while this place may be a reasonably modern building, the toilet is still outside! $

HIKING AROUND XINALIQ

The surrounding mountains make for **excellent hiking** opportunities, but note that this is only 15 miles from the border with Russia and there is a military presence. Hikes may need to be authorised and **permits** issued some weeks in advance – you can do this by contacting the fantastic Azeri Mountaineering company at ⓦ mountaineering.az. Short hikes in the area include a walk to a fire temple about 3 kilometres in the direction of the border, or to the local waterfall. Longer options include the multi-day trek to the even more remote village of Laza.

Qusar

Qusar is a town north of Quba, the last major settlement before the road heads into the mountains. It's not in itself a worthy destination, but from here you can access one of Azerbaijan's two major ski resorts.

Shahdag Mountain Resort

Shahdag Ski Rd, Qusar • Charge • ⓦ shahdag.az

Most people probably don't immediately think of Azerbaijan when planning a skiing holiday, but perhaps they should. The resorts here boast 17km worth of slopes (12km blue runs, 5km reds), and there are 11 ski lifts to whisk you around. There's a skiing village of plush hotels, and it's all very affordable and picturesque.

The easiest way to get here is with your own car: it's a straightforward drive on a good road. On public transport, your best bet is to take a bus to Qusar from Quba (half hourly 8am–6pm, 30 minutes) or direct from Baku (half hourly 7am–6pm, three hours), and then pick up a taxi to take you the rest of the way.

ACCOMMODATION | **QUSAR**

Shahdag Hotel & Spa ⓦ shahdag.az/en/hotel/shahdag-hotel-spa. Very smart and swish international standard hotel, equipped with inclusive hammam and pool facilities. Spa treatments are available for an extra cost. A shuttle bus runs every hour to the cable car for the ski slopes and it's possible to take skiing lessons. The rooms – all with balcony – are spotless and classy, and some have great views of Mount Shahdag. The restaurant isn't bad either. **$$$**

Xacmaz

Plenty of towns in Azerbaijan are decorated with a bizarre sculpture here and there, but **Xacmaz** has upped the game. As the main road between Baku and Derbent (in Russia) runs through town, it passes endless examples of the genre: colourful Russian-style fairy tale castles, teapots suspended in mid-air, an entire menagerie of animals (giraffes seem particularly popular) and an utterly inexplicable replica of London's Tower Bridge.

If you venture off the main road into town, you'll probably find yourself at Heydar Aliyev Park, a perfectly manicured square overlooked by a vast white palatial structure and a statue of the man himself. The only sight in town, except for the crazy sculptures, is the **Aziz Aliyev Museum** (Nariman Narimanov St, free). Aziz Aliyev – the grandfather of the current president, Ilham, and the father-in-law of Heydar – had a colourful career in Soviet politics, including a successful stint as the Secretary of the Dagestani Regional Committee. This museum covers his career with unexpectedly good English signage, though the exhibits are limited in number.

DERBENT, RUSSIA

Just across Azerbaijan's northern border lies **Derbent**, an ancient city that dates back as far as the eighth century BC. It's only been Russian territory since the nineteenth century, prior to which it was under Persian rule or independent. According to legend, it was the site of an enormous **wall** that extended for some distance into the Caspian Sea to protect the Persian Empire from invaders from the north. Its citadel, fortress and old town have been designated a UNESCO World Heritage Site and it's the most obvious tourist destination in the territory of Dagestan.

Due to the war in Ukraine, travelling to Russia is not recommended at time of writing, and even if Russia weren't off-limits, the Dagestan region probably would be: it's long been regarded as probably the most **dangerous** part of Russia to travel due to potential terrorist activity and a heavy Russian police presence. One day, it may open up again, but for now it's best to be a Dagestani armchair traveller.

South of Baku

There's little to distract you between Baku and Qobustan, except perhaps the stalled **Khazar Islands** development, which was an attempt to rival Dubai's artificial Palm Island by building into the Caspian Sea. Building commenced and a considerable amount of work was done, but in 2014 the islands' financier was implicated in a corruption case, and work ceased. Noises have been made about resuming work, but for now nothing appears to be happening, and you'll probably be prevented from getting anywhere near the site.

Qobustan

Two of Azerbaijan's most unusual sights can be found in the barren dry landscape about 60km south of Baku. As such the area makes for a good day trip from Baku.

Qobustan Rock Art Cultural Landscape

Qobustan, signposted from the E119 Baku-Lankaran Highway • Charge • Ⓦ gobustan-rockart.az/en/main • Bus 195 from Baku, but best visited with own transport or as day trip from Baku

One of Azerbaijan's three UNESCO World Heritage Sites, the **Qobustan petroglyph reserve** is a fantastic display of ancient rock art. Thought to date back up to 20,000 years, there are depictions here of people and animals, boats and hunting scenes, all of which provide valuable clues to life here in the period before written history.

You'll kick off your visit in the museum, which is excellent and well-presented – albeit with some silly sound effects – and covers Azerbaijan's and other global petroglyphs with engaging information panels. There are also some fun interactive displays which make a valiant effort to be engaging to children. All in all, it's one of the best local museums in the Caucasus and whets your appetite to see the petroglyphs themselves.

After the museum, you'll need to drive up to the second car park, then follow the set walking route through the petroglyphs. Some of the most famous – the ten dancing figures and the boat – can be seen if you follow the left path when the route forks at a rock. You'll also find a faint aurochs here, and further round are two very clear bison-type animals, accompanied by more dancing figures.

Also on site is the easternmost Roman inscription yet discovered. Dating from the reign of the Emperor Domitian (81–96 AD), it's evidence of the presence of a Roman legion in this territory far beyond the Empire's limits. Domitian made frequent campaigns against tribes on the Empire's northern edges and it's been theorised that a Roman legion was sent here to assist the kingdoms of Iberia and Caucasian Albania in such struggles.

Mud volcanoes

Off the E119 Baku-Lankaran Highway • Free • No public transport, best visited by taxi

It's a fair bet that you won't have seen anything like this before: a collection of small mounds – up to 6 or 7ft high – bubbling and spitting with cold mud. This may not sound that enticing, but it's a thoroughly bizarre sight: you can find yourself mesmerised by watching the mud pools and listening to their glooping sounds. There's an information board here that makes an attempt to explain the geology, but you'll probably be more interested by the largest of the mud volcanoes, where locals frequently bathe. Visitors are welcome to join them, but you might not be allowed back in the taxi afterwards.

The route to the volcanoes is very rough, especially the final push up to the hilltop, and it's best to leave it to the taxi drivers in their indestructible Ladas unless you have a 4WD or are incredibly confident/foolhardy. You can pick up a taxi at the highway junction by the Alat Ailevi Liman restaurant, and drivers will take you up to the volcanoes, wait for you as long as you like, then bring you back.

ARRIVAL AND DEPARTURE

QOBUSTAN

Tour operators in Baku will bring you to both the Qobustan Rock Art Cultural Landscape and the mud volcanoes, though such tours can be a little rushed – if you want more time consider hiring a taxi for the day from Baku (though for the mud volcanoes you'll need to transfer into another taxi to tackle the off road bit). Those determined to use public transport will need to take bus number 125 to the end of its line, where you can pick up bus number 195 (every 20 minutes) down the highway and get off at Qobustan for the petroglyphs or Alat for the mud volcanoes. Even then, you'll probably want a taxi for the last few kilometres to save the long and tedious walk.

South of Qobustan

Southern Azerbaijan, especially from Lankaran down to Astara and across to Lerik, is beautifully lush with a subtropical feel to it, which is a remarkable contrast to much of the rest of the country. The wetlands area of Ghizil-Aghaj State Reserve is included on the Ramsar Convention's list of internationally important wetlands and is home to much of Azerbaijan's birdlife, including flamingos, pelican and storks. It's also thought that rare beasties like the Persian leopard still prowl the Talysh Mountains.

Lankaran

The principal city in the south of Azerbaijan is **Lankaran**, a pleasant little place to base yourself for a couple of nights. There are no world-beating sights here, but a couple of minor attractions will keep you occupied for an afternoon, and it's a good spot from which to visit the Talysh Mountains

Begin your visit at the Hazi Aslanov square, where you'll see a statue of Lankaran's most famous son, Hazi Aslanov. From here you can also see Lankaran's eighteenth-century lighthouse, which is now some distance from the coast, indicating the extent

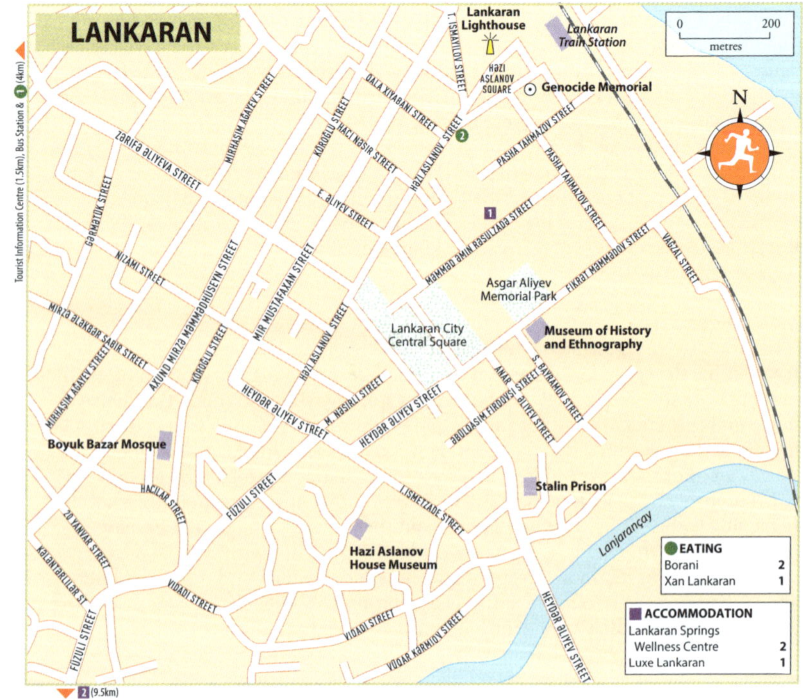

HAZI ASLANOV

Born in 1910, **Hazi Aslanov** joined the Soviet military in the 1920s, attending the Leningrad Cavalry School. During the 1930s he rose through the army's ranks and served with distinction in the **Great Patriotic War**, being awarded the title of Hero of the Soviet Union twice – firstly for his bravery at Stalingrad and secondly for his success in crossing the Berezina River in Belarus and liberating surrounding towns. His second award was issued in 1991, many years after his death. He's remembered with pride in his hometown of Lankaran, across Azerbaijan and in many of the former countries of the Soviet Union.

to which the Caspian Sea has shrunk over the last few centuries. Round the corner on Pasha Tahmasov Street you'll find a memorial to the victims of the Khojaly massacre.

Museum of History and Ethnography

Fikrat Mammadov St • Charge • 994 25 2550829

The range of exhibits in this museum is quite sparse but it's worth a visit to see the interior of the building itself, which is a sumptuous French-designed 1913 mansion built for Ahmed Khan, the descendant of the khans of Talysh.

Stalin Prison

Heydar Aliyev St • Free

A round brick tower that's seen better days, this was once a Tsarist prison that hosted a certain Mr Josef Stalin. You can't go in so you can only look at it from outside, and in all honesty, unless you're a fervent Stalin completist, you probably won't get much from it.

Hazi Aslanov House Museum

19 Ismat Gayibov • Free • 994 25 2553720

Hazi Aslanov, one of Azerbaijan's most prominent heroes of the Great Patriotic War, was born in this house in 1910. Visitors can now view photos of him, as well as war memorabilia and some fabulous socialist realist art. There's no English labelling, but the friendly staff will communicate through translation apps and, if you're lucky, by doing impressions of tanks.

Boyuk Bazar Mosque

Koroglu St • Free

This is an attractive red-brick building, with stained glass windows through which the sun shines beautifully in the mornings. Pillars inside are wooden and the arches are also of red brick. If the door doesn't open, it's probably bolted from inside – if this is the case someone will open it to let you in. While you're in the vicinity, a wander round the neighbouring bazaar is chaotic but great fun.

ARRIVAL AND DEPARTURE LANKARAN

By train Lankaran is connected to Baku on the train line that runs down the Caspian coast. There's one train per day, departing at 10.15pm and arriving at 5.50am the following day. If you're heading the other way, to Astara, you'll need to be at the station for the 7.05am train, which takes 55 minutes. The station is just to the east of Hazi Aslanov Square.

By bus The bus station is outside the town centre at the roundabout between Sahidler Xiyabani Street and the E119 highway. Buses to Baku depart hourly from 8.30am, with a journey time of five hours. Marshrutkas to Astara depart when full from the bazaar; the journey is about 40 minutes. There's no bus service to Lerik, but you can pick up shared taxis from southwest of town at the crossroads by Lankaran's airport.

By car Lankaran's town centre can be surprisingly busy so be prepared to sit in traffic for a short while if driving in. Parking is easy enough. Note that there is a one-way system in operation and that it isn't signposted terribly well.

GETTING AROUND AND INFORMATION

You'll probably want a taxi to take you to and from the bus station but otherwise, Lankaran is compact enough that your feet will be all you need.

Tourist Information Centre 99 Zarifa Aliyeva St, ☎ 994 25 2541753. Lankaran's official tourist information service is friendly, can recommend hotels and hands out leaflets. The staff can also put you in touch with guides for hiking in the Talysh Mountains. Daily 9am–5pm.

ACCOMMODATION
SEE MAP PAGE 282

Lankaran Springs Wellness Centre 1 Sultan Aliyev St, Haftoni village ⓦ lankaransprings.az. The *Lankaran Springs* brings an international level spa hotel experience to southern Azerbaijan. Service is great (if occasionally a little quirky), rooms are very smart, and there's a good choice of bars and restaurants. It's some way out of the town centre, in a pleasant rural setting. ₻₻₻

Luxe Lankaran 11 Qala Xiyabanı St ⓦ luxelankaran.az/lang.en. It's aiming smart and falling slightly short with its faded aesthetic, but it's very conveniently positioned at the centre of town and prices are reasonable, so it can be forgiven. Try to get a room at the back as it can be noisy at night. ₻₻

EATING
SEE MAP PAGE 282

Lankaran isn't exactly blessed with a thriving culinary scene, but there are a couple of reasonable choices.

Borani Qala Xiyabanı St ☎ 994 51 5850909. A glossy place popular with the young and hip crowd, *Borani* is bang in the centre of town and serves up good fast food options including pide, lahmacun, pizzas and burgers. ₻

★ **Xan Lankaran** Corner of E119 highway and Sahidlar Xiyabani St ⓦ khanlankaran.com. A rustically decorated place adjoining the bus station, *Xan Lankaran* has a wide-ranging menu of Azerbaijani cuisine including an excellent take on the local speciality, lavangi – a dish of chicken or fish stuffed with plum and walnut. It's also a good hotel. ₻₻

DIRECTORY

Banks You'll find banks and ATMs aplenty in the town centre, around the Central Square or down Mir Mustafaxan St.

Pharmacies There aren't as many pharmacies as you might expect in a city of Lankaran's size; try Heyat Aptek on Hazi Aslanov St.

Post office The local branch of Azerpost is on the central square; it's open Mon–Fri 9am–5pm.

Lerik

Lerik is a small and friendly town in the Talysh Mountains, about an hour's drive from Lankaran along a very pretty, but at times rough, road. It's a great starting point for hikes, and it also boasts a pleasant, if over-manicured, central square. You can get a good view over town and the surrounding mountains by climbing the stairs to the left of the requisite Heydar Aliyev statue.

If you're wanting to hike, a good place to start is with the Mountain Host company (23 Uzeyir Hajibeyov St, Baku, ⓦ facebook.com/mountainhost.az) who run regular trips to Lerik and may be able to arrange a guide for longer treks. Alternatively, the Lankaran Tourist Information Centre (ⓔ ilqarazimov@gmail.com) can connect you with guides.

Aside from the obligatory and none-too-exciting Heydar Aliyev Museum, the only specific sight in town is the **Museum of Longevity** (22 Arzuman Asadullayev St, free). Lerik is famous for its long-lived residents and this little museum offers photographs and newspaper articles about some of the most prominent, including Muslunov Farziali, who is listed as having lived to the age of 168! Many of the museum's subjects were apparently born in the early 1800s and lived through to the 1970s. More recent long-lived individuals seem to make it to the more plausible 110 years of age or thereabouts. There's no English labelling in the museum, but there is some in French.

Shared taxis leave Lankaran for Lerik from the crossroads by the airport. Shared taxis back can be found at the eastern edge of town.

Archivan

Archivan – about 6km north of Astara – is an entirely forgettable village save for one interesting sight – **Yanar Bulag** (Alat-Astara Highway, free), a fountain dispensing water

CROSSING TO IRAN

So long as your visas are in order, the **crossing to Astara in Iran** – and vice-versa – is a simple procedure. The border is open 24/7 and the guards are efficient – you'll probably find the Azerbaijan border slower than the Iranian. Moneychangers here (on both sides) have a reputation for ripping travellers off – including with tricks relying on travellers not knowing the difference between Iranian rial and toman – so it's best to avoid changing large amounts of cash with them. Note that several nationalities (including British, Americans and Canadians) cannot travel independently in Iran and will need to arrange to be met by their tour guide.

This northwestern corner of Iran is often overlooked by tourists, but has many interesting sights. It's often referred to as 'South Azerbaijan' and contains more ethnic Azeris than the Republic of Azerbaijan does. For those interested in Azeri history and culture, a visit to **Babak Castle** is a must: a starkly beautiful fortress perched atop a rocky crag, it was the HQ of the eighth-century Azeri folk hero Babak, who resisted the expansion of the Abbasid Caliphate into Persia, but eventually was betrayed and suffered an extremely unpleasant death. He's considered a national hero in Azerbaijan, but the Iranian authorities are less fond of his legacy.

that will catch fire if prompted with matches or a cigarette lighter. There are usually locals present who will be happy to demonstrate. The water is drinkable, albeit sulphurous.

Astara

You will probably only visit **Astara** if you're going to or from Iran, but it's not an unpleasant place should you choose to visit. The border crossing is at the south end of the coastal road, adjacent to the attractive Bulvar walkway along the seafront, which is punctuated with an enormous flagpole and some fake castle walls of the sort of which Azerbaijan is so fond.

At the north end of the Bulvar, you'll find the reasonably popular town beach, which is considerably cleaner than most Caspian beaches, though you probably still won't be tempted.

ARRIVAL AND DEPARTURE

ASTARA

By train Astara is the end of the train line from Baku – there have long been mutterings about linking Azerbaijan and Iran's rail networks, but nothing's come of it yet. The daily train to Baku leaves at 9.25pm to arrive the following day at 5.50am. This train also stops at Lankaran en route, at 10.15pm. Note that the train station is about 4km north of Astara's centre.

By bus You can pick up a marshrutka to Lankaran from the southern end of Azerbaijan Prospect; from Lankaran you can transfer onto a Baku-bound bus.

By car Astara is a sleepy place and it's easy to drive in – so easy, in fact, that you may not realise you've reached the Iranian border until you nearly cross it.

ACCOMMODATION

Maricel 39 Cabbarli St ⓦ maricelresort.az/en. A resort hotel on the seafront, Maricel has been built in a rather ostentatious style, and has some very unusual interior design choices – the blue carpet gracing most rooms is bold, to say the least. It's clean and friendly, though, and has a good pool for lesiurely afternoons and a decent restaurant. $$

EATING

All along the Bulvar and on the beachfront you'll find a selection of cafés that all serve decent Azerbaijani tea but for some reason decent coffee universally alludes them. You have been forewarned.

Lem Restaurant Bulvar ☎ 994 51 687 21 11. The *Lem Restaurant*, easily identifiable by its ridiculous fake turreted castle, is located just off the Bulvar and offers unremarkable but decent Azerbaijani fare. Some outdoor seating is available. $

Internal Azerbaijan

Internal Azerbaijan

While much of the interior of Azerbaijan is composed of semi-desert, the road that runs west from Baku towards the Georgian border passes some of the country's most outstanding cultural highlights. Take the opportunity to explore Azerbaijan's metal-working traditions in Lahıc, its early Christian heritage at Qabala and Kiş, and the history of its fractured khanate era in the beautiful city of Sheki. Further south, you'll find Ganja, the country's third city, an island of cosmopolitanism isolated in the barren countryside. Miss this area and you'll miss a real sense of Azerbaijan and its history.

11

A trip into Azerbaijan's interior is a journey into the real face of the country, away from the glossy modernism of Baku. Glimpses of Azerbaijan's extensive history can be seen along the road running west from Baku, from the few remains of the mysterious **Caucasian Albanian** civilisation (unrelated to modern-day Albania – see box, page 297) to the stunning **palace** left behind by the Khans of Sheki in the eighteenth century. In the idyllic village of **Lahıc**, delicate copper-working is still practised as it has been for centuries. A visit rewards both souvenir shoppers and those seeking to get away for a relaxing stay in the gorgeous mountains. The country's third city, **Ganja**, is a little out on a limb in desert-like surrounds, but those who make the effort to visit will find a relaxed and cosmopolitan town with low-key but fascinating historical sights.

Brief history

In antiquity, this part of Azerbaijan was ruled by the Persians for 250 years, a period that was followed by a Greek invasion under Alexander the Great. By the first century BC, however, the area was more locally ruled, with the River Kura (near Ganja) being the boundary between Greater Armenia and Caucasian Albania. Armenia and Albania shared much common culture – the Albanians adopted Christianity shortly after Armenia, and their churches were closely linked.

Northern Azerbaijan remained under Albanian control until the Arab conquest in 667, and in the subsequent centuries was subjected to further conquests by Turks, Mongols and Timurids. Local rulers the Shirvanshahs originated in Shamakhi in the ninth century but moved their capital to Baku following devastating earthquakes. Other principal cities in the region became centres of their own khanates in the eighteenth century, notably Sheki, which found time in between fighting with the Quba Khanate to build beautiful palaces in their capital.

The region was the subject of dispute between Qajar Iran and Tsarist Russia in the early nineteenth century, suffering greatly in the Russo-Persian War of 1804–13, which resulted in the area being incorporated into the Russian Empire. Independence came briefly after World War I, as part of the short-lived Democratic Republic of Azerbaijan, before the Soviet period. Since the fall of the USSR, the region has embraced the boost that tourism offers to its economy, which is otherwise mainly industrial.

Shamakhi

Your first sight of **Shamakhi** is likely to be a line of castle walls along the main road, decorated with sculpted books bearing the images and quotes of prominent Azerbaijani writers. It's an example of Azerbaijan's preoccupation with tidying up its history and producing medieval-style castles which are so shiny and new that you can't tell what's authentic and what isn't.

Highlights

❶ **Wine tours** Azerbaijan isn't known for its wines like the other Caucasian nations are, but the vineyards around Shamakhi and Qabala are seeking to change that. See page 292

❷ **Lahıc** A small village in the Caucasus foothills, Lahıc's sweet cobbled streets are home to expert copper workers producing gorgeous handicrafts. See page 293

❸ **Caucasian Albania** In its early history, much of northern Azerbaijan was home to the Caucasian Albanians, a Christian civilisation whose legacy can still be seen at Kiş and Qabala. See page 297

❹ **Ski slopes** The hills above Qabala are perfect for skiing in winter or hiking come summer. See page 295

❺ **Khan's Palace, Sheki** Hands down one of the best sights in Azerbaijan, the eighteenth-century Khan's Palace is a beautiful masterpiece. See page 298

❻ **Shah Abbas Square, Ganja** The ensemble of buildings in Ganja's central square encapsulates much of Azerbaijan's history: a mosque, a mausoleum, a hammam and a monolithic Soviet town hall. See page 305

HIGHLIGHTS ARE MARKED ON THE MAP ON PAGE 290

GEORGIA
Rustavi
Gurjaani
Sighnaghi
Balakän
Zaqatala
Dedopolis Tskaro
GARA-YAZ
NATIONAL PARK
Qazax
Tovuz
Semkir
Reservoir
Yenikend
Reservoir
Mingechevi
Reservoir
Ijevan
DILIJAN
NATIONAL
PARK
Ganja
6
Imamzade
Nizami
Mausoleum
Sevan
Shahumyan
GOYGOL
NATIONAL
PARK
Gavar
Lake Sevan
Vardenis
Martuni
KHOSROV
NATURE
RESERVE
ARMENIA
NAGORNO-KARABAKH
Jermuk
Yeghegnadzor
Stepanakert
Areni
0
20
kilometres

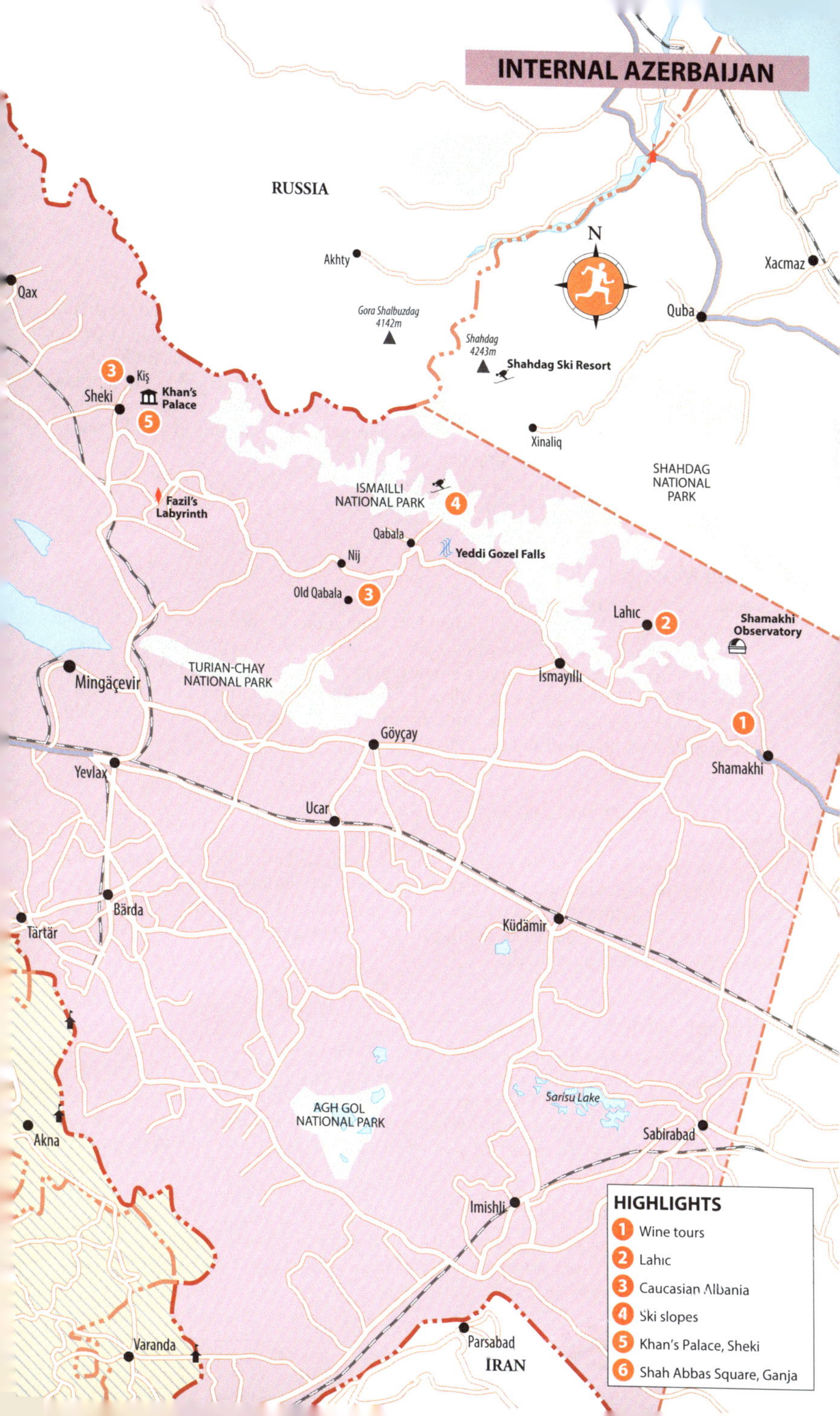

INTERNAL AZERBAIJAN
N
RUSSIA
Akhty
Xacmaz
Qax
Gora Shalbuzdag 4142m
Shahdag 4243m
Shahdag Ski Resort
Quba
Kiş
Sheki
Khan's Palace
Xinaliq
SHAHDAG NATIONAL PARK
Fazil's Labyrinth
ISMAILLI NATIONAL PARK
Qabala
Nij
Yeddi Gozel Falls
Old Qabala
Lahıc
Shamakhi Observatory
Mingäçevir
TURIAN-CHAY NATIONAL PARK
Ismayıllı
Göyçay
Shamakhi
Yevlax
Ucar
Bärda
Küdämir
Tärtär
Sarisu Lake
Akna
AGH GOL NATIONAL PARK
Sabirabad
Imishli
HIGHLIGHTS
1 Wine tours
2 Lahıc
3 Caucasian Albania
4 Ski slopes
5 Khan's Palace, Sheki
6 Shah Abbas Square, Ganja
Varanda
Parsabad
IRAN

> ### STARGAZING IN SHAMAKHI
>
> Around 20km north of Shamakhi, in Pirkuli village, is the **Shamakhi Observatory**, built in 1960 and equipped with one of the biggest telescopes in the former USSR – its mirror has a diameter of 2m. There are up to two hundred cloud-free nights per year here, making it an ideal place to gaze at the heavens. It's possible to arrange stargazing visits, and sometimes to stay at the observatory –or contact via the website at Ⓦ shao.az/en.

This is unnecessary, since Shamakhi has enough to recommend it without resorting to creating more history. The town was the original home of the Shirvan dynasty, who ruled their state from here between 861 and 1192, when Shamakhi was hit by an earthquake and the capital was moved to Baku. Shamakhi re-emerged as the capital of the Shirvan Khanate in the eighteenth century, and after the Russian occupation was the centre of government in the region until another earthquake hit in 1859. Following this the town went into something of a decline.

There are several sites of interest to the tourist, making it a very worthwhile – and off-the-beaten-track – stop if you're journeying from Baku to Sheki.

Juma Mosque

Seyid Azim Şirvani St • Free • ☎ 994 55 7879870

Originally built in 743, Shamakhi's **Juma Mosque** is one of the oldest mosques in the Caucasus, second only to Derbent's. Owing to the numerous earthquakes over the years, the current building is largely a new construction – it was restored most recently in the early 2010s, but sympathetically. The interior is a calm, quiet place with a magnificent portal and lovely tile work. From outside the mosque is an elegant, white-yellow edifice with beautifully maintained gardens.

Yeddi Gumbaz Tombs

Dada Qorqud St • Free

The last representatives of the Shirvan dynasty are buried on this hillside overlooking Shamakhi, in attractive domed mausoleums, the oldest dating to 1810. There were once seven such domes here but earthquakes have reduced the number to three. You can venture inside the domes to see the attractive gravestones. It's a pleasant site that you're likely to have to yourself.

Shirvan Wines

M4 Baku-Shamakhi Highway • Charge • Ⓦ meysariwines.az • No public transport

Azerbaijan has a long wine-making tradition, but in the Soviet years the art was largely abandoned. **Shirvan Wines** is seeking to re-establish Azeri wines on the world stage. This may be ambitious, but visiting the vineyard and enjoying a wine-tasting session is no bad way to spend an afternoon. There's a pleasant restaurant on site too.

ARRIVAL AND DEPARTURE

SHAMAKHI

By bus İsmayıllı-bound buses from Baku will drop you here. It's harder getting on a bus to move on from here, as they're often full of passengers from Sheki or İsmayıllı.

By car Shamakhi is on the main highway between Baku and Sheki and poses no problems if you're driving yourself.

ACCOMMODATION

Shamakhy Sport Villas Baku-Shamakhi Highway ☎ 994 10 3160056. Shamakhi's accommodation options are extremely limited. The best – indeed, pretty much the only – choice is this large complex, which offers pleasant rooms and decent spa facilities. The downside is that it's some 2km from the town centre. $\overline{\$\$}$

EATING

The dining scene in Shamakhi is less than inspiring. The best option is probably to take a taxi the 5km out of town to *Abqora Restaurant and Wine Club*, the restaurant attached to the Shirvan Wines vineyard, which offers good Azeri food accompanied by the vineyard's wines.

İsmayıllı

The industrial town of **İsmayıllı** is, like Shamakhi, equipped with a long line of not even vaguely authentic castle walls, which surround the town centre. At one corner, the Azerbaijan-France Friendship Park, with its attractive fountain, is a pleasant spot at sunset. Otherwise, İsmayıllı is short on sights, but it's not a bad place to break your journey or base yourself for a trip to Lahıc.

ARRIVAL AND DEPARTURE

By bus Two buses leave to Baku daily, one at 8am and the other at 6pm, taking 2.5 hours. There are more regular buses to Qabala, the cost of which varies, depending seemingly on whether the driver likes the look of you. Additionally, buses leave to Lahic at 8am and 11am, taking 45 minutes.

By car Self-drivers won't have any issues with İsmayıllı. The roads are wide – though sometimes potholed – and it's not very busy, except right in the centre. Parking is easy.

INFORMATION

Tourist Information Centre Qaramaryam-İsmayıllı-Şaki yolu, ☎ 994 20 2853145. The enormously friendly staff at the tourist information centre will be pleased – if surprised – to see you, and you'll likely be asked to sign their visitors' book and pose for pictures with them. The office has a wealth of informative leaflets about attractions in the area and they can advise about onward transport.

ACCOMMODATION

İsmayıllı Guest House Mican kandi St ⓦfacebook.com/GuestHouseIsmayilli. It's not right in the town centre, but the friendly welcome accorded by the family here more than makes up for being out of whatever action İsmayıllı offers. The property has four rooms – a double, a single, a twin and a quad – and shared bathrooms. A good dinner can be provided, and you may be lucky enough to meet their pretty grey cat. There's no sign outside; it's through the grey metal door underneath the large red and white cylinder. If you get lost ask someone on the street for directions. $\overline{\$}$

EATING

İsmayıllı has very few places to eat, but the restaurant in the *İsmayıllı Resort Hotel* (Cavanşir Street) has a decent menu. If you're staying in a guesthouse, it's recommended that you ask your hosts to supply dinner.

Lahıc

The delightful village of **Lahıc**, in the foothills of the Caucasus mountains, is famous across Azerbaijan for its handicrafts, especially copper-working. It's one of the most touristy places in this part of the country, with day trips running from Baku often filling the main street with sightseers. At times the place can border on cutesy, but it just about manages to maintain its charm, in part due to the friendly locals who all seem very keen for a chat in English. If you stay the night and explore after tour groups have left, you'll get a more authentic experience of this lovely settlement.

Hüseynov Küç – the main street – is beautifully cobbled and lined with old stone houses, many with overhanging traditional balconies. The buildings are now primarily souvenir shops rather than the traditional copper workshops, but a few still retain their original function, such as number 27 **Hüseynov Küç**. There's also an interesting workshop a few doors up from the history museum where you can see the craftsman in action, as well as being able to buy souvenirs direct.

The streets are well signposted, with principal sights such as the tourist information office and the museum pointed out regularly, making it easy to find your way around.

History Museum

Nizami Küç • Free, donation expected

Housed in an old mosque, the **museum** is packed to the gills with a mishmash of local historical items. In pride of place is an enormous pair of bellows for use in copper work, and – as you might expect – there are also plenty of examples of copper products.

Hiking

Lahıc is a good starting point for pleasant **walking** options. One day hike leads up the ridge to the west of the village where a ruined castle sits, and then back down into the valley on the other side. There's also a trip to a waterfall some distance up the river. Ask at your accommodation, the Tourist Information Centre or in the History Museum for directions, or to arrange a guide.

ARRIVAL AND DEPARTURE

By bus Buses leave from İsmayıllı at 8am, 11am and 2pm, taking 45 minutes, and return from Lahıc at 10am, noon and 4pm. The bus will deposit you at the crossroads opposite the post office.

By car It's easy to pick up a taxi in İsmayıllı to bring you to Lahıc, while for the return trip, your best chance of picking one up is from the car park at the entrance to the village. If you're driving yourself, note that the beautiful road is a little hair-raising at times as it climbs the valley and gets narrower, particularly after you pass the village of Namazgah. It's relatively well-paved all the way, but it's recommended less confident drivers take the bus or a taxi.

INFORMATION

Tourist Information Centre Nizami Küç, ☎ 994 50 6777517. The tourist office, located next to the History Museum, keeps sporadic hours. If you need something organised it may be wise to call ahead of time. They can arrange guides and homestays.

ACCOMMODATION

Evim Otel Unnamed road, central Lahıc ☎ 994 51 8800010. In a hugely convenient location, the *Evim's* 23 clean rooms, some with balcony, are a great choice. Breakfast is served in the garden and is created entirely from local produce. The friendly management will help with hiking and horseriding arrangements. ⑂⑂

Lahıc Guesthouse Unnamed road, east end of Lahıc ☎ 994 17 877344. With its nine rooms (two doubles and seven twins, all en suite), *Rustam's* has been getting consistently great reviews for years. Try to stay in room 2.5 which has its own private balcony and beautiful river view. Rustam himself is a friendly and chatty soul who speaks excellent English and can arrange a guide for numerous hikes around the area. ⑂

EATING

Asma Korpu Restaurant Lahıc yolu. In a peaceful location by the river – opposite the silver war memorial – this garden restaurant serves great barbecued meat, accompanied by chips and salad. There's no menu but you will be enthusiastically beckoned into the kitchen to point out what you want. ⑂

Lahıc Qartal Hotel Unnamed road, central Lahıc ☎ 994 50 6761444. With an upstairs veranda offering a nice, if not incredible, view, this is a pleasant place for coffee, tea or a snacky meal. It's nice and close to the bus departure point too so it's ideal for waiting if you're a bit early. ⑂

Old Tea House Hüseynov Küç ☎ 994 55 4297128. A lovely retreat in a gorgeous flowery garden serving good tea and strong Turkish coffee. ⑂

SHOPPING

Copper goods are the souvenir of choice here, of course – you can buy cups, bowls, plates, jugs and whatever else you may want, from any of the souvenir shops along **Hüseynov Küç**. If you locate copper workshops – often in the back streets – you can buy direct for marginally better prices. Expect prices to start from 20 manat for cups, or 40 manat for dishes and bowls.

Unexpectedly, there's an ATM on Hüseynov Küç, which is handy as most of the vendors here will take cash only.

Qabala

Now one of Azerbaijan's top ski resorts, and hugely popular especially with Arab and Indian tourists, **Qabala** was known as Kutkashen until the end of the Soviet period, but post-independence it took the name of Qabala after the ancient capital of Caucasian Albania (see box, page 297). The original Qabala is now known as Old Qabala and is some 20km to the west of the newer town.

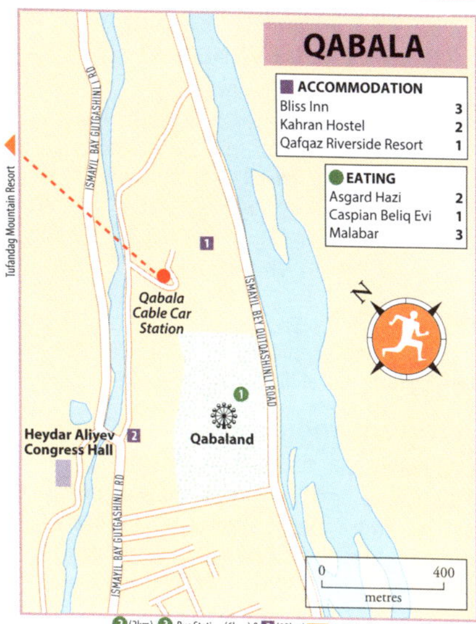

Tufandag Mountain Resort

I Qutqashinli St • Charge • W tufandag.az

A series of cable car routes up the mountains behind Qabala offer great views and, in appropriate weather, the chance to ski. It's also possible to undertake other activities including paragliding. If you don't have your equipment with you there are numerous shops selling and renting ski paraphernalia around the cable car station.

Heydar Aliyev Congress Hall

Ismayil bay Gutgashinli Rd • Free

Worth a quick glance from the outside, this structure is a palatial building attractively set beneath wooded hills. There's an adjoining well-manicured riverside park which is nice for a short stroll. Just watch out for the random rhino.

Yeddi-Gozel Falls

Off the İsmayıllı-Qabala highway • Free

This series of small waterfalls is about 3.5 km off the main road, about 13km from Qabala in the direction of İsmayıllı. Access requires a short but sweaty hike up a staircase that runs through a forest that would be pretty if it hadn't been overdeveloped with tea houses. The access road is quite rough and they are unlikely to be the best waterfalls you've ever seen, so they are only recommended if you're desperate for distraction.

ARRIVAL AND DEPARTURE

QABALA

By bus The bus station is unhelpfully at the opposite end of town to everything else, on the highway to Sheki. Buses run to Baku every hour, to Sheki at 9am and noon, to İsmayıllı every hour, and to Ganja at 8am, 10am and 3pm.

By car Anyone driving the main road between Baku and Sheki will need to traverse Qabala. It's not a difficult place to navigate, with a wide, well-maintained bypass, and an easily negotiable town centre.

By plane Qabala has an airport, which allegedly offers flights to Baku with Azerbaijan Airlines, but there never seem to be tickets available, leading to a suspicion that these flights do not in fact exist.

JEAN-CLAUDE VANDAM?

Fans of the Muscles from Brussels may wish to make a quick stop at the small village of Vandam, just to the southeast of Qabala, where a lifesize statue of **Jean-Claude Van Damme** – doing the splits across two logs, with an extremely impassive expression on his face – was erected in late 2019. The only connection between the actor and the village is the similarity in their names, but the statue has proved something of a hit with local tourists - and even resulted in an appreciate Facebook post from Jean-Claude himself.

INFORMATION

There's no tourist information centre in Qabala. You could try speaking to the staff at the Qafqaz Riverside Resort if you want to know about transport options; they will at least try to be helpful.

ACCOMMODATION

SEE MAP PAGE 295

Bliss Inn İsmayıllı-Qabala highway ⓦfacebook.com/BlissInnGabala. On the İsmayıllı-Qabala highway, the *Bliss Inn* is very much a motel. Its rooms are perfectly pleasant and there's a swimming pool and restaurant in the grounds, but it doesn't elevate itself above just being a place to lay your head, and for that it's expensive. $$

Kahran Hostel Ismayil bay Gutgashinli Rd ☏994 24 2054036. Shiny clean hostel up near the ropeway, with kitchen facilities and 18 beds across three dorms. Enter via the gateway to the left of the perfume shop, then follow the building round to find the entrance at the back. $

Qafqaz Riverside Resort Qabala-Laza road ⓦriverside.qafqazhotels.com. Ideally situated for those wishing to use the ropeway, this large international standard hotel is probably the smartest option in town. The rooms are immaculate and it boasts the usual array of pool, spa, gym and restaurant. $$$

EATING

SEE MAP PAGE 295

Asgard Hazi Aslanov St ☏994 50 2900379. Aiming at and only slightly missing a German beer hall ambience, Asgard has an extensive menu of international options, running from Georgian khinkali to Indian tikka masala, via the usual pizzas and burgers. There's also a well-stocked bar. $$

Caspian Beliq Evi 2120 Demiraparan chai ⓦfacebook.com/caspianbaliqevi. Proudly proclaiming itself to be the "new taste of the Caspian", the reality is you'll find nothing out of the ordinary on the menu here. It's worth a visit though to enjoy its remarkably tacky white and blue cabin booths accessed via wooden walkways over an artificial lake full of fish and the occasional demented sculpture. It's mad as a box of frogs, a bit expensive for what it is, and the service is interminably slow, but despite all that it's somehow still unmissable. $$

Malabar Heydar Aliyev St ⓦmalabarrestaurantqabala.com. There are quite a few curry houses in town, and this one is arguably the pick of the bunch: it's not 100% authentic, but it certainly gives it a good go. The butter chicken is probably the best choice. $$

ENTERTAINMENT

Qabaland 1 Ismayil bay Gutgashinli Rd ☏994 50 2900138. The small theme park of *Qabaland* may provide an hour or two's distraction if you have kids in tow. Daily 10am–9pm.

DIRECTORY

Banks There are a few banks with ATMs along Ismayil bay Gutgashinli Road, including the reliable Kapital and AFB Banks.

Pharmacies A couple of pharmacies can be found around the crossroads where Ismayil bay Gutgashinli Rd meets Heydar Aliyev St.

Post office Qabala's big central post office is at 26 Heydar Aliyev St.

Qabala to Sheki

The journey from **Qabala to Sheki** passes through the heart of the ancient realm of Caucasian Albania and includes a couple of sights that are worth a quick stop if you're driving and have the time.

CAUCASIAN ALBANIA

Caucasian Albanian – in no way linked with Albania in the Balkans – was an ancient state covering much of what is now western Azerbaijan and areas of eastern Georgia. It seems to have spent much of its history as a vassal state of various neighbouring powers – the Achaemenids, the Roman Empire, the Persian Sassanids, and Greater Armenia all held sway here at various times.

Originally following paganism or Zoroastrianism, the Caucasian Albanians converted to Christianity soon after Armenia did, possibly after the Caucasian Albanian king Urnayr visited St Gregory the Illuminator and was baptised by him. The Caucasian Albanian church was independent at first, but became subservient to the Patriarch of Armenia in 705 AD. The region was conquered in the seventh century by Arabs spreading Islam, and by the following century the name of Albania was used only to denote a geographical region: the state of Albania was no more.

Soviet and post-Soviet Azerbaijani historians have often used the name of Caucasian Albania to promote a revisionist history which asserts that the Caucasian Albanians are the ancestors of modern Azeris. By re-labelling any **Armenian heritage** as Caucasian Albanian they aim to suggest that Armenians have no ancestral right to certain territories (Nagorno-Karabakh in particular). This revisionism has led in some cases to cultural vandalism – in the church of Kiş, for example, ancient Armenian engravings have been erased. It also forms the basis for Azerbaijan's attempt to claim the monastery of Davit Gareja in Georgia. Approach references to Caucasian Albania in Azerbaijan with caution, as this ancient kingdom is the centre of modern spin.

Old Qabala

Off R9 Qabala-Sheki highway • Charge • ☎ 994 24 2021257

It's likely that this archaeological site, thought to date back to the fourth century BC, is the original city of **Qabala**, the capital of the Caucasian Albanian kingdom. It's thought that it was destroyed in the eighteenth century invasion of the Persian Nader Shah and was only rediscovered in 1959. The site consists of three separate areas: two archaeological sites and one museum.

The first site is the ruins of the former settlement of Salbir, which is still undergoing excavation. The visible remains consist of low walls, catacombs and – perhaps most interestingly – ancient water pipes. On the opposite hill is the second site, where two towers and a short stretch of walls are all that is left of the gates of the original Qabala. Other indistinct tumuli on the plateau suggest further remains are waiting to be unearthed.

The museum houses finds from the archaeological sites, including beautiful pottery and some remarkable little figurines from the second or third century AD. Labelling is limited and there's little explaining the context of the finds or even who the Caucasian Albanians were.

Nij

The small village of **Nij** is home to the Udi, a Christian people who may be descended from the Caucasian Albanians. Once more widespread in the region, many of the Udi fled along with local Armenians during the Nagorno-Karabakh war, and the community in Nij is all that remains of them in Azerbaijan.

Church of St Elisha

Nij village, off Qabala-Sheki highway • Free • ☎ 994 51 6097285, ⓦ udi.az

Dating from the eighteenth century, the church was restored in the mid-2000s. The interior is relatively plain with images of St George and the Dragon, and Jesus holding a Caucasian Albanian church in his hand. The churchyard is peaceful, and if you walk to the back you'll find an interesting photo display of the Udi people demonstrating their links to the Caucasian Albanians.

Udi Ocagi Ethnographic Centre
Nij village, off Qabala-Sheki highway • Free • ☎ 994 50 7762801

Let's be honest, this is more of a restaurant complex than a genuine ethnographic museum, and, as such, it's a sanitised Udi Disneyland rather than a truly insightful Skansen. Even so, the wooden houses, carts and barrels set around a small pond are nice enough for a little wander, although in all honesty it's probably not worth the drive up the unpaved road from St Elisha. The food isn't bad, and it's one of the few places in Azerbaijan where you can order an entire sheep, though this is only advised if you're really hungry.

Fazil's Labyrinth

Off the main road, in Fazil village, about 20km before you reach Sheki is a complex of interesting underground graves, which have been excavated by a team of volunteers. A museum has been established but opening hours are very erratic. Before setting off, consider checking on the current situation at Sheki's tourist office.

Sheki

The pleasant city of **Sheki** is home to one of the historical highlights of Azerbaijan: the Palace of the Sheki Khans, a beautifully preserved eighteenth-century gem. The palace itself is reason enough to visit, but it's not all Sheki has to offer. The attractive old town rewards casual wandering, and just outside the city limits is the lovely Caucasian Albanian church of Kiş. Sheki is also known as a silk production centre and is famous for its sweets, so the town offers good souvenir shopping opportunities.

A major centre in the Caucasian Albanian era, the city came to prominence in the eighteenth century under the Sheki khanate. The original town of Sheki – further up the river valley – was destroyed in a flood in the 1770s, and the population relocated here, to what was then known as Nukha. The khanate burned bright in the late eighteenth century, engaging in both alliances and conflict with the powerful Quba khanate, but was subordinated and abolished by the Russians in 1819. Nukha was renamed Sheki in 1968.

Khan Palace complex
Mirza Fatali Akhundov St • Free

Fortress walls surround the complex, which houses a variety of museums as well as the star attraction, the Khan's Palace. Each museum is charged separately, and some give you more for your money than others.

Khan's Palace
Palace complex • Charge • ☎ 994 51 6185973

Completed in the late 1700s, the UNESCO-listed **Khan's Palace** is a masterpiece of eighteenth-century architecture. The exterior is beautiful, with elaborate patterns snaking over every wall, but it's the gorgeous interior that will make the greatest impression. Sunlight shines through remarkably intricate stained-glass windows, casting multicoloured patterns on the ornate wall decorations. If that isn't enough, the palace also contains magnificent painted miniatures depicting hunting and battle scenes. It took two just years to build, but a full eight years to complete the decoration.

You cannot take photos inside the palace, and guards are extremely vigilant – to the point of officiousness – about this.

House of Craftsmen

Palace complex • Free

This is a souvenir shopping outlet, with goods such as scarves, bags, faux antiques, and quite a lot of generally tacky stuff. The tourist information centre can be found on the upper floor.

State Art Gallery

Palace complex • Charge

To the left as you enter the main palace gates, this small building hosts a selection of pretty unremarkable paintings.

Sheki City Museum of Local History

Palace complex • Charge

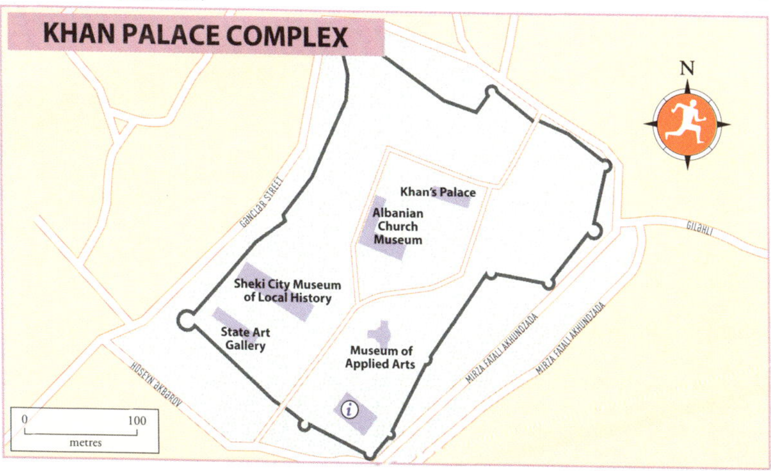

NAGORNO-KARABAKH

The territory of **Nagorno-Karabakh** has been ruled by all the usual political entities that feature in the history of the Caucasus – including, but not limited to, Greater Armenia, the Persians, the Turks, the Mongols and the Russians – as well as a stint in the eighteenth century as an independent khanate, ruled from the city of Shusha. In the wake of the collapse of Tsarist Russia, the nascent Republics of Armenia and Azerbaijan both claimed the region and fighting continued until both countries were subdued by **Soviet Russia's Red Army**.

In his role as Commissar for Nationalities, Josef Stalin attempted to resolve the issue by granting the territory – along with that of Nakhchivan – to Azerbaijan. This was so unpopular with the Armenian inhabitants that a rethink was required, and the area became the **Nagorno-Karabakh Autonomous Oblast**, with the city of Stepanakert as its capital.

During the Soviet period, ethnic tensions lay dormant – though signs of discontent were there, if anyone had been looking for them – until 1988, when ethnic Armenians gathered in the central square to demand unification of the Oblast with Armenia, unwittingly setting the wheels in motion for the devastating Nagorno-Karabakh War, breaking out three years later in the wake of the disintegration of the Soviet Union.

The war lasted three years, during which time both sides committed atrocities against civilian populations, the most notorious being the Armenians' massacre of Azerbaijanis at Khojaly. The war ground to a halt with a grudging ceasefire in 1994 leaving Armenia in de facto control of Nagorno-Karabakh, which became the self-declared independent Republic of Artsakh.

The situation remained largely frozen until September 2020, when the **conflict** erupted again. Azerbaijan quickly gained the upper hand due to its use of drone warfare, and the war eventually ended, via a Russian-negotiated ceasefire, with Azerbaijan now in control of much of the territory, including the town of Shusha, which holds symbolic importance to both Armenia and Azerbaijan.

This new status quo didn't last long: although the Republic of Artsakh remained in control of Stepanakert and its surrounding area, access to the Republic was only possible along the road from the Armenian border which ran through Azerbaijani-controlled territory. With the Russian peacekeeping force seemingly distracted by Putin's war in Ukraine, in December 2022 Azerbaijan blockaded the road, refusing to allow crucial supplies to reach Stepanakert. After nine months of this, Azerbaijan launched a new offensive, quickly taking the remaining territory of Nagorno-Karabakh. Most of the Armenian population fled, with one hundred thousand refugees entering Armenia.

Depressingly if predictably, the war was punctuated by atrocities, perpetuated by decades of demonisation of each other. Both sides have submitted complaints to the International Court

---

A great model of the town as it was in 1772 is the first thing you see as you enter this old-style museum, which is otherwise packed to the gills with a variety of interesting objects, including beautiful copperware and an amazing phaeton that was used to ferry around Nariman Narimanov in the 1920s. The stained-glass windows inside are also beautiful in their own right, but if you've already been inside the palace you'll probably be a bit jaded on this front by now. Note that there's no English labelling on anything (except for a bit of impassioned text about the Nagorno-Karabakh conflict), but the entry fee does include a guided tour, which ends with a sampling of traditional Sheki sweets.

Albanian Church Museum

Palace complex • Charge

This fifth-century church now houses a fair few ethnographic artefacts, including pots, carpets, animal skins, stained glass windows, clothes and a spinning wheel. There's no English labelling and no apparent reason why this place couldn't be combined with the Museum of Local History.

of Justice, and there are concerns that Azerbaijan intends to erase Armenian heritage in the region: the Ghazanchetsots Cathedral in Shusha has been remodelled to replace its Armenian spire with a dome. Gandzasar and Dadivank Monasteries are at risk of being termed Caucasian Albanian churches as part of Azerbaijan's historical revisionism. Azerbaijan maintains that Armenia did the same during the years between 1994 and 2020.

Following the conflict, the Armenian government appears to have accepted that **Azerbaijan** now controls the region, and is now concentrated on the need to normalise relations after 35 years of conflict. Although some promising steps have been taken, including a prisoner exchange in December 2023, there remains relatively little progress at time of writing.

Until 2020, it was easy to visit Nagorno-Karabakh from Armenia, either via the road from Goris in the south or the road from Vardenis in the north. With Azerbaijan's recovery of the territory, however, the situation is now considerably more complicated. Baku has big plans for redevelopment of Nagorno-Karabakh, particularly Shusha, as tourist destinations, but at time of writing **foreign visitors are not permitted to travel into the territory** independently. The regime does run infrequent propaganda-heavy tours of the area, but these appear to be with the express purpose of legitimising Azerbaijan's actions in the war and its current political position, which may make visitors uncomfortable.

At present, therefore, visiting Nagorno-Karabakh is a challenging proposition. Hopefully, this will change in the future, as in peacetime the region is well worth a trip, including the following highlights:

Papik Tatik This sculpture, officially entitled "We Are Our Mountains", was installed on the outskirts of Stepanakert in 1967. It's the single most recognisable sight in Nagorno-Karabakh: it represents an old couple, intended to symbolise the famously long-lived people of this area and their connection with the land.

Hunot Gorge A lovely short walk through some of the region's most spectacular scenery, passing an eighteenth century stone bridge and an abandoned 1930s village to reach the Zontik Waterfall.

Tigranakert One of Armenia's early rulers, Tigran the Great, established a city here more than 2000 years ago. The ruins, including a fifth-century town square and a medieval three-arched building, are well worth exploring.

Gandzasar Monastery Meaning "hilltop treasure", this is one of the finest Armenian monasteries in the entire Caucasus. A beautiful building, enhanced by its fantastic position at the top of a hill surrounded by gorgeous mountains, it's elevated to the next level by the abundance of exquisite carving that covers its surface

Vank village Architecture in the Caucasus is often "innovative", but the projects found in Vank – particularly the former Eclectica and Seastone Hotels – are completely barking. Think enormous stone lions, Greek pillars supporting classic cars, and a wall covered in car number plates. There's probably a very good reason for it all, but it's not obvious.

Abad Pottery Centre

Palace complex • Free

For all its grand posturing about "restoring the historical pottery traditions of Sheki", this is essentially a souvenir shop, albeit one in a beautiful building.

Other sights

Although Sheki's most obvious attraction is the Khan's Palace, that's not all the city has to offer. In particular you'll want to take a bit of extra time to check out the under-visited Winter Palace, a small-scale version of its more famous near neighbour.

Winter Palace

Hikmat Alakbarzada kuc • Charge

It comes as a surprise to many visitors that there are in fact two palaces in Sheki. The smaller **Winter Palace** is hidden away in the back streets but well worth seeking out, perhaps as an appetizer to the more famous Khan's Palace. There are six rooms but only one of interest, which contains mind-blowingly beautiful, detailed paintings on the walls and door contrasting with the elegant simplicity of the four-colour stained-glass windows.

You can take photos inside but you are requested not to post them online. The ticket office is not always manned, so if no one appears to be about, wander round the garden for a few minutes and the caretaker should appear.

Juma Mosque

20 Yanvar kuc • Free

The attractive red-brick nineteenth-century **mosque** rewards a quick look inside. The antechamber is carpeted a deep red while the main prayer room contrasts this with predominant greens. The mihrab is pleasingly, if unremarkably, tiled.

ARRIVAL AND DEPARTURE
SHEKI

By bus The bus station is on Mammadamin Rasulzada Prospect, about 1.5km south from the central Baxtiyar Vahabzada Park. There are up to 25 buses and marshrutkas per day to Baku, starting at 6.30am, which take between four and six hours. Other options include the seven daily buses to Qax (where you can pick up a bus to Tbilisi), which take 45 minutes, the three daily buses to Qabala (1hr 30min), and the five daily buses to Ganja (2hrs 30min). The tourist information centre can supply you with an up-to-date bus timetable.

By train There's one train per day to Baku, which leaves at 11.15pm. However, as the train station is some 17km out of town, this is not an enormously convenient option.

By car Sheki is easily reached by the main Baku-Georgia road, but it's not the easiest city to drive in, owing to a frankly infuriating one-way system that will frequently divert you on enormous detours. Note that mapping apps are not always programmed with the one-way system, so don't just follow their instructions blindly. Many streets are quite narrow too. There are no parking restrictions, except for a fee if you park near the Palace.

GETTING AROUND

By foot It's easiest to traverse Sheki on foot, and you shouldn't ever need to walk for more than half an hour, unless you're staying a very long way out of the centre. The main sights are all clustered within a 15-minute walk of each other.

INFORMATION

Tourist Information Centre House of Craftsmen, Palace Complex, ☎ 994 24 2446095, ⓦ sheki.heritage.org.az. The friendly and helpful tourist office is on the upper floor of the House of Craftsmen. The staff all speak English, and there are also German, Russian and Italian speakers among them. As well as being able to advise on transport, accommodation, restaurants and local tourist attractions across the towns of Sheki, Qak, Zaqatala and Balakan, they can put you in touch with guides for hiking in the local area or arrange experiences such as halva-making classes and the chance to make, and dye, your own silk scarf. Perhaps most importantly, they can book the Karavanserai hotel for you. Daily 9am–6pm (from 10am weekends).

ACCOMMODATION
SEE MAP PAGE 299

Central Hostel 5 Heydar Aliyev Ave ⓦ centralhostel.az/en. True to its name, the Central Hostel is found in the centre of town, with easy access to restaurants and a 20-minute walk to the palace complex. It's a sleek and confident addition to Sheki's accommodation scene, offering four sparkly clean dorms, some mixed and some female only. There's also a good café here, which serves arguably Sheki's best coffee. ⓢ

Karavanserai 185 Mirza Fatali Akhundov St ☎ 994 55 7555570. A stay here is to emulate the ancient Silk Road traders: this is a genuine caravanserai, dating back to the eighteenth century. The rooms are all en suite but otherwise they're as no frills as you would hope for such an old building. The central courtyard, with its arches, is beautiful. Note that some rooms have no hot water so do check when booking. It's not the easiest place to book in advance; if you have no luck calling them, try contacting the tourist office, or just turn up and hope. ⓢⓢ

MinAli Boutique Hotel 11/15 Mirza Fatali Akhundov St ⓦ minaliotel.business.site. The building dates from 1896 but has been restored and extended to create this delightful 12-room hotel. The rooms at the back are all original and the ones at the front are modern. There are various ethnographic exhibits on display in reception and in the corridors, including musical instruments and the ubiquitous copperware. The top floor has a restaurant with good views

over Sheki and the hills beyond. $$
★ **Old House Guesthouse** 4 Shafiqa Akhundova St ⓦ facebook.com/oldhouseguesthouse. There are six rooms available in this beautifully rambling 200-year-old townhouse, each of them different and still sporting their original decorations and furniture. Bathrooms are shared one bathroom to three bedrooms. There's also a hostel on the grounds in a separate building with a four-bed dorm. $$
Sheki Palace Hotel Akhundzada Ave ⓦ shekipalacehotel.business.site. Eyes on the prize – Sheki Palace Hotel aims to be the slickest game in town,

and it's making a decent job of it. Most rooms are smartly decorated – though some are looking a bit tired – and the spa facilities are pretty good. The on-site restaurant, with lovely terrace, is excellent too, and there's an extremely well-stocked and tempting wine cellar. $$
Sheki Saray Hotel 187 Mammadamin Rasulzada Pr ⓦ en.shekisaray.com. A 40-room hotel with friendly staff, the *Sheki Saray* is well placed for restaurants and is only 20 minutes' walk or so from the Khan's Palace. Rooms offer hints of old Sheki style with the shape of the alcoves, but otherwise are international standard. $$

EATING AND DRINKING

SEE MAP PAGE 299

★ **Calabi Xan** Baxtiyar Vahabzada Park ☎ 994 50 5334763, ⓦ celebixan.az. This popular establishment on the main square is Sheki's top dog restaurant for a reason. Beside its interesting modern-meets-traditional façade and pleasing garden, the food – which covers the full range of Azerbaijani cuisine – is excellent. The saj is particularly good, and if you fancy a change from the standard options, you can get a great Turkish pide or a passable pizza here. $$
Illy Espresso House Mirza Fatali Axundov St. In an old room, with a wooden-beamed ceiling, decorated with carpets, pottery and other paraphernalia, authentic Turkish tea and coffee are served up by the smiley owner. $
Limon 4 Axundov St ☎ 994 50 5576643. This fast-food joint, with bright orange walls and tables, and several slightly odd wooden booths, is a reliable place for fast, filling and fantastic Turkish staples such as pide, lahmucun, doner kebabs and pizzas. $

Qafqaz Restaurant 20 Yanvar kuc ☎ 994 24 2444463. This garden restaurant has no menu, but the friendly owner will list options. It's a good place to try Sheki's speciality, piti (a mutton and vegetable soup infused with saffron and served with a piece of lamb fat). $$
Qaqarin Azadliq kuc ☎ 994 50 6237350. Named after the cosmonaut Gagarin, and decorated with a charmingly inept picture of him at the entrance, this restaurant near the palace serves up reliably good Azerbaijani fare: the piti and the kebabs are particularly good choices. $$
SM Pub Mirza Fatali Axundov St ☎ 994 70 8088889. Heralded by locals as the only pub in Sheki, this welcoming – if male-dominated and smoky – place has two draft beers and a range of spirits. Despite laser lights seemingly attempting to generate a nightclub atmosphere, it remains a chilled place. $

ENTERTAINMENT

Chingiz Klub 185 Mirza Fatali Akhundov St ☎ 994 50 2567444. If you're desperate to go to the cinema, this place imports a selection of recent blockbusters. They're

sometimes subtitled and sometimes dubbed, so check in advance.

SHOPPING

Sheki is a good place to pick up a souvenir. It's famous for both silk and sweets, especially halva. There are any number of places along Mirza Fatali Akhundov Street selling halva, and you can watch it being made too.
The best place to buy silk scarves is the silk factory, on the

corner of F. Khoyski Street and Mammadamin Rasulzada Prospect. The factory itself is sadly no longer open to visitors but has an excellent shop. Prices vary wildly depending on colour, size and quality.

DIRECTORY

Banks Banks and ATMs are mostly found along Mammadamin Rasulzada Prospect, just south of the Sheki Saray Hotel.
Pharmacies There are plenty of pharmacies at the newer

end of town; Tebessum Aptek on Mammadamin Rasulzada Prospect is open 8am–midnight.
Post office Sheki's main post office is on Mammadamin Rasulzada Prospect, south of the Sheki Saray Hotel.

Kiş

Kiş village, an attractive rambling settlement of cobbled streets on a hill a few kilometres north of Sheki, is home to a **Caucasian Albanian church** (unnamed road,

☎ 994 24 2498833, charge), which allegedly dates from the first century AD and is thought to be the oldest church in the entire Caucasus. The church was built atop an even older moon worship temple and some of the earlier remains can be seen in the church's courtyard. You'll also see glass-topped open graves in the courtyard, still containing skeletons.

Inside, the church is now an informative museum about the Caucasian Albanians, including English-language information panels and a range of artefacts. Pride of place goes to a replica of a large stone with an Albanian inscription on it; the original is in Baku's Historical Museum.

There are guides who hover around the entrance, but they aren't all terribly informative, and some operate by rushing you round and spinning tall stories involving Jesus Christ, Attila the Hun and 2.5-metre-tall, blonde-haired, blue-eyed Caucasian Albanian warrior women. Exciting as this may be, you'll probably get more from the visit by politely fending the guides off and looking at the exhibition for yourself.

By the entrance, there's a souvenir stand which mostly sells tat: steer clear and instead head for the tea house opposite, which serves highly recommended tea and rose jam. To reach Kiş by public transport you can take bus number 15 from Sheki, which takes about 25 minutes.

Qax

Qax, aside from being an absolute belter if you happen to be playing Azerbaijani Town Name Scrabble, is notable primarily for the attractive nineteenth-century Georgian **Kurmukhi church** (free) which sits atop a hill just outside town, easily visible from the Qax-Sheki highway. It's thought to have been built on the site of an older Caucasian Albanian church. There are a further two churches in town, but **St George** is of little interest architecturally and the **Allaverdi church** has fallen into disrepair.

You can pick up a bus to Tbilisi from Qax at 8.30am, 10.30am and 1pm, which will take 5.5 hours.

Zaqatala

Zaqatala is a sleepy little town that may well be your first stop in Azerbaijan if you're coming from Georgia. It's got a vaguely alpine feel about it, with many buildings particularly around the central **Meydan Park** having a cottagey style. This impression is furthered with the chalet-style verandas dotted around the park, though the fake castle towers can make you feel like you're in a medieval Disneyland.

Castle walls

28 May kuc • Free

A line of old fortress wall hugs the hill to the north of Meydan Square. There's a grand staircase leading up, punctuated by fake towers and the occasional silly statue. Once you're at the top, there's not much more to see.

Rus Kilisasi

28 May kuc • Free

The ruined nineteenth-century church is visible from Meydan Square and is accessible via the road to the left of the castle steps. It's got a melancholy dignity from outside but has been shamefully mistreated inside. Entry is only possible via a window, which is clearly how locals access it, but the floor is covered in broken glass, the walls are graffitied, and it smells rather unsavoury.

ARRIVAL AND DEPARTURE ZAQATALA

By bus Four buses per day leave Zaqatala for Sheki, taking two hours. There's also one daily bus to Tbilisi at 8.30am, which takes four hours. The bus station is on Faiq Amirov St, about 1.5km southwest of Meydan Park.

ACCOMMODATION

In all honesty, if you've got the time and means to do so, it's advised to press on to Sheki or to Georgia (depending which way you're going) instead of spending the night. If you do get stuck here, the following is acceptable:

Grata Hotel 100 Heydar Aliyev Prospect ☎ 994 24 2253353. A reasonably smart choice on the roundabout by the bus station, with 36 rooms, garden, restaurant and a remarkably temperamental lift. There are great views from the rooms at the back, which are also the quieter choices. Note that you can only pay cash – or, as the staff slightly inexplicably say, "no cash, only money". $$

EATING

Zaqatala's culinary scene is limited, but you won't go hungry. There's a string of teahouses/fast food places/shisha lounges along Heydar Aliyev Prospect, the best of which is probably *Meydan Ali Kafe* in the Meydan Square. It is equipped with colourful seating and parasols, making it a relaxed place for people-watching over a fast-foody lunch – expect pizzas, burgers and the like.

Ganja

While unlikely to ever hit the Top 10 Must-See Destinations list, **Ganja** – Azerbaijan's third largest city – is not an unattractive place. If you're heading to or from Georgia on this route instead of the Sheki road, you could do much worse than stopping for an overnight stay to check out the town's handful of sights and pleasantly chilled vibe.

It's a newer city than many in the Caucasus, dating back to the ninth century, when it was founded by Muhammad ibn Khalid, the local governor for the Abbasid Caliphate. Aside from a brief wobble when it was taken by the Georgians (the town gates were carried away as trophies and can now be seen at Gelati Monastery near Kutaisi), Ganja remained in Persian hands for most of its history. As an independent khanate in the eighteenth century, the city attempted to repel Russian encroachment without success. During the Soviet era, it was renamed Kirovabad, but reverted to Ganja post-independence. The city suffered damage in the Second Karabakh War in October 2020, with Armenian missile attacks killing more than thirty people and destroying infrastructure, but – though reconstruction in the outskirts has been slow – the centre is largely unaffected.

Shah Abbas Square

Most of Ganja's principal sights are to be found on or around the central **Shah Abbas Square**, which litterally has something for everyone: there's a mosque, a mausoleum, a glitzy shopping mall, grand hotels, a ridiculously overblown Soviet town hall… and a pub.

Shah Abbas Mosque

Shah Abbas Sq • Free

Built in 1603 by the Safavid Shah Abbas, the **mosque** has a silver dome and a pair of brick minarets which stand apart from the main building. It's of little interest inside, but it makes an impressive centrepiece for the square.

Tomb of Javed Khan

Shah Abbas Sq • Free

Javed Khan was a khan of Ganja in the eighteenth century, whose attempts to keep the city out of the grasp of Russian hands were ultimately doomed to failure. You can't go inside the mausoleum, but you can peer through the stained-glass windows for a sight of his tomb.

Chokak Bathhouse

Shah Abbas Sq • Free entry, charge for use of baths • ☎ 994 22 2640182

This still operating, attractive red-brick domed bathhouse was built in 1606, potentially by Baha' al-Din, the master architect who designed and built the beautiful Imam Square in Isfahan in Iran.

Ganja City Executive Building

Shah Abbas Sq • Free

The city hall is an utterly monumental Neoclassical Soviet-era building. The bas-reliefs above and around its doors extol the virtues of collectivisation. You can only admire it from the outside as there's no public access.

Shah Abbas Caravanserai

61 Şeyx Bahaddin • Free • ☎ 994 51 4028468

This seventeenth-century caravanserai enjoyed an extensive restoration during the 2010s, and now operates as a hotel. Even if you're not staying here, visitors are welcome to enter the courtyard and have a look around.

Elsewhere in the town centre

The sights on Shah Abbas Square are Ganja's main attractions, but it's worth exploring further, a block or two to the square's west. Here you'll find a pleasingly old-school museum, a reasonably pleasant park, and the outstandingly bizarre but aptly named Bottle House.

Museum of Local Lore

244 Mustafa Kemal Ataturk Ave • Charge

Housed in a crumbling nineteenth-century mansion, this museum takes the visitor through an old-fashioned, but reasonably well-presented, chronological look at Ganja's history, starting with fossils of elephants and ancient pottery, moving on to an exhibition on Javed Khan and finishing with a nice Heydar Aliyev personality cult room. It was closed for refurbishment at time of research, with no anticipated reopening date.

Khan Baghi

Gala St • Free

The khan's gardens are a popular place for local men to gather for tea or soft drinks on hot summer evenings. The gardens are also the home to a very small remaining section of Ganja's sixteenth-century red-brick fortress.

Bottle House

Corner of Huseyn Cavid and Qamber Huseynli • Free

Seemingly for no reason other than the whimsical pleasure of it, this house is constructed with a great many bottles as well as more standard building material. It's worth wandering the short distance from the main square for a quick glance. If the owner spots you, he might offer to take a photo of you on the balcony for a small charge.

Outside town centre

On the city's outskirts are a pair of interesting attractions: an impressive Islamic complex and the mausoleum of Nizami Ganjevi, one of Azerbaijan's most revered poets.

THE OIL SPAS OF NAFTALAN

About 50km southeast of Ganja is the small city of **Naftalan**, which has been on the tourism map since the 1930s, when its first sanatorium was built. Its popularity increased throughout the Soviet era, and has continued to develop during independence, after a brief lull in the 1990s. So far, so Soviet, but Naftalan's **sanatoria** are a little different: here, guests immerse themselves in bathtubs filled with the local naftalan oil. Advocates of naftalan oil bathing insist it can treat numerous health conditions, from eczema to musculoskeletal diseases; the World Health Organisation, on the other hand, has designated naphthalene (which is present in high concentrations in naftalan oil) a potential carcinogen. This doesn't deter local tourists, who come for treatment programmes involving multiple immersions over the course of several weeks. If you decide to indulge, you'll probably find that just once is more than enough.

Imamzade

Ganja-Samukh Rd • Free • Bus 4 or 18 from city centre

This is a heavily restored large Central Asian-style mosque with adjoining buildings. Quite unusually, the mosque has been constructed around the mausoleum of one of the sons of the eighth-century imam al-Baqir, so when you go inside, you'll be confronted by another building almost immediately. The carpets underfoot are gloriously soft.

Nizami Mausoleum

R51 Ganja-Shirvan Highway • Charge • Bus 4 from city centre

Ganja's favourite son, the twelfth-century poet Nizami Ganjevi, has rested in various mausoleums on this spot for centuries. The current mausoleum dates from 1991, after the previous incarnation collapsed in the late 1980s. There's also a museum here which contains manuscripts, books and carpets relating to Nizami, though the lack of English labelling or speakers on site does mean it's difficult to get much out of it.

About 3km from the mausoleum are the **Gates of Ganja**, a massive brick fortress constructed in 2014 in an effort to replace the city gates captured by Demetrius I of Georgia in 1139.

ARRIVAL AND DEPARTURE GANJA

By train The train station is about 4km to the north of town. Services include two daily trains to Baku (the faster, slightly more expensive, train leaves at 6pm and arrives at 10.15pm, while the slower leaves at 11.40pm and arrives at 6.30am). Before the Covid-19 pandemic, there was also a daily train to Tbilisi, but this service remained suspended at time of writing.

By bus Buses leave the Yevlax bus station for Baku hourly between 7am and 7pm. The trip takes seven hours. Yevlax is also the place to get a marshrutka to Sheki, which leave at 1.30pm and 4.30pm, or earlier if they fill up.

By plane Ganja's airport, about 10km northwest of town, is served by Azerbaijan Airlines, which offers weekly flights to Nakhchivan, as well as connections to Moscow Vnukovo four times a week. Oddly, there are no direct flights to Baku. There are also regular flights to Istanbul with Turkish Airlines and Pegasus.

GETTING AROUND

By bus To get to the train station, you'll need bus number 1, 4 or 12 from the town centre. Bus numbers 17 and 23 run from the centre of town to the Yevlax bus station.

By taxi Most of the sights in Ganja's town centre are within walking distance, but you may want a taxi for some of the outliers – it may be sensible to combine a trip to the Imamzade and the Nizami Mausoleum and negotiate some waiting time.

INFORMATION

Tourist Information Centre 31 Hasan Aliyev Street, ☎ 994 51 3102383, ✉ ganja@tourism.gov.az. Ganja's tourist information centre is a friendly and reasonably helpful office which can advise on transport links and find you a hotel. Daily 10am–5pm.

ACCOMMODATION SEE MAP PAGE 306

Cinema Boutique Hotel 2 Cavadkhan St ⓦ facebook.com/cinemaboutiquehotel. There are 17 smartly decorated and well-kept rooms in this delightful place, a few minutes' walk from the main square. Breakfast is served in the adjoining Kolorit restaurant. $$

Hotel Ganja Shah Ismayil Khetayi Ave ⓦ gancahotel.com. This Soviet-era relic has a great location on the town square, but it's also got a gloomy aura and rude/borderline aggressive staff, so it's perhaps only a good choice if you can't get a room elsewhere. $$

Vego Hotel Shah Abbas Sq ☎ 994 22 2640182, ⓦ vegohotel.com. A grand building in a perfect location right on the town square, the *Vego* is a plush hotel with large, semi-suite rooms, though some are beginning to look a little tired. Still, the beds are comfortable, breakfast is good, and – though they don't advertise it – there's access to the Chokak Hammam via an underground tunnel; ask reception to show you the way. $$$

VM Hostel 42 Rustaveli St ☎ 994 50 7932127 ⓦ vm-hostel.business.site. It's not in an enormously convenient location, and it could do with a sign outside, but the *VM* makes up for being a bit out-of-the-way with a friendly welcoming owner, sparkling clean rooms (with seven beds across two dorms) and kitchen, and free coffee and tea on tap. Not much English spoken. $

EATING
SEE MAP PAGE 306

If you find yourself desperate for familiar fast food, the food court of Ganja Mall has a *KFC* and a *McDonalds*, as well as a sweet waffle house and two international style coffee shops. Of these, *Coffeemania* has the edge because of its marginally better view over the main square, but *Coffee House* is quieter and more peaceful.

Aşxana Muzey 36 Attarlar St ☎ 994 55 2597026. Packed to the gills with carpets and antiques, the Aşxana Muzey restaurant is a lovely evocative place to tuck into tasty Azerbaijani food. The pilaf in particular is very good. $$

Kolorit 135 Attarlar St ☎ 994 70 5561313. True to its name it's colourful. The outdoor seating area has sofas and chairs in bright red and yellow, and indoors there are pop art photos adorning the walls. It's popular with Azerbaijani families. The cheap and good food is a variety of international options including pizzas, pasta, steak and salads. $

London Coffee Shop 10 Cavadxan St ⓦ facebook.com/londoncoffeeshopco. Decorated with photos and artwork of London, this friendly little place does great coffee and incredibly generously sized slices of cake. There's indoor and outdoor seating, with the indoors attempting to evoke an English tearoom and the outdoor being a great place to people-watch on the pedestrianised Cavadkhan Street. $

DRINKING
SEE MAP PAGE 306

Qala Pub 258 Mustafa Kemal Ataturk Ave ☎ 994 55 2127452. Evocative underground pub with an arched roof, popular with locals for alcoholic beverages and shisha. It's a bit smoky, but otherwise pleasant enough. $

ENTERTAINMENT

Ganja Mall is a large and modern shopping mall. If you're looking to entertain kids, the food court level is home to **Ganjaland**, an indoor entertainment centre involving a carousel, dodgems, soft play and computer games. It's quite boring for grown-ups but at least you will be able to confuse and alarm the grandparents by telling them you've taken the kids to Ganjaland. Ganja Mall also contains a cinema on the floor above the food court.

DIRECTORY

Banks There are several banks with ATMs along the pedestrianised shopping Cavadkhan St, and a couple along Ataturk Ave too.

Hospital Ganja International Hospital (60 Shah Ismayil Khetayi Ave, ☎ 994 55 5007100, ⓦ gbx.az)

Pharmacies Most of Ganja's pharmacy shops can be found along Ataturk Ave.

Post office The central post office is on Mirza Abbas Abbaszade.

Nakhchivan

BATABAT LAKE

Nakhchivan

Isolated from the rest of the country by Armenia's Syunik Province – a quirk of geography courtesy of post-World War I chaos and the ensuing Soviet administration – Nakhchivan has long been a sensitive border area and correspondingly unwelcoming to tourists. Since the mid-2010s, however, the administration here has become considerably more relaxed, making it a perfect time to explore this unique corner of the country.

Completely separated from the rest of Azerbaijan, the autonomous enclave of **Nakhchivan** is wedged uncomfortably between Armenia to the north and east, and Iran to the south and west, with a very small border with Turkey at its western extremity. A visit to the region is a richly rewarding, if bizarre, experience. Towns across Azerbaijan have a habit of reinventing themselves – and their history – to justify the current status quo, but nowhere is this so apparent as in Nakhchivan, where ancient monuments are routinely spruced up to look shiny and new. This may be blatant historical and archaeological vandalism, but it's presented with such a straight face that it can only be regarded as a fascinating cultural experience in itself.

Brief history

Allegedly first settled by Noah and his family following their descent from nearby Ararat, Nakhchivan spent much of its earlier history as part of the **Kingdom of Armenia**, and it may even have been the location where Mesrop Mashtots invented the Armenian alphabet. However, Arab, Turkish and Persian rule over the centuries led to many Armenians fleeing or being deported from the region. Ethnic violence between Armenians and Azeris became particularly vicious in the years between the collapse of Tsarist authority in 1917 and the establishment of Soviet rule in 1920. In 1921, the Bolsheviks designated the territory as the Nakhchivan Autonomous Soviet Socialist Republic; three years later, it formally became part of the **Azerbaijan SSR**.

The Soviet era brought modernisation to the area, with education and healthcare seeing vast improvement. At the same time, the demographics of the enclave changed dramatically. The population of Armenians in the 1920s was 15 percent, but by the 1980s the percentage was negligible. Following independence, the **Nagorno-Karabakh war** saw Armenia attempting to cut Nakhchivan off entirely from Azerbaijan. Tensions ran particularly high in late 1993 when Turkey and Iran sided with Azerbaijan while Russia backed the Armenians, resulting in fears that the standoff between these major world players could lead to World War III. Luckily, the situation was defused when the Armenians backed down.

Following Azerbaijan's recovery of Nagorno-Karabakh in the early 2020s, access to Nakhchivan from the rest of Azerbaijan became something of a political hot potato. Initially, Azerbaijan advocated the establishment of a "Zangezur Corridor" through Armenia's Syunik Province, a proposal that was not met with overwhelming approval by Armenia. After some initial talks focusing on the reconstruction of a Soviet-era rail line, however, Azerbaijan dropped the Zangezur Corridor idea in favour of establishing a similar corridor through neighbouring Iran. Whichever, if either, approach is eventually taken, it is likely to be some time before any material progress is made.

In the meantime, Nakhchivan can still be reached by flights from Baku, and once the country's land borders reopen, it will also be accessible from Turkey and Iran. The enclave is today celebrated as the home of Heydar Aliyev, Azerbaijan's post-Soviet president, who is revered here with a particularly sycophantic museum. The enclave's

Highlights

❶ **Nakhchivan City** A bizarre "showcase" city, the obsessively clean and tidy capital is home to a huge range of museums, not to mention the Tomb of Noah himself. See page 314

❷ **Qarabaglar Mausoleum** Nakhchivan is home to several medieval mausoleums in this distinctive style, but Qarabaglar's is perhaps the most elegant and beautiful. See page 322

❸ **Batabat** Head up into the hills in Nakhchivan's north to make the most of the gorgeous scenery around these high lakes. See page 322

❹ **Alinja Castle** Often referred to as Azerbaijan's Machu Picchu, Alinja Castle occupies a dramatic position providing stunning views of Nakhchivan's barren south. See page 323

HIGHLIGHTS ARE MARKED ON THE MAP ON PAGE 314

most regular tourists are Iranians, who come over the border at Jolfa to take advantage of Azerbaijan's more liberal drinking laws. Westerners are less frequently seen, but are becoming more common. This is perhaps due to the change of attitude in Nakhchivan's police force, who no longer seem to harbour such deep suspicions of foreign travellers as they once did.

Nakhchivan City

The enclave's capital city, also known as **Nakhchivan**, has a lengthy history, which – according to local historians – begins with Noah, who apparently descended from Mount Ararat and established a city here. Be that as it may, Nakhchivan City is known to have existed as far back as the second century BC, and went through the usual procession of invaders including Persians, Arabs, Armenians, Timurids and Russians, before becoming the capital of the Autonomous Soviet Socialist Republic of Nakhchivan in 1924.

Post-independence, Nakhchivan has received significant investment from Azerbaijan's central government. This is partly due to its special status as the home of Heydar Aliyev, but the desire to keep it prosperous after being cut off from the rest of the country also plays a part. The result is an obsessively clean and neat city with enormous wide avenues, shiny hotels and expensive restaurants – with barely any population

HIGHLIGHTS

1 Nakhchivan City
2 Qarabaglar Mausoleum
3 Batabat
4 Alinja Castle

to make use of them. Despite this dearth of people, the city somehow avoids feeling sterile and has a very welcoming feel about it. It's by far the best place to base yourself to explore the area.

People in the rest of Azerbaijan regard Nakhchivanis as overly privileged, brash and arrogant – "like Texans", according to one Ganjan – and it's certainly true that the level of education and other public services here are noticeably superior to what you'll encounter elsewhere in Azerbaijan. That being said, your chances of finding English speakers in these parts are fairly limited in comparison to other areas of the country so be prepared.

Yezidabad Fortress

Off Calil Mammadquluzada St • Free

Until the mid-2010s there was little to be seen of Nakhchivan's castle. This has changed with an enthusiastic reconstruction programme in the last decade and there's now a perfect 'medieval' **fort** on the site, which is just a short walk south of the town centre. It's a lovely place for a sunset stroll around the crenellated walls framing a large courtyard – with luck, you'll see both Mount Ararat and İlan Dağ – and it certainly brings in the tourists, but those concerned about historical authenticity may wish to look away.

Qala Museum

Yezidabad Fortress courtyard • Free

The ceiling of this round museum has been painted with a blue sky and clouds for some reason – possibly to distract from the exhibits, which are certainly nothing out of the ordinary compared to other Azeri museums, though the intricate gravestones are momentarily interesting. Most of the pieces on display here date from the first and second millennia BC, and many of them were only discovered during the extensive castle renovations.

Noah's Tomb

Off Calil Mammadquluzada St • Free

Just outside the fortress walls, on a platform overlooking the valley below, stands a modern tower constructed in Central Asian style which claims to house the remains of Noah of biblical fame. You can choose to believe this or not, but it must be noted that the **tomb chamber** at the bottom is suspiciously empty. Interestingly, Turkey, Iraq and Jordan all also lay claim to being home to his tomb.

In the upper chamber, you'll find a mixed bag of exhibits on display, including some fossils which apparently prove the presence of the sea in Nakhchivan and by extension the truth of the Noah business. The foundations of the tower are thought to date from the eighth century.

Elsewhere on this platform further domes were under construction at the time of research. Presumably these are for the intended tombs of other hitherto elusive biblical figures.

> ### NOAH, THE ARK, AND İLAN DAĞ
>
> Nakhchivan is very proud of its association with **Noah**. Although Ararat, the Ark's alleged final resting place, is in Turkey, locals assert that the Ark crashed through the Nakhchivan mountain of İlan Dağ on its way to Ararat – this is apparently why İlan Dağ has a cleft in its summit. Moreover, the name Nakhchivan itself can be translated (in Armenian) as "the place of descent", because Noah came down from Ararat and settled here.

Imamzade

Azadlig St • Free

Below the castle, a collection of brightly coloured domes lure the visitor toward these tombs, dating from the 1730s. Like much else in Nakhchivan City, they have been heavily restored. They are usually kept locked.

Yusif ibn Kuseyir Mausoleum

Off Calil Mammadquluzada St • Free

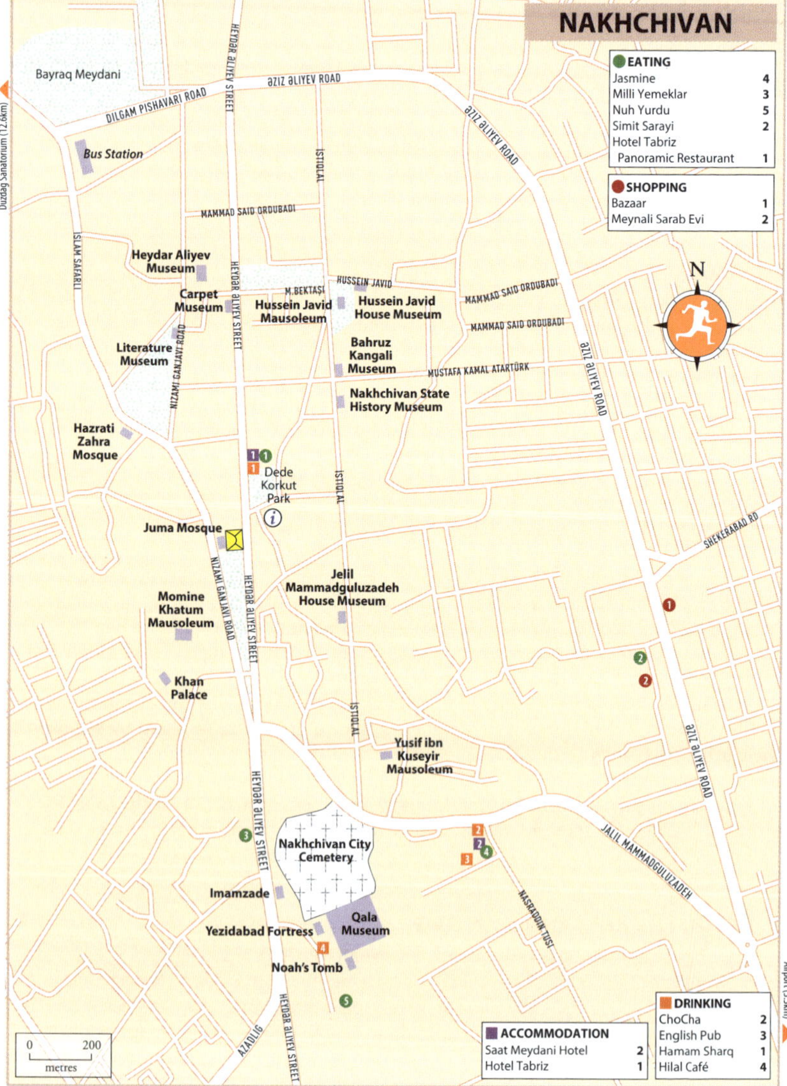

This beautiful and elegant little tomb was built in 1161. Like most of Nakhchivan's other monuments, it has enjoyed the attentions of an enthusiastic restoration team, but it's still an extremely attractive building, with a striking conical roof and geometric decoration on the exterior.

Jelil Mammadguluzadeh House Museum

Mammadov St • Free

Jelil Mammadguluzadeh, who was born in this house in 1869, was a political writer and satirist, considered to be one of the first Middle Eastern **feminists**. His magazine, *Molla Nasreddin*, was a generally progressive publication that denounced social inequalities and religious fanaticism. As such, it was not popular with either Tsarist or Soviet authorities. In 1931, the magazine was forced to close down after 25 years, and Mammadguluzadeh died in Baku the following year. The house museum is small and mainly filled with copies of his magazine.

Momine Khatum Mausoleum

Off İslam Safarli St • Free

This tomb was built in the twelfth century by the Seljuk atabeg Shamseddin Eldeniz – who ruled over a large territory, stretching from Georgia to Iraq – for his wife, Momine. The exterior of the mausoleum is beautifully decorated with interlocking shapes, while the inside features an exhibition of photos and artwork of the complex. These are diverting enough, but it's more interesting to gaze up at the impressive high dome. Don't miss the lower chamber with its excellent vaulting brickwork.

Khan Palace

Off İslam Safarli St • Free • ☎ 994 77 5450637

It may be overly restored, and not as spectacular as the palaces in Sheki, but nonetheless it's interesting to take a quick wander through the rooms of the palace of the Nakhchivani Khanate. Look out in particular for the excessively **mirrored hall**. The building was used for some time as a carpet museum – and is sometimes still described as such online – but is now more of an ethnographic museum.

Juma Mosque

Nizami Gancavi St • Free

It's thought there's been a mosque on this site since the twelfth century, but the current incarnation – an attractive red-brick building – dates from the eighteenth. It's particularly pleasant to visit towards sunset when the light streams in through the stained-glass windows.

Hazrati Zahra Mosque

İslam Safarli St • Free

This huge silver-domed and Central-Asian-tiled mosque sits on the western edge of town. Entry is, unusually, from the first floor via the steps opposite the main gate. It boasts a splendid mihrab. Segregated entrances ensure women get a worse view of the mihrab than men.

Dede Korkut Park

Dede Korkut Park • Free

DEDE KORKUT

The *Book of Dede Korkut* is a collection of **Turkic myths** set in the Caucasus, principally Azerbaijan. Varying between prose and poetry, the twelve stories tell of heroes, battles, infidels and villains. The only major link between the tales is the presence of the titular **Dede Korkut**, who fulfils the role of wise man and religious leader.

The epic, which is likely to have been composed over many years, drawing on oral traditions, is thought to have been first written down in the fifteenth century. It has been described as being an enormously important resource concerning "Turkish history, literature, identity, science and spirit", as well as being influential in "the formation of their national memory". It was not well-regarded by authorities during the Soviet period due to its potential for fomenting nationalism among the Azeris, but since independence, the epic has gained in popularity and, as of 2018, has been added to UNESCO's List of Intangible Cultural Heritage of Humanity.

In the centre of town, the small **Dede Korkut Park** contains the Sharq Hammam, a gold-domed hammam now in use as a teahouse, and a statue of Dede Korkut on a star-shaped plinth. Just down the unnamed street to the south is a small, octagonal sandstone building with a conical roof. Inside it is extensively decorated with carpets, some of which are lovely and some of which are tacky as you like.

Nakhchivan State History Museum

90 İstiqlal St • Free • ☎ 994 36 5450130

Those familiar with Azerbaijan's museums will recognise the format here – a mishmash of mildly diverting historical artefacts stretching from prehistory through to the twentieth century. Highlights are probably the fifteenth-century intricately carved gravestones, but there's also a great model of the Yusif ibn Kuseyir Mausoleum prior to its recent restoration, and some decent ethnographic exhibits.

Bahruz Kangali Museum

20 Atatürk St • Free • ⓦ behruzkengerli.nakhchivan.az/en

Bahruz Kangali was an early **twentieth-century artist** and this large museum hosts artefacts of his life, photos of his family and examples of his work. The ground floor includes some beautiful sketches of refugee children, while upstairs are more oil paintings and watercolours. The staff are friendly and eager to give a tour in English, though be prepared for the occasional rant about Armenia.

Though the artworks are impressive, perhaps the most interesting thing about the museum is that it's housed in the college that Heydar Aliyev attended, and there's a room full of photos of his schooldays. Look out for his (naturally excellent) school report, which records his high marks in subjects as diverse as trigonometry, geography and USSR Constitution Studies.

Carpet Museum

21 Heydar Aliyev Prospekt • Free

This museum is home to a vast array of exclusively Nakhchivani carpets, with very little contextual information. If you've already been to Baku's Carpet Museum, you don't need to come to this one as well unless you're wildly enthusiastic about carpets.

Literature Museum

19 Nizami Gancavi St • Free • ☎ 994 36 5451686

You'll have to try pretty hard if you want to get anything out of this museum. There are books and illustrations from famous Azerbaijani works, but unfortunately, there's no contextual English labelling you'll probably be lost immediately.

Heydar Aliyev Museum

Heydar Aliyev Prospekt • Free • ☏ 994 36 5459298

Dedicated to the life of **Azerbaijan's post-Soviet president**, this huge shrine of a museum has more Aliyev memorabilia than you can shake a stick at, including commemorative stamps, medals, family photos, gold busts, carpets, and even a very nice picture of Heydar's face beaming out of the sky instead of the sun. It's a very interesting experience, but you'll probably be followed around by the staff to ensure you don't snigger.

Hussein Javid House Museum and Mausoleum

Hussein Javid St • Free

The prominent poet and playwright Hussein Javid, who eventually met his end amid Stalin's purges, was born in this house in 1882. The fascinating museum contains photos of his plays in action and artefacts of his life. It's also a great opportunity to see a traditional Nakhchivan dwelling.

Around the corner there's an attractive white marble mausoleum which is a sensitive and elegant modern take on Nakhchivan's traditional tomb towers. Hussein Javid's remains were laid to rest here in 1996.

Bayraq Meydani (Flag Park)

Dilgam Pishavari Rd • Free

Typically over-the-top park featuring geometrically patterned astroturf sloping up a terraced hill to an enormous Azerbaijani flag atop the Museum of the National Flag. The museum is about as exciting as its name suggests, but the beautifully maintained park is a lovely place for an evening stroll, with great views over the city and beyond to Iran.

Duzdağ Sanatorium

Duzdağ Yolu • Free

About ten minutes' drive out of town is this truly bizarre place, a former salt mine which has now been converted into a dormitory for those suffering breathing afflictions. Walking down the 500-metre-long corridor with walls of salt you'll begin to understand why it helps to improve breathing. It does smell strong, though, and staying overnight is perhaps not recommended.

As it is a working medical establishment you can't just wander in, but if you're here with a guide they should be able to arrange a quick look around.

Military Park

Heydar Aliyev Prospekt • Free

On the R49 road out of town towards Batabat is a park displaying military hardware, including jeeps, tanks, planes and missiles. There is plenty of information about each of them, though you'll need to read Azeri to understand it.

ARRIVAL AND DEPARTURE   **NAKHCHIVAN**

By plane The easiest way to get to Nakhchivan is on a flight   from Baku with Azerbaijan Airlines. Given there are at least

NAKHCHIVAN'S INTERNATIONAL BORDERS

At time of writing, Azerbaijan's international land borders were closed, but when they reopen to travellers, there are two routes into Nakhchivan from neighbouring countries.

To/from Turkey Iğdır bus company run five buses a day to Istanbul via Iğdır and Erzurum in Eastern Turkey, which is certainly a good value way of getting to/from Turkey. Do bear in mind that the Iğdır company seems to have a special relationship with a petrol garage about 10 minutes from the border, and whether you're coming or going you will doubtless get to spend an indeterminate amount of time at this magical place.

The Turkey–Nakhchivan border was once notorious for the guards extracting bribes from travellers – stories abound of passports going walkies until wallets come out – and though the crossing has improved substantially since around 2010, you should be aware that there may be fun and games of this sort here.

Guards at the border crossing into Nakhchivan from Turkey are a little suspicious of foreign travellers and passport stamps from Armenia will be scrutinised thoroughly, but the process is reasonably quick. Police will want to know your travel plans so have them down pat.

Coming out of Nakhchivan into Turkey is another matter altogether. The Turkish border guards here seem entirely unaware of their country's visa regulations. Eventually, they will be able to figure their regulations out but you could be in for a long wait. **To/from Iran** Officials on both sides will probably be surprised to see you, but it's perfectly possible to cross the border that separates the Nakhchivani and Iranian towns of Julfa/Jolfa, so long as you have the requisite visas. If you're heading to Iran and are British, Canadian, American or any other nationality that requires you to be on a tour, you'll need to arrange for your guide to meet you there.

four a day, you would expect getting a ticket to be easy, but surprisingly, they do sell out several days in advance, so make sure you plan ahead. The flight, which departs from Baku's Terminal 2, takes 1.5 hours. There are also twice-weekly flights with Turkish Airlines from Istanbul. Nakhchivan's airport is only just outside the city and a taxi to the centre will be easy to pick up.

By bus Buses run to Baku daily at 7.30pm, arriving the following day at 9am, and cost 25 manat, but since this involves transiting in Iran you'll need a lot of visas. If the Zangezur Corridor proposition ever gets off the ground, this may change, but for now getting to Nakhchivan by bus is not a particularly viable option.

By train There's a faint chance that a train route from Azerbaijan to Nakhchivan through Armenia's Syunik Province may be opened at some point, but at time of writing this was not an option.

GETTING AROUND

By bus Marshrutkas run from the bus station (opposite Bayraq Meydani, on Dilgam Pishavari Road) all around the enclave, but there's no set timetable and they leave when full, so you'll need to turn up and ask what's going where. If you're tight for time the flexibility and affordability of hiring a driver for the day make this a better option – you should be able to arrange this by asking in your hotel.

By taxi Nakhchivan City's taxis charge a low flat fee to go anywhere within town, making them an enormously affordable way of getting from one end of the city to the other. Taxis tend to congregate around Bayraq Meydani and can also be picked up at Dede Korkut Park.

By foot The town centre is walkable. It's 3.5km from Bayraq Meydani to Noah's Tomb, which are the most northerly and southerly points you're likely to visit. Starting at one and walking to the other will take you past all the town's principal sights.

INFORMATION

Tourist Information Centre Dede Korkut Park. Nakhchivan's tourist information centre is in the little red-brick domed building just across the road from the south end of Dede Korkut Park. The staff are welcoming and will enthusiastically ply you with leaflets about Nakhchivan's various attractions, and then ask you to sign the visitor's book. At a push they can arrange drivers to take you around the enclave, but don't expect much in the way of practical help about transport or any actual knowledge about Nakhchivan's historical buildings. You'll probably get more

useful information on the official tourist website ⓦturizm. nakhchivan.az/en. Daily 9am–6pm, closed 1pm–2pm.
Listings Set up for Nakhchivan's tenure as Capital of Islamic Culture 2018, the website ⓦimp.nakhchivan.az/en offers some in-depth information about tourist sights across the enclave.

ACCOMMODATION
SEE MAP PAGE 316

Nakhchivan hasn't embraced the concept of hostels and it's not a place to find budget accommodation. On the other hand, its smattering of hotels – while not actively cheap – are still a bargain bucket price when taking into consideration the high standard of service and quality of the rooms.

Saat Meydani Hotel Saat Meydani Sq ⓦsaatmeydani. com. A very smart hotel – clearly aiming, with some success, to be Nakhchivan's top choice – with rooms around the top floor of the Saat Meydani square. The rooms are large, clean and impressively quiet, while the corridors are stylishly irregularly angled and decorated with entertaining and occasionally terrifying artwork. The sparse breakfast buffet is served next door in the Batumi restaurant. $$

★ **Hotel Tabriz** 17 Heydar Aliyev Prospekt ☏994 36 5447701. Nice and central with fantastic views from the opulent rooms and the panoramic restaurant on the top floor, the *Tabriz* is an excellent option. It's very cheap for such a well-located and smart hotel, and English is spoken to some extent by most staff. In the basement there's a spa and swimming pool, as well as a bizarre little 'museum' of ancient radios and TVs alongside some entertaining taxidermy. $$

EATING
SEE MAP PAGE 316

With the completion of Saat Meydani Square in 2019, Nakhchivan doubled the number of restaurants in town at a stroke. The places here are upmarket, with a Western outlook and prices to match. Away from Saat Meydani you can find cheaper and more traditional Azeri eateries.

There are also plenty of other upmarket eateries in Saat Meydani Square, including the Georgian restaurant *Batumi*, the fast-food *Chef* and the Anatolian *Kosebasi*.

Jasmine Saat Meydani Sq. Smart pan-Asian place offering a range of very good Chinese, Thai and sushi, though not everything is always available. Be aware that ordering wine by the glass seems to be a thoroughly unfamiliar concept and it's a good idea to check carefully for any unwanted extras (like, for instance, an entire bottle of Smirnoff vodka that you haven't drunk) mysteriously appearing on your bill. $$$

Milli Yemeklar 6 Azadlig St ☏994 36 5545858. Closed for renovation at time of research, this restaurant housed in Nakhchivan's old ice-house reputedly serves good Azeri food. $

Nuh Yurdu 2 Heydar Aliyev St ☏994 55 9734655. On the hillside just below Noah's tomb you'll find Noah's ark – or at least a silly facsimile of it – where visitors can eat decent Azeri food, including good kebabs, as well as good international options. There are also tables around a fish-filled pool, where there are good views of the fortress. Unfortunately, service is hit-and-miss and it's best to avoid the plov – it's just a bowl of plain, cold rice. $

Simit Sarayi 20 Aziz Aliyev Rd. Outlet of the Turkish bakery chain offering pastries and fast food. The bagel with egg and cheese is a calorific treat. Sadly the coffee is not great. It's conveniently located right next to the bazaar. $

Hotel Tabriz Panoramic Restaurant Hotel Tabriz, 17 Heydar Aliyev Prospekt ☏994 36 5447701. The fantastic view from this 13th-floor restaurant is probably the best reason to eat here. The service may be a little slow but the food is good and there's a considerable range of options on the menu. $

DRINKING
SEE MAP PAGE 316

ChoCha Saat Meydani Sq ☏994 60 2040066. A European-style coffee shop within the clock tower in Saat Meydani Square, with a balcony terrace overlooking the square. It's popular with the young and hip local crowd in the evenings.

★ **English Pub** Saat Meydani Sq. "Pub" is a bit of a misnomer – it's more like a trendy Brighton bar. Quibbling about the name aside, it's very stylish with an industrial hipster vibe, offering a short international menu, as well as a decent wine selection, beer on tap and the best-stocked spirits bar you'll find In Nakhchivan.

★ **Hamam Sharq** Dede Korkut Park. The gold-domed building in front of the Hotel Tabriz, this eighteenth-century bathhouse is now in service as a chaikhana (tea house). It's worth a visit to take a look around the well-restored features of the hammam, and it's a very atmospheric place to drink a glass of tea.

Hilal Café Yezidabad Fortress courtyard. In the castle walls, Hilal is a relaxing and welcoming place for a pot of tea – though in summer, it'll have to be after dark, as the courtyard is roasting during the day.

ENTERTAINMENT

There's an outlet of the Azeri cinema chain **Cinema Plus** at the Saat Meydani Square, showing recent Hollywood blockbusters (usually dubbed) as well as Azeri and Iranian films.

Nakhchivan boasts several theatres, including the **Musical State Drama Theatre** (26 Heydar Aliyev St, ☎ 994 55 2419863) and the **Nakhchivan Puppet Theatre** (3 Heydar Aliyev St, ☎ 994 36 5453423). Performances are irregular and not advertised online; ask at the ticket office what's on.

SHOPPING
SEE MAP PAGE 316

Bazaar Aliz Aliyev Rd. A world away from Nakhchivan's usual obsessive orderliness, the bazaar offers a welcome splash of minor chaos. It sells everything from spices to electrical goods and the fresh fruit and vegetable market is a particularly colourful and friendly place for a quick wander.

Meynali Sarab Evi 20 Aziz Aliyev Rd ☎ 994 36 5458558. Excellent selection of Azerbaijani wines – including one from Nakhchivan – with friendly English-speaking staff to help you make a choice.

DIRECTORY

Banks Banks and ATMs can be found primarily around Dede Korkut Park. There is an ATM in Saat Meydani Sq but it doesn't always have cash in it and can be quite temperamental.

Hospital Central Hospital (Aziz Aliyev Rd).

Mobile phone shops SIM cards from the rest of Azerbaijan don't always work here, and you'll be hard pressed to find a mobile phone shop willing to sell you a local card. You will probably have to resign yourself to being out of contact when you're not on the wi-fi.

Pharmacies The most central pharmacy is İffat Aptek, 5 Atatürk Prospect, ☎ 994 60 2130002. Several others can be found around Istiqlal St in the north of the city.

Post offices Nakhchivan has a veritable plethora of post offices. The central one is at 1 Atatürk Prospect, ☎ 994 36 5450765, and is open daily 9am–7pm (to 5pm Sun).

Outside Nakhchivan City

It's worth getting out of Nakhchivan City and into the smaller towns and villages of the enclave. You'll find some fascinating cultural sights, as well as areas of outstanding natural beauty. Outside the capital, Nakhchivan isn't quite as neat and tidy, but most of the tourist sites have been obsessively cleaned up and enthusiastically restored.

Northern Nakhchivan

The main reason to venture north of Nakhchivan City is the Qarabaglar Mausoleum, an impressive Mongol-era burial site. Also worth a visit are the pretty Batabat lakes, which if the political situation with Armenia were a little less tense would make great start points for hiking.

Qarabaglar Mausoleum

Qarabaglar village • Free • 35-minute drive from Nakhchivan City

This seven hundred-year-old mausoleum, which dates from the **Mongol period**, is thought to have been built for the wife of Abaqa Khan, one of Genghis' great-grandsons. It's a beautiful and elegant building, bedecked with Central Asian style tilework. Its state of perfect preservation is a tad suspect – it's clearly been visited by Nakhchivan's ever busy army of restoration workers, who have also attached a new museum (containing an unremarkable array of artefacts) to the former caravanserai, which has had its minarets rebuilt. The lower chamber, with its vaulted brickwork, feels the most authentic remaining part of the complex.

If you have a driver, he may opt to take you on a long loop north of Qarabaglar through attractively barren hills and a couple of pristine villages so he can point out the delightful Nakhchivan cement works, at which point you will rejoin the main road back towards the city.

Batabat

Batabat Rd • Free • One-hour drive from Nakhchivan City

The road to **Batabat** takes you through the town of **Shahbuz**, which is grand and pristine like Nakhchivan City. The flag park on the main road is probably the most interesting sight, consisting of immaculately tended lawns and intermittent mosaics of tanks, helicopters and the like. There's also a tank in pride of place atop a small hill adjacent to the enormous flag. It's only worth a stop if you have time to kill.

Past Shahbuz, the road becomes prettier and prettier, tracing a lush green river valley between stark hills, until eventually you begin to climb a switchback road. At the top is a series of deep, cold lakes set in very attractive mountainous scenery. This area is very popular with picnicking families in the summer and has the potential to be ideal hiking country if it weren't right on the Armenian border. Needless to say, you shouldn't go wandering too far from the lakes.

Southern Nakhchivan

The mountainous landscape south of Nakhchivan City hides some of the enclave's top sights, primary among them the gorgeously-sited Alinja Castle, a stiff but extremely worthwhile climb. This area also contains an interesting Islamic place of pilgrimage and the Iranian border town of Julfa.

Ashab-i Kehf

Ashab-i Kehf Rd • Free • 20-minute drive from Nakhchivan City

A popular and **important pilgrimage site** for Muslims, this red-coloured cliff houses the Cave of the Seven Sleepers as described in the Qur'an. There's now a whole complex here, with clearly defined paths leading up the cliffs. The Sleepers' Cave itself is small and of interest largely only for the allegedly magnetic rock – if your faith is strong as you pray, you can get a pebble to stick to the cave wall.

Continuing up the staircase, you'll reach a rock pillar, around which it's customary to walk three times, squeezing through the narrow gap to show your devotion and faith. After this, the path splits. Taking the right-hand way leads up a metal staircase to a viewpoint, while the left route brings you to an interesting open-air mosque and a staircase leading to a larger cave offering good views over the canyon. Here, devotees sit and pray, hoping for a drop of water from above to land on their heads as a sign of divine favour.

Back at the car park, there are picnic benches, tea stalls, toilets and a gift shop – the latter is a rarity in Nakhchivan, so if you want a fridge magnet this is the best place to buy one.

Nearby, there's a turn-off from the road leading to a small spring where water bubbles up for five minutes or so every half hour. The water is prized for its healing powers.

Alinja Castle

Alinja-Bayahmed Rd • Free • 30-minute drive from Nakhchivan City

Frequently optimistically described as Azerbaijan's Machu Picchu, **Alinja Castle** sits atop a hill in the barren landscape to the east of Nakhchivan City. The castle dates back at least as far as the seventh century – perhaps further – and spent a good part of its early existence as a stronghold of Greater Armenia, though this is unlikely to be mentioned on your visit. It was certainly the site of a 13-year siege by Tamerlane's armies in the late fourteenth century, after which the castle took a less prominent role in local history.

The fortress has been restored to within an inch of its life, so there's little historical authenticity on offer, but the views of the castle site and the mountains and valleys beyond are breathtaking. It's a hefty 30-minute walk along a well-paved path to the castle's main courtyard. For those with superhuman energy reserves or the desperate urge to see some genuine castle remains, you can climb further to an unrestored tower base overlooking the main castle and offering a striking view of İlan Dağ.

12

The small one-room museum at the base includes artefacts from the castle and surrounding area, including an ingenious fifth-century water filtration system.

Nakhchivan City to Ordubud

The road from **Nakhchivan City** down to **Ordubud** traverses several differing attractive landscapes. Early on, you'll pass through semi-desert, with big red rock bluffs by the side of the road. Further on, the mountains that surround the enclave come into clearer view and you travel through greener, almost lush, landscape, though still with bare yellow crags on either side of the road.

You'll pass Nakhchivan's most iconic mountain on this road –İlan Dağ, which translates as Snake Mountain. Local explanations for the name are somewhat lacking: on enquiring, you're likely to be met with a moment of silent reflection before being told "once there was a snake there", which is logical but not enormously helpful. The huge cleft in the summit was allegedly caused by Noah's Ark crashing through the mountain – presumably they were letting one of the animals drive at this point.

The town of Julfa is only worth visiting if you are heading to or from Iran. The border crossing is reasonably trouble-free, assuming you have the requisite visas. The town was once a thriving Armenian settlement, but in the seventeenth century the majority of the population was deported by the Persian Shah Abbas to Isfahan. They left behind the world's largest Armenian cemetery, which has since been entirely demolished by the Azeri authorities. You will find it difficult to get anyone in town to acknowledge there was ever an Armenian community here, and it's not a great idea to pursue this topic.

Ordubud

Nestled in the southeast corner of Nakhchivan, immediately bordering Iran and Armenia, **Ordubud** is the textbook definition of "end of the road". That doesn't mean it's an unpleasant place, though: on the contrary, it's a friendly little town with an excellent museum. Police were once notoriously suspicious of tourists here but have eased up considerably.

History Museum

Emin Sadliq Sarayi • Free

One of the best-presented museums of its type in Azerbaijan, the Ordubud **History Museum** is housed in a seventeenth-century market building and exhibits a wide range of local items, from prehistoric artefacts to Soviet era publications. English is sometimes spoken, and guided tours in some language will be provided.

This museum is the best place to get information about the remarkable petroglyphs at nearby **Gamigaya**, which, sadly, are very difficult to visit due to their position near the Armenian border. Try to arrange a trip by emailing ✉ gemiqaya@nakhchivan.az.

Juma Mosque

Emin Sadliq Sarayi • Free

The **Juma Mosque**, dating from at least 1604, is the largest of Ordubud's many mosques. The entrance is round the back on the unnamed street between Samad Vurgun and Sarsehar streets. Inside, it houses an attractive mihrab and pleasant stained-glass windows.

Buzxana

Emin Sadliq Sarayi • Free

This gold-domed building on the main street was originally constructed as an icehouse for keeping food cool in Nakhchivan's hot summers. It's much deeper inside than it appears from outside. It now operates as a restaurant and teahouse but the owners don't seem to mind tourists coming in for a quick look.

MammadAliyev House Museum

7 Yusif MammadAliyev St • Free

This museum is the birthplace and former home of the Soviet chemist pivotal in the development of the oil extraction processes in the 1940s and 50s, earning the Order of Lenin award for his contribution to the Great Patriotic War.

EATING AND DRINKING   **ORDUBUD**

Dubandi Teahouse Yusif MammadAliyev St. Pop round behind the History Museum and you'll find an enormous teahouse which has tables on and around bridges over a small gorge with a not enormously attractive waterfall. The tea with (allegedly) famous Ordubud lemons and spiced murabba sweets is very good here, though not particularly cheap. $$

Manzara Heydar Aliyev Prospekt. On the outskirts of town, *Manzara* is a no frills, outdoor restaurant serving up tasty kebab-based options. Manzara means "view" but the view in question is of a yard of broken stones, so don't get too excited. $

12

ARMENIAN WOMEN WITH SPINNING WHEELS, CA. 1915-21

Contents

History

Despite their close geographical location – or perhaps because of it – the three Caucasian countries have often taken wildly different paths. Their history is peppered with periods of invasion and suppression by outside powers – the Turks, Persians, Byzantines, Russians and Mongols all have a part to play – but when independence was gained, each country followed its own direction. The only time they tried to forge a common path, independent of any other power, was in 1918 with the Transcaucasian Democratic Federative Republic, a union which dissolved just over a month after formation owing to an apparent inability of the peoples to work together. This section will approach each country independently or collectively, dependent on their relationships at each point in history.

Pre-history

There is evidence of prehistoric human habitation in the **Caucasus** dating back millions of years. Archaeological finds at Dmanisi in Georgia include a set of skulls (now on display in Tbilisi's National Museum) thought to be 1.8 million years old, while finds at Azokh Cave in Nagorno-Karabakh suggest the presence of proto-humans, including Neanderthals, up to 0.7 million years ago. While little is known of these early people, it's thought that the Caucasus region, between the Black and Caspian seas, was an important passage for early migrations of humans into Northern Asia.

Urartu

Today's Armenian people are thought to descend from the **Urartians**, a group that formed a political entity centred around Lake Van, now in Eastern Turkey. The Kingdom of Urartu was at its height in the mid-eighth century BC, with territory reaching as far as Lake Sevan and south Georgia. It was in this period that King Argishtu I founded the fortress of Erebuni, which in later years became the city of Yerevan. However, the Urartian Kingdom came under pressure from raiding Cimmerians in the north and attacks from the Medes in the southeast. By the year 590 BC, Urartu was no more.

Colchis

Around 1300 BC, a major power had emerged in western Georgia based at today's Kutaisi, then known as **Colchis**. Known to the Ancient Greeks as the mythical destination of Jason and the Argonauts, Colchis was not so much in the business of

c. 18,000–3,000 BC	c. 6000 BC	c. 1300 BC
Prehistoric peoples carve petroglyphs in Qobustan and other sites around the Caucasus.	Wine-making process discovered in Georgia or Armenia; the two nations will forever each claim that they invented wine.	Kingdom of Colchis established in Georgia; Jason and the Argonauts visit on the Quest for the Golden Fleece.

INSTAGLYPH?

Perhaps an early version of social media, the ancient peoples of the Caucasus seem to have shared our interest in recording daily activities and lifestyles, but they did so in the less transient form of **petroglyphs** – carved images on rocks. The most famous examples in the Caucasus are those found at Qobustan National Park in Azerbaijan, where pictures of animals, dancers, warriors and boats – among many other topics – were carved in the period between twenty thousand and five thousand years ago.

The Norwegian anthropologist Thor Heyerdahl studied the Qobustan petroglyphs in depth, even suggesting they offer corroboration for his theory – based on a study of linguistics – that the Vikings originated here and sailed up the River Don, eventually reaching Scandinavia. This theory has not met with widespread acceptance.

Viking or not, the prehistoric Caucasian peoples inscribed their petroglyphs in other parts of the region too. You'll find particularly fine examples around Ughtasar Lake, near Sisian in Armenia, and Gamigaya in Nakhchivan, which is not so easy to reach due to the political situation. Visiting these remote spots is a great opportunity to catch a glimpse of what was important to these ancient cultures – and to reflect on whether our own social media postings will be as perfectly preserved in twenty thousand years' time…

producing golden sheep but developing sophisticated agricultural techniques. When Urartu fell to the Cimmerians and Medes, the Colchians were similarly overrun, but threw off their conquerors and achieved independence around 300 BC.

The Median Empire

The territory that is now Azerbaijan had been home to many peoples, including Scythians and Caucasian Albanians, but the first time these groups had coalesced into a political state seems to have been under the Medes. The **Medes**, who held an empire covering the entirety of modern-day Iran and beyond, traced their ancestry back to the mythological witch-queen Medea of Colchis, and were responsible for the fall of Urartu. In Azerbaijan, they held sway until the sixth century BC, when the Persian Cyrus the Great conquered them, leading to the establishment of Zoroastrianism as the predominant local religion.

The Achaemenids

Under Cyrus the Great, who came to power in Persia in 559 BC, much of what is now Azerbaijan and Armenia was incorporated into his **Achaemenid Empire**. The territory of Georgia followed about fifty years later, under Cyrus' successor, Darius the Great, but his rule there seems to have been nominal. Achaemenid rule was generally light-touch, with subject territories required to pay tax and send tribute – a carving of an Armenian bringing tribute can be seen on the Wall of Peoples at the Iranian ruin of Persepolis. Religious tolerance was practiced, with Zoroastrianism reaching Azerbaijan under the Achaemenids, but there seem to have been no efforts to impose it on Georgia or Armenia.

782 BC	**Sixth century BC**	**301**
Yerevan founded (as Erebuni Fortress) by the Urartian King Argishti I.	Northern Azerbaijan known as Caucasian Albania.	St Gregory the Illuminator converts Tiridates III to Christianity; Armenia becomes the world's first Christian state.

THE GATES OF ALEXANDER

Alexander the Great is credited with the construction of enormous iron **gates** in the Caucasus mountains to keep out northern invaders, including the savage mythological tribes of Gog and Magog. The location of these gates is disputed. Varying sources – as diverse as the Qu'ran and Marco Polo – suggest either Derbent (now in Dagestan, Russia) or the Dariali Gorge at the north end of Georgia's Military Highway. It seems unlikely that Alexander ever put in the effort to safeguard the Caucasus, but there is evidence that the Persian Sasanian dynasty erected a wall of defensive towers near Derbent, which may be the origin of the legend.

Alexander the Great

The conflict between the Macedonian **Alexander the Great** and his rival, the Achaemenid Darius III, reached a critical point in 334 BC, when Alexander invaded Persia. In the subsequent campaign, Alexander subdued all Achaemenid resistance and forced the surrender of the Empire, thus resulting in independence for the Caucasian regions. After Alexander's death, the former Achaemenid Empire was divided, with the Caucasus coming under the nominal control of the Seleucid Greek dynasty, but their rule was generally weak.

Greater Armenia

In the wake of the collapse of the Achaemenids, Armenia established an independent kingdom, during which time **Zoroastrianism** became the predominant religion. Known as Greater Armenia, this was a period of prosperity and power for the country, especially under the rule of Tigran the Great (95–55 BC). Tigran's strength and diplomacy led to Armenia becoming one of the strongest states east of Rome, with boundaries that stretched all the way from the Caspian Sea to the Mediterranean, even as far south as Damascus.

Tigran founded four cities bearing his name – all called **Tigranakert** – including a capital for his empire somewhere near Diyarbakır, Turkey. The only one of these cities that now remains is in the Nagorno-Karabakh region and largely ruined, especially following damage in the 2020 war. Armenians still remember Tigran with pride, and it's not uncommon to meet Armenians named Tigran in honour of this king, under which Armenia achieved one of its golden ages.

Tigran was defeated by the Romans in the Battle of Tigranocerta in 69 BC, after which Greater Armenia was brought under the sway of the **Roman Empire** when client kings were installed. For about a century, the territory was frequently disputed by the Parthians (a significant Persian power) and had to be regularly retaken. By the time of the accession of Tiridates I in 66 AD, the Parthians had effectively ejected the Romans, though Rome still regarded Armenia as their territory.

Caucasian Albania

The Caucasian Albanians (see box, page 331) were a people occupying northwest Azerbaijan from around the sixth century BC, with their power base near the modern town of Qabala and, later, around Barda. Despite

326	Late 400s	c. 645
St Nino converts King Mirian of Iberia; Christianity is established as Iberia's state religion.	Tbilisi founded by King Vakhtang Gorgasali of Iberia.	Caucasus conquered by Arabs and divided into emirates under the Umayyad caliphate.

> ## IMPERATOR
>
> The Armenian government surprised computer gamers in 2019 by using the country's official Twitter account to tweet their excitement about an upcoming PC strategy game entitled **Imperator: Rome**. The reason was soon clear: the game is set in the period of Greater Armenia and the country is a playable power. There was no follow-up after Imperator's release, but since it's a long-running game, perhaps the government is still playing?

Azerbaijani claims that they were the very first inhabitants of the Caucasus, historiography of this group is vague, but it's clear they were tributary to the Achaemenid Empire in their time, as well as to Greater Armenia under Tigran the Great. Caucasian Albania became part of the Roman Empire in the mid-first century BC, and – at Qobustan – was the site of the easternmost Roman inscription ever found.

Roman decline

From 65 BC, Colchis was occupied by the Romans, who were following up their successes in Greater Armenia with a conquest of the wider Caucasus. Colchis seems to have had a good relationship with its Roman overlords, but by the early second century AD, Roman influence on the region was waning. Greater Armenia and Caucasian Albania were already **Parthian client states** rather than Roman. Under King Pharsman II of Iberia, much of what is now Georgia achieved independence from Rome too. Despite attempts to regain power in the region, the Roman period was largely over.

The Advent of Christianity

Since the death of Christ, missionaries had journeyed to the Caucasus preaching and attempting conversions. They'd usually either failed or met unpleasant ends – the nun St Hripsime was burned alive. However, in the year 297 **St Gregory the Illuminator**, who had been imprisoned in a pit in Khor Virap for thirteen years, was released to cure the Armenian King Tiridates III of a mental illness. Tiridates was evidently satisfied with the cure since in 301 he converted to Christianity and allowed Gregory to baptise him and other members of his court. He then went further and declared Christianity to be Armenia's state religion, the first country in the world to do so.

   Christianity spread quickly throughout the region. The Caucasian Albanians seem to have adopted it shortly afterward – though it has been known for tour guides at Kiş Church near Sheki to suggest that Christianity came to Azerbaijan first, spread by Jesus Christ himself, with the unexpected assistance of Attila the Hun – while in Georgia, St Nino converted Queen Nana and then King Mirian, who made Christianity the state religion in 326.

Christianisation in Armenia

A wave of Christianisation followed, with the **establishment of churches and monasteries** all over the region. At Echmiadzin, St Gregory saw a vision of Christ

961	**1045**
Armenia's Golden Age begins with the crowning of Ashot III as the king of Bagratid Armenia, with its capital at Ani.	Bagratid Armenia falls to the Byzantine Empire.

> ## A DIFFERENT ALBANIA AND IBERIA
>
> To Westerners, **Albania** tends to mean the Balkan country and Iberia refers to Spain and Portugal. In the Caucasus, these names refer to entirely different political entities, which seem to have shared the names. Caucasian Albania was a kingdom in what is now Azerbaijan, while Iberia was the name for the early Georgian kingdom. While no link between the two Albanias seems to have been proposed, medieval Georgian writers were interested in the notion that the two Iberias shared a common origin.

descending from the heavens and a cathedral was duly constructed on the site. Echmiadzin subsequently became the centre of Armenia's religious life and the seat of the Catholicos. The seat transferred to several different locations through history, but from 1441 onwards it returned to Echmiadzin and has remained there ever since.

The establishment of other monasteries across Armenia ushered in an era of learning and scholarship, particularly after the monk, **Mesrop Mashtots** (see box, page 160), invented the Armenian alphabet in the early fifth century, allowing for the translation of religious texts into the Armenian language, and the composition of original literature. Despite invasions from Persia – which included attempts to forcibly reconvert the population back to Zoroastrianism – Christianity maintained its grip, and following the Battle of Avarayr in 451 Armenians were granted the right to continue to practice their religion.

The founding of Tbilisi

The adoption of Christianity by King Mirian in 326 brought Iberia culturally into alignment with the Byzantine Empire, which was establishing itself at the other end of the Black Sea around this time. After a defeat at the hands of the Persians, however, Byzantium left Iberia to become a Persian vassal state. Initially, Christianity was tolerated, but under the Sasanians in the fifth century, **Zoroastrianism** was heavily promoted and became a second state religion.

In the late fifth century, however, King Vakhtang Gorgasali, to whom the foundation of Tiflis (Tbilisi) is legendarily attributed, came to power. According to the story, while out hunting, he came across hot springs and ordered the construction of a city on the spot. He is likely to have regarded this as less important than his struggle for independence against the Sasanians, which led him into alliance with the Byzantines. He achieved his goal and established himself as the head of the Iberian state, but the kingdom he left behind lasted no more than twenty years as an independent entity. By 580 it had been abolished altogether, becoming no more than a Persian province.

Sasanian Azerbaijan

The Sasanians – who had conquered Armenia and Georgia – occupied Azerbaijan from the mid-third century. They tolerated Christianity at first, but by the fifth century they began to fear Christian subjects would naturally align with Byzantium, and an effort to convert the Caucasian Albanians to Zoroastrianism began. Resistance to the **Sasanians** centred around the territory now known as **Nagorno-Karabakh**, and Christianity survived despite

1071

Armenia conquered by the Seljuk Turks in the aftermath of the Byzantine defeat at the Battle of Manzikert.

1121

Georgia's Golden Age begins when King David the Builder expels the Turks from Georgian territory.

> ## BABAK KHORRAMDIN
>
> Now regarded as something of a folk hero in Azerbaijan, **Babak Khorramdin** lived in the early ninth century in northwest Iran. Under his leadership and based at the impregnable castle that now bears his name, the native Persians fought back against the Arab conquests, until Babak's eventual defeat, capture and predictably grisly execution. Despite his Persian ancestry and field of operation, he was claimed by Soviet historians as an Azerbaijani national hero, a status which he has retained in post-Soviet Azerbaijan. The government of Iran is perhaps less keen on him. As a **nationalist symbol** for the 15 million Azerbaijanis now living in northwest Iran it's feared Babak could be a focus for discontent.

continued suppression by the Sasanians, as well as frequent incursions by Turkic tribes from the north. But, by the early seventh century, the world was about to change.

The Arab Conquest

It's not exactly clear when the armies of **Islam** first reached the Caucasus – the first expedition may have been in 639 or 640, but if so, it was defeated and forced to retreat. Subsequent encounters were more decisive. By 654, it seems certain that the Arabs had successfully conquered the region following several years of invasions. Armenia, Iberia and Caucasian Albania were all grouped together as the province of Arminiya under the **Umayyad Caliphate**.

The terms of the Caucasian capitulation were generous. The region's rulers were obliged to pay taxes and supply men in times of war, but in return were left in nominal control and were entitled to Arab protection in the event of an attack from another power, such as the Byzantines. This period saw the disappearance of the Caucasian Albanian state, but both the Iberians and the Armenians eventually emerged as new political entities as the Arab hold on the territory weakened over the subsequent two hundred years.

Independence

By the latter half of the eighth century, the Georgian noble Bagrationi family was increasing in power. In 808, when the Emir of Tiflis declared his **independence from the Abbasid Caliphate**, he sought the support of the Bagrationis. This independence seems to have been initially tolerated, but by the mid-850s the Armenians were also in rebellion, resulting in a putative expedition by the Abbasids resulting in the destruction of Tiflis and the suppression of the revolt. However, by the end of the ninth century, Arab rule in the Caucasus was in decline, replaced in Azerbaijan by a succession of Iranian conquerors, but in Armenia and Georgia with the establishment of Christian kingdoms, headed in Georgia by the Bagrationis and in Armenia by the related Bagratid family.

Bagratid Armenia and the Golden Age

In 884, the **Bagratid Ashot I** became the first King of Armenia since the Persian invasions in 428. He attained this position by playing the Byzantines and Arabs off

1184

1191

Tamar the Great becomes queen of Georgia, overseeing the apogee of the medieval kingdom.

Baku becomes capital of the Shirvanshah dynasty.

EMPEROR BASIL I

Known as '**Basil the Macedonian**', the Byzantine Emperor Basil I was in fact most likely an Armenian, whose remarkable rise to power in Constantinople took him from the position of stable-boy to emperor in just nine years. Coming to the attention of the Emperor Michael (the Drunkard) for his remarkable way with horses, he was brought into the Emperor's palace so that he could marry Michael's mistress, Eudocia, thus providing an excuse for Eudocia to be at court. Once installed, Basil inveigled his way to the top of the food chain, persuaded Michael to crown him co-Emperor, and then had Michael murdered. It's convoluted plots like this that give us the adjective 'byzantine'.

against each other, securing alliances with each empire and eventually being sent a crown by both the Byzantine Emperor Basil I and the Caliph Al-Mu'tamid. Ashot's son and successor Smbat I was less fortunate. Embroiled in wars against the resurgent caliphate in 914, he was captured at Alinja Castle in today's Nakhchivan and tortured to death by Emir Yusuf Ibn Abi'l-Saj.

Smbat's violent death had the effect of uniting all Armenian princes behind his son, Ashot II, who oversaw the transition from Arab rule to independent Armenia. The tenth century saw the kingdom achieve peace and prosperity in the Armenian Golden Age, from the capital of Ani, Armenia's territory included most of Eastern Anatolia, as well as reaching as far as Ganja to the east. This was a period of scholastic learning, magnificent architecture, and political, diplomatic and economic success.

By the mid-eleventh century, however, internal strife had weakened Armenia sufficiently for the **Byzantine Empire** to make its move. Perceiving Armenia as a rival and seeking to subsume it into the empire, Emperors Basil II and Constantine IX made successive attacks on Ani, which eventually surrendered in 1045. Armenia's Golden Age was over.

The Restoration of Iberia

The Iberian monarchy had been abolished during the Sasanian period, but with the help of Armenia's Ashot I, the Bagrationi prince Adarnase IV managed to restore the institution with himself as the king. Arranging for himself to be crowned at the ancient capital of Mtskheta, Adarnase swiftly achieved Byzantine recognition for his new status and secured his family's position. His descendants styled themselves Kings of Iberia until Bagrat III, who in 1010 united the **kingdoms of Iberia** and Abkhazia and the Principality of Kakheti, in effect becoming the first king of a united Georgia. Bagrat, who founded the Bagrati Monastery in Kutaisi, was canonised by the Georgian Church in 2016. His successors, George I and Bagrat IV, spent much of their reigns defending the nascent Georgian state from Byzantine incursions, which continued until the political landscape underwent a major upheaval.

The Seljuk Conquest

The new kids on the block, the **Seljuk Turks** originated in Central Asia in the 950s and began to press into the Caucasus and Anatolia from around the 1040s onward.

1220 and 1230s	**1555**
Mongol incursions into the Caucasus.	Greater Armenia is divided between Turks and Safavid Iranians.

THE BATTLE OF MANZIKERT

Described by the historian John Julius Norwich as "the greatest disaster suffered by the Byzantine Empire in its seven and a half centuries of existence", the **Battle of Manzikert** in 1071 was an encounter in which the Byzantines, under Emperor Romanus Diogenes, were roundly defeated by the Seljuk army of Alp Arslan. The battle ensued after Romanus rejected an offer of peace in the hope that he would be able to rid Eastern Anatolia of the Turks.

The **Byzantines** spent the day of the battle attempting to engage the **Seljuks**, but the Seljuks simply used archers around the Byzantine fringes to harass and provoke the army. Only when the sun was setting, and Romanus turned to retreat to his camp, did the Seljuks attack. In the ensuing conflict, the treachery of a Byzantine noble named Andronicus Ducas ensured the defeat of Romanus, resulting in a decisive Seljuk victory.

Romanus was taken prisoner and treated with courtesy and respect by Alp Arslan. They negotiated peace terms, and it is possible that had these been adhered to, the Byzantine Empire could have quickly recovered. However, Romanus was captured by Andronicus Ducas before he could return to Constantinople. He was deposed immediately and then brutally blinded, dying shortly after. His successor, Michael VII, refused to stick to the terms of the agreement with Arslan. As a result, the Seljuks continued their incursions into the already dangerously weakened Byzantine Empire.

Already reeling from their 1045 submission to Byzantium, the Armenians were utterly unprepared for the arrival of the Seljuk Turks, who swept in and took Ani in 1064. Shortly after this, in 1071, came the disastrous Battle of Manzikert, when the Seljuks defeated the Byzantines, paving the way for the rest of the Armenian kingdom to be swiftly brought into the Seljuk Empire. One result of this was a wave of migration, leading to the establishment of the separate **Armenian Kingdom of Cilicia** in the Middle East, which lasted until 1375. Close links remain between Armenia and the Middle East today.

The Georgian king Bagrat IV managed to put off Turkic invasion for some time by marrying his niece to the Seljuk ruler, Alp Arslan – a man who reportedly had a moustache so long that it needed to be tied behind him when he was hunting. The marriage was only a temporary solution and under Bagrat's successor George II, the Seljuks overran the Georgian kingdom.

In Azerbaijan, the Seljuks had already achieved dominance by 1055. Unlike Georgia and Armenia, which eventually expelled the Turks, the Seljuks remained in the territory that is now Azerbaijan, and it's thought that the native peoples – of Caucasian Albanian and Iranian origin – were 'Turkified' in terms of language and culture. Udi, spoken by a small community now found only around the Qabala and Sheki region, is considered the last remnant of the region's pre-Turkic language.

In any case, Azerbaijan's Seljuk period is considered a **time of peace**, when science, architecture and literature were prized. Ganja's most famous native son, the poet Nizami Ganjavi, composed his works at this time, and it was during this period that the local Shirvan dynasty established Baku as its capital. It's quite possible that Baku's iconic Maiden Tower is of Seljuk construction.

1604	1744
Shah Abbas of Iran forcibly relocates Armenian population of Jolfa, Nakhchivan, to Isfahan.	Erakle II begins his reign as King of Kartli-Kakheti, aligning Georgia with Russia.

The Golden Age of Georgia

Georgia's George II had entirely failed to stave off the invasions of the Seljuks and the country became a Turkic possession in 1083. In 1089, George appears to have surrendered the throne in favour of his 16-year-old son David IV, and though some evidence suggests he lived on for another twenty years or so, he certainly played no further part in Georgia's political life. David, on the other hand, was set upon reuniting the Georgian kingdom and expelling the Seljuks. He set about this goal with energy and determination.

He was fortunate that the Seljuks were distracted at this crucial moment by the beginning of the Crusades, when western armies poured into Turkic territories on their way to the Holy Land. With the Seljuks occupied, David spent much of the first thirty years of his reign engaged in warfare, culminating in the Battle of Didgori in 1121, when his army utterly defeated a much larger Seljuk force. By the time of his death in 1125, David had taken Georgia back, and even expanded its borders as far as Ani in the west and Qabala in the east.

David's successes – particularly the **victory at Didgoni** – are considered the greatest military victories in Georgian history, but warfare was not the only focus of his reign. He was a generous patron of the church, establishing schools and monasteries, including Gelati in Kutaisi, where he is buried. He also composed a number of hymns, and it was under him that Tiflis (Tbilisi) became Georgia's capital. In subsequent centuries, he became known as David the Builder in acknowledgement of his work restoring Georgia's statehood.

David's immediate successors, Demetrius I and George III, were no slouches either. The reign of Demetrius I, although beset by resurgent Seljuks, saw Georgian victories over Ani and Ganja. Demetrius even carried off the magnificent city gates from the latter: they have never been returned and can be seen at Gelati Monastery. Demetrius also meddled in the powerful Shirvanshah dynasty in Azerbaijan's Shamakhi, installing his preferred candidate to their seat of power and insisting on a beneficial alliance. George III's reign was primarily occupied with putting down a rebellion of his own nobles and endless conflict with the atabeg Eldeniz, the Islamic ruler to the south who built the beautiful Momine Khatum mausoleum in Nakhchivan City.

The peak of **the Golden Age**, however, came with the reign of George's daughter, **Queen Tamar**, who oversaw a period of flourishing cultural achievements, including the construction of beautiful monasteries and the composition of Georgia's most famous poem, Shota Rustaveli's *The Knight in the Panther Skin*. Tamar was also hugely successful in her campaigns against the Seljuks, and under her rule, Georgia reached its largest territorial extent.

Tamar is revered in Georgia to this day. Her position as a successful female medieval monarch has led to the romanticising of her image, and there's a degree of mystery about her. Her place of burial is yet to be discovered, with possibilities including options as widely strewn as Mtskheta, Ushguli and even Jerusalem. It's also possible her reign is looked back upon with such reverence because her achievements were swiftly undone, when Georgia's Golden Age – and the peace of the entire Caucasus – came crashing to an end just two decades after Tamar's death in 1213.

1758   **1801**

Fatali Khan becomes ruler of Quba Khanate, ushering   Russia annexes Georgia.
in Quba's brief predominance in Azerbaijan.

TAMERLANE

Coming to power in 1370, **Tamerlane** was the last of the great Central Asian conquerors, and quite possibly the bloodiest. It's estimated that his campaigns resulted in the deaths of approximately five percent of the world's population at the time. His invasions of the Caucasus were largely due to his desire to use the region to pass between the targets of the Persian Ilkhanate and the Golden Horde, but they were utterly devastating for the inhabitants of the region, particularly Georgia, where he is not remembered with kindness.

The Mongol invasions

Initial Mongol armies reached the Caucasus in the 1220s, clashing several times with combined Georgian-Armenian armies and always winning, but acting as passing raiders instead of an occupying force. This changed in the 1230s. The Mongols conquered Azerbaijan early in the decade, destroying many towns and killing the ruling Khwarazmian shah Jalal ad-Din. Jalal ad-Din had spent much of the preceding decade attacking Georgia, which meant that when the Mongols invaded in 1236 Georgia was in no position to defend itself. Georgia and Armenia both submitted to Mongol overlordship and agreed to pay annual tribute and supply men for the Mongol armies.

Georgia's relationship with the Mongols was rocky, involving frequent rebellions and short-lived declarations of independence, but the Armenians seem to have stayed on relatively good terms with the Mongols. In 1254, the Armenian king, Hethum I, travelled through Central Asia to Karakorum to meet the Great Khan, and later in the century there were joint Mongol-Armenian expeditions against the Mamluks in the Holy Land.

As part of the **Mongol Ilkhanate of Persia**, the Caucasus was on the front lines of the Ilkhanate's ongoing wars against the Golden Horde – a rival Mongol state otherwise known as the Kipchak Khanate – to the north. The two Mongol states clashed regularly, until both were conquered and overrun by the armies of Tamerlane in the late fourteenth century. Tamerlane's invasions finally shattered Caucasian unity, and the countries of the region spent the next several hundred years as small independent principalities, often under the rule of larger neighbours.

The Shirvanshahs

The longest-lasting dynasty in Islamic history, **Azerbaijan's Shirvanshahs** originated in the region around Shamakhi at some point in the ninth century. For much of their history they were vassals to other rulers – the Seljuks and the Georgians, primarily – but achieved a couple of periods of independence. The first of these was in the late 1100s, under Akhsitan I, who moved the Shirvan capital to Baku after Shamakhi was destroyed by an earthquake. The second began in the reign of Ibrahim I (1382–1417), who managed to appease Tamerlane and spare the country from his ravages, and then seized the opportunity after Tamerlane's death to consolidate the Shirvanshah state.

Under Ibrahim, the Shirvanshahs extended their rule to Derbent in Dagestan and as far south as Ganja and Nagorno-Karabakh. Ibrahim's son Khalilullah I further expanded the Shirvanshah territory and began the construction of the Shirvanshah Palace in Baku, but the dynasty wasn't destined to last much longer. The next ruler,

---

1828

1846

Russo-Persian War concludes, with Russia occupying the entire Caucasus region.

First oil well drilled in Azerbaijan; large scale oil exploitation begins in the 1870s.

SHAH ABBAS

Shah Abbas (ruled 1588–1629) is generally considered the greatest of the Safavid rulers, but you'd probably be hard-pressed to find a Georgian or Armenian who's that keen on him. In Georgia, he ruthlessly suppressed a number of rebellions and deported thousands of people to Iran. Deportation was also the name of the game in Armenia, with Abbas destroying the entire town of Jolfa (in today's Nakhchivan) simply to deny his Ottoman opponent a place to spend the winter. The population was forcibly relocated to Abbas' new capital of **Isfahan**, with thousands dying en route. Once the survivors arrived, however, they were permitted to establish their own district, with considerable religious liberty and relief from heavier taxes. There's still a sizeable Armenian minority in Isfahan's New Jolfa community today.

Farrukh Yassar was defeated in battle by the Safavid invader Ismail I in 1500. The Shirvanshahs were permitted to continue as a Safavid client state until 1538, when Azerbaijan was made a province of the Safavid Empire.

Turks and Safavids

The **fall of the Byzantine Empire** to the Turks in 1453 left Georgia and Armenia surrounded by hostile states with no obvious local allies. Already weakened by Tamerlane's invasions, they were in no position to defend themselves against the Turks and Safavids. The entire Caucasus became a front line in the incessant wars between these two powerful empires. For the most part, Azerbaijan remained under the control of the Safavids, but Georgia and Armenia were taken and retaken continuously for the next couple of centuries.

During this period, Azerbaijan became fully converted to the Shi'a branch of Islam, as practiced by the Safavids. Many Georgian and Armenian nobles also converted to Islam – either Shi'a or Sunni, depending on which power was then in charge – but Christianity was tolerated in general. On the other hand, social conditions were poor. The region was often devastated by warfare, the economy slumped, and population levels fell.

The **Safavid Empire collapsed** in the early eighteenth century due to pressure from outside influences – such as raids from Central Asian tribes and wars with Peter the Great's Russia – as well as a long succession of ineffectual rulers. In the wake of the collapse, the 1724 **Treaty of Constantinople** divided the Caucasus between the **Ottoman Empire and Russia**, with most of the territory of modern-day Georgia and Armenia being ceded to the Ottomans, while Azerbaijan came under Russia's sphere of influence.

The Khans and the King

The agreement reached in the Treaty of Constantinople swiftly became null and void when a resurgent Iran emerged in the 1730s under the first Qajar, Nader Shah, who reconquered the entire Caucasus by 1735. Nader's assassination in 1747 brought this short period of Iranian dominance to an end, with the Caucasus once again splintering into disparate small principalities.

1878

Josef Stalin is born Josef Djugashvili in Gori, Georgia.

1896

Construction of Baku-Batumi oil pipeline begins.

THE ARMENIAN LIBERATION MOVEMENT

During the period of Persian rule, there were several individuals who dreamed of an independent Armenia. **Israel Ori** – a native of Sisian – was one of the first. In the 1680s and 1690s he travelled around western European courts attempting to drum up support. Eventually, in the early 1700s, Peter the Great of Russia agreed to help, but Ori died before any plans could be set in stone.

Ori's spiritual successor was Joseph Emin, born to Armenian parents living in Persia in 1726. Emin's attempts to secure Armenia's independence began with travelling to London and befriending the British aristocracy, then proceeded through visiting the Russian court at St Petersburg and gaining an introduction to Georgia's King Erekle II. Unfortunately, Erekle seems to have disliked Emin and before long he was told in no uncertain terms to leave Georgia. Emin concluded his career in the British Army, serving in India.

Ori and Emin had tried to **liberate Armenia** by persuading nobles and kings, but perhaps the most effective of the early Armenian nationalists was David Bek, a nobleman who took matters into his own hands. His campaigns in the 1720s against the Safavids and the Ottomans gained considerable popular support, so much so that the Safavid ruler Tahmasp could only defuse matters by appointing David the local governor. David died in 1728, and with the murder of his successor Mkhitar Sparapet, it's considered that the armed Armenian liberation struggle came to an end.

In Azerbaijan and Armenia, this was the period of the khanates: small independent states ruled by local khans from Quba, Baku, Sheki, Karabakh, Yerevan, Nakhchivan, Ganja, and many more. The latter half of the eighteenth century was turbulent, with these khanates jostling each other for supremacy, only occasionally allying themselves with each other to defend the region against external threats.

Meanwhile, in Georgia, King Erekle II had become the ruler of the eastern Georgian states of Kartli and Kakheti – the first time these regions had been unified in several hundred years. His policy of opposition to Iran steered Georgia towards the Russians, and in 1783 he signed the **Treaty of Georgievsk**, and Kartli-Kakheti became a Russian protectorate. This status didn't save Georgia from the Persian Agha Mohammed Khan, who invaded in 1795 and burned Tiflis to the ground.

Russian wars

When King Erekle II died in 1798, his kingdom passed to his son George XII, who was fated to be the last king of Georgia. Seeking aid against his enemies, George began negotiating a treaty with Russia, and during these negotiations Tsar Paul I made up his mind to incorporate Georgia into the **Russian Empire**. George died in 1801, at which point the new Tsar Alexander I formally annexed the country. The Georgian nobility were herded into Tiflis' Sioni Cathedral and forced to take oaths of loyalty to the Russian crown.

Over the next ten years, the Russians advanced through the Caucasus. The Azerbaijani khanates became protectorates between 1802 and 1806 and were subsequently absorbed, while the western regions of Georgia were annexed by 1810.

1915	1918
The Ottoman Empire embarks on programme of genocide against ethnic Armenians in Eastern Anatolia.	Georgia, Armenia and Azerbaijan unite as the Transcaucasian Democratic Federative Republic; the Republic dissolves just over a month later.

THE GEORGIAN CONSPIRACY

Born in 1795 in Georgia, **Prince Okropir** was six years old when his father, King George XII, died and Georgia was annexed by the Russians. He was taken to St Petersburg, where he received an education as befitted his noble status. He became an officer in the Russian Chevalier Guard at the age of 17 and then retired in 1816 when he was 21. It could be argued that this is young for retirement, but Okropir didn't lapse into indolence. Instead he spent his time trying to set the scene for the **restoration of the Georgian monarchy**.

Banned from Georgian territory, Okropir visited Tiflis in secret in 1830 to scout out potential support – and found plenty among the Georgian nobility and intellectuals, including the poets Alexander Chavchavadze and Grigor Orbeliani. By 1832, a plan had come together. The chiefs of the Russian administration in Georgia would be invited to a ball, where they would be assassinated, and the road into Georgia through the Dariali Gorge would be seized to prevent Russian reinforcements arriving. Meanwhile, Prince Alexander – Okropir's brother and the heir to the throne – would be invited back from his exile in Persia to become the new Georgian king.

The plot came to nothing. The plan was betrayed to the Russians, and the conspirators were all arrested. The Russian authorities were surprisingly lenient. Sentences of death were handed down but immediately reprieved to exile, and in many cases even this was quietly forgotten after a couple of years. Okropir was permitted to return to Moscow, where he lived until his death in 1857.

The Erivan khanate – roughly covering the territory of today's Armenia – held out longest but was invaded by the Russians in 1827.

The Caucasus had long been a fault line between Russia and Persia and the invasion of Erivan set in motion what proved to be the last major confrontation between these two powers. It ended in a decisive victory for the Russians, who took control of the Erivan and Nakhchivan khanates. The Araxes river, which formed the southern border of these territories, has ever since remained the dividing line between the Caucasian states and Iran.

The **1828–9 war** between the Russians and the Ottoman Empire resulted in Russia's acquisition of all remaining Caucasian territory, as far as Kars in modern Turkey. The new regime was not enormously popular. In Armenia and Azerbaijan, which both had large Muslim populations, the Russian authorities alienated their new peoples due to some discriminatory practices against non-Christians, as well as a more general unawareness of local customs. In Georgia, meanwhile, their high-handed rule led to several rebellions and aristocratic plots aiming to unseat them.

Russian rule

In 1844, the Russian Napoleonic War veteran Prince Mikhail Vorontsev was appointed viceroy of the Caucasus. His primary task was putting down the rebellion of Imam Shamil in Dagestan, but in Georgia, Armenia and Azerbaijan he was sympathetic to local issues, leading to the region becoming better integrated into the Russian Empire. In Georgia, the nobility became more sympathetic to the Russians under Vorontsev.

1922

The independent Republics of Georgia, Armenia and Azerbaijan are incorporated into the Soviet Union.

1941

Germany invades Russia; the Great Patriotic War begins.

ILYA CHAVCHAVADZE

Of noble birth, **Ilya Chavchavadze** hailed from the Kakheti region of Georgia. Educated in St Petersburg in the 1850s, he became inspired by the revolutions that took place in Europe of that decade and returned to Georgia with the hope of liberating his native country from Russian rule. His ideas for Georgia, however, were at odds with those of many other revolutionaries at the time – Chavchavadze envisaged a **bourgeois liberal state**, which was not in line with the plans of the Georgian Social Democrats, who preferred a more radical approach. He was assassinated in 1907. His murder remains unsolved, but it's very likely to have been the work of the Bolshevik wing of the Social Democrats, and possible that he was an early victim of Stalin.

Chavchavadze's **prolific writings** and opinions on the subject of Georgia's independence and national identity have cemented him as a hugely popular figure in Georgia ever since. His name was invoked as a figurehead by anti-Soviet dissidents throughout the life of the USSR, and in the early 2000s the United National Movement of Mikheil Saakashvili claimed to have adopted Chavchavadze's legacy. Saakashvili's political opponent Eduard Shevardnadze, meanwhile, once described Chavchavadze as the "**father of the nation**".

The relationship became more strained in 1861, when Tsar Alexander II abolished serfdom throughout the Russian Empire. In Georgia, this resulted in considerable disquiet. The newly-freed peasants found themselves in dire economic straits, while the nobles resented the loss of their serfs and also considered themselves threatened by the growing Armenian middle class. In these conditions, a nationalist Georgian **liberation movement** began to grow, spearheaded by intellectuals such as Ilya Chavchavadze, Alexander Kazbegi and Giorgi Tsereteli.

Azerbaijan's oil boom

People had been aware of the Caucasus' **oil reserves** for hundreds of years – Marco Polo, in the thirteenth century, had described a stream of oil which, though "not good to eat … is good for burning" – and there had been limited exploitation of the oil fields as far back as the sixteenth century, but it wasn't until the Russian period that full-scale oil extraction began. The world's first oil well was drilled in 1846 just south of Baku, and by the 1870s, Azerbaijan was experiencing a major boom.

Foreign investors – including the Rothschild and Nobel families – set up companies alongside locally-owned businesses. Baku became one of the fastest growing cities on earth and was soon a major industrial centre where over one hundred oil companies operated. The city quickly developed more extensive connections with the outside world. Telegraph wires, telephone lines and a railway link all appeared in the latter half of the nineteenth century, and the world's longest oil pipeline was opened between Baku and Batumi in 1907.

The oil magnates built extravagant houses for themselves in Baku – one such palace, nationalised under the Soviets, is now the National Museum of Azerbaijan – and many engaged in extensive philanthropy. Murtuza Mukhtarov, for example, funded the establishment of mosques across the Russian Empire, while Shamsi Asadullayev set up schools and paid for the education of talented pupils. An Armenian oil magnate named

1942–3	**1945**
German offensive heads into the North Caucasus in an effort to reach Baku's oil fields; eventually forced to retreat.	USSR defeats Germany; Great Patriotic War ends.

Alexander Mantashyants – who owned one of Baku's most prosperous companies – funded the construction of the Catholicos' residence in Echmiadzin as well as churches and education for Armenians across the globe.

Despite this ostentatious philanthropy from the wealthy magnates, conditions for the oil workers were poor. Twelve-hour working days, 360 days a year were not unusual, and workers lived in prison-like barracks, or even for long periods down in the mines. Injuries were common: in the period 1887–97 there were 309 accidents reported in the oil industry, resulting in 108 deaths, and it's likely that the genuine figures were higher. Unsurprisingly, the workers weren't well compensated for this difficult, dangerous work. Wages were often ridiculously low – up to five times less than equivalent pay packets in the USA during this period. Bearing these industrial conditions in mind, it's easy to see how social revolutionaries would see the need to institute serious change.

Home-grown revolutionaries

The late nineteenth and early twentieth centuries saw the rise of **the revolutionaries**. Often followers of the theories of Karl Marx, these individuals wanted to replace the Tsarist state with a socialist model. The Caucasus produced a fair number of such revolutionaries. The most famous was Josef Stalin, born in 1878 in Georgia's town of Gori but others such as Stepan Shahumyan and Noe Zhordania also made names for themselves in the years that followed.

Zhordania was one of the leading firebrands in the Caucasus. An intellectual who had travelled around Europe absorbing and propounding Marxist theory, in the 1890s he became a leader of the Georgian Social Democratic Party and was sentenced to prison for his role in inciting clashes between workers and the army in 1901. While he was imprisoned, the Georgian and Russian Social Democrats merged into one party, and Zhordania aligned himself with the moderate Menshevik faction in the new organisation, opposing the more radical Bolsheviks.

The 1905 **Russian Revolution** – sparked by a strike in St Petersburg – spread to the Caucasus, where factory and oil workers went on strike. Tragically, during the strikes, ethnic violence broke out between Armenians and Azerbaijanis in numerous locations, including Baku, Shusha and Nakhchivan – the first time, but by no means the last, these groups would clash over the course of the twentieth century.

War and genocide

Throughout the nineteenth century, Armenians in the Russian Empire had agitated for further Russian expansion into eastern Anatolia, then an Ottoman-owned province but inhabited by a considerable number of Armenians. At the outbreak of **World War I**, the Russians – who harboured ambitions to take Constantinople itself – were bolstered by considerable numbers of Armenian volunteers joining the army in the hope of unifying the Armenian people. Meanwhile, one of Turkey's objectives was the recovery of the territory it had lost during the Russian-Turkish wars of the nineteenth century, including the cities of Kars and Batumi. The stage was thus set for a clash of empires.

The Russians launched the first campaign in November 1914, advancing as far as the city of Doğubayazıt. The subsequent Battle of Sarikamish resulted in a heavy

1988

1988

Protestors in Armenia and Nagorno-Karabakh demand that Nagorno-Karabakh become part of the Armenian SSR rather than the Azerbaijani.

Devastating earthquake hits Spitak, Armenia, in December; worldwide international campaign sends aid.

defeat for the Turks, thanks in part to the performance of the Armenian volunteer units. The Turkish commander, Enver Pasha, claimed that his defeat was due to local Armenians assisting the Russians. This tied in with anti-Armenian propaganda the Turks had produced earlier in the year and paved the way for the **Armenian Genocide**.

From February 1915, citing fears of collaboration with the Russians, the Turks removed all ethnic Armenians holding posts in the Ottoman army. This was only the beginning. On April 24, the Turks imprisoned the leading Armenian intellectuals in Constantinople, then from May onwards they began to deport Armenians from Turkey into the Syrian desert. The deportations took the form of brutal death marches which the Armenians were not expected to survive. Elsewhere in Turkey, Armenian villages were burned and the people were massacred. Now considered to be one of the modern world's first genocides, it's estimated that up to 1.5 million people died as a direct and intended result of the Ottoman government's policy.

Revolution and unification

Though Russia's World War I campaigns in Turkey met with a fair degree of success, the same could not be said of its performance in the central European arena, where the army's heavy losses proved enormously demoralising. By 1917, the combination of military defeats and economic devastation led to mutinies and revolts, sparking the February Revolution that toppled the Tsar, followed by the October Revolution when Vladimir Lenin and the Bolsheviks swept aside the provisional government and proclaimed Russia a Soviet Socialist Republic.

This development ushered in a period of considerable chaos in the Caucasus. A body calling itself the **Transcaucasian Commissariat** was established on November 11, 1917 to govern the region. This institution, which initially intended for the Caucasus to remain part of Russia, signed the Armistice of Erzincan on December 18, pausing the war against the Ottomans. In February 1918, however, Soviet Russia signed the Treaty of Brest-Litovsk, ceding Batumi, Kars and Ardahan to the Turks, despite the fact that these territories were now under the control of the Transcaucasian Commissariat rather than Russia.

The Commissariat took exception to this and, declaring independence from Russia, proclaimed the existence of the **Transcaucasian Democratic Federative Republic (TDFR)** on April 22, 1918. This new country covered the territory that now makes up Georgia, Armenia and Azerbaijan, and its government, based in Tiflis, was headed by a Menshevik politician called Akaki Chkhenkeli. Unfortunately, it was a fragile coalition of peoples right from the start, and the strain of the ongoing war with Turkey proved too much. Though Armenian forces successfully halted the Turkish advance during battles at Sardarapat and Karakilisa, the TDFR lasted just over a month before Georgia declared independence on May 26, followed by Armenia and Azerbaijan two days later.

Post-war independence

Following the **dissolution of the TDFR**, the three Caucasian countries entered a period of independence. They were beset with a number of internal and external problems. The Republic of Armenia was under considerable social strain from the influx of

1989	1990
Anti-government protests in Tbilisi lead to the deaths of twenty demonstrators; ethnic violence in Abkhazia; tensions rise further in Nagorno-Karabakh.	Ethnic violence breaks out in Baku; Moscow's attempts to regain control result in further violence and considerable anti-Soviet feeling.

THE BAKU COMMISSARS

Led by **Stepan Shahumyan**, an ethnic Armenian Bolshevik revolutionary, a short-lived Marxist commune was established in Baku in 1918. After the collapse of the commune, its leaders attempted to escape across the Caspian Sea to Astrakhan but were intercepted by anti-Bolshevik forces and taken to Ashgabat in Turkmenistan instead. On September 20, 1918, the 26 commissars were taken out of Ashgabat on the Trans-Caspian Railway and shot in the desert. The only survivor was Anastas Mikoyan, who seems to have led a charmed existence – he later became the only Soviet politician to remain in power under every leader from Lenin to Brezhnev.

It remains unclear who ordered the executions but in the 1920s the Soviet authorities blamed British agents, and recriminations over the incident were a sticking point between the UK and the USSR for several years. The commissars themselves were regarded as Bolshevik martyrs and an enormous concrete memorial was later erected for them in Baku. This was demolished by the Azerbaijani government in 2009 amid whispers that the authorities did not want ethnic Armenians such as Shahumyan to be held in honour.

refugees from the Armenian Genocide, as well as occupying itself in short wars with Georgia, Azerbaijan and Turkey over territorial disputes. This left the nascent country in no shape to resist the arrival of the Red Army, which brought **Armenia** under the control of Soviet Russia in December 1920. An uprising in 1921, when the south of the country briefly regained independence as the Republic of Mountainous Armenia, proved ultimately unsuccessful, and the country became the Armenian Soviet Socialist Republic.

The Republic of Azerbaijan fared little better. Already in a chaotic state after the devastating ethnic violence that broke out across the country in the March Days (see box, page 254), the government went through five cabinets in the space of two years and engaged in wars over territory with Armenia and Georgia. Foreign relations were stabilised by the presence of a British military force, which arrived in November 1918 to attempt to secure Baku's oilfields from both the Bolsheviks and the Turks, and a fair degree of social progress was made. Azerbaijan was the first Islamic country to extend the vote to women and the county remains proud of his achievement. However, occasional uprisings in favour of the Bolsheviks, combined with Soviet Russia's desperate need for oil, made the Republic too tempting a target for the Red Army to resist, and Azerbaijan was invaded in spring 1920.

The **Democratic Republic of Georgia** lasted the longest of the three, and initially appeared to have the best chance of long-term survival. Allying itself with the Germans at the tail-end of World War I gave Georgia the strength it needed to repel Red Army incursions from the north, and after the war the British replaced the Germans as peacekeepers in the region.

The former revolutionary Noe Zhordania became the country's president and instituted what is quite possibly history's only example of a genuinely democratic socialist **Marxist state**. Land was redistributed more fairly between the peasantry and nobility, urban industrial workers were empowered and economic cooperatives were established. A delegation of prominent Western European socialists – including

1991

Georgia, Armenia and Azerbaijan secede from the USSR; by December, USSR has ceased to exist.

1991

Military action between Armenia and Azerbaijan over the Nagorno-Karabakh issue breaks out.

the future British Labour Prime Minister Ramsay MacDonald – visited to see this innovative state in action and came away impressed.

The American trade unionist Eric Lee has described the democratic socialism of Georgia's post-war republic as a great experiment and notes that the experiment did not end in failure: it ended because the Bolsheviks invaded and imposed their own brand of authoritarian socialism upon the country. Zhordania and the rest of his government were forced to flee in early 1921 after the **Red Army's invasion** and maintained a government-in-exile until Zhordania's death in 1953.

The Soviet Era

In March 1922, with all three Caucasian republics now in Soviet Russia's orbit, Lenin proposed they form one political entity, with the catchy name of the **Federative Union of Soviet Socialist Republics of Transcaucasia (TSFSR)**. The TSFSR was one of the four founding members of the Soviet Union, which was instituted on December 30, 1922.

Despite its unity, the three countries of the TSFSR maintained a degree of autonomy from each other and the seeds of future discord were planted early on. As Commissar for Nationalities, Josef Stalin (see box, page 87) drew the borders between the three republics, placing the territory of **Nagorno-Karabakh** within the Azerbaijan SSR despite a promise that had been made to the Armenian SSR in 1920. This was to cause considerable bloodshed in later years, but at the time, it was the Georgians who rose up in rebellion against Soviet rule, in the August Uprising of 1924, which was suppressed by Stalin and other prominent Bolsheviks.

The Soviets further developed Azerbaijan's **oil industry**, introducing subsurface pumps and increasing exports by 1928 to four times the level they had been under Tsarist Russia in 1913. In the 1930s, the Caucasus republics were modernised under Stalin's Five Year Plans resulting in economic expansion, but they were also subjected to fierce political and religious repression. Many of the surviving early Caucasian revolutionaries perished in Stalin's purges, as did intellectuals such as the Armenian writer Axel Bakunts and the Azerbaijani poet Hussein Javid.

In 1936, the TSFSR was disbanded, with each republic becoming an **autonomous Soviet Socialist Republic**. It was also in this year that Tiflis was renamed Tbilisi, in an effort to bring its name closer to the linguistics of the Georgian language.

The Great Patriotic War

One of the primary targets of Nazi Germany's invasion of the Soviet Union was the oilfields of Baku, but owing to fierce fighting with the Russian Army in the North Caucasus, Hitler's armies never crossed into Georgia or Azerbaijan, and the Transcaucasian republics were spared the devastation that affected much of the USSR's European territory. Even so, the Caucasus felt the effects of the War, particularly in the large number of men who went off to fight and never returned. All three nations produced Heroes of the Soviet Union, including Armenia's Major General Hmayak Babayan, killed in action in Berlin, Azerbaijan's Major General Hazi Aslanov, killed during reconnaissance in Latvia, and Georgia's Lieutenant General Vladmir Dzhandzhgava, who survived the War and went on to have a successful career in Tbilisi's State University.

1991–3	**1992**
Georgian civil war between supporters of Eduard Shevardnadze and Zviad Gamsakhurdia; Shevardnadze emerges victorious, but the regions of Abkhazia and South Ossetia have effectively seceded from Georgia.	Nagorno-Karabakh tensions escalate into all-out war. Both sides commit atrocities in attempts to take control of the territory.

Stagnation

Following **Stalin's death** in 1953, a power struggle ensued at the highest levels of the Communist Party. **Nikita Khrushchev** emerged as the General Secretary and the leader of the USSR. Khrushchev embarked on a programme of 'de-Stalinisation', dismantling the personality cult that the former dictator had built and reversing several of Stalin's more ruinous economic policies. The Caucasian countries enjoyed an economic revival, as well as greater religious and social freedoms. Even so, in Georgia, protests against de-Stalinisation erupted in 1956, accompanied by renewed demands for Georgian independence. The protests were violently suppressed, resulting in several hundred deaths.

Khrushchev's era came to an end in 1964. He was replaced in the Kremlin by **Leonid Brezhnev**, under whom the USSR entered a period of economic stagnation and decline. In Azerbaijan, the on-shore oil reserves were now largely depleted and off-shore extraction was not thought to be as efficient as the use of oilfields in other parts of the USSR. The result was a concerning lack of economic growth. In 1969, a politician named **Heydar Aliyev** was appointed the head of Azerbaijan's government. Aliyev instituted changes including expanding Azerbaijan's cotton industry in an effort to kick-start productivity.

All three republics were subject to the high levels of inefficiency that characterised the USSR at this time. Georgia, in particular, was notorious for corruption. Some improvements were made when Eduard Shevardnadze became the country's First Secretary in 1972, instituting reforms and rooting out corrupt officials. However, the country saw substantial protests in Tbilisi in 1978 when Moscow attempted to designate Russian as an official state language alongside Georgian. This provoked a nationalist outcry against the change, forcing Moscow to back down.

The fall of the USSR

Brezhnev died in 1982. By 1985 he had been replaced by **Mikhail Gorbachev**, a leader who saw the need for major reform across the Soviet Union. His twin policies of glasnost and perestroika (openness and restructuring) led to greater freedom of speech and economic revival. One consequence of the former was that the long suppressed issue of Nagorno-Karabakh was able to rise to the surface.

In 1923, Stalin had drawn up borders between the Armenian and Azerbaijani SSRs to include the territory of **Nagorno-Karabakh** within Azerbaijan. However, the majority of the population of the territory were Armenian, and over the course of the 1980s they considered that the authorities of the region had been engaging in 'forced Azerification'. In 1987, a petition was raised by the Armenian populace of Nagorno-Karabakh and sent to Gorbachev, asking for the territory to be transferred to the Armenian SSR.

Gorbachev denied the petition, but the issue was not laid to rest. In February 1988, mass demonstrations began in Nagorno's capital, Stepanakert, and the regional soviet voted to unify with Armenia. Moscow refused to accede to the vote's result and violent skirmishes began to break out between Azerbaijanis and Armenians in the region. Tensions rose further with an anti-Armenian pogrom occurring in Sumqayit just north of Baku.

1993

Azerbaijani internal political situation deteriorates; former Soviet leader Heydar Aliyev becomes Azerbaijan's president.

1994

Nagorno-Karabakh ceasefire comes into effect; the conflict is regarded as frozen.

The devastating earthquake in Spitak in late 1988 brought widespread destruction to a large portion of northern Armenia, and in the aftermath Gorbachev made his only visit to the Caucasus. While in Yerevan, much to his fury, he was asked about the Nagorno-Karabakh issue. Shortly afterwards he ordered the arrest of the Karabakh Committee, firmly turning Armenian popular opinion against him.

With the situation deteriorating further throughout 1989, ethnic Armenians and Azerbaijanis fled the Azerbaijani and Armenian SSRs respectively. In early 1990, in what is now known as **Black January**, horrific ethnic violence erupted in Baku, with at least 90 Armenians killed and hundreds more subjected to terrible abuse. The Azerbaijani authorities did nothing to intervene and in desperation Gorbachev sent in the Soviet military to restore control in the city. This resulted in 130 Azerbaijani deaths and turned Azerbaijani hearts irrevocably against the USSR.

The Soviet army had also intervened – with equally disastrous results – in a nationalist demonstration held in Tbilisi in April 1989, when 20 Georgians were killed and many hundreds were injured. This event set Georgia down the path of **independence** and two years later, on April 9,1991, the country formally declared its secession from the USSR. Azerbaijan and Armenia followed on August 30 and September 21 respectively. By the end of the year, the Soviet Union itself had dissolved.

Independence and war

The early years of the 1990s were extremely difficult for all three newly independent countries. The war between Armenia and Azerbaijan escalated into three years of intense fighting over Nagorno-Karabakh, using weaponry that had been abandoned by the departure of the Soviet army. Initially, Azerbaijan had the advantage, but following the Armenian army's capture of the town of Shusha in May 1992 the war turned against them. Eventually they were forced to retreat. Exhausted by the years of fighting, a ceasefire line was agreed in 1994, which remained the de facto border until 2020.

The **Nagorno-Karabakh War** poisoned Armenian-Azerbaijani relations, seemingly irrevocably. Both sides accuse the other of human rights abuses, each of them with good reason. Armenian troops committed a massacre in Khojaly, while Azerbaijan engaged in indiscriminate shelling in its major assault on Stepanakert, as well as killing large numbers of civilians in the village of Maraga.

Georgia faced problems of its own in the immediate post-independence period. Having elected the former Soviet dissident Zhiad Gamsakhurdia as president, the country found itself in a state of economic collapse governed by an increasingly authoritarian regime. A civil war erupted, ousting Gamsakhurdia from power, but not before his uncompromising approach had provoked a needless war in South Ossetia.

The next president was a familiar figure, Eduard Shevardnadze, who had been an effective and respected leader of Georgia in the Soviet era. He took quick steps to resolve the situation in South Ossetia but was unable to prevent a subsequent war when the region of Abkhazia in Georgia's northwest effectively seceded amid horrific human rights abuses and the expulsion of all ethnic Georgians. A ceasefire was declared in 1994, after which the status quo was maintained for some fourteen years.

2003	**2003**
Heydar Aliyev dies; his son Ilham Aliyev succeeds him as president of Azerbaijan.	Eduard Shevardnadze resigns as Georgia's president in the Rose Revolution.

Rebuilding

The second half of the 1990s were calmer for all three new countries. Under Shevardnadze, Georgia aligned itself with the West amid increasing tensions with Russia. In Armenia, the former member of the Karabakh Committee Levon Ter-Petrosyan became president, but faced extensive economic issues due to the country's closed borders with both Azerbaijan and Turkey. In Azerbaijan, meanwhile, the former Soviet leader Heydar Aliyev had assumed power in 1993 and was engaged in consolidating his power base as well as strengthening Azerbaijan's economy with the expansion of the oil industry.

Aliyev died in 2003, having unquestionably restored stability to Azerbaijan, which in the immediate post-independence years was at risk of descending into chaos. His domestic, foreign and economic policies were, on the whole, successful and his time in office saw no violations of the Nagorno-Karabakh **ceasefire agreement**. On the other hand, he has been accused of establishing a police state where elections were rigged while individual and press freedoms were curtailed, and there's still a cult of personality around him. Most towns in Azerbaijan feature a Heydar Aliyev Museum and the day he took office in 1993 –June 15 – is now celebrated as the **Day of National Salvation** of the Azerbaijani People. Following Heydar's death, his son Ilham became president in an election not noted for being free of fraud and abuse.

Georgia's Saakashvili government

Shortly after Ilham Aliyev assumed power in Azerbaijan, there was a similarly momentous change in government in Georgia. Shevardnadze had been re-elected as president in November 2003, but the contest was denounced as rigged by Georgia's rising political star, Mikheil Saakashvili. Saakashvili led peaceful demonstrations, attracting mass support, culminating in his storming of the Georgian Parliament Building clutching a bunch of red roses. These events subsequently became known as the Rose Revolution.

Shevardnadze resigned as president and in 2004 Saakashvili was elected in his place. His presidency steered Georgia on an ever more pro-Western course, adopting domestic policies designed to modernise the country – in particular cutting down the considerable corruption in officialdom. He also brought the breakaway region of Adjara back under Tbilisi's governance, but was less successful in his efforts to regain control over South Ossetia. In 2008, when separatists attacked Georgian military targets, Saakashvili responded with an invasion of the South Ossetian capital, Tskhinvali. The situation quickly escalated, with the South Ossetians calling on Vladimir Putin's Russia for assistance. Russia – already unhappy with Georgia's pro-Western outlook – responded quickly and the **Six Day War** erupted. Russia occupied several Georgian cities, including Gori, where an assault on Tbilisi could easily have been mounted. Saakashvili, who had expected support from his Western allies, was forced to sign a ceasefire. Ever since, Georgia has regarded South Ossetia and Abkhazia as Russian-occupied Georgian territory.

Saakashvili's popularity waned over the following years amid protests against his government, concerns around human rights violations and corruption and a failed army mutiny. In 2012, his United National Movement party was defeated by the new Georgian Dream coalition in parliamentary elections, and the following year he lost the presidential election. The Saakashvili years were over.

2004	**2008**
Mikheil Saakashvili becomes Georgia's president; begins campaign to reduce corruption and modernise economy.	Georgia's attempt to reassert control over South Ossetia leads to the Six-Day War with Russia.

MIKHEIL SAAKASHVILI

The flamboyant **Mikheil Saakashvili** is one of the more colourful characters of Georgia's recent history. Born in Tbilisi in 1967, he took higher education courses in the United States and France in the field of human rights. In 1995, at the age of 28, he was elected to Georgia's parliament in Shevardnadze's government, but resigned in 2001 claiming that he could not morally continue in the post. Instead, he launched his own party, the United National Movement, and ran against Shevardnadze in the 2003 elections.

Shevardnadze won the election, but it was widely considered to have been unfair and after mass protests, Saakashvili came to power in the peaceful Rose Revolution. He embarked on a major modernisation of the domestic economy, raising wages and building Public Services Halls in Georgia's major towns, so that citizen-government business could take place in the open, thus reducing the risk of corruption and bribery. Living conditions in the country soared and infrastructure saw vast improvement. Large-scale new building projects began, with modern structures such as Tbilisi's Peace Bridge and Kutaisi's Parliament Building dotting the landscape.

Saakashvili also charmed foreign powers, befriending US President George W Bush, as well as other US politicians including Joe Biden and John McCain. His first meeting with Vladimir Putin did not go so well: Saakashvili was late, having overestimated how much time he could spend in the hotel swimming pool before he needed to set off for the Kremlin. Even so, initially, it seemed the two hit it off, though before long Russia and Georgia found themselves on opposite sides of the South Ossetian conflict.

It seems that Saakashvili expected his NATO allies to support his action in South Ossetia, and the lack of response when Russia invaded Georgia left him in an awkward position. Many Georgians today still consider that the West erred in failing to come to Georgia's aid, opining that if Russia had been tackled in Georgia in 2008, it would not have gone on to invade Crimea in 2014 or, perhaps, Ukraine in 2022.

After two terms as **president**, Saakashvili was ineligible to run for a third time when his office came to an end in 2013. He left Georgia very swiftly, embarking on a further career which has been nothing if not eventful. Initially accepting a lectureship post at Tufts University in the United States, he moved to Ukraine in 2015 to become governor of Odessa but resigned this post the following year claiming that the Ukrainian government was corrupt.

In 2017 he became involved in **protests** against the Ukrainian government, was stripped of his Ukrainian citizenship and was dramatically detained by police on the roof of his apartment building in Kyiv. He was deported and became a stateless person, having given up his Georgian citizenship in 2015. The Georgian government, meanwhile, tried and convicted Saakashvili in absentia for a variety of crimes allegedly committed during his period in power, including the use of public funds for personal projects and the cover-up of human rights abuses. Claiming these charges were politically motivated, Saakashvili returned to Georgia in October 2021, where he was arrested. He remains in prison serving a six-year sentence.

Georgia, Armenia and Azerbaijan in the 2010s

Post-Saakashvili, the **Georgian Dream coalition** came to power in Georgia, led by the billionaire Bidzina Ivanishvili, who served as prime minister for one year before stepping aside in favour of his colleague Irakli Garibashvili. Georgian Dream, made up of a wide range of disparate parties with differing principles, struggled to find an

2013	**2018**
Saakashvili loses presidency to Georgian Dream candidate Giorgi Margvelashvili.	Nikol Pashinyan leads Velvet Revolution in Armenia, ousts Serzh Sargsyan, and becomes prime minister.

ideology of its own. It identifies as left-wing, and certainly some of its policies – such as the passing of legislation to end discrimination against LGBTQ+ people – reflect that direction.

Protests in 2019 accused Georgian Dream of being subservient to Russia. In response to the anti-Russian sentiment, Putin banned all flights between Russia and Georgia, and increased the duty on Georgian wine imports, with the apparent intention of squeezing Georgia economically.

Armenia's 2008 presidential elections were marred by protests and violence. The winning candidate, Serzh Sargsyan, was accused of rigging the vote, but he was able to consolidate his position and was confirmed as president. He remained in power for ten years, overseeing **renewed tensions** with Azerbaijan over the Nagorno-Karabakh issue, including an outbreak of fighting in 2016, the worst clashes since the ceasefire in 1994. When Sargsyan was elected prime minister in 2018, protestors considered that he was attempting to cling on to power and he was ousted by the charismatic Nikol Pashinyan in the Velvet Revolution.

Azerbaijan continued since 2003 under the presidency of Ilham Aliyev, despite international concerns over rigged elections and an increasingly disaffected younger population. The country has experienced an economic surge, with Baku in particular seeing innovative modern architecture springing up. Internationally, Azerbaijan has hosted several high profile events, including the 2012 Eurovision contest. Even so, despite the wealth that the country has amassed from its energy industry, there's a good deal of inequality here. One taxi driver summed the situation up succinctly with the phrase, "Oil – yes; gas – yes; money – nyet!"

Pandemic and war

The outbreak of **Covid-19** in early 2020 forced all three Caucasian nations into lockdowns of varying severity, with Georgia reacting fastest to the emerging crisis and thus escaping the high death rate of the pandemic's first wave. Covid proved calamitous to the region's tourist industry, given the worldwide travel restrictions, and all three countries were keen to reopen to visitors as soon as possible. Georgia in particular slashed hotel prices in an effort to bring tourists back into the country. Vaccine uptake in all three nations was relatively slow, with scepticism particularly high in Armenia, resulting that many of the nation's vaccines were instead administered to Iranians who crossed the border seeking immunisation.

However, Covid-19 wasn't the only problem the region faced in 2020: in September, war broke out when Azerbaijan began an operation to retake Nagorno-Karabakh, which had been under Armenian control since the 1990s. Making effective use of drone technology, and aided by Turkey, Azerbaijan made significant inroads into Karabakh, including the recapture of Shusha. A Russian-brokered ceasefire took effect in late November, leaving Azerbaijan in control of much of the territory, though the self-proclaimed Republic of Artsakh retained Stepanakert and a portion of the region.

Armenia suffered a subsequent period of minor instability, with protests against Pashinyan labelling him a traitor for signing the ceasefire. A snap election held in 2021 returned Pashinyan to the post of prime minister, following which criticism of him

2020	**2022**
Covid-19 pandemic hits Georgia, Armenia and Azerbaijan; Second Karabakh War between Armenia and Azerbaijan results in significant Azerbaijani territorial gains.	In wake of the Russian invasion of Ukraine, Georgia submits application to join EU; Azerbaijan begins blockade of remaining Armenian-controlled Nagorno-Karabakh territory.

subsided somewhat. One positive side effect to the war is a relaxing in tensions between Armenia and Turkey: flights have resumed between Yerevan and Istanbul, and there is talk of reopening the closed border.

Despite the ceasefire, it was clear that neither side regarded the conflict as over. From December 2022, Azerbaijan blockaded access to Stepanakert, preventing supplies from reaching the remaining Armenian-held parts of Nagorno-Karabakh. The Russian peacekeeping force that had been installed in the region following the 2020 conflict did not intervene, and Azerbaijan ignored calls from international organisations including the European Court of Human Rights to lift the blockade.

In September 2023, Azerbaijan launched a new offensive against the remaining territory held by the Republic of Artsakh, and over the space of two days succeeded in capturing the entirety of **Nagorno-Karabakh**. Despite Aliyev's assurances that the rights of Armenians living in Karabakh would be protected, the vast majority of the population opted to depart, with more than 100,000 refugees crossing the border into Armenia amid fears of genocide.

Following the conflict, Armenia's government has acknowledged Azerbaijan's sovereignty over Nagorno-Karabakh and has not voiced any intent to attempt to recapture it, instead putting its efforts into normalising relations between the two countries. Since December 2023, delegations from the two countries have met several times but at time of writing are yet to come to any meaningful agreement.

Meanwhile, Georgia maintains cordial relations with both Armenia and Azerbaijan, though tensions have flared with the latter over a border dispute concerning the monastery of Davit Gareja and with the former in a slightly bizarre spat over who invented yoghurt first. Georgia's main preoccupation, however, remains the potential threat of Russia on its northern border: memories of the 2008 invasion remain keen, and the Russian invasion of Ukraine in February 2022 prompted Georgia to formally **apply for entry into the European Union**. In December 2023, it was granted candidate status, and its next steps towards full membership are reliant on progress made towards administrative and economic reform, as well as closer alignment with the EU on foreign policy issues. This process suffered a setback in spring 2024, when the Georgian Dream government attempted to pass a law requiring groups receiving more than 20 percent of their funding from abroad as 'foreign agents': immediately condemned as a step towards authoritarianism, the law resulted in mass protests which were violently suppressed by the police. Brussels issued strong criticism of the crackdown, and warned that it cast doubts on Georgia's suitability for EU membership. Georgia's path to the EU, therefore, remains rocky.

2023

Azerbaijani offensive captures Stepanakert and remainder of Nagorno-Karabakh; more than 100,000 ethnic Armenians flee the territory; Georgia is granted EU candidate status.

2024

Azerbaijan's presidential elections result in Ilham Aliyev winning his fifth term as president, with 92.12 percent of the vote.

Peoples

"The high peaks of the Caucasus cover such a large area that it would take two months or more to traverse their length or breadth. Only the Creator can number the peoples that live there."

Mas'udi, tenth-century Iraqi historian

It's common to hear places described as being home to a **melting pot** of people, but there are very few regions where this applies as much as the **Caucasus**. The diversity of an already wide range of indigenous peoples has been expanded by the arrival throughout history of a considerable number of conquerors, including Persians, Turks, Mongols and Russians. Sadly, the Caucasus has also regularly been the scene of considerable ethnic violence which, combined with mass deportations of various ethnicities during the Stalinist era, has led to some regions becoming more homogenous. Even so, an incredible array of peoples still exists in the Caucasus. Listing all the ethnicities found here would be next to impossible, but the following encompass some of the larger populations.

Georgians

The largest ethnic group in Georgia is the Georgians, also known as the **Kartvelians**. This group seem to have inhabited the region since the Neolithic era, formed of the proto-Georgian groups known as the Iberians and the Colchians. There have been a number of explanations presented for the origin of the word 'Georgian'. These include either from the root of the Persian 'gurg' meaning 'wolf', or the Greek 'georgos' meaning 'earth-worker'. The medieval claim that the name is due to a particular reverence for St George can most likely be rejected.

Georgians make up nearly 87 percent of the population of Georgia. The country has become considerably more homogenous since the fall of the Soviet Union, with the departure of high numbers of Russians, Armenians and Azerbaijanis – among other groups – since the declaration of independence. In the years since 1989 the percentage of the population belonging to an ethnic minority has decreased from 30 percent to 13 percent. Though Georgia is tolerant of its minorities and has launched programmes to minimise unemployment in minority communities, governmental representation remains heavily dominated by ethnic Georgians and civic participation by minorities is low.

The Georgian ethnic group can be broken down into further subgroups, including the Svans, Khevsurs and Tush of the mountainous northern regions, the Mingrelians, Meskhetians and Imereti of the west, and the Kakhetians of the east. Each of these subdivisions tends to have its own dialect of Georgian, and in some cases – the Mingrelians, for example – an entirely separate, if related, language.

THE 'CAUCASIAN RACE'

'**Caucasian**' is now frequently used as a catch-all term for racial origin, meaning 'white' and generally encompassing people of European origin. This originated in the 1780s in the theories of race scientists at the University of Göttingen, who claimed there were three 'types' of human – 'Caucasoid', 'Mongoloid' and 'Negroid' – the Caucasoids included West Asians and North Africans as well as white Europeans. This view – developed by the German polygenist Christoph Meiners, the proponent of a number of repugnant racial ideas – was the basis for a considerable degree of scientific racism throughout the nineteenth and twentieth centuries, over which time the term 'Caucasian' came to be used as a synonym for 'white'. Thus it remains: though at a very early stage of its use it was meant to refer to the peoples of the Caucasus, it now primarily means 'white' rather than Georgian, Armenian or Azerbaijani.

Abkhaz

As of the 2014 census, there are approximately 4500 **Abkhazians** reported as living in Georgia. This does not include the population count in the breakaway region of Abkhazia, which amounts to roughly 125,000. Known to the Ancient Greeks and Romans as a warlike people, the Abkhaz have been considered an ethnically distinct group for thousands of years. Their history includes a period as part of the Byzantine Empire, followed by a distinct Kingdom of Abkhazia which eventually became part of the unified Georgian kingdom. In the nineteenth century, Russia invaded and deported enormous numbers of Muslim Abkhaz to the Ottoman Empire and in the Soviet era Abkhazia became an autonomous republic within the Georgian SSR.

The break-up of the USSR saw the secession of Abkhazia from Georgia. It's now a self-declared independent republic, unrecognised by most nations other than Russia. During the 1992–3 Abkhazian War, up to 10,000 resident Georgians were killed and a further 250,000 expelled from their homes in a programme of ethnic cleansing. Dislike of ethnic Georgians remains high in Abkhazia, and Georgia considers Abkhazia as illegally occupied territory.

There's a wide mix of religions in Abkhazia. Orthodox Christianity and Sunni Islam are the most frequently practiced, but there's also a substantial number of adherents of Abkhaz neopaganism, an apparent revival of the pre-Christian and -Islam religious system of the region. Economically, the Abkhaz rely on tourism – mostly from Russia – though agriculture is also a notable source of income.

Ossetians

The **Ossetian** people are of **Iranian descent**, though interestingly their closest ethnic relations are to be found among the Jász people of Hungary. They inhabit areas of the Caucasus mountains that are now split between Georgia and Russia. The North Ossetian Republic is one of Russia's Caucasian provinces, while South Ossetia is a self-declared independent republic in Georgia's north and regarded by Tbilisi as an illegal occupation of Georgian territory.

Approximately 50,000 Ossetians live in South Ossetia, with a further 14,000 or so in Georgia proper. The most prevalent religious practice among the Ossetians is Russian Orthodox Christianity, but the pagan faith of Assianism is also widespread, particularly among the Russian Ossetians.

Georgia and South Ossetia have engaged in two wars since the fall of the USSR. Despite this, a report in 2009 by the European Centre for Minority Issues stated that Ossetians have been better integrated into Georgian society since the Soviet period than any other ethnic group. However, there has been a reported increase in Georgian hostility towards Ossetians, though there is no evidence of an organised governmental anti-Ossetian policy.

Caucasus Greeks

There were small communities of Greeks in the Caucasus along the Black Sea for centuries, but the most substantial Greek migrations to the region came in the Ottoman era, possibly seeking refuge from the risk of Turkish reprisal following the Russo-Turkish War of the late eighteenth century. Settling primarily in Georgia and Armenia, these Caucasian Greeks integrated into the local Russian-dominated culture. By 1989 there were approximately 100,000 **Caucasian Greeks** living in Georgia. However, in the post-Soviet period the vast majority chose to emigrate to Greece and there have been claims that the Georgian government has deliberately attempted to move the Greek communities on, in favour of ethnic Georgians. Today, no more than 6000 Greeks remain in Georgia.

Meskhetian Turks

The early history of the ethnic group known as the **Meskhetian Turks** is not entirely clear. Dependent on one's view – and, to some extent, what political point one is trying to make – the Meskhetian Turks are either Turkish settlers who arrived in

Georgia during the sixteenth century, or Georgians who converted to Islam during the Ottoman period. What is certain, however, is that in 1944 Josef Stalin, planning a potential offensive into Turkey, formed misgivings about where the loyalty of the Meskhetian Turks might lie in such an event. Consequently, he ordered their deportation. One hundred and fifteen thousand people were driven from their homes and shipped off to Central Asia, a horrific journey which resulted in the death of up to half the deportees. There are now very few Meskhetian Turks in their original homeland of Georgia, where they face a fair degree of discrimination. However, there's a sizeable population in Azerbaijan, which became home to about 70,000 refugees in 1989 after violence broke out in the Fergana Valley between the native Uzbeks and the Meskhetian Turks who had been living there since the 1940s.

Assyrians

An ethnically Semitic group originating in the Middle East, **Assyrian** migration to the Caucasus has a long history, but the largest numbers arrived fleeing genocide inflicted on them by the Ottoman Turks in World War I. There's a sizeable minority of Assyrians in Georgia today, as well as smaller numbers in Armenia and Azerbaijan.

Laz

The **Laz** people, historically found along the Black Sea coast of Georgia and northeast Turkey, now form a very small minority of the population of Georgia, numbering perhaps 2000 and largely considering themselves Georgian rather than Laz. There is, however, an annual festival of Laz customs called Kolkhoba held in Sarpi village. In Turkey, the national identity is more comprehensively maintained, with Laz people identifying as Laz before – and often instead of – Turkish.

Armenians

The origin of the **Armenian people** has been the subject of considerable debate. It has been suggested that they are the descendants of a proto-Greek community that migrated south from the North Caucasus, some of whom continued on to Greece and became today's Greek people, while others remained in Eastern Anatolia and became the Armenians. An alternative theory has the Armenians being of Western Anatolian origin and migrating eastward. However, genetic studies – combined with the Armenians' own origin myths – suggest that the people originated in the region around Mount Ararat.

As of the 2011 census, Armenia's population is made up of 98 percent Armenians. The proportion of Armenians in the country has always been high – it was 93 percent in 1989 – but since the collapse of the Soviet Union, many Russian, Georgian and Azerbaijani minorities have departed, leaving only very small non-Armenian populations. It's therefore not enormously surprising that Armenians dominate in all areas of civic life.

In large part due to the Armenian Genocide in the early twentieth century, Armenia has a widespread diaspora. While there are three million Armenians in Armenia, there are a further eight million living in other countries around the world. Russia, the United States and France have the largest Armenian communities outside Armenia, with a sizeable population also living in Georgia and Ukraine. Notable members of the Armenian Diaspora include the Kardashian family, the singer Cher, the actor Andy Serkis, and the presenter of the BBC show Bargain Hunt, David Dickinson.

Kurds

Originating in Iraq and Eastern Turkey, the **Kurds** have a long and complex history with the Armenians. The two groups appear to have had good relations, especially when both were minorities in the Ottoman Empire, though tensions rose in the late nineteenth century. Kurds were also targeted by the Turks during the Armenian Genocide and subsequently a sizeable minority population of Kurds were to be found in the Armenian,

Georgian and Azerbaijani SSRs, including in an area of Nagorno-Karabakh that was for a time known as 'Red Kurdistan'. However, persecution under Stalin led to the deportation of many Kurds from the Caucasus, but after Stalin's era, Armenia became the Soviet Union's centre of Kurdish culture. Today, there remains a population of approximately 40,000 Kurds in Armenia, 15,000 in Georgia and roughly 6,000 in Azerbaijan.

Often included under the banner of Armenia's Kurds are the Yazidis, a distinct ethnic group with their own religion who have faced persecution across the Middle East, most recently at the hands of the Isis terrorist organisation. In Armenia, the Yazidis have freedom to practice their religion – and the world's largest Yazidi temple can be found here – but there have been some reports of discriminatory practices against them.

Azerbaijanis

Considered a Turkic people, **Azerbaijanis** have a complex ethnic makeup that can be traced back to the Oghuz Turks, as well as Persians and the Caucasian Albanians, an ethnically Iranian people that lived in what is now northwest Azerbaijan. It is thought that the Turkic invasions from the eleventh century onwards resulted in substantial 'Turkification' of the already existing populations. Certainly, Azerbaijanis themselves now tend to regard themselves as Turkic.

Azerbaijan's population, which is composed of roughly 92 percent ethnic Azerbaijanis, officially hit 10 million in April 2019. The growing population is a matter of pride to the country, but it's far from clear whether the figure is in fact accurate – though that didn't stop cities and towns holding official celebrations of the birth of the 10 millionth citizen.

The borders drawn in the aftermath of the Russian-Persian wars of the nineteenth century resulted in the world's Azerbaijanis being split in two: there's a population in northwest Iran of approximately 15 million Azerbaijanis, more than in the Republic of Azerbaijan itself. The borders between Azerbaijan and Iran are well-travelled, with the majority of tourists in the enclave of Nakhchivan being Iranian.

The Azerbaijani people can be subdivided into smaller ethnic groups, including the Ayrums, who live primarily in the northwest of Azerbaijan, the Terekeme of Azerbaijan's southern regions, and the Padars, who are thought to be more of Mongol origin than Turkic.

Lezgins

Azerbaijan's largest ethnic minority, the **Lezgin** people straddle the northern border and are also a minority in Russia's Dagestan region. They are thought to descend from Bronze-Age peoples who inhabited the area prior to the arrival of Persian invaders in the sixth century BC. They converted to Sunni Islam as late as the fifteenth century and have remained an integral part of Azerbaijan and Russia since the nineteenth century, aside from a brief attempt to set up an autonomous independent Lezgin Republic in 1991.

Though officially there are approximately 180,000 Lezgins in Azerbaijan, making up about two percent of the population, it is generally considered that the true figure is much higher – possibly up to 700,000. Lezgins frequently identify as Azerbaijani in order to circumvent potential discrimination in the jobs market, as well as avoiding potential persecution based on the government's mid-2000s assertion that Islamic fundamentalism was particularly prevalent among the Lezgins. In addition, Lezgins are underrepresented in the Azerbaijani government and many Lezgins think they are being pressured to assimilate into Azerbaijani culture.

Related to the Lezgins, both closely and more distantly, are a number of peoples considered indigenous to the Caucasus, including the Shahdags, the Kryts and the Budukhs, all of whom live mainly in the mountains in north of Azerbaijan.

Talysh

Occupying a territory in the southeast of Azerbaijan, in the vicinity of the mountains of the same name, the **Talysh** people are an ethnically distinct group practicing Shia Islam and claiming descent from the ancient Cadusian people. Thought to consist of up to 300,000 people, the Talysh were encouraged during the Soviet era to re-identify as Azerbaijani rather than Talysh and post-independence this appears to have remained the policy of the Azerbaijani government. In the early 1990s a separatist Talysh Autonomous Republic was established, but when Heydar Aliyev came to power, the republic was reintegrated into Azerbaijan and its leaders imprisoned. In the years since, Talysh leaders have accused Azerbaijan's government of attempting to create a single Azerbaijani culture and, in doing so, suppressing the Talysh people.

Tats

The **Tats**, a people of Persian origin who once made up a sizeable proportion of the inhabitants of eastern Azerbaijan, now number about 25,000 across the country, making up less than 0.3 percent of the population. This decline appears to have originated in the Soviet era, when Tats began to identify as Azerbaijani rather than Tat. They shared a similar language with the Mountain Jews of the same region, but there appears to be no ethnic link between the two peoples.

Mountain Jews

Jews had been present in Persia from at least the eighth century BC onwards and it's thought they travelled from Persia to settle in the Caucasus in about the fifth century AD. Becoming known as **Mountain Jews** – owing to their homes being in the Caucasus mountains – they lived primarily in Dagestan and Chechnya but after persecution in these territories in the eighteenth century, large numbers fled and established a substantial settlement in Quba. They lived here under the tolerant regime of Fatali Khan. During the Soviet years, the population was about 18,000, but this has diminished since independence, with emigration increasing to Israel and the United States. The Jewish population of Azerbaijan was approximately 9,000 as of the 2009 census.

There was once also a distinct and substantial population of Jews in Georgia who enjoyed a history of considerable toleration for nearly 2,600 years. The Soviet years, however, were not kind to this community and, from independence onward, Georgia's Jews have largely emigrated to Israel.

Udi

Considered the descendants of the Caucasian Albanians, the **Udi** are Azerbaijan's principal Christian minority. They primarily live in the village of Nij, in the northwest of the country. Before 1991, there were more settlements but many were expelled during the Nagorno-Karabakh War due to their adherence to the Armenian Apostolic Church. More recently, however, Azerbaijan has taken pride in the Udi heritage as being derived from Caucasian Albania. As a result, the Udi maintain their traditions with the support of the Azerbaijani government.

Russians

Georgia, Armenia and Azerbaijan all maintain a substantial Russian minority, though in all three republics the number of Russian inhabitants has shrunk since the fall of the Soviet Union. Populations have particularly fallen in Azerbaijan and Georgia, both partly due to strained relations with Russia leading to a degree of ethnic tension. In Azerbaijan, this is as a result of the violence of Black January in 1990, when Soviet troops violently put down civil unrest in Baku, while in Georgia it was caused largely by the Six Day War in 2008. Despite these tensions, the **Russian population** in the Caucasus has risen in the 2020s, with Russians who object to the war in Ukraine choosing to resettle here. They haven't always been welcomed: especially in Tbilisi, you'll see graffiti across the city denouncing Russia as a terrorist state, and Georgians often consider that if Russians are unhappy with their country's leadership, they should return home and try to do something about it.

Wildlife

Thanks to its geographical position and variety of landscapes, which range from harsh mountains to verdant forest via semi-desert, the Caucasus is home to many species of both flora and fauna. They're not always easy to spot, but with luck, you may catch a glimpse of some of the region's elusive inhabitants.

Fauna

While you probably wouldn't travel to the Caucasus specifically on a wildlife-watching expedition, there's certainly a wide range of species here. Tbilisi's National Museum is a good place to get an introduction to the animal life of the Caucasus – there's an exhibition of taxidermy on the ground floor including most varieties of fauna found in this region. You'd probably prefer to see the animals alive and in their natural habitats, which is possible if you go off the beaten track.

Starting with the larger and rarer animals, the Caucasus is home to populations of the **brown bear** and the smaller subspecies, the **Caucasian bear**, both of which live in forested or mountainous regions and try to avoid humans. Similarly evasive is the Caucasian **leopard**, which is thought to have a range stretching from Turkey through Georgia, Armenia and Azerbaijan to Iran. You'd have to be supernaturally lucky to catch sight of one of these magnificent animals, who are thought to number no more than twenty-five in the entire region, and keep themselves very much to themselves.

In forested areas the **grey wolf** still has a decent range, as does the **Eurasian lynx**, **golden jackal** and the **red fox**. In eastern areas, there's even a small population of striped **hyena**. A couple of species of the goat-like **tur** are exclusively found in the Caucasus: the Western Caucasian tur lives at, yes, the western end of the mountain range, while the Eastern Caucasian tur is native to Dagestan and North Azerbaijan.

If you're lucky, you might spot the **Armenian mouflon**, the goitered **gazelle** or the critically endangered **saiga antelope** with its unique, refined nose. Smaller mammals endemic to the region include the European **badger**, the **jungle cat**, the **pine marten**, and – in Azerbaijan's Talysh mountains – Indian crested **porcupine**. In the extreme south, on the border with Iran, there have been reports of sightings of manuls, which in December 2020 were also spotted for the first time in over a century in Armenia.

The Caucasus has also long been known for its magnificent horses, particularly the **Karabakh horse** which is known for its beauty – in the novel *Ali & Nino*, they are described as the most beautiful thing in the country of Karabakh. These horses are also reputed to have good temperament and remarkable speed – in 2004, one such horse covered a kilometre in a little over a minute. They are now endangered, with only about 1,000 thought to still exist.

Of course, the one animal encounter you don't want is sadly one of the most likely – the shepherd's dog. Caucasian **sheepdogs** are big and aggressive for a reason, and you should avoid giving them any reason to suspect you're a sheep rustler. If you meet a sheepdog while out hiking, retreat from the sheep and look around for the shepherd.

Some animals that once roamed here can no longer be found. A few, like cheetahs and Asiatic lions, can still be seen elsewhere in the world, but others, including the Caucasian moose, the Caucasian wisent and the Caspian tiger are sadly extinct due to overhunting and poaching. The last Caspian tiger in Georgia was shot in 1922, with no confirmed sightings of the species anywhere since the 1970s. It was declared extinct in 2003.

The Caucasus is a good destination for **birdwatchers**. Endemic species include the Caucasian grouse and the Caucasian snowcock. It's also possible to see birds of prey such as the Eurasian imperial eagle and the steppe eagle. The Debed Canyon in

Armenia is a good place to see eagles, as are the Caucasus mountains – for example around Stepantsminda. Migratory species that pass through include lammergeyers, Egyptian vultures and pelicans. There are a number of companies offering dedicated birdwatching tours in the Caucasus; try Birdfinders (wbirdfinders.co.uk) or Nature Trek (wnaturetrek.co.uk).

With its position between the Black Sea and the Caspian Sea, and being home to the large freshwater Lake Sevan, it's hardly surprising that there's a fair range of **aquatic life** that calls the Caucasus home. The Sevan trout – sadly favoured at barbecue restaurants – is endangered, as are many of the various endemic sturgeon. The Caspian (beluga) sturgeon – which is considered the largest freshwater fish – is in a critical position as it's long been favoured for the production of caviar. Needless to say, you should avoid purchasing any beluga product.

It's likely that you'll see some **reptile** life during your trip to the Caucasus. One of the most attractive is the small Caucasus Emerald Lizard, which, as the name suggests, is bright green. Other examples include the Caucasian lizard, the Armenian rock lizard and the Dagestan lizard. There are also a fair number of snakes that call this region home. Some are venomous, including the Caucasian viper, Dinnik's viper and the spotted whip snake, but most snakes are not aggressive and will not attack if you do not threaten them.

On the **insect** level, the region is home to a variety of creepy-crawlies. You'll probably enjoy seeing the wide range of butterflies, which include beautiful species such as the Glanville Fritillary and the Damon blue, while you may be less enthusiastic about venomous individuals such as the steppe spider and the yellow deathstalker scorpion. Luckily, these wee beasties are rarely seen, and you'd have to be very unlucky to fall foul of them. Mosquitoes are a more likely pest. Consider insect repellent if you're near water in summer, especially in the evening.

Flora

There are a considerable number of different topographical landscapes in the Caucasus, ranging from desert to wetlands, via steppe and subalpine meadowland, and more besides. With many different zones comes a wealth of **diversity in plant life** throughout the region.

In the years following independence from the USSR, all three countries have suffered a degree of deforestation and overexploitation of their resources. Efforts are now underway to bring this under control, with a considerable number of protected areas. Trees endemic to the region include the Caucasian and Georgian oaks, the Oriental beech and the Caucasian fir. National parks, such as Borjomi and Dilijan, are heavily forested and make ideal hiking territory.

Spring flowers are hugely abundant in the region and can enhance the already beautiful sights. Amberd Fortress in Armenia, for example, is utterly magnificent when surrounded by the colourful wildflowers scattered across the site. Some such flowers that you're likely to see include the gladiolus atroviolaceus and the helichrysum rubicundum.

Language

With so many different ethnic groups, it's no surprise to find that the Caucasus region is also home to an astonishing **variety of languages**: one estimate counts almost fifty tongues in use here. That being said, each of the three nations has its own official language, which is spoken by the vast majority of the population. Despite their geographical proximity, the **Georgian, Armenian and Azeri** languages are not related to one another – and, in the case of Georgian and Armenian, are distinct from all other world languages too – so learning one of them will avail you little in the neighbouring countries. In particular, trying to speak Azeri in Armenia, or vice versa, will not be appreciated. Among young people, particularly in Georgia and in the larger cities, **English** is commonly spoken, and **Russian** is also a lingua franca across the region, though depending on the political situation, it's not always a popular default. It's certainly worth attempting a few words in the local language: your efforts are usually appreciated, and a badly-pronounced "shnorhakalut'yun" or "madlobt" is an almost guaranteed way to bring a smile to the face of whoever you're talking to.

Georgian

Georgian, the first language of approximately 90 percent of the Georgian population, is the most commonly spoken member of the **Kartvelian language** family. Kartvelian languages originated in the southern Caucasus and have no apparent links to other world languages. Boasting its own distinct alphabet, the Georgian language's early history is obscure, with the first known reference to it being a mention by a Roman author in the second century AD. It is first known as a written language two centuries later, with the earliest surviving piece of Georgian literature being *The Martyrdom of Queen Shushanik*, written in the fifth century.

Although the individual **alphabet** isn't the easiest to follow for those familiar with Latin scripts, once Georgian is transliterated into the English alphabet, pronunciation presents few problems. For those wishing a deeper dive, there are a couple of dictionaries and phrasebooks available: the Hippocrene *Georgian-English/English-Georgian Dictionary and Phrasebook* by Nicholas Awde and Thea Khitarishvili is perhaps the most accessible.

Georgian words and phrases

English Transliterated Georgian

Hello Gamarjoba გამარჯობა

Goodbye Nakhvamdis ნახვამდის

Please Gtkhovt გთხოვთ

Thank you Madlobt გმადლობთ

You're welcome Arapris არაფრის

Okay K'argi კარგი

I don't understand Ar mesmis არ მესმის

Sorry Bodishi ბოდიში

Do you speak English? Inglisurad lap'arak'ob? ინგლისურად ლაპარაკობ?

Yes Diakh დიახ

No Ara არა

How much is it? Ramdeni? რამდენი?

Menu Meniu მენიუ

Bill Angarishi ანგარიში

Today Dghes დღეს

Tomorrow Khval ხვალ

Where is the… Sad aris… სად არის…

Bus station Avt'obusis gachereba ავტობუსის გაჩერება

Train station Mat'areblis sadguri მატარებლის სადგური

Airport Aeroporti აეროპორტი

Museum Muzeumi მუზეუმი

Toilet Tualeti ტუალეტი

Hospital Saavadmq'opo საავადმყოფო

Please call a… Gtkhovt darek'ot a… გთხოვთ დარეკოთ ა…

Doctor Ekimi ექიმი

Police Politsia პოლიცია

Taxi Taksi ტაქსი

One Erti ერთი

Two Ori ორი

Three Sami სამი

Four Otkhi ოთხი

Five Khuti ხუთი

Six Ekvsi ექვსი

Seven Shvidi შვიდი

Eight Rva რვა

Nine Tskhra ცხრა

Ten Ati ათი

Twenty Otsi ოცი

Thirty Otsdaati ოცდაათი

Forty Ormotsi ორმოცი

Fifty Ormotsdaati ორმოცდაათი

One hundred Asi ასი

Monday Orshabati ორშაბათი

Tuesday Samshabati სამშაბათი

Wednesday Otkhshabati ოთხშაბათი

Thursday Khutshabati ხუთშაბათი

Friday Paraskevi პარასკევი

Saturday Shabati შაბათი

Sunday Kvira კვირა

Common menu items

Georgian cuisine is extremely wide-ranging, but some of the most items most often seen on menus are listed below.

English Transliterated Georgian

Tomato and aubergine stew Ajapsandal აჯაფსანდალი

Meat and plum stew Chakapuli ჩაქაფული

Tomato and chicken stew Chakokhbili ჩახოხბილი

Cheese bread Khachapuri ხაჭაპური

Beef, tomato and walnut soup Kharcho ხარჩო

Dumplings containing meat, cheese or potatoes Khinkali ხინკალი

Spicy bean stew Lobio ლობიო

Barbecued meat, usually pork Mtsvadi მწვადი

Vine leaves stuffed with rice or meat Tolma ტოლმა

Wine Vvino ღვინო

Armenian

Spoken by the vast majority of the population of Armenia, the **Armenian** language occupies a distinct branch of the Indo-European language family. It is almost entirely unique, though it potentially had early links with Greek, Albanian and the Indo-Iranian language group. Its distinct alphabet was developed by the monk Mesrop Mashtots in the fifth century AD, and written texts in Armenian have survived from that time. From the nineteenth century onward, with the traditional Armenian homelands split between the Russian and Ottoman Empires, the language split into two distinct forms: Eastern and Western Armenian. Eastern Armenian is the language now spoken in Armenia itself, while much of the diaspora uses the Western Armenian form. There are enough similarities between the two to be largely mutually understood.

If you're used to Latin alphabets, the Armenian alphabet can look intimidating, but once the language is presented in Latin script, it presents few pronunciation issues, although the length of some common words can lead to you tripping over your tongue. Dictionaries and phrasebooks are few and far between: try *Eastern Armenian: Dictionary and Phrasebook* by Nicholas Awde and Peter Maghdashyan if you want to get a handle on the language.

Armenian words and phrases

English Transliterated Armenian

Hello Barev Բարեւ

Goodbye Ts'tesut'yun Ցտեսություն

Please Khndrum yem խնդրում եմ

Thank you Shnorhakalut'yun Շնորհակալություն

You're welcome Khndrum Խնդրեմ

Okay Lav Լավ

I don't understand Yes ch'em haskanum Ես չեմ հասկանում

Sorry Neroghut'yun Ներողություն

Do you speak English? Du khosum yes angleren? Դու խոսում ես անգլերեն?

Yes Ayo Այո

No Voch Ոչ

How much is it? Inch' arzhe ayn? Ինչ արժե այս?

Menu Menyu Մենյու

Bill Hashive Հաշիվ՛ը

Today Aysor Այսոր

Tomorrow Vaghy Վաղը

Where is the… Vortegh e… Որտեղ է…

Bus station Avtobusi kangarr Ավտոբուսի կանգառ

Train station Yerkat'gtsi kayaran Երկաթգծի կայարան

Airport Odanavakayan Օդանավակայան

Museum T'angaran թանգարան

Toilet Zugaran զուգարան

Hospital Hivandanots հիվանդանոց

Please call a… Khndrum yem zangaharel… Խնդրում եմ զանգահարել…

Doctor Bzhishk Բժիշկ

Police Vostikanut'yun Ոստիկանութjուն

Taxi Taksi տաքսի

One Mek մեկ

Two Yerku երկու

Three Yerek երեք

Four Ch'vors Չորս

Five Hing Հինգ

Six Vets Վեց

Seven Yot Յոթ

Eight Ut Ութ

Nine Iny Ինը

Ten Tasy Տասը

Twenty K'san Քսան

Thirty Yeresun Երեսուն

Forty Karrasun Քառասուն

Fifty Hisun Հիսուն

One hundred Haryur Հարjուր

Monday Yerkushabti երկուշաբթի

Tuesday Yerekshabti երեքշաբթի

Wednesday Ch'vorek'shabti Չորեքշաբթի

Thursday Hingshabti Հինգշաբթի

Friday Urbat Ուրբաթ

Saturday Shabti ory շաբաթ օրը

Sunday Kiraki Կիրակի

Common menu items

The list below covers several of the most frequently available dishes on Armenian menus.

English Transliterated Armenian

Vine leaves stuffed with rice or meat Dolma Տոլմա

Pastry, stuffed with sweet or savoury fillings Gata գաթա

Wine Gini գինի

Soup made from various parts of a cow, including the head, feet and stomach Khash խաշ

Lamb and vegetable stew Khashlama Խաշլամա

Barbecued meat, usually pork Khorovats Խորոված

Brandy Konyak կոնjակ

Flatbread Lavash լավաշ

Whitefish from Lake Sevan Sig սիգ

Flatbread stuffed with herbs and greens Zhingyalov hats Ժինգjալով հաց

Azeri

Azeri, or **Azerbaijani**, is the official language of Azerbaijan. It is a Turkic language which reached the region during the medieval Turkic migrations, and it can for the most part be understood by speakers of modern Turkish. Owing to the division of Azerbaijan between the Russian and Persian Empires in the nineteenth century, there are now two varieties of the language: North Azerbaijani is spoken in Azerbaijan, as well as in the Dagestan region of Russia, while South Azerbaijani is spoken in northern Iran.

With a few minor changes, Azeri uses the Turkish Latin alphabet, which is largely the same as the Roman alphabet, although there are a couple of variations: primary among these is the existence of the ə character, which for the most part is pronounced similarly to the English 'e' sound. Note that the presence of a cedilla (written as a comma) beneath a letter creates an 'h' sound – for example, 'Şark' would be pronounced 'Shark'. For a reasonably extensive dictionary and phrasebook, try Hippocrene's *Azerbaijani-English/English-Azerbaijani Dictionary & Phrasebook* by Nicholas Awde and Famil Ismailov.

Azeri words and phrases

English Azeri

Hello Salam

Goodbye Sağol

Please Lutfen

Thank you Teşekkür ederim

You're welcome Buyurun

Okay Tamam

I don't understand Men anlamıram

Sorry Bağışlayın

Do you speak English? İngilis dilinda danışırsınız?

Yes Bali

No Yox

How much is it? Na qadar?

Menu Menyu

Bill Hesabı alabilir miyim?

Today Bu gün

Tomorrow Sabah

Where is the… Haradadır…

Bus station Avtobus dayanacağı
Train station Damir yolu stansiyası
Airport Hava limanı
Museum Muzey
Toilet Tualet
Hospital Xastaxana
Please call a… Zang edin
Doctor Doktor
Police Polis
Taxi Taksi
One Bir
Two Iki
Three Üç
Four Dörd
Five Beş
Six Altı
Seven Yeddi
Eight Sakkiz
Nine Doqquz
Ten On
Twenty Iyirmi
Thirty Otuz
Forty Qırx
Fifty Elli
One hundred Yüz
Monday Bazar ertasi
Tuesday Çarşanba axşamı
Wednesday Çarşanba
Thursday Çuma axşamı
Friday Çuma
Saturday Şanba
Sunday Bazar

Common menu items

Frequently seen items on Azerbaijan's menus include those on the list below.

Azeri English
Bakhlava Sweet dessert made from hazelnuts and cardamom
Balıq Grilled fish
Dolma Vine leaves stuffed with rice or meat
Lavangi Chicken stuffed with herbs, spices and walnuts
Piti Mutton soup, served with bread, onions, sumac, and a lump of lamb fat
Plov Rice with meat and vegetables
Shashlik Barbecued meat, usually chicken or mutton

Books

There are a growing number of books concerning the Caucasus. Travel accounts and histories are particularly well represented, and fiction writers – both local and Western – have long known of the region's potential for great stories. There are a number of titles on other subjects such as cookery and architecture, but sadly coverage of the region's rich environment and natural history is sparse.

TRAVEL AND GENERAL INTEREST

Tony Anderson *Bread and Ashes: A Walk Through the Mountains of Georgia*. In 1998, Anderson set himself the task of walking through the Caucasus on Georgia's northern border, visiting the peoples of this region. His account of the journey is full of fantastic bits of historical and geographical detail, as well as providing great cultural insight.

Alexandre Dumas *Adventures in the Caucasus*. The French author of *The Three Musketeers* undertook a journey to the Caucasus in the 1850s, but his account of his journey – which took him through Azerbaijan and Georgia – is only available in English in a truncated form. If you're a French reader, you can enjoy the full account.

Douglas Freshfield *The Exploration of the Caucasus*. Published in the late nineteenth century and now difficult to locate in hard copy, this description by the President of the British Geographical Association of the peaks, culture and history of the Georgian Caucasus, is available to read online for free at ⓦ archive.org/details/explorationofcau01fres.

Philip Marsden *The Crossing Place*. An account of the author's travels across the countries of the Armenian Diaspora, and eventually Armenia itself, this book gets under the skin of Armenian national identity.

Stephen Powell *The First Toast is to Peace*. The Welsh journalist Stephen Powell travelled across all the countries of the South Caucasus to write this book, which covers his journey as well as an analysis of the history, culture and landscapes of Georgia, Armenia and Azerbaijan.

Colin Thubron *Among the Russians*. In 1983, Colin Thubron travelled alone by car through the USSR from St Petersburg to Georgia and Armenia – alone, of course, except for the KGB tailing him all the way. This account of his journey offers some great insight into the culture of Georgia and Armenia in the Brezhnev era.

HISTORY AND POLITICS

Lasha Bugadze *Georgia v Joseph Stalin*. A bestseller in Georgia, this book examines the worrying trend towards lionising Stalin in his home country in the years since his death, and attempts to dispel myths and correct the historical record. At time of writing, it was not available in English, but a translation is due in late 2024.

Tanar Akçam *A Shameful Act*. The first Turkish scholar to refer to the 1915 Armenian massacres as genocide, Akçam's 2007 work draws on extensive use of the Turkish state's archives to examine the Ottoman Empire's motives in this dark period of history.

John Antal *Seven Seconds to Die: A Military Analysis of the Second Nagorno-Karabakh War and the Future of Warfighting*. One of the only accounts of the 2020 Karabakh War written to date, this tome focuses on the Azerbaijani use of drone warfare.

Lesley Blanch *The Sabres of Paradise*. A biography of Imam Shamil, the Dagestani warlord who resisted Russian advances into the Northern Caucasus in the mid-nineteenth century. Among the incidents recounted is Shamil's kidnap of a pair of Georgian princesses.

Suha Bolukbasi *Azerbaijan: A Political History*. Not a particularly easy read, this history text focuses heavily on the last few years of the Soviet era and the Nagorno-Karabakh conflict.

Eric Lee *The Experiment*. A clearly written and sympathetic account of Georgia's post-World War I republic and its efforts to build a genuinely democratic socialist state. It's an overlooked period in Georgia's history, and this is an excellent way to rediscover it.

Markar Melkonian *My Brother's Road*. An account of the life of Monte Melkonian, a complicated figure considered a terrorist by the West but a hero of the First Nagorno-Karabakh War by Armenians.

Simon Sebag Montifiore *Young Stalin*. There are plenty of biographies of Georgia's most (in)famous son to choose from, but this one specifically concentrates on his early life and experiences. As such, it's a great resource for those interested not only in Stalin, but also in the world of small-town Georgia under Tsarist Russia.

Donald Rayfield *Edge of Empires: A History of Georgia*. A fantastic, succinct and readable one-volume history of Georgia from its earliest beginnings right through to the Saakashvili era. Definitely a great place to start for those wishing to understand how Georgia's past affects its present.

Geoffrey Robertson *An Inconvenient Genocide: Who Now Remembers the Armenians?* Published in 2015, shortly before the centenaryof the Armenian Genocide, this volume by the QC Geoffrey Robertson is a thorough analysis of the events of 1915 making a compelling case for the massacres to be considered a genocide.

Joseph Roth *'Saint Petroleum',* in *The Hotel Years.* The German Joseph Roth travelled extensively in Europe in the 1920s and 30s, and his 1926 account of Baku's oilfields and the surrounding town is an evocative portrait of the industrial life of early USSR.

Ronald Grigor Suny *"They Can Live in the Desert but Nowhere Else: A History of the Armenian Genocide".* Perhaps the definitive historical account of the Armenian Genocide, Suny's well-researched book is an essential work for anyone hoping to understand the massacres. It's wordy so be prepared.

Ronald Grigor Suny *The Making of the Georgian Nation.* Written in 1994, this study of the Georgian people is now a little dated but still a good resource for anyone hoping to learn more about the country's national consciousness throughout its history.

Thomas de Waal *The Caucasus: An Introduction.* An essential first stop for anyone hoping to understand the tangled politics of the modern Caucasus, de Waal's volume is lucidly written and approaches challenging topics without prejudice.

Thomas de Waal *Black Garden: Armenia and Azerbaijan Through Peace and War.* De Waal's in-depth account of the First Nagorno-Karabakh War, including its origins and subsequent attempts to resolve it, is probably the most lucid and comprehensive work on the subject.

CULTURE AND SOCIETY

Banine *Days in the Caucasus.* Banine – or Ummulbanu Asadullayeva – was born in 1905 into a Baku family who had grown tremendously wealthy on oil money. Following the Soviet takeover, she fled Azerbaijan for Paris, where this volume of her memoirs was published in 1945. It's a fabulous and evocative portrait of a now-vanished world.

Maia Barkaia *Gender in Georgia: Feminist Perspectives on Culture, Nation and History in the South Caucasus.* Essays by a number of Georgian and international researchers focusing on gender dynamics in Georgia from the nineteenth century to the present day.

Vasily Grossman *An Armenian Sketchbook.* Vasily Grossman, the author of the classic Russian novel *Life and Fate,* travelled to Armenia in the 1960s. This fantastic book details his experiences there, which are quirky, funny and moving.

Mehran Kamrava *The Great Game in Western Asia.* A series of essays exploring the influence of Iran and Turkey on the countries of the Caucasus. The opening essay is an excellent summary of the political state of play across the region.

Peter Nasmyth *Georgia: In the Mountains of Poetry.* An in-depth and beautifully written look at Georgia since the end of the Soviet era, Peter Nasmyth's lovely book is essential for understanding the country's current situation.

Wendell Steavenson *Stories I Stole from Georgia.* Wendell Steavenson lived in Georgia in the late 1990s and early 2000s and this book is a fantastic account of her experiences there during this difficult period in the country's recent past.

FOOD AND COOKERY

Carla Capalbo *Tasting Georgia: A Food and Wine Journey in the Caucasus.* Easy to follow and excellent recipes, as well as gorgeous photography and cultural information on Georgia.

Olia Hercules *Kaukasis the Cookbook: The Culinary Journey through Georgia, Azerbaijan and Beyond.* A splendid cookbook full of delightful recipes from the region, punctuated by beautiful photography and reminiscences from the author. It even tells you how to make *tklapi* – the flat dried fruits that you'll see for sale by every roadside along your trip.

Kate Leahy *Lavash: The Bread That Launched 1000 Meals.* Focusing on Armenian cooking, particularly on lavash bread, this lovely recipe book is also part travelogue.

Tiko Tuskadze *Supra: A Feast of Georgian Cooking.* Dedicated to the excellent culinary traditions of Georgia, this recipe book, by the owner of London's *Little Georgia* restaurant, includes all the favourites such as *khinkali* and *khachapuri,* as well as more unusual dishes.

NATURAL HISTORY AND THE ENVIRONMENT

Eberhard Fischer, Andreas Gröger and Wolfram Lobin *Illustrated Field Guide to the Flora of Georgia (South Caucasus).* This does exactly what it says on the tin and is an excellent resource for botanists travelling in Georgia. At 830 pages though it's unwieldy if you're intending to use it as a field guide.

ART AND ARCHITECTURE

Eve Blau *Baku: Oil and Urbanism.* An exploration of the connection between the oil industry and the architecture and town planning of Baku, this probably isn't for casual readers, but anyone with an interest in the topic will find it fascinating.

Chorgolashvili, Ana *Tbilisi Architecture Map.* A fold-out map of Tbilisi that focuses on its most innovative architecture, including introductory text for fifty of the city's buildings.

Antony Eastmond *Royal Imagery in Medieval Georgia.* It's very scholarly and hardly an easy read, but if you want information on how medieval Georgia's kings represented themselves in architecture, this is probably the best source.

Helen Evans *Armenia: Art, Religion and Trade in the Middle Ages.* A beautiful coffee table book on Armenia's medieval art and architecture, this weighty tome is readable, extremely informative and stacked with fantastic photos.

Owen Hatherley *The Adventures of Owen Hatherley in the Post-Soviet Space.* A quirky and brilliant exploration of Soviet and post-Soviet architecture covering much of the former USSR, this accessible volume includes fantastic chapters on Tbilisi, Kutaisi, Yerevan and Sevan.

Christopher Herwig *Soviet Bus Stops.* A coffee table book of photography, featuring examples of innovative bus stop architecture from across the former USSR. Of the Caucasian republics, Armenia and Abkhazia are the best represented. The examples from Abkhazia are particularly remarkable.

Adriano Alpago Novello *Art and Architecture in Medieval Georgia.* Long out of print and now hard to find, this 1980s text offers a decent introduction to medieval Georgia's rich cultural heritage.

FICTION

Viken Berberian *The Structure is Rotten, Comrade!* This quirky graphic novel about a young man intent on becoming a legendary architect and transforming Yerevan's cityscape is an intelligent and angry political satire.

Michael Berman *Georgia Through Earth, Air, Fire and Water.* A collection of Georgian folk tales, some of which are translated here into English for the first time. The book also contains some scholarly discussion concerning the meaning of the stories.

Nicola Davies *The Leopard's Tail.* This children's book is set in Armenia and revolves around the adventures of a boy called Malik as he attempts to prevent poachers from killing a leopard. It's a great little story with an important conservation message.

Nino Haratischvili *The Eighth Life* Translated into English in 2019 and billed as the Georgian 'War and Peace', this hefty and critically acclaimed novel tells the story of one Georgian family from 1917 through the turbulent years of the twentieth century until the present day.

Eve Makis *The Spice Box Letters.* A young lady named Katerina on holiday in Cyprus meets an Armenian named Ara and begins to unearth a tragic family history that leads her to confront the horrific events of the Armenian Genocide.

Andy McNab *Aggressor.* This instalment of the Nick Stone series is set in Georgia, but largely features scenes of people beating up/being beaten up by Georgian gangsters, and as such is unlikely to give you much of an idea about Georgian culture.

Aka Morchiladze *Journey to Karabakh.* The first book by one of Georgia's most popular and prolific post-Soviet novelists, this tells the story of two young Georgians who accidentally get caught up in the First Nagorno-Karabakh War when a drugs deal goes awry.

Aline Orhanesian *Orhan's Inheritance.* When a Turkish rug-maker dies and leaves his family estate to an Armenian woman now living in California, his family investigate and uncover uncomfortable truths about their history. This debut novel by Aline Orhanesian is an excellent work of historical fiction set against the backdrop of the Armenian Genocide.

Alexander Pushkin *The Prisoner in the Caucasus.* Written by Pushkin during his exile in the Caucasus, this poem depicts an army officer seeking escape from a tedious life by taking up with Circassian tribesmen. It was one of Pushkin's most popular works and bears some resemblance to the later novella of the same name by Leo Tolstoy.

Shota Rustaveli *The Knight in the Panther Skin.* This epic poem composed in the twelfth century tells the tale of a pair of chivalric heroes – Avtandil and Tariel – and their quest to find Tariel's love, Nestan, who is thought to be an allegorical representation of Queen Tamar. It was first translated into English in the early twentieth century by Marjory Wardrop.

Kurban Said *Ali and Nino.* Considered Azerbaijan's national novel, but also held in high regard in Georgia, *Ali and Nino* tells the story of a love affair between a noble Azerbaijani boy and a Georgian girl. Set in Baku, Tbilisi, Nagorno-Karabakh, Dagestan and Persia in the years around World War I, it's a tale of high drama which paints a remarkable picture of the pre-Soviet Caucasus.

Leo Vardiashvili *Hard by a Great Forest.* Leo Vardiashvili was picked as one of the Observer's best new novelists of 2024. His debut novel tells the story of a young man returning to Georgia for the first time since fleeing the 1990s civil war, seeking his father and brother who have gone missing.

Various *The Book of Tbilisi.* A collection of short stories set in Tbilisi by some of Georgia's leading authors, this anthology is a great introduction to the varying styles of contemporary Georgian fiction writers.

Franz Werfel *The Forty Days of Musa Dagh.* Published in 1933, this novel was one of the first to tackle the subject of the Armenian Genocide. It's set in the village of Musa Dagh, where the Armenian populace successfully resisted Turkish attacks. The English translation has long been abridged, but a full version was published in 2018.

Small print and index

ABOUT THE AUTHOR

Owen Morton has been travelling for twenty years, with a particular affinity for the former Soviet world and the Middle East. Based in Yorkshire, he's worked for Rough Guides on guidebooks ranging from Pembrokeshire to the Philippines, and was delighted to take the opportunity to write this guide to the Caucasus. When not exploring the world, he entertains himself by writing a blog about 1980s cartoons. His favourite animal is the wonderfully expressive and permanently furious manul, native to Central Asia and occasionally sighted in the Caucasus. Follow him on Instagram at owenmortonmanul.

Adam Prince lives in Hampshire, but has been travelling since his university days. He's found himself repeatedly returning to the Caucasus, particularly Armenia, which he loves for its fantastic scenery, history, food and people. This is his first published work for Rough Guides.

Natalie Taylor is a keen traveller and photographer, with a special interest in Eastern Europe and post-Soviet spaces. She particularly enjoyed exploring Azerbaijan for this guide, and considers Baku one of the wordl's most fascinating cities.

A ROUGH GUIDE TO ROUGH GUIDES

Rough Guide credits

Editor: Kate Drynan
Cartography: Katie Bennett
Picture editor: Piotr Kala
Picture Manager: Tom Smyth

Layout: Pradeep Thapliyal
Head of DTP and Pre-Press: Rebeka Davies
Head of Publishing: Sarah Clark

Publishing information

First edition 2024

Distribution

UK, Ireland and Europe
Apa Publications (UK) Ltd; mail@roughguides.com
United States and Canada
Two Rivers; ips@ingramcontent.com
Australia and New Zealand
Woodslane; info@woodslane.com.au
Worldwide
Apa Publications (UK) Ltd; mail@roughguides.com

Special Sales, Content Licensing and CoPublishing
Rough Guides can be purchased in bulk quantities
at discounted prices. We can create special editions,
personalized jackets and corporate imprints tailored to
your needs. mail@roughguides.com.

roughguides.com

EU Representative

LOGOS EUROPE, 9 rue Nicolas Poussin, 17000,
LA ROCHELLE, France; Contact@logoseurope.eu;
+33 (0) 667937378

Printed by Finidr in Czech Republic

ISBN: 9781835291610

Help us update

We've gone to a lot of effort to ensure that this edition of
The Rough Guide to Georgia, Armenia & Azerbaijan is
accurate and up-to-date. However, things change – places
get "discovered", transport routes are altered, restaurants
and hotels raise prices or lower standards, and businesses
cease trading. If you feel we've got it wrong or left
something out, we'd like to know, and if you can direct us
to the web address, so much the better.

Please send your comments with the subject line "**Rough
Guide Georgia, Armenia & Azerbaijan Update**" to mail@
roughguides.com. We'll send a copy of the next edition (or
any other Rough Guide if you prefer) for the very best emails.

Acknowledgements

The authors would like to thank the fantastic team at Rough Guides, particularly Kate Drynan, Sarah Clark, Rachel
Lawrence, Katie Bennett and Tom Smyth. Also Tom Fleming, Zara Sekhavati and Sian Marsh. On the road, among many
others, Gaga Mumladze, Giorgi Bakuridze, Sabina, Vasila, Ilqar and Karine provided invaluable help, and Adam would like
to extend particular gratitude to the family who leapt to his aid when his car broke down in Haykadzor. Tips from Hyerin
Eom, Anna Clarke, Kirsty Landles, Jasper and Acacia, Pawal and Alina, and the Snell family were all greatly appreciated,
and Martin Brasher's proofreading was invaluable. Thanks (or blame, depending on your perspective) are due to Jay
Leadbetter for a particularly appalling pun in Chapter 6. Thanks also to Kerry Appleby and Mike Kaye for supporting this
endeavour, and Owen would like to extend special thanks to Magnus Bartlett for showing that this was possible. Finally,
thanks to all family, particularly Katherine Morton.

Photo credits

(Key: T-top; C-centre; B-bottom; L-left; R-right)

All images **Shutterstock** except **Owen Morton** 13B, 16B, 18L, 18T, 19BR, 20/21M, 21C, 22TL, 24, 106/107, 108/109,
176/177, 194/195, 270/271, 310/311

Cover: Ruins of the Temple of Zvartnots with the Mount Ararat in the background, Yerevan, Armenia **Shutterstock**

Index

A

B

YOUR TAILOR-MADE TRIP
STARTS HERE

Tailor-made trips and unique adventures crafted by local experts

Rough Guides has been inspiring travellers with lively and thought-provoking guidebooks for more than 35 years. Now we're linking you up with selected local experts to craft your dream trip. They will put together your perfect itinerary and book it at local rates.

Don't follow the crowd – find your own path.

HOW ROUGHGUIDES.COM/TRIPS WORKS

Pick your dream destination, tell us what you want and submit an enquiry.

Fill in a short form to tell your local expert about your dream trip and preferences.

Our local expert will craft your tailor-made itinerary. You'll be able to tweak and refine it until you're completely satisfied.

Book online with ease, pack your bags and enjoy the trip! Our local expert will be on hand 24/7 while you're on the road.

Map symbols

The symbols below are used on maps throughout the book

International boundary	Point of interest	Zoo
State boundary	Mountain peak	Temple
Chapter division boundary	Statue	Museum
Pedestrian street	Transport stop	Ski area
Motorway	Bus station	Cave
Street	Train station	Lighthouse
Footpath	Palace	Waterfall
Steps	Information office	Hospital
Railway	Post office	Metro station
Ferry route	Fortress	Synagogue
Wall	Monastery	Church (regional maps)
Cable car	Castle	Stadium
Zip line	Amusement park	Church
Funicular	Observatory	Building
Main border crossing	Brandy factory	Park
Other border crossing	Gardens	Beach
Airport	Viewpoint	Cemetery

Listings key

Accommodation	
Eating	
Drinking & nightlife	
Shopping	

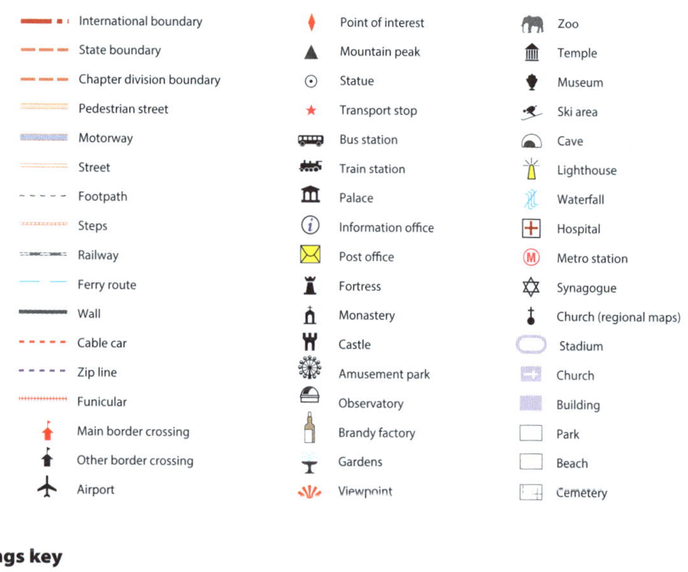

BENEFITS OF PLANNING AND BOOKING AT ROUGHGUIDES.COM/TRIPS

PLAN YOUR ADVENTURE WITH LOCAL EXPERTS

Rough Guides' English-speaking local experts are hand-picked, based on their experience in the travel industry and their impeccable standards of customer service.

SAVE TIME AND GET ACCESS TO LOCAL KNOWLEDGE

When a local expert plans your trip, you save time and money when you book, even during high season. You won't be charged for using a credit card either.

MAKE TRAVEL A BREEZE: BOOK WITH PEACE OF MIND

Enjoy stress-free travel when you use Rough Guides' secure online booking platform. All bookings come with a money-back guarantee.

WHAT DO OTHER TRAVELLERS THINK ABOUT ROUGH GUIDES TRIPS?

This Spain tour company did a fantastic job to make our dream trip perfect. We gave them our travel budget, told them where we would like to go, and they did all of the planning. Our drivers and tour guides were always on time and very knowledgable. The hotel accommodations were better than we would have found on our own. Only one time did we end up in a location that we had not intended to be in. We called the 24 hour phone number, and they immediately fixed the situation.

Don A, USA ★★★★★

Our trip was fantastic! Transportation, accommodations, guides – all were well chosen! The hotels were well situated, well appointed and had helpful, friendly staff. All of the guides we had were very knowledgeable, patient, and flexible with our varied interests in the different sites. We particularly enjoyed the side trip to Tangier! Well done! The itinerary you arranged for us allowed maximum coverage of the country with time in each city for seeing the important places.

Sharon, USA ★★★★★

PLAN AND BOOK YOUR TRIP AT ROUGHGUIDES.COM/TRIPS